EUROPEAN STUDIES SERIES

General Editor   Colin Jones
                               Richard Overy

Series Advisers   Joe Bergin
                               John Breuilly
                               Ruth Harris

This series marks a major initiative in European history publishing aimed primarily, though not exclusively, at an undergraduate audience. It encompasses a wide variety of books on aspects of European history since 1500, with particular emphasis on France and Germany, although no country is excluded and a special effort made to cover previously neglected areas, such as Scandinavia, Eastern Europe and Southern Europe.

The series includes political accounts and broad thematic treatments, both of a comparative kind and studies of a single country, and lays particular emphasis on a social and cultural history where this opens up fruitful new ways of examining the past. The aim of the series is to make available a wide range of titles in areas where there is now an obvious gap or where the existing historical literature is out of date or narrowly focused. The series also includes translations of important books published elsewhere in Europe.

Interest in European affairs and history has never been greater; *European Studies* helps make that European heritage closer, richer and more comprehensible.

Nationalism in Germany, 1848–1866

Revolutionary Nation

MARK HEWITSON

First published 2010 by
PALGRAVE MACMILLAN

Palgrave Macmillan in the UK is an imprint of Macmillan Publishers Limited, registered in England, company number 785998, of Houndmills, Basingstoke, Hampshire RG21 6XS.

Palgrave Macmillan in the US is a division of St Martin's Press LLC, 175 Fifth Avenue, New York, NY 10010.

Palgrave Macmillan is the global academic imprint of the above companies and has companies and representatives throughout the world.

Palgrave® and Macmillan® are registered trademarks in the United States, the United Kingdom, Europe and other countries

ISBN 978-1-4039-1329-6   hardback
ISBN 978-1-4039-1330-2   paperback

This book is printed on paper suitable for recycling and made from fully managed and sustained forest sources. Logging, pulping and manufacturing processes are expected to conform to the environmental regulations of the country of origin.

A catalogue record for this book is available from the British Library.

A catalog record for this book is available from the Library of Congress.

10 9 8 7 6 5 4 3 2 1
19 18 17 16 15 14 13 12 11 10

Printed in Great Britain by CPI Antony Rowe, Chippenham and Eastbourne

To Anna and Camille

Contents

Figures, Maps and Tables

Acknowledgements

The author and publishers wish to thank the following for the use of copyright material:

Maps 1 and 2 adapted from H. Best, *Die Männer von Bildung und Besitz* (Düsseldorf, 1990), 250 and 289, reproduced with permission of Droste and the Kommission für die Geschichte des Parlamentarismus und der politischen Parteien.

Map 3 adapted from R. Okey, *The Habsburg Monarchy, c. 1765–1918* (Basingstoke, 2001), xii, reproduced with permission of Palgrave.

Figure 4.1 adapted from H. Brandt, *Parlamentarismus in Württemberg 1819-1870* (Düsseldorf, 1987), reproduced with permission of Droste and the Kommission für die Geschichte des Parlamentarismus und der politischen Parteien.

Tables 1.1, 1.2 and 1.3 from W. Siemann, *The German Revolution of 1848–49* (Basingstoke, 1998), 113, 122, 124, reproduced with permission of Palgrave Macmillan.

Tables 5.1, 5.2 and 5.3 from A. Biefang, *Politisches Bürgertum in Deutschland 1857–1868* (Düsseldorf, 1994), 104, 245, and 304, reproduced with permission of Droste and the Kommission für die Geschichte des Parlamentarismus und der politischen Parteien.

Every effort has been made to trace the copyright holders, but if any have been inadvertently overlooked the publishers will be pleased to make the necessary arrangements at the first opportunity.

Preface

This book, although now self-standing, started out as part of a much broader project on nationalism – especially liberal nationalism – in Germany between 1848 and the early 1930s. I am still working on the other parts, and the debts that I have incurred are correspondingly large and open-ended.

I wrote much of the volume on a year's sabbatical funded by UCL and the Arts and Humanities Research Council, as part of its Research Leave Scheme. I am very grateful to both for giving me the opportunity to write for an extended period, rather than for the usual snatched moments during vacations and term, and to concentrate on the minutiae of research instead of the minutiae of departmental and college administration. In a period when funding is increasingly 'applied' and 'collaborative', the AHRC scheme has continued to provide scholars in the Humanities with time to do what they should, in terms of research, be doing. I hope – but doubt – that the successor scheme will be as successful. I am also indebted, in a much more personal sense, to Matthew D'Auria, Jan Vermeiren and Daniel Laqua for providing teaching cover over the course of my sabbatical and for doing such an excellent job. My colleagues in the German Department and in European Social and Political Studies at UCL have picked up much of the rest of the work that this and other sabbaticals have occasioned, as well as putting up with sporadic moaning about lack of progress. Without such departmental backing (and lack of complaint), I am not sure that I could have completed this volume – certainly not within the decade.

The nature of the subject of the volume (the 1850s and 1860s) has necessarily made the research for it somewhat solitary at times. I am therefore all the more indebted to Rudolf Muhs and John

Breuilly, two of a small number of UK scholars who have continued to treat the period seriously, for taking an interest in the project: the former for reading the typescript in its entirety and giving such helpful advice; the latter for his engagement, as an editor and colleague, with all aspects of the book, providing detailed and challenging criticism (in the best sense) of its arguments and evidence. In different ways, both have served as models, at different times, during the difficult transition from the early twentieth to the mid-nineteenth century. In a wider sense, whether with reference to German history or nationalism in Europe, I have also benefited greatly from the comments and help of Tim Baycroft, Stefan Berger, Mary Fulbrook, Egbert Klautke, Eckard Michels, James Retallack, Bernhard Rieger, Jill Stephenson, and all of my Ph.D. students at UCL, especially – in this regard – those working on the national question – Jan, Matthew, and Mark Tilse. Finally, I am thankful for the very constructive suggestions of the anonymous referee and for those of the editorial staff at Palgrave who did not give up the project despite its changing shape.

My main debt, as will always be the case with work that so often 'comes home', is to my family. The research and writing of this book has spanned the birth of my two daughters, Anna and Camille. For their support during a very busy time and their toleration of too many working holidays and visits, I wish to thank my own parents and sister, and the parents and family of my partner, Cécile Laborde. Their help has not only made it possible for Cécile and I to continue to research (perhaps more often than we should), it has also enabled us to see each other from time to time. It is principally those times, and our time together with Anna and Camille, that have given me sustenance when confronted with the unwieldier and more tiring aspects of writing, research and teaching. I have dedicated this book to our girls, for their good-natured acceptance of the metaphysics of 'work' and for their unstinting energy, affection and inspiration.

MH
London, 2010

Introduction

The revolution of 1848–49 altered the history of politics and the nation in Germany. 'The idea of unity became historical – that is the great result of 1848, which cannot be turned back by any means of violence or cunning,' wrote the liberal publicist Ludwig August von Rochau in 1853: 'By becoming historical, the idea of unity entered the same stage of development in which designs for internal reform in the individual states have existed for a long period of time.'[1] In *Grundsätze der Realpolitik* (1853), the former insurrectionary, who had fled life-long imprisonment in Frankfurt in 1833 and had only returned to Germany in 1848, purportedly helped to usher in a realistic age spanning the reaction of the 1850s and Bismarck's wars of unification in the 1860s, after the 'failure' of the revolution. He was joined by Hermann Baumgarten, a neighbour in Heidelberg before 1861, whose 'self-critique' had supposedly exposed the fatal weaknesses of German liberalism in 1866, outmanoeuvred by the Prussian Minister-President. Even if it 'had to fail', wrote the journalist and academic, 1848 had been 'the first attempt to solve the German question'.[2] The Reich constitution of 1849 was 'a considerable advance', albeit an unreliable one, 'on our politicisation until that date'.[3] 'Its main merit consisted in … casting the first bright light into the night of our political dreams and indicating the path which could lead us out of the labyrinth of German fragmentation,' Baumgarten admitted, despite his intention of highlighting the naivety and inefficacy of his fellow liberals during and after the revolution.[4] Like Rochau, the Karlsruhe academic was anxious to debunk liberal myths of the *Vormärz* and revolutionary periods, yet he, too, understood 1848–49 as estab-

1

lishing a long-lasting nexus of the nation, politics and, especially, liberalism.

This study examines such a nexus, in conjunction and conflict with other emerging political milieux and parties. It argues that many of the elements of the case for a *kleindeutsch* (small German) solution to the 'German question' had been decided by 1849, most notably through the discussion and enactment of the Reich constitution in March. These elements were defining features of political debate and activity over the next two decades. Contemporaries were right, of course, to doubt whether a constitutional, federal and democratic *Kleindeutschland* (small German state) was attainable in or after 1849. A powerful coalition of states and conservative political interests had blocked its realisation during the revolution itself and it had successfully resurrected a reactionary German Confederation, backed by most small and middling states and by the largest and most forceful German Great Power, the Habsburg monarchy. Despite such obvious obstacles, the revolutionary model of a German nation-state remained influential in the 1850s and, it is proposed, became decisive in the 1860s, as the principal alternatives to a small German state, which had already been partially discredited in 1848–49, proved not to be feasible. Since unification continued to be a political priority for many parties, especially those in the critical areas of the third Germany, the narrowing of the range of 'national' options available to ministers and policy-makers was highly significant, even for Austrian and Prussian statesmen, whose pursuit of their own state's interests forced them to take account of 'public opinion' and party preferences in Saxony, Bavaria, Hanover, Württemberg, Baden and other principalities. The effective preclusion of national alternatives to *Kleindeutschland* within some of the most prominent political debates of the previous 18 years helped to ease the very difficult transition towards a Prussian-dominated North German Confederation in 1867 and German Empire in 1871. The fact that so many features of the *Reichsverfassung* of 1849 seemed to have been retained made the new German states acceptable to most liberals and many democrats.

The transition towards *Kleindeutschland* was by no means inevitable. The forces – or balance of powers in a changing set of historical conditions – working against the formation of a small German state were considerable, dominating the 1850s and early 1860s. Recent historical accounts, correctly seeking to revise the persistent pro-Prussian orthodoxy of pre-war 'Borussian' historiography, have emphasised the significance of such hindrances to the creation of a 'small German' polity. Historians like Heinrich Lutz and Helmut Rumpler have underlined the continuing predominance of the Habsburg monarchy in German affairs.[5] From their point of view, the most pressing question concerns the timing of and reasons for the withdrawal of Austria from Germany. Lutz's answer, in contrast to those of the majority of authors who concentrate on the Austro-Prussian War (1866), points to the period after 1866, suggesting that Austrian policy-makers gave up their German ambitions more slowly than previously assumed, renouncing them definitively only in 1879 with the signature of the Dual Alliance.[6] Other historians have focused on the Habsburg monarchy's main allies in the third Germany before 1871. Abigail Green, Manfred Hanisch, Andreas Neemann, Dieter Langewiesche, Lothar Gall and Michael John have demonstrated the extent to which the *Mittelstaaten* served as an alternative point of identification and loyalty after 1848.[7] As a consequence, any solution to the German question had to pay attention to the wishes of governments in Munich, Dresden, Stuttgart, Karlsruhe and Hanover and to the affiliations of the German 'tribes'. It would also have to confront the German Confederation, which had become the principal diplomatic framework of the middling states and the main legal obstacle to unification according to the revolutionary small German model. How far could the Bund be reformed through the initiatives of the *Mittelstaaten* and of Austria in order to become a workable political structure for the German nation? This is the question posed by scholars such as Jürgen Müller, Jonas Flöter, Anselm Doering-Manteuffel and Jürgen Angelow, lending new credence to the Confederation as a political and legal framework for very disparate German states.[8] A confederal solution appeared more attractive because of the unpopularity of a Prussian alternative, with widespread antipathy to the Hohenzollern monarchy, especially in the South German states. In this respect, perceived geographical, cultural and religious differences were exacerbated by internal divisions within Prussia itself.[9] Amongst other things, recent research has revealed just how ambivalent Prussian conservatives and courtiers were towards *kleindeutsch* nationalism.[10]

The barriers to the realisation of the national settlement outlined in the Reich constitution of 1849 rested on existing powers, institutions and conditions – restored political elites, the borders of 1815, the Confederation, regional economies, the armies of the German Great Powers – which were the product of the 'reaction' rather than the revolution. It is contended here, however, that more or less continuous debates about a German nation-state after 1848 had a decisive impact on such powers, institutions and conditions, not least because the 'public sphere', the press and 'public opinion', which were often referred to collectively as '*die Öffentlichkeit*', were heeded by governments in the aftermath of 1848, particularly in the third Germany. It is true that relatively little was – and is – known of the opinions, beliefs and assumptions of the majority of subjects, but it can be argued that what mattered most in the formulation and execution of policy was ministers' evaluation and understanding of 'opinion', as it was interpreted and shaped by journalists, academics, and politicians. For the public sphere was, at the same time, a rapidly evolving political forum, connected to emerging political parties, networks and milieux. Thus, 'opposition' groups, whose parliamentary activities were regularly reported in the press, existed in virtually all German states during the 1850s and 1860s, playing an important part in political debate, if only through their public protestations, and in sanctioning and blocking legislation and ministerial actions, most famously – if also unsuccessfully – during the Prussian constitutional crisis after 1862. Two years earlier, in Baden, liberals from the opposition had even entered government. This study examines the relationship between ministers and policy-makers, on the one hand, and politicians, journalists and other publicists, on the other. It proposes that, when statesmen addressed the German question, they did so partly – and increasingly – on terms established by liberals in the public sphere. Policy-makers kept returning to the national question because it constituted a priority of the dominant liberal parties, which figured in the domestic deliberations of the governments of the small and middling German states and, in part as a result, in the external calculations of the German Great Powers. Prussian ministers and diplomats, in particular, sought to court parties and opinion-makers in the third Germany in order to avoid the Austrian-engineered machinery of the Bund.

Such arguments about the linkages between nationalism and politics are necessarily framed in the wider context of debates, which have been central to the controversy about a German *Sonderweg*, concerning the putative failure of revolution in 1848, the weakness of liberalism, the circumscribed role of representative assemblies, and the formation of contradictory, authoritarian or sham-democratic systems of government in the individual states, the North

German Confederation and the *Kaiserreich*, with far-reaching consequences for later, twentieth-century German regimes.[11] Critics and defenders of the thesis about a 'special path' have already qualified most of these claims – and others relating to the Prussian Chancellor's 'Bonapartism', the position of Junkers or the 'feudalisation' of the *Bürgertum*, for example – in respect of Bismarckian and Wilhelmine Germany, but they have paid less attention to the decade or so after 1848, when many of the critical political and national questions first surfaced. This study seeks, in common with other research into specific political constituencies, to reassess the legacy of 1848 and the continuities of public debate and party organisation.[12] Like recent works on individual German states, it investigates and evaluates the tenacity, variety and extent of associational life and politics. Unlike these works, it also explores the reciprocal relationship between local politics and the formation of national political networks, nationalist ideologies and a German public sphere, revealing how such political activity fostered the emergence of a small German state.

Parties and the Public Sphere

From a national perspective, the period examined here connected the first and second attempts to unify the German lands. Despite significant diplomatic, military, political, social and economic changes, the ways in which politics and the nation were conceptualised remained remarkably constant between 1848–49 and 1866–67, with many of the tentative questions and answers of the revolution being confirmed over the succeeding two decades. The first unification of Germany was inaugurated in 1848, establishing a nation-state on paper and many elements of one in practice by early 1849, including the Central Power and National Assembly in Frankfurt. Clearly, such a unification – or the nationally legitimated formation of a single nation-state from several existing states – remained incomplete, with Friedrich Wilhelm IV eventually rejecting the Frankfurt Parliament's offer to become 'Kaiser of the Germans' in April 1849, yet the process was at an advanced stage, with the creation of an executive, assembly and constitution, and it enjoyed broad legitimacy in the third Germany and in Prussia, especially in the period before the appointment of the conservative Brandenburg ministry in November 1848.[13] Twenty-eight German states had jointly accepted the Reich constitution on 14 April 1849, with King Wilhelm I of Württemberg forced by his own ministry to join them on 24 April and with the lower chambers of Hanover, Saxony and Bavaria putting pressure on their own monarchs – ultimately unsuccessfully – to do the same.[14] Although the Reich constitution was never implemented, it was seen to be legitimate by the majority of deputies and much of the political nation. From their point of view, a German nation-state had been illegally suppressed by a small minority of reactionaries.

As contemporaries, but not all later historians, seem to have been aware, debates about a polity, constitution and nation-state had coincided during the revolution. This remained the case after 1848–49. Even a sceptical Bavarian and Catholic periodical such as the *Historisch-politische Blätter* was still confident, a decade later, that 'the movements of 1848 had two great ideas as their foundation': 'These were the ideas of *nationality* and *inner freedom*; the best part of the nation (*Nation*) took them up, and they handed power to public opinion, on which the uprising foundered.'[15] The convergence of politics and nationalism in Germany already had a long history by the time of the revolution, deriving from opposition to petty or absolutist German states and from criticism of a German Confederation dominated by the Great Powers.[16] The perceived collapse of existing polities in 1848 appeared to have cleared the way for the construction of a new regime, a product of the revolution in which political and national imperatives seemed to be combined unconditionally. This type of 'revolutionary nationalism', where political elements were seen to play an essential part in the formation or perpetuation of a nation-state, was accompanied by – and depended on – a series of transformations which altered the scope and significance of political and national debates and actions.[17]

The revolution had created the conditions for a reorganisation of institutions and for the realisation of ideas which had been discussed within the limited, sometimes persecuted, circles of the *Bildungsbürgertum* since the French Revolution and, in some instances, beforehand. To the majority of commentators from the middling strata of the larger towns, the nation seemed a natural framework for such institutions. Many creeds – liberalism, conservatism and 'democracy' – were transformed and redefined during the revolution, creating a ferment of ideas in which politics and the nation were 'naturally' and intimately combined.[18] Political parties, although existing in some localities and within a web of regional associations, changed fundamentally after 1848 and extended beyond individual cities and states, developing from pre-revolutionary regional networks of politicians, journalists and officials and from the informal groups of deputies who met regularly at taverns and hotels – the Café Milani, the Deutscher Hof, the Westendhalle – in Frankfurt.[19] Partly as a result of the creation of mass political organisations with connections to parties, such as the democratic *Zentralmärzverein*, conservative 'King and Fatherland' associations and Catholic Pius Associations, the public sphere expanded dramatically, informing as well as enfranchising significant numbers of citizens – up to 75 per cent of men – across the German lands. The revolution, recalled the novelist and publicist Gustav Freytag, 'was a wonderful apprenticeship for German journalism, and it is no coincidence that many capable editors of our greatest political newspapers emerged from 1848, clever, worldly-wise, skilful, of sure judgement in great questions, not fully matched by a younger generation'.[20] To journalists like Freytag, many of whom spent time in Frankfurt during the revolution, *Politik*, in the full sense of the German word, was being discussed and acted on: as a set of specific policies, the character of which had not been determined; as the concentration and distribution of power within a state; as a territory at the centre of Europe, whose borders were negotiable for the first time since 1815; and as a power within a collapsing states' system. These political debates impinged on, and were affected by, assumptions about the nature and extent of the German nation.

Debates about a new – or revolutionary – German nation-state or national polity were dominated by political 'parties' after 1848. The revolution was critical in creating the conditions necessary for party politics, introducing representative assemblies for the first time in Prussia and Austria, reinstalling them in states such as Hanover and Kurhessen, and briefly granting freedom to assemble, to form political associations, to vote and to express political opinions in the press, all of which extended across the traditional barriers of state borders. Political *Vereine* (associations) had been outlawed in the lands of the Confederation before 1848, though tolerated in states with more liberal constitutions and more established *Landtage* such as Baden and Württemberg.[21] Parties in the sense of organised groups distinguished by their shared political convictions, not occupational interests, and designed to return their representatives to a parliament and to influence state decision-making and public opinion over an extended period of time had, at most, existed in an inchoate form in the South German *Mittelstaaten*.[22] In Württemberg in 1847, lamented one of the mouthpieces of the opposition, the *Beobachter*, there were 'no political parties, but at most political opinions': 'Party is nothing other than a vitally integrated organisation of common strivings.'[23] In most localities, there were merely overlapping associations, with a variety of public functions – civic improvement, the coordination of occupational or economic interests, scientific endeavour and cultural activity – but with little more than concealed and unarticulated political purposes, frequently lacking a focus in the form of a powerful *Landtag* opposition.[24] Where state assemblies existed, usually with highly restricted or corporate franchises, the opposition was, in effect, 'a great liberal party, if one could use the term "party" for a strange mixture of all possible elements of opposition against the government without a specifically formulated programme', wrote one correspondent of the *Deutsche Monatsschrift* in 1851 of the era 'before March 1848'.[25] Where *Landtage* did not exist, in most of North Germany, *Vereine* constituted the principal forum of political organisation and activity. They remained essential during and after the revolution but their objectives and membership differed from the overtly political purposes and activities of parties.[26]

In 1848–49, the organised factions of the Frankfurt Parliament crystallised into identifiable parties with programmes and close connections to an extensive network of associations. The main impulse for such organisation came from the democratic party (Donnersberg, Deutscher Hof and parts of the Westendhalle), which was instrumental in the formation of the *Zentralmärzverein*, but it also had an effect on conservatives, Catholics and liberals, all of whom formed ties with their own associations in spite of residual resistance to the very notion of what Brockhaus's *Conversationslexikon* had bemoaned in 1846 as 'organised, consciously calculating parties'.[27] 'Let us learn from our enemy!' proclaimed the liberal *Darmstädter Journal* in August 1849: 'It is already organised! Democratic associations and their transparent reflection, the loyally genuflecting *Märzvereine*, are the majority in our Hessian land and, indeed, a well-disciplined majority, bound together by the unified business of the opposition.'[28] Within the next year or so, most party organisations had been dissolved. According to the confederal law of association of 13 July 1854, which formalised on a national level what had already occurred in many states, political *Vereine* were not allowed to affiliate with each other, effectively preventing the creation of anything other than purely local organisations. Such legislation ensured that parties remained, as the Social Democratic leader Wilhelm Liebknecht later put it, organisational 'embryos', without the classic features – party agents, a central committee, a national conference, a political programme, voting discipline, affiliations, membership dues and a large budget – of the SPD and Centre Party during the imperial era.[29]

Nevertheless, political groupings were organised as self-evident 'parties' – the term was now used universally, in contrast to the period before 1848 – in localities and in *Landtage* throughout the German lands, except in Austria and enclaves of 'absolutism' like Mecklenburg. Whereas theories of 'party' had earlier been contested, if not rejected outright, even by liberal supporters of 'opposition' to the government, they were advanced and discussed across the political spectrum during the 1850s and 1860s.[30] 1848 had demonstrated the possibility of party organisation on a national level and had created enduring memories of party affiliation – as an element of a wider revolutionary mythology – which many contemporaries aimed to revive after the 'reaction'. The speed with which national and party organisations such as the Progressives and the *Nationalverein* were established after 1859 owed much to liberals' and democrats' experiences, recollections, acquaintances and myths of 1848–49.[31] What was more, much of the structure of associational life, which had been so important during the revolution, continued to develop after it, with cultural, civic, professional and economic *Vereine* multiplying and expanding, partly as a consequence of urbanisation and industrialisation.[32] The combination of such local milieux and national networks of politicians and journalists consolidated by the revolution – the connotations of 'political culture' or 'sub-cultures' are too exclusive, fixed or small-scale to describe these networks – allowed the survival and rapid reconstruction of nationwide or, at least, inter-state party organisations during the post-revolutionary decades.[33]

Debates about a German nation-state and polity, initiated and shaped by parties, could take place because of the continuing existence of national and state-wide public spheres. The German term for such a sphere, '*die Öffentlichkeit*', or openness, was less ambiguous and much older than its English equivalent, dating from the eighteenth century.[34] It described an open or public space between absolutist states and their successors, on the one hand, and a developing private sphere, on the other.[35] Although it continued to co-exist with corporations, to overlap with sectional and family interests, to be characterised by distinctions of status and to be subject to state interference and control, it became the principal locus, comprised of associations and the press, of civic progress and sociability in towns, and sometimes beyond them, during the late eighteenth and the nineteenth century, cultivating a degree of equality, individualism and freedom of expression.[36] It was at once a political and a communicative sphere. Political discussion and criticism seemed to have many different causes and contexts, including the intervention of the state in supposedly autonomous markets, competition between officials and *Vereine* in areas of civic improvement, free scientific enquiry, and the habit of reading and finding out about the wider world via books, almanacs, periodicals and newspapers. *Die Obrigkeit* (authority), both local and state-wide, had become, in important instances, less personal, no longer as closely connected to kin, guilds and orders. States were conceived, in part, as fulfilling public functions and administering public goods, subjecting themselves in the process to public scrutiny and approval. The fact that officials played such a prominent role in the advent of politics in the German lands during the early nineteenth century, as the exponents of 'official liberalism', evinced the extent to which the public sphere was taken for granted as well as blurring the edges between state and 'society', for civil servants engaged in politics as citizens not just as agents of the state.[37] Over half of the deputies of the Frankfurt Parliament were officials, despite the assembly's revolutionary role and reputation. Their criticism of the individual states and their willingness to form a new German nation-state were founded on interlinking notions of impersonality, reason, legality, legitimacy and utility, which appalled conservative nobles more accustomed to patriarchalism, patrimony and reciprocal, hierarchical, personal bonds. Whereas Ernst Ludwig von Gerlach viewed Prussia and the Confederation as he viewed his family or his father-land, admitting and chiding their 'faults', liberals and democrats seemed to treat them impersonally, with the result that they were willing to 'pulverise' them.[38]

Such distance, impartiality and ruthlessness were features of a communicative sphere which encouraged the conceptualisation of – and gave a sense of familiarity with – far-away events. Through a regular reading of the press, large and distant institutions could be imagined and understood, in a literary, discursive and purportedly factual form, separate from the physical, visual, symbolic and ritual-istic ways of conceiving of authority at close quarters in towns and villages, which, of course, continued to exist.[39] National festivals, as Heinrich von Treitschke acknowledged, were, amongst other things, an attempt to recreate the immediate, physical proximity and visual symbolism of local politics on a grand scale, yet most impressions of German and state affairs came from the press, which continued to grow throughout the nineteenth century.[40] In 1826, there were 371 separate German-language newspapers, 688 in 1848, 845 in 1858, and 1,217 in 1867.[41] The thirst for news on the part of readers was commonly remarked upon at the time, most obviously as momentous events – such as the outbreak of revolution – unfolded. 'We have been living here recently in great excitement,' wrote Clothilde Koch-Gontard from Frankfurt in March 1848: 'Political news (*Neuigkeiten*) is awaited with incredible impatience'.[42] In quieter times, too, a reading public avidly read reports and formed views of occurrences beyond their locality. Even a counter-revolutionary sceptic like the Saxon minister Ferdinand von Beust accepted, in 1857, that 'the best way to attract readers is through good news reporting'.[43] The words and opinions of the press allowed contemporaries to define, comprehend and evaluate the actions of leaders and the characteristics of institutions, notwith-standing the shifting focus of reportage, from the frank exchanges about domestic politics of 1848–49 and the New Era to the coverage of foreign politics in the 1850s. In certain circumstances, they appear to have prompted readers to envisage a different future.[44]

The public sphere was numerically small, with the readership of individual newspapers and periodicals numbering only thousands; it was socially restricted, with at least 70 per cent of readers of the *Deutsche Zeitung* during the revolution coming from the civil service (21.5 per cent), educated professions (35.8 per cent) and commerce (12 per cent); and it was personal, with readers identify-ing closely with 'their' publication and appealing to the editor with a collective 'we'.[45] It was also subject to government censorship and influence, although this was much more successful in some states – for instance, in Hanover, where 'most of [the press] is in the hands of the government or otherwise influenced', in the estimation of the *Deutsche Reichszeitung* in 1864 – than in others, where the retro-spective seizure of editions and placement of articles proved relatively ineffective.[46] In most regions, large-circulation liberal and even democratic newspapers and periodicals – the *Kölnische Zeitung*, the *Frankfurter Journal*, the *National-Zeitung*, the Berlin *Volks-Zeitung*, the *Münchner Neueste Nachrichten*, the *Allgemeine Zeitung*, the *Schwäbischer Merkur*, the *Hamburger Correspondent*, the *Hamburger Nachrichten*, the *Grenzboten* and *Kladderadatsch* – were dominant, extending from Berlin, Frankfurt, Munich, Stuttgart, Hamburg and Cologne into their hinterlands.[47] It is notable that reactionary governments felt unable, after a rapid expansion of the press and the public sphere in 1848–49, to return to pre-revolutionary practices of censorship, resigning themselves to intimidation, the retrospective impounding of offending copy, the control of information, the establishment of more effective official publications and the insertion of articles in 'independent' newspapers. Such tactics undoubtedly led to self-censorship and a frequent muzzling of the press, but they failed to destroy the dominant liberal publications and the expression of unwelcome opinions and reportage, partly because of the contiguity of more and less liberal German states and the inefficacy of the Bund.

Governments regularly found themselves following rather than leading the press, in the manner of Württemberg's ministry in 1851, seeking to ensure that the official '*Staats-Anzeiger* is able to compete with the *Schwäbischer Merkur*, through providing the interesting daily news items, which secure the large readership of the latter'.[48] The readers of such newspapers, who came preponderantly from the liberal milieux of the larger, pivotal cities, were seen, even by the chief of the Hanoverian Press Bureau Oskar Meding, to be unsusceptible to government influence.[49] To this limited but significant reading public, the press was a bridge to the rest of Germany and beyond, fostering political reflection and discussion, even under conditions of censorship. Some titles were read throughout the German lands, including the *Deutsche Zeitung*, published by Georg Gottfried Gervinus in Heidelberg and with 36.5 per cent of its readers in the South, 20.3 per cent in the North, 26.2 per cent in Prussia, and 17 per cent in Central Germany.[50] Most titles instilled in readers some sense of 'Germany', creating a discursive political sphere which was connected to the oral cultures of the locality, via discussions within families, reading societies (597 founded 1770–1820), lending libraries (656 in Prussia by 1846) and coffee houses, and which extended to a calendar and almanac-reading public – encompassing a significant part of the literate 80 per cent or so of men and 50 per cent or more of women of early nineteenth-century West German towns, for example – even if it also excluded the lower orders from regular daily or weekly exposure to state or national politics.[51] In this national public sphere, characterised by a literary rather than visual culture and by the dense parliamentary reports of the press, which were supplemented but not contradicted by mass-circulation 'entertainment' periodicals such as *Die Gartenlaube* with its circulation of 100,000 by 1860, the 'German question' and the future German nation-state were described and debated.

Liberalism and Nation-Building

The public sphere before 1866 was shaped above all by liberalism. Opposition newspapers and periodicals, factions and parties, associations and national organisations were preponderantly liberal after the persecution and exile of radicals and democrats in 1849. In the beginning, noted the conservative commentator Friedrich Julius Stahl, 'liberal' had denoted everyone belonging to the 'party of movement', irrespective of faction.[52] Although different party creeds and groupings had emerged before the revolution, liberals had largely been followed by democrats and socialists until the present, Stahl asserted in 1862.[53] Many democrats had joined the Progressive Party in the previous year. The first workers' party, the *Allgemeiner Deutscher Arbeiterverein* (*ADAV*) was founded in Leipzig in May 1863 from a small minority of liberal-dominated *Arbeiterbildungsvereine*, but it only counted 4,600 members by the end of 1864. It was overshadowed by liberal–democratic workers' education associations, which formed the *Verband Deutscher Arbeitervereine* (*VDAV*) in response to the establishment of the *ADAV*. Because of restricted franchises, workers' parties remained insignificant in electoral terms until the imperial era. Political Catholicism was better represented, yet it lacked either a party organisation or programme before 1866: in the Prussian *Landtag* elections of that year, only 15 clerical deputies were elected from a Catholic population comprising about a third of the kingdom's population.[54] As a consequence, liberals remained dominant, controlling many of the 'March ministries' and the majority of the Frankfurt National Assembly in 1848, before being challenged briefly by radicals in the following year, dictating much of the content of the *Reichsverfassung* (1849), constituting the majority of the 'opposition' – albeit an initially small, undefined one – in most states in the 1850s, and making up the larger part of the national organisations – the *Nationalverein, Abgeordnetentag, Handelstag,* and *Fortschrittspartei* – of the 1860s.[55] The liberal 'party' during this period derived from a persisting set of demarcations and self-definitions, which often used other labels such as 'Gotha' and 'constitutional' interchangeably, and it was built on a series of well-established local milieux, which left liberals such as Otto Elben in Stuttgart in no doubt of their political affiliation or background, having spent their youth – in Elben's case – under the 'star of liberalism' with a father who was 'a dyed-in-the-wool liberal'.[56] The party was also based on a shared political programme and doctrine.

Liberalism as a creed in mid-nineteenth-century Germany was a collection of ideas from varied sources. Although it had been distinguished before 1848 – and routinely after that date – from 'democracy' in particular, it remained flexible enough to serve as a rallying-point for opposition to existing German states and support for a new nation-state.[57] The premise of attaining individual freedoms and removing unnecessary constraints on such liberties remained attractive during and after the reaction, with Catholics, democrats and socialists agreeing with the basic rights of free association, assembly, expression and conscience which had occupied such a prominent place in the revolution and the Reich constitution, and which was taken up explicitly by the *Nationalverein* when it officially adopted the *Reichsverfassung* in the 1860s.[58] Until the late 1860s, at the earliest, secularism and anti-Catholicism played a relatively minor role in liberal and national politics, aided by the existence of powerful 'Catholic' states (Austria and Bavaria), a largely secular state tradition, the weak ties of the Protestant and Catholic churches beyond the borders of the states, and the absence of a Catholic party. Notwithstanding resentment at the frequent charge of 'ultramontanism' and occasional attacks on liberal 'absolutism', 'intolerant, ruthless centralisation' and the deification of the state, in the words of Wilhelm Emmanuel von Ketteler, Catholics proved capable of cooperating with liberals in elections and on questions such as disestablishment and the separation of church and state.[59] Similarly, doctrinaire economic liberalism, even if more salient in the 1850s than the 1840s, continued to be overlooked by most contemporaries, for whom the gradual extension of freer trade within the *Zollverein* was a point of agreement rather than division.[60] Almost by default, the principal liberal questions still concerned the state, in defence of individuals' rights against state interference and coercion, in the championing of state-led reform, especially in the field of social policy, or in the actual restructuring of the state and the creation of a nation-state. The apparent ubiquity of reactionary governments in Germany during the 1850s made continued support for basic rights comparatively uncontroversial. Likewise, the need to address the 'social question' was barely questioned by liberals or, indeed, others – even conservatives such as Hermann Wagener and Victor Aimé Huber – since the problem appeared unavoidable before and after 1848, although there was no agreement about how to solve it.[61] The restructuring of the state was more divisive, with many radicals harbouring a desire for a republic and many liberals fearing the consequences of universal suffrage. Nonetheless, a majority on both sides came to accept the necessity of a 'federal' and 'constitutional' – rather than 'parliamentary' – monarchy, at least temporarily, and of manhood suffrage, underpinned by a common belief in popular sovereignty.[62] The influence of the 'historical school' of law and a distancing of German liberals from the 'French' model had prepared the ground for such moderate 'constitutionalism' in the 1830s and 40s.[63] Yet they did not prevent liberals openly countenancing 'revolution' and seeking to construct a nation-state from scratch, even if legitimately or legally, in and after 1848.

To the Saxon historian Heinrich von Treitschke, who was rare amongst scholars-cum-publicists in not having experienced 1848 as an adult, the attempt to create a constitutional *Bundesstaat* within the Confederation was 'simply a revolutionary step'.[64] In 1848–49, few, if any, liberals had balked at this revolutionary course of action. Although some subsequently altered their position, most upheld the rectitude of the Frankfurt Parliament's 'national revolution'. Many were fearful of what the young deputy Rudolf Haym described as 'the descent into the terrorism of the masses and the ruin of any reasonable development of the state', but they usually believed, like Haym, that 'reasonable development' was possible.[65] The academic lawyer Georg Beseler, travelling to Frankfurt from Greifswald, where his 'circle' had taken 'a most lively interest in public affairs', was aware that 'order, public tranquillity, even personal security and property were in danger in many places, especially in the South West, where the parliament had its seat', yet he was also confident that the assembly 'in its majority was ready to back not only freedom, but also order and law', as 'it became the focal point for the consolidation of the profoundly shaken legal conditions of Germany'.[66] The majority of deputies maintained that the transfer of power from the German Confederation to the National Assembly was a legal one, with the *Bundesversammlung* in Beseler's account simply 'dissolving itself, after it had passed all its powers to the *Reichsverweser*', who had just been appointed by the parliament to head a provisional executive.[67] 'Everyone saw that the *Bundestag* no longer worked', he went on, arguing that the King of Prussia himself 'wanted to escape from [its] misery'.[68] In Saxony, another academic deputy, Karl Biedermann, likewise justified his actions in part by revealing the complicity of his government, which the Confederation supposedly served, in setting up 'a *Bundesstaat* with a head of state' and in accepting the 'necessity of "a limitation of the independence of the individual members of the (future) federal state for the benefit of unity"', which was 'completely in the spirit of the words spoken to me by His Majesty'.[69] Excitedly taking the stagecoach with Friedrich Christoph Dahlmann to Frankfurt along with a crowd of other deputies, a 24-hour journey from Saxony since the railway line terminated at Eisenach, Biedermann was expectant, not anxious.[70] Throughout the revolution, he and most of his counterparts felt that they were in control of events and that they could maintain law and order.

Legality in the conditions of 1848–49 meant due process. It was not perceived to preclude a change in the ultimate grounds of the legal order, not least because the dynastic, confederal and, often, absolutist basis of the old order was held to be illegitimate. The new constitutional regime was justified in part because it replaced arbitrariness with the reasonable, predictable precepts of the law. More importantly, it was founded on the sovereignty of the nation, with citizens deserving a clear, codified statement of constitutional principles and individual freedoms and duties. As Haym explained to his voters on 1 May 1848, proud of his 'great and pure love of the fatherland, an unshakeable confidence in the creation of a Germany powerful in its freedom and unity, and trust in the eternal idea of right and truth', the transformation which was taking place was a national one:

> I am of the opinion that one cannot bind the spirit of nations and achieve the happiness of states through the rigid orders of an artificial system of government, but that the particular form and nature of each individual nation deserves sensible and caring

attention. It is a question now, at the time of the great divisions of the peoples, of imbuing forms of government created and consolidated over centuries with a newly-awoken national feeling and of consciously doing justice to the instinct of the *Völker* about what they need.[71]

Although the 'constitution of Germany could only be that of its individual states', 'the constitutional system with all its consequences is to be transferred from the parts to the whole', with 'the life of the individual parts' rooted 'in the greater body of the constitution'.[72] The 'conflict of the dynasties' would dissolve 'in the unanimity of the tribes' and the Bund could be abolished almost as an afterthought, as Haym put it to the Prussian Finance Minister David Hansemann in June.[73] The notion that the constitution needed to be agreed by treaty with the princes, which was put forward by Georg von Vincke and – on 'the extreme right' – by Heinrich von Arnim-Boitzenburg, was 'a highly unfortunate and fully discredited position'.[74] What counted was the approval or disapproval of the *Volk*.[75] In this sense, a moderate liberal such as Haym was ready to swear allegiance to 'the revolution', even if it required 'nerves of a kind which I don't have'.[76] His allegiance went back to the very start of the revolution, as he had celebrated the fall of Metternich, 'the last bulwark of reaction in Germany', and had welcomed the Austrian statesman's opponents as 'the liberators of the fatherland': 'a single, general, German development of our history has become possible, and I no longer hold anything, not even a German parliament in a popular sense, to be impossible.'[77] Most of the Greifswald lawyer's liberal colleagues concurred.[78] Within the limits of a novel constitutional order, which would guarantee legal process and outlaw violence, liberals were 'revolutionary nationalists', willing to create a new system of government on the dual foundation of freedom and unity, if necessary against the wishes of the representatives – individual governments or the *Bundestag* – of an illegitimate old regime. Despite the fact, as conservative critics later pointed out, that there was no natural affinity between liberalism and nationalism, the German revolution had helped to create an enduring historical one. The emancipatory political components of such revolutionary or liberal nationalism proved resilient.[79]

In the nineteenth century, nation-building constituted an important part of politics. National movements in Poland, Ireland, Hungary, Italy and Germany and the national independence of

Greece (1821) and Belgium (1830) had helped to legitimise the nation-state. By 1848, it seemed obvious to the majority of German commentators that a national culture and political structure should coincide. 'Up until a few decades ago, the common inherited particularity (*Stammeseigenthümlichkeit*) of a population was only viewed by statecraft in a very secondary way', wrote the Badenese academic and diplomat Robert von Mohl in 1860: 'One was almost proud to be able to show a great exemplary map of nationalities.'[80] This had 'altered radically,' he went on:

> Conditions and demands based on nationality have taken up one of the most important places in practical policy. Acquisitions and partitions of lands, which in part have existed for centuries, are now fought over because they do not correspond to the borders of nationalities. The formation of individual states is demanded solely on the basis of the descent of their populations, even at the expense of secession from – and the destruction of – a great whole, or through the merger of hitherto divided fragments.[81]

By the mid-nineteenth century, argued the former deputy of the Frankfurt Parliament, nothing could stand in the way of 'claims resting on the observance of the particularity of the *Volk*'.[82] The elements making up nationality were barely contested: to Mohl, these were the 'facts' of 'race' and 'tribe', 'climate, the fertility of the soil and its products, historical events too, religion, important personalities', 'a bodily and mental individuality, which manifests itself externally in physique, mentally above all in language, but also in manners and morals, which ultimately rest on innate and constant natural attributes, but which are then determined more closely by historical events and are cultivated in the individual'.[83] For most of human history, states – or 'inclusion in a certain state organism' – had not been 'a significant feature' of nationality, but as the state ceased to be 'an end in itself' and began to exist 'only to further the purposes of the *Volk*', it was forced to take nationality into account.[84] To liberals such as Mohl, nations did not coincide with the old borders of dynastic states and they had rightly complicated, in a more representative era, state-building and politics.

The converse was also true, however. After 1848, the most important feature of a nationality, even a democratic proponent of federalism such as Julius Fröbel conceded, was its will and ability to form a state. 'A nationality, according to the linguistic usage of the revolutionary law of states and *Völker* of our days, is a group of people which grounds a claim, on the basis of its historical character, to form a state for itself', wrote the former forty-eighter in 1864.[85] The most powerful national groups deserved to create their own states, with 'the right of a group of people to build a state' resting 'on the power to do so'.[86] Although, in contrast to most of his contemporaries, the former revolutionary was prepared to question the role of race, culture and language in the definition of nations, he still believed in the existence and significance of the principle of nationality, emphasising territory and history, as well as descent and character. Nevertheless, many aspiring nations did not become states, and those which had succeeded had been obliged to conform to – and had been affected by – the existing configuration of states:

> Do you want to split from us and found a state for yourselves?' existing powers typically asked of national movements: 'Very well, try it. We shall seek to prevent it with all the means at our disposal!' – Or: 'Do you desire violently to unite us with yourselves and your state? Come and try it! We shall defend ourselves![87]

The ineluctable relationship in the revolutionary era between statehood and nationality, power and culture, had led to a confusion of terms, so that *Nationalität* meant 'something other than race, something other than *Volk*, something other than *Nation*'.[88] 'What does nation mean?' asked the liberal politician and academic Johann Caspar Bluntschli on the eve of the Franco-German war in 1870.[89] The English and French very often understood 'nation' to mean what 'we understand by *Volk* (*populus*), i.e. the political totality of citizens', and they used '*peuple*' or 'people' to denote 'what we mean, according to the origin of the word, by *Nation*, i.e. the natural racial community (*Rassegemeinschaft*), separate from the state'.[90] Yet the terms were rarely so unambiguous, not least because the entity itself was amorphous: 'It is not easy to agree about the concept of the nation (*Nation*), since usage varies, and the expressions *Nation* and *Volk* are sometimes held to be, and valued as, the same thing, and are sometimes used in a different sense.'[91] Subjects of the German states were both citizens and nationals. A future German nation-state would be both an expression of a national character and a political structure, designed to represent a national will and safeguard national interests, and fashioned from existing relations of power. It was this combination of national and political objectives, threatening respectively to sweep away individual dynastic states and to pull down traditional institutions, which proved so explosive in Germany during the revolution, as contemporary onlookers realised. 'In 1848 the Germans prepared a surprise for the world, in that they wanted to become a nation (*Volk*) again, and not only in the ethnographic sense of a species of people (*Menschenart*) bound by language and descent, not only in the literary field, as they had been to an eminent degree for a hundred years, but in the political sense,' wrote Baumgarten in 1870: 'They wanted to have a state again, to be a power again, to bring their national interests emphatically to bear in the world, as their neighbours, organised in states, had done for a long time.'[92] The revolution in Germany was not merely an attempt to establish a new system of government or to install different political elites, it was the establishment, which remained incomplete, of a national polity, with novel borders and an uncertain relationship with existing German states and neighbouring powers.

To some contemporaries, it seemed that unresolved national questions – the inclusion or exclusion of Poles in Posen and Danes in Schleswig, competition between advocates of *Kleindeutschland* and *Grossdeutschland*, conflicts with hostile powers – posed the greatest menace to the Central Power and National Assembly in Frankfurt. Others, including Baumgarten, believed that political disagreements proved most decisive, with Germans finding, despite 'unanimous' support for unification, that 'the attempt to establish their national unity led to the most sensitive division': 'All desired the same end of German power and greatness, but the ways to it ran hopelessly apart.'[93] This study explores the insight of Baumgarten and other forty-eighters, treating German unification primarily as an interconnecting series of political problems which first manifested themselves to a wider public in 1848. Nationalism here was principally a form of politics, with 'voluntary' considerations giving substance to the process of unification and causing the greatest difficulty for contemporaries.[94] As a political movement, it relied on an extensive public sphere and emerging party milieux, as well as on parliamentary assemblies, the existence of well-defined bureaucracies, and co-ordinated reactions to state intervention.[95] The ways in which the nation was conceived of – its putatively 'organic' nature – changed far less during and after the revolution and had correspondingly little impact on the content of unification in 1848–49 and after 1866.[96] The 'facts' of a common descent and national character were widely accepted, and they constituted a precondition of unification, explaining why large numbers of liberals, democrats and others looked to a nation-state rather than to a supranational *Mitteleuropa*, a confederation or to their own individual states or localities as the main locus of political reform. National sentiment was a significant source of motivation and mobilisation, helping to create revolutionary zeal and self-sacrifice, but it was open political questions which proved most troublesome and time-consuming in and after 1848–49 and which played the largest part in determining the precise nature of the nation-state. What form should a national polity take – a republic or a monarchy, federal or unitary, with a universally and directly elected National Assembly or not? How centralised should a nation-state's executive and bureaucracy be, and what type of army should it have? How should it define and treat German citizens, national minorities and foreigners? How extensive should the territory of the nation-state be, and was such a territorial nation-state militarily and diplomatically defensible within the states' system?

Plan of the Book

Revolutionaries had arrived at answers to these questions with the passing of the Reich constitution and the offering of the title of 'Kaiser of the Germans' to the King of Prussia on 28 March 1849. The study begins with the debates and actions of such revolutionaries, leading to the production of a blueprint of a German nation-state which remained influential in liberal and democratic circles during the following decades and which was incorporated into the programme of the *Nationalverein* in the 1860s. It ends in 1866 with the definitive expulsion of Austria from Germany, the dissolution of the German Confederation for the second time, after it had been replaced by the revolutionary *Reich* in 1848–49, and Bismarck's drafting of the constitution of the North German Confederation, which contained important elements of the *Reichsverfassung* and which became the basis of the constitution of the *Kaiserreich* in 1871. My intention is to re-evaluate the national legacy of the revolution, treating it as a first unification of Germany, and to investigate its effect on the politics of the 'missing' decade and a half between the end of the revolution and the 'wars of unification', examining the articulation of intertwined party programmes and national ideas prior to the second unification of Germany after the Austro-Prussian war.[97]

The study investigates the impact of nationalism and politics on each other in order to answer the question – which is still open – of when, how and why the process of unification began in Germany. It looks, in Chapter 2, at the diplomatic conditions in which decisions about unification were made. It asks how the German question was viewed by the governments of the Great Powers, including those of the Habsburg monarchy, which – backed by majority opinion – usually kept 'Austria' separate from 'Germany', even if they continued to pursue putatively vital interests in the German lands. Conversely, how were international conditions and constraints, including those imposed by Vienna, understood by German observers? Chapter 3 examines party and press depictions of the Habsburg monarchy in light of such Austrian detachment and self-exclusion from most plans for German unification. It was widely assumed that the governments of the individual states were prepared to support Vienna out of self-interest, but what did their compatriot politicians and journalists make of Austria and its role in German politics? Chapter 4 assesses the stance of the governments and publics of the third Germany in more detail, as well as investigating external opinions and judgements of the position and role of the *Mittelstaaten*. It analyses the limits of the 'reaction' in the 1850s, especially in the smaller and middling states, and of attempts to reform the Confederation in the 1850s and 1860s. Chapter 5 enquires how Prussia was perceived during the New Era and the years of constitutional crisis after 1862, focusing on the relationship between the Prussian government and liberals. Finally, Chapter 6 determines how far opinion of Prussia shifted as a result of the diplomatic and military conflict in Schleswig-Holstein between 1863 and 1866, which served as a dress-rehearsal for the military unification of Germany in and after 1866, not least because it came to hinge on Berlin's relations with Vienna and the Bund.

By assessing the national ideas and actions of those in dominant liberal milieux, in conjunction with those of other parties, it is intended, first, to question the existence of a broad shift from liberal to conservative nationalism; second, to challenge the notion that cultural and ethnic forms of nationalism were particularly pronounced in Germany as a result of late unification; and, third, to qualify the idea of a 'revolution from above' and the supposed neglect and manipulation of weak political parties, a muzzled or intimidated press, and a fragmented and immature electorate, all of which have been connected to a traditional concentration and undue emphasis on Bismarck.[98] Arguably, the Prussian Minister-President was constrained by parties and a public sphere produced or consolidated by the German revolution, which had obliged newly formed political elites hastily to design both a new polity and a German nation-state. The first chapter investigates how revolutionaries reconciled these two – often clashing – imperatives.

1 A German Revolution

Revolution in 1848–49 revealed on a new scale and in an incontrovertible fashion what had already become familiar to narrow circles of political notables, publicists and academics before 1848; that the advent of 'politics', in the form of party, press and public debate about government and state affairs, was closely tied to the articulation of national aspirations and the founding of national contacts and associations. It is impossible to separate nationalism in Germany during the first half of the nineteenth century and the formation of parties, the consolidation of a public sphere, and the emergence of distinct political milieux. In virtually all the German states, liberalism – in a variety of guises – was central to such political milieux.

Most liberal – and many democratic – leaders accepted the primacy of the national question. 'The first and, at the same time, the most comprehensive thing that the German nation (*Volk*) desires is unity,' declared the *National-Zeitung* at the end of April 1849, after the revolution was said to have 'failed'.[1] All other reforms, including the constitution of the Reich, which had been promulgated on 28 March, rested on national foundations. Indeed, much of the Frankfurt Parliament's legislation was inseparable from the idea of national unity, since it served to constitute a German nation-state and to cement the principle of popular participation in government. 'In order to found a constitutional government in Germany, unity must come from the popular will and be grounded in a constitutional way, as decided by the representatives of the nation,' continued the same article:

That is what the German people wants from the constitution decided by its representatives: the demand for unity in the service of freedom, material and social well-being; the insight that unity cannot be created by princes, but only by the people itself; the conviction that the constitution does justice to the political demands of the nation (*Nation*); and an awareness that honour, freedom and peace demand that the constitution should be respected and brought into effect.[2]

A year earlier, on its first day of publication, the same publication, which had quickly become one of the major liberal newspapers in Germany, had declared 'what we want', which consisted above all in the consolidation and elaboration of a German state, since 'The German too has at last become, what man is by nature, a state-being (*Staatswesen*); he has entered onto the highest field of human endeavour, politics, with self-conscious freedom.'[3] Championing 'progress from a national point of view', the paper concluded that Germany was 'most deeply gripped' by the national revolution because it had, in this respect, been 'left behind for longest'.[4] Germans had long had a 'feeling of unity', a 'feeling of Germanness', but without power and a political superstructure such unity had collapsed and decayed.[5] The new polity, recorded the *Kölnische Zeitung* in May 1848, had rightly been based on the principle of nationality, which was dearer to Germans now because it had been ignored in the past, internally and externally.[6]

From the standpoint of the political leaders who emerged in 1848, the path to German unity appeared natural, from a meeting on 5 March in Heidelberg of 51 deputies from the chambers of the South West, via the 'Committee of Seven' appointed in Heidelberg to invite deputies to a 'Vorparlament' in Frankfurt on 30 March, to the 'Committee of Seventeen' and the 'Committee of Fifty' which helped to organise the May elections of the National Assembly. Thus, the fact that the 51 deputies were not even representative of their own *Landtage*, not to mention those of Germany as a whole, was justified by those involved as an inescapably temporary means to a defensible national end. The 51 deputies, 'unanimous in the struggle for the freedom, unity, independence and honour of the German nation', resolved that 'the establishment and defence of these most valuable goods must be striven for in conjunction with all the German tribes (*Volksstämme*) and with their governments – so long as salvation (*Rettung*) is still possible in this way.'[7] The Committee of

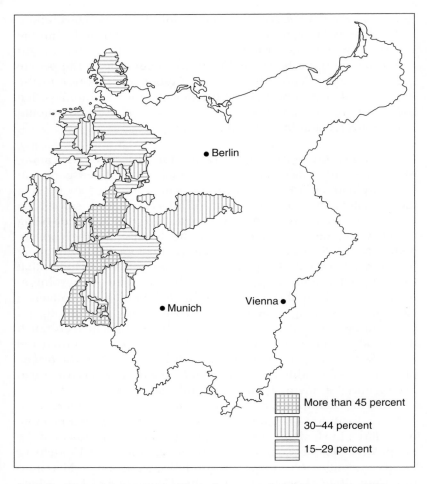

Map 1   Participation in the Vorparlament and the Committee of Fifty in 1848–49.
Source: Adapted from *H. Best,* Die Männer von Bildung und Besitz *(Düsseldorf, 1990), 250*

Seven, made up of constitutionally minded notables, was then entrusted to establish 'a more complete assembly of trusted men from all the German peoples'.[8] Although the Vorparlament which it convened from Germany's *Landtage* – by means of newspaper announcements – contained only 2 deputies from Austria, 141 from

Prussia, 44 from Bavaria, 26 from Saxony and 9 from Hanover, compared to 84 from Hesse-Darmstadt, 72 from Baden and 52 from Wurttemberg, out of a total of 574, it was hailed, even by the Prussian envoy to the Bundestag August Graf von Dönhoff, as an 'actual national parliament'.[9] The regional and other biases of the early institutions of the first all-German political movement were overlooked in the name of a greater national good to be realised in the imminent future. The National Assembly in Frankfurt, which went on to establish a Central Power on its own authority, was seen as the legitimate 'German' outcome of necessarily imperfect national antecedents.

It would be wrong, of course, to imply that the only concern of revolutionaries was to establish a German nation-state, even though unification was a priority of most liberals and many democrats. The February revolution in France had triggered a series of uprisings in South West Germany, spreading unevenly but rapidly to many other German lands and aiming to replace perceived injustices of the old, existing order. Popular grievances, which sustained the insurrections, differed from state to state in accordance with diverse conditions, but they usually included economic deprivation, a desire to abolish seigneurial dues and privileges, resentment of taxes, criticism of officialdom, an expectation of legality and equality before the law, a call for political rights of free assembly, association, speech and conscience, and the demand for a representative government and assembly. Some cultural questions such as the separation of church and state, as well as economic questions such as the reform of the guilds and corporations, proved more divisive, yet there were many basic 'liberties' which were widely supported in 1848 and which revolutionaries worked to achieve on both a local and a national level. Many contemporaries were aware solely of their locality, guided by notables – as in the first round of the joint elections to the Berlin and Frankfurt National Assemblies in one village in Westphalia – to 'elect thoughtful men who would conscientiously vote for the most worthy candidates'.[10] The vitality and independence of state legislatures, the adoption of long-standing matters of contention in towns and villages, the adaptation of rituals like 'cat music' – in which youths had policed sexual and other moral codes – to new political ends, and a general shift in the second wave of the revolution from cities to the countryside – in Baden, Württemberg, the Bavarian Palatinate, the Rhineland and Saxony – all underlined the continuing importance of localities.[11]

Most revolutionaries would probably have been content with the granting of 'liberties' without the creation of a German nation-state. In the event, however, they did not have to choose between the two, for the counter-revolution, which had achieved its first successes with Prince Alfred zu Windischgrätz's suppression of unrest in Prague in June 1848, was enforced by Austria and, especially, by Prussia in the individual states at the same time as in Frankfurt and Stuttgart, to which the 'rump' National Assembly had fled in June 1849. In the context of this general clampdown on revolutionary freedoms, many forty-eighters continued to believe that the state and the nation, politics and culture, citizenship, individual rights and nationality could and – if only for the defence of the revolution – should be combined. They were nevertheless left facing a shifting array of reactionary forces, with which they were obliged to compromise. Austrian troops began to recapture northern Italy after defeating Piedmont at Custozza in July 1848, they put down the uprising in Vienna in late October, and they suppressed the Polish insurrection in Galicia in November, ushering in the counter-revolutionary ministry of Felix zu Schwarzenberg on 21 November and forcing the abdication of the mentally retarded Emperor Ferdinand in favour of an eighteen-year-old Franz Joseph, who was more amenable and predictable, on 2 December. For its part, Prussia had withdrawn from the 'national' war against Denmark through the armistice of Malmö in August 1848, without consulting the Provisional Central Power in Frankfurt although with the backing of liberal ministers such as David Hansemann; it had quashed the attempt of radicals to overthrow the Frankfurt National Assembly in September, albeit at the request of the Central Power; and it had witnessed the installation of the reactionary ministry of Friedrich Wilhelm Graf von Brandenburg on 2 November, with counter-revolutionaries making use of the King of Prussia's power of appointment. A more conservative constitution was subsequently imposed on 5 December.

By this time, it was already clear to national-minded liberals in Frankfurt and the state capitals that the counter-revolution was gaining strength, threatening the achievements of 1848. How far did they alter their policies to take account of such changing realities? To a degree, the willingness of revolutionaries to include at least the German-speaking parts of the Habsburg monarchy previously belonging to the Bund in a new German Reich – or to exclude them from it – was influenced, respectively, by the prospect of the monarchy's collapse in early and mid-1848 and by the spectre of a successful counter-revolution from late 1848 onwards. Yet it is worth noting that such contingent arguments do not in themselves explain deputies' shifting conceptions of 'Germany' and 'Austria': the Frankfurt Parliament's Constitutional Committee drafted Articles 2 and 3, which would have severed Austria's 'German' lands administratively, legally and even militarily from the rest of the monarchy in a fashion known to be unacceptable to Habsburg political elites, in October 1848, before Schwarzenberg came to power or the radical Frankfurt deputy Robert Blum was executed in early November. The Habsburg monarchy's exclusion from a German nation-state would not have been accepted so quickly if it had not seemed to make sense in other than power–political terms. Certainly, many proponents of Prussia had not altered their stance as a result of the onset of reaction there from November onwards, and a large number of deputies – initially a majority – had continued to support the Reich constitution, even after it had effectively been rejected by Prussia's reactionary elites in April 1849, when Friedrich Wilhelm IV had turned down Frankfurt's offer of becoming 'Kaiser of the Germans'. Despite the increasing strength of the 'reaction', liberals remained remarkably confident and their political deliberations surprisingly constant during 1848–49. Given the growth of democratic constituencies and organisations, however, to what extent can it be said that they were still in control of the 'revolution' itself? The next section examines this question.

A Political Nation

For German liberals, who were also known as 'constitutionalists', political freedom and national unity were natural bedfellows in early 1848. Indeed, some, such as the historian and newspaper editor Georg Gottfried Gervinus, specifically emphasised their constitutionalism – rather than the less-inhibited liberty implied by 'liberalism' – in order to make their creed fully compatible with the rational and emotional limitation and self-sacrifice required by a *Rechtsstaat* (law-governed state) and a nation-state.[12] In a memorandum written over Christmas 1848, the historian Johann Gustav Droysen, who had served on the Committee of Seventeen and remained one of the principal liberal publicists of the revolution, looked back to the spring and summer: 'We began with the idea of national unity.'[13] Although the fatherland was 'creaking and shaking' by May, he assured his readers that they should not fear, for only 'the old forms are breaking up', and not at the hands of foreigners, but by 'the enormous force of the increasingly heartened German people': 'From the truth of our German being, from the "primordial spirit" of the united German people, from the sovereignty of the nation, our new Germany is rebuilding itself.'[14] As nationality conflicts began to surface during the course of the year, 'the principle of democratic freedom seemed to be able to become all the more unifying'.[15] Soon, it became obvious, Droysen continued, that freedom could take on 'wild forms', frightening and disgusting even those who had been 'mad about it'.[16] In truth, many liberals had always harboured reservations about excessive liberties leading to anarchy and extremism. Far fewer had worried about the possible dangers of the national idea, which had seemed, in the historian's words, 'so great, simple and convincing', despite later being unable to conceal its weaknesses.[17] Virtually no one in liberal circles, however, had believed that national unity and freedom, properly conceived, stood in tension with one other. The cautious aims formulated by the Württemberg publicist and liberal deputy Paul Pfizer in his article on 'liberalism' in Rotteck and Welcker's *Staatslexikon* – equality before the law, constitutional government, political representation, extended but limited franchises, education and property at the expense of the old corporations, emancipation and progress – all appeared to be reinforced by the nation-state.[18] Nationhood, it seemed to liberals like Droysen, had redeemed freedom and safeguarded politics:

> Of course, it was revolution that raged from palace to palace in the month of March and that stirred up the otherwise dumb and dull masses. But the magic word of German unity drowned out the wildest roar; where it rang out there was an immediate … joyful confidence, a good conscience resulting from a just desire. In this spirit of unity the constitution-granting Reichstag convened; and its first sign was that it put the most German man [Heinrich von Gagern], the proved statesman of the unity of the fatherland, at its head.[19]

In the opinion of prominent liberals, democrats often favoured liberty at the expense of the nation. 'For at least a year, the liberals of Germany, the liberals of education and national sentiment

(*Vaterlandsliebe*), had been not only internally but also externally split from the radicals, for whom ... an abstract concept – democracy, republic or whatever else – was the main thing,' wrote Heinrich Laube in his history of the 'first German parliament' in 1849.[20] Yet democrats themselves were much less willing to forfeit the national idea than their critics claimed, even if the *Neue Rheinische Zeitung* – the largest radical paper, with a circulation of 6,000 – and a minority of literary and philosophical revolutionaries or workers' representatives – including a more or less indifferent Karl Marx – were more stridently international in outlook.[21] Recalling the early days of the revolution, Hermann Schulze-Delitzsch pleaded for a return to unambiguous national feeling in a National Assembly speech in July 1848: 'In this respect, the call for German unity was the first and leading idea, the password (*Losungswort*), as the great movement of peoples came to us. The movement will only be complete when it returns to this, its starting point.'[22] Not only were unity and freedom linked rhetorically, with deputies such as Johann Jacoby declaring in 1848 that 'Germany should from now on be a free and united Reich', but they were also connected historically, since weak and divided German states, under a system of external relations and internal repression characterised by the Treaty of Westphalia (1648) and the Congress of Vienna (1815), seemed to have been unable to foster and defend constitutional liberties.[23] 'Germany's fragmentation piled shame and poverty on us for centuries', wrote Jacoby: 'Only unity can bring us salvation.'[24] The whole generation which had grown up with the Vienna Congress saw in the name 'German Confederation', and the divided territories and states of which it was made up, 'the by-word for all political baseness and wretchedness', remembered Ludwig Bamberger.[25]

The unassailable power of national unity would protect liberty. Although there were manifest dangers in pairing unity and freedom, which radical critics like the Hegelian Arnold Ruge continued to point out, there seemed for most democrats to be little alternative. Ruge had stated in his study of *Der Patriotismus* in 1847 that 'Freedom is not national', for nationality itself merely implied particularity, yet he continued to combine the two concepts throughout 1848, believing that the former would remove the feelings of superiority and mysticism commonly attached to the latter.[26] For this reason, he went on supporting Prussia as the guarantor of the revolution: 'Prussia will be free of Russia if it wins Germany; and the Prussian government necessarily remains democratic – to remain powerful.'[27] There

seemed to be a dialectical logic to events in Germany in 1848, resulting from the insight that states required popular participation in
order to be powerful and that participation and rights could only be
safeguarded by a strong state. It was widely assumed by democrats
that the 'unity of peoples' was possible and that, in Robert Blum's
words, all peoples would live 'with one another'.[28]

Before the revolution, the boundary between nationalists, liberals
and democrats such as Blum was blurred, with a single and indistinct
'opposition' – or 'representatives of a brave German people', in
Welcker's words – characterising politics in most German states.[29]
Blum himself had been active in the Leipzig Schiller Association in
the 1830s, had founded the 'constitutional' journal *Der
Verfassungsfreund* in 1840, and had worked for the *Sächsische
Vaterlandsblätter* during the 1840s.[30] In 1846, he was one of the 'politically effective men from different German states' who made the
pilgrimage to Baden in order to meet national-minded liberals such
as Johann Adam von Itzstein.[31] Although distinguishing themselves
to an extent semantically and ideologically by the 1840s, democrats
or radicals remained close to liberal organisations and milieux.[32] To
the *Staatswissenschaftler* and prominent liberal Robert von Mohl, 'the
poorest', along with their political representatives, 'had to rely on the
German liberal party' until 1848, even if they subsequently turned
against it during the revolution itself.[33] According to Mohl in 1855,
examining liberal mistakes during and after the revolution, democrats and radicals had only managed to detach themselves in 1848–49,
renaming themselves '*die Volkspartei*'. Until then, they had still had to
cope with the enduring influence of the dichotomy between 'liberal'
and 'servile' parties first established in the 1820s.[34] 'Who would not
have been "liberal", who would have wanted it to be said or even to
have wanted to admit to oneself that one was servile?' Mohl asked
rhetorically.[35] Before 1848, liberals were generally confident that
they were representatives of the German nation, not a sectional
'opposition' in the English sense of the word.[36] If the ancient historian and later Progressive Theodor Mommsen were to be believed,
the main political shift in the pre-revolutionary period was from
'abstract' to 'concrete' liberalism, as self-ordained representatives of
the people began to organise informal networks and associations, to
contribute to a German public sphere, and to formulate and influence policy.[37] Despite often owing their reputation to their position
as notables – or publicists – in their own city or state, their aims – and
their organisations – usually included a significant national element.

Table 1.1 Breakdown of the Frankfurt National Assembly by profession

Senior civil servants, *Landräte*	115	
Middle-ranking civil servants	37	
Mayors, local government officers	21	
Judges, public prosecutors	110	
Officers	18	
Diplomats	11	
University teachers (49), *Gymnasium* teachers	94	
Other teachers	30	
Total civil servants		**436**
Lawyers, advocates	106	
Doctors	23	
Writers and journalists	20	
Total freelance professions		**149**
Large merchants, merchants	35	
Manufacturers	14	
Publishers and booksellers	7	
Total commercial middle class		**56**
Large landowners, farmers (3)		**46**
Craftsmen		**4**
Members with a doctorate, no profession given		**35**
Other professions		**3**
No details known		**44**
Total		**812**

Source: Siemann, *The German Revolution of 1848–49,* (London, 1998), 122.

Together, national-minded democrats and liberals constituted the principal representatives of a rapidly expanding political public in 1848–49. Over 75 per cent of adult male Germans were allowed to vote in the elections to the Frankfurt National Assembly in April 1848, with a turnout of between 40 (Saxony and Holstein) and 75 per cent (Württemberg).[38] They voted overwhelmingly – as can be seen in Table 1.1 – for educated, middle-class notables with national aspirations. Of the 812 deputies who were elected to the National Assembly in Frankfurt between May 1848 and June 1849, at least 718 were civil servants (436), lawyers (106), clergymen (39), doctors

(23), writers and journalists (20) and merchants (35). Details of
another 44 are not known. The figures for the Prussian National
Assembly, with 74.7 per cent of deputies belonging to middle-class
professions, and the Prussian second chamber, with 81.3 per cent,
are similar, as are those for other German *Landtage* such as those of
Baden, with 71.8 per cent, and Bavaria, with 58.8 per cent.[39] Given
the inchoate nature of political parties in 1848–49, it is difficult to
determine the political views of such deputies with certainty. One of
the best estimates for the Frankfurt Parliament, based on the hotels
and taverns where deputies met, assigns 6 per cent of seats to the
right (Café Milani), 34 per cent to the centre right (Casino,
Landsberg, Augsburger Hof), 13 per cent to the centre left
(Württemberger Hof, Westendhalle, Deutscher Hof), 15 per cent to
the left (Deutscher Hof, Donnersberg), and 32 per cent to no
faction (see Table 1.2).[40] Beyond the various assemblies, most of the
leaders of Germany's estimated 1 to 1.5 million members of associations in 1848–49 were bourgeois, with a larger number of under-
employed journalists, academics and students among the leadership
of democratic clubs.[41] According to a conservative calculation, 300
of Prussia's 700 political associations in October 1848 were consti-
tutionalist, 250 democratic, 50 conservative, 12 working-class and 6
Catholic.[42] Although relatively little is known in detail of the political opinions of such mass memberships, with up to 10 per cent of
men organised in associations and more than half voting in national
and state elections, the personal testimonies and speeches of their
leaders suggest that only a small minority actively opposed the idea
of a German nation-state. Most were strongly in favour.

   The national political elites which emerged in 1848 owed their
prominence to a number of overlapping milieux. First, the majority
had originated from the *Bürgertum* of the principal cities of
Germany, which still only constituted less than 5 per cent of the
population as a whole. They enjoyed both the respectability and
security of their localities and the broader, more exciting prospects
and benefits of a shared German culture. Second, many had been
to university, frequently studying outside their state, forming life-
long circles of friends from other cities, and involving themselves in
the national politics of the *Burschenschaften*. Third, they formed part
of the German public sphere, subscribing and contributing to a
small but critical array of newspapers and journals, through which
they could communicate with their counterparts in other German
lands and imagine themselves participating in broader national

Table 1.2 The factions of the Frankfurt National Assembly

Café Milani	Casino	Landsberg	Augsburger Hof	Württemberger Hof	Westend-hall	Deutscher Hof	Donners-berg	In no faction
6%	21%	6%	7%	6%	7%	8%	7%	32%
'Right'		'Centre Right'		'Centre Left'	'Centre Left'	'Left'	'Left'	
Conservative		constitutionalist-liberal		parliamentary-liberal		democratic		

Source: W. Siemann, The German Revolution of 1848–49 (Basingstoke, 1998), 124

causes. The circulation of publications like the *Kölnische Zeitung*, which was Germany's largest newspaper with 17,000 subscribers, and the newly founded *Deutsche Zeitung*, with up to 4,000 subscribers, hinted at how narrow the new political elites were. Their number and scope mushroomed – as is shown in Table 1.3 – during the revolutionary era, with Prussia counting 404 newspapers, *Intelligenzblätter* and *Volksblätter* in 1847 and 622 in 1849, and Austria 79 in 1847 and 215 in 1849. Fourth, notables were usually active in a wide range of associations, from local self-help organisations to national occupational, cultural, gymnastics, shooting and choral societies. The burgeoning of political associations after 1848, with the *Zentralmärzverein* boasting more than five hundred thousand members, was based on the practices and networks of these clubs. Fifth, the elites were founded on participation in – and reportage of – existing *Landtage*, particularly those of the South and West, where politicians and incipient parties debated policies and affected legislation. Thus, a figure such as Heinrich von Gagern was already 'well-known and popular' 'in the widest circles' for his legislative activity and ministerial programme in Darmstadt.[43] Likewise, assemblies such as that of Baden had already established a national reputation in the 1840s: 'many came as far as Karlsruhe in order to be present at the sessions of our chamber,' recorded the Badenese liberal Daniel Bassermann, 'which at that time was perceived and visited as the prototype of political activity and the university of practical state wisdom in the whole of Germany'.[44] Political elites were being formed whose outlook and ambitions were national.

Through the course of 1848 and 1849 the narrow and loosely connected milieux of an incipient German political culture were extended and transformed. This had a direct impact on the scope, content and impact of nationalism. Millions of politically active citizens, wrote the *Kölnische Zeitung* in April 1848, had been united within a new German nation-state.[45] The question was: what was the basis of the nation and how were its institutions to be invested with moral legitimacy?[46] 'Public life was a new thing for us', Elben remembered, 'now it was a question of reporting meetings and popular movements daily.'[47] Whereas 'until now, the old liberals, who formed the March Ministries, were almost alone decisive', he went on, they were quickly subsumed by a broader mass, the aims of which were generally unifying, but also more diverse and less predictable.[48] It was in such circumstances that the first parties began to crystallise, the programmes of which, to a significant but

Table 1.3   Numbers of newspapers, Intelligenzblätter and Volksblätter in
individual German states in 1847 and 1849

	1847	1849
Prussia	404	622
Austria	79	215
Saxony	153	183
Bavaria	110	127
Württemberg	60	67
Baden	63	55
Hesse-Darmstadt	22	34
Hanover	23	34
Hamburg	18	24
Frankfurt a. M.	10	17

Source: Siemann, The German Revolution of 1848–49, 113.

far from exclusive degree, rested on competing conceptions of a
German nation-state.[49] 'Parties', of course, had been identified in
the period before 1848, often by their critics, but laws of association
under the Congress system – most notably the Federal Decree of 5
July 1832 – had formally prevented their existence, prohibiting
membership and meetings of political organisations.

The replacement of these provisions during the revolution by
much more liberal legislation concerning the press, public meetings, associations and elections gave an unprecedented fillip to
party organisation, which was acknowledged across the political
spectrum.[50] Even Heinrich von Gagern, the President of the
Frankfurt National Assembly, came to realise that it was difficult, if
not impossible, to pass and implement policies without the backing
of a party: 'An isolated position is always a weak one; one can only
have or attain political influence at the head of a political party.'[51]
Similarly, Ernst Ludwig von Gerlach, the de facto leader of the
Prussian reactionaries, was forced to accept by mid-1848 that
conservatives would only be effective 'as a party (Parthey)': 'party
elections are alone practicable'.[52] Political associations were established which assumed the features of modern parties – a constitution, an elected committee, regular meetings for a fixed
membership, a political programme, a national umbrella organisation – but they did not coincide precisely with either the early
groupings in the Frankfurt National Assembly, named after their

meeting places, or the broader constellations of constitutionalists, democrats, conservatives and, to a more limited extent, Catholics and workers, which emerged later in 1848 and early in 1849. Such a patchwork of organisations – with some regional, such as the moderate liberal *Deutscher Verein* and the radical *Vaterlandsverein* in Saxony, and others national, such as the largely democratic *Zentralmärzverein* and the Catholic Pius Associations – extended and mobilised a German political public, with members of the *Mittelstand* and lower orders constituting up to 40 per cent of conservative and constitutional or liberal associations and more than 60 per cent of democratic and Catholic ones.[53] The patchwork failed to create clarity over important questions of policy, however. Inexperienced deputies formed parties from issue to issue, reported Biedermann, with many failed coalitions and false unions.[54] This was especially true of the national question. All parties were in favour of a united German fatherland, reported one deputy to the rump National Assembly in May 1849, but disagreed over the means to achieve it.[55]

Constituting Germany

The main disputes about the means of realising a German nation-state were political. Notoriously, the Central Power and the National Assembly in Frankfurt were preoccupied with the minutiae of the constitution, including its prefatory declaration of basic rights, but they were, in effect, debating the form which the new *Nationalstaat* – the term was used in 1848, though rarely – should take.[56] These debates, in turn, affected – and were affected by – the borders, territory, regional and confessional composition, national 'character' and international position of the German Reich envisaged and partially enacted by the Frankfurt authorities. Between March 1848 and April 1849, such authorities enjoyed national legitimacy, backed by a large majority of *Landtag* deputies and their electors, with the exception of the members of the Austrian Reichstag, which had been convened in July 1848 and was dissolved permanently in March 1849. Although their agreement was tentative, with many questions unanswered and most radicals still opposed, a majority of deputies eventually came to support the political and national principles and compromises embodied in the *Reichsverfassung* of 1849.

The constitutional and political solution of March 1849 was made easier – even, perhaps, rendered possible – by the legitimating force of national unity. The creation of a nation-state, it was widely believed, required the erection of a suitable political superstructure to suit a pre-existing national culture. A state was needed to harness the creativity, energy and power of the nation, permitting a more harmonious and productive coexistence at home and necessary protection from enemies abroad. Most contemporaries accepted that the 'German question' was a political one. Few were 'unpolitical', pitting the law, state or nation against the corrupting sectionalism of 'politics', as some Germans were wont to do in the years after unification.[57] The revolution itself, following a long period of liberal 'opposition', had ensured that the nation had become integral to politics, constituting a new source of legitimacy for the Frankfurt Parliament beyond the law, history or religion. To liberals, as the *National-Zeitung* spelled out in January 1849, 'the trust of the nation' legitimised the actions of the *Vorparlament* and the various committees which had led to the National Assembly in the first half of 1848, pushing the Bundestag and the princes to refashion the constitution of the Bund, which in turn ensured the legality of the transfer of power from the institutions of the German Confederation to the Frankfurt Parliament.[58] The movement of history towards unification seemed inevitable and natural. Since the February revolution, 'another feeling had dominated the German people which made itself felt as strongly as the urge for freedom,' the newspaper continued: 'The nation believed the time had come when they could make real an idea which had captivated the most noble minds since the wars of freedom of 1813–15, then was taken up by the academic youth and, fostered more and more, was carried forth into the most recent times. This idea was – the unity of Germany.'[59]

Many conservatives challenged such an interpretation, denouncing the Frankfurt Assembly for leaving the 'ground of given legal relations' and drawing 'a thick line through our history' by failing to reform the existing national structure of the German Confederation from within.[60] At the same time, however, they usually acknowledged the legitimising, if not pre-eminent, force of the nation, sometimes placed within a national understanding of recent history, as the *Kreuzzeitung* revealed in a retrospective article on 'The German Question and the Frankfurt Decisions' in March 1849: 'There is no question that Germany's peoples demanded unity ... The tributaries of German life had frozen over under Metternich's biting diplomatic cold.'[61] In another article in the

same newspaper, Stahl similarly opposed the inundations of the
revolution and the decision of the National Assembly to rely on
revolutionary methods, yet he, too, as he explained elsewhere,
believed that 'the idea of German unity is a true and exalted one',
before adding: 'we are not sorry about the German business, just
the revolutionary one'.[62] In his opinion,

> the Frankfurt Assembly was convened to bring the constitution of
> Germany into being through the governments and the nation
> (*Volk*), and that is obviously the task of a mediating activity ...
> True, the expression 'constituent assembly' appeared in later
> decisions of the Bund, but nothing follows from this alone ... the
> National Assembly in Frankfurt has up until now stuck to its
> claim, irrespective of the contradictions of prominent members,
> that it has the sovereign decision over the constitution . . . This
> principle of popular sovereignty, however, is not only an
> infringement of the legal ground, but an infringement of the
> deepest moral foundations of the states.[63]

The National Assembly, in Stahl's opinion, had a political role as the
representative of the nation, but had overstepped its legitimate and
legal function in the name of a one-sided principle of national
sovereignty. All the same, even to conservative sceptics, the nation
had become an important part of politics.

The public in Germany was 'more politically mature', remarked
the *Kölnische Zeitung* in May 1848, 'than is believed in certain
circles'.[64] Although parties remained in vestigial form, with another
'national' paper arguing that 'in the people itself no sharp delin-
eation of parties has occurred', deputies and journalists did reach
agreement on many questions.[65] First, the use of national rhetoric,
which was barely contested by 1848, tended to imply acceptance of
popular participation, however limited, in government. Even
conservatives such as Stahl, for all their dislike of 'revolution' as a
form of political rationalism going back to 1789, admitted that the
National Assembly had been legitimate before it went on to countenance illegal acts, most notably failing to consult the princes and to
resurrect the old machinery of the Bund in its drafting and enactment of the 1849 Reich constitution. Stahl's work on *Die deutsche
Reichsverfassung* (1849) demonstrated his commitment in principle
to German unity, helping to maintain and strengthen his belief,
dating back to the pre-revolutionary period, that the old conserva-

tive notion of 'estates', representing corporations, should be replaced by a more modern assembly, representing the *Volk*, with some say over legislation. Such powers, especially the right to scrutinise the budget, constituted one of 'the demands of the times'.[66] Friedrich Wilhelm IV's issuing of patents on 18 March, which instituted a constitutional system of government and agreed to the convocation of the United Diet (*Vereinigter Landtag*) on 2 April, proved to Stahl 'that the people (*Volk*), as a whole, itself has a part in the rule of the highest echelons, and is a joint carrier of the one public power, and that its representation is not just a representation of the independent circles, the estates, but at the same time also of people, of individuals in these estates, and thus – save for the hereditary chamber – issues from a vote. This is the archetype of the new state.'[67] Stahl's programme for the 'Conservative Party' in the elections to the Prussian assembly during the spring of 1849 contained seven points, starting with an acknowledgement that 'We recognise the *new order in the state*', and continuing with assurances that 'We want the unity of Germany' and 'We seek the power of preservation (the conservative element) not in an outstanding estate, but in all estates through well reinforced institutions, which unite them, and bind the individual and his interests to the whole and to its order.'[68]

The new 'facts' of the situation after 1848, recognised quickly by Stahl and more haltingly by Ludwig von Gerlach, had been largely shaped by Friedrich Wilhelm IV, who helped to create the close linkage in conservatives' minds between nationalism and popular participation in government, having been obliged to parade through the streets of Berlin behind a black, red and gold flag and to deliver his proclamation 'An Mein Volk und an die deutsche Nation' in late March 1848, at the same time as promising electoral reform and repeating his acceptance of constitutional government. From his later correspondence and actions, it is evident that Friedrich Wilhelm IV had felt forced into such precipitate statements and decisions, raising the possibility of 'dictatorship' as early as July and backing the counter-revolutionary government of Brandenburg on 2 November.[69] Having concurred in the imposition of a conservative Prussian constitution on 5 December, the King proceeded on 28 April 1849 to reject the title of 'Kaiser of the Germans', which he had already confided privately had a 'whorish smell of revolution'.[70] However, throughout the early months of the revolution, Friedrich Wilhelm IV linked constitutional and parliamentary concessions to the greater cause of the German nation, explaining the former through reference to the latter. As Leopold von Gerlach recorded in his diary on 13 April 1848, 'the king excused his weakness and his concessions; constitutionalism had had to be acknowledged *because of Germany*'.[71] The King had acted, as he announced to the veteran nationalist Ernst Moritz Arndt in March 1849, 'as a German (*teutsch*) man and prince'.[72] He could argue that, by making concessions to the people and its representatives, he was helping to unite the German nation. Conservatives' belief in this national mission, which had widely been associated with the work of the assemblies in the early months of the revolution, helps to explain how much of the right in Prussia came to accept, through the imposed constitution of December 1848, the establishment of a second chamber, elected by universal manhood suffrage, which had important budgetary powers and a sanction over legislation, unlike in Austria, where the Reichstag was dissolved and 'absolutism' resurfaced.[73] Many Prussian conservatives also accepted Joseph Maria von Radowitz's call for a German *Volkshaus*, with a three-class franchise, as part of the courtier's Erfurt Union plan.[74]

A representative assembly was a necessary component of a constitutional monarchy, which became a second point of agreement in debates about a German nation-state. The right's changing understanding of constitutions was related to shifting notions of government. In contrast to the pre-revolutionary era, when opponents of constitutionalism such as Carl von Voss, Carl von Canitz, Carl Wilhelm von Lancizolle, Carl Ernst Jarcke and Victor Aimé Huber were prominent at the Prussian Court, Friedrich Wilhelm IV's and the government's main legal advisers in 1848, in addition to Radowitz and Ludwig von Gerlach, who was the only lawyer in the preponderantly military camarilla, were Stahl and the Berlin jurist Friedrich Ludwig Keller, both of whom championed constitutions. Indeed, Stahl was introduced to the Minister-President Brandenburg as someone who would be 'very useful', being 'experienced in constitutionalism, since he has been a deputy in the Bavarian chamber'.[75] His work on the 'monarchical principle', published while he was at Erlangen in 1845, outlined how 'the innermost urge of the age' was 'the progress ... from the patrimonial character of the constitution (*Verfassung*) to a state or constitutional (*constitutionell*) one'.[76] This transition had entailed the definition and specification of the King's powers, which had become central to the monarchical principle, but it had also allowed a strengthening of the Crown's position vis-à-vis an opposing parliamentary principle, where there were no constitutional or other checks on an assembly's jurisdiction.[77] By 1848, Ludwig von Gerlach and Radowitz concurred with much of Stahl's interpretation, with the latter, who had previously advocated a 'monarchy of estates (*ständische Monarchie*)' in preference to an 'absolute monarchy' or 'parliamentary' or 'republican' government, now contending that 'the momentum towards a constitutional system of representation' was 'ineluctable', since the concept of estates had 'increasingly gone into decline' 'in the majority of those living'.[78] Like Stahl, Radowitz understood representation to refer to the whole *Volk*, not merely to particular corporations. Such representation required, on a German as well as on a Prussian level, a constitution to keep it in check.

Arguably, the role of representation within a system of constitutional government was challenged more fundamentally by the left than by the right. 'This left believed that it was there by the grace of God more than anyone,' declared Carl Theodor Welcker to laughter from democrats and cheers from the centre of the Frankfurt Parliament in December 1848, during a debate about an absolute veto for the Reich's head of state: 'This left believed that it could do everything it wants, and one cannot place a veto in its way.'[79] Both the centre and the right were worried by what the latter called democratic 'absolutism'. Certainly, democratic rhetoric gave the impression that checks on the principle of popular or national sovereignty were unjustifiable, as Johann Jacoby explained to Prussian deputies in May 1848: 'Whoever wants the unity of Germany should back the power of the popular parliament (*Volksparlament*). Whoever stands against this power, whoever restricts or weakens it, is an enemy of the fatherland.'[80] A significant number of radicals seemed to be against the monarchy altogether: 'Can the German people (*Volk*) want a constitutional monarchy?' asked Julius Fröbel at the start of the revolution: '*No!* Does it want absolute monarchy? *No!* Does it want a feudal monarchy? *No!* What is left for it to want? *The republic!*'[81] This potential opposition to a monarchical form of government was vital because of the growing strength of the radical camp: 20 per cent of Frankfurt deputies belonged to the left in Prussia, 29 per cent in Austria, 62 per cent in Württemberg and more than 75 per cent in Baden and Saxony.[82] The question of radical attitudes to monarchy came to a head during the tortured debate about the title and nature of the 'Kaiser of the Germans' in March 1849, on which the entire Reich constitution came to depend. In December, against the backdrop of a 'coup' in Berlin leading to the imposition of the Prussian constitution on 5 December, democrats had refused to grant an absolute veto to the head of state, despite having agreed to do so in the realm of consti-tutional affairs during the first reading. In March, with the rest of the constitution complete, radicals and some spoilers on the right voted down a bill to make the emperorship hereditary by 263 to 211. The constitution only passed in its entirety at the second reading, by 267 votes to 263, because Heinrich von Gagern, the leader of the *Erbkaiserlichen*, had formed a pact with Heinrich Simon and his faction of democrats, according to which 114 supporters of the *Erbkaisertum* pledged that they would back a suspensive veto even in matters concerning the law and suffrage in exchange for a written promise by 15 followers of Simon to back the hereditary principle.

Such figures on their own, however, gave a misleading impression of the strength of republicanism, since they were mixed with anti-Prussian sentiment and miscellaneous other points of principle, as Radowitz observed.[83] North German democrats had been largely in favour of constitutional monarchy from the start, remarked Biedermann in Frankfurt.[84] Thus, it was natural for the Hamburg radical Gabriel Riesser, even though he came from an oligarchical republican city-state, that the head of the Reich should be a monarch, since the population was monarchical.[85] Of the South German radicals, the republicans were concentrated above all in Baden and Württemberg, which together provided only 42 democ-rats out of the 812 deputies elected to the National Assembly in 1848–49. Some of these, as Ludwig Simon, from Trier, explained to the parliament on 27 April 1849, had had to accept the King of Prussia as hereditary head of a monarchical system of government in order to pass the constitution and safeguard a German nation-state.[86] Others such as Friedrich Hecker, claimed Gagern, had given backword and reverted to republicanism, leading to their exclusion – by a majority – from the National Assembly.[87] Hecker, who had been elected – and then re-elected – to a Badenese constituency of the Frankfurt Parliament, had been refused the right by other deputies of taking up his mandate. 'It is of great importance', wrote Droysen, that the insurrection in Baden, led by Hecker, failed, with the result that followers 'left the Paulskirche in masses', once their hero had been repudiated, and they did not declare a republic.[88] Subsequently, the goal of the revolution – republic or monarchy – was not in doubt, unlike in France; what was in dispute were the means to achieve desired reforms within the framework of a national and constitutional monarchy.[89]

The dispute between republicans and monarchists was judged by radicals such as Ludwig Bamberger, who remained agnostic, to be subordinate to the federal question.[90] Although Bamberger himself, at least retrospectively, believed that it had been necessary to let the federal state 'fall as an unavoidable sacrifice on the altar of a German rebirth', many of his democratic colleagues remained wedded to the idea of a German *Bundesstaat*, to the extent that it became a third point of agreement in the debate about the future political form of a German nation-state.[91] To a minority of radicals, of which Fröbel was the most well-known, 'the democratic republic rests on the principle of brotherhood (federation). The *Bundesstaat* is its form.'[92] Switzerland and the United States were important models, although Fröbel himself became convinced during the revolution that constitutional or 'parliamentary monarchy' was more suited to German conditions, at least temporarily.[93] Other democrats and radicals were influenced more by the French model and were more inclined to demand unitary government in the name of the German people, yet they, too, were obliged to moderate their demands during the course of the revolution, as they came to terms with the local sympathies of their voters, the continuing existence of the German states and the difficulty of integrating Austria. Facing a barrage of petitions – 9,000 in Leipzig alone – in favour of monarchy and the integrity of the Saxon state, Blum was forced to admit, after much prevarication, that state rights were threatened by the right, not the left.[94] Likewise, Riesser put himself forward as a mediator between the centre and the states, and between republicans, who 'pursued unity more crudely and ruthlessly than us' and particularists, who 'do not desire ideas of unity, because they do not want to let the independence, the particular life of the individual states, especially the power of the princes, be limited in any way'.[95]

By contrast, during the final debates about the *Reichsverfassung*, Riesser was less worried about the sensibilities of his own electors than about the necessity of maintaining links with Austria and integrating Prussia. In his opinion, it was obvious that Germany would be a federal state, attracting Austrian Germans over the longer term, even if they had had to be excluded for the meantime: 'We harbour the confident hope that precisely then, when our *Bundesstaat* has come strongly and powerfully into being, Austria will enter into as close an alliance (*Bündnis*) as possible with a united Germany of equal status for their mutual well-being.'[96] Only a federal state could accommodate Prussia, whose power and political framework was needed for German unification, and other anti-Prussian populations. Like Riesser, the Cologne radical Franz Raveaux was convinced that Prussia was the active element in Germany: 'there, they act, and here, we wait'.[97] Unlike Riesser, he believed that Prussia had to be resisted, yet his goal of establishing a federal state arguably remained the same: 'Prussia has a different policy from you', he warned Bassermann: 'Prussia wants to be the central point, the sun around which all the small planets should turn; it wants to fashion Germany in this way, and not otherwise, and if you don't counter Prussian arrogance preventatively, you won't ever succeed in realising the *Bundesstaat* that you have set out in the constitution.'[98] Here, Raveaux agreed with Ludwig Simon, one of the most radical deputies, a critic of 'weedy liberalism' and a defender to the death of the Provisional Central Power in Frankfurt: in late April 1849, a call to the *Volk*, rather than reliance on 'inimical governments' to pass the Reich constitution, did not imply the desire for an *Einheitsstaat*, he declared, against the charge put forward by moderate liberals such as Karl Mathy; in the same way, the Reich ministry's earlier seizure of power and use of violence did not betray a desire for 'a constitutional unitary state', 'only a constitutional *Bundesstaat*'.[99] Simon could not be said to be a supporter of a decentralised federal state, but nor was he prepared to be labelled an advocate of a unitary state.

The left, claimed Raveaux, was often accused by liberals of being in coalition with the right against the constitution of a national *Bundesstaat*. This was not true, he protested.[100] Similarly, the right objected to such charges and displayed its support for a federal state. Conservatives, proclaimed the *Neue Preussische Zeitung* as late as March 1849, were in favour of a German *Bundesstaat*, not a French-inspired *Einheitsstaat*: 'Germans wanted a *Bundesstaat*, but not an *Einheitsstaat*, for they had absolutely no talent for creating one – it thoroughly contradicts a German sense of independence which, in spite of long dilution through the aping of France, is still so strong.'[101] In order to work, a German nation-state needed some sort of central authority, as Reich ministers rightly insisted, but one based on the real powers of existing German states, not merely described in words, as in Frankfurt: 'A central power must be strong, and Germany in particular needed a genuinely strong central power for many reasons; but it will not become strong by increasing competencies to the point of omnipotence on paper (just as one doesn't knock out a single man with an army on paper), but by being granted such power in reality by all sides, by being raised and carried by all the individual states.'[102] Only Prussia could underwrite such a design, since it was by far the largest power in Germany, with 16 million inhabitants, of whom 14 million were 'of German descent'.[103] The other 27 princes and 10 million Germans would join the national effort, as soon as Prussia gave its consent and agreed to act.[104] Many contemporaries from various parties and different individual states had reservations about the federal, constitutional and representative nation-state agreed in Frankfurt, but it had nevertheless been enacted with majority support in the *Reichsverfassung* of March 1849.

Unifying Germany

The national ramifications of the Reich constitution threatened to derail it. In addition to his conservative and legitimist disdain for a product of the revolution, Friedrich Wilhelm IV was unwilling in April 1849, as he rejected the National Assembly's offer to become 'Kaiser of the Germans', to frame a smaller German nation-state to exclude the Austrian monarch and a dynasty of former emperors of the Holy Roman Empire of the German Nation. Yet the King of Prussia's later reluctant backing of Radowitz's smaller German 'Erfurt Union' plan, put forward between June 1849 (Gotha) and November 1850 (Olmütz), suggests that he was motivated more by political reasons – especially hatred of the revolution – than by national ones.[105] In this sense, the 'temporary' exclusion of German-speaking parts of the Habsburg monarchy foreseen by the constitution might, in itself, have been acceptable to the monarch, as might the borders discussed in the debates of the Frankfurt parliament in 1848.

Liberal expectations of a German nation-state – the coincidence of politics and culture, the integration of other nationalities, the peaceful coexistence of Europe's nations and the existence of uncontested borders – were soon challenged and resisted, after briefly holding sway during the 'March days'. The ensuing debates about territory and culture, or nationality, arguably always shaped – and often dominated – those concerning the constitution, polity,

rights and citizenship. The question of who was a citizen, with full
political and legal rights, was linked from the start of the revolution
to the question of who was a German, which in turn rested on definitions of German culture, descent and territory. All the parliamentary discussions of basic rights and systems of government took
place against the backdrop of a war with Denmark over Schleswig-
Holstein, a long-standing national cause, which had begun with the
Danish annexation decree of 21 March 1848. In May, Prussian
troops suppressed the Polish uprising in Posen, leading to the
creation of 'German Posen' by the Prussian government commissioner on 4 June, a decision later sanctioned by the Frankfurt
Parliament. In the Austrian *Kaiserreich*, meanwhile, national
conflicts flared up constantly: in Prague on 12–16 June, in Northern
Italy between June and August, and in Hungary and Croatia in
October 1848. Opinions on the viability of different forms of
government and the territorial extent of a German nation-state
were critically affected by these conflicts.

National conflicts also had an impact on definitions of citizenship.
From the *Vorparlament*, which jettisoned the phrase 'every German'
in favour of 'every citizen (*Staatsangehörige*)' from its election regulations at the behest of Anton Wiesner, via Titus Mareck's proclamation in support of group rights and the extension of Germans' rights
to non-German citizens in the National Assembly in May 1848, and
Johann Fritsch's attempt once more to replace 'German' with
'citizen' in the June draft of the basic rights, to Alois Boczek's and
Carlo Esterle's objections to different aspects of Paragraph 47's
nationality rights in the final constitutional debates of February
1849, it was above all Austrians who brought up the questions of citizenship and belonging, mindful of the likelihood of further national
uprisings in the Habsburg lands. The decision of the Constitutional
Committee in the summer of 1848 to omit a citizenship clause guaranteeing rights to non-Germans and to avoid constitutional provisions concerning naturalisation can only be understood in this
context. As a result, citizenship remained, temporarily at least,
within the preserve of the individual German states. The provision
was only altered on 6 November 1848, when the Constitutional
Committee agreed to add the qualification that 'The German
people consists of the citizens of the states that form the German
Empire' to the existing statement about 'every German' possessing
citizenship and, therefore, rights. The addition was made in order to
facilitate the entry of Austria, with its many non-German citizens,

into the German nation-state, after the Frankfurt Parliament had asked the Habsburg monarchy to make its intentions clear in late October. It was legally and diplomatically convenient, and in accordance with liberal tenets concerning participatory government, to grant citizenship rights to all responsible residents. Such an account, however, does not explain why parliamentarians refused to replace references to '*jeder Deutsche*', which lay at the heart of the basic rights and constitution, with '*jeder Staatsangehörige*', as they were asked to do on repeated occasions. Arguably, a significant number wanted to make Germans – in a cultural sense – of all citizens and to consolidate the national foundations of the new state. At the very least, a nation-state required a *lingua franca* to make it work and to ensure social and political cohesion.

Very few deputies or commentators doubted that German would be the language of state in the new Germany, to be used by all citizens on the national level, for example within the Frankfurt Parliament, and by officials in most instances, particularly those relating to the activities of a 'central power'. 'German is, indeed, the language of state', ran the original version of Mareck's proclamation.[106] For Georg Beseler and other North and West German liberals, this predicate was obvious, since there was no doubt 'who is the dominant people in Germany'.[107] For most South Germans and many Austrians, however, the need for a common, 'national' language was also accepted, partly because of the perceived menace of the dissolution of the multilingual Habsburg monarchy. It was probably for this reason, in addition to scepticism about parliaments generally, that the Austrian Prime Minister Prince Felix Schwarzenberg avoided the creation of a genuine *Volkshaus* in his plans for Germany in early 1849. Anton von Schmerling, the leader of the Austrian delegation in the Frankurt Parliament, rejected such plans, on the grounds that they were too reactionary, paying too little attention to the necessary German foundation of any new order, but he, too, found it difficult to envisage Rhinelanders and Ruthenians sitting together in an assembly without a *lingua franca*.[108] Likewise, the Austrian reform conservative Count Friedrich Deym could only imagine the 'Babylonian confusion' of a single multilingual German–Habsburg parliament, preferring instead two separate but linked assemblies.[109] For Germans outside Austria, including the Bavarian deputy Johann Eisenmann, it was better for Germany to detach itself from the Habsburg monarchy's Poles, Italians, Croats, Slovaks and Hungarians altogether, because of the danger that they posed to the linguistic and cultural unity of the new state.[110] For his part, the liberal leader Carl Welcker labelled the idea of a multilingual Austrian *Reichstag*, effectively giving up a language of state, as 'crazy'.[111] Even radicals, who went furthest in their defence of language rights, usually admitted that a common German language was nevertheless required. The Bohemian left liberal Gustav Gross supported the language rights of 'Slavs', but 'when this principle is given a broader extension in a German state, then I must declare myself against it'.[112] Esterle, the South Tyrolean democrat who argued for greater political and administrative autonomy, continued to accept that 'The borders of Germany are to be found where the German tongue ceases to be heard.'[113] For this reason, he preferred the name 'German Reich' – a largely but not exclusively German territory and state – to 'Germany'.[114] North and West German radicals were much less guarded. How could Schmerling's concept of a German–Habsburg *Volkshaus* possibly work, given the deputies' different languages, asked Ludwig Simon? 'We are finally acting in earnest against the attempts of the nationality-lets to seek an independent existence among us and, like parasitic growths, to annihilate our own existence', resounded the opinion of the left-wing Hegelian Wilhelm Jordan.[115]

The majority of deputies, it could be contended, believed that a superior German culture would prevail in the long run. This could be seen in Schleswig-Holstein, the oldest and most prominent of Germany's national causes. On 21 March 1848, King Frederik VII of Denmark had announced his intention of annexing Schleswig in order to forestall the full independence of the duchy, along with the Duchy of Holstein, and in order to appease Danish nationalists, for the monarch had ceded absolute power and promulgated a constitution on his accession in February 1848.[116] For the majority of deputies and newspapers in Germany, Denmark had acted in contravention of history and international law, according to which the two duchies were to remain in tandem and Schleswig was never to be taken by Denmark – a provision dating back to 1326 in the opinion of the *Grenzboten*.[117] The populations of the duchies had rightly called for German aid, with black, red and gold colours quickly replacing the red, white and blue of Schleswig-Holstein in the major towns: on 18 March, the estates of Schleswig-Holstein, meeting in Rendsburg, had called for a separate constitution for the duchies and for Schleswig to join Holstein in the German Confederation; on 23 March, a provisional government was set up by conservatives, national liberals and radicals to protect the rights of the duchies against the 'unfree duke', who had been constrained, as King of Denmark, by Danish nationalists.[118] At this stage, the course of history, legality, local patriotism and German nationalism appeared to be complementary. In this spirit, Friedrich Wilhelm IV, prompted by Christian August, the Duke of Augustenburg, who was a contender in the succession to the duchies, issued a proclamation on 24 March pledging his support for the duchies against a Danish attack in accordance with the Confederation's decision in September 1846. On 12 April, the *Bundesversammlung*, which had previously recognised the provisional government of Schleswig-Holstein, as had other German states, declared that the war between Denmark, the duchies and Prussia, which had begun at the end of March, was a *Bundeskrieg*, involving Germany as a whole, through the Confederation. Accordingly, the Tenth Federal Army Corps, with troops from Hanover, Mecklenburg, Oldenburg, Brunswick and the Hansa towns, was deployed alongside the Prussian army. With the demise of the Bund, the Provisional Central Power and the National Assembly in Frankfurt formally endorsed the conflict as a 'German' or 'Reich' war. Deputies from both Schleswig and Holstein were elected in May to the Frankfurt National Assembly, despite the fact that the former territory lay outside the old Confederation. Even liberal-minded, cosmopolitan conservatives sceptical of the German cause, such as Karl August Varnhagen von Ense, believed that 'Our war against Denmark is a just war.'[119]

The 'German' parties involved in the conflict soon fell out. Prussia had entered the war without the formal approval of the Bund, the March ministries or the Heidelberg 'Committee of Seven'. When Friedrich Wilhelm IV and the Prussian government, under pressure from Britain and Russia, unilaterally ended the war with the truce of Malmö on 26 August 1848, in contravention of the Central Power's conditions, the Frankfurt Parliament voted against it by 238 votes to 221 in early September, but General Friedrich von Wrangel, the Prussian commander of all German troops in Schleswig-Holstein, had already begun a withdrawal. Under such circumstances, with history and law read by Danes and Germans in different ways, given that Schleswig was outside the German Confederation but was indissolubly linked to the confederal state of Holstein, the principle of nationality quickly became pivotal. It was predicated on the existence of unambiguous cultural and territorial boundaries between nations, which did not, in fact, exist. A division of Schleswig-Holstein on national grounds would benefit Germany, it was widely assumed. The population of the duchies 'only wants to be German'; 'the majority, not only of a head count, but also of the educated, the majority of education is in Schleswig-Holstein decisively German', claimed the *Grenzboten* in June 1848.[120]

One of the main reasons given by liberals for refusing to split Schleswig in early 1848 was their doubt about the viability of Denmark as a small state – giving only the 'appearance of an independent state', according to one article – and about the attractiveness of 'Danishness': 'How would one partition? According to sympathies and antipathies? That is not possible, for only a small part will want to become Danes ... Or according to language? The language which is spoken in the northern districts can be called Danish as little as it can be called German; it is a poor bastard', declared the *Grenzboten*.[121] Even here, it was obvious to the same publication, the 'educated part of the population', to which one had to turn 'if one wants to research true opinion', was German: 'all who are educated in Schleswig (with the exception of certain Flensburg merchants) belong to the German element'.[122] What was more, whereas German Schleswiger were 'chained to Holstein through the links of the law, all state institutions, the material interests of trade, and so on, Danish Schleswiger are connected to Denmark through none of these things', went on the periodical.[123] Other liberal newspapers made similar claims.[124] Most agreed that all of Holstein was German and that 'two-thirds of the population [of Schleswig] are German, one third Danish', in the words of the *Grenzboten*. Such figures were based on misleading statistics about language of worship, yet figures for popular usage of German in Schleswig lay between 120,000 and 128,000 people, Danish approximately 145,000, and Frisian about 26,000 people.[125] No language predominated in central Schleswig, where between 47,000 and 60,000 people lived. Even if Frisians, on the North Sea coast, were held to be 'German', which was usually the case, about half of Schleswigers spoke Danish as their main language.[126] This fact was routinely ignored by German liberals, and others, who called for the incorporation of the larger – and most populous – part of Schleswig and the whole of Holstein by the new German nation-state.

A similar set of assumptions about the cultural superiority of the Germans underpinned most commentators' responses to the national dispute in Posen. National self-determination, it was widely believed, would benefit Germans in the territory. On 4 June 1848, the Prussian government commissioner General Ernst von Pfuel had divided two-thirds of the territory from the province, calling it 'German Posen'. The Poles were simply not able to swallow half a million Germans argued the *Regierungsrat* and Posen deputy Ernst Viebig.[127] His liberal compatriot Adolph Goeden agreed, arguing that the existence of half a million Germans left no other option than to split the province in Germany's favour.[128] According to the *Kölnische Zeitung*, in the Grand Duchy, there were 790,000 Poles, 420,000 Germans and 80,000 Jews in 1843; in the province of Prussia, there were 560,000 Poles and 1,666,000 Germans; and in Silesia only Oppeln had an overwhelmingly Polish population from a total of 518,000 inhabitants.[129] 'It is a key result of these figures that as a consequence of a reorganisation on a national basis – the only one that can be acknowledged as justified – not the present provincial borders but the borders of the nations must be definitive,' continued the same publication:

> Still we must also add that the Poles in Prussia and Silesia, notably also in East Prussia, are already so alienated from the nationality of the Poles, and partly from religion, that the desire for a division of Germany will come from them only reluctantly; we must add that, if one leaves these stretches of land to themselves, without any pressure, Germanisation would soon have succeeded.[130]

The newspaper ignored the implications of its own figures – the fact that Poles were preponderant in 15 *Kreise* and Germans in 16 *Kreise* in the mixed areas of the province of Prussia – and refused to reconsider the earlier inclusion of East and West Prussia in the German Bund. Like other publications, the newspaper concentrated exclusively on Posen, refusing to sacrifice the 500,000 Germans there who had defended Germany for so long against the East.[131] On 27 July 1848, 342 Frankfurt deputies to 31 voted for Prussia's division of Posen and retrospectively sanctioned the *Bundestag*'s inclusion – on 22 April and 4 May – of this western part in the German Confederation. The bill put forward by the left, criticising the division of Poland as an 'ignominious injustice' and calling for the 'recreation of an independent Poland', was defeated by 331 votes to 101.[132] The majority of deputies had not been willing to compromise Germany's national interests, it could be suggested, for the sake of culturally inferior Poles. As in Schleswig-Holstein, a maximising interpretation of 'national interest' was only likely to be compromised because of the opposition of a Great Power.[133]

Such opposition and compromise were most salient in the National Assembly's treatment of the nationality principle in Austria, especially in the Bund lands of Bohemia and Moravia. Here, confronted by 2.6 million Czechs, the representatives of Bohemia's 1.7 million Germans recognised that they were in a weaker position than Germans in Posen and East and West Prussia, not least because their Czech counterparts – together with other Czechs in Moravia (4 million in total) – were able to exploit the traditions of Bohemia as a semi-independent crown land and to champion the monarchy itself, which permitted them to act in concert with other nationalities in the Habsburg lands such as the Slovaks (almost 2 million), Croats (1.5 million), Serbs (1.5 million), Slovenians (1 million), Ruthenians (3 million) and Poles (2 million) against the representatives of the territory's 8 million Germans and 5 million Hungarians. The Pan-Slav Congress in Prague during April, May, and June 1848, which issued in the refusal of Frantisek Palacky, the author of the celebrated *History of Bohemia* (1836 onwards), to participate in the preparations for the Frankfurt Parliament as 'a Bohemian of Slav race', combined with the re-establishment of a Bohemian provisional government under the governorship of the supposedly Slavophile Count Leo Thun on 29 May and the convocation of the Bohemian *Landtag* on 7 June, not only suggested to German onlookers the seriousness of Czech resistance – with the radical *Constitution* commenting that 'the Czechs have thrown off the mask, showing the grimacing face of their national hate' more than a month before the Prague uprising – but also the complexity of the national question in the Habsburg monarchy as a whole.[134] Palacky's own recommendation to the Reichstag at Kremsier identified eight national units of territory – German Austria, Czech Austria, Poland, Illyria, Italy, the lands of the southern Slavs, Hungary, Romania – which were themselves to be divided into national administrative *Kreise* in areas of mixed settlement. The final constitutional draft adopted in March 1849 by the Kremsier Reichstag, based on the proposals of the German Moravian Cajetan Mayer, retained the crown lands rather than adopting Palacky's national units, but it divided such lands into national *Kreise* – nine in Bohemia, ten in Galicia, four in Moravia, three in Lower Austria, two in the Tyrol, and two in Styria – and it foresaw an Upper Chamber of the Lands made up of representatives of both crown-land diets, with six deputies each, and the *Kreise*, with one deputy for every two units. The imposed constitution of March 1849, devised by Franz Graf von Stadion, likewise emphasised *Kreise*, as well strengthening the central power of the Habsburg monarchy at the expense of the autonomy of the crown lands. In all these intricate designs, there was no room for cross-cutting obligations to *Grossdeutschland*.[135] 'Germany can never come to an understanding with Austria,' proclaimed Ludwig von Löhner, one of the leaders of the German Austrians and a former advocate of *Grossdeutschland*: 'Let us take Austria out of Germany to make at least an agreement between the others possible.'[136]

At some point between December 1848 and March 1849, the majority of deputies in the National Assembly – and, arguably, most commentators and much of public opinion – came to accept the exclusion of Austria from Germany on national and political grounds. By 12 March, as he put forward his bill to pass the constitution and offer Friedrich Wilhelm IV the title of Kaiser, the leading liberal Welcker was sure, 'on objective grounds', that Austria did 'not want to enter a German *Bundesstaat*'.[137] It was now evident to the editor of the *Staatslexikon* that 'we may not expect the unification of Austria within a German federal state', not least because of 'the work of the ministers with their own hands' and because of 'their Babylonian constitution'.[138] For Welcker, mindful of the sensibilities of governments and public opinion in the South German states, blame should be attached to 'the Austrian cabinet, not the Austrian people, us, our work or our crowned heads'.[139] By 20 March, Gagern, too, had publicly accepted that Austria would not join Germany in the near future. The alternatives were now: 'should a German *Bundesstaat* completely separate itself from Austria, or can a wider alliance with the *Gesamtmonarchie* exist?'[140] The liberal Minister-President could 'not follow those who, from an historical standpoint, set their sights on distant possibilities, and derive conclusions from them; from a political point of view, one must stick to present facts, and a constitution must adapt to these facts'.[141] Other liberal deputies such as Karl Mathy and Friedrich Römer agreed: Austria would only enter a '*Bundesstaat*' of its own choosing – that is, not a real one acceptable to the Frankfurt Parliament.[142] In truth, Austrians has only played a minor role – in terms of office-holding (see Map 2) - in the decisions of the Reich Central Power and the German National Assembly.

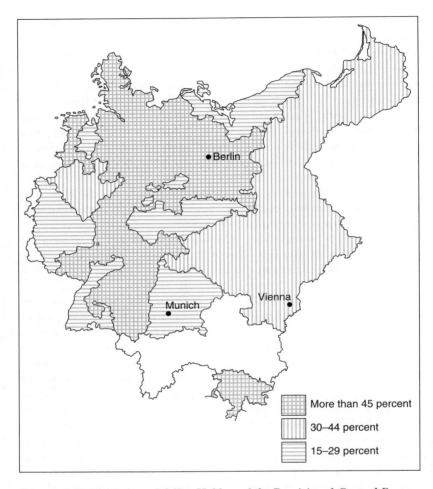

Map 2   Participation of Office-Holders of the Provisional Central Power and Members of Committees of the Frankfurt Parliament.
Source: Adapted from H. Best, Die Männer von Bildung und Besitz *(Düsseldorf, 1990),* 289

Deputies and journalists from radical, Catholic and conservative camps remained more ambivalent and divided about the 'Austrian question', with significant numbers still supporting either *Grossdeutschland* or a looser German confederation. Nevertheless, most radicals were critical of Schwarzenberg, who was associated with the execution of Robert Blum on 9 November 1848, and they shared Ludwig Simon's belief in March 1849 – even if they disputed his conclusion that '*Kleindeutschland* is here' – that 'we truly stuck it out with our German brothers in Austria, we (pointing to the Left) offered them the hand of a brother until the last flicker of a possibility; we lost one of our best and most noble for them'.[143] Schmerling, declared Simon, was a hypocrite, who had supported a united Germany in Frankfurt but had placed the Austrian *Gesamtmonarchie* above everything in Vienna.[144] Austrian deputies had been prohibited from taking part in the constitutional deliberations of Frankfurt by their own government, asserted the radical deputy a month later: with such a government no cooperation was possible, especially given that the Schwarzenberg Ministry had made clear that the German Bund continued to exist and the National Assembly was illegal, that an Austrian Kaiser would 'never and under no conditions subject himself to a foreign legislative power' and that 'the Austrian government will not enter a *Bundesstaat* with a representative constitution'.[145]

Catholic deputies, such as the Rhineland leader August Reichensperger, disagreed fundamentally with the premises of radicals' arguments, viewing the opening paragraphs of the *Reichsverfassung*, which democrats perceived to be necessary foundations of a nation-state, as an act of war against the Habsburg monarchy, making the constitution unworkable.[146] Yet even Reichensperger conceded that many mistakes had been made by the Austrian government, although not as many as by the Frankfurt authorities, as a result of its 'ignorance of the nature of this assembly and of German conditions'.[147] Austria had been left to adopt the idea of 'a separate constitution' and had been prevented from joining 'a rejuvenated Germany' at a later date – the chance of founding a German nation-state with the other German states was ruled out by the Catholic politician.[148] Reichensperger appears to have concurred with Prussian conservatives that, in 1848, Austria was too distant from German affairs – 'put on another course by its composition and its position in the world' – 'to be a part of a German *Bundesstaat*' from the outset.[149] Though there was vacillation on the part of Catholics and conservatives over the political elements of the Austrian question, there were also doubts about the possibility, nature and likelihood of Austrian involvement in German state-building.[150]

The principle of nationality, seen by many commentators as the fundamental principle of the revolution in Germany, initially overrode other considerations, obscuring complications and conflicts of interest. Although the Habsburg monarchy was eventually excluded from Germany on national grounds, in conjunction with other political, constitutional, military and diplomatic obstructions to incorporation, it was assumed for much of 1848 by the majority of deputies and journalists that Austria's German-speaking lands would be included in the new nation-state. Such inclusion was championed most ardently by democrats and Catholics, but it was also accepted by liberals and conservatives.[151] From the start of the revolution, commentators and politicians of all affiliations had given voice to their dreams of a German nation-state extending at least as far as the old Confederation and, if possible, beyond, in keeping with Arndt's famous *Lied* – still the most widely cited text amongst nationalists in 1848 – 'Des Deutschen Vaterland' (1813). Austria was the main site of such dreams: after asking 'What is the German's fatherland?', each stanza of Arndt's song suggests another set of territories, starting from '*Preussenland*' and ending – tellingly – with Austria, before culminating in the conclusion towards the end of the song that the German fatherland should extend 'As far as the German tongue is spoken'.[152] From the call of the Viennese deputy Karl Moering for an '*Anschluss* with the territories of Austria not belonging to the German Bund' and the creation of 'a power-ful, united, free *Mitteleuropa*' a week after the National Assembly had been inaugurated in May 1848, a large number of deputies and jour-nalists – with Austrians most prominent – put forward their plans for the consolidation of German culture and a German state in the territories of the Habsburg monarchy.[153] It went unquestioned by most deputies in the spring and summer of 1848 that Germany would stretch at least to the borders of the German Confederation. This aspiration persisted in Paragraph 1 of the *Reichsverfassung*, passed by a coalition of liberal *Kleindeutschen* and radicals, which continued to maintain that the territory of the German Reich included, in theory, Bohemia, Moravia and 'old Austria' as lands of the old Bund. The clause was supposed, recalled Reichensperger, to give us 'a claim on German Austria'.[154]

By October 1848, when Paragraph 1 was passed by a large major-ity, it was already apparent, before Schwarzenberg's counter-revolu-tion, that such undefined national yearnings might come into conflict with each other and with the interests of the individual states, especially those of the largest and least German state, Austria. Reichensperger was critical of Paragraph 1 precisely because it constituted a 'sleeping lion', unacceptable to the Habsburg monarchy. The lion 'sleeps on the condition that it will be woken up when circumstances allow it to seem appropriate'.[155] Some Catholics and South Germans, who felt closer to Austria than to Prussia, continued to support the Habsburg monarchy even at the cost of rejecting the Reich constitution. The 'Austrian' question had, as Biedermann later wrote, altered national politics: alongside the 'Austrian party', which met at the Hotel Schröder, were 'the so-called "Grossdeutsche", a mixture of ultramontanes, particularists and several ideologues who ... wanted solely to keep Austria in Germany at any price – even at the price of this "Grossdeutschland" receiving as loose a form as that which the German Bund had had.'[156] In October 1848, the Bavarian deputies Ernst von Lassaulx and Hermann von Rotenhan were amongst four dissenting voices in the Constitutional Committee to Paragraphs 2 and 3, which insisted that the administration and 'constitutional government' of the 'German' parts of a multi-national entity belonging to the Reich must be separate from those of the non-German parts, and the head of state – the Habsburg monarch – should either reside in the German parts or formally split his role.[157] The constitution and legislation of the Reich were to have binding force in the German parts of the monarchy.

In the subsequent National Assembly debates, Lassaulx and Rotenhan were joined by the Munich church historian Johann Nepomuk Sepp, who argued for the union of Germany and Austria within *Mitteleuropa*, creating an ascendancy over France and Russia, and permitting the peaceful Germanisation of the Habsburg lands. In December, not only the Austrians opposed Gagern, wrote Duncker to his wife, 'there are also ultramontanes, who do not want a Prussian *Kaisertum*, there are Bavarians, for the most part stirred up by the Austrians – it is the whole fear of the South of the North'.[158] In January 1849, Duncker estimated that Gagern was already opposed by 'all the Austrians, three-quarters of the Bavarians, three-quarters of the ultramontanes'.[159] The opinions of the latter were represented during the constitutional debates of March 1849 by the Catholic politician Franz Josef Buss, who contended that only the incorporation of the whole of the Habsburg monarchy into Germany would strengthen it sufficiently to play a mediating role between the 'Slavs' and the 'Romance' peoples.[160] 'Only when we have Austria, which is now educating the Slavs through its free constitution and which draws them to it through German freedom and education, will we neutralise the dangers with which Pan-Slavism threatens us.'[161] Throughout the revolution, deputies such as Sepp and Buss were backed by Catholic and South German publicists and officials such as the Bavarian Minister-President Ludwig von Öttingen-Wallerstein, who wrote of Germany dominating Central Europe with Vienna as its capital, and the Württemberg national economist and deputy, Moriz Mohl, who outlined his vision of a Reich of 70 million inhabitants, uniting Germany and the whole of Austria in one state, 'if Germany wants to be the most powerful state in the world'.[162] Many South Germans, in particular, were reluctant to sever ties to Austria, with which they had greater religious, cultural and, in some cases, economic affinities than with Prussia and North Germany.

Despite enduring scepticism of Prussia, however, many liberals and democrats in the most receptive South German states of Württemberg and Bavaria accepted Gagern's verdict and opposed their pro-Austrian monarchs. In the former, the majority of deputies and the public had supported the Frankfurt Parliament until at least September, when radicals' loyalty was weakened by the National Assembly's perceived weakness over Schleswig-Holstein and the truce of Malmö. The democrats, though, maintained their backing of Frankfurt – perceived by the *Beobachter* as the wish for 'unity at any price' at the time of Archduke Johann's election as *Reichsverweser* and the implicit sanctioning of a German nation-state as a constitutional monarchy – and they voted, along with liberals, for Welcker's and Gagern's Prussian hereditary *Kaisertum*, jettisoning their call at the mass meeting of Ulm on 24 February for an elected head of state and the incorporation of German Austria in a German Reich.[163] As the radical Friedrich Theodor Vischer put it after the vote, 'I have fought a terrible inner battle', resolving 'not to help the bloke [Friedrich Wilhelm IV], but also not to hinder him, but only, like dear God with evil, to allow it'.[164] The liberal Minister-President Friedrich Römer was able to use such public opinion and political support to force King Wilhelm of Württemberg to accept the *Reichsverfassung* and the offer of the title of Kaiser to the King of Prussia. The governments and monarchs of Bavaria and other refractory states would be required by their populations to come to the same decision, claimed Römer. In the event, the Minister-President was wrong. Maximilian II and the Bavarian government, guided by the conservative Foreign Minister Ludwig von der Pfordten, rejected the Reich Constitution in April 1849. Yet

Bavaria's second chamber, dominated after elections in December 1848 by the left and centre, refused to endorse the government's decision. Pro-Austrian monarchs in other states in the 'third Germany' such as Saxony and Hanover, where Ernst August insisted on decorating the counter-revolutionary Austrian generals Windischgrätz and Jelacic, were likewise countered by assembly majorities and public opinion, which came to countenance the possibility of Germany without Austria.[165]

The corresponding shift towards Prussia and, after the turn of the year, what came to be known as '*Kleindeutschland*' was, of course, neither inevitable nor irreversible. It took place against a background of national awakening in 1848 during which virtually all protagonists – except the old ruling elites – believed in the unproblematic application of the principle of nationality and, as a consequence, in a German nation-state which stretched at least as far as the borders of the old Bund. Such expectations and hopes proved difficult for many forty-eighters to relinquish and were retained even in the *Reichsverfassung* of 1849. They make the turn towards *Kleindeutschland* all the more remarkable, especially in the context of contemporaries' many-sided scepticism of Prussia. Friedrich Oetker, a deputy from Kurhessen, testified to the unexpectedness of the change in his memoirs: Gagern's programme, introduced a few days after taking office on 15 December, was the first 'official' formulation of a solution to the German question based on Prussia.[166] Gagern's five sentences, 'according to which Prussia and the smaller states should in future form a *Bundesstaat* and stand in an "indissoluble alliance" (*Bundesverhältniss*) with Austria', thus caused a sensation.[167] Franz Duncker wrote to his wife on 20 December of the session that 'the ship is breaking up and the waves are crashing down'.[168] The left, in particular, rose up 'lividly, with Jakob Venedey the dreamer at their head': 'From right and left the applause rang out – one no longer knew who was a friend and who a foe', he concluded.[169] After a four-day debate, the new Minister President's programme was passed by 261 votes to 224 on 13 January. By most accounts, changing position to vote for the programme was difficult. Amongst many conversions, Arndt's was the most famous, remarked Oetker: 'Old Arndt voted for it, whereupon the left, amidst great agitation in the Assembly, called out to him: "Das ganze Deutschland soll es sein"', from his song 'Des Deutschen Vaterland'.[170]

The shock was comparable on 12 March 1849 when Welcker, possibly Germany's most well-known national liberal as editor of the

Staatslexikon and a prominent advocate of *Grossdeutschland* in the debates initiated by Gagern's Ministry, put forward a bill declaring that the National Assembly 'is ready to preserve existing national and fraternal relations, but not to the detriment of the independence of the German Reich constitution, as long as difficulties still stand in the way of a definitive realisation of the full entry of the German–Austrian lands into the German Reich constitution'.[171] The pronouncement produced, in the words of the official record, 'a great, enduring sensation and movement in the Assembly'.[172] In the entire speech, Welcker concentrated almost entirely on Austria, which had proved unwilling to join the Reich, omitting to mention Prussia at all, other than by implication, through 'the transfer' of 'the hereditary title of Kaiser' to the King of Prussia.[173] Welcker, from Baden, was mainly concerned to demonstrate that there was no alternative to a *Bundesstaat* without Austria, to be created immediately because 'the fatherland is in danger'.[174] 'Public opinion will therefore be for us', he concluded, since 'our brothers in South Germany, which this division touches especially painfully', knew that Germany had not been torn up 'hastily or selfishly': 'I am convinced the Bavarians, and even the Austrians, and the Catholic Württemberger and Badenese, too, are all suffused with the conviction that the saving of the fatherland can no longer be postponed.'[175] In the same way, just over a week later, Gagern was anxious to prove his South German credentials and to deny any relation with or predilection for Prussia, concealing the fact that he had written about a Prussian-led Germany even before the revolution. Yet, given Austrian opposition, he declared in his speech to the National Assembly, there was no alternative to *Kleindeutschland*, 'as it is called'.[176] Prussia would not be the centre of the new German nation-state – although it would obviously be the biggest single component of it – and it would experience 'decentralisation' and 'a fusion with Germany' as a 'necessary, gradual consequence' of joining the Reich.[177] The Prussian state was composite in nature, containing a 'South German' Rhine province, many from the Saxon 'tribe' and the Austrian border land of Silesia, and it had already 'fully flowed into the main stream of German life', contrary to the claims of anti-Prussian commentators.[178] 'We cannot imagine it separate from us', asserted the Minister-President, implicitly contrasting an integral Prussia with an excluded Austria.[179]

To Gagern's Pomeranian collaborator on the Reich constitution Droysen, who went on to found the 'Prussian school' of history with his *Geschichte der preussischen Politik* (1855–86) but who was more critical of Prussia as a professor in Kiel until the 1850s, Austria had ruled itself out of Germany, since it could not, as a multi-ethnic monarchy, enter a German nation-state. *De facto*, the will of Germany to unite in 1848 had reversed the historical relationship of the Habsburg monarchy and the German lands, by which the former had ensured for 300 years that the latter were 'rotten', 'fragmented' and 'impotent'.[180] 'Granted, the Austrian monarchy is a form of geographical or ethnographic necessity', wrote Droysen in October 1848: 'But look more closely: only the standstill of all maintains the whole; every movement endangers the edifice.'[181] For its part, Prussia had become 'the standard-bearer' of a 'new spirit in the nation', partly because it had become more 'western' in 1815, with the acquisition of the Rhineland, at the same time as Austria had become more 'eastern', giving up lands in Belgium and western Germany, or 'the old territories through which it was rooted deeply in western Europe'.[182] With the establishment of Frankfurt as an ideal, national centre of Germany, and with the weakening of Austria, Prussia now had the power, unlike before 1848, to decide 'the fate of Germany within a few weeks, and in the most salutary way', if it agreed to reshape Germany 'into a true *Bundesstaat*' and to defend that state militarily.[183] Prussia might balk at such collaboration with the new idea of national unity, preferring to revert to the Bund, which 'was nothing other than the Confederation of the Rhine, now with the double protectorate of Austria and Prussia', admitted Droysen in a memorandum from Christmas 1848.[184] Yet such a restored *Staatenbund* would be bound to fail, after the national and democratic changes of 1848.[185] The only remaining option was collaboration between Frankfurt and Berlin. The point, in Droysen's opinion, was that Prussia was in a position for the first time, after several failed initiatives from 1840 onwards, to become a central part of a federal German nation-state.

The revolution of 1848–49 had altered the geographical, political and cultural foundations of the German question, raising unexpected difficulties and suggesting novel solutions concerning the creation of a German nation-state. The most pressing issue was how revolutionaries' vision of the Hohenzollern monarchy's central role in any solution to the German question, given the political exclusion of Austria, would fare after Friedrich Wilhelm IV had refused the title of Kaiser, the revolution had been replaced by reaction, and Prussia had been forced to give up any notion of a Prussian-led

Kleindeutschland at Olmütz on 29 November 1850. The following chapters explore different aspects of this question: what would happen to the national settlement – or blueprint – of the revolution during the years of an Austrian-led counter-revolution?

2 The Great Powers and the Austrian Question

Two cartoons summarised the end of the revolution and the start of a new era in Germany. One, appearing in the *Düsseldorfer Monatshefte* in 1849, depicted three gigantic figures towering over a map of Europe. Napoleon III and Prussia were sweeping revolutionaries, respectively, into the Atlantic and towards Switzerland. Austria was slashing at Italy and Hungary with a large sword. From the margins of the picture, Queen Victoria looked on through glasses, cradling a baby.[1] The other cartoon, in the Berlin *Buddelmeyer-Zeitung* in February 1851, showed 'A Political Hen-House'. Franz Joseph, a two-headed turkey in royal regalia, stood in the centre of the scene, accepting the ingratiating homage of Friedrich Wilhelm IV, a cockerel with its head bowed to the ground. The monarchs of Bavaria, Württemberg, Hanover and Saxony were represented as small ducks, clucking amongst the tail feathers of Austria. The other German princes, imagined as hens, scratched around for grain, unconcerned.[2] The caricatures appeared to bear witness to the common view that the old Austrian-led system, backed by the monarchs of Europe and the princes of Germany, had been reinstalled and would dominate the domestic and foreign affairs of the German states.

Prussia, which had best been able to defend the 'national development of Germany against Austria', had joined forces with the Habsburg monarchy and with Russia, wrote the pro-Prussian liberal Droysen in October 1850, before the meeting at Olmütz on 29 November, at which Otto van Manteuffel was forced to back down by Schwarzenberg in a stand-off over Hesse-Kassel.[3] Berlin had been in a position to decide 'the European question', preventing the return of the 'unbearable aspects of the system of 1815' which had led to 'the disorder (*Unheil*) of 1848', but it had failed to act, leaving reactionaries in Austria and elsewhere to dictate the course of events.[4] 'Instead of securing educated Western Europe against the assault of barbarity, in league with the national strengthening of Germany, they have allied themselves precisely with such barbarity in order to hinder the national movement of Germany,' he went on: 'As if it is not enough that they have again proclaimed the organised disunity of Germany, the old Bundestag, they have killed off every point of political crystallisation, they push towards the maddest despotism, they will soon also smother German science, and they will, where possible, kill off Protestantism.'[5] The Prussian government had supported such reactionaries, concluded Droysen, in the belief that the principle on which Tsar Alexander had claimed to ground the European states' system in 1815 still obtained; 'that all governments have a common interest in moments of danger'.[6] 'Reaction' in Germany and Europe, of which the government in Berlin had become part, was significant above all because 'it has tried to work against a powerfully acting European crisis, to remove from Prussia, Germany and, where possible, Europe, those extensive changes of conditions and attitudes which have already established themselves, to dam the breaches in the dykes and to prevent inundation'.[7] To this end, Prussian reactionaries believed, 'in respect of Prussia's foreign policy', that they should 'assuage Austria's envy of Prussia at any price' and abide by 'Russia's arrogant strictness', so that 'Prussia, in a sincere league with them, could maintain the declining world order and entrench it for a long time to come'.[8] As a result, Manteuffel could no longer say, as he once had, that the whole people (*Volk*) was for him, but he could argue that 'Austria and Russia, perhaps also Bavaria,' were for him.[9] In the opinion of liberals such as Droysen, the German states, including Prussia, had tied their own fortunes to those of an absolutist Austria and a despotic and barbaric Russia at the expense of German unity and unification.

Many historians, from differing points of view, have subscribed to Droysen's analysis, implying that any change in the German order would come from 'above', as shifts of power affecting Austria, Prussia and the third Germany coincided with those involving the European states' system.[10] Such narratives tend to stress the success of Schwarzenberg and his successors in resurrecting the Concert of Europe and imposing reaction in Germany. The turning-point then becomes the Habsburg monarchy's defeat by France and Italy – both associated with nationalism – in 1859, provoking financial ruin – with Austria's and Prussia's debts by 1865 amounting to 1,670 million and 290 million Thaler respectively – and initiating a series of domestic concessions, including the introduction by Schmerling of a new centralised constitution in February 1861, which precipitated a series of protests by Hungarians, Czechs and others and which eventually led to the creation of a formal Dual Monarchy, split between Austria and Hungary, in 1867.[11] Vienna, it is held, had managed to recover after the revolution, quelling opposition, appeasing its national minorities, promoting economic growth and adjusting the states' system during the Crimean War (1854–56), breaking with St Petersburg as the conservative hub of the Concert and, *de facto*, backing London and Paris in order to stifle Russia's ambitions in the Balkans.[12] The permanent weakening of Austria in 1859 in Italy, where it lost Lombardy to Piedmont, allowed Prussia to challenge it in Germany from 1862 onwards under Bismarck, it is implied. By contrast, the argument presented here stresses the destabilising effects of the revolution and the Crimean War, only four years after the post-revolutionary conflicts of Vienna and Berlin, and the openness of the international system throughout the 1850s and 1860s, limiting its ramifications for German politics.

In most accounts, the principal point of articulation between the states' system and Germany remained Austria and Prussia, the 'German' Great Powers. The negotiations between the two powers at Olmütz are usually taken to be pivotal. The Austrian Minister-President, Schwarzenberg, had travelled to the largely German-speaking town in Moravia, the site of Emperor Ferdinand's abdication in 1848, in order to meet the new Prussian Foreign Minister, Otto von Manteuffel, for talks about an impasse between Prussia and the Habsburg monarchy in Holstein and Hesse-Kassel. The disputes dated back to 1849 and the aftermath of the German revolutions. While Austrian troops were occupied by the struggle against Hungarian insurgents, Radowitz had established the *Dreikönigsbündnis* with Saxony and Hanover in May 1849, having seen Prussia's promise of assistance against Hungary – in return for Austrian acceptance of Gagern's plan of a narrower union and a provisional Prussian *Reichsverweser* – rejected by Schwarzenberg in the same month. Twenty-six German states joined the league in

1849, partly as a guarantee against revolution. The constitution that the league put forward was, in turn, endorsed by 130 former Frankfurt deputies, mainly moderate liberals, who had met at Gotha in June 1849. The states and the parliament, which met at Erfurt in March 1850, formed the basis of the Erfurt Union. It was vehemently opposed, after the defeat of the Hungarians in August 1849, by the Austrian government, which had obliged Berlin to sign the 'interim agreement' in September, providing for joint Austrian and Prussian control of Germany until May 1850. When the interim agreement lapsed, Vienna restored the Bund in Frankfurt under an Austrian presidency, inviting all German states to send representatives to discuss the reform of the old Confederation and the formation of a central German authority. Bavaria, Württemberg, Saxony and Hanover, which had formed the *Vierkönigsbündnis* on 27 February 1850, sent delegates, along with six other states. One of the principal reasons given by Saxony and Hanover for leaving the union was its failure to incorporate the whole of the Habsburg monarchy, a condition which Radowitz had conceded in May 1849.

Under the auspices of the revived Bund, Austria and its allies sought to impose important elements of the old, repressive external and internal order. The two flashpoints were Holstein and Hesse-Kassel. In the former, the Danish King appealed to the Confederation, according to the terms of the Russian-sponsored peace treaty with Prussia in July 1850, to act against German 'insurgents', dissolve the 'revolutionary' *Landesversammlung* and depose Friedrich von Reventlow-Preetz, the conservative German *Statthalter*. In the latter, the Elector, having fled to Frankfurt, petitioned for the Bund's support, even though formerly a member of the Erfurt Union, in his attempt to remove the financial powers invested in the Estates in 1831, which had provoked the resistance and dissolution of the assembly, the refusal of civil servants to collect taxes and the resignation of most army officers in order to avoid complying with their ruler's call to use force against the population. In both cases, Schwarzenberg promised support via the Confederation in vital spheres of Prussian interest, with Hesse-Kassel forming a bridge between Austria and North Germany, and between the Prussian Rhineland and the Prussian heartland. At Olmütz, Schwarzenberg demanded that Prussia back down. The primacy of Austria and the princely states, and the imposition of 'reaction' at home, seemed to hinge on the meeting in Moravia.

Prussian – or 'Borussian' – historians interpreted Manteuffel's signature of the Olmütz Punctation, by which settlement of the conflicts in Holstein and Hesse-Kassel were entrusted to the Confederation, as a humiliating turning-point, reversing most of the national aspirations and achievements of the German revolutions and assuring the predominance of the Habsburg monarchy and the Bund until the era of Bismarck after 1862.[13] Many subsequent historians, even those emphasising the successes of Schwarzenberg and his predecessors or of Beust, Pfordten and the other leaders of the third Germany, have been influenced by such an interpretation.[14] It appeared that the secret negotiations of courtiers had thwarted the national-minded projects of liberals, democrats, and moderate conservatives or, in the Borussian reading of events, that the national aims of Prussia had been quashed by Austria and the forces of the Restoration. The national significance of Olmütz, however, was not so clear-cut. The meeting itself, which was held in the Hotel Zur Krone during the evening of 29 November and the morning of the next day, went unnoticed in the press at the time, even in the pro-Austrian Augsburg *Allgemeine Zeitung*, according to Leopold von Gerlach.[15] Manteuffel was accompanied only by his secretary, returning to Berlin inconspicuously on the 5 o'clock train on 30 November.[16] Schwarzenberg, who had only decided to go to Olmütz on 26 November at the insistence of Franz Joseph, went with the Russian envoy in Vienna, Peter Freiherr von Meyendorff, but his visit attracted little comment on the part of well-informed insiders such as the Viennese Inspector-General of the Gendarmerie, Johann Freiherr Kempen von Fichtenstamm, even if the Minister-President was subsequently granted the freedom of Vienna and other Austrian cities in recognition of his mission to Moravia.[17] Neither minister had an unambiguous set of instructions, with Schwarzenberg warned by his Emperor against his will to keep the peace and Manteuffel trying to reconcile his King's last-minute decision to mobilise troops over Hesse-Kassel and his own desire for conciliation. The consequences of their decisions were ambiguous.

Prussia backed down and agreed to the replacement of its troops in Hesse-Kassel by Habsburg forces and to full demobilisation, compared to Austria's agreement merely to partial disarmament. None of the leaders, including Schwarzenberg, wanted war in November 1850, with the stand-off coming at the end of a complicated series of military crises, interventions, retreats, ceasefires and peace treaties beginning in 1848.[18] 'War between Prussia and

Austria would be like an ancient Japanese duel in which each of the participants ripped open his own bowels', remarked Manteuffel.[19] What was more, such leaders shared many other aims, not least the need to defeat 'revolution' at home and abroad. In these circumstances, Olmütz was unlikely to redefine the terms of the German question.[20] The Prussian version of events in the press, wrote Schwarzenberg, tried to conceal the nature of the agreements reached and compromises made. 'We at least are more candid and tell the world: yes, we have made concessions in order to arrive at an understanding with an old ally and to maintain peace, and because we hope that Germany will be the gainer thereby.'[21] For Austrian diplomats such as Anton von Prokesch, the Habsburg ambassador in Berlin, it was obvious by 1 December 1850 that Prussia had compromised – 'what Prussia can and does view as concessions are for us just as many guarantees of a conservative course that she gives us' – but it was not evident where these compromises would lead.[22] As the Austrian ambassador in Paris, Alexander von Hübner, confided to Metternich, Prussia seemed to have committed itself to the Confederation, acting 'as policeman in the duchies and in Hesse' and marking 'a break with the revolution', but the question remained: 'have we arranged it so that a necessary consequence of this convention must be a total and basic change of system in Berlin?'[23]

Manteuffel denied that the change was necessary, maintaining that the choice 'between an alliance with the Great Powers of Europe or with the revolution' was 'not in doubt' in Prussia.[24] The acting Foreign Minister, who was confirmed in his post and as Minister-President on 4 December 1850, 'now gained the reputation of a great diplomat', wrote Leopold von Gerlach on 7 December: 'the punctations of Olmütz are seen as one of the most successful and honourable negotiations for Prussia'.[25] The minister's own reading of the meeting's outcome was that Schwarzenberg had 'conceded a great deal': the joint handling of Holstein and Hesse, the occupation of Cassel by a Prussian and Austrian battalion, and the hasty convocation of a conference to decide matters, 'not in Vienna, but in Dresden'.[26] To Friedrich Wilhelm IV, in his forthright response to the resignation letter of the *Kultusminister* Adalbert von Ladenberg, 'Austria gives us, after 18 months, what we all, including the excellent Radowitz, have not ceased for a single moment since May 1849 to demand of Austria, in the name of Prussia and in its good right, in the name of the good rights of

Germany (*Teutschland*), its princes, its people (*Volk*), its history, in the name of healthy human reason, of logic, of genuine German national feeling: "*The reconstruction of Germany by the entirety of its states under the united auspices of its two Great Powers.*"'[27]

Despite retrospective accounts of the 'humiliation' of Olmütz, many liberals and other members of the political 'opposition' in Prussia did not, at the time, disagree publicly with this positive reading of events. In an article in the *Constitutionelle Zeitung* on 12 December criticising the 'system of 1815', Droysen continued to champion the Hohenzollern state as a self-contained power, 'not like certain others' which needed '"the solidarity of conservative interests" in order to impose themselves on their own constituent parts (*Glieder*) with suicidal barbarity'.[28] Prussia, the liberal historian implied, had not given way to, and connived in, the re-establishment of domestic reaction and a repressive Austrian-led Confederation. Indeed, according to the liberal editor of the *Constitutionelle Zeitung* Ludwig Karl Aegidi, rather than Prussia having been defeated in Germany by Austria at Olmütz, the Habsburg monarchy had revealed itself, from the point of view of the 'common man', to be 'foreign' to German affairs.[29] Liberal deputies in the Prussian chambers were undecided about the significance of the meeting and the government's policy towards Holstein and Hesse-Kassel. Duncker, together with Simson, Beseler and the conservative Vincke, wanted to give up their seats in protest against Manteuffel's 'reaction', but Auerswald, Beckerath, Schwerin and Camphausen were strongly opposed to this course of action. For its part, 'the mass of the party has no conviction or opinion in this regard at all,' wrote Duncker on 8 January 1851: 'that is, it never even thought about it on its own'.[30] On 10 January, Gagern, the former leader of the National Assembly, predicted a Prussian-led future for Germany, characterised by enduring political struggles and eventual constitutional reform, entailing 'a gradual progression towards unity and freedom'.[31]

This chapter extends such a reading of events, revealing the fragility and openness of the international order after the revolutions of 1848–49, and it explores the restrictions imposed, externally and internally, on the various actions of statesmen in the Habsburg monarchy and the other German states. As subsequent chapters demonstrate, public debates about a German nation-state did not disappear during the 1850s and early 1860s. What is more, many of the tentative answers to the 'German question' arrived at in

1848–49 – tellingly, the very phrase dates from the latter stages of the revolution in recognition of the existence of an unsolved problem – proved surprisingly persistent, shaping the assumptions of the most resistant ministers and diplomats of a supposedly reactionary age.[32]

Unholy Alliances

In contemporary mythology, which linked the Treaty of Westphalia to the Congress of Vienna, and in much subsequent historiography, Germany posed a question for European diplomats precisely because of the divisions and weaknesses of the German states. The German lands, it has been maintained, constituted a necessary buffer zone at the centre of the European pentarchy. It could be argued, however, that the shortcomings of the German states exposed in 1848–49, together with the new sources of international disagreement and uncertainty resulting from the revolutions, prompted the Great Powers to look more favourably on some form of German unification or cooperation. 'A German Union embracing all the smaller states, with Prussia at its head, would have been a very good European arrangement', declared Palmerston in November 1850.[33] 'Instead of this', he continued, 'Prussia went on pottering about an Erfurth Union, which never could end in anything but smoke, and then she chose deliberately to expose herself to the humiliation of being obliged, by military threats, to retreat step by step from all the positions she had taken up in regard to almost all pending affairs.'[34] Writing two days before Schwarzenberg's and Manteuffel's meeting at Olmütz, the British Foreign Secretary contended that 'the interest of England and I should say of Europe generally would be that out of such a war Prussia should come unscathed and if possible enlarged and strengthened'.[35] Although 'Russia on one side and France on the other ... must be inwardly chuckling at seeing Germany come down in so short a time from *Einheit* to intense exasperation and to the brink of Civil War', he speculated, such instability was detrimental to the balance of power.[36] In fact, Russia had initially, in the wake of Olmütz, gone so far as to accept Schwarzenberg's plan of incorporating the whole of the Habsburg monarchy in the German Confederation, not least because of the Tsar's 'consideration for Austria', in the opinion of Meyendorff, the Russian ambassador in

Vienna.[37] Britain remained opposed to this plan throughout the 1850s and 1860s on the grounds that 'the whole mass might in the name of the Confederation be used against France or Belgium', making it 'inconsistent with the balance of power in Europe', but it was unlikely that London would have intervened militarily to prevent it.[38] Even at the height of the European 'reaction' to the revolutions of 1848–1849, the Great Powers lacked the will, resources and unity either to provide a solution to the German question, however it was defined, or to prevent the German states, parties and public opinion from searching for one on their own.

Britain, in particular, had attempted to find a solution which was consonant with the requirements of the states' system. In contrast to its position during the German revolutions, when it had remained formally neutral, the Foreign Office openly endorsed Prussia's plan for a reorganisation of Germany's institutions from July 1849 onwards, since the Erfurt Union promised to be less democratic, centralised and speculative than its revolutionary predecessor. 'The Central Power at Frankfort, which was to have been the nucleus around which German unity was to have been formed seems to have crumbled to pieces,' wrote Palmerston on 13 July 1849 in a despatch that was sent to all British embassies on the Continent:

The scheme of German unity which has led to no result at Frankfort has been taken up at Berlin and ... has, provisionally at least, been worked into a practical measure ... Such an extensive organization of Germany would no doubt be advantageous to the German people, with reference both to their internal interests and to their foreign relations, and it would consequently on that account be advantageous to Europe at large.[39]

Nevertheless, the government quickly altered its position as the other Great Powers and the German states resisted Prussia's initiatives. 'It has long been clear to me that Prussia having to contend against the open hostility of Russia and Austria, the covert hostility of France and the jealousy of the principal German sovereigns ... would not succeed', wrote Russell to Prince Albert on 9 April 1850.[40] Unlike Queen Victoria and the Prince Consort, both of whom were more supportive of Prussia and the duchies, Palmerston and Russell became increasingly critical of Berlin's designs in Schleswig-Holstein, which appeared to have issued in the frank admission of Alexander von Schleinitz, the Prussian Foreign

Minister, in August 1850 that the dismemberment of Denmark was being considered.[41] Despite repeated royal attempts to reverse the proclivity of British policy, Palmerston put forward the London Protocol on 4 July 1850, according to which the Great Powers agreed to preserve the integrity of the Danish monarchy, in the face of vehement Prussian opposition. When Radowitz was sent to London to enquire about the possibility of an Anglo-Prussian alliance, partly to shore up the monarchy in its dispute with Austria over Schleswig-Holstein, he was refused. Britain had effectively reverted to its earlier policy of non-intervention in German affairs, ruling out the idea that Austria or the states of the third Germany, which according to the attaché in Berlin in 1861 had 'for ten years ... used the protectorate of Austria to secure impunity to their own execrable misgovernment and to emasculate the national spirit of Germany', could proffer a workable alternative to a Prussian-led national union.[42] 'I confess I do not see my way as to the future organisation of Germany,' Russell wrote to Prince Albert in April 1850: 'If it is declared at Erfurt that Austria cannot by her constitution enter into the confederation, and at Vienna that she must enter with all her states, there appears no room for negotiation.'[43] British statesmen would not have intervened to block attempts to reorganise Germany after 1850, but they could not see how this could be done.

The Foreign Office had intervened in an attempt to foil Schwarzenberg's aim of incorporating the entire Habsburg monarchy in the Bund, with the prospect of forming an anti-British customs union, by insisting on the terms of the Treaty of Vienna: 'the Germanic Confederation is not a Union formed solely by the voluntary association of the states that compose it, and which therefore can be altered and modified at the absolute will of those States ... The German Confederation ... is the result and creation of a European Treaty concluded at Vienna in 1815, and it forms part of the general Settlement of Europe which that Treaty established and regulated.'[44] Neither Britain and the other Great Powers nor the German states belonging to the Erfurt Union had consented to Schwarzenberg's scheme. Yet Britain's insistence on the European character of the German settlement in 1850 was largely pragmatic. When the Austrian Minister-President re-formed the *Bundesversammlung* in September 1850 out of a conference attended by only ten German states, Cowley noted that the procedure was '*strictly speaking* illegal', but the British government failed to act, partly because it favoured the reconstitution of the German Confederation *faute de mieux*.[45]

After the instability of 1848, Palmerston desired a 'closer union of the German states (perhaps with the exception of Austria, Württemberg and Bavaria) under the patronage of Prussia' as 'a solid barrier between the great states of the continent', rather than an Austrian-led German 'mass', but his own growing opposition to Berlin's policy towards Schleswig-Holstein, the principal national question in Germany, worked against such a desire.[46] In any event, as the Foreign Secretary recognised in November 1850, Britain lacked the means to intervene militarily, even if it had wanted to do so:

> To send a land force to cooperate with the Prussians against Austria would be out of the question, and our naval cooperation would be of small assistance. If our alliance is sought for with reference to such a conflict we should probably say that we could not promise it without the consent of Parliament; that Parliament would not be likely to give its consent.[47]

Even more importantly, Britain had little chance of gaining the consistent support of the other Great Powers for any European settlement of the German question, given the disparity of their aims and the virtual collapse of the states' system in 1848, after Prussia, Austria and France had succumbed to revolution. As a liberal power unscathed by revolution and founded on the frightening and unstable basis of industrial growth on display at the Crystal Palace of the World Exhibition in 1851, Britain itself was a major cause of uncertainty in Europe, unwilling to fit into a reconstituted 'Holy Alliance' of conservative powers.[48] Despite adhering to a rhetoric of 'balance' and 'legality', the United Kingdom was unable and unwilling to oversee and enforce the old 'system of 1815' in Germany after 1849. Partly for this reason, public opinion and the press in the German lands rarely, if ever, saw Britain as a member of a reactionary alliance of oppressive Great Powers.[49]

France, too, was not usually held to be part of a refashioned conservative international order. In the conservative press especially, the Napoleonic regime was seen as the successor of the revolution, 'an exemplary warning' which had 'ended in moral bankruptcy after a series of increasingly humiliating revolutions and reactions', remarked the moderate conservative *Preussisches Wochenblatt* in 1853.[50] Napoleon III was often viewed as a 'parvenu'

or a 'French Caesar', but his 'imperialist' regime – an 'Empire' or
'*Kaiserreich*', not to be confused with the German tradition of
'*Kaisertum*' – appeared to be more deeply rooted, associated with
modernity, the army and 'French national life (*Volksart*)', threatening to reduce Germany to the status of a vassal.[51] In the Crimean and
Italian wars of 1854–56 and 1859, the Napoleonic regime had
exploited the national question in a revolutionary way in order to
pursue its own interests, making it imperative to reform the Bund
and establish a 'dam against the supremacy' of France.[52] Even before
these wars, the European states' system seemed to have lost its 'rally-
ing point', lamented the *Wochenblatt*, with a 'solidarity of conservative interests' no longer existing on an international stage.[53] To the
reactionary *Neue Preussische Zeitung*, Napoleon III had deliberately
sought to undermine the entire system, acting 'not for the freedom
and independence of Italy' in 1859, but 'to honour each state and
each city in Italy with Napoleonic institutions and laws', 'to turn
dualism in Germany into an open, long-running wound' and 'to
suffocate the threat of an Anglo-German coalition'.[54]

From differing religious and political points of view, liberal and
Catholic publications agreed with such an analysis. Dictatorship
appeared likely in France once Napoleon's presidential mandate
had expired, with the prospect that the crisis could spread from
France to Germany, as in 1848, forewarned the *Grenzboten* in 1850.[55]
Such a 'military' regime pursued its own interests opportunistically
and ruthlessly, manufacturing an 'Italian question' in 1859 to suit its
own ends.[56] Although it had fought against the outbreak of war, the
Grenzboten had now given up its opposition, fearing a French plan
'to isolate and weaken Austria in order in its next campaign, backed
by Russia and unhindered by Austria, to throw itself on Prussia with
all its might': 'it is more about the Rhine border for France than
about Italy'.[57] All parts of Germany were anxious about a French
attack, even though they had not joined Austria in the conflict
against Italy and France: 'The Bavarians are already picturing the
possibility of a French occupation of the Palatinate, the
Württemberger are already complaining about the hardships of war,
the Hanoverians are reminding themselves that we do not possess a
fleet to keep the French army of invasion from the coast.'[58] German
weakness, it was widely assumed, would eventually be exploited by
an unscrupulous, dictatorial or revolutionary French neighbour, as
had occurred in the era of German humiliation at the hands of
Napoleon I after 1806. For this reason, even in the peacetime of

1863, a Bavarian, Catholic periodical such as the *Historisch-politische Blätter* preferred Prussia to the spectre of another Confederation of the Rhine.[59] Nothing was more despicable, implied the same publication, than to admit that 'Germany is disunited', to 'wash our hands in innocence' and to 'go over to France', for the German lands would again become vassal states.[60] The implication throughout such analyses was that Europe existed in a phase of international disorder and self-interest akin to that of the revolutionary and Napoleonic periods. Germany would not be protected from France by international law or the states' system.

Napoleon III refused to accept the settlement of 1815, helping to prevent the reconstitution of the international order after 1848.[61] France's revolutionary heritage, its uneven support of nationalities, its desire to expand eastwards, and its inconsistency constituted a direct threat to the German lands at the same time as undermining the states' system, as the Russian Foreign Minister made plain in 1863. 'Prince Gortchakov affirms that the Imperial Government of France allied with the revolutionary forces in Europe is a constant source of anxiety and disturbance to the other Powers,' Napier reported to Russell: 'The bulwark against French ascendancy in the Monarchies of Austria, Prussia and the German Confederation is profoundly shaken and may at any moment be laid in ruins.'[62] Gorchakov had already warned the French ambassador Montebello in 1860: 'If you continue periodically to disturb that peace you will gradually end by inspiring everybody with a certain mistrust. In the end, your best friends will break away from you.'[63] Prior to the Crimean War, Edouard Drouyn de Lhuys, the French Foreign Minister, was driven to form an alliance in part to bring about the collapse of the system of Nicholas I, 'the main object of which', according to one British diplomat in 1854, had been 'to keep France in check'.[64] During the Italian war, France was ready to weaken Austria, a Great Power, in the name of Italian nationalism and in pursuit of the annexation of Nice and Savoy. At the time of the Polish insurrection, pushed by the anti-Russian sentiment of public opinion, 'The French hint Threats which we are not prepared to make and we appeal to the Treaty of Vienna which the French would wish to tear to Tatters', asserted Palmerston in 1863.[65] Finally, after initial quiescence during the Prusso-Danish war over Schleswig-Holstein, Napoleon grew impatient, threatening – in the British Foreign Secretary's view – to drag 'us into a war, in which she would claim the Rhine, and possibly revolutionise the whole of

Italy'.[66] Even to British policy-makers, who had been in favour of the
Anglo-French alliance that had existed from the Crimean War to the
insurrection in Poland, France constituted an unpredictable
element, variously menacing Germany, defeating Austria, opposing
Russia and hindering the reconstruction of the states' system.

The system was propped up, it was widely believed, by a tsarist
autocracy which had escaped revolution in 1848 and which had
intervened to re-establish the power of the Habsburgs through the
suppression of the Hungarian insurrection in 1849. Yet St
Petersburg enjoyed a precarious relationship with the two other
'conservative' powers, Prussia and Austria, disagreeing with Berlin
over Schleswig-Holstein and the German question, and with Vienna
over the Balkans and the Near East. Schwarzenberg himself, at the
height of counter-revolutionary cooperation between Russia and
the Habsburg monarchy, was alleged to have warned of Austria's
future 'ingratitude' to its eastern neighbour.[67] As Vienna joined
London and Paris in opposing Russia's occupation of the Ottoman
Principalities of Moldavia and Wallachia in defence of Christians'
rights on 3 July 1853, the Austrian Foreign Minister Karl Ferdinand
von Buol-Schauenstein reiterated Schwarzenberg's argument about
the monarchy's strategic interests: 'My conduct with regard to the
Eastern question is inscribed on the map.'[68] Austria's 'vital interests', in the words of Franz Joseph, clashed with those of Russia.[69]
Having broken definitively with St Petersburg in the summer of
1854, insisting on the unconditional evacuation of the Principalities
and consorting with France and Britain, eventually mobilising
troops on the Russian border although formally neutral, Vienna was
never to reassume its position as a bulwark of the 'Holy Alliance'.
For this reason, Franz Joseph was anxious that 'the present war
should not end by a mere Treaty of Peace,' wrote the British Prime
Minister in 1855: 'He thought Russia would long bear ill-will to
Austria for the part she had taken, and he wished to be united in a
Treaty with the Maritime Powers, with a view to a permanent political system.'[70] As Nicholas I told the Austrian ambassador coldly in
July 1854, 'the trust which had existed until now between the two
sovereigns for the happiness of their empires being destroyed, the
same intimate relations could never exist again'.[71]

This long-standing sense of betrayal seems to have pervaded the
majority of Russia's elites, whose 'language not only of exasperation
and hatred but even of menace' could be heard in Europe's spas:
'Many of them give it to be understood in an indirect but significant

manner that not long will elapse before Austria will be made to pay severely for what in the apparently official language of Russia is termed "her unparalleled treachery".[72] In 1860, as Austria searched desperately for allies after defeat in its war against France and Italy, the Russian Foreign Minister Gorchakov, a former ambassador in Vienna, remarked in private that he was not inclined to look for alliances 'in rotting debris'.[73] Russia did not have to ally itself to 'those in agony', he went on elsewhere, which would be 'too blind a policy' and one which St Petersburg could avoid, 'thank God', since it did not have 'cataracts'.[74] Although, in 1866, Alexander deplored 'the extinction of the small German States, several of whose Princes were connected by ties of kindred with the Imperial family of Russia', and he regretted 'the total exclusion of Austria from Germany', he did not consider supporting the Habsburg monarchy militarily – or by threat of force – against Prussia.[75] During the 1850s and 1860s, the rift between the two main conservative powers proved unbridgeable. By 13 August 1866, Gorchakov saw no alternative, after the failure of his initiatives first to avert war and then to mitigate the effects of Austria's defeat, 'but to restrict ourselves to a *purely Russian* policy', since 'we have not been listened to'.[76]

Russia refused to intervene in the German question in the years between Olmütz and Königgrätz. It generally backed Denmark and opposed Prussia over Schleswig-Holstein, most notably between 1848 and 1850 and in 1863–64, but its interest 'on behalf of Denmark', although 'sincere' in the estimation of one British diplomat, was 'secondary'.[77] 'We have already done and will continue to do *morally* everything that can be done for the defence of Danish rights,' wrote the Tsar in February 1864: 'As for material intervention, that is not to be thought of.'[78] After the Crimean War, in which it had been opposed by the armies of Austria and offended by the neutrality of Prussia and the other German states, Russia repeatedly refrained from offering more than moral support in Germany, even to the Court in Berlin, to which it remained, as Alexander II assured Bismarck in his first audience as Prussian ambassador in St Petersburg in June 1859, personally and politically most attached.[79] Such sentiments of attachment 'are for me an inalienable inheritance that I have received from my father and from my mother', who was Friedrich Wilhelm IV's sister, but they were distinct from the official relations of the two states, which could blow hot and cold.[80] After 1856, Russia faced 'an almost absolute necessity of dealing with its own internal affairs and developing its moral and material forces', wrote the former Russian Foreign Minister Nesselrode in his outgoing memorandum of February 1856, having resigned in November of the previous year.[81] This necessity, together with the perceived duplicity of the German states, helped to ensure that 'for us the German conflict is only of interest if it results in a general conflagration', noted the Tsar in 1863.[82]

At most, Russia aimed to unite the other powers in an ad hoc fashion against the revolutionary designs of Napoleon III, 'a constant source of anxiety and disturbance', and 'to lay cautiously and quietly the basis of a common policy the objects of which should be to support the two great German Powers and give them courage to resist the elements of internal dissolution and the menace of foreign aggression', reported the British ambassador in St Petersburg in December of the same year.[83] Over Schleswig-Holstein, Gorchakov 'merely proposes that the four powers should mutually acknowledge their common interests in this matter and avow to each other the formation of a sort of moral coalition against revolutionary conspiracy, Ultra-Democracy, exaggerated national-ism and Military Bonapartist France', he continued.[84] In fact, the Russian Foreign Minister had already confessed privately that the tsarist regime could count on no other power, not even in a moral sense rather than a legally or diplomatically binding one: 'It is a sad age, the one in which we are destined to live and act! At the present time, there is not a single power of the first rank which can, by its intrinsic value or the invariable character of its convictions, serve as a source of support for a probate and honest government such as our own.'[85] Russia had neither the means nor the intention of resur-recting a Holy Alliance to preside over discussion of the German question.

The Crimean War demonstrated that the Holy Alliance had been hollowed out by the revolutions of 1848–49, despite Nicholas I's apparent certainty as late as 1853 that 'when I speak of Russia, I speak of Austria as well'.[86] As Karl Friedrich Kübeck von Kübau remarked of the plan of his mentor Metternich to keep to the tenets of the Vienna system of 1815, manoeuvring Russia out of the Principalities through the concerted actions of the other powers while refusing to become entangled in any conflict, supported by an alliance with Prussia and the German Bund, the pursuit of Austria's traditional foreign policy was no longer feasible: 'The Prince spoke wisdom – but it will not work!'[87] Even Buol, who worked hardest in 1854–56 to preserve some of the bases of the international order, seems to have believed that a new system was needed in the changed circumstances of post-revolutionary Europe. In 1813, argued the Foreign Minister in an emergency meeting of the Austrian *Ministerrat* on 22 March 1854, Austria had acted decisively at the right time 'to give a definite direction and solid foundation to European politics, on which the general peace and political balance of power had rested in surety for 40 years'.[88] 'That the building which was erected at the time threatened to collapse into rubble before our eyes was certainly not Austria's fault', he continued.[89] In occupying the Principalities, Russia had committed 'a hostile act which contravened all the treaties' concerning the Eastern question and comprising an essential part of the states' system.[90]

If the props of the Concert of Europe consisted of its 'conservative spirit', opposing revolution and imperialism on the Continent, and its common rules of Great Power behaviour, including abstention from territorial wars in Europe, avoidance of confrontations between the powers and the requirement of states' consent over questions touching on their vital interests, they were shown by the Crimean War to be inadequate.[91] Britain and France had threatened Austria with the incitement of revolution in Italy, if it failed to confront the tsarist regime, and Russia, the principal conservative power, had deliberately countenanced 'the collapse of the Turkish Empire', in Buol's opinion.[92] Little other than the internal preoccupations of destabilised states and the coincidental absence of significant flashpoints had maintained the integrity of the Concert of Europe between 1848 and 1854. In particular, the agreement of the powers over effective Austrian hegemony in Italy and Germany, the critical centre of the pentarchy and arguably the pivot of the states' system, had been challenged by Prussia in the latter and France in the former, and had been virtually ignored by Britain, which had been sympathetic to Italian nationalism and Prussian-led German unification. Ironically, Vienna's decision to side with the maritime powers against Russia in 1854, juggling a desire to maintain the Concert against Russian aggression and the need to defend Austrian interests in the Balkans, served to undermine its own hold, with support from St Petersburg, over the German core of the European system.

Unlike its Austrian counterpart, the Prussian government managed to uphold an uneasy neutrality during the 'oriental crisis'. In part, such a stance was dictated by the indecisiveness of Friedrich Wilhelm IV, who was caught between criticism of Russia, whose illegal occupation of Moldavia and Wallachia through an act of 'arrogance and error' had caused 'the terrible mess' in the first place, and support for St Petersburg, since the tsarist regime had come to symbolise conservatism and had occupied the Principalities in the purported defence of Christians' rights against Islam and the Ottoman Empire.[93] 'The War that is breaking out is an *unjust* one on both sides,' declared the King early in 1854: 'And *I will not let Prussia be forced into an unjust war.*'[94] The Tsar was less charitable: 'My dear brother-in-law goes to bed a Russian every evening and gets up every morning an Englishman.'[95] In part, Berlin's position was forced on Manteuffel's administration by the eventual ascendancy of the camarilla, which wanted 'nothing more sincerely than the good friendship of *Prussia, Austria* and *Russia*'.[96] Although the Gerlach brothers were not 'Spree Cossacks', as moderate conservatives claimed at the time, they were consistently opposed to the western powers, which they associated with revolution: '*My* opinion of the foreign policy of the era', wrote Ernst Ludwig von Gerlach retrospectively, 'was not to attack England and France, not to be enthusiastic about Russia, as were almost all conservatives of the age, but still to be decisively against the western alliance, of which liberalism in its entirety was in favour, and to be for friendship with Russia and a brokering neutrality, hand in hand with Austria.'[97] Yet, despite championing the Holy Alliance, the camarilla began to falter once 'the disclosure of the immoral, egotistical and Bonapartist ... Austrian policy' of rapprochement with the maritime powers was made in Berlin in October 1854.[98]

The reactionary right's victory over moderates in 1854 had, in any event, long been precarious. The pro-British 'Wochenblatt' party of Moritz August von Bethmann-Hollweg, a Frankfurt academic and editor of the *Preussisches Wochenblatt*, included influential figures at Court and in the administration such as the War Minister Eduard von Bonin, the diplomats Christian Carl Josias Bunsen, Albert von Pourtalès, Robert von der Goltz and Guido von Usedom, and the King's brother, heir and effective head of the army, Prince Wilhelm. The group was openly critical of Russia and Austria, and viewed the Crimean War as a 'liberation' from the existing system at home and abroad, as Usedom termed it at the end of 1853.[99] As the proceedings against Bunsen, the Prussian ambassador in London, revealed in March 1854, when he sent a memorandum to Manteuffel outlining the territorial aggrandisement of Prussia in the East at the expense of Russia, moderate conservatives did not feel bound by the traditions of the Concert of Europe. Although Bunsen was forced to resign in May, as was Bonin, which precipitated the Prince of Prussia's standing down as first officer of the army and his controversial and angry departure from Prussian soil for Baden, it was evident that moderate conservatism in Prussia, as in the era of Radowitz, remained a significant force, not least because of the position and likely regency of Prince Wilhelm, who returned to Prussia in June 1854. At the start of the conflict, the Minister-President Manteuffel had himself toyed with anti-Russian, pro-western ideas. From an external standpoint, it was not at all obvious which policy Berlin would adopt. Prussia was widely seen to be opportunistic and self-interested, with 'a double-dealing treacherous cowardly court' in the British Foreign Secretary's view, rather than being cooperative and supportive of the international order.[100]

The press and public opinion, in Prussia as in the rest of Germany, rarely seem to have assumed that the states' system, either in the form of a conservative Holy Alliance or a looser Concert of Europe, was sufficiently coherent and powerful to inhibit German unification. Even in the autumn of 1850, as Austria and Russia imposed the London Protocol on Schleswig-Holstein in the face of Prussian opposition and liberal uproar throughout Germany, the *National-Zeitung* still ridiculed the idea that 'the Great Powers have spoken': 'We can answer that diplomats have only found the courage to interfere because of our impotence and inactivity. Everywhere, they only impose their laws on the weak, whilst they always rush, faced with the strong, to recognise *faits accomplis.*'[101] The 'old system of a European balance of power' had lost much of its relevance, commented the *Preussisches Wochenblatt* in 1852: the Holy Alliance was 'very nice in theory', but in reality it had 'mostly turned into its very unholy opposite'.[102] It is true that there were references to the interference of reactionary powers such as Russia. Thus, when Austria resurrected the *Bundestag*, openly backed by Alexander II, the *National-Zeitung* mockingly lamented the fact that 'the most important decision in the German constitutional question' had slipped out of 'the hands of the German National Assembly into those of the Tsar of Russia'.[103] It is also true that significant sections of the press and public genuinely feared foreign enemies on political and, in the case of Russia, racial grounds.[104] In both the French and Russian 'characters' lay a powerful 'drive towards territorial expansion' which might lead to the destruction of Prussia in the same manner as Poland, Sweden and Turkey, warned the *Wochenblatt*.[105] However, foes were usually identified singly and inconsistently.

During the Crimean War, claimed the *Kölnische Zeitung*, 'both conflicting parties in Germany look towards "Russia's dominance", one hopefully and faithfully, the other fearfully but sceptically'.[106] Liberal publications were usually critical of St Petersburg and reactionary ones approving, though with qualifications.[107] Their attitudes to France and Britain tended to be reversed. Catholic, South German and Austrian newspapers and periodicals tended to follow the movement of the Habsburg monarchy away from the tsarist regime and towards the western powers. The *Augsburger Allgemeine Zeitung* accordingly interpreted the oriental crisis in early 1854 as a struggle against the Ottoman Empire, the 'hereditary and imperial enemy' of the West (*Abendland*), with Russia defending a 'national and religious idea' held by 'all peoples and princes of Christendom'.[108] In contrast, by the end of 1854, the same newspaper could be found discussing a 'racial conflict' between 'Slavs' and 'Germans': 'Austria not only has a neighbour to fear but also the national character of this Great Power. Between the compact masses of the North and South Slavs, German elements have pushed their way between, in the Austrian duchies on the Danube down to the mouth of the March.'[109] Despite referring to long-lasting stereotypes, Germans' views of their 'enemies' were diverse and unstable. Few contemporaries placed such enemies in a durable international system. Indeed, wrote the *Historisch-politische Blätter*, Europe had undergone a revolution in the relations between states between 1854 and 1856.[110] In these uncertain conditions, the best defence seemed to be greater German unity vis-à-vis the outside world, contended the Catholic periodical, against the charge that it was 'ultramontane' and 'un-German'.[111] A similar pattern could be observed during the wars of 1859 and 1864, both of which overturned previous inter-state allegiances and assumed affinities, planting further doubts in many contemporaries' minds about the validity and relevance of a European 'states' system'. Rather than perceiving a domestic and international 'reaction' which had re-established political fault lines through and beyond the German lands, in the manner of the Metternichian order of 1815, most commentators in the 1850s appear to have viewed foreign affairs in a national way, distinguishing between 'Germany', however defined, and a changing array of external allies and enemies.

Austrians and the *Vielvölkerreich*

The main point of contact between 'Germany' and the states' system appeared to be Austria, which had dominated the German lands until 1848 and which had played a vital part in the Concert of Europe. Thus, a 36-year-old Otto von Bismarck-Schönhausen, Prussia's new envoy to the reconvened Bundestag in Frankfurt, made one of his first tasks a visit to Metternich, who was staying on the family estates at Johannisberg on the Rhine in 1851, after returning from exile in Britain. The two men got on well, discussing the previous half-century of European history and meeting again in Vienna a year later. Twelve days after Bismarck's first visit, the Austrian elder statesman – 'the hero of the day' – was unexpectedly called on by Friedrich Wilhelm IV, on his way down the Rhine from Coblenz to Mainz.[112] As in Metternich's time, much of the Habsburg monarchy's status and leverage as a Great Power continued to derive from its position as the principal German power and its ability to mobilise other states via the Bund. It was therefore imperative that the governments and, to a varying extent, the presses, parties and publics of the German states accepted that Austria was 'German'. After 1848–49, such acceptance was by no means straightforward. Moreover, German Austrians themselves seemed during the revolution to have put their loyalty to the monarchy above their cultural affiliations with Germany. The continuing existence of this 'Austrian question', at least in southern Germany and in certain political milieux, largely dictated the terms of the debate about German territory and borders.

The competing notions of *Kleindeutschland* and *Grossdeutschland*, which had only emerged in the latter stages of the revolution and continued to be used only sporadically, fail to do justice to the complexities of such a debate, which resulted from the intertwining of the rivalry of Austria and Prussia, attempts at mediation and reform on the part of medium-sized German states, and an ongoing public debate about a German nation-state. Whereas the boundaries of *Kleindeutschland* were more or less fixed, with the exception of Schleswig-Holstein and Bavaria, those of *Grossdeutschland* remained open: the word usually described the inclusion of the old 'German' lands of the Confederation in a new German entity, but the constitutional form and territorial extent of that entity – particularly with regard to Bohemia and Moravia, which had belonged to the Bund – had been left undefined. In any event, the actions of the

Austrian government after October 1848, Austrian deputies in the Frankfurt Parliament and 'German–Austrian' public opinion, as far as it could be determined, had suggested that *Grossdeutschland* on this basis, which threatened the integrity of the Habsburg state, was unacceptable. Contemporaries were faced with the inclusion of Austria's non-German lands as well as the old confederal ones, the exclusion of Austria in its entirety, or the quest for a constitutional arrangement which was sufficiently flexible to avoid the dichotomy between inclusion and exclusion.[113] The question seemed to hinge less on the extent of Germany – whether it was to be 'great' or 'small' – than on the attitude of the Austrian government and public opinion to German affairs, and on the willingness of the governments and publics of the individual states to view the Habsburg monarchy as a 'German' power.

Austrian leaders certainly wanted to preserve the Habsburg monarchy's role in Germany after 1848–49. Schwarzenberg was not ready to allow Austria to be forced out of the German sphere: his goal was 'an externally solid and powerful, internally strong and free, organically integrated and, yes, united Germany,' he wrote to Schmerling on 4 February 1849:

> Confident of the view that there exists no contradiction between the interwoven, if also sometimes apparently diverging, interests of the German and non-German parts of the monarchy, on the one hand, and of these and the rest of Germany, on the other, the government in no way underestimates the difficulty of an inner unification (*Vereinigung*), but it also has no doubt, if the work is done impartially and without other motives, of the successful resolution of the great task.[114]

As early as December 1848, the Austrian Minister-President had mooted the possibility of the whole of the Habsburg monarchy entering an historically 'German' Confederation, despite the likely objections of the non-German nationalities. He adhered to this position throughout 1849 and 1850, in opposition to Radowitz's Union plan, first floated in the spring of 1849 and opposed by Schwarzenberg in a fit of rage as a contravention of the 1815 settlement, and in the wake of the stand-off with Berlin over Kurhessen and Schleswig-Holstein in the autumn of 1850.[115] After the Prussian government had refused to give up the Union and to discuss a reform of a reconstituted Bund in July 1850, Schwarzenberg again put forward the idea of Germany as a Bund of 70 millions in his 'six-point programme' of the same month, which outlined the entry of the Austrian *Gesamtstaat* and the institution of a common *Zollunion*.[116] When this initiative was also rejected, he went ahead and reconvened the Bundestag independently of Berlin in August, but nevertheless continued to articulate his 'desire for an agreement with Prussia, without which a definitive and reasonable constitution (*Konstituierung*) of Germany is not to be achieved'.[117]

Prussia, of course, was obliged to acknowledge the Confederation at Olmütz in November 1850, agreeing to discuss a reform of the Bund at the Dresden Conferences of January 1851, yet Austria's 'German' rhetoric remained unchanged by the reversal of the two states' positions of power, as the joint invitation to the other states on behalf of Vienna and Berlin made plain: a revision of the constitution of the Bund was required because 'otherwise the German lands would be reduced to complete insignificance in the context of the European family of nations'.[118] The implication was that Austria was a 'German' power, with an inalienable right to remain in Germany. Thus, as the Frankfurt Parliament had begun to discuss offering Friedrich Wilhelm IV the title 'Kaiser of the Germans' in January 1849, Schwarzenberg, who believed that the Prussian King might be obliged to accept, had insisted that the Austrian Emperor was 'the first German prince': 'This is a right, made sacred by tradition and the passing of centuries, by the political power of Austria and by the wording of the treaties on which the still-undissolved ties of the Bund are founded.'[119] In this sense, Prussia's acceptance of the Bund seemed to imply recognition of Austria's continued presence in Germany.

Karl von Buol-Schauenstein and Bernhard von Rechberg, Schwarzenberg's successors as Foreign Minister in 1852–59 and 1859–64, followed a similar course, insisting on Austria's legal entitlements and historical friendships within the German Confederation. Thus, on 21 March 1854, as Britain and France joined Turkey in its war against Russia, Buol proposed Austrian intervention to Franz Joseph on the grounds that passivity or neutrality would either lead to Russian predominance in the Near East or French and British incitement of revolution in Italy in order to force Vienna's hand; if Austria occupied Moldavia, Wallachia and Serbia, Prussia and the Bund could be relied upon to back Vienna in the event of war or the use of force.[120] During the following day's ministerial conference, the Foreign Minister declared, against criti-

cism from military members of the meeting such as Heinrich von
Hess and Karl von Grünne, that Prussia had already offered a defensive alliance, eventually signed on 20 April 1854, that 'started from
the premise that Austria might need to occupy certain Turkish
provinces and that, if this brought with it a Russian attack on
Austrian territory, we would have a full claim on the support of the
projected alliance': 'It would therefore simply be a question of
agreeing expressly with Prussia that, if we were to move into the
Danube principalities with the agreement of the Porte in order to
force their evacuation, the help of the Bund for us would be
assured.'[121] After it had signed alliances with London and Paris in
December 1854, Vienna attempted in vain to instigate a resolution
in favour of the mobilisation of the Bund's forces by sending a circular to the larger German states except Prussia on 14 January 1855.
Buol adopted the same 'German' tactic in 1859, contending in
February that Germany 'as a power in its entirety (*Gesamtmacht*)' was
threatened by the war against France and Italy, and in May that
Austria's 'power relations' were intertwined with 'the security of the
whole Confederation'.[122] Buol again asked the *Bundesversammlung*
to mobilise federal troops on 7 July, the day before a ceasefire was
agreed. Austria, of course, had been defeated in a war for whose
preparation – and 'the assurance of a favourable outcome' – 'next
to nothing was done', in the opinion of Rechberg, Buol's replacement.[123]

Defeat, however, did not prompt a revision of the administration's
German policy. Although Prussia and the other German states had
refused to back Austria in 1859, Rechberg's answer was to court
them more determinedly, not to give in to those calls in Vienna to
reduce Prussia, perhaps through an alliance with France, to a
second- or third-ranking power: 'Quite aside from the standpoint of
legality, it would be accompanied by the most disastrous consequences,' wrote the new Foreign Minister: 'Germany would be weakened and Austria would stand alone against a preponderant
France.'[124] Rechberg's aim was to 'act calmly but firmly in the
defence of our legitimate rights, and collect the other German
governments around us' so that 'Prussia will perceive the impossibility of achieving her plans and this will facilitate the victory of the
calmer and more sensible party in Berlin'.[125] Germany could be
persuaded to rally around Austria, the principal German power.
Rechberg asked of Prussia 'only that for her part she respect our
dignity and the position we have in Germany as a Great Power and

as the heir of a glorious past'.[126] His policy towards Schleswig-Holstein in 1863–64 was likewise marked by a willingness to concili-ate Berlin and to maintain Austria's position in Germany, a position which – he held in 1866 – he would not have lost through a disas-trous war with the other German Great Power.[127] Such claims were consistent with his pedigree, as the son of a Bavarian Foreign Minister, and his reputation as a German specialist, with Metternich asserting as early as 1855, when he became Austrian envoy in Frankfurt, that 'Rechberg knows German conditions; in that regard he stands almost alone there.'[128] Both Buol and Rechberg followed a broadly Metternichian policy in support of Austria's continuing role in Germany, its maintenance of the Confederation and its linkage of the German question and the European states' system.

Critics, however, claimed that Vienna usually placed its European interests above its German responsibilities and that it proved inca-pable of adapting to public demands for a German nation-state in and after 1848. To Anton von Schmerling, one of the most well-known representatives of German–Austrian liberals and the Austrian *Staatsminister* (Prime Minister) from December 1860 to 1865, the Habsburg monarchy had failed to take the initiative in Germany: 'Alone from the highly insignificant Graf Buol, who led the affairs of state from the death of Minister Schwarzenberg to 1859, and just as little from Graf Rechberg, no decisive act at all was to be expected.'[129] The appointment of Schmerling, the former head of the Central Power in Frankfurt and champion of constitu-tional reform in Austria, had appeared to signal a change in Vienna's German policy, leading to Austrian-led attempts to reform the Bund from within through the deliberations of the *Bundesversammlung* in 1862 and from without at the Frankfurt *Fürstentag* in August 1863. Through the machinery of the *Bund*, Rechberg and Ludwig von Biegeleben, the Hessian-born head of the German section of the Austrian Foreign Ministry, adopted the plan of Reinhard von Dalwigk zu Lichtenfels, the Minister-President of Hesse-Darmstadt, advocating the establishment of a confederal court, a tripartite executive and an assembly of delegates of the state assemblies.[130] At the *Fürstentag*, Franz Joseph proposed a 5-person executive, a federal Bundesrat of 17, a federal court, an assembly of 302 delegates of state parliaments, and an assembly of princes and heads of state, all of which were held, in an Austrian memorandum enclosed with the invitation to the conference of princes on 31 July, to constitute 'a new shaping of the political constitution' of 'the

German nation (*Nation*) in its entirety'.[131] The former initiative was defeated by 9 votes to 8 in the *Engerer Rat* of the *Bundesversammlung* in January 1863; the latter foundered on Wilhelm I's refusal to attend the meeting of the princes, with the heads of the individual states subsequently insisting in a signed declaration that their support for the Austrian project was valid only 'until the members of the Bund not represented [that is, Prussia] either definitively reject the disclosed plan or have shown us their counter-proposals'.[132]

Berlin, of course, scuppered the plan, putting forward its own scheme, which included a Prussian and Austrian veto over the declaration of wars other than those in defence of confederal territory, full Prussian parity with Austria in the leadership of the Bund, and the institution of a directly elected national parliament. Yet even before the defeating of Austrian proposals, there were justified doubts about Vienna's commitment and freedom of manoeuvre. In the discussions with Franz Joseph prior to the *Fürstentag*, Rechberg had been sceptical, in Schmerling's view:

> the honourable gentleman shook his head and said that nothing would come of the affair, that Prussia would never allow itself to be present and to accept such a reform because, as everyone knew, the Prussian government had other plans altogether. But quite apart from this, the idea that an agenda for the reform of the German Bund could even be formulated and that he would be in a position to represent it was anything but agreeable to him.[133]

For his part, Franz Joseph insisted on taking Rechberg to Frankfurt with him rather than Schmerling, despite the objection of Hungarian ministers that such a step would 'inflict very significant damage' and 'that the impact of Graf Rechberg in this matter would amount to nought', resulting in a 'fiasco'.[134] The dominant view in government, court and army circles in Vienna was that constitutional reform in Germany posed difficulties, thought by many to be insurmountable, for the political and administrative structure of the Habsburg monarchy.

Many Austrian statesmen and officials could not see how a multinational Habsburg state could be integrated into a German polity.[135] Their objections usually focused on attempts to create a confederal or German assembly. For conservatives, especially during the period of neo-absolutism between 1849 and 1861 when

Austria lacked a parliament, the very notion of an assembly was problematic. Even in 1863, two years after the February Patent had re-established a parliamentary *Reichsrat* with legislative and budgetary powers, Franz Joseph was still averse to the term 'popular representation' to describe the German assembly of delegates discussed at the *Fürstentag*. Correspondingly, the chamber was to be purely consultative, was subject to the veto of an assembly of princes, and was only to meet every three years. In his initial meeting with Schmerling, the Emperor barely attempted to conceal the distasteful fact that, according to the briefing which he had received about Austria's espousal of 'a reform of the German Acts of Confederation', not only a powerful executive had to be created, 'but also of course a representative assembly (*Vertretung*) must be contemplated'.[136]

Schmerling himself was much more enthusiastic about representative government, believing that its return in the Habsburg monarchy in 1861 had ended the 'mistrust of Austria which had been harboured in the whole of Germany, the view that it was only to be seen as a bulwark of absolutism'.[137] He went on to produce a plan, in conjunction with Biegeleben and the federalist publicist and his close acquaintance Julius Fröbel, which included a shared executive and an assembly of *Landtag* delegates, since 'the integrity of the individual states must be preserved, so that a directly elected parliament was not called into being, but as much as possible was allowed to come from the individual representative bodies, whereby the necessary linkage with German popular representative assemblies was made and the possibility was created that laws agreed in this Reich representative assembly would also be introduced without resistance in the individual states.'[138] The *Staatsminister*'s hope by the time of the *Fürstentag* was that state and Reich governments and assemblies would agree over important pieces of legislation and policy. In his first meeting with Franz Joseph, however, Schmerling had conceded that such convergence and cooperation was far from guaranteed, particularly on the part of the multi-national Austrian assembly, by which 'German' laws were to be sanctioned or rejected:

> Whenever a law comes into being it must be referred to the Austrian *Reichsrat* for constitutional consideration, and it is to be considered there whether a law agreed in Germany may also be introduced in Austria ... Admittedly, there exists the difficulty, which does not exist in other German states, that not only

deputies from the so-called German federal lands, but also those from other Austrian territories such as Galicia, Dalmatia, and Venice take up their seats in the Austrian *Reichsrat.* It is simply to be hoped that laws accepted in Germany will also be accepted here.[139]

Few, if any, other Austrian ministers and officials were so confident that the non-German nationalities of the monarchy would cooperate within such a constitutional framework. As early as December 1848, in response to Schmerling's demand that Austria should agree to a constitution suited to Germany in the first instance and then add special clauses to make it acceptable to the Habsburg monarchy, Schwarzenberg had warned that such a modus operandi threatened further to undermine the trust of Austria's other nationalities: Croatia wanted to become Austrian not German, he cautioned.[140] Since the Minister-President was opposed to the idea of a *grossdeutsch* constitution, sending its proponents from the Frankfurt Parliament back home in the spring of 1849 without even meeting them, it soon became apparent that his conception of the Bund, which required the so-called '*Gesamteintritt*' of Austria, was not national at all, but rather, as he put it to the ministerial conference of 8 October 1849, a '*Mitteleuropäischer Staatenbund*' of three blocs – the Habsburg monarchy, Prussia, and the middling and smaller German states within a narrower Bund – united by an indissoluble agreement in international law and by a common customs' union.[141] In response, the Bavarian Minister-President Pfordten devised an alternative scheme, which was accepted by Vienna in January 1850 except for the exclusion of Lombardy and Venice. Once again, Schwarzenberg's 'Central European' concept took precedence over his German loyalties:

The German land of Austria, which supports Germany but which does not want for this reason to give up its whole body (*Gesamtkörper*), acquired in the course of centuries, steps forth as one of the major factors in the international Bund which is to be formed and fulfils in this way one of the natural and justified desires which have been voiced since 1848; namely, the corresponding position of power of a great Central European body. The incorporation of the Italian provinces of Austria in the common customs' area can only be an advantage for Germany.[142]

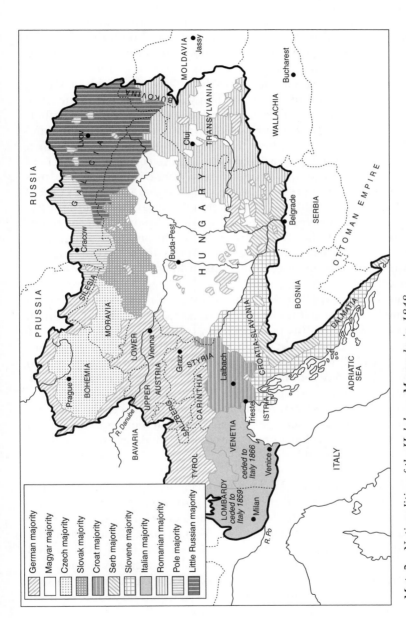

Map 3 *Nationalities of the Habsburg Monarchy in 1848.*

Source: Adapted from R. Okey, The Habsburg Monarchy, c. 1765–1918 (Basingstoke, 2001), xii

Partly as a consequence, but also because of a deep-rooted antipathy to 'democracy', Schwarzenberg eschewed the introduction of representative assemblies, which would have underlined – and would have been weakened by – national differences. Austria had only accepted the 'absurd' and 'unnecessary' representative elements of the Bavarian plan in 1850, the minister noted in March, in order not to be isolated in Germany and not to leave 'the revolution and Prussia jointly a free field and easy hand in the fatherland as a whole (*Gesamtvaterland*)'.[143] In his 'six-point programme' of July 1850, Schwarzenberg ruled out a popular assembly in a reformed *Bund* altogether. Finally, during the Dresden Conferences in January 1851, he was accused by the King of Württemberg, in a letter leaked to the press, of being against the creation of a confederal parliament. Although he recognised that a 'purely administrative and military form of rule' corresponded neither 'to the needs and relations of the monarchy' nor 'to the general situation in Europe', the Austrian Minister-President was unable to find an alternative solution to meet the demands of liberals and nationalists in Germany.[144]

Buol likewise spelled out, after a flurry of press reports about a planned Austrian reform of the Bund in 1855, that he had no intention of introducing 'the parliamentary principle' or any other measures 'in the sense of liberal doctrines'.[145] His successor Rechberg wanted, with Prussia, 'to nip German democracy in the bud' and to keep the Confederation in its old form: Austrians could not risk 'dismantling the existing edifice without assuring ourselves of the construction of another comfortable one'.[146] Even the restored Austrian *Reichsrat*, much less a German parliament, he remarked in 1861, would be divided along national lines, making Austrian policy in Germany impossible:

The majority of the *Reichsrat* would by no means belong to the German race. Should the imperial government find itself in the situation of having to defend its German policy in order to fulfil its confederal obligations to the German Bund, then the Hungarians, the south Slavs, the Poles, and the Italians would unite in the dictum that they would reject any policy that required sacrifices of money and blood for Germany. As a result of such a vote the imperial government would be unable to assert its rights and its position in Germany.[147]

In important respects, Buol's and Rechberg's well-documented desire to champion historical rights and international treaties, which were held to underpin the Bund, derived from a fear of the principle of nationality and the pursuit of national interest. Austria had to adhere to 'the basis of legality and the treaties, which are, in the final analysis, the only foundation of European society,' wrote Hübner to Rechberg in November 1862: 'Perhaps the day is not far off when a deluded public opinion will recognise this. But, near or far, the policy of legality and of principles – one can laugh over this word as much as one wants (and he who laughs last, laughs best) – is the only useful one for Austria.'[148] To Habsburg ministers and diplomats, nationality, international law, popular representation and the German question often seemed to be incompatible. The monarchy seemed to be at odds with a Continent characterised by national movements and national conflicts. In such circumstances, it was tempting for Austrian leaders to resurrect many of the conservative foreign and domestic policies favoured by Metternich, emphasising dynasty, history and legality. As Buol warned the ministerial council in March 1854, 'in politics nothing seems more dangerous than experimentation'.[149]

Austria's defence of its rights appeared to conflict with the interests of a German nation-state. For a short period, Schwarzenberg had seemed to avoid the dilemma of his successors, hinting that a Central European Confederation could at once retain a German core and make use of an extended periphery, enhancing the power of the whole. By such reasoning, Germany benefited from the inclusion of non-German nationalities within its borders and from the coexistence of Great Powers within a powerful *Staatenbund*. On 9 March 1849, Schwarzenberg had written to Schmerling privately that Frankfurt had to 'give up the nonsense that the weakening of Austria was the strengthening of Germany'.[150] If the German lands were to be divided up 'organically' in accordance with its 'tribes', 'Austria has advantages to offer such a Germany: in holding open Reich citizenship, in terms of settlement, in respect of tariffs, in conjunction with the Mediterranean and the Black Sea etc. – advantages which will bring about close ties and true unity in a shorter time and for the greater use of Germany than can be achieved in any other way.'[151] The incorporation of the whole of the Habsburg monarchy in the Bund remained Schwarzenberg's aim at the Dresden Conferences in January 1851, after he had forced Prussia to back down militarily in November of the previous year. Yet the Austrian Minister-President failed to achieve Austria's *Gesamteintritt*, even though Prussia and Russia had stated in 1850 that they would not oppose it.[152]

From accounts of both Olmütz – at which even Manteuffel's own private secretary thought the Austrian aristocrat 'a splendid man, noble through and through,' whom he would have preferred as Prussia's own minister – and of Dresden, where the Austrian Minister-President occupied the first floor of the royal palace with silverware and champagne glasses while his Prussian counterpart was allotted the floor above with water glasses, Schwarzenberg dominated proceedings and arguably had the means to enforce his will. That he chose not to was the result of many overlapping considerations: the wish of Franz Joseph to avoid war and court Berlin; Russia's divided loyalties; fear of public reaction in Germany, especially if Russia were to become involved; the need to gain the support of the western powers in the Near East; scepticism of the steadfastness of Austria's allies in the third Germany; and uncertainty about Austria's military superiority over Prussia. Above all, however, the Minister-President seems not to have valued the monarchy's *Gesamteintritt* in the Bund highly enough to risk war after Olmütz or to offer Prussia full parity in Dresden. His instructions to Vienna's representatives at the Dresden Conference were conservative: Austria should portray itself as a defender of legality and should back the old Bund, reassuring the German states and European Great Powers, which 'may well consider what a guarantee of the peace the German Confederation offers them under its present constitution, and what a danger a militarised state, such as would be established by Prussia, would bring for them'.[153] The restoration of the Confederation, contemplated here before the conferences had begun, militated against incorporation and the establishment of a 'Bund of 70 millions' – a phrase which was avoided by Schwarzenberg and other diplomats, despite its use in the Austrian press. When challenged by Prussia, Vienna proved less interested in setting up a new type of government and territorial settlement for Germany than in shoring up Austria's position as a Great Power, cultivating its relations with other European powers, and ensuring the continuity and legality of existing German institutions.

The idea of a Central European economic bloc, which surfaced during the Schwarzenberg and Schmerling eras, seemed – like the *Mitteleuropäischer Staatenbund* – to contradict such conservatism, yet it found few supporters in government and was quickly jettisoned. Between 1849 and 1851, Karl Ludwig von Bruck, the Minister of Trade and founder of the Austrian Lloyd, presented the case for a gradual reduction of tariffs to merge the three trading areas of Germany – Austria, the *Zollverein* and the North German coastal states – in order, 'regardless of all obstacles and prejudices, the scale of which we do not hide from ourselves, to fulfil all the needs of the peoples (*Völker*) and to ground a truly fixed and rewarding order of things with the new political construction of Germany and Austria.'[154] Schwarzenberg initially sponsored Bruck's proposals only to drop them at Dresden in favour of the overriding foreign-policy goal of restoring the Bund. In his letters to Metternich, Prokesch and Buol during 1850, he tellingly never mentioned a German customs' union or, indeed, other *Mitteleuropa* schemes or a Bund of 70 millions.[155] The Minister-President's instructions to Buol in Dresden suggest that he wanted to put any *Zolleinigung* to immediate political use as a means of securing the agreement of Prussia more generally. The levels of the tariffs could be decided later.[156] Like Schwarzenberg, Buol appears to have had little interest in the complicated negotiation of a customs' union, seeing it increasingly as an obstacle to better relations with Berlin. The trade and customs agreement that he signed with Prussia in February 1853 failed to secure the Habsburg monarchy's eventual entry into the *Zollverein*, merely noting that negotiations should begin again in 1860.

When talks actually recommenced in 1862, the commission into tariffs advised ministers only to revive the pursuit of a *Gesamteintritt* into the *Zollverein* if Prussia did not conclude its free-trade agreement with France. Since Rechberg asserted to the council of ministers on 23 April 1862 that 'a unification of tariffs (*Zolleinigung*) with the entire *Zollverein* is obviously not to be achieved', the main question was whether Austria could set up an alternative Central European customs' union to rival that of Prussia, composed of South German states and the Habsburg monarchy, or whether it would be saddled with 'the political disadvantages connected to isolation'.[157] As in 1849–51, Austria had considerable leverage, with many members of the *Zollverein* resistant to the removal of tariffs on French goods and with some willing to profit from Bismarck's lack of popularity in Germany: 'If we succeed in moving a greater number of these states, and namely those on which the maintenance of the continuity of its customs' area depends such as

Hanover, Braunschweig, Hesse etc., not to accept the Prussian treaty with France, then there is a hope of pushing Prussia towards compromise.'[158] Yet Austrian ministers remained cautious and disorganised. As late as 11 April 1862, Rechberg belatedly asked what policy to pursue: it was necessary to know 'what the intentions of the imperial government were, which direction he should go in and whether he should attempt to effect the entry of Austria into the *Zollverein* or not'.[159] Repeatedly, the Foreign, Trade and Finance Ministries complained of a lack of coordination.[160] On 22 July 1863, Biegeleben lamented that Austria had still not managed to settle on a tariff level and was therefore unable to persuade individual states to leave the *Zollverein*.[161] Even at the start of negotiations with other German states, Rechberg had acknowledged the possibility 'that only Bavaria and Württemberg [would] join Austria', although he noted the tariff commission's advice that this would be better than nothing.[162] Throughout, ministers' expectations were limited. They seemed to be jockeying for position in Germany, usually against Prussia, rather than attempting to construct a new order or system of government there. In 1865, Vienna signed a treaty with the *Zollverein* which simply left open the question of a general unification of tariffs. Albrecht von Bernstorff reported to the council of ministers that it was 'the most advantageous that could be arrived at under the prevailing conditions'.[163] The Austrian government's plans for a Central European or a new German customs' union had been largely defensive, designed to cajole or threaten Prussia into moderating its own aims. It is doubtful whether they corresponded in any meaningful way to an alternative Austrian vision of a new German order.

Austrian leaders saw Germany as a sphere of Great Power politics and as one of the sources of the Habsburg monarchy's Great Power status. Despite paying lip service on occasion to the reform or replacement of the Bund's political institutions, Vienna preferred to deal directly with Berlin in order to achieve its ends. Even at the height of the conflict between the two powers in 1850, Schwarzenberg was certain that 'our desire for agreement with Prussia ... remains the same'.[164] In August, the Minister-President's 'six-point programme' had called for an executive and *Bundesversammlung* composed exclusively of Prussian and Austrian representatives. From Dresden, the Minister-President wrote to Franz Joseph on 1 January 1851 that any reform of the organs of the Confederation would require Prussian cooperation: 'That agreement with Prussia is above all necessary to this end is unmistakable. It is necessary not only because of the indispensable sanction of Prussia, but also because only when we bring in our suggestions together with the Berlin cabinet, and indeed in a decisive fashion, will all the claims, objections and doubts be removed which are to be expected in this matter from the side of almost all our allies in the Bund.'[165] When the small states refused Austrian proposals in Dresden in March, Schwarzenberg blamed Prussia, but he nevertheless went on to sign a defensive alliance with Berlin in April. Buol's priorities were similar. During the Crimean War, Vienna had to gain the explicit consent of Prussia to the Austrian occupation of the Principalities and, the Foreign Minister assumed, 'the help of the Bund is assured us'.[166] Buol's rivals at the ministerial council, most notably Hess, were still more emphatic: 'the absolute necessity of eventual Prussian help' had to be 'completely certain' before Austria acted.[167] During the war against France and Italy in 1859, the same considerations prevented Austria trying to enlist the support of the Confederation until it was too late, notwithstanding the fact that – in Bruck's words of 28 May – 'Austria wins more and more friends in Germany': Rechberg explained on 28 June 1859 that Austria had not turned 'to the German Bund simply in order to avoid a misunderstanding with Prussia'.[168]

Buol's replacement believed throughout his period of office that 'a truly German and conservative policy is only possible through the unity and under the leadership of Austria and Prussia'.[169] The unity of the two powers was the 'natural course of German affairs'.[170] There were, he assured other ministers at the time of Berlin's offer of a defensive alliance in April 1861, 'some elements in Berlin in the highest sphere friendly to Austria, alongside inimical ones'.[171] 'If we act calmly but firmly in the defence of our legitimate rights and collect the other German governments around us,' he advised the Bavarian Foreign Minister in January 1862 during the struggle with Berlin over the *Zollverein* and reform of the Bund, 'Prussia will perceive the impossibility of achieving her plans and this will facilitate the victory of the calmer and more sensible party in Berlin.'[172] Although Rechberg's long-standing opponent, Bismarck, proved to be 'hair-raising', not calm and sensible, the Foreign Minister nonetheless preferred to deal with him directly in the war against Denmark in 1864 rather than attempting to work with the Confederation or rally the German states.[173] Prussia and Austria, acting as Great Powers, needed to take Schleswig as security against the future actions not only of Denmark, but also those of the Confederation, whose resolutions on the succession in the duchies contravened international law and the London Protocols agreed by the powers in 1852: 'It is very pressing that Austria and Prussia take steps towards this security because otherwise the Bund could make an incompetent decision and the collision with England could be made unavoidable.'[174] It was much more important 'not to disturb the political waters' of the states' system, remarked Rechberg in February 1864, 'than to disturb unjustified expectations here and there in Germany'.[175] Although Prussia was Austria's main rival in Germany, it alone could be expected to act sensibly and effectively.

Habsburg ministers' dogged pursuit of Prussia was the consequence of scepticism about the third Germany, making it difficult for them to imagine a new German order, even if they had wanted to. In general, the medium-sized German states were viewed in Vienna as a means of tipping the balance of the Confederation in Austria's favour. Thus, most of Schwarzenberg's plans for reforming the Bund relied on the pro-Austrian sympathies of the monarchies of Bavaria, Saxony, Hanover and Württemberg: in December 1848, the Minister-President had outlined the reorganisation of Germany into six military 'duchies', with the 'quasi-mediatisation of all the non-monarchical state bodies of Germany', including the pro-Prussian Grand Duchy of Baden; in May 1849, he put forward the idea of a 'trias', or tripartite executive, with Bavaria – although unmentioned – intended for the decisive third seat in the executive; in October 1849, he envisaged that the directory of his *Mitteleuropäischer Staatenbund* would likewise be composed of the representatives of the Habsburg monarchy, Prussia and the rest of Germany, with Austria acting as chair; in January 1850, he accepted a seven-person directory – the six monarchies and both Hessian states – together with a tripartite Volkshaus of 100 Austrian, 100 Prussian and 100 other German deputies; finally, in January 1851 at Dresden, he first suggested a nine-person executive which was then expanded to eleven with Austria and Prussia having two representatives each, and then, after these suggestions had been stymied, he proposed a trias again. After a decade of inactivity, in which Vienna followed but did not actively support the reform initiatives of Bavaria, Saxony and other states, Franz Joseph, Rechberg and Schmerling took up the idea of a five-person executive – Austria, Prussia, Bavaria, and two places in rotation – together with the '*Engerer Rat*' of the *Bundesversammlung* as a federal organ and an assembly of 302 delegates of the states' parliaments at the Frankfurt *Fürstentag* in August 1863.

All these plans were designed to give Austria and its allies a majority over Prussia. They were not founded on an attachment to the Bund in itself, which Schwarzenberg had branded an 'old , thoroughly shaky, and very wobbly boutique, ready to collapse at the next blow from inside or outside'.[176] Buol blamed the Confederation for failing to mobilise during the Crimean and Italian Wars in 1854–56 and 1859, and Rechberg castigated it for flirting with popular nationalism in the war against Denmark in 1864. In response to the claim of Bruck, who was serving as ambassador to the Ottoman Empire, that Austria and the German states should unite in 1854 to make them more independent of both Russia and the maritime powers, Buol declared that 'A great union with Germany in order to decide the issue vis-à-vis both East and West is a beautiful but empty dream. Prussia feels nothing but hatred and envy toward us and the small states can only at best be compelled to do what they feel like doing. To rely on such allies would simply be too naïve.'[177] On returning from Vienna in November 1854, Pfordten described Buol's mistrust of Prussia, which had 'until now obstructed Austria step by step', and his 'indifference towards the rest of Germany, which he calls many-headed'.[178] In a similar vein, Rechberg, who had served as an envoy to the Bund between 1855 and 1859, thought that it would be 'very healthy' in February 1864 to give 'a good lesson to the middle states'.[179] He had departed for Frankfurt in the 1850s, reported Kempen, 'with a heavy heart': 'he holds the entire German soil to be undermined by democracy'.[180] Any attempt to force the individual states to act against their particular interests, especially Prussia, was likely revive their defeatist, treasonous '*Rheinbund*' tendencies'.[181] Such comments were redolent of Schwarzenberg's repeated lament that the German states, whose 'life cannot be extended by artificial means over the long term', had proved unable to resist revolution in 1848 and to function independently after that date.[182] As far as Austrian policy-makers were concerned, the structure of the Bund was prone to deadlock and inactivity – a fact that Prussia was able to exploit – and the states of the third Germany were inclined to squabble and contradict each other. Neither circumstance encouraged already sceptical and distant Habsburg ministers to see the third Germany as an amenable basis for a reorganisation along national lines.

The loyalty of Austrian ministers and diplomats to the Habsburg monarchy tended to rule out strong support for 'Germany', not least because the reorganisation of the latter usually seemed to undermine the former. Although most policy-makers saw themselves as 'German' Austrians, with Schwarzenberg coming from Bohemia, Buol and Rechberg from Bavaria, and Biegeleben from Hesse, they were also the products of the Habsburg civil service and army. From their memoirs and correspondence, their overriding affiliation was to the Emperor and the state, which bound Austria together.[183] 'No state was in such danger of being shaken by the fever of nationality as Austria, which is composed of so many peoples (*Volksstämme*) that hold the balance of power one after the other according to their number', wrote Carl von Czoernig, a head of section in the Ministry for Trade, in 1858.[184] Only Austria's Emperor, he went on, had allowed the monarchy 'to end its internal disorder, to guide the conflicting forces onto concentric paths, to ground the unity of the Reich solidly, to achieve a previously unimaginable progress on the path of civilisation, to open the sources of well-being', and to regain 'its foremost place in the ranks of the Great Powers, its old, justified influence on Germany regained' and its role as 'arbiter of Europe' in the 'momentous oriental struggle' re-established.[185] As Czoernig indicated in his characterisation of the monarchy, dividing it into distinct geographical and ethnically mixed territories (German, Slav, Hungarian, Italian), the whole was more than the sum of the parts.

Most officials had been transferred from region to region, with the Chief of Police Johann Freiherr Kempen von Fichtenstamm, for instance, passing from the military academy in Vienna (1803–09) to the mobile armies of the Napoleonic wars (1813–15), to the Bavarian border and Galicia before moving back to the General Staff in the capital (1818–30), and then on to Znaim (1830–32), Iglau (1836–44) and Petrinja (1844–48).[186] Diplomats had seen less of the monarchy in the course of their service, but had often spent extensive periods in Vienna and had been groomed by Metternich. They were part of what Prokesch termed 'the world of the few', linked by marriage and belonging to a largely aristocratic Viennese society of salons and balls.[187] Some, such as Buol, had served in Germany, as envoy to Württemberg (1838–44), Baden and Hesse-Darmstadt (1828–38); others, such as Rechberg, had worked further afield, in London, Brussels, Stockholm (1841–43), Rio de Janeiro (1843–47) and Constantinople (1851–53). As ministers,

they were habitually preoccupied with regions and spheres of interest beyond Germany: Schwarzenberg in Hungary and Italy, where
he had acted as envoy (1844–48 in Piedmont) before commanding
a brigade in Radetzky's army in 1848; Buol in the Balkans and then
in Italy; and Rechberg in Italy and Galicia at the time of the Polish
uprising in Russia in 1863. The Habsburg monarchy of Metternich,
who remained personally influential until his death in 1859, was
primarily a European power and dynastic empire, balancing its
different interests as a matter of survival. From this point of view,
the reorganisation of Germany – especially, in the form of a threatening nation-state – could not be a priority of Austrian statesmen.

In many respects, Anton Prokesch von Osten was not typical of
the diplomatic caste. Labelled 'half Turk' by Bruck, he had been
appointed a professor in maths at the *Kadettenschule* in Olmütz at the
age of 21 and had gone on to become an acclaimed orientalist
during his time in the Austrian navy (1824–30) and as a diplomat in
Greece and the Ottoman Empire (1834–49, 1855–71).[188] In the
words of Schwarzenberg, Prokesch was 'an unusual person: soldier,
academic, seafarer, diplomat. Each of these many-sided ways of life
have left behind a rich treasure of experiences, and an inex-
haustible pile of living pictures for his fantasy.'[189] 'A long, interesting stay in the Levant during the remarkable epoch of the Hellenic
wars and the Turkish reforms, many sea expeditions and diplomatic
missions, personal acquaintanceship with the most influential men,
especially with Mehmet Ali and Ibrahim Pasha, have given him a
deep, fundamental and complete knowledge of the Orient and its
conditions, which even Prince M. thought fit to value,'
Schwarzenberg continued: 'Rarely in one person are such a wonderful poetic spirit, such a rich treasure of knowledge, such a clear
reason, such an outstanding talent for description, and such a
sharp-sighted logic combined.'[190] Notwithstanding its uncharacter-
istic trajectory, Prokesch's life showed how Austrian diplomats, even
those born in 'old', German-speaking Austria, were tied to the
empire and its southern and eastern spheres of interest. Born in
1795 in Graz into a minor aristocratic family on his maternal side,
Prokesch lost his mother at the age of nine, and his father, a distant
figure, at sixteen. His life from the earliest years was overseen by a
series of official sponsors, from his teacher Julius Franz Schneller at
the Lyzeum in Graz, via Karl von Schwarzenberg, whom he had
served as an ordnance officer in 1815 and whom he had cared for
in illness and death in 1820, and Sigmund Heinrich von Kavanagh,

his supporter in the *Hofkriegsrat* in the 1820s, to Metternich himself, into whose 'most intimate circles he was drawn' in the 1830s, as one contemporary put it, and by whom he was sent to Italy in 1831–32 and then to the Near East.[191] Prokesch's invitation from Metternich to the marriage of Melanie, his daughter, was considered more prestigious and important for the young diplomat's career than his ennoblement in 1830. Although far from Vienna for most of the 1830s and 1840s, Prokesch was closely linked by correspondence and trips home, during which he visited Metternich and the Ballhausplatz.

In spite of being 'the most intimate friend' of Alexander von Humboldt and an admirer of Goethe, whom he met in 1820, the diplomat viewed Berlin between 1849 and 1852 as 'the most disagreeable posting in the world' and the Bundestag in Frankfurt as 'juridical pedantry and narrow calculations of interest'.[192] A shared culture seemed to have fostered few shared sympathies. Germany appeared to be little more than a fiction, as could be seen at Frankfurt: 'What will I be in a position to make out of this fundamentally flawed institution? Prussia full of envy and jealousy, represented by a ruthless, petty man [Bismarck]. Each of the states insisting on their equal rights, separate interests ... and single line. Jurists not politicians. In none a German heart, each only a Bavarian, a Württemberger etc., with the jealousy of the states amongst themselves ... Seventeen views on each question to take into account, with these dependent on each ... Court.'[193] Set against such fragmentation and division was Prokesch's straightforward sense of loyalty to and identification with the Habsburg monarchy, despite its obvious political shortcomings. 'I bore the false and unworthy position into which I was brought by the absurd system of the modern period only out of love for the Kaiser as the cornerstone of the monarchy,' he wrote retrospectively in 1872: 'What I had to bear was not nearly as much as was imposed on him, and I thought: as long as I believe that I can be useful to the state, it is my duty not to ask how often and to ask about the sacrifices involved, but to persevere.'[194] Like his colleagues, Prokesch identified with 'Austria': as soon as he thought that Austria seemed incompatible with the reorganisation of 'Germany', or that Germany was incapable of reorganisation, he had little difficulty leaving the latter to its own devices.[195]

Habsburg officials were generally wary of plans to refashion the German order and discouraged or prevented Austrians from taking part in many of the discussions to this end. Thus, when Schmerling received an invitation from the liberal Grand Duke Ernst of Saxe-Coburg in 1862 to discuss reform, Franz Joseph refused to give him permission to visit the ruler. In fact, the *Staatsminister* went on to meet the Grand Duke privately in Vienna, expressing his opinion 'that it is certainly desirable to undertake a reform of the German *Bundesverfassung* and that I could not imagine it other than that a moderate representation came into being in the Bund and that it is inescapably necessary to cater for a stronger executive than the previous Bundestag possessed.'[196] Schmerling's conviction that a liberal Austria could play a constitutional part in Germany was quite widely shared by German Austrians, many of whom only gave up such a hope in 1866. Yet it was not obvious how this hope could be realised, for it seemed to be contradicted by the support of the German–Austrian liberal majority for centralism in the tradition of Joseph II, which in turn was considered by the other nationalities as a form of German colonisation under the auspices of the Habsburg state. 'Germanising' officials despatched to Hungary, for instance, were dismissed as 'Bach's hussars', lowly civil servants dressed up in aristocratic uniforms with swords at the behest of Alexander Bach, the bourgeois liberal Interior Minister who had formerly supported the revolution. 'Two years of parliamentary activity have sufficed to bring forth a very respectable opposition from the midst of those who belonged to the so-called German liberal party, of which one could have rightly said that they strongly defended my system and supported me in carrying it out,' wrote Schmerling: 'They were, on the whole, in agreement with the principles of the February consti-tution, called themselves Austrians and supporters of a centralised state, and vigorously fought those, like the Czechs and Poles, who wanted to know nothing of the general parliament. On the contrary, it was always their aim to extend the power of the parliament as much as possible and also to draw the lands of the Hungarian crown into the representation of the Reich.'[197] The problem for German–Austrian liberals was that the other nationalities became even more disaffected as a consequence of such 'Germanising' poli-cies: eventually all nationalities except the Transylvanian Romanians boycotted the *Reichsrat*, making Austrian involvement in Germany even more unpopular amongst the non-German majority, which accounted for 78.4 per cent of the population in 1851. Combined with the difficulty of reconciling centralism in the Habsburg monarchy with cooperation between the German-speaking parts of Austria and the German lands, the nationality question was recognised by many liberals as an obstacle to Vienna's full participation in the reshaping of Germany.

Political opinion in Austria during the 1850s, because of censorship and restrictions on associations and meetings, was difficult to assess and was correspondingly less influential, but the opinions on the German question which surfaced during the 1860s were similar to those of 1848–49 and had probably not changed much in the intervening years.[198] The positions which had been visible in 1848–49 still seemed valid: the idea of a German-dominated Central Europe, popular in Vienna, Niederösterreich and Moravia, and championed by Bruck, Schwarzenberg, Schmerling, Perthaler and Fröbel; the concept of 'greater Austria', based on international treaties, the Habsburg dynasty and a *Staatenbund*, and put forward by Karl von Mühlfeld in the Frankfurt Parliament and by conservatives later on; the notion of *Grossdeutschland* or 'union', which had been supported by republicans and democrats such as Karl Giskra and Johann Berger in 1848–49 and especially by Bohemian Germans after the revolution; and 'autonomy' or particularism, limited largely to Steiermark and Oberösterreich.[199] The boundaries between the positions were ill-defined, however: it was possible to be a '*Grossdeutscher*' and an Austrian 'autonomist' and 'dualist' in the manner of Karl Rechbauer, noted one observer, just as one could be a '*Grossdeutscher*' and a strict 'centralist' and '*Grossösterreicher*'.[200] Moreover, all except republican proponents of *Grossdeutschland* remained loyal to the Habsburg monarchy and refused to countenance the break-up of Austria, along the lines prescribed by Franz Joseph during a famous appearance at the conference of German jurists in 1862: 'I am above all an Austrian, but decisively German and desire the most intimate connection of Austria to Germany.'[201] Such attachment to Austria had dictated the actions of the majority of deputies in the Frankfurt National Assembly in 1849 and arguably became more defensive and more pronounced during the 1850s and 1860s. As the main Viennese newspaper *Die Presse* put it in a seminal article on 'Die Deutschen in Österreich' in 1860, German Austrians had been obliged to look for support from other Germans by the hostility of Hungarians, Czechs and Poles in the Habsburg monarchy, but their advances had been rejected as a result of the popularity of a 'shimmering liberal political doctrine' in Germany which taught 'that Germany could only be united on the debris of Austria'.[202] The '*Kleindeutschen*' in particular were 'Austrophobic', sympathising with the Italians and other 'oppressed' nationalities in the monarchy while regarding the German Austrians with 'accents of contempt'.[203]

Austrian commentators were not very successful in countering the '*kleindeutsch*' case. The main problem facing them was how to combine the integrity of the Habsburg monarchy and Austria's full participation in Germany. Even the prominent theorist of federalism Julius Fröbel, who collaborated with the government in Vienna during the early 1860s, was not certain how it was to be done. Schmerling looked to the former radical and forty-eighter for 'interesting information about events in Germany' and asked him, with Biegeleben, to draught a proposal for the reform of the Bund, to be presented to the *Fürstentag* in 1863.[204] The resulting plan, Schmerling hinted, was a compromise, implicitly falling short of the National Assembly's constitution of 1849: 'We could not conceal from ourselves that the German *Reichsverfassung* worked out in Frankfurt, with a Kaiser at its head and a Reich parliament with a two-chamber system, could not be realised under existing conditions, given the integrity of the individual members of the Bund, and that an altered form in every sense would have to be chosen in order to have any prospect of success.'[205]

Of necessity, the idea of a directly elected parliament had had to be given up because of the need to protect individual states from its overriding authority; similarly, 'the thought of a unified head was ruled out of house because it could be imagined that neither of the Great Powers would concede primacy to the other, and that not even the middling states would allow themselves to be deprived of the chance of exercising influence in the executive'.[206] Such provisions ran against the grain of liberal thought and, as Fröbel had admitted in 1859, militated against the principle of nationality, which would have meant the destruction of the Austrian *Gesamtstaat*.[207] Fröbel's assurance that 'democracy is synonymous with the federal system carried out from below to above' found little resonance in the commentaries of other liberals or democrats.[208] Moreover, his insistence that 'the German Confederation acts like a Great Power' seemed to be contradicted by his advocacy of a 'trias'.[209] His claim that 'a single German state can never, even from a patriotic point of view, take over German politics on its own and for itself' was explicitly framed against the case articulated by the *Nationalverein*, in which Prussia was designated – in Fröbel's opinion – precisely this role: 'should Prussia merge with Germany in name, in fact it would be and would remain a Prussian occupation'.[210] For its part, Austria might be prevented from acting, not least by its internal divisions and nationality conflicts – an inhibition that the publicist was anxious, but by no means certain, to overcome. 'The principle that Austria must have ordered its own affairs before it can get involved in German ones is, consciously or unconsciously, the programme of an Austrian Gothaism, which has as its aim the giving up of Germany to Prussia.'[211] Fröbel's priority was to ensure that a powerful German power emerged, preferably in the form of a colonising empire, which could defend itself as the pentarchy was replaced by a 'world system of states'.[212] How that power might be created constitutionally was arguably secondary.

The Habsburg monarchy, although championing 'national affairs' in Italy and in the East, was routinely perceived to be separate from the German sphere. Germany had 'the most decisive and important interest in a powerful, flourishing, enlightened state, in the closest possible alliance with Austria, continuing to exist on the territory currently occupied by Austria', wrote Fröbel.[213] Although closely tied to the German lands, the Habsburg monarchy was needed in its own right. Indeed, it was the aim of Schmerling's reforms, wrote another of his advisers, the constitutional lawyer Hans von Perthaler, to 'create Austrians, understood as a political nationality'.[214] Other commentators were more forthright, with some, such as the historians Ottokar Lorenz, Wilhelm Scherer and Anton Springer, backing the creation of *Kleindeutschland* and the exclusion of Austria for its own good.[215] Such exclusion did not alter the fact that Austria was a German power, defending Germans' interests in Italy and elsewhere, but it did mean that the role of the Habsburg monarchy as a strong, colonising empire derived from its multi-ethnic and centralised character, which ensured that it remained distinct from a reorganised Germany. 'Austria and Germany' faced similar threats, but remained discrete.[216] 'We ourselves pursue no German policy, we harbour no black, red and gold dream, we do not gaze beyond Austria, because we are convinced that German Austria, if Austria in its entirety is to exist, cannot be integrated and must not let itself be integrated in a newly constructed Germany', wrote the German–Austrian journalist Heinrich Reschauer.[217]

To the newspaper editor and German 'autonomist' Bernhard Friedmann, 'our political system must become a new, *whole* and *unified one*', restricted to the monarchy alone and external to the

German Confederation, which had cut across Germany and Austria, weakening both.[218] Only in a unified Austrian political system 'can the totality of interests and the unity of the empire find a firm guarantee for the future', he went on:

> Reform of the previous confederal legal relationship to Germany, and its transformation into a purely *international alliance* (*völkerrechtliches Bündnis*), as is only possible between two fully independent, unified, self-contained and complete states – it is *this German reform* alone that can protect Austria and Germany from internal civil wars and foreign entanglements. The new alliance will unite all the advantages of the former one without bringing back the disadvantages of the latter one ... The greater German idea, as far as it has any political worth or practical significance at all, can only come into being *in this way* and *in this form* of an international alliance between a German Union and an Austrian Union.[219]

To this end, Prussia should be encouraged to place itself in the middle, although not at the head, of the German movement in order to solve 'the problem of German unity' and overcome 'statist, particularist sentiment in previously sovereign federal states (*Bundesstaaten*)'.[220] Of necessity, such a development would entail the self-exclusion of Austria, other than through an alliance, from German affairs: 'The demand of the German nation for unified representation abroad and for a German parliament are impossible to meet without either Austria leaving the Confederation or decreeing its own dissolution', which was to be avoided at all costs.[221]

The background to such support for the monarchy was the perceived threat posed by the other nationalities in Austria, which had issued in an Italian war in 1859, the cross-border ramifications of the Polish uprising in 1863 and an on-going boycott of central political institutions by Czechs and Hungarians.[222] According to the ex-radical deputy and German autonomist Johann Berger, defeat in Italy at Solferino had been so catastrophic and national disunity so great that the convening of a strengthened *Reichsrat*, the October Diploma and the February Patent had all come at least two years too late and were incapable of maintaining the *Gesamtstaat*. Only the constitutional dualism of 'old Austria' and Hungary, together with more federalism, was now realistic, given Austrian conditions. In a unitary, constitutional Habsburg state, German Austrians could be outvoted by the other nationalities and isolated from other Germans in the Confederation. It was therefore desirable for them 'to accentuate their national character and to keep their national linkages with the German nation intact', seeking, 'not political hegemony, but a hegemony of culture amongst the peoples of Austria'.[223] Such affiliations and links, however, were to be coeval with the strengthening and restructuring of the Habsburg monarchy, in which a directly elected constituent assembly was to safeguard 'the necessary measure of unity between both halves of the Reich'.[224]

Berger's fellow radical proponent of *Grossdeutschland* in 1848, Carl Giskra, was moved by a similar assessment of political conditions towards Austrian centralism, having become an advocate of so-called '*Grossösterreich*' by the 1860s. There was 'no longer any question of the dissolution of Austria in Germany' by 1861; rather, it was necessary 'for now and for a long time' 'to have and to maintain Austria as a great state', even though 'German culture' remained 'the moral, ennobling element in our union of peoples (*Völkerverband*)'.[225] 'My political statement of faith can be summarised in a few words,' wrote the parliamentary leader of the 'greater Austrian' faction of the liberal *Verfassungspartei*:

> I believe in and recognise, I hope for and desire a great, free Austria ... I believe in the mission of Austria to bind together in one *Gesamtstaat*, so that all receive the blessings of a great state at the same time as the cultivation of their national life, the different tribes which live on its territory, of which each is large enough and is entitled to lead its own national life, but none is large enough and strong enough to be able to be independent as a state. Because the first part of the mission is not complete and the second part – now as then – is a necessity, I believe in the maintenance and continuance of Austria.[226]

A 'greater German unitary state' was unachievable.[227] All that could be hoped for was a common front against the hereditary enemy in the West, similar weights, measures and legal principles, the same arrangements for the institutions of high culture, and improvements in business and personal exchanges between Austria and Germany.

Conservative and liberal German Austrians – and many others – doubted that even such minimal convergence was possible. Officials wrote articles in support of a common customs' union, with *Mitteleuropa* heralded as 'an historical and natural unity, created by the power of the world order and dictated by its position in the world', but it became apparent to ministers that significant sections of Austrian industry were resistant to the idea.[228] Like Bruck in 1851, Schmerling, Biegeleben and Rechberg in the early 1860s were obliged to acknowledge the reluctance of the majority of industrialists and businessmen, whose position was thought to be 'besieged', to accept lower tariffs.[229] The Minister of Commerce himself believed that support for a customs' union was 'to gamble with industry in Austria for the sake of competition with Prussia'.[230] To the Ballhausplatz, failure to join the *Zollverein* or to design an alternative union constituted a major obstacle to an Austrian-led effort to achieve German unity.[231] This helped to reinforce the inward-looking proclivities of many contemporaries, who tended to be preoccupied by the Habsburg state's various endeavours to preserve the monarchy.

Even an unorthodox and pro-German liberal such as Franz Schuselka, the editor of *Reform*, argued that the government 'must completely banish the suspicion that it intends, by the defence of the German position, to subjugate the non-German peoples by a German power. Only when Austria has carried out this duty will it be in a position to acquire its German rights'.[232] Internal reform was needed before external intervention in Germany. Despite favouring 'a solid organic unity (*Einigung*) of the whole of Germany' with a common executive and directly elected parliament, Schuselka also retained his conviction that a restoration of the Austrian constitution of 1849 was required in order to avoid the collapse of the monarchy.[233] The objective of any Austrian reform was to create 'autonomous lands, tied together by a strong central power'.[234] Existing conditions in the Habsburg monarchy called for pluralism rather than dualism, and a real union between the different parts of Austria rather than a purely personal, dynastic union.[235] Schuselka's emphasis throughout was on the survival and consolidation of the Austrian monarchy in the face of significant threats from within. He stayed loyal to a wider German nation, supporting its interests against the Great Power manoeuvring of Vienna and Berlin in Schleswig-Holstein for example, but he also prioritised state-building in Austria, sharing – notwithstanding his own protestations – the ultimate goals of an Austrian centralist majority in the *Reichsrat*.[236] To both centralists and federalists, Austria came before Germany. Such loyalties, combined with other constitutional, diplomatic and territorial sources of conflict between the Habsburg monarchy and the German lands, made it harder for proponents of *Grossdeutschland* outside Austria to win over public opinion.

3 The Habsburg Monarchy and the Germans

Some sections of public opinion in the third Germany, especially southern Germany, were receptive to Austrian advances. To the Prussian democrat Hermann Schulze-Delitzsch, writing on behalf of the *Nationalverein*, the gulf between North and South Germany was a profound one, even if it had been bridged by the reappearance of France as a common enemy in the Italian war of 1859.[1] Likewise, to the historian and publicist Heinrich von Sybel, who had become one of the principal champions of *Kleindeutschland* in the 1850s and early 1860s, it was incontestable that the 'German South' was still strongly pro-Austrian. 'Sympathy for an Austrian national character is just as strong there as antipathy towards the self-confident behaviour of the Prussians', he lamented in 1862, drawing on his experience as a professor at the university of Munich.[2] Historical links, geographical proximity, Catholicism, cultural contiguity, the perceived warmth of southern manners, dynastic ties – with Franz Joseph's mother and wife both coming from the Bavarian Wittelsbachs – and the prominence of German-born officials in Vienna – including Metternich, Rechberg, Biegeleben and Buol – all contributed to the reluctance of many southerners – and others in Hanover and Saxony – to exclude Austria from the German lands.

The significance and power of the Habsburg monarchy during the 1850s and 1860s purportedly led to the maintenance of strong historical links between Austria and South Germany. Certainly, the monarchy's continuing presence in German affairs was required by the governments of the *Mittelstaaten*, as a bulwark of the Bund and a counterweight to Prussia. Although it was true that Vienna was 'using the middling states for its own ends', it was necessary to consider 'what to do in order to protect Austria, the weakening or decline of which would inevitably bring the collapse of the individual German governments in its wake', warned Reinhard von Dalwigk zu Lichtenfels, the first minister of Hessen-Darmstadt, in 1861.[3] The power and reputation of the Habsburg monarchy in Germany rested entirely on 'the trust and dependency of the governments' of the middling and smaller states, wrote the Saxon minister Richard von Friesen retrospectively of the mid-1860s, yet even the ministries of the *Mittelstaaten* had become 'mistrustful'.[4] The decisive element as far as the Habsburg monarchy was concerned was 'public opinion' and party support, which had greater weight in the third Germany as a consequence of the perceived precariousness of the individual states after 1848. In Friesen's view, the inconsistency of Austria's policy after 1849 had alienated 'the public opinion (*öffentliche Meinung*) of Germany', making it receptive, in prospect, to Prussian advances.[5] This chapter investigates the extent to which such alienation actually existed.

Germany in the Presses of the *Mittelstaaten*

The struggle in the third Germany between different conceptions of *Grossdeutschland* and *Kleindeutschland* reached its peak in the early 1860s, after the formation of the *Nationalverein* in 1859, the Progressive Party (*Fortschrittspartei*) in 1861 and the *Deutsche Abgeordnetentag* in 1862. Formally, at least, the adoption of the Reich constitution of 1849 by the National Association in 1860 met, in Sybel's opinion, 'the wishes of German Austrians' and it gave to 'the *Grossdeutsche* the inclusion of Austria'.[6] The question of the inclusion or exclusion of Austria was 'in fact the point at which the opinion of North and South German liberals typically divides,' continued Sybel, writing from Munich in February 1861: 'to the former, the splitting off of Austria has been the most common view since 1849; the latter are of the view that it would be faint-hearted not to want to draw Austria to them and to regenerate it. There is only one opinion on the matter in the whole of Württemberg, Bavaria and the greatest part of Baden.'[7] Liberals in the southern German states only joined the *Nationalverein* in small numbers, put off largely because of its purportedly pro-Prussian and anti-Austrian stance.[8]

In Hanover, where the founders of the National Association faced a powerful group of opponents, the historian Onno Klopp, reporting from the '*grossdeutscher Verein*', proclaimed that Austria was a defensive, protective, conservative power, traditionally repelling Ottoman and Slav invaders from the East, whereas Prussia was a foreign-backed conqueror-state.[9] Vienna had defended Germany against France during the revolutionary and Napoleonic wars, and again in 1859.[10] Austria alone was strong enough to stand up to France; Prussia was 'scarcely half as strong'.[11] Moreover, the Habsburg monarchy could co-exist with the other German states, continuing the precedent of the Holy Roman Emperors of never intervening 'in the internal affairs of the German territories', since it was not 'centralising, and could not be such because of its natural conditions'.[12] By contrast, the Hohenzollern state, to which the leaders of the *Nationalverein* wanted 'to transfer the military and diplomatic command of German affairs', was a 'military monarchy, with centralisation and uniformity ruthlessly enforced', making it a threat to the third Germany.[13] 'We want a Germany which keeps to already-acquired extra-German positions, particularly in the East, which has the greatest land mass and the greatest military power, with which we have the fate of the world in our hands,' wrote Klopp's fellow Hanoverian and historical writer Heinrich Langwerth von Simmern: 'We want the extension of the Bund with the retention of the independence of its parts ... We do not want a displacement of Germany's centre of gravity to the North or even to the Germanised North-East.'[14] The 'small German party', wrote Klopp in 1863, 'wants to satisfy the German nation's need for unity through the loosening and tearing up of existing law and existing legal powers and, after the exclusion of Austria, wants to put the other states together under Prussian rule in the form of a so-called *Bundesstaat*', which would lead to civil war.[15] The *grossdeutsch* party, for its part, would avoid internal strife 'by tightening the ties which already exist' and by including the Habsburg monarchy.

Such opinions were shared by South German commentators like Albert Schäffle, the prominent economist and government-backed publicist from Tübingen. Attitudes towards Austria rested on 'the contradiction between Protestantism and Catholicism, of the old *Kaisertum* of the Reich and the new *Kaiseridee* of Gotha, of historical law and modern state-building, of constitutionalism and the absolutist or estates' system', wrote the later founder of the *Reformverein* – the main counter-organisation of the *Nationalverein* – in 1859.[16] The role of the middling German states was to mediate between the two powers and integrate them into a reformed Confederation. 'The two Great Powers truly have a place in a *Föderation* of Germany, but not in a *Bundesstaat*', he warned; and whereas the 'new Gotha' party attempted 'to banish whole-German federalism through unitarism under Prussia's auspices and with Austria's marginalisation', supporters of the Habsburg monarchy in the southern German states were able to emphasise the affinity between legality, local patriotism and confederation, benefiting from fear of Prussian hegemony and civil war in the medium-sized and small German states.[17] The concepts of nation, nationality, historical law, sovereignty and autonomy had been misused, contended the sociologist, ignoring the fact that cultures and relations between individuals were varied and organic.[18] A reformed Confederation incorporating the whole of the Habsburg monarchy would accommodate the German nation's 'entire cultural life' and its extended areas of settlement.[19]

An overburdening of the concept of nationality was ill-advised, he wrote in 1863, because it concentrated on institutional structures of power at a time of movement towards an international sphere in which the fortunes of a nation would rest on 'the richness of the inner, natural unfolding of its spiritual and material cultural life'.[20] For this reason, as well as for purely economic ones, Schäffle backed the Habsburg monarchy's entry into the *Zollverein*, pointing out the North's dependency on the South and designating the role of broker between Prussia and Austria to the economically independent states of South West Germany.[21] The inclusion of Austria in a common customs' union and a reformed Bund offered the prospect of a larger German-dominated economy and a more powerful and extensive 'German' territory from the Adriatic to the Baltic and from the Rhine to the mouth of the Danube. In the words of the inaugural statement of the *Wochenblatt des Deutschen Reformvereins*, of which Schäffle was a correspondent, the aim was to pursue everything which 'can increase the greatness, power and reputation of Germany abroad and its material or spiritual development, its harmony and strength at home'.[22] 'Germany should not become smaller and mutilated; it should remain strong enough to be able for once to play the role in Europe which it deserves', it continued.[23] As a consequence, declared Schäffle in the *Augsburger Allgemeine Zeitung* in September 1859, the *kleindeutsch Nationalverein* would be unsuccessful in convincing proponents of *Grossdeutschland* to support it: 'The South German people (*Volk*), in an overwhelming majority not only according to a head-count but also its intelligentsia and its educated and influential classes, will not be made, by inducements and restrictions, to incline towards the programme.'[24] To the sociologist and later Austrian minister, significant sections of public opinion in South Germany would not accept the idea of *Kleindeutschland*.

Some newspapers and periodicals in the South and in other parts of the third Germany gave a similar impression, especially during the wars of the 1850s.[25] During the Crimean War, many publications had backed Vienna. The *Allgemeine Zeitung, Casseler Zeitung, Frankfurter Postzeitung, Hamburger Correspondent, Hannoversche Zeitung, Leipziger Illustrierte Zeitung, Mainzer Journal, Augsburger Postzeitung, Weser Zeitung,* and *Deutsches Volksblatt,* published in Stuttgart, had all supported Austria's stance, aided by its alliance with the more liberal western powers.[26] Similarly, during the Italian War, much of the press and public opinion sympathised with the Habsburg monarchy's supposed defence of German interests against France. 'There are only a few partially developed schoolboys who still doubt whether there will be a separate Austria, Prussia and Bavaria in the case of war, or simply Germany,' wrote one former South German deputy from the Frankfurt parliament to Georg Cotta, the owner of the *Allgemeine Zeitung*, in February 1859: 'No neutral German government would have strong enough shoulders to bear the curses of their people and the contempt of Europe.'[27] Even the pro-Prussian periodical the *Grenzboten*, edited by Gustav Freytag in Leipzig, conceded that much of the public supported Austria.[28] Vienna, wrote a 'South German democrat' in *Stimmen der Zeit*, was leading the call of the German nation for unification: 'The breaking of the constraints of the territorial state and the rise of the nation towards unity (*Einigkeit*), with the support of Austria, which has been drawn onto the path of German development, that is the true sense of the national movement, which we see emerging following the threat of war.'[29]

The Habsburg monarchy had a legal right to remain in Italy, asserted the *Bayrische Wochenschrift*, notwithstanding its links with liberals and the government in Berlin: Italy was simply 'the ground on which Austria and France fought for dominance; it has been so for centuries and it will remain so until Italy gains the moral force for regeneration from within, of which there are still no noticeable signs'.[30] The German lands should support Vienna because we see the political direction of Austria as a transitory one, just as the Manteuffel-Westphalen way of governing was a transitory one in Prussia, and because we do not assess the development of our people in decades; also because we – to declare our deepest and ultimate ground – esteem the national integrity of Germany more highly than one more or one less political freedom, which over the long term cannot be denied to any people that has shown itself, through its education and moral seriousness, as worthy as the German one.[31]

Economically, too, it was essential, noted the Saxon weekly *Glocke*, that Germany in its entirety fought alongside the monarchy 'for the sake of Germany's well-being and its commercial significance for the East', that it kept 'the Danube free for Germany, Austria and Hungary's right to the sea, and that possession of its Adriatic lands be assured to the Kaiser state'.[32] The free-trade *Bremer Handelsblatt* and the Frankfurt *Deutsche Blätter* made a similar economic case for an Austrian war against France in Italy.[33] With the re-establishment of Austria as the greatest power in Germany and with its defence of German causes during the 1850s, many commentators in the third Germany refused to write it off.

The largest and most reputable newspaper in the South, the *Allgemeine Zeitung*, was also widely believed to be the most pro-Austrian.[34] In 1855, the Habsburg *Presseleitungskomitee*, which had been founded two years earlier to monitor and influence the press in Germany, claimed that the 'importance of the paper' not only encouraged governments to place articles, but also 'to maintain the most agreeable relationships in person'.[35] 'In certain people's eyes', the publication was famous for 'its bias towards Austria in the entire field of foreign policy'.[36] The editor, Gustav Kolb, was said to be 'inclined towards Austria', as were many of the journalists.[37] These biases were thought by some to have worsened by 1859. Thus, immediately after the signature of Austria's armistice with France in July, Sybel attacked the publication for its 'support, not of the Reich and the people of Austria, but for the Austrian constitutional system'.[38] Other treatises defended the paper, but accepted its backing of the Habsburg monarchy.[39]

By this time, Hermann Orges, who had risen to prominence after Kolb succumbed to illness in the mid-1850s, had moved the paper further towards Vienna's point of view, allowing himself 'to be beaten to death for Austria' and channelling his 'Austrianness into a

Table 3.1 Circulation, readership and political tendency of major newspapers

Newspaper	Political Direction	Circulation	Readership	Date of figure
Prussia				
Preuss Staats-Anzeiger	Official	3,093–4,300	Officials	1852–54
Die Zeit	Semi-official	2,020–4,200	Officials	1852–61
Kreuzzeitung	Conservative	4,000–7,610	Prussian nobility	1852–61
Königsberg Hart Zeitung	Semi-official	4,175	East Prussia	1854
Stralsundische Zeitung	Semi-official	3,000	Baltic	1854
Vossische Zeitung	Independent	11,000–15,500	Middle classes	1852–61
Kölnische Zeitung	Liberal	10,200–15,700	Rhineland, Germany	1852–61
National-Zeitung	Liberal	5,000–10,000	Prussia, esp. Berlin	1852–61
Spenersche Zeitung	Liberal	8,000–5,860	Prussia, upper middle classes, officials	1852–61
Kladderadatsch	Liberal	24,550	Middle classes, Germany	1854
Volkszeitung	Democratic	6,100–26,450	Popular, Berlin	1852–61
Elberfelder Zeitung	Liberal	3,200	Rhineland	1854
Elberfelder Kreisblatt	Liberal	3,200	Rhineland	
Schlesische Zeitung	Liberal	4,600–9,000	Silesia	1852–61
Magdeburger Zeitung	Liberal	4,980–7,350	Brandenburg	1852–61
Ostsee Zeitung	Liberal	2,533	Baltic	1854
Volkshalle	Catholic	3,600	Rhineland, Westfalia, Posen, Silesia	1854

(continued overleaf)

Table 3.1   continued

Newspaper	Political Direction	Circulation	Readership	Date of figure
Bavaria				
Neue Münchner Zeitung	Semi-official	2,450–2,300	Bavarian officials	1849–54
Allgemeine Zeitung	Independent liberal; pro-Austria		South Germany	1854
Münchner Volksbote	Democratic/popular	6,000	Popular, Bavaria, Württ., Tyrol	1854
Münchner Neueste Nachrichten	Liberal	15,000	Middle-class, popular, Bavaria	1854
Nürnberger Correspond	Liberal	5,000	Bav., Württ., Austria	1854
Augsburger Postztg	Catholic	1,700–5,000	Clergy, Bavaria, Tyrol	1854
Württemberg				
Staats-Anzeiger	Official	1,000–4,000	Officials/elites	1851–54
Schwäbischer Merkur	Liberal	7,500–9,000	Württemberg	1854–58
Beobachter	Democratic	1,000–2,000	Popular	1854–58
Ulmer Schnellpost	Liberal/democratic	1,800	Mixed	1854
Stuttgarter Neues Tagblatt	Liberal	3,800–7,600	Middle classes	1850–65
Volksblatt	Catholic	1,400	Clergy, conservatives	1854
Saxony				
Dresdner Journal	Official	801–1,188	Officials/elites	1854–62
Leipziger Zeitung	Semi-official	5,500–1,188	Officials and middle classes, Saxony/Thur.	1854–62
Constitutionelle Zeitung	Liberal	996–1,208	Middle classes	1858–62
Allg Deutsche Zeitung	Liberal; pro-Prussia	1,100–1,292	Mixed	1854–62

Hanover				
Neue Hannoversche Zeitung	Semi-official	1,600–2,500	Conservatives	1854–66
Deutsche Nordsee Zeitung	Semi-official	2,140–2,500	Official circles	1865–66
Zeitung fur Norddeutschland	Liberal	2,425–3,000	Official circles	1865–66
Hannoversches Tageblatt	Independent	7,375–9,200	Middle classes	1865–66
Casseler Zeitung	Semi-official	1,000	Hanover	1854
Frankfurt and Hesse				
Frankfurter Postzeitung	Pro-Austria	3,000	'Reich', Hesse, Rhineland, Hesse-Darm, South West	1854
Frankfurter Journal	Liberal	10,000		1854
Mainzer Journal	Catholic	1,000–1,200	Hesse, Nassau	1854
Hansa Cities				
Hamburger Börsenhalle	Independent liberal	2,600	Finance, business	1854
Hamb. Correspondent	Liberal; pro-Prussia	5,000	Business	1854
Hamburger Nachrichten	Liberal; pro-Prussia	11,000–12,000	North Germany	1854
Weser-Zeitung	Liberal	5,000–6,000	Bremen, Hanover, Pr.	1854
Baden				
Badische Landesztg	Semi-official	2,000		1854
Karlsruher Zeitung	Semi-official, Catholic	1,500	Officials	1854
Freiburger Zeitung	Catholic, pro-Austria	2,000	Catholic circles	1854
Mannheimer Journal	Liberal	2,000	Middle classes	1854

Note: Highest and lowest figures are given, when disputed.

Source: A. Green, *Fatherlands* (Cambridge, 2001), 182; K. Paupié, *Handbuch der österreichischen Pressegeschichte* (Vienna, 1960), vol. 2, 23–53; K. Wappler, *Regierung und Presse in Preussen* (Leipzig, 1935), 46–47, 62–76; O. Groth, *Die Zeitung* (Mannheim, 1928), vol. 1, 249–50.

complete system', in the editor's estimation.[40] 'You cannot deny that this shift in the nature of the A.Z. has been brought about by me with some skill,' wrote Orges to Georg Cotta in June 1859: 'I let no opportunity pass to act as if this has been the natural development of the paper, the latent aim of its founding. As you consented to my programme, you gave your indirect authorisation for this shift.'[41] To Orges, the Habsburg monarchy had become a German state after the Frankfurt Parliament had shown the redundancy of the unitary 'small German' model. [42] The monarchy guaranteed the continuance of the Bund and the individual states, underpinned by international law. It also defended German interests in the East: 'We say openly that, if a member of the German Confederation, if Austria did not already possess these extra-German lands, the German people would have to conquer them at any cost as absolutely necessary for its development and its position as a world power', commented the journalist in January 1859.[43] As the Habsburg monarchy began to lose its war against France, the newspaper's partisanship became a talking point amongst its opponents, with Carl Vogt, for instance, singling out Orges as the 'clever inventor of that truly colossal sentence' in praise of Austria's evacuation of Milan and its retreat to the Mincio line.[44]

When the journalist left the newspaper in 1860, denounced as 'thoroughly incapable' by Kolb, the publication toned down rather than altered its attitude to Vienna.[45] In the opinion of the deputy editor in 1861, the newspaper's line should be an 'unconcealed preference for Austria, but not inaccessible to other confederal and specifically greater German views concerning the powerful reorganisation of Germany'.[46] Looking back from the vantage point of 1863, Kolb admitted that his championing of Austria had been long-lived and public. 'If we wanted to change, the idea of a Prussian Union shows us the path that we would have to tread,' he warned Cotta's son, who had just become the owner of the paper: 'But after we have defended the connection (*Anschluss*) to Austria for fourteen years, and had to defend it in my strongly-held opinion, how could we now suddenly change? Wouldn't everyone point the finger at us, and wouldn't we meet with justified mistrust on one side and complete contempt on the other?'[47] The *Allgemeine Zeitung* neither should nor could repudiate its long-standing predilection for Austria, for it was part of a cultural and geographical southern sphere which included the German-speaking lands of the Habsburg monarchy.

The most important cultural characteristic of the 'South' was arguably Catholicism, notwithstanding the haziness of confessional boundaries in areas of mixed settlement. To opponents such as the radical Heinrich Simon, writing from Zurich in 1859, the belligerent support of southern Germans for Austria rested on 'Ultramontanes" fear of isolation if Prussia were to come to dominate Germany.[48] Contemporaries were aware that the inclusion of the Habsburg monarchy in a reorganised German Confederation would have guaranteed a Catholic majority: in 1855, even discounting Austrian lands outside the Bund, 23 out of 43 million inhabitants of the Confederation, or 52.5 per cent, were Catholics.[49] If the Austrian confederal lands were removed to create a small German state, 11 million Catholics would have been outnumbered by 20 million Protestants. The main Catholic periodical, the *Historisch-politische Blätter*, denied that it was part of an 'Austrian party', as was often claimed, but admitted, 'we are convinced that the integrity of Germany can only be saved through the most intimate connection of Austria to our fate ... The French Emperor does not want to destroy the Habsburg monarchy, but he does want to destroy its connection to Germany; we want the exact opposite for national and ... religious reasons.'[50] The Bavarian publication did not accept that Catholicism, nationalism and Austria's involvement in Germany were incompatible.[51]

Whereas liberal proponents of *Grossdeutschland* viewed the German question 'as a domestic constitutional question', Catholics saw it as 'the great world-question of the century', which involved Austria as a Great Power and would require 'a violent upheaval of Europe' for its solution, warned the *Historisch-politische Blätter* in 1863.[52] Prussia was criticised for its 'un-German stance', seeking to dominate or annex the third Germany.[53] 'In the 17th century, the Protestant princes wanted to make Gustavus Adolphus Kaiser, and in the 19th century our great fatherland should be ruled by a parliamentary regime and Prussia, as a Protestant power, should be its head,' noted an article in 1866: 'Austria was an obstacle to this transformation as a result of its composition and its power, but it was an obstacle principally as a *Catholic* power.'[54] The *Nationalverein*, North German liberals and the Prussian state were equated by the *Historisch-politische Blätter* as a common threat to Catholics; Austria was perceived as a means of self-defence. The *Nationalverein*'s criticism, therefore, 'that Catholics carried their confessional sympathies and antipathies into their politics of the fatherland' had an element of truth in it, but only as a reaction to the aggression of Protestants, 'for, as the unification of Germany should lead to the domination of

Protestantism, a natural feeling was bound to lead Catholic Germany back to an historical, that is to a Catholic, head of the Reich'.[55]

The Habsburgs, of course, had traditionally assumed the role of Kaiser of the Holy Roman Empire, to which the Catholic publication alluded. With the Concordat in place, Austria seemed to have chosen the historical path of a 'Christian-Germanic *Rechtsstaat*', which promised self-government, freedom, legality and the old form of Christian civilisation, prophesied the periodical in 1856.[56] It allowed the 'German people (*Volksthum*)' to stand between East and West: it was 'Austria once more' which defended 'its mission' and 'defends it up to the present'.[57] In Prussia, everything was intertwined with 'the purposes of the state', promoting 'despotic arbitrariness' and the 'caprices of particularism'.[58] Austria pursued German interests in the Alps, in Eastern Europe, in Schleswig-Holstein and in Europe in general.[59] The Habsburg monarchy, the *Historisch-politische Blätter* repeated, was a 'German Great Power' and was much less threatening than Prussia.[60] 'If Germany must merge into a great state, the South German individual peoples (*Völkerschaften*) would much prefer to be unified with Austria,' declared an article on 'The German Question' in 1862: 'The relationship of descent (*Stammesverwandtschaft*) with the Germans in Austria draws them to the latter, the acceptance of a constitutional form of government has removed an inequality of conditions, and with the Diploma of 20 October Austria can grant to the Bund lands their autonomous standing to a far greater extent than Prussia can.'[61] For southern Germans, contended the *Historisch-politische Blätter*, Austria was closer to Germany than Prussia was: it consequently had to be included in any reorganisation of the German lands.

Despite such goodwill towards Austria, and fear of Prussia, in the third Germany, it was difficult to envisage exactly how the Habsburg monarchy could be incorporated into a German nation-state, which most commentators believed was necessary in some form or other. The *Historisch-politische Blätter*, which had backed Austria strongly during the Crimean and Italian wars, demonstrated many of the difficulties facing supporters of Vienna in the German lands. 'The revolution had inherited the omnipotence of monarchy and its institutions, and it had stretched both to their outer limits,' remarked the federalist Catholic publication in 1861, regretting that these French-inspired centralising traditions had remained in place: 'As the revolution was defeated in 1849, unfortunately with the help of the Russians, the idea of a unitary (*einheitlich*) state and a strongly concentrated government seemed to be completely natural and simple, and it was scarcely asked whether the necessary conditions existed for its realisation.'[62] The national idea had been pursued in an extreme way at the urging of a French Empire which would eventually become 'the shadow of a memory'.[63] Italy might attain 'a certain unity', but it would quickly collapse, with the Vatican reacquiring its former territories and Austria Lombardy.[64] Nevertheless, although 'the old territorial settlement can perhaps again be made good', 'the old order' never could: 'After a generation the ideas of nationality and popular sovereignty will no longer blind people, they will no longer drive them to dizzying giddiness and they will no longer serve the quest to dominate in the face of existing laws – but they will also not completely disappear, they will take on other forms and they will be expressed more mildly in public law,' predicted the *Historisch-politische Blätter*, accepting the irreversibility of nationalism in Germany, Austria and elsewhere: 'At first, these ideas were mocked, then they were feared, and now they have become facts.'[65] The challenge for Vienna was to unite 'the elements of the monarchy into one great body', given that a 'bureaucracy can never carry out such a work ... less so in Austria than in any other land'.[66] Since Germans held the pursuit of 'the unification of the tribes in a nation' to be an absolute right, they could 'not deny the natural justification of other nationalities'.[67] In the Habsburg monarchy, this meant that the 'administration of the bureaucratic central state' – the 'system' of 'the modern state' – could 'never again balance the variety of its parts'.[68] Whereas 'in most countries, descent and language create a natural equality of relations, which collect the inhabitants of a state territory together in a particular unity, in the Austrian monarchy descent and languages are elements of division'.[69] The periodical's solution of 'self-government' on the British model seemed unconvincing, especially when extended to Austria's role in the reorganisation of Germany.

Many purported to have the solution to the Habsburg monarchy's difficulties, claimed the *Historisch-politische Blätter* in 1861, but they ignored the external aspects of the question, which had rendered the terms of an internal debate about federalism and centralisation, nationalities and state interests, autonomy and constitutionalism inadequate.[70] Initially, the publication linked its advocacy of federalism at home to the cause of *Grossdeutschland* abroad, since a greater

Germany would cross the border between Austria and the South German states. Favouring Fröbel's prediction that the transition from 'small' to 'greater' Germany was inevitable, the *Historisch-politische Blätter* was reassured that Schmerling had appeared to switch to the 'greater German' camp.[71] All the same, it acknowledged that many of the Minister of State's former 'greater Austrian' colleagues had not changed allegiances, threatening to leave the 'small Germans' a free hand in Germany.[72] 'Nowhere are there as many "Gothaer" in Germany as in Austria, especially unconscious ones', noted a New Year's survey in 1863.[73] Although the fact that everything was 'provisional' in the Habsburg monarchy seemed to offer an unusual opportunity for the establishment of *Grossdeutschland* across traditional state borders and against the grain of existing constitutional theory, it also pointed to the monarchy's instability and possible demise.[74]

Austrians had reached a crossroads, unable to justify their continuing presence in Germany at the same time as consolidating a system with so many non-German interests: 'If Austria wants to remain German, then it must again become as German as it was once was; otherwise, it must rest completely on a non-German basis. The artificial halfway-house, a relationship and non-relationship, can only last if the status quo in the German Bund were forever assured, but who can believe in that?'[75] The Confederation had proved difficult to reform and had an uncertain future, with many advocates of 'autonomy' in the third Germany simply using Austria for their own ends, wrote the Munich periodical.[76] By 1863, it seemed obvious that the Bund was in 'crisis' and that the notion of *Grossdeutschland* was problematic: 'It is time to say a few serious words about the position of those organs, outside the two German great states, which are termed and known to be 'Catholic'... May they identify without reservation with the greater German Toms, Dicks and Harrys? We say a decisive "no".'[77] The 'greater German' party had declined and the *Reformverein* was weak by the mid-1860s, admitted the *Historisch-politische Blätter*.[78] Austrians preferred Great Power politics to entanglements in Germany, and Germans saw the Habsburg monarchy as '*das Ausland*'.[79] Given such entrenched positions, in addition to the perceived obstinacy of Berlin, the periodical increasingly asserted that a reorganisation of Germany which included Austria could only follow a vaguely defined foreign-policy 'catastrophe', most probably a civil war.[80]

South German liberal proponents of *Grossdeutschland* were less apocalyptic, perhaps because they were less convinced by the

Austrian model. Published in Bavaria and owned by the Stuttgart Cotta family, the Augsburg *Allgemeine Zeitung* was arguably the main South German repository of greater German liberal points of view. Although it was broadly pro-Austrian, it continued to be a 'forum' (*Sprechsaal*), as even Orges recognised.[81] 'The *Allgemeine Zeitung* should, according to its original programme, be "unpartisan", i.e. to let all (at any rate, permissible) views and interests be represented in its columns', recorded the Austrian *Presseleitungskomitee* in 1855.[82] Whereas the newspaper had sold half of its copies in the Habsburg monarchy until 1848–49, acting as an organ for the German-speaking lands of the South, it had witnessed its Austrian circulation drop to only one-sixth of the total by the early 1850s.[83] The owner and editors saw their publication as the mouthpiece of the southern German lands, which had become increasingly separate from the Habsburg monarchy during the 1850s and 1860s. When Lorenz Stein approached Cotta at the request of the Austrian government in 1862 to try to convince him to move the newspaper to Vienna, he was politely turned down, with the owner prophesying that a Viennese *Allgemeine Zeitung* would be seen as 'the foreigners' or Swabians' paper' in Austria and that it would 'lose touch with Germany and all its good German colleagues'.[84] Throughout the period, the publication was criticised by Austrian correspondents for being anti-Austrian. During the 1850s, Johann Christoph von Zedlitz, who had worked for the paper in the 1830s, wrote a series of letters to Cotta deploring the lack of energy with which the newspaper had mediated between Austria and Germany.[85] Schwarzenberg, reported Zedlitz, had been disappointed that the *Allgemeine Zeitung* had supported Gagern's solution to the German question, even if it had 'never been for a Prussian *Kaisertum* nor a separatist *Klein-Deutschland*'.[86] Although the publication was lauded for supporting Vienna in the Crimean and Italian wars, its outlook seemed, to Zedlitz, to be insufficiently 'Austrian', partly because it did not take into account the diplomat's own strictures.[87] In the early 1860s, the pro-Austrian articles of the Viennese academic and *Allgemeine Zeitung* correspondent Karl von Hock were likewise regularly overlooked.[88]

In some respects, it had proved easier for the South German newspaper to support the Habsburg monarchy during the wars of the 1850s, when the majority of public opinion seemed to back Vienna's defence of German interests, than during the period of constitutionalism in the 1860s, when the Austrian government attempted to reform the Bund and to work with Prussia: Vienna's attempts at reform appeared half-hearted, leaving Schäffle 'in no way satisfied', and its flirtation with Prussia, most notably in the war with Denmark over Schleswig-Holstein in 1864, seemed to ignore the national feelings of the public in favour of the reasons of state of the two Great Powers.[89] Furthermore, with Belcredi's suspension of the constitution in 1865, Vienna's endeavour to unite domestic and German reform had effectively come to an end, as Gustav von Lerchenfeld, the leader of the moderate Bavarian liberals and an *Allgemeine Zeitung* correspondent, conceded in October 1865: 'Austria places itself not only before the impossibility of having any success in Germany, it also goes to great efforts to destroy from the bottom up the last residue of sympathy which remains for it … If the decline and fall is unavoidable, one must know how to let it happen in silence.'[90] Like August Joseph Altenhöfer, the long-standing deputy-editor of the *Allgemeine Zeitung*, Lerchenfeld was still opposed to Prussia, but found it hard to support Austria: 'Not that I personally like the Berliners; I am a South German, and Bavarians, Austrians etc. are much closer to me in temperament than Pomeranians and Brandenburgers, but I recognise a logic of facts and rights in the existence of North German power and in its advances.'[91] For most correspondents of the *Allgemeine Zeitung*, sympathy for Austria had to be balanced against a desire for German unification, which the Habsburg monarchy increasingly seemed to obstruct.

Gustav Kolb, the editor of the *Allgemeine Zeitung* between 1837 and 1865, showed the strength of liberals' commitment to the national cause, despite being accused of serving Austria. In fact, Kolb, who had been born in 1798 in Stuttgart, had spent much of his early life evading the police forces of the Metternichian Confederation. A member of a nationalist *Burschenschaft* at the university of Tübingen, he travelled to Piedmont as a 23-year-old, sending back reports to a local newspaper about the uprising in Turin. On his return from Italy, he joined a secret society – again, largely motivated by national sentiment – and began, along with other members of the *Geheimbund*, to write for the *Allgemeine Zeitung* in the 1820s. In the middle of the decade, he was imprisoned by the confederal *Zentraluntersuchungskommission* in Mainz, only to be released in 1826. During the 1830s and 1840s, he was close to the Young Germany movement. He also became the friend of the national economist Friedrich List, who worked on the *Allgemeine Zeitung* before he committed suicide in 1846. His principal ambitions appear to have been the achievement of journalistic impartiality and the creation of a German nation in the tradition of 1813, which usually prevented him from taking the side of either Prussia or Austria. In a world of censorship, persecution and political agitation, it was necessary to stand apart, as 'an impartial observer', from the confusion of events: 'how many had failed as a result of their own action in this period, how many hundred times had the reputation and position of parties altered, only to collapse and disappear after a short spell of domination, as if they had never existed'.[92]

In Kolb's opinion, 'Germany' stood apart from such changing political constellations and shifting state interests. In this context, it was even more important to oppose Berlin, which had acted aggressively to impose Prussian hegemony in 1848–50, 1854–56, 1859 and under Bismarck after 1862, than it was to oppose Austria, which often seemed to act defensively. 'Orges and I are certainly German (*deutsch gesinnt*), not remotely Austrian,' he wrote to one of his opponents in May 1859: 'but this mistaking of a living spirit in Germany only in order to put Prussia at the helm and to marginalise Austria has shocked us.'[93] On Georg Cotta's death in 1863, Kolb was anxious to impress on Lerchenfeld that he would 'never' 'defend the small German business and vote in the same sense as the *Süddeutschen*'.[94] 'I am convinced,' he wrote to Cotta's pro-Prussian son in June of the same year, 'that you hold sacred the principles of your father, who wanted a whole Germany, not a Prussian one.'[95] As one contemporary remarked of Kolb, he had little contact with North Germany and little liking of high politics: 'he was a completely Swabian, but very appealing, person who, although diplomats and statesmen often came to court him, preferred to be with his own kind, and showed himself to be unusually undemanding and modest in their company'.[96] As such, he was reluctant to exclude Austria altogether and to accede to Prussia's policy of *force majeure*, which seemed to militate against the interests of 'Germany'. Yet Kolb was not, by the same token, a strong supporter of Vienna's German policy.

Parties in the Third Germany

The pro-Austrian standpoint of the various 'greater German' parties and the *Reformverein* proved unpopular in the third Germany. The Reform Association, for instance, only counted 1,500 members, compared to the 25,000 members of the *Nationalverein*.[97] A thousand members, or two-thirds of the total, came from Munich, yet even here support for the Habsburg monarchy was ambiguous. Liberals and democrats counted 80 out of 140 seats between 1849 and 1855 in the Bavarian *Landtag*, and liberals alone comprised 113 out of 148 seats between 1855 and 1859, and 84 out of 140 between 1859 and 1863. Conservatives and '*Klerikale*', who made up the bulk of the 'greater German' organisations, accounted for 60 (1849), 35 (1855) and 60 seats (1859) in the three legislative periods, despite Catholics outnumbering Protestants by almost three to one. For the Bavarian aristocrat and later first minister Chlodwig zu Hohenlohe-Schillingsfürst, it was obvious that the idea of a 'small German' *Bundesstaat* had 'foundered because of the resistance of the Catholic party', yet it was equally evident that the minority Catholic party prevented 'reform, through its attachment to the *grossdeutsch* party and its maintenance of the greater German programme, without any prospect of realising its own wishes'.[98] The majority of public opinion in Bavaria was not, in Hohenlohe's view, in favour of Prussia or *Kleindeutschland*, but it was also rightly sceptical of Austria, whose links to Germany were best maintained through an alliance, as Radowitz and Gagern had envisaged in 1848–50.[99] While the founders of the *Fortschrittspartei* in Bavaria, which was widely seen as the small German successor of the *Nationalverein*, decided not to set up an overarching Bavarian party or to call for the establishment of local associations, since they had little chance of succeeding before 1866, greater German and pro-Austrian associations also failed to recruit members or attract mass support.[100] From the 1850s onwards, the press in Bavaria divided equally for – as in the case of the Augsburger *Allgemeine Zeitung* (7,800 subscribers), the *Augsburger Postzeitung* (1,700) and the *Volksbote* (6,000) – and against Austria – in the form of the *Münchner Neueste Nachrichten* (15,000), the *Nürnberger Correspondent* (5,000) and the *Süddeutsche Zeitung*.[101]

In the only other 'Catholic' state, Baden, which had almost twice as many Catholics as Evangelicals, the press was similarly split between 'ultramontane' or pro-Austrian papers, such as the official *Karlsruher Zeitung* (1,500) and the *Freiburger Zeitung* (2,000), and liberal ones, such as the *Mannheimer Journal* (2,000) and the *Frankfurter Journal* (10,000), which was published in the neighbouring city-state. By contrast, the political balance in Baden tipped much more pronouncedly towards the 'liberal party': at least 32 out of 63 deputies were liberals in 1850 and 1859, rising to 48 in 1861, 54 in 1863, and 59 in 1865.[102] As in Bavaria, many liberals were not in favour of *Kleindeutschland*, with the majority undecided and a smaller number – above all in the largely Catholic southern *Oberland* – supportive of *Grossdeutschland*, but they were more inclined than their Bavarian counterparts towards a constitutional, federal nation-state, which was difficult to reconcile with the policy of the Austrian government and the structure of the Habsburg monarchy.[103] 'It is a known fact', wrote Hohenlohe in 1862, 'that "German unity" nowhere enjoys greater popularity than in the South-West German states.'[104] At the *Fürstentag* of 1863, the Grand Duke of Baden had, according to his father-in-law the King of Saxony, 'agitated against the entire project' of the Austrians: 'Behind the Grand Duke stands the Gotha party with Ludwig Häusser and Johann Caspar Bluntschli at its head, which wants to oppose Austria.'[105] Although the Badenese liberal leader and, from 1861, effective first minister Franz von Roggenbach refused for the sake of party unity to force liberals to choose between a small and a greater Germany, he was himself, like many graduates of Heidelberg, a critic of Austria and an advocate of *Kleindeutschland*, to the extent that the Crown Prince of Prussia expressed 'his joy' over his 'activity'.[106] In a meeting with Hohenlohe in September 1862, Roggenbach had explained that 'now Austria starts with the idea of destroying Prussia and putting itself at the head of a Reich of the *Mitte*. By opening the German-national question, Austria is playing a dangerous game, since it is awakening the national sympathies of its German population for Germany, for which there is no form and over which the unitary state [that is, Austria] will collapse.'[107] To Badenese liberals, it was difficult to imagine how the Habsburg monarchy could be accommodated within a German nation-state.

The states surrounding Frankfurt – the Duchy of Nassau, the Electorate and Grand Duchy of Hesse – demonstrated the weakness of any Austrian-backed 'alternative to German unification'.[108] In Frankfurt itself, there had seemed briefly to be the possibility of an alliance between democratic *Grossdeutsche* and the '*Geldaristokratie*' of financiers, who – in the words of a police report of July 1862 – 'were rather Austrian-minded as a result of their interests'.[109] On his tour of Germany in 1861, designed to assess the strength of the greater German cause, Fröbel estimated that 'in Frankfurt am Main the *grossdeutsch* view is by far the preponderant one', yet his evaluation proved to be wildly over-optimistic, with the democrats failing to cooperate with the city's financial elites and with the *Reformverein* failing to find a foothold before disappearing completely by the end of 1863.[110] As L. W. Fischer-Goullet, the editor of the *Deutsche Stimmen* and the Austrian-sponsored *Frankfurter Postzeitung*, put it in March 1863, 'The great influence of "new Gothaism" rests above all on its domination of journalism in its entirety. This gives it the means not only to dictate the political opinion of the people, but also to dominate science, art and literature as a whole.'[111] The *Frankfurter Journal*, with its circulation of 10,000 in 1862 outstripping the combined total of 1,600 copies of the pro-*Reformverein Postzeitung* and the democratic *Volksfreund für das mittlere Deutschland*, remained the dominant newspaper in the region and was, in the opinion of the Viennese *Presseleitungskomitee*, pro-Prussian, Protestant and nationalistic, publishing 'systematic attacks on the *Kaiserstaat*, its conditions and government, and against the maintenance of the Confederation with Austria'.[112] Together with the *Mainzer Zeitung*, the *Mainzer Anzeiger*, the *Rhein-Lahn-Zeitung*, the *Rheinischer Kurier*, the *Mittelrheinischer Zeitung*, the *Hessischer Morgenzeitung* and the *Zeit*, the *Frankfurter Journal* eclipsed clerical publications such as the *Mainzer Journal* and official ones such as the *Darmstädter Zeitung*. To Ketteler, the pro-Austrian bishop of Mainz, 'the press, a very large majority of which serves the Devil, is now the highest power in Germany which fights against the kingdom (*Reich*) of God'.[113]

The proponents of different versions of *Grossdeutschland* within the *Reformverein* were small in number and came largely from Catholic and government circles, seen by opponents as 'a religious – a priests' – association (*Pfaffenverein*)', as Ludwig Heydenreich, the founder of the Nassau *Reformverein*, conceded.[114] Such perceptions were significant because Catholics constituted a minority, with 217,405 (1858) compared to 595,541 Protestants in the 'mixed' Grand Duchy of Hesse, and 204,771 Catholics (1859) to 331,545 Protestants in Nassau. It was imperative, held one Frankfurt supporter of the association, to keep meetings 'free of all suspect colleagues from the ultramontane and absolutist-aristocratic camp', but it proved impossible.[115] Despite state backing for 'greater German' candidates and the outlawing of the *Nationalverein*, the Progressive Party won 32 of the 50 seats in the Grand Duchy of Hesse's Landtag in September 1862, with a further 6 seats going to the old liberals. In elections in the Duchy of Nassau in November 1863, the Progressives won three-quarters of the seats in the second chamber and all those in the first chamber; and in the Electorate of Hesse, the withdrawal of whose constitution had triggered the Prussian–Austrian confrontation at

Olmütz in 1850, the liberals gained a large majority in the elections of 1860 and went on by 45 votes to 3 in May 1861 to defend their declaration of December of the previous year that the constitution was illegal. The third dissolution of the *Landtag* by the Elector yielded another large liberal majority in January 1862. Liberals and Progressives, most of whom were sceptical of Austria, had overshadowed the anti-Prussian party of the *Reformverein*.

The pro-Austrian party would have been strengthened, as Fröbel recognised, if it had been supported consistently by greater German democrats. Radical circles, supported by sections of working-class, lower middle-class, and middle-class opinion in the larger cities, had been powerful in 1848–49 and were believed by Fröbel to be strong – as the representatives of 'the true *Volksmasse* or democracy' – and 'decisively *grossdeutsch*' in Frankfurt during the early 1860s.[116] The democratic *Neue Frankfurter Zeitung*, which later became simply the *Frankfurter Zeitung* and was edited by Leopold Sonnemann and ex-National Assembly radical Georg Friedrich Kolb, was listed by the pro-Austrian publicist as the second most important Frankfurt newspaper after the *Frankfurter Journal* and was labelled '*grossdeutsch*', if 'Jewish and negative'.[117] Yet the newspaper, although it had supported the Habsburg monarchy in 1859, was generally critical of both Vienna and Berlin, as its commentaries on the *Fürstentag* made plain in 1863: 'It is the same to us whether the northern state coerces the southern monarchy, or whether the latter overpowers the former.'[118] 'We are almost daily in a position to report scandals from Prussia and scold Prussian particularism,' recorded the publication in May 1861: 'But it doesn't at all follow that we are speaking specifically for Austriandom or that we want to give the impression that the piling up of terrible conditions in the *Kaiserstaat* is anything other than it is.'[119] The meetings of the German *Reformverein* in Frankfurt were discounted from the start by the radical *Volksfreund*, edited by Nikolaus Hadermann, for their 'aristocratic, ultra-conservative physiognomy'.[120] 'Democratic elements' were 'very weak' at such gatherings, not least because radicals fundamentally disagreed with the Reform Association's espousal of an indirectly elected confederal chamber and an executive directory which left to the individual states many of their old prerogatives.[121] German Austria, wrote Kolb in the *Neue Frankfurter Zeitung*, could only be an organic part of a federal, republican Germany on the model of Switzerland if it harmonised 'its internal constitution with the national ideas of freedom and rights'.[122]

For its part, the *Deutsche Volkspartei*, which was established in 1865 after a secession of left-wing democrats from the *Nationalverein* and which later became the principal left-liberal party of Württemberg, declared in its provisional programme that Germany should have 'no Prussian and no Austrian head'.[123] It was preposterous, asserted Ludwig Büchner, one of the leaders of the *Volkspartei* in Frankfurt and Hesse, to expect

> Guarantees from Austria!! A guarantee for the sovereign rights of those princes which help it – a guarantee of the continuation of absolutism and German fragmentation – there will be a guarantee of the domination of the sword and priests, but no other; and the abysmal business of reaction will probably flourish more luxuriantly in Germany under the protective hand of Austria, once Prussia has been torn down, than ever before. Who has not yet understood that German unity and freedom belongs in the realm of fantasy as long as Austria contemplates it in its present form and position as a Great Power, just as with Prussia.[124]

To such democrats, the Habsburg monarchy was no better than its Hohenzollern counterpart.

A good example of radical ambivalence towards Austria was furnished by Johann Baptist von Schweitzer. The son of a wealthy, established Frankfurt family of Italian origin and Roman Catholic faith, Schweitzer was one of the most pro-Austrian democrats, the grandson of the editor of the *Oberpostamtszeitung*, which was owned by the Thurn and Taxis family. Educated by Jesuits and then by Stahl, Gneist and Mittermaier at Berlin and Heidelberg, he was also a friend of Arthur Schopenhauer and an admirer of Kant and the Enlightenment, which helped to push him towards radical politics, where he was suspected by working-class colleagues such as August Bebel of foppishness and dilettantism. His antipathy towards Prussia and his attachment to *Grossdeutschland* remained constant, even if relatively weaker, after he turned to social democracy in the mid-1860s. 'It should be the whole of Germany!' he proclaimed in a treatise *Zur Deutschen Frage* in 1862, echoing Arndt: 'If the mercenaries and toadies of the small German press praise the instruments of Hohenzollern domestic politics as German heroes, independent and reasonable men simply say: riff-raff, just like the others!'[125] 'Free of any special interests, we and our colleagues will always use our spiritual weapons in the most disinterested way for the unity and freedom of Germany,' declared the editorial of *Nordstern*, on which Schweitzer collaborated, in April 1861:

> We didn't and don't belong to those false prophets who seek to lead our people astray by speaking for *Grossdeutschland* or *Kleindeutschland*; we want the whole of Germany in its natural borders from the Königsau to the Alps and the Adriatic, from the Ardennes to Memel and the March. We shall also continue to hold our black, red and gold banner high, for all Germans must gather under this banner alone when it is a question of fighting for the unity and freedom of the fatherland.[126]

Schweitzer's view of Austria's role in such fantasies of greater Germany changed. When he entered politics at the age of 26 in 1859, he argued – in *Österreichs Sache ist Deutschlands Sache* and *Widerlegung von Carl Vogt's Studien zur gegenwärtigen Lage Europas* – that Austrians were safeguarding the legal treaties of the international order, defending German interests against Italy and France, and calling on natural ties of kinship: 'Where is the cornerstone of a unified national form to be found? Not there, where we calmly look on as the common enemy attacks our fraternal tribe, but there, where we feel ourselves to be a nation (*Nation*) and recognise in the injury of our brotherly tribe the injury of all.'[127] With the Habsburg monarchy's rapid capitulation after two defeats in battle, however, the Frankfurt radical abandoned the weak, supposedly unreformable state in favour of a mass national movement founded on associations of gymnasts and riflemen. *Der einzige Weg zur Einheit*, published in 1860, described how the 'old' German powers confronted the 'new' revolutionary potential of the German people, with the 'traditions of 1848' having established deep roots.[128] 'The democratic party is in Germany at the same time the national one,' he went on: 'From the graves of 1848 comes the call: not the Habsburgs, not the Hohenzollern! A united Germany.'[129] Finally, as a successful mass national movement came to seem unlikely, Schweitzer briefly reverted to support for Austria in *Die österreichische Spitze* in 1863, but only 'to nullify a greater evil by a lesser one, to still Prussian and small German agitation by an Austrian and greater German one; in short, to seek to drive out the devil with the devil'.[130] 'Since every strengthening and extension of a specific Prussiandom is nothing more than the amplification of an evil, which is already large enough, evidence is mustered at the same time that the small German agitation for Prussia is to be seen as a generally destructive evil', he continued.[131] If a German Reich of 70 millions could be achieved through Austria's offices, 'it would be the heartbeat of this part of the world, it would be the bulwark of civilisation and humanity', but it was not evident how Austria, which was 'internally disunited', would be able to realise such a 'political dream'.[132] As the editor of the *Social-Demokrat*, he advised his readers to fight against both Prussia and Austria by 1865 in order to achieve German unity, which would be 'a new work, only possible on the rubble of the old'.[133] Even Schweitzer, with his increasing hatred of Prussia under Bismarck and of an 'extra-clever Gotha half-humanity', refrained from explaining how the Habsburg monarchy fitted into his republican, democratic and national conception of Germany. Austria merely stood closer to 'Germany as a whole' than did Prussia or the 'bourgeois' Gotha and Progressive parties.[134]

Like other opponents of Berlin in the third Germany, Schweitzer tacitly acknowledged that he was swimming against a tide of scepticism about the Habsburg monarchy in the German public sphere, especially in the North German lands. Internal reform in the monarchy appeared impossible, he admitted in 1860: 'Even a cabinet composed of Richelieu, Colbert, Pitt, and Machiavelli, with Cicero as the director of the official press, would run its head against a wall in view of this impossible task.'[135] Most radicals, including Schweitzer's opponent Carl Vogt, agreed with this diagnosis. Austria's defeat in Italy was both likely and desirable, since it would reduce Vienna's nefarious influence in Germany, wrote Vogt in his *Studien zur gegenwärtigen Lage Europas* (1859). Since the entire history of the Habsburg monarchy was 'a concatenation of heinous crimes against Germany's unity, honour, worth, security, freedom, power and greatness', it was necessary to banish it from German affairs and, possibly, to break it up.[136] Unlike Prussia, Austria was an extra-German power: 'Thus, raise the cry for a new structuring of the German Confederation in all organs of the press, all chambers and amongst the people as a whole. No more extra-German provinces in the Bund! No guarantee for the extra-German possessions of a ruler! ... A German popular assembly! A political whole to face the wider world! One people! One power! One army!'[137] Any support for war in South Germany, wrote the radical forty-eighter Heinrich Simon in 1859, derived less from national motives than from the fear of ultramontanes, particularists and reactionaries that Austria's defeat would mean Prussian hegemony. As long as France did not attack Germany, Berlin should either act against those German states agitating for 'an un-German war' that was nothing to do with them or reinstate the Reich constitution of 1849 through a call to the people.[138] In order to rise, Germany needed to be split from Austria and to be constituted in full before the Germans in Austria could be given a helping hand.[139]

Ludwig Bamberger was even more blunt:

> The best thing that could now be written for the enlightenment of Germany would be a short, handy, popular history of the Habsburg dynasty. If only they knew their history! It has been said often enough how poor German literature is in great historical talents, but it has seldom led to an awareness of just how intimately this poor historical education is entangled with the misfortune of the German nation … Is this nation (*Volk*) really to be helped? A nation which doesn't break out into laughter when the Habsburgs talk of German brothers, a nation which doesn't become suspicious when Jesuits preach about nationality, a nation which doesn't resist when petty despots declare the fatherland in danger? Do you not see what is in danger? The Austrian royal house is in danger, the evil pole of Germany, and everything linked to this evil pole – the rule of the many, fragmentation, obscurity, Jesuitism, backwardness and the corruption of a patriarchal police regime at all levels and in all its forms.[140]

The working-class leader Ferdinand Lassalle, still a 'voice from democracy' in 1859, likewise traced the failure of German unity to the independent Great Power status of Austria, which rested on its extra-German territories.[141] A German reawakening depended on the destruction of the Austrian *Gesamtstaat*, which would allow the merger of Prussia and Germany: 'With the dismemberment of Austria, the particularity of Prussia disappears by itself, just as an assertion disappears along with its opposite.'[142] In 1866, the *Social-Demokrat* recalled Lassalle's position in 1859 as a guide to current events: Austria, it affirmed, was not a German power; Prussia was, even if also an absolutist one.[143] Despite the greater German past and anti-Prussian attitude of the majority of radicals, most viewed the Habsburg monarchy with suspicion or contempt.

Liberals generally shared such feelings, with fewer of them worrying about Prussian 'absolutism', in the opinion of the *Social-Demokrat*.[144] There was, of course, a split between 'North' and

'South'. 'In relation to the power of Austria, there are two views,'
wrote Heinrich von Gagern to the Cassel liberal Friedrich Oetker in
the early 1860s, having given up his earlier position from 1849:
'According to one, and this is mine, Austria in its position of power
is not just a European necessity, but also a bulwark of Germany ...
The adherents of this opinion, who want to maintain Austria in
Germany and Germany in Austria and who cannot think of a
Germany without Austria, have only endeavoured until now to find
a solution for the special relationship of Austria to Germany.'[145]
'According to the other view, Austria is merely a great obstacle to
the unitary construction of Germany under Prussian leadership,
and its dissolution can only be welcome, the sooner the better,' he
continued: 'In its most extreme outgrowths, this view goes as far as
to suggest that it would be better to strive for a northern, predominantly Protestant Germany, unconcerned about the rest, and to
throw overboard southern, predominantly Catholic ballast, which
hangs on the tails of the enlightened and ambitious North.'[146]
Although Gagern doubted that the latter point of view was
'national', his own rendering of the former rested on a continuing
distinction between 'Austria' and 'Germany', which required a
'special relationship' and a novel, unspecified constitutional
arrangement in order to co-exist.[147] By the time that Gagern
outlined this case in September 1862 at the *Abgeordnetentag* in
Weimar, he was, in Oetker's estimation, 'a "dead man" for
Germany', listened to politely but coldly for over an hour.[148] On
returning to Frankfurt, the former liberal leader joined the
Reformverein: 'From then on, Gagern was forgotten.'[149]

From his vantage point in Saxony, Biedermann shared Gagern's
diagnosis, if not his inclinations, noting that 'public opinion at that
time was very divided' between those – 'almost universally in the
South and partly in the North, too' – who wanted Germany and
Prussia to support the Habsburg monarchy and those, like himself,
who wanted to act 'in the well-understood interests of the German
nation' and to avoid being 'dragged along by Austria'.[150] For the
Saxon liberal, 'the whole logic of relationships led to the result of
taking up again the idea of 1848; namely, unification of non-
Austrian Germany under the leadership of Prussia'.[151] In Prussia
itself, it seemed, such a belief had been taken to the point where 'a
thorough-going understanding or even a lively, active interest in the
German question' was not to be found, with contemporaries feeling
untouched by Austrian affairs, enjoying the 'humiliation of Austria'

in 1859 as a 'sort of nemesis for Olmütz' or concentrating entirely on domestic politics.[152] Sybel, with his experience of Bavaria, detected a similar incomprehension amongst Prussian liberals and conservatives, with Vincke arguing that the fate of Austria did not concern him, since only a fifth of its population was German and its government was opposed to Berlin. This, he went on, remained a divide between North and South German liberals, with northerners having wanted to expel the Habsburg monarchy from Germany since 1849 and southerners wanting to draw it towards them in order to reinvigorate it.[153] The need for regeneration was not questioned, however, and the means to include Austria in Germany were not specified. For Sybel, as for Biedermann and Gagern, such southern sentiments did not imply that Austria should be fused with Germany, but rather that it should retain strong links with it. The very terms that Sybel attributed to southern liberals suggested that '*Österreich*' and '*Deutschland*' were separate from each other.

The Case against Austria

Most liberals – and many others – were swayed by the 'northern' case against the Habsburg monarchy. 'The recognition of the necessity of Austria's exclusion from Germany, which wants to unite itself on a constitutional basis ... has almost become a common good of the nation', wrote the Rhineland liberal Gustav von Mevissen in February 1850.[154] In a tract which had a run of 50,000 and was sent to leaders of the opposition in all the individual German states in 1859, the publicist and academic Ludwig Karl Aegidi claimed that Austria had attempted to make Prussia and Germany into instruments for the pursuit of its own interests outside Germany. By referring to diplomatic documents, he sought to show that Prussia, not Austria, was 'the only defender of national forces and power abroad, and the only defender of political and religious freedom at home': 'Germany has not identified with Austria, from a feeling of its own independence. We are the German nation and we do not mount Austrian wars, only our own.'[155] The philosopher and journalist Constantin Rössler, writing before the Italian war, agreed: 'To raise the German world into a state is the task of Prussia by the grace of God and by right.'[156] 'Austria will not budge an inch from its sphere of power in Germany and from the prospect of extending it', he continued:

as a consequence, 'we should only leave our South German sphere of influence to Austria on pain of death'.[157] Austria's interests, which would be defended by force, were different from those of Germany.

North German liberals like Aegidi, Rössler and Georg Beseler were fundamentally opposed to the Habsburg monarchy, wrote Ludwig Häusser from Heidelberg to Hermann Baumgarten, who had just returned from Berlin after a tour of the South in May 1859: 'Beseler hates Austria with all his heart; I have nothing against this. But, in my opinion, he underestimates the ease with which it can be gobbled up and killed off. For him there can be no German future at all without the fall of Austria; thus, he is too indifferent to the dangers which threaten it.'[158] Notwithstanding exceptions such as Gervinus, who blamed the Italian war on 'Austria's bellicosity' and hoped for its 'defeat and misfortune in the highest measure', liberals in the third Germany, held Häusser, backed the Habsburg monarchy in the defence of its territory and of wider 'German interests', though without changing their view of Austria's role in Germany itself.[159] The Hanoverian liberal Johannes Miquel exemplified this position in his speech to the second general meeting of the *Nationalverein* in Heidelberg in 1861. The Habsburg monarchy would survive in a more or less centralised form and it would retain its German core, he proclaimed, but it would remain separate from Germany, fulfilling its mission of colonisation in the East:

> Is the construction of a German *Bundesstaat* incompatible with the strengthening of Austria? Do the interests of both contradict each other? In an Austrian *Gesamtstaat*, in my view, the Germans will ultimately remain the rulers in fact; at least insofar as they have a forceful and powerfully organised German *Bundesstaat* behind them ... Now, gentlemen, it has already been raised in the committee report that an Austrian *Gesamtstaat* cannot, now or ever, and certainly not the one presently being built, be incorporated in a German *Bundesstaat* ... nevertheless the building of such a *Bundesstaat* is in the interest of Germans in Austria. For they will have a powerful, organised brother-tribe (*Bruderstamm*) at their back.[160]

For its own good, Austria had to remain outside Germany, but in a close alliance with it, as in Gagern's plan of a narrower and a wider union from 1849.

Many southern liberals appear to have agreed with such a position. Like Miquel, the Württemberg publicist and former Frankfurt deputy Paul Pfizer, although sensitive to Gagern's later refusal – in the 1850s and 1860s – to rule out Austria altogether, remained convinced that the Habsburg monarchy would be peripheral in the process of German unification.[161] Throughout, he claimed in 1862, he had doubted that Austria could join a German state.[162] In its own constitutional deliberations in 1849, the monarchy had 'ignored Germany and failed to mention it in a single syllable'.[163] Germany, therefore, was justified in replying in kind and excluding all Austrians.[164] 'Full unification with Austria', wrote Pfizer in the *Schwäbische Chronik* in January 1850, 'meets insuperable obstacles.'[165] On the one hand, Austrian leaders tended to think of their state as a European power, for it was 'big enough without Germany to exist independently', taking 'little notice of those, as is well-known, which it does not necessarily need'; Prussia, by contrast, relied on 'the rest of Germany', which was strong enough together to defend itself against the Prussian army, but not against the Austrian one.[166] In the 'German' wars against Denmark over Schleswig-Holstein between 1848 and 1850, Vienna had not even withdrawn its envoy from Copenhagen.[167] Its main focus was the Near East, looking to Germany largely as a source of compensation when its eastern ambitions were frustrated.[168] The German Austrians felt themselves to be 'part, and indeed the dominant part, of a great whole [that is, the Habsburg monarchy]', making Germany – historically labelled 'out there in the Reich' – seem like 'a purely external work and appendage of Austria'.[169]

On the other hand, it was difficult to see how the Habsburg monarchy could be united with Germany, even if Vienna had desired it:

However necessary a narrow alliance of friendship between Germany and the Austrian *Gesamtstaat* is, however desirable and worthy of sacrifice the participation of Austria in many of the confederal institutions of Germany may be, Austria – which is a powerful and fully independent state without Germany because of its possessions outside the Bund – appears all the less suited to the leadership of the Confederation because it is increasingly losing its character as a German power, given the scope and the mass imbalance of its extra-German territory and the daily increasing demands of its Magyar and Slav population.[170]

Austrian governments had consistently opposed the establishment of a united German state, Pfizer went on, because they feared that it might attract German Austrians, splitting the Habsburg monarchy:

> The German hereditary lands still constitute the kernel or the roots of Austrian power, as well as the dominant element in the whole, extensive Austrian territory; but this is without doubt one of the main reasons for Austria always opposing any plans and demands in favour of the unity of a German state and German national law, just as it was always against a more unified structuring of Germany because of the power of attraction which this could have over Germans in Austria.[171]

The Habsburg monarchy, concluded the Swabian publicist, was at once an extra-German power and an opponent of a German nation-state, 'which the people demand'.[172] Since dualism within the Bund was no longer feasible and the incorporation of Austria in a 'unified Germany' impossible, Germans were left no choice but to opt for Prussia.[173]

The principal liberal periodical, the *Grenzboten*, illustrated the evolution and range of charges against Austria from a national point of view. The Habsburg monarchy, commented one article in 1860, had not been 'German' for 200 years.[174] 'The task, on which all others rest, is to free Germany from the political influence of the Austrian dynasty,' continued the correspondent: 'This liberation is necessary, and it is also possible without much sacrifice', since Vienna's hold over the German lands was tenuous.[175] Even immediately after Olmütz in 1850, Austria was perceived to be 'losing' Germany, in spite of the fact that Schwarzenberg's victory had appeared to be a 'great' and 'complete' one.[176] Whereas reactionaries in the German lands supported Austria, the 'constitutional' party generally backed Prussia because it appeared to embody the 'principle of movement' and of 'reform', noted the publication in 1851.[177] When the Habsburg monarchy became a constitutional state in 1861 and sought to reform the Confederation a year later, its actions caused only confusion in the rest of Germany, since they ran against the grain of the monarchy's German policy until that date: 'That the whole thing is a hollow form, that it can in fact yield no results, that it would further aggravate the chaos and fragmentation of the parties in the German states is no doubt one more reason for the government of the imperial state to pursue its plan.'[178]

Even if the Austrian administration were serious about reform of the Bund, it had put forward its proposals too late, asserted the *Grenzboten* in 1863: the 'national party', which was opposed to Vienna, was already dominant in three-quarters of Germany.[179] Although part of the national party wished to use 'a German parliament convoked by Austria as a starting-point', others feared 'the repetition of the struggle of 1848' between conservative Habsburg forces and parliamentary ones.[180] The 'ultimate end' of both factions – 'a new construction of Germany' – in any event ran counter to Vienna's aims: for this reason, 'the Austrian government could only count on a cold acknowledgement, not at all on the heart-felt applause, of the national party for its plans, however liberal they might seem. For that, Germany has already been revolutionised to too great an extent, if we are not mistaken in our characterisation of the existing state of affairs.'[181] By the end of 1863, it was undeniable that the Austrian plan to reform the Bund and regain a hold over Germany had failed.[182] The Habsburg monarchy was held to be incompatible with the *Zollverein* when treaties were renegotiated in the early 1850s, notwithstanding its need for rapprochement with Prussia as a consequence of bankruptcy, and it remained so in the early 1860s, it appeared, despite broad acceptance by this time of Friedrich List's argument that politics and economics were closely connected and that the removal of tariffs within a large, protected, national market would stimulate German industry and create the foundation of German power in the world:

> However imposingly and energetically Austria puts itself forward, it can only be the loyal ally of a unified Germany; our spirit, our interests, our education, our hopes and wishes do not fit in with the structure of the *Kaiserstaat*; it can only be a question of a closer connection of the two trading bodies, not full unification. Our hopes rest on Prussia.[183]

Because of its constitutional form and its diverse nationalities, the existence of which pushed the government to oppose nationalism, the Habsburg monarchy could not play a part in the political reorganisation of Germany.[184] To the *Grenzboten*, Austria was simply not a German state.[185]

Prussian conservatives were more convinced by and less interested in the Habsburg monarchy's 'German' credentials. Vienna was seen by the camarilla as Berlin's main ally in the counter-revolution, with Ernst Ludwig von Gerlach going so far as to represent Olmütz – in a retrospective essay – as the saving of Prussia, Austria and Germany, which had been 'standing on the edge of an abyss'.[186] As the reactionary leader wrote in the *Neue Preussische Zeitung* during the death throes of the revolution: 'The soul of the *German* Bund is the unity (*Einigkeit*) of *Austria* and *Prussia*.'[187] However, even in the immediate aftermath of the revolutionary events in Germany and Austria, the Gerlachs were anxious not to be seen as 'Austrian', telling Wagener – the editor of the *Kreuzzeitung* – in September 1850, for instance, to emphasise the 'pettiness and myopia of Austrian policy'.[188] All conservatives in Prussia, as Bismarck-Schönhausen spelled out in September 1849, put their *Preussentum* before any counter-revolutionary or national affiliation with Austria. 'What preserved us [in 1848–49] was that which constitutes the real Prussia,' he proclaimed: 'It was what remains of that much stigmatized *Stockpreussentum*, which outlasted the revolution: that is, the Prussian army, the Prussian treasury, the fruits of an intelligent Prussian administration of many years' standing, and that vigorous spirit of cooperation between king and people which exists in Prussia ... You will not find in the army, any more than in the rest of the Prussian people, any need for a national rebirth. They are satisfied with the name Prussia and proud of the name Prussia.'[189]

This degree of loyalty to the Prussian dynasty, army and state distanced most conservatives from the Habsburg monarchy, especially during the turbulent years of the Erfurt Union, Olmütz and Dresden between 1849 and 1851, when the ministries of Brandenburg and Radowitz and of Manteuffel came into conflict with Vienna. Although such conservative administrations were divided in their attitude to Austria, the two Minister-Presidents and the Foreign Minister, together with other colleagues, were all sceptical of the Ballhausplatz's intentions. 'The relationship of Austria to Prussia constitutes a particular difficulty in the judgement of the state of the German business,' wrote Manteuffel in July 1850, despite having come to oppose Radowitz's Union by that date:

It seems to me that the persisting difference between the two states has a more profound cause than mutual insults and sensitivity to insults; there is in my opinion really a considerable split present, for which one can find different forms of expression, but which I shall limit myself to characterising: Prussia wants the organic formation of all or some of the German lands into a genuine whole, Austria notably negates this aim, insofar as it is a question, in the sphere concerned, of a radius capable of expansion and thus touching on the Austrian–German states. Both states seek to find justification for their demands from the old laws and rights of the Bund. The negative position of Austria gives it the advantage that it is backed overwhelmingly abroad, whereas in Prussian leanings the transformation of existing relations and possible complications are feared.[190]

Reinforced by the actions of the ministry and the attitude of Friedrich Wilhelm IV, who railed that 'Austrian scandal sheets have never ridiculed Prussia' as much as Ludwig von Gerlach had in 1850, the wider 'party' of conservatives generally avoided the pro-Austrian sentiments of the camarilla, leaving the latter feeling isolated and weak.[191] Radowitz, who was the main target of the Gerlach circle's criticism, quipped after the Erfurt parliament elections of February 1850 that the *Kreuzzeitungspartei* and the 'ultramontanes' had won only a sixth of the seats, meaning that 'the entire party of the *Kreuzzeitung* has enough space in just *one* room'.[192] By far the biggest faction at Erfurt, with 120 seats out of a total of 222 in the *Volkshaus*, was the *Bahnhofspartei*, which was largely liberal but also contained a handful of moderate conservatives such as Vincke and Ernst von Bodelschwingh-Velmede. To its right was the so-called '*Klemme*', with about 40 seats, and the main conservative grouping, the *Schlehdornpartei*, which counted only 35 deputies, including the Catholic representative Peter Reichensperger. The former tended to follow the line of the Prussian government.[193] The latter was led by Stahl, who supported most aspects of the Union and was labelled 'Radowitzian' by Gerlach.[194] On 12 April, Stahl outlined his programme to the parliament, basing his case on 'German' values and implicitly accepting the exclusion of Austria from the narrower union: Prussia and Austria were to be two pillars of monarchism, but the Prussian-led Union was only to be tied to the Habsburg monarchy by a lasting and extensive agreement, not by a merger.[195] A month later, the conservative politician reiterated the point that Prussia had to work closely with the German princes in order 'strongly to resist both the attacks of Austria and the endeavours of the liberal (Gotha) party to absorb monarchical powers'.[196] For Stahl, as for Manteuffel, Austria was a rival and even an 'enemy' by 1850.[197]

Although the 'Stahl faction' was effectively dissolved as a consequence of the abandonment of the Erfurt Union and parliament at
Olmütz, the reactionary right, under Hans Hugo von Kleist-Retzow,
was unable to profit in the Prussian *Landtag*, counting merely 64
seats out of 352 by early 1851. The 50 deputies of the 'pure' right,
led by Adolf Heinrich von Arnim-Boitzenburg and Ernst Albert von
Bodelschwingh, and the 85 of the 'centre', which was in effect the
centre-right and drew most of its members from the Rhineland,
Westphalia and Silesia, were less likely to sympathise with the pro-
Austrian stance of the Gerlach brothers.[198] The left, Poles and 'wild
ones' had 153 seats between them. The upshot of such a balance of
forces in the Prussian and Erfurt parliaments made ultra-conservatives around the Gerlach brothers all the more dependent on the
favour of Friedrich Wilhelm IV. Even here, though, they were not
entirely successful, with Leopold reporting the monarch's claim in
October 1850 'that I recognise Austria ... all too much'.[199] After the
majority of the Prussian administration had opposed Radowitz's
brinkmanship with Austrian-backed Bavarian and Hanoverian
troops in Hesse-Kassel in October 1850, leading to the Foreign
Minister's resignation in early November, the King of Prussia criticised ministers' 'un-Prussian, craven attitude': 'Under no circumstances did they want to mobilise the army; they wanted to deliver us
without defences to the Austrians.'[200] When Brandenburg died a
few days later, the monarch blamed his death on Schwarzenberg's
treachery.[201] The King, noted Leopold von Gerlach, had been
brought by Radowitz 'into contradiction with himself', believing in
a German nation, the extension of Prussian power and the restoration of the Reich with an Austrian Emperor at its head.[202] His attitude to the Habsburg monarch was, at best, unpredictable.

The pro- and anti-Austrian sentiments of conservatives were
subjected to conflicting forces in the 1850s. During the Crimean
War, the camarilla sided with Russia against Austria and the western
powers, with Varnhagen going so far as to spread the false rumour
that 'the Russian government is giving huge sums of money to the
Kreuzzeitung people so that their scandal sheet eagerly takes Russia's
side'.[203] 'Of this money', he went on, 'Wagener, Goedsche, Stahl
and Gerlach received the greater part.'[204] Leopold von Gerlach
ignored such defamation, but nevertheless was critical of Austria,
contending that it had desperately and wrongly sought France's aid
in order to protect its weak position in Italy, bringing it into conflict
with Russia, 'which alone shares its policy'.[205] The Habsburg monar-

chy's position was again 'negative', 'lacking the courage to undertake a struggle of the Germans, i.e. of Austrian institutions, against
the Slav-Greek-and-Turkish, especially since (*viribus unitis*) Austria is
ruled largely by gendarmes'.[206] The monarchy's precarious internal
order seemed to have led it to act against the political interests of
the 'reaction' and against its own interests abroad. The Manteuffel
administration, however, was much more cautious, maintaining an
armed neutrality which alienated both St Petersburg and Vienna.
According to Prokesch, who had served as Austrian ambassador to
Prussia in the early 1850s, this anti-Austrian party was 'the strongest
in Berlin'.[207] 'Since all the people in Berlin are the same as during
my time there,' he remarked in August 1854, 'I cannot get rid of my
conviction that all the thoughts and endeavours of Pruss. policy
have the sole purpose of diminishing the position of power of
Austria and its prestigious influence in all spheres, and that this
purpose is the only one which exists in Berlin during the present
crisis.'[208]

The other main strand of conservatism by 1854, the
Wochenblattspartei led by Bethmann-Hollweg, eventually advised
Prussia to support Austria, but only as an ally of the maritime
powers, having initially asserted that, 'if we must go to war, it would
be more advantageous for us to have Austria as an enemy rather
than as a friend'.[209] Bunsen, a prominent member of Bethmann-
Hollweg's party and the Prussian ambassador in London, had even
written a memorandum in 1854, before Vienna had allied itself with
London and Paris, in which he contemplated backing the maritime
powers and expanding Prussia at Austria's expense. He also recommended the formation of a German *Bundesstaat*, 'as demanded by
Prussia and Germany, as desired by England, and as tolerated by
France'.[210] Although he was subsequently pushed to resign by
Friedrich Wilhelm IV, who thought he had had a nervous breakdown, Bunsen's actions had demonstrated the confusion of conser-
vatives' allegiances, exacerbated by Austria's abandonment of
Russia and its alliance with Britain and France.

The Habsburg monarchy's war against the Bonapartist regime in
1859 found broader support amongst conservatives, with even the
Preussisches Wochenblatt deploring the 'revolutionary' purpose of the
Second Empire and portraying Prussia as the 'last hope' of nullifying it.[211] Unfortunately, the newspaper's stance was not universally
shared in conservative circles: diplomats such as Pourtalès and
Usedom on the left of such circles and *Realpolitiker* such as Bismarck-

Schönhausen on the right were openly anti-Austrian; a second group, which contained liberals such as Waitz and Droysen and conservatives like Wagener and Stahl, aimed for compensation for Prussia in return for support for Austria; and a third group, including Gerlach and Gagern, was voluntarily pro-Austrian, at least until the government started to champion armed neutrality rather than alliance and war. After the 'New Era' administration had adopted this posture, profound splits re-emerged in the conservative camp, with the *Kreuzzeitung* complaining of ministers' liberal Gotha-inspired *Tendenzpolitik* and accusing them of being motivated by a single ideology, opposed to a reactionary Austria.[212] The Prussian government had made serious errors in the war and was guilty of producing an 'apology' for Napeolonic self-interest in Italy.[213] Once again, the reactionary right disagreed about Austria with the Prussian ministry and other sections of conservative opinion.

The rise of Bismarck to power in 1862 increased the isolation of Austrian supporters amongst the ranks of Prussian conservatives. From the early 1850s, during his time as Prussian envoy to the Bundestag, Bismarck had been known as a cynical defender of Prussian interests and opponent of Vienna. Prokesch, his Austrian counterpart in Frankfurt, was certain that 'the party to which Herr v. Bismarck belongs has no other aim in view than the reduction of Austria's position of power. This seems to them to be the key to Prussia's greatness.'[214] Bismarck's sponsorship of confederal neutrality in the Crimean War, wrote the Austrian envoy in July 1854, rested 'not so much on love of Russia as envy of Austria, not so much on any conservative principle as on a ravenous appetite for more power in Germany'.[215] Rechberg, who had served opposite Bismarck in Frankfurt and had become embroiled in a mutual antagonism with him during the mid-1850s, was appalled by Bismarck's *Realpolitik*, even in the wake of Austrian and Prussian cooperation in the Danish war of 1864, since it seemed to contradict many of the principles – legality, preservation of the status quo, the Concert of Europe – on which Vienna's policy was founded:

> when one has to deal with a man who displays his political cyni-
> cism so openly that he replies to that part of my letter – that we
> must make the maintenance of the Confederation and the hered-
> itary rights of the German princes the foundation of our policy –
> with the hair-raising phrase that both of us must place ourselves
> on the practical terrain of cabinet policy and not let the situation

be obscured by the fog that derives from the doctrines of a German policy of sentiment. Such language is worthy of a Cavour. Adherence to the basis of legality is a nebulous policy of sentiment! The task of keeping this man in bounds, of dissuading him from his expansionistic policy of utility ... surpasses human powers.[216]

From Bismarck's own point of view, Vienna sought unjustifiably to maintain its position of superiority in Germany and in its other spheres of interest. Although Bismarck had eventually praised Olmütz in public, he had contemplated war as late as 13 November 1850, if 'Prussia, our black and white Prussia, is not assured by clear and conclusive treaties of rights in Germany that are everywhere on a par with Austria's'.[217] He resented the complacent sense of Friedrich von Thun, the Austrian envoy in Frankfurt in November 1851, that 'a predominant Austrian influence in Germany was in the nature of things'.[218]

Such an innate sense of superiority had to be countered 'with facts, not with ideals': 'a Prussia that, as Bismarck put it, "renounced the inheritance of Frederick the Great" in order to be able to dedicate itself to its true destiny as Lord High Chamberlain to the Emperor did not exist in Europe, and before I sent home a recommendation for such a policy the issue would have to be decided by the sword'.[219] Prussia was at least Austria's equal, in Bismarck's opinion, and it should maintain an independent sphere in Germany and insist on parity within joint German institutions. Thus, at the start of the Crimean War, he warned against 'binding our spruce and seaworthy frigate to the wormy old warship of Austria' and, in the aftermath of the Franco-Austrian war, he repeated that 'I am neither Austrian, nor French, nor Russian, but Prussian, and that I see our welfare only in trust in our own strength and that of the German national movement'.[220] After becoming Minister-President, Bismarck stated his position baldly to Alois von Karolyi, the Austrian ambassador, avoiding the meaningless notion of Austrian–German brotherhood and acknowledging 'only the uncomfortable politics of self-interest', before going on to argue that the period between 1815 and 1848 had been characterised by Austrian concentration on its European role and Prussia's free hand in Germany.[221] If Vienna would give up Schwarzenberg's policy of seeking hegemony in Central Europe and would 'shift [its] centre of gravity to Ofen [Buda, in Hungary]', 'instead of looking for its centre of gravity in

Germany' and administering its non-German territory, particularly Hungary, 'as an appendage', Berlin would cooperate with the Habsburg monarchy.[222] Such brusque disregard of Austria, labelled 'insane' by some contemporaries after the Hofburg leaked the details of the Minister-President's conversations with Karolyi, directly contradicted the pro-Austrian outlook of the Gerlach circle, but found support in other sections – bureaucratic and Junker – of conservative opinion in Prussia.[223] Whether or not Austria was 'German', it should refrain from interfering in Germany.

The wars of the 1850s, especially the Franco-Austrian war, appeared to belie the claim that Austria stood outside Germany, with many newspapers and a flood of pamphlets coming to the aid of the Habsburg state.[224] However, support for Austria's 'national' wars was conditional and limited. Of the 32 German newspapers surveyed by the Austrian *Presseleitungskomitee* in 1855, 14 supported Vienna's stance in the Crimean War and 10 opposed it, yet the majority of publications continued to back Prussia (17) rather than Austria (8) and to criticise the Habsburg monarchy in more general terms.[225] There was a similar response in 1859, with much of the press and public opinion initially on Austria's side. 'There are no longer democrats and ultramontanes, backward-looking men and a revolutionary party, only Germans who are ready to mount a common defence when danger and disadvantage threaten the whole fatherland', commented the *Freiburger Zeitung* in January 1859, while the *Badische Landeszeitung* was impressed by 'the patriotic spirit' infusing 'the whole of Germany'.[226] Even leading pro-Prussian publications such as the *National-Zeitung* and the *Grenzboten* could not deny the existence of an 'agitated mood that today grips the German people', as it sought 'a significant role for our great nation in this European drama'.[227] Guido von Usedom, the Prussian delegate at the Bundestag, was convinced that 'the whole of South Germany is mad about Austria' and 'identifies Austria with Germany', making it difficult even for reluctant governments such as those of Bavaria and Württemberg to avoid entering the war.[228]

Yet the meaning of such national feeling was contested. According to the *Grenzboten*, 'public opinion', which in 'quiet times is a matter of indifference' but which 'now begins to become a serious and dangerous power', had experienced an 'awakening of German national sentiment' largely because of deep-rooted animosity towards France and identification with national struggles of the past, recalling 'Germany's shame in the years 1805–1813' and 'hapless reminiscences of 1847 and 1848'.[229] 'By far the larger part of the German public' seemed to support Austria *faute de mieux*, since its 'flags at least give the impression of representing the German cause'.[230] In fact, 'the masses' were 'still completely unclear about what they wanted', the article asserted.[231] After Vienna had allegedly ignored British and Prussian efforts to keep the peace, nullifying the treaty rights granted to Austria in Italy by the Congress of Vienna, the *Grenzboten* began to denounce the Austrian campaign as dynastic rather than national, even though the South German states continued to support the monarchy.[232] The Leipzig periodical was joined by other important North German publications such as the *Preussische Jahrbücher* and the *Preussisches Wochenblatt*.[233] Even before Austria's defeat, opinion in Germany was divided. Whereas Buol, who resigned part way through the conflict in May 1859, was confident that 'the whole of Germany' would 'gather round a hard-pressed Austria', if it lost the war, Kempen thought 'this hope ... merely a chimera'.[234] Once the Habsburg monarchy had been vanquished, there was a rapid reappraisal of Austria and its role in Germany which suggested that the police chief's scepticism had been well-founded. By 1860, 'the view in Germany that participation in the Italian war would have been a great national misfortune, that we would have sacrificed our national and free interests for an Austrian retreat', was now 'overwhelmingly' accepted, wrote the North German liberal politician and publicist Wilhelm Beseler.[235] National support for Austria in its war against France did not imply backing for its activities in Germany itself.

Many commentators, especially those in the North, had little sympathy for the Habsburg monarchy in the Italian war. For radicals such as Arnold Ruge, with their memory of persecution under Metternich and counter-revolution under Schwarzenberg, Prussia, 'with its objectionable love affair with the police', was 'the only salvation for Germany from Jesuits and reactionaries in politics', who were associated with Austria: 'If Germany is not now capable of using this position to free itself from Austrian tyranny, it will be wasting another great opportunity ... German freedom means separation from Austria.'[236] In Bamberger's opinion, the Habsburg monarchy was 'a hundred times deadlier' than France for German freedom and unity.[237] 'By declaring ourselves against Parisian tyrants, we are not preaching sympathy for tyrants in Vienna', declared Karl Blind in a confiscated treatise, before going on to welcome the day when Lombardy, Venice, Hungary and Galicia demanded their freedom from Austria.[238] Jakob Venedey went even further, arguing at first for support for Vienna against Napoleon III, but then switching allegiances after the peace of Villafranca to Prussia as the only defence against both Austria and France.[239] The spectre of Austrian tyranny was usually present in radicals' response to the Franco-Austrian war, sometimes mixed with sympathy for Italian nationalism.[240]

In comparison, liberals were less worried by the former and less attracted to the latter, even though the *Società Nazionale Italiana* served as the model for the *Nationalverein*. Droysen, despite harbouring 'all imaginable sympathies' for the 'unfortunate' Italians, wanted Austria to 'have and rule Italy' so that it was not tempted to 'put even more pressure on Germany', the interests of which were his 'first concern'.[241] 'That the war which has been started in Italy is directly a German affair has not even been claimed by those who have taken it up, notwithstanding the fact that, where Germans fight, the sympathy of all other Germans will always be on their side', proclaimed the rector of Berlin University Heinrich Wilhelm Dove in August 1859.[242] Austria's war, insinuated Rössler, was the corollary of its unnatural, imperial character, contradicting the imperatives of nation-building: 'Austria hinders natural development. But its nemesis stands before the door ... The Schwarzenberg system has been judged and made forever impossible.'[243] Prussia should not be misled into joining Habsburg wars in Italy and the Near East, but should assume the leadership of Germany, after the withdrawal of Austria, and solve the 'German' problem of Schleswig-Holstein, concluded the publicist.[244]

The liberal historian and military commentator Theodor von Bernhardi, writing in the *Preussische Jahrbücher*, went so far as to blame Austria for attacking France as a means of propping up its ailing imperial system of rule and re-establishing a conservative order in Europe: 'What it was actually about was the entanglement of Germany and especially Prussia in a war, the shifting of the war to the Rhine, the invasion of France with a powerful, superior military force, the destruction and banishment of the Napoleonists, and the return of Heinrich V and his befriended clerical coterie to the throne of his ancestors.'[245] Austria's intentions were 'very easy to see through', he explained to Usedom in April 1859: Vienna wanted 'to transfer the war to Germany at any price', meaning that the decisive battles would be fought on the Rhine and that the 'main

burden of the war' would pass from Austria to Prussia.[246] 1859 was
the last episode in a long history of Habsburg exploitation of both
Italy and Germany, according to Wilhelm Beseler. Such anti-
Austrian rather than pro-Italian sentiment was what linked Italian
and German nationalism, in the view of many liberals:

> The German nation has no interest at all in seeing the territorial
> possessions and influence of the House of Habsburg-Lorraine
> maintained or even increased. It must be admitted, however diffi-
> cult this is for many Germans, who have become accustomed –
> with no reason whatsoever – to looking down on the Italians, that
> Germany and Italy are largely in the same position vis-à-vis
> Austria, and that we scarcely suffer less under Austrian pressure
> in Germany than do our neighbours on the other side of the Alps
> as a result of the Austrian position in Italy.[247]

In Beseler's view, Prussia had to lead Germany, not Austria. Some
North German old liberals – Waitz, Droysen and Duncker – were
less openly against the Habsburg monarchy in 1859, but few were
for it. For their part, conservatives were divided between outright
supporters of Austria in the camarilla around the Gerlach brothers,
a handful of opponents such as Bismarck-Schönhausen, and an
uncomfortable majority, including Stahl and Wagener, who backed
the Prussian government's policy of armed neutrality.[248]

The Habsburg monarchy, as the Italian war of 1859 had demonstrated, was not a predominantly German power in the eyes of many
observers. As Austrian commentators themselves made plain, the
existence of increasingly powerful nationalities in the Habsburg
lands meant that the German minority could only exercise a 'hegemony of culture' not politics and that it was tempted to espouse
centralisation as a defensive mechanism and as a means of creating
what Hans von Perthaler termed an Austrian 'political nationality'.[249] Combined with the centrifugal proclivities of its non-German
nationalities, which forced Austria to look to Italy and the Balkans
rather than Germany, the state-supporting reflexes of German
Austrians helped to reinforce 'the political dividing wall which separates Austria from the rest of Germany', in the words of the pro-
German Minister of Commerce Karl von Bruck in 1860.[250] The
Habsburg monarchy seemed to be trapped by the principle of
nationality: if it championed the principle, it would strengthen the
position of Prussia in Germany and weaken its own hold over its own

diverse nationalities; if it opposed the principle, it would lose 'the residue of its influence in Germany', since most of the German political public saw the nation as the necessary underpinning of the modern state.[251]

Even supporters of Austria in Germany such as the journalists associated with the *Historisch-politische Blätter* and the *Stimmen der Zeit*, edited by the Viennese émigré Adolph Kolatschek in Gotha and then Leipzig, were obliged to admit that nationality obstructed a merger between German and Austrian lands, with non-German interests in the latter and Prussian aims in the former relying on each other: 'Germany will never become Greater Prussia without a Magyarised and Slavicised Austria, and vice versa.'[252] Because of the threat posed by its nationalities, recorded the *Stimmen der Zeit* in 1861, German Austrians had to concentrate the powers of the Habsburg state, despite aggravating the division between Austria and Germany: 'Although Austria, like Germany, can only exist as a federal state, the attainment of unity must be emphasised here, where the tendency of the nationalities towards independence has achieved a sudden and dangerous breakthrough.'[253] If Austria did not leave Germany, commented Joseph Edmund Jörg, the editor of the *Historisch-politische Blätter*, a year later, it was possible that the Habsburg dynasty would fall, so great was nationalist opposition to 'Germans' in the monarchy.[254]

Many North German liberals agreed with this diagnosis. 'As long as Germany wishes to be more than nothing,' wrote Aegidi, 'German Austria must either separate itself as a state from non-German Austria – that is, the Austrian monarchy must collapse – or, since it cannot belong to two states at once, it must take up a privileged position in Germany, namely remain part of the Bund, without becoming part of the *Bundesstaat*, so that, as I have said, the German Confederation is comprised of a *Bundesstaat* and of Austria.'[255] Personally, Aegidi preferred to maintain the Habsburg monarchy intact as 'a colony of Germany', but it could not therefore be fused with the other German lands.[256] Wilhelm Beseler went further: 'Austria is in its innermost being not a German state but a Reich, which has its own spheres of interest that are mostly foreign to Germany and often inimical. Germany has no obligation to defend the existence of Austria, just as it has none to defend the existence of France or Russia.'[257] Austria as a multi-national empire seemed to be alien to Germany, in which the modern principle of nationality had become one of the driving forces of politics.

Behind such analyses lay the possibility of Austria's collapse. According to Beseler, writing in 1860, it was difficult to predict whether this would happen rapidly or slowly.[258] The 'insoluble' problem was that the Habsburg monarchy's nationalities, with the exception of particular groups of Slavs, had become too independent to maintain the dynastic empire:

> If one ignores specific Slav tribes in the Austrian population, whose cultural level will tolerate an absolute regime and the rule of priests for a long time, the other nationalities are, in accordance with their natural situation and with their advanced development, no longer to be governed exclusively by the interests and whims of princely rule ... think of a Reichstag for the whole monarchy with the inclusion of Magyar and Latin tongues; it must certainly be held to be completely impossible that all the greater and smaller nationalities make themselves understood, not to mention coming to an agreement in the representation of the Austrian monarchy over the common interests of the Reich, over the division of its burdens, over the treatment of claimed special rights and provincial needs, over the necessary limitation of strivings and desires, over the taming of passions and prejudices on the part of individual lands and races.[259]

The old unlimited regime was no longer sustainable, Beseler went on: 'Austria is only to be saved, if appearances do not deceive, if it draws new and revitalising force from the awakening of a public spirit and from the participation of its peoples in the administration of the state.'[260] Yet how could this occur, given the monarchy's patchwork of different nationalities? Everyone accepted that 'a great state which is built on the broad and deep foundation of an exclusive nationality can, under certain circumstances, experience violent shocks and changes in its form of government, but not be threatened in its very existence, as long as the nation (*Volk*) still has the will to live'.[261] The Habsburg monarchy was not based on a national foundation, meaning that 'Germany would, in attempting to help Austria ... exhaust its energies in a hopeless undertaking, perhaps bleed to death in the process and, by tying its fate to that of a declining Reich, at best rob itself for a long time of any hope of remedying its own weaknesses and fragmentation.'[262] Since merely a quarter of Habsburg territory was German, it was not in Germany's interest or part of its legal obligation to defend the monarchy, contended Beseler. If the Austrian regime were to collapse, Germany might even benefit in the Near East, with 'a number of larger and smaller states' being formed and with Hungary becoming the dominant power in the Balkans and Italy south of the Alps. Despite the fact that 'a strong national opposition to the Germans has been created in these lands' by Austrian rule, 'it is not to be doubted that, as soon as the grounds for this aversion are removed, it will itself disappear'.[263] Beseler not only imagined the disappearance of the Habsburg monarchy, he also foresaw advantages for Germany as a result of such a disappearance.

Although premonitions of Austria's collapse were offset by assessments of its military strength, population and territory, they were nonetheless common amongst commentators across the political spectrum. Liberals like Beseler and Rössler were quick to condemn the Habsburg monarchy's backwardness, arguing that it hindered the 'natural development' of Germany and that its 'nemesis' was imminent, with the 'Schwarzenberg system' having become forever unrealisable.[264] Both small and greater German liberalism, by agitating for a parliamentary German *Bundesstaat*, had promoted the separation of Austria and Germany, and had made possible the Habsburg monarchy's collapse, claimed Jörg in 1862.[265] The monarchy's nationalities were fragmentary, argued Miquel, threatening to 'reinstall old Austrian absolutism or destroy Austria'.[266] 'I can imagine', he continued to the delegates of the *Nationalverein* in 1861, 'that quite a few of us desire the latter outcome ... I openly confess that I previously had this point of view.'[267] Although Miquel had changed his mind, believing that a 'lasting refashioning of Austria' could take place 'under the predominant influence of the German race (*Rasse*) and of the German Austrians', he had no inhibitions in considering the future collapse of the Habsburg monarchy, which still seemed likely if Austria were not fundamentally restructured.[268] Such a collapse appeared to menace Germany, too, according to a pamphlet co-authored by the liberal-minded Ernst II of Coburg. By 1860, Austria faced a revolution 'which not only endangered the system of government, constitution and dynasty, but also the integrity of the *Kaiserstaat*'.[269]

Many radicals and democrats actively welcomed such an outcome, delighted to envisage the end of a reactionary system and contemplating what would happen to its various parts.[270] Catholics, conservatives and southerners were much less willing to portray the Habsburg monarchy as a likely victim of revolution or collapse, but

they regularly discussed the 'future of Austria', with the implication
that it might not have one.[271] To the Hessian liberal Oetker, there
were two sets of opinions concerning Austria: one set saw the necessity of retaining the Habsburg monarchy as a bulwark against the
East; the other wanted to exclude it completely from Germany,
leaving it to become weaker and eventually to unravel.[272] Like other
'empires' in the East, most notably the Ottoman Empire, the
Austrian 'Reich' appeared to have an uncertain future because it
contradicted the modern state-building principle of nationality.
Although many commentators in Germany believed that the significance of such a principle had been overstated, few were prepared
to deny its importance altogether. It was in these circumstances that
prophecies of the Habsburg monarchy's decline and fall, which had
seemed so improbable before 1848, gained a purchase and further
weakened the case for Austria's inclusion in a reorganised Germany.

The Austrian *Vielvölkerreich*, it was held, lacked the internal
strength and external compatibility required to sustain its role in
Germany. To the majority of German commentators, it seemed
impossible to reconcile the multinational empire with the nation-
state. 'The unclear, perpetually vacillating policy which Austria
followed after 1849, abroad as well as in its own interior,' wrote the
Saxon minister Richard von Friesen in his memoirs, 'all this had
destroyed almost every sympathy for Austria in the public opinion
of Germany, and led, more than all the efforts of Prussia, to the
alienation of the German *Volk* from Austria and its delivery into the
hands of Prussia, which one alone wanted to credit with the capa-
bility of reasonably furthering the material interests of Germany
and to entrust with the power for the realisation of the national
idea.'[273] Many southerners, in particular, were still fearful and critical of Prussia, but few thought that Austria could take its place as
the main sponsor of national unity. This left the German
Confederation as the main alternative to Prussian-led unification.

4 The Third Germany and the Bund

In *Die Naturgeschichte des deutschen Volkes*, published between 1851 and 1855 in Leipzig, Wilhelm Heinrich Riehl described the contours of Germany, dividing it into three zones: the German flatlands (*Tiefland*), reaching south from the North Sea and the Baltic; the central hilly plateau (*mittelgebirgiges Deutschland*), stretching from the wall of mountains from the western Carpathians and the source of the Oder to the Ardennes in the North down to the Danube in the South; and the mountainous region (*hochgebirgiges Deutschland*) of the Alps and beyond, encompassing the German lands of the South and South East. Marked out by its climate and geography, the central plateau of the 'third Germany' was in many respects the core of the German lands as a whole, bounded by the harsh North German plain with its 'heavy, damp air, strong, relentless winds, and storms and mist', and by the mountains of the South with their 'thin, dry air, brutal changes of temperature, sharply contrasting seasons, and dreadful downpours and hailstorms'.[1] 'Das mittelgebirgige Deutschland' knew 'little of this struggle' of weather and environment: 'Here, the climatic opposites cancel each other out, and the mild, moist air of the valleys also helped to make people placid, rounded and soft.'[2] Whereas the North and South were characterised by extensive, uniform forests, vast expanses of potato fields and heath, and a crude three-field system, central Germany (*Mitteldeutschland*) had an 'agriculture of garden-like diversity' and 'the most developed agrarian businesses'.[3] It was no coincidence, Riehl continued, that Charlemagne established the centre of his 'world power' in the western part of *Mitteldeutschland*, leaving the 'very mixed German

Kulturvolk of the Franks, including the Swabians, the Alemannen and the Bavarians', opposite the 'so roughly German-fashioned *Naturvolk* of the Saxons' in the North and the 'barbarians' pouring out of Hungary in the South East: 'in the religious and national struggles of Karl der Grosse in the German North and South East, it was the prototypes of the more and more powerfully developed threefold division of the German people which came into conflict'.[4] In these struggles, *Mitteldeutschland* – the basis of the third Germany – became 'powerful first'.[5] To Riehl, it was the natural, historical and cultural centre of the German lands and the German people.

As contemporaries asked themselves how to redefine German territory and reconfigure German political institutions, the states and populations of the third Germany figured prominently in their plans, aided by the marginalisation of Austria. Recently, historians have resurrected certain contemporaries' arguments in their quest to revise a long-standing narrative of particularism, reactionary rule, petty court politics, and weakness in the face of the two German Great Powers. Some scholars have emphasised the successes of local patriotism and state-building in Saxony, Württemberg and Bavaria; others have reassessed attempts to reform the German Confederation as a workable alternative to Prussian-led unification.[6] In terms of population, territory and economic activity, the states of the third Germany were potentially significant if they could act in concert, but they were negligible alone (see Table 4.1). This was one reason why the governments of the *Mittelstaaten* paid so much attention to the Confederation. It could be argued, however, that the smaller and middling states were significant, not as weights in a German balance of power, but as a source of public opposition to state-imposed 'reaction' and of public discussion of German unification during the 1850s and early 1860s. This chapter assesses the role and importance of such discourses about a German nation and state in the light of power-political, territorial and constitutional questions first broached in 1848–49. It casts doubt on the significance of state-based identities, at least as an alternative to German nationalism, and on the viability of the German Bund, which was the principal focus of national debate between 1849 and 1863. In the political milieux and public spheres of the post-revolutionary era, national identification remained a crucial component of politics, especially in the critical forums of the third Germany.

Reaction and Opposition

'Reaction', promoted by Prussia and Austria, undeniably placed limits on political debate and stunted the growth of political parties. In the last redoubts of the 'revolution', prosecutions and emigration were commonplace. In Baden, where the democratic Central Committee of the People's Associations had led an uprising in May 1849, spreading to soldiers and precipitating the flight of the Archduke on 14 May before being put down by Prussian and 'Imperial' troops in June and July, 6,000 prisoners were taken at the fortress of Rastatt alone. Some were executed, more than 1,000 were prosecuted, and an estimated 80,000 emigrated, which amounted to five per cent of the population as a whole or almost 20 per cent of men under 60. In Saxony, where the provisional government and its forces under the Mayor of Dresden Karl Gotthelf Todt were put down in early May 1849, more than 6,000 were indicted and 727 received long sentences. Large numbers of left-wing deputies, most of whom had gone on to the Rump Parliament in Stuttgart, were tried for treason or other political 'crimes'; 49 per cent of left-wing National Assembly deputies from Prussia, 54 per cent of those from Württemberg, 62 per cent from Saxony, 67 per cent from Bavaria and 75 per cent from Baden. Amongst the factions of the 'left' ('Donnersberg' and 'Deutscher Hof'), between 64 and 75 per cent of deputies were prosecuted, and in those of the 'centre left' ('Westendhall' and 'Württemberger Hof') between 21 and 41 per cent. 44 per cent of radical Prussian deputies went into exile, 58 per cent of Bavarian and 69 per cent of radical Badenese deputies.[7]

Beyond the left, which was much more open to persecution because of its willingness to defend the constitution by force during the later stages of the revolution, a much broader political spectrum in all German states was subjected to repression as a consequence of the *Bundesreaktionsbeschluss*, or reactionary decree, passed by the Confederal Diet in August 1851. The actions of the resulting *Reaktionsausschuss*, or 'reactionary committee', which clamped down in some smaller states on democratic franchises, the budgetary powers of assemblies, and freedom of assembly and expression, were supplemented by the independent efforts of the individual states. The *Polizeiverein deutscher Staaten*, established by the seven largest states, pooled information about political dissidents across Germany. At the height of such surveillance in 1853, Prussia posted information about 558 individual cases, Saxony 234 cases, and

Table 4.1   The Third Germany, Prussia, Austria and the Bund

	Third Germany	Prussia	*Bundesgebiet* of Austria	*Bund*
Population (1865)	19,039,000 Bavaria 4.815 m. Saxony 2.354 m. Hanover 1.926 m. Württbg 1.752 m. Baden 1.429 m.	14,785,000	13,865,000	47,689,000
Territory (km²)	325,457 (excl. Hamburg and Bremen)	273,796	198,924	628,443
Pig iron and steel Production (1867)	935,355 tons	915,363 tons	460,000 tons (pig iron only)	–
Armies	–	214,000 (1866)	275,000 (1866)	506,725 (1855+) Austria = 3 corps Prussia = 3 corps Bavaria = 1 corps Rest = 3 corps

Source: J. Angelow, Der Deutsche Bund (Darmstadt, 2003), 16–17, 117; Breuilly, Austria, Prussia and Germany, 100–102; www.hgis-germany.de

Bavaria 74.[8] Berlin collected files in this period on up to six thousand political suspects per annum, monitoring travel, publication, house searches and political agitation throughout the monarchy.[9] Political activity was allowed in most German states, but elections were routinely fixed, since they were open, indirect and limited, in the Prussian case in accordance with the three-class franchise. Saxony dissolved its 'democratic' assembly and returned to its pre-March 'corporate' *Landtag* in 1850, Württemberg in 1851, and

Hanover, with the backing of the confederal *Reaktionsausschuss*, in 1855. The disbelief of Biedermann's circle, with one friend uttering 'That must be a bad joke', was widely shared.[10] What was more, if such electoral and constitutional restrictions proved inadequate, a state of siege could easily be declared – in Prussia, by the *Staatsministerium* in the name of the King – with the effect that articles concerning personal liberty (Art. 5 in the Prussian Constitution of 1850), the independence of judges (Art. 7), press freedom (Arts 27 and 28), and freedom of association (Arts 30 and 31) were suspended. The state of siege declared in 1849 lasted in Baden until 1852 and in Kurhessen until 1854. Under such circumstances, it proved much more difficult than in 1848–49 to form political parties and maintain political debate.

It is worth remembering, however, that the barely restricted freedoms of the revolutionary period, not the constraints of the 1850s, were anomalous, when compared to the conditions of the nineteenth century as a whole, in Germany and beyond. Contemporaries from different 'parties' certainly accepted that the 'reaction' was counter-revolutionary, reversing the worst excesses or major advances of the March Ministries and the National Assembly, but they rarely, even in conservative circles, saw it as a restoration of an unchanging order. To Ernst Ludwig von Gerlach, reaction was a 'dual struggle' against 'a defeated but not extinguished radicalism and against bureaucracy and absolutism'.[11] 'A greater participation of subjects in public affairs' was to be welcomed as 'a true achievement of March', he declared in October 1851, since 'we, although reactionaries, are not retrograde'.[12] In the opinion of the Prussian commentator Varnhagen von Ense, who was well connected to both conservative and liberal circles, reaction would not succeed, as Gerlach hoped, in expunging other more objectionable aspects of the revolution and in silencing political opposition. 'The movement of 1848 cannot be revived according to a plan or randomly; its ramifications endure, however, and continue to work without our doing anything,' Varnhagen wrote in his diary in September 1856: 'Reaction makes the greatest efforts, piles one institution on another, and pushes its vigilance to extremes … What they have built and supported for centuries, all their works, can be brought down in one moment, in one breath of wind. Until then our opposition exists in internal strengthening, in the winning of the greatest possible independence of intellectual and civic life.'[13]

From this point of view, governments and conservatives were reacting against the revolution, with some success over the short term, but with little intention or prospect of destroying many of the political gains of 1848–49, even if it made sense, in Varnhagen's view, for an 'honourable, principled man' to 'hold himself back and tend to his character and creed' in 'times like the present ones'.[14] Such times, he implied, would soon be over. This was certainly the sense of other, arguably more committed liberals, especially those outside Prussia.[15] Otto Elben, in Stuttgart, went so far as to contend that experience of reaction reinforced and simplified party affiliations, when seen from the vantage point of 1900:

> They were certainly bad times that the new decade brought to Germany: the failure of all hopes and the return to the Bundestag, and at home experiments with backward-looking laws as well as the disciplining and persecution of out-of-favour men. [Yet] in the fight against reaction, in the belief in the approach of better days, in its serious striving to go forwards, the period was filled with more idealism than the present … The party system was extremely simple: a liberal *Bürgertum* against a victorious reaction – that was the position. One recovered gradually from defeat, the *Bürgertum* slowly reunited, one took up again old ties, local elections initially gathered together friends once more, and younger forces, as revealed in 1848, joined the old liberals. The newly strengthened party acted under different names, sometimes called liberal, sometimes called the Progressive Party (*Fortschrittspartei*).[16]

The *coups d'état* and constitutional modifications of 1849–51 left space for party politics. All save three German states retained representative assemblies in some form, usually with a veto over legislation and with budgetary powers, in keeping with the precepts of 'constitutional monarchy'.[17] To the liberal historian Georg Waitz, whose *Grundzüge der Politik* was published in 1862, 'the essence' of 'constitutional monarchy' – or any 'constitution-based order' – was 'the participation of the *Volk* or entitled sections of it in the life of the state'.[18] Looking back on the 1850s, it was obvious 'that we have entered a period in which no one will doubt that our state's life can only develop on the basis of a constitutional order'.[19] How exactly this constitution was to be set up 'or, in other words, how the cooperation of king and people, the participation of the people in the state and the life of the state' was to take place remained to be decided, but that such participation was the foundation of the existing and future order went unquestioned by Waitz.[20] Even to more sceptical academic commentators like Robert von Mohl, who asserted in *Staatsrecht, Völkerrecht und Politik* (1860) that the 'constitutional system' had failed, representative assemblies still played an essential part in the German states, despite apparently being incompatible with the power of the monarch: 'In this way, there are two powers in the constitutional state which are fundamentally independent of each other: the prince in possession of state power; the representatives of the people with the right of appeal and, with exceptions, with the inalienable right to take part in certain government business. Undeniably, a dualism has been created which extends as far as the rights of representation go.'[21]

Most German states maintained such a dual system of government after 1849, albeit with the narrow franchises and indirect voting systems which had characterised the pre-revolutionary period. Württemberg, for instance, reverted to its old electoral law and *Landtag*, the second chamber of which contained representatives of traditional constituencies, those of seven 'good' towns and of the universities, six Protestant superintendants, three Catholic bishops and deacons, and thirteen nobles. About 250,000 men – more than half the adult male population – were eligible to vote in the first round of elections to the second chamber, but under 40,000 – less than 10 per cent of men – could vote in the critical second round. Prussia, which had had no regular *Landtag* before 1848, kept in place its 'revolutionary' one, but with a modified and restrictive – but still comparatively 'modern' – three-class franchise of taxpayers imposed in May 1849, in which 4.7 per cent of voters belonged to the first class, 12.6 per cent to the second, and 82.7 per cent to the third, with each class having an equal electoral weight. As in other states, elections were open and indirect, allowing manipulation and necessitating wealth and social standing on the part of deputies, who were voted in by 57,809 notable *Wahlmänner.*[22] Like the Prussian constitution of February 1850, this electoral law was much less liberal than the manhood suffrage of 1848, but it did allow political participation and the existence of political parties, just as the King's oath to the constitution, ministerial counter-signature and accountability before the *Landtag*, and the right of the *Abgeordnetenhaus* to initiate legislation and reject the budget, created the conditions for party politics.

In such circumstances, parliamentary factions continued to exist in most German states during the 1850s, permitting the emergence or refashioning of parties and the possibility of 'opposition' to reactionary governments. The terms 'party' and 'opposition' were used by commentators from different backgrounds as if they were self-evident.[23] In Bavaria and Baden, liberals were preponderant throughout the post-revolutionary period.[24] In Elben's state of Württemberg, in which the administration of Joseph von Linden had illegally reconvened an Assembly of the Estates, liberals – who had accepted the change – gained 35–40 seats in 1851, democrats 18 seats, and the 'government' party just over 30 seats. Under government pressure, the united front of liberals and democrats gained fewer seats in 1855 – 39–40 out of 93 – and were outnumbered by 'government' deputies, but they nevertheless constituted an important 'opposition' (see Figure 4.1).[25] The President of the Chamber from 1851 to 1863 was Friedrich Römer, the national-minded, liberal Minister-President of the revolutionary epoch.

In Saxony, where a complicated voting system of four estates (towns, nobility, farmers and commerce) had made 'parties' more difficult to identify, the free professions and commerce, from which liberals were usually drawn, gained between 34.2 (1851–52) and 45.3 per cent (1863–64) of seats in the second chamber, together with between 15.5 (1851–52) and 22.8 per cent (1857–58) of civil servants, officers, judges and mayors, which divided between state-supporting conservatives and oppositional liberals.[26] Noble landowners and farmers, which formed the backbone of the conservatives, gained between 44.7 (1851–52) and 38.6 per cent (1863–64) of seats. Although the *coup d'état* in Dresden had reinstated an electoral system weighted towards agriculture and office-holders, the opposition remained, at the very least, a large minority. The same was true of Hanover, where a mixed bloc of support for the moderate governments of Johann Carl Bertram Stüve (1848–50) and Alexander von Münchhausen (1850–51) was roughly balanced by that of a liberal-dominated opposition, whose numbers had sunk from 41 to 33 seats out of 70 over the course of 1850.[27] As the administration moved to the right under Eduard von Schele, the son of the architect of the 1837 coup against the Hanoverian constitution, liberal opposition increased, confirmed by the elections of 1853. Even after the ministry of Wilhelm Friedrich Otto von Borries and Eduard von Kielmannsegg had dissolved the second chamber in 1855 and had reimposed the more restrictive constitution and

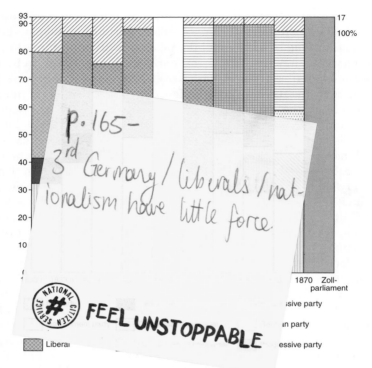

Figure 4.1   *The Strength of Factions in the Second Chamber in Württemberg, 1833–70, and in the* Zollparlament *of 1868.*

Source: Adapted from H. Brandt, Parlamentarismus in Württemberg 1819–1870 (Düsseldorf, 1987), 807.

electoral law of 1840, pro-government factions failed to gain an overwhelming victory – 40 against 30 – over the opposition.[28] In spite of a notorious Bund-backed coup, liberal elites were still firmly entrenched in Hanover's *Landtag*, municipal councils and local associations.[29] Finally, in Prussia, the conservative vote grew until 1855, declining after that date. Even in this period, though, there was a sizeable minority in the *Abgeordnetenhaus* opposed to the Manteuffel administration. In 1851, the 'centre' (85), the left (70) and the Poles (15) won 170 out of 352 seats in 1851, against 114 on the right; in 1853, with greater official interference, the pro-government groups of the right gained 182 seats, with moderate conservatives winning 28 seats, Catholics 65, the left 65 and Poles 12, or 170 seats altogether; in 1855, conservatives and ministerial groups won 218 seats, against 131 in the opposition or unaligned; and in 1857, the pro-government right gained 174 seats, against 172 in the opposition or unaligned.[30] As elsewhere in Germany, reaction in Prussia had not stifled parliamentary activity or political debate.

The prosecutions, surveillance and restrictions of the 1850s had most impact on radical and democratic milieux, many of which were disrupted. Exile, imprisonment and persecution served to break up the largest and most powerful factions and associations of the revolutionary period. Even in the most liberal German state, Sachsen-Weimar, the democrat Christian Schüler wrote in 1853 that '1848 has destroyed my previous ties': 'Since we failed to improve the life of the German state, I devote myself to the improvement of apple and pear trees, peaches and apricots.'[31] Likewise, the Leipzig historian Heinrich Wuttke, who also escaped prosecution, found himself 'pushed to one side at the university, just as in public affairs, as is natural for a forty-eighter'.[32] Many others, as Ludwig Uhland noted in 1853, lost 'their *Heimat*, their freedom and civic honour, and even succumbed to the death sentence'.[33] More than half of democratic deputies in the Frankfurt Parliament – 136 out of 261 – were tried. Karl Biedermann was imprisoned for four months in Saxony; Georg Friedrich Kolb was sentenced to six months in the Palatinate; and Adolf Rösler received a four-month sentence in Prussia. Ludwig Bamberger (Hesse), Lorenz Brentano (Baden), Karl Nauwerck (Prussia), Franz Raveaux (Prussia), Ludwig Simon (Prussia), Franz Zitz (Hesse) and Hugo Wesendonck (Prussia) were all condemned, in their absence, to death. Many went into exile in Switzerland, Belgium, Britain and the United States, where they suffered impoverishment, isolation and despair, as Ludwig Simon explained in his widely circulated work *Aus dem Exil*, published in 1855. The early deaths of previously prominent figures, such as Franz Raveaux at the age of 41, were blamed by colleagues on the disappointments of their banishment and the daily privations of their existence.

Such experiences often appeared to have kept alive democrats' longing for German unity, but their views rarely reached a wide audience in Germany during the post-revolutionary decade. Radicals like Carl Vogt, Brentano, Zitz and Bamberger huddled around tables in the *Bärenleist* bar in Berne or listened to lectures at the *Kornhaus*, largely cut off from their own lands. 'The circle which is gathered here largely consists of men who have sacrificed everything for their fatherland,' proclaimed the Württemberger Carl

Mayer in one of a series of lectures at the *Kornhaus* at the end of 1849:

> The burning desire to see it finally free, united and great has driven us from the comforts of peace, from secure careers and from civic activity away to the speaking platforms of the *Volk*, into the tumult of meetings and onto the battlefield ... Nowhere is there a circle of German men who can look back on the past with greater self-confidence and a better conscience. And now you are here, pursued, banished, in destitution and, what is hardest for noble men, living from the hospitality of a neighbouring people for which we are a burden.[34]

It was essential, wrote Bamberger, still in exile in 1867, to keep abreast of events in Germany and Europe from afar, 'for all those who fail to do the latter become dry and old extraordinarily quickly here.[35] For Ruge, referred to in a *Gartenlaube* article in 1863 as 'Der Verbannte von Brighton', exile proved demoralising and alienating, with little opportunity of publishing under his own name in Germany despite his reputation as a thinker and writer.[36] Closely monitored, to the point where Jodokus Temme believed that half of his letters were opened by the authorities and subsequently went 'missing', radicals and democrats remained for the most part a beleaguered and silenced minority until the early 1860s, when forty-eighters began to be pardoned and to return to Germany, at the same time as new democrats took advantage of emerging party structures and looser restrictions on their activity. Until then, they were a 'small parliamentary bunch', in Ludwig Simon's words, which 'stays loyally and courageously together' under adverse circumstances.[37]

In rare instances, liberals faced similar adversity. Oetker was forced to flee Kurhessen during the stand-off between Prussia and Austria in October 1850, for example, left 'for long years' only with the image of his wife and child 'laughing and crying as I entered the room' prior to his departure for Helgoland and Belgium. When he sought to contact fellow liberals again in 1856 – after the military court's judgment against him had been rescinded – in order to organise a campaign in Kurhessen to restore the constitution of 1831, he was amazed to find one of his oldest friends, a government counsellor, competing 'to bury [the matter] in the sand' and to be greeted by others 'extremely coolly or smilingly and negatively'.[38]

Most liberals, although they fared better and faced no judicial proceedings, were frequently ostracised and disappointed as they returned to precarious or mundane existences in the professions. In Mannheim, one of the birthplaces of the German revolution, Friedrich Daniel Bassermann, weakened by the exertions of the revolution, shot himself at the age of 44 in 1855; Alexander von Soiron, former Vice-President of the National Assembly but now impecunious and embittered, died early – at 49 – in the same year; and Karl Mathy, more robust but also lacking funds, was obliged to leave for a job, found for him by Gustav von Mevissen, in the Schaffhausenschen Bankverein in Cologne in 1854.[39] In Halle, the struggling academic Rudolf Haym talked in 1852 of the town as 'a miserable little hole' and of his life 'as little worth living'.[40] As early as January 1851, the liberal had expressed his envy of the democrats, whom the reactionaries had at least 'vanquished', whereas 'they are slowly sucking the blood out of us'.[41] In Frankfurt, the parliament had had to be destroyed but, in Erfurt, the assembly was 'already destroyed', with the result that liberals were in a perilous position.[42] 'Everything rests on the fact that our party cannot get used to understanding itself outside the effective sphere of present-day influence', warned Haym.[43] In his knowingly overstated 'self-criticism' of German liberalism published in 1866, Hermann Baumgarten understood such individual fates as a much broader form of internal exile and parochialism, which had led contemporaries to ignore the 'great movement' of liberalism and nationalism in Europe as a whole, especially in Italy during the 1850s: 'In government for just a year, [our liberalism] was everywhere pushed aside again, thrown back to private posts, from which only scarce and thin threads reached to the regions in which it would have been possible to an extent to oversee European politics.'[44] The fragmentation of liberals during an era of reaction seemed to have blinded them to the progress of the wider liberal movement outside Germany.

Baumgarten conceded, however, that German liberals had retained 'valuable positions in all states' and that they 'had an infinitely widened horizon' compared to that of the 1840s: 'in Prussia, the constitution had been saved, press freedom, jury courts and much else was still standing in most states, albeit under great pressure'.[45] In general, once the Erfurt parliament had been abandoned by Prussia at the end of 1850, liberals retreated to their own states and localities, where they continued to participate in assemblies and associations and to write for and read newspapers and periodicals. Even if they had desired to do so, the medium-sized and smaller states lacked the means to monitor or persecute such moderates: Saxony had a mere 173 policemen for a population of over two million, Württemberg 431, and Hanover 415.[46] By 1854, Baden reported only 12 cases to the *Polizeiverein deutscher Staaten*, Württemberg 24, Bavaria 59 and Hanover 70.[47]

In Baden, where Carl Joseph Anton Mittermaier, Johann Baptist Bekk, Karl Theodor Welcker, Franz Peter Buhl and Adam von Itzstein had all left the chamber after 1849, in addition to Bassermann, Soiron and Mathy, others such as Ludwig Häusser, who became the new leader, remained *in situ*, joined by younger liberals like Bernhard August Prestinari, a merchant's son and *Ministerialrat* in the Justice Ministry, Ludwig Achenbach, an *Obergerichtsadvocat* born in 1812, Ludwig Kirsner, who had been elected in 1850 after inheriting the *Hofapotheke* in Donaueschingen, the two innkeepers Ludwig Paravicini and Karl Friedrich, Philipp Artaria, the son of a wealthy art dealer, Eduard Kölle, a banker from Karlsruhe, and the 30-year-old August Lamey, the son of the founder of the *Mannheimer Zeitung* and the *Badische Staatszeitung*. For these liberals, it was a question, as Lamey put it later, of 'achieving something better through steady but also slow steps forward, through sober patience and undeterred persistence, with modest hopes and demands, conciliating and coming to terms with the overwhelming influence of the powers and directions which had been brought to our otherwise so mildly and liberally administered *Heimatland* mainly by the imbecilities and excesses of the revolutionary movement'.[48] Contacts between notables, resting on the factions of the *Landtag*, church, family gatherings and marriages, commerce, the law and the state, town councils, cultural and philanthropic associations, and the press, formed the basis of 'politics' after the national institutions of the Frankfurt Parliament and the Provisional Power, together with an incipient set of umbrella associations, had been brought to an end in 1849–50.

Like Baden, Hanover – the later cradle of the *Nationalverein* – showed how these notable networks endured in the 1850s, in spite of increasing repression. Shooting and gymnastics associations, the campaign in the early 1850s to set up the Thalia Theatre in opposition to the Court Theatre in Hanover, the Athenäum Club, credit associations, local government involvement in poor relief, housing, public health, education and other public works, as exemplified by

Johannes Miquel in his capacity as mayor of Osnabrück, liberal newspapers like the *Hannoversche Courier* and the *Zeitung für Norddeutschland*, upper middle-class and aristocratic 'society' in the handful of larger towns (Hanover, Harburg, Hildesheim, Göttingen and Osnabrück), and the *Landtag* itself all helped to maintain the fabric of liberal politics, even in a state ruled by a reactionary, blind, irascible, 'English' monarch and composed of a new western part granted in 1815 (East Friesland and part of Westphalia) and an old eastern part, linked only by a narrow strip of land.[49] Similar forms of local, notable and liberal politics were discernible in Württemberg, Saxony, Bavaria, and Prussia.[50]

Such regional political organisation did not imply that the national aspirations of 1848–49 had been abandoned, merely that vestigial national institutions had been destroyed. In a letter to Haym, the Badenese liberal Alexander von Soiron was not unusual at the start of the 1850s in believing that the liberal – or 'constitutional' – party would again become dominant in Germany through its triumph in Prussia. Although it would 'remain a minority in the chambers for a certain time', since it commanded only minority support within the limited political '*Volk*' of the three-class franchise in Prussia, 'this must change over time': 'it truly does not need to despair of victory'.[51] Liberalism, or constitutionalism, would succeed, via a constitutional Prussia, in a united Germany. Seven years later, at the end of 1857, Haym still trusted in the victory of 'the resolute constitutional party' and in its ability to unify Germany, notwithstanding his experiences of reaction in 'miserable' Halle.[52] From here, he kept alive many of his Prussian and German contacts and prepared the ground for the re-emergence of national politics. During the reactionary era between 1849 and 1858, Haym corresponded with at least thirty prominent liberals from different German states.[53]

Rudolf von Bennigsen, a founder of the *Nationalverein* in 1859, demonstrated how national hopes and local politics could be combined during the years of reaction. Part of the aristocracy with a family seat two miles south of Hanover and related to a series of generals and the Premier and Foreign Minister during the revolution Alexander von Bennigsen, the later National Liberal leader seemed to come from a background different from that of most of his liberal counterparts. As Stüve recalled, nobles 'had opposed necessary reforms, insisting on their privileges' before 1848 and they bore 'the odium of the coup of 1837 in public opinion'.[54]

Bennigsen himself had been willing to take advantage of noble privileges, as he sought to benefit from an aristocratic quota of positions
in the judiciary in the early 1850s.[55] Yet it was already known, he
held, that he was 'almost the only younger aristocrat who is fundamentally against the pretensions of the aristocracy, including their
expected interference with the constitution'.[56] His noble pedigree
did not prevent him associating with, and sharing many of the views
of, the Hanoverian *Bürgertum* in the succession of towns –
Lüneburg, Hameln and Hanover – to which his father, an officer,
was posted and in which he was educated alongside the sons of
largely middle-class families. His experiences at Göttingen, where
he enrolled as a law student in 1842, were similar, notwithstanding
the fact that much of his life there revolved around the *Korps
Hannovera*, to which Bismarck had belonged ten years earlier. As
Bennigsen wrote to his mother, virtually all students joined a corps
or *Landsmannschaft*, with the latter being reserved mainly for
theologians and medical students: 'If I am to join a club … so I must
choose the side on which I have the most and dearest acquaintances. And that is the corps. Many of my former school friends are
in the corps.'[57] The friends whom he mentioned all came from the
Bürgertum, although he went on to befriend a mixture of bourgeois
and noble students in the corps itself.[58] His experiences in
Heidelberg, to which he had transferred in 1843 in order to remain
close to his family after his ailing father had been sent to Frankfurt
and its surrounding spas, were likewise 'liberal', alternating
between the cultural history lectures of Gervinus, attended by 150
students, and the drinking and duelling of the *Korps Vandalia*, which
– as he reassured his father – had 'nearly cost him his life'.[59]
Bennigsen's subsequent decision to enter the civil service as a
lawyer, and later a judge, having rejected the army as the only other
alternative open to noble offspring, placed him in a position akin to
that of many liberal contemporaries, concerned with public affairs
but exposed to state manipulation.

Bennigsen, who was born in 1824, was representative of a younger
generation of liberals which had not played an active part in the
revolution of 1848 but which was influenced by it. 'True, they are no
longer asking, they are demanding with a shrill voice, but they are
merely asking for what all previous peoples of history have already
taken,' wrote the 24-year-old to his father in March 1848: 'The
danger for Germany will first come, if at all, several years from now,
when, on one side, what has been granted develops consequences

and, on the other, when regret perhaps emerges over what was agreed in a moment of fear.'[60] As the revolution proceeded, Bennigsen was convinced that a republic was likely, given 'the energy of the democratic spirit, which is growing daily in geometrical progression'.[61] His preference, though, remained a constitutional monarchy, which led him to support the *Reichsverfassung* of 1849, along with 'almost all Germany exc. Austria', as he put it to his mother in June 1849.[62] Governments such as that of Hanover would not dare to oppose the Reich constitution, he predicted in March of the same year, because the Ministry would be faced with a flood of popular petitions and would 'no longer dare to dissolve the chambers'.[63] Even after the second chamber had been dissolved by Georg V on 25 April, the authorities were careful to give assurances of their support for the creation of a German *Bundesstaat*.[64] Although Bennigsen was sceptical of ministers' intentions, warning in 1850 that 'we younger ones', critical of government action over Schleswig-Holstein, 'will not allow ourselves to be deceived by threadbare promises made in moments of despair', he was prepared to continue to work as a civil servant throughout the early 1850s and to treat the Hanoverian state as a moderate constitutional monarchy.[65]

Only after the coup of 1855 did Bennigsen begin to talk of abuses of power and to contemplate resigning from his post as a judge, which he did the following year. Nevertheless, Hanoverian 'reaction' was understood as a momentary deviation from the established 'constitutional tracks' of the German states, along which Prussia, too, had started to proceed: 'Do they really believe', he asked in a *Landtag* debate of April 1858, 'that they can uphold such a state of emergency in the face of the institutions of the rest of Germany and the resistance of our own population?'[66] In 1855, he had depicted the change as a temporary one, lasting for 'perhaps another year', which 'a handful of unscrupulous people' had forced on 'a quiet land, for which nothing was lacking for its prosperous advancement'.[67] This was a point that Bennigsen made repeatedly in the reconvened *Landtag*, to which he was elected, in spite of government electoral interference, in 1857. The Ministry, he declared in a *Landtag* speech addressed to a wider audience in Germany after Austria's defeat by France and Italy in July 1859, lacked public backing: ministers themselves 'would not speak with too much confidence of their following amongst burghers and farmers'.[68] In Germany as a whole, he went on, the movement was still very raw and immature in 1848; disunity was not to be avoided. The Prussian ruler did not find in himself the necessary strength to take up the position of power offered to him. It could now be the case that both had changed; that the Prussian government sees itself called on, through its whole position in Europe, to take the head of the German reform movement, and that in the German *Volk* disunity is no longer so great, the hatred of the parties has rather disappeared, youthful fantasies have been put to one side, and the febrile haste of renewal has been transformed into a steady and reliable decisiveness. There is already rare agreement between constitutionalists and democrats. A practical tendency has gained the upper hand. Vanities and schoolboys' opinions retreat into the background. As difficult as it might be for the governments, they will have to decide to act in accordance with the movement. The Bavarian and Saxon governments appear in private to have done so; and perhaps even the Hanoverian one will eventually give way to the current of opinion. If you only trust in the nation itself, there is no reason to despair of German conditions ... the nation is rising as powerfully and with as much vitality as it ever has done, and it will finally also carry along resistant governments with it.[69]

During the second, 'reactionary' half of the 1850s in Hanover, Bennigsen had used the *Landtag* and had cultivated his party connections in the state and in Germany as a whole to criticise repressive governments and to put forward German unification as a better alternative. As he 'broke with his whole past, with his entire social milieu ... in full contradiction with the state government and the King of Hanover', the 32-year-old liberal did so in the conviction that 'the time must finally return when, in the face of a successful reaction in almost the whole of Germany since the suppression of the movement of 1848, civic rights will again come back into force'.[70] Finally, he went on, 'the time and happy conditions must come when we succeed in taking up again the interrupted and temporarily disturbed national movement of the Frankfurt parliament in 1848–49, and in giving Germany the political constitution which such a great people, in its entire make-up, deserves'.[71] In the most unpropitious of circumstances, with the Hanoverian state's increasing restrictions running counter to the loosening of controls in most of its neighbours, nationalist politics continued: its main reference point was 1848.

An important component of national – and occasionally opposi-tional – politics during the 1850s was to be found in conservative milieux. Even in Hanover, where the aristocracy was widely blamed for the reaction of the government, the *Ritterschaft* had turned against the 'arbitrary measures' of the government by 1856, in Bennigsen's view.[72] In most other medium-sized states, conserva-tives had either merged with political Catholicism, as in Bavaria, or moderate liberalism, as in Saxony, or they had retreated into politi-cal insignificance.[73] In such circumstances, the best that the govern-ment could expect, wrote the former Bavarian Minister-President Pfordten in 1859, was 'that the nobility did not oppose it with enmity, and that is enough'.[74] By default, Prussia constituted both the main exemplar and the principal site of organised conservatism in Germany as a whole, with aristocrats and ministries in other states looking admiringly at the *Kreuzzeitung* and at the various right-wing factions – which Gerlach had termed a 'conservative party' as early as 1848 – in the Prussian *Landtag*.[75] Yet it was evident to most observers – including Karl von Bennigsen, who likened his son Rudolf to Georg von Vincke – that Prussia's conservative camp was diverse and often refractory.[76] The monarch, who was supposedly the hub of conservative forces in Prussia, was weak and dilatory after 1848, admitting to Edwin von Manteuffel that he was 'really a harmless creature', 'harassed' and with 'nerves'.[77] After difficult decisions, Friedrich Wilhelm IV 'fell apart physically', wrote Ernst II, Duke of Saxe-Coburg-Gotha, 'dragging his hand over his sweat-drenched brow, while his countenance assumed an expression of utter ruin'.[78] Usually, such inactivity or inconsistency left the Minister-President and other 'bureaucrats' such as the Police President Carl Ludwig von Hinckeldey – the 'second king', as Varnhagen put it – in charge of the legitimate government and, in their own estimation, at the heart of Prussian conservatism.[79]

The Manteuffel administration, however, was attacked on two flanks throughout its life from 1850 to 1858. On the right, romantic reactionaries around the Gerlach brothers, who favoured greater autonomy and broader jurisdictions for nobles, labelled the govern-ment 'absolutist' and 'Bonapartist'.[80] Despite their initial proximity within a common front against Radowitz, the Gerlachs were already warning that 'the absolutist Manteuffel is not to be trusted' by mid-1851: 'the domination of a crass absolutism is already in train', recorded Ernst Ludwig von Gerlach in the July *Rundschau* of the *Kreuzzeitung* in 1851, having made 'enormous steps' since 1848.[81] As

early as the spring of 1850, the conservative newspaper had accused
Manteuffel of introducing revolution into the 'heart-blood' of
Prussia.[82] Within the ministry, in the form of reactionaries such as
the Minister of the Interior Ferdinand von Westphalen and the
Kultusminister Karl Otto von Raumer, and at Court, especially in the
person of Friedrich Wilhelm IV's secretary Marcus Niebuhr, the
camarilla attempted to counter the influence of the Minister-
President, to the point where the latter employed a spy, Carl
Techen, to steal and transcribe the letters of Niebuhr and Leopold
von Gerlach in order to monitor their activity. As Techen confessed
in January 1856, 'the Minister-President believed that these persons
were constantly intriguing against him'.[83] What was more, the ultra
right was also prepared to use its mouthpiece, the *Neue Preussische
Zeitung*, to reinforce its 'opposition' to the government, provoking
'the repeated attacks of the bureaucrats against it', which in turn
threatened the leadership of the 'conservative party in the land', as
Leopold explained to the King in February 1853.[84] On the orders of
the head of the *Zentralstelle für Pressangelegenheiten* Rhyno Quehl,
anti-government editions of the *Kreuzzeitung* were seized on
repeated occasions in the years up to 1853. In the opinion of the
newspaper's editor Hermann Wagener, Manteuffel was a 'liar whose
own aim is to destroy all parties' and set up an 'absolutist
Bonapartism' in Prussia.[85] Ludwig von Gerlach's reply to the editor
was 'to remain in place and hold our party together in order to fight
Manteuffel's Bonapartism', which was 'exactly what we are doing,
and not without success'.[86] In addition to intrigues at Court, the
camarilla was quite willing to make its 'party' criticism of the
government public.

The '*Kreuzzeitung* party' arguably provided the model for the left
wing of Prussian conservatism, led by Moritz August von Bethmann-
Hollweg and founded on the *Preussisches Wochenblatt*. Like the ultra
right, the supporters of Bethmann claimed that they were not part
of any 'opposition' to the government, but that they were advisers
of Friedrich Wilhelm IV: 'No route which stands in contradiction to
the innermost being of the king can lead to our goal', warned the
constitutional lawyer Clemens Theodor Perthes, a colleague of
Bethmann in Bonn, in March 1852.[87] The '*Kammerverein Stadt
London*', which counted 15 deputies in the second chamber of the
Prussian *Landtag* by 1852 and which grew steadily until the Crimean
War in 1854, purported to be 'neither oppositional nor ministerial'
and 'to be limited by no factional or other external ties' in the exer-

cise of 'its free, independent opinions', true to the 'king, fatherland and constitution'.[88] Bethmann-Hollweg himself had been a leading member of the counter-revolutionary *Verein für König und Vaterland*, a participant in the reactionary *Junkerparlament* in 1848 and a constitutional lawyer in the 'historical school' of Friedrich Carl von Savigny, who was close to the Gerlachs. Yet in the aftermath of the revolution, it became clear to the Bonn academic and his supporters that they differed fundamentally from the camarilla in their attachment to the 'holy' constitution of January 1850, in their support for the parity of Catholicism and Protestantism, in their criticism of the Bund, in their leanings towards the West rather than the East, and in their opposition to the police measures of the 1850s, 'put forward and defended by the bearers of an anachronistic, inflexible system – Metternich's – introduced and maintained by the overwhelming influence of two European Great Powers (Austria and Prussia), supported by the cowardice of second-rank German princes and not fought against by the sleeping German nation', in the words of the diplomat Robert von der Goltz.[89] Above all, the '*Wochenblatt* party', which drew most support from the 'new' western territories of Prussia and from Anglophile and Francophile diplomatic circles, was wedded to the national idea: Bethmann-Hollweg was, he declared in his treatise on *Reaktion und Sondertümelei* (1848), the son of a patrician family of the 'free' *Reichstadt* of Frankfurt who had joined Prussia voluntarily because he believed that it was the main pillar of the German fatherland.[90] As Goltz had written in the same year, 'the nation must at last stand as a whole before the outside world, and it must as such gain the means to maintain the position that it deserves amongst the peoples of the earth'.[91]

Although Perthes had contended at one of the founding meetings of the *Wochenblatt* in 1851 that 'there will be an important party with us, through the significance of its head, if we only attack the *Kreuzzeitungspartei*, and against us, if we immediately attack the ministry', the followers of Bethmann were seen to be critical of Manteuffel's administration from the start.[92] 'The contributors to the *Neue Preussische Zeitung* and the clique of literati behind the *Preussisches Wochenblatt* speak in public places in a similar fashion, and what I have reported to Your Excellency previously has been fully confirmed – that there exists an agreement between Herr Wagner [*sic*] and Herr Jasmund [the editor of the *Wochenblatt*] that it is above all things a question of removing Your Excellency', reported Quehl in November 1852.[93] Between 1851 and 1855, editions of the *Wochenblatt* were seized on 16 separate occasions for expressing 'principles and views ... which seemed not to be suitable for general dissemination and recognition, which may indeed increase the tendency amongst those who are still undecided to oppose the decrees of the authorities', in the words of the *Polizeipräsidium*.[94] The 'Bethmann-Goltz opposition and newspaper' appeared to have defied Bismarck-Schönhausen's prediction in 1851 that 'a conservative opposition can only be led with and by the King, so that H. M. is drawn towards interests which are against his own ministers, not through public papers, but through personal influence at the Court'.[95] 'With us, every other opposition has no grounds', he went on, 'or it must become radical.'[96] To Friedrich Wilhelm IV, as to many other conservatives, such opposition seemed to mean that 'the ministry would not be able to maintain itself, the conservatives would join the constitutionalists, and no one would be for the ministry'.[97] Conservatives and liberals appeared to have colluded in the re-emergence of party politics in Prussia after 1849–50.

In most states, liberals were more commonly joined by Catholics than by conservatives, despite their mutual reservations.[98] Although contemporaries would have heard 'as much as nothing' of 'our doings and strivings here, of our Catholic faction, our bills and debates', a Catholic party was forming in several states during the 1850s, suggested August Reichensperger, after the emancipating events of the revolution.[99] In Prussia, he noted in 1852, a 'Catholic faction of about 60 members has already been constituted'.[100] By 1858, contended his brother Peter Reichensperger, the Catholic party in the Prussian *Abgeordnetenhaus* was the single largest element of the moderate 'Left', with 51 seats, together with 20 seats of the Mathis-Bethmann-Hollweg faction, and 28 members of Schwerin-Putzar's group: 'The numerically strongest faction, namely the Catholic one, consisted in its majority of Rhenish, Westphalian and Silesian deputies, and these provinces monitored their effectiveness in such a way, as a whole and individually, that there was least need for them to support and further the aims of the faction in large numbers and by the act of voting.'[101] In the localities, there was a strong correlation between confession and voting, with most Catholic deputies receiving between 75 and 90 per cent of the votes of the electors in the predominantly Catholic areas of the Rhineland and Westphalia.[102] With a low turnout in the 1850s, typically around 10 per cent, priests, landowners, peasants and petty officials were able to dominate electoral colleges, regularly voting in their co-religionists. In Paderborn, for example, in 1855, such groups made up 68.2 per cent of electors.[103] Voters in other states with large Catholic populations were slower to form confessional milieux, with most voting either for liberal or governmental candidates in Baden and Württemberg throughout the 1850s and early 1860s, partly hindered by indirect voting, which meant that Catholics only gained three seats in the 1867 election to the Badenese *Landtag* instead of the 27 seats out of 63 that they would have won in a direct vote.[104] In Bavaria, the influence of confession, although still largely submerged, was more visible, with the 'opposition between Catholics and Evangelicals' playing a distinct role, in the opinion of Hugo Lerchenfeld-Köfering: most of the 35–60 deputies not belonging to the liberal and democratic parties in the 1850s were labelled 'clericals', although few openly challenged the Bavarian state's control of the Catholic church, which had been one of the most contentious questions during the revolution.[105]

Political Catholicism continued to exist as an element of the 'opposition' in the post-revolutionary decade, especially in Prussia, because the sources of confessional difference and discrimination remained in place. As one 'important personality' put it in the *Kölnische Zeitung* in 1853, reprinted in the Catholic *Deutsche Volkshalle*, 'the formation of the Catholic faction has not been brought about by an indeterminate confessional interest, but by a distinct, existing infraction of the constitutional rights and freedoms of the Catholic church'.[106] The press had labelled the faction the 'ultramontane party', and later the 'Catholic party or faction', which was a name justifiably adopted by Catholic deputies themselves to represent their main purpose: if Bavaria had encroached on the constitutional freedom of Protestants, no one would object to them adopting the name 'Evangelical faction', concluded the correspondent.[107] 'Over centuries, Prussia was an Evangelical state', wrote one deputy in 1852, after the *Kultusminister* Karl Otto von Raumer had placed restrictions on Jesuit missions and on Catholic theologians studying in Rome, 'and in this Evangelical character of the state, as well as through its resulting influence over the smaller Protestant states of the Continent, lay the centre of gravity of its political position, just as much as through the personal significance of its ruler and more than through its material power.'[108] With 7 million Catholics, compared to 10 million Protestants, wrote another deputy on the same occasion, Prussia should not be an 'Evangelical state'.[109]

Such 'facts', asserted the Catholic grandee Joseph zu Stolberg-Westheim, 'lead us back to a deep wound, they lead us back to the position of Catholics in Prussia', who lacked 'parity' or 'equality of opportunity' (*Gleichberechtigung*).[110] Many Prussian provinces, he continued, did not contain 'a single Catholic' civil servant: in the upper echelons of the administration, 'from ministers to the *Landrat*', there were a mere 108 Catholics out of a total of 1,227 officials.[111] Unsurprisingly, this level of discrimination had led to political resentment and party mobilisation, even if instances of cooperation between administrators and Catholics remained common in individual constituencies. Such grievances, argued Peter Reichensperger in 1858, had the potential to unite Catholics throughout Germany, constituting one of the bases of unification rather than a source of division, as some Protestants claimed:

> From that moment on, when all confessions in Germany have complete security that their constitutional rights will be equally guaranteed in the individual states, that a difference of religion will underpin no difference of state entitlement or favour, from that moment on the political unity and power of Germany will rest on the firmest foundations, and an opposition of conscience will only act and clash in a sphere which knows no political boundary disputes, in the sphere of teaching, example and spiritual competition.[112]

In a much more limited form and in fewer regions, Catholic politics, like its liberal counterpart, had a national set of aspirations during the era of 'reaction'.

The principal means by which such aspirations reached a broader public was the press, which printed the proceedings of the *Landtag* as well as its own reportage of events at home and abroad. Even Manteuffel admitted that 'each century has seen new spiritual powers step into the circle of traditional life which were not to be destroyed but to be worked with, and our generation recognises the press as such a power. Its importance has increased with the widened participation of the *Volk* in public affairs, which the daily press in part gives expression to and in part feeds and gives a direction to.'[113] There were, of course, restrictions on press reporting, which varied from state to state, since the watered-down Bund Press Law of 1854 was not implemented by most of the larger states. Seizure of individual editions of newspapers, collective liability for the contents of a publication on the part of authors, publishers, printers and sellers, the withdrawal of licences to publish or sell, sizeable deposits and interference with postal subscriptions, the banning of 'foreign' papers, the establishment of 'government' papers and the placement of articles were all widely practised.[114] However, there were many signs that governments failed to control or stifle the press in the 1850s.

Some states such as Saxe-Coburg-Gotha and Sachsen-Weimar, to which Biedermann moved in 1855 to edit the *Weimarer Zeitung*, were like 'a happy oasis in the middle of the political desert that covered the greater part of Germany', where politics could be discussed openly.[115] Other states such as Bavaria did not have a system of deposits and had retained jury trials for cases involving the press, which had been introduced in 1848. Pfordten confessed in 1857 that 'the judgement of charges against the press by juries does not safeguard effective repression of the excesses of the press'.[116] This left seizure of copies of newspapers as the government's main deterrent, which Karl Brater, the Bavarian deputy and newspaper publisher, estimated had been used on 2,520 occasions between 1850 and 1858, making it virtually a daily occurrence; yet it generally took place without further penalty or charge.[117] The Bavarian Ministry of Justice itself seemed to doubt the efficacy of press controls, most notably in a 15-page memorandum published in 1869 and looking back to the 1850s and 1860s:

> At different times, and namely at times of agitation, the demand resurfaced to again exercise influence over the press, which was usual in the old legal order. The permissibility of confiscation gave a helping hand towards this end. There was at times the fullest and, it cannot be denied, also a barely permitted use of this method. With what success? Individual evil-intentioned voices in the press were silenced, and the admirers of the past were almost and temporarily satisfied, but only by summoning forth in this fashion, and giving actual credence to, new storms and, at the same time, by making the well-intentioned institution of confiscation, which was not incidentally intended to extend beyond the sphere of penal legislation, into the object of unanimous antipathy.[118]

Officials in other states had similar experiences. In Hanover, the government professed its continuing support for 'the basic principle of press freedom' in 1851; in Baden, the Foreign Minister asserted that 'there can be no talk, as is self-evident, of a reintroduction of censorship'.[119] Even in Prussia, Friedrich Wilhelm IV regularly became 'very agitated over the direction of public opinion', which refused 'blindly to trust in his policy', but wanted 'to make itself independent', in Varnhagen von Ense's words.[120] When the King was attacked by the *Vossische Zeitung* for sacking Gustav von Bonin as War Minister in 1854, Hinckeldey reportedly shrugged his shoulders and said that the courts usually acquitted journalists in such circumstances.[121] With 1,160,214 newspapers sold every week in Prussia by 1855, the Prussian state lacked the means to control the press.[122]

Despite censorship, a diverse and large press continued to exist in Germany, abetted by the patchwork of individual states with their 27 different sets of press laws.[123] In Prussia, it has been estimated that weekly newspaper sales amounted to more than a third of the electorate.[124] The actual number of readers of newspapers and periodicals was probably between three and five times this figure.[125] In the mid-1850s, 34.3 per cent of newspapers were 'oppositional', mainly liberal or democratic, 4.4 per cent Catholic, 6.7 per cent neutral, and 14.2 per cent conservative.[126] 40.4 per cent of titles were 'governmental'. In terms of circulation and influence, it is likely that liberal publications played an even more significant role than a simple count of titles suggests: in the Rhineland and much of Westphalia, the liberal *Kölnische Zeitung* (12,250 copies in 1854), the Catholic *Deutsche Volkshalle* (3,225) and the Protestant and liberal *Elberfelder Zeitung* (3,200) were dominant; in Berlin and much of Brandenburg and Posen, the *Vossische Zeitung* (12,950) was usually supportive of the government, along with *Die Zeit* (6,800) and *Die Neue Preussische Zeitung* (5,650), but they were confronted by the liberal satirical journal *Kladderadatsch* (24,550), the *National-Zeitung* (6,750), the *Volkszeitung* (7,200), the *Magdeburger Zeitung* (5,550), the *Hallesche Zeitung* (3,138), the broadly liberal *Spenersche Zeitung* (7,860) and the moderate conservative *Preussisches Wochenblatt* (1,100).[127] In other regions of Prussia, which were largely agrarian and accounted for only 27 per cent of titles, conservative and governmental papers were preponderant, constituting 89.6 per cent of publications in the province of Prussia, 72.2 per cent in Silesia, and 48.6 per cent in Pomerania, compared to 34.7 per cent in the Rhineland and Westphalia. In Bavaria, the *Allgemeine Zeitung* (7,800), the Catholic *Augsburger Postzeitung* (5,000), the Prussian-leaning and formerly democratic *Münchner Neueste Nachrichten* (15,000), the popular *Münchner Volksbote* (6,000) and the liberal, Prussian-leaning *Nürnberger Correspondent* (5,000) overshadowed 'particularist' papers like the *Bayrischer Volksblatt* (4,000) or official ones such as the *Pfälzer Zeitung* (500) and the *Neue Münchener Zeitung* (3,000). A similar pattern could be observed in Württemberg, where the pro-Prussian and liberal *Schwäbischer Merkur* (5,000) and the democratic *Stuttgarter Beobachter* (1,000) and *Ulmer Schnellpost* (1,800) stood opposite the official *Württemberger Anzeiger* (1,000), and in the Hansa towns and surrounding areas, which were dominated by the broadly liberal *Weser-Zeitung* (5,000), the *Hamburger Correspondent* (5,000), the *Hamburger Nachrichten* (11,000) and the *Hamburger Börsenhalle* (2,600). In Saxony and Baden, the official press was more prominent, but was nevertheless matched by more independent publications: in the former, the liberal *Allgemeine Deutsche Zeitung* (1,100) and the unaligned *Leipziger Illustrierte Zeitung* (10,000) faced the official *Dresdner Journal* (1,200) and *Leipziger Zeitung* (5,500); in the latter, the liberal *Mannheimer Journal* (2,000) and Catholic *Freiburger Zeitung* (2,000) were opposed by the pro-government *Badische Landeszeitung* (2,000) and the official *Karlsruher Zeitung* (1,500). Throughout Germany, a more or less independent press and a set of inchoate political parties, together with their readers and voters, existed in 'opposition' to official candidates, publications and policies. This public sphere proved decisive in the transfer and modification of the set of national ideas formulated in 1848–49.

Heimat and Nation

In the 1850s, 'public opinion' and 'politics' were largely confined to the representative institutions, associations and presses of individual states, or a conglomeration of states, yet they frequently continued to hinge on the national question. At the very least, local authorities proved unable to prevent debates about German unity and a German nation-state taking place. Identification with individual states, their dynasties, their traditions and their good fortune was, of course, common. It was fostered by government-backed newspapers, schools, public monuments and state ceremonies, which were designed to consolidate support for weakened monarchical regimes and to counter the national experiments of

1848–49. A Bavarian Interior Ministry memorandum of 4 December 1849 indicated how such loyalty to the state and dynasty could be cultivated:

> Above all, it is essential that civil servants of all categories devote themselves sincerely to the system and interests of the state, as a powerful lever for the self-consciousness of a *Volk*, and that each says with just as much passion and pride: 'I am a Bavarian' (as one often hears in Prussia: 'I am a Prussian').
>
> As subordinate means, the following should be considered: the reawakening of provincial and also local *Volksfeste*, the celebration of festivals which recall the popular (*volksthümlich*) government measures of Max I, and also, for example, the refashioning of the *Oktoberfest* into a more effective national festival for the whole of Bavaria – in addition, careful respect for monuments to which commercial and legendary recollections are tied; the maintenance of popular elements of ritual and domestic *mores* ... and furthering of what is already in place.
>
> Particularly important is, finally, care for the material advantages of the rural population ... and care for workers and the poor.[128]

There were recurrent characteristics of state-sponsored allegiance and identity. First, individual states were habitually equated with particular *Volksstämme*, or 'tribes', dating back to the '*Völkerwanderung*'; Württemberg with the Swabians, Saxony with the Saxons, Hanover with the Lower Saxons, and Bavaria with the Bavarians. Every German tribe had the right to its own customs, attributes and, even, language, asserted the semi-official *Leipziger Zeitung* in 1861.[129] The newspaper's editor had argued as early as March 1850 that the German question could only be solved 'if every German *Stamm* ... is true to itself, does not abandon its own interests and independently unites with the greater whole'.[130] For this reason, wrote the *Neue Hannoversche Zeitung* in 1859, the German was an 'enemy of centralisation', preferring 'to observe his own morals at home, his own customs in his towns and his own law in his country'.[131] The governments of the *Mittelstaaten* had 'been supported by their people for centuries in the struggle for their independence', remarked the *Staats-Anzeiger für Württemberg* two years later.[132] It was 'natural', implied the individual governments, that every *Stamm* had its own state.

Second, the histories of the *Mittelstaaten*, and many smaller states, were held to be unique, resting on long-established and heroic dynasties. Ernst August (1771–1851) was praised in the press as the military liberator of Hanover from the French in 1813, the sponsor of the limited constitution of 1840, and the defender of the relative tranquillity of the kingdom in 1848–49; Wilhelm I of Württemberg (1781–1864) was known for his military defeats of the French in the 'Wars of Liberation', for his granting of the constitution in 1819, and for safeguarding the 'prosperity and happiness' of his state for most of his reign; and Friedrich August 'the Just' of Saxony (1750–1827) was portrayed as an elder statesman, respected by Prussia, as a servant of his people, remaining in Saxony during the difficult years of the Napoleonic wars, and as a pious, fair and gentle monarch.[133] Such rulers were held to have fought for the independence of their states in an age of revolution, foreign occupation and threats from the Great Powers.

Third, the middling German states were depicted as havens of prosperity and culture, more than compensating for their lack of power. Railways, manufacture (Saxony), agricultural improvement (Württemberg and Bavaria), maritime trade (Hanover), education and culture were all seen to have flourished in the 1850s. History 'has demonstrated repeatedly that vitality, strength and influence on human development is manifested less often in large states than in states of a moderate size,' recorded the *Staats-Anzeiger für Württemberg* in July 1860: 'It may well be true that the fragmentation of Germany into a myriad of *Stämme* and states has hitherto prevented her from making her political power felt as it should be; it is at least equally true that precisely because of this, Germany has become a country second to none with regard to the dissemination of culture and knowledge, even among the very lowest classes of the population.'[134]

Fourth, governments and official publications took pride in their states' constitutional liberties, when compared to the restrictions and military burdens of Prussia and Austria. This public espousal of constitutionalism went furthest in states such as Württemberg, which was said by the *Staats-Anzeiger* in 1850 to have outdone 'the other German *Stämme* by forging ahead in creating a healthy political life' after 1819, and Saxony, where the *Dresdner Journal* could declare in 1859 that the state could 'look with heart-felt satisfaction upon its constitutional situation, in comparison with other states, whose constitutions still seem so uncertain and incomplete'.[135] It

was hindered in Hanover by the coups of 1837 and 1855, and in
Bavaria by divisions within the government itself, with Max II and
the reactionary Interior Minister after 1852, August Lothar Graf von
Reigersberg, opposing official 'constitutionalism' and the more
reform-minded Minister-President Pfordten and Reigersberg's
predecessor, Theodor von Zwehl, in favour of it.[136] In all such
repeated catalogues of local patriotism, there was an implied opposition to an *Einheitsstaat* and a preference for a *Staatenbund*, which
could alone accommodate such rich and rewarding diversity.

Loyalty to one's state and identification with one's local *Heimat*,
however, were rarely seen to exclude German unity or to require the
continuation of the German Bund. Even a 'realist' such as Ludwig
August von Rochau, one of the most ardent supporters of a
Prussian-led nation-state and a critic of 'anti-national' particularists
in the third Germany, admitted that the four monarchies of Bavaria,
Hanover, Saxony and Württemberg, together with Baden and the
two Hessian states, which were 'quite suitably given the name
Mittelstaaten', had been obliged publicly to acknowledge the
national idea, even if insincerely: 'In order ... not to antagonise
national sentiment openly, the middling states occasionally and
gladly associate themselves with a certain German disposition or
signal, which is all the less troubling because the obligations which
could be derived from it regularly find their limit in the dualism of
the two great states, which prevents them from passing from theory
to practice.'[137] For their part, the small states willingly countenanced the national cause, since 'national patriotism
(*Nationalpatriotismus*) demanded of them no notable sacrifice in
terms of state policy' and all could be given 'to the nation ...
because what they had was not worth much for them and was a
highly precarious possession'.[138] Although Rochau was sceptical of
treaties and legal constraints on sovereignty, believing that it was
won, lost or shared 'only through violence', he conceded that the
Mittelstaaten had acquired 'a type of independence', which made
them impossible to ignore in the construction of a single German
nation-state, despite the fact that 'the sharpest corners and edges of
particularism have been noticeably ground down through the
history of the last centuries and especially of the last generation'
and that 'the German states' system' had been 'simplified' by the
unlamented passing over the previous 50 years of 'the religious principalities, a pile of small ruling houses, the majority of the Reich
cities, and the *Reichsritterschaft*'.[139]

Particular loyalties in the third Germany persisted, reinforced in the 'most recent era by the political advantages which the populations of most individual states believed themselves to have compared to their neighbours': 'Often, instead of all the other advantages, petty political habits, which one had got used to, sufficed or, in an emergency, the custom of being ruled from this or that capital city and of seeing these or those colours and uniforms around. In the South German states, it was constitutions and the chambers, in particular, which produced the feeling of a certain political superiority.'[140] At the same time, the unification of Germany by the *Volk* was inevitable: 'The *when* and *how* of the fulfilment of its historical vocation can remain in doubt for a people, but never the *if*. And that Germany *is called* to unify itself, in whatever form, that is a statement which every German carries, as a feeling, or as consciousness, as a conviction, as a belief, as a hope or as a desire, at least.'[141] Modernity was characterised by the 'dissolution of the tribal constitutions, the fragmentation of the *Stämme* themselves, the regular mixture of blood, the balancing effects of a communal culture, a better understanding of the conditions of public security and welfare, the manifold improvement of communication, the multifarious overlapping of material interests through trade and change', all of which had tamed 'the oppositions in the character of the different sub-divisions of the German people'.[142] If continuing attachments to individual states and their traditions prevented the straightforward emergence of a unitary German state, implied Rochau, it might be possible to reconcile them with the institutions of a *Bundesstaat*.[143] The German Confederation, a *Staatenbund*, was, in any event, not suited to such a task, having 'achieved too little in the course of 33 years' before 1848.[144]

Most proponents of *Kleindeutschland* were more optimistic about the flexibility and longevity of a German *Bundesstaat* and more appreciative of Germany's geographical, cultural and political variety than was Rochau. The writers and journalists of the *Grenzboten* were a case in point. Gustav Freytag, the journal's editor since 1848, was a strong advocate of Prussian ascendancy in Germany, a conviction cemented by his upbringing in the borderlands of Silesia, but he denied that loyalty to Prussia excluded feelings for his *Heimat* or a belief in a German nation-state:

I was born as a Prussian, a Protestant and a Silesian not far from the Polish border. As a child of the frontier I learned to love my

German essence early in opposition to a foreign national identity
(*Volksthum*), as a Protestant I won a quick entry into science and
learning without painful circumspection, and as a Prussian I grew
up in a state in which the dedication of the individual to the
fatherland was self-evident.[145]

In 1847, Freytag moved to Saxony, editing the *Grenzboten* in Leipzig
from 1848 until 1870, and purchasing a house in Saxe-Coburg-
Gotha in 1850. As he recalled in his memoirs, he had quickly settled
in Saxony, with 'a great circle of good acquaintances', alongside the
Austrian and other exiles working on the periodical.[146] His journal,
although stressing – like Freytag himself – that Prussia was 'present
and indispensable' for German unification, did not underestimate
the distinctiveness and independence of the other German
states.[147] There were, as the *Grenzboten* noted in 1854, many local
differences in Germany: each city tended to be divided into 'three
circles' – an exclusive one, an oppositional one, and one in the
middle trying to mediate – but these 'local circles, from which the
parties constitute themselves, receive their direction from the
central point of the party, which is in turn subordinated to local
conditions'.[148] From 1848 onwards, after 'unrest' had created 'an
extraordinary confusion' of 'political concepts', 'true party formation' had taken place in those places in which parliamentary assemblies had gathered, encouraging tensions between the national
locus of Frankfurt, where the 'middle party' of liberals and constitutionalists had been dominant, and the individual states, where
local variations had affected the emergence of parties.[149] In Leipzig,
which had avoided a noble reaction, class divisions rather than
different political aims determined the establishment of factions; in
Königsberg, which had seen government and aristocrats unite in
1848, there was no *Mittelpartei*, only a democratic opposition. In
general, the 'middle party' had done well in 1848–49 in smaller
states and democrats in the less liberal larger states, with consequences for the post-revolutionary period.[150]

Given the *Grenzboten*'s strong support for national unification, the
periodical naturally assumed that all Germans were fundamentally
similar. The strength of Germany was greatest, the publication
asserted in 1859, when 'all the individual governments are united
with their peoples': 'This is only possible because, in spite of all
their patriotism (*Patriotismus*), which exists rather in forms of
speech, symbols, flags and provincialisms, all German *Völker* want

the same at bottom.'[151] Although some contemporaries claimed to back Austria, few, if any, would think of becoming 'Austrian'.[152] The problem lay not with the 'peoples' of Germany, but with their leaders: in Bavaria, 'a brave, loyal *Volk*' and a well-intentioned monarch faced an illiberal, anti-Prussian government; in Hanover, Stüve had, with some success, mobilised liberals against Prussia and behind the government in its attempt to reform the Bund, but only temporarily, since Hanoverians did not live 'on an island' – 'progress and regression are linked together in all German states' and 'a solidarity of interests exists'.[153] The division of Germany into 'two halves' in the North and South, which were 'geographically split regions', was the corollary of 'extraordinary historical conditions' and could be overcome through an overarching assembly, noted another article in the same year.[154] Germany's diverse but integral culture was, as one correspondent had maintained in 1850, 300 years old.[155] It would not collapse during a period of transitional and unstable politics after the revolution. It could be incorporated not in a unitary 'Prussian' state but in a federal German one, as the *Grenzboten* repeatedly pointed out.[156] A German *Bundesstaat* would harness the individual states and *Völker* without stifling them, it was implied; a *Staatenbund* was too loose a structure and would fail to contain 'particularism'.[157]

Widespread suspicion of '*Particularismus*' and '*Kleinstaaterei*' worked against the establishment of local patriotisms in competition with German nationalism.[158] Such suspicion was especially pronounced in *kleindeutsch* publications such as the *Grenzboten* and the *Preussische Jahrbücher*, which had been set up in 1858 by 'the decisively constitutional party' as 'a national matter' in the belief that 'Prussia sooner or later is destined to take the lead in Germany', in the words of its founder, Haym.[159] To the former periodical, looking back on the 1850s, industrialisation had pushed 'our smaller, domestic states' towards the 'movement of the rest of the world for the first time' and had witnessed the passage of 'the life of our nation' to another 'phase', yet it had also created the 'selfishly material' and a 'one-sided spirit of accumulation and speculation', which – as types of 'particularism' – reinforced the traditional particularism of the German states and undermined the 'earlier, still one-sidedly ideal life of the nation'.[160] 'The particularism of the bourgeois social elements, i. e. their spirit of privacy, which is still mired in crude private law, one-sided acquisition and possession, and their correspondingly atomistically fragmented condition, also

upholds the particularism of the German states against each other',
recorded the same article in 1861.[161] Both forms of 'crude particu-
laristic entity', aggravated by the external, bureaucratic nature of
the modern state, 'stand in the way of our national unification'.[162]
This 'in no way' meant that 'all the national endeavours, with whose
final reawakening the nation again first begins to breathe' were 'in
vain or meaningless'.[163] Indeed, 'in the national task we Germans
are again given considerable means to counter the soporific and
self-seeking power of a mere material spirit of acquisition', continued the correspondent.[164] Rather, it was necessary to replace the
'higher ideal tie which once kept Germany together in the medieval
Kaisertum' with 'independent statehood', 'the development of an
organic, legal *Bürgertum* and its professions', 'the maturity of a
general historical and human development', which together would
create a 'lasting form of national unity and strength'.[165] Given these
general forces, particular loyalties would be overcome. The
Preussische Jahrbücher came up with a similar diagnosis. It was impossible to imagine the sovereignty of French departments and cities;
yet such circumstances actually existed in Germany, wrote one
contributor in 1858.[166] Even in 1848–49, 'particular interests' had
persisted, with opposition to the creation of a powerful German
fleet.[167] 'If such particular interests opposed an acknowledged
unitary central government during a period of national upturn,
how much more must this have occurred during a period of down-
turn, as the *Bundesversammlung* once again pushed aside the Central
Power', noted another article in the same periodical in 1860.[168]
Particularism continued to exist, serving as a foil for the national
aspirations and projects of its opponents.

Occasionally, conservative publications challenged or ignored the
negative connotations of 'particularism'. Thus, the *Neue Preussische
Zeitung* argued in September 1863, at the time of the *Fürstentag* in
Frankfurt, that the German *Volk*, 'i.e. the ethnic nation (*das völkische
Volk*)', had always been diverse, although containing 'from its
origins until today a richer interior than the French and English'.[169]
'For this particularism of the German tribes in Germany, small entities must be maintained; that is, one must give them the means to
maintain themselves, but also one must impress upon them the
necessity of bowing, as a matter of principle, to that which sustains
those means – for example, protection from the external world,
which would otherwise break them', continued the article.[170] The
Bund and the Holy Roman Empire, which were understood as

loose, free 'republics', alone safeguarded German particularism, which was the source of its strength and richness.[171]

In the immediate aftermath of the revolution, the *Historisch-politische Blätter*, the principal Bavarian and Catholic periodical, agreed with the *Neue Preussische Zeitung*'s opposition to the Erfurt Union, which it saw as a French-inspired attempt to create a unitary state and to trammel the independence of the German 'tribes'.[172] In an article on 'Nationality' in 1850, the journal sought to protect particularity in Germany from the standardising impulses of the 1848 revolution, which had redirected the cosmopolitan egotism of the French Revolution of 1789 towards an uncompromising, unitary nation-state.[173] In this revolutionary form, nation-states had become self-contained and exclusive, breaking ties in a Machiavellian fashion with a common God-given humanity and portraying traditional 'love of the [local] fatherland as one-sidedness'.[174] The old Christian order had allowed diversity and particularity; the modern nation-state did not. In 1850, amidst the backlash against the revolution, the preservation of Germany's cultural and political particularity was the priority of the *Historisch-politische Blätter*, although the periodical also conceded that particularity could easily become a damaging source of division:

> Germany's fate is close to that of Greece; we are one in terms of our descent, language and historical ties; but we are politically separate, and not just in recent times ... We have in Germany a natural, genetic, historical and literary fatherland, and we have loved it, perhaps most recently with less hue and cry, but with greater introspection, than any other *Volk* has loved its own. But we do not have a political fatherland, and whoever wants to impose it on us in this sense does at once violence and injustice to nature, to facts, to the whole *Volk* and to the individual states which comprise it. Politically ... we are Austrians, Prussians, Bavarians and so forth, according to our tribes and our circumstances, not just by the form and existence of our governments, but as the result of an age-old customary community (*Gemeinschaft*) of our public existences, our morals and attributes, our fates and matters of honour, our suffering and joy.[175]

Despite seeking to maintain diversity and to defend the individual states and the Bund, the *Historisch-politische Blätter* was wary of being labelled 'particularist'. Instead of attempting to contest the meaning of the term, the periodical sought to use it against Prussia, whose 'particularism' had been manifested in the pursuit of its own interests, even during the national emergency of the Crimean War.[176] In an article surveying the 1850s as 'the Interregnum of the Reaction', the Bavarian publication pointed to the damaging legacy of political divisions in Germany since the Reformation and a subsequent age of absolutist princes, each fighting for their own sovereignty. 'The being rather than the concept of civic and political freedom has passed into the spiritual life of the peoples,' noted the article in 1858:

> If this has taken longer amongst Germans than amongst other nations, the cause lies in their fragmentation. Each of the small state structures in Germany was split from the others, in each small land the inhabitants lived together like the tenants of a great estate; the little people (*Völkchen*) became old with its ruler, it could only think of its own existence in conjunction with the family of this ruler; it had no need of political freedom, and therefore the concept could not emerge.[177]

It was obvious, went on the same correspondent, that 'no German state can see itself today as cut off; each must recognise common affairs, as the nation has long recognised them as such. More and more, Germans see their salvation in the unified handling of these affairs. The *Bund*, as it is now, no longer suffices.'[178] If Germans wanted the affairs of the Bund to be 'concentrated' and dealt with more effectively by a central body, 'this desire has resulted from a re-awakened national sentiment', a feeling 'more general than any other', making it impossible for even 'the fastidious servant of the Court' to 'parade his particularism'.[179] The German nation had woken again, in spite of attempts to thwart it over the previous 100 years, confirmed the periodical in 1859 at the time of the Franco-Austrian War. The 'crudest sectional system (*Sonderwesen*)' had existed, paradoxically bolstered by 'the constitutions of the German states', which at the same time pushed the 'life of the state into the public sphere (*Öffentlichkeit*) and awoke civic sentiment', creating the conditions for national criticism of particularism.[180] The actions of the individual governments before 1848 had convinced the *Volk* that 'a powerful institution for the unification of our fatherland' would never be constructed by the states themselves, but by free institutions.[181] 'Thousands of the best men' who joined the national movement were united in their recognition of 'the weakness of the *Bund* and the wretchedness of its authorities' and in the belief 'that the individual states should give up a small part of their sovereignty' and 'that alone the devoted caring for national interests' guaranteed the survival of the individual states.[182] 'The great majority of the nation shared this opinion', concluded the correspondent.[183] The fear of appearing to be a 'particularist' prevented significant sections of the population, even in the patriotic South West, from arguing for the sovereignty of the smaller and medium-sized states, remarked the *Historisch-politische Blätter* in 1865.[184] In retrospect, Joseph Görres himself, the spiritual father of the publication and son of the German fatherland who had died in 1848, was purported to have opposed particularism on the grounds that it had deprived Germany of its just desserts after national liberation in 1813–15.[185]

After the unsettling events of the 1848 revolution, no state in the third Germany except perhaps Bavaria, whose government alone sometimes sought to popularise the idea of a Bavarian nation, considered itself popular or strong enough to exist in its own right, independently of a German *Staatenbund* or *Bundesstaat*. Against the threat of revolution and invasion, it was necessary for the individual states to cooperate and to sacrifice some of their sovereign powers, noted the Minister-President of Hesse-Darmstadt, Reinhard von Dalwigk zu Lichtenfels in 1861: 'The purely German monarchies, whether great or small, are on their own vis-à-vis the enormous danger that confronts them. They can only save themselves through firm, honest solidarity, by discarding all particularist interests.'[186] The 'organisation of their military forces' was needed to defend the states 'against revolutionary attacks' 'in view of the growing boldness of organised revolution', and a united position was required 'against Prussia and Austria in the Confederation' and 'against *das Ausland*', especially if Austria were threatened.[187] If the Habsburg monarchy were distracted, as seemed likely throughout the 1850s, or were weakened, as was the case after 1859, it 'would inevitably bring the collapse of the German individual governments in its wake', warned Dalwigk.[188] For their defence, the German states had traditionally relied on Prussia and, in particular, Austria as Great Powers, but such reliance was dangerous by the 1850s, given Berlin's and Vienna's rivalry and pursuit of their own interests after 1848–49. 'The *Mittelstaaten* have another enemy apart from democracy,' wrote Dalwigk in a memorandum on the reform of the *Bund* in 1861: 'This is the dualism of the two German Great Powers.'[189]

Most other German leaders shared the Hessian Minister-President's mistrust and his sense of his own state's weakness: even Ludwig von der Pfordten, the former and future Bavarian Foreign Minister, believed that, 'in fifty years, all German middling and small states will be mediatised'.[190] To Beust, the Saxon first minister, the single-minded antagonism of Prussia and Austria, which frequently blinded them to the other German states, could be compared to that of North and South in the approaching American Civil War.[191] From Olmütz and Dresden onwards, when Germany seemed to be 'on the brink of a *Bürgerkrieg*', through the Crimean and Franco-Austrian Wars, to the *Fürstentag* and the Gastein Convention of 1865, the third Germany seemed to have been tossed around by the currents of Great Power diplomacy and Austro-Prussian rivalry.[192] Since 'the times were, thank God, over when a German state could seriously think of separating itself from the German land of brothers', proclaimed Beust in 1863, the governments of the individual states had little choice but to join forces.[193] For the Saxon Minister-President, as for the ministers of all the medium-sized states except Baden, the German Confederation constituted the most likely framework for such cooperation: to this end, he put forward proposals to reform the Bund at the Dresden conferences of 1851, at the Bamberg conference of 1854 and at other points during and after the Crimean War in 1855, 1856 and 1857, at the Würzburg conferences of 1859 and 1860, at the Saxon *Gesamtministerium* of October 1861, at the Frankfurt *Fürstentag* of 1863, at the Nuremberg conference of ministers in the same year, and at a similar conference in Augsburg in 1866.[194] This reforming zeal derived, as Dalwigk made plain in his commentary on Beust's plan of 1861, from a frank assessment of a medium-sized state's options during the 1850s and early 1860s:

Those German states which, like the Grand Duchy of Hesse, are not in a position, as a result of their political, historical and geographical relations, to step forward as independent powers in the European states' system, find in the German *Bund*, which ensures for all its members internal and external security, independence and inviolability, the best guarantee of their existence and prosperous development. The dissolution of the Confederation would expose these states' requirements for life to the greatest dangers.[195]

The individual states seemed to have little alternative, even in the opinion of particularist ministers, but to cooperate with each other in the Bund.

Reform of the Confederation

The majority of ministers in the third Germany saw the Bund as a conservative structure. Fearing the outbreak of 'a great struggle between revolution and the legitimate order, which has been prepared for a long time', Dalwigk believed that 'the particular interests of the individual states, the relations of governments with each other, the disputes between governments and estates, the desires of peoples' all had merged with 'this terrible question': 'Arguments, negotiations and wars are only conducted in the service of revolution or the conservative principle.'[196] The overriding need of the *Mittelstaaten* was 'to fortify themselves for violent shocks' by reforming the German Confederation, which had been 'so eagerly undermined in recent times' but which would be needed to defend the individual states.[197] 'After a European catastrophe, it might easily be too late for a reform of the *Bund*!' warned the Minister-President:

> And when one looks carefully at the current political situation, not only in its momentary meaning but in conjunction with the history of the last decades, certain aspects stand out, which make it seem like the task of a conservative policy aiming to preserve the monarchical principle in the individual German states to search for the solution of the problem of how, on the foundations of the existing order of things, the desire of the German people for a more powerful, long-lasting representation of its interests as a whole can be satisfied more fully.[198]

Most of the protagonists in the reform of the Bund – Beust (Foreign Minister, 1849–66) in Saxony, Pfordten (1849–59) and Karl von Schrenk (1859–64) in Bavaria, Dalwigk in the Grand Duchy of Hesse (1850–71), Eduard August von Schele (1851–53) and Adolf von Platen-Hallermund (1855–66) in Hanover, Joseph von Linden (1850–51 and 1854–55) and Karl Eugen von Hügel (1855–64) in Württemberg – stuck rigidly to the idea, established by the revolution, that the Bund was a *Staatenbund* rather than a

Bundesstaat, which limited the amount of power to be invested in a refashioned executive and the extent to which they were prepared to countenance a representative assembly. Reform was to be carried out on the 'existing foundation of the Confederation', since the *Staatenbund* constituted 'the form which corresponds to the historical and legal relations' of Germany, declared a memorandum by the Badenese envoy to Berlin in 1855.[199] By 1863, Baden's official newspaper, the *Karlsruher Zeitung*, remarked that 'only the transformation of the *Staatenbund* into a parliamentary *Bundesstaat* truly helps', but no other medium-sized state government was willing to back this Badenese reading of events.[200] 'The national consciousness of the Germans in no way demands a unitary state,' objected Dalwigk:

> It does not exclude the feeling of tribal particularity and uniqueness, for it flows from the same source as these.
>
> One should not, above all, mix up the consciousness of *national* unity, i.e. of belonging together through the same descent, language, morality, and so forth, with the demand of *political* unity. It is this demand which brings the independence of the individual states into question and which might exclude Austria; any consciousness of the counter-case, as for example has been thoroughly announced at the *Volksfesten* of recent years, takes the individual German states *as such* and entwines them as a whole with a confederal (*föderativ*) tie.[201]

Proposals to reform the Bund were limited in nature, especially on the questions of executive power and the creation of a representative assembly, which together constituted the main focus of press and party criticism. Some plans did little more than tinker with the existing structure of the *Bundesversammlung*, or *Bundestag*, which was divided into an infrequently convened *Plenum* of all states' delegates, with votes apportioned according to population and requiring unanimity, and an *Engerer Rat* – a form of standing committee working by majority vote – from the 17 delegates of the two Great Powers, the seven *Mittelstaaten*, Holstein and Lauenburg, Luxembourg and Limburg, and the six 'curia' of the small states, presided over by Austria (see Table 4.2). Other plans were slightly more audacious. Most settled on some form of directory or trias for the 'highest power of the Bund' – it was rarely, if ever, termed an 'executive' – if they addressed the question at all. At the Dresden conferences in 1851, Beust put forward a directory of five, with Austria and Prussia holding two votes each of the total of seven, and Schwarzenberg and Manteuffel proposed a body of seven, with the Great Powers having two votes each of nine; in the Munich agreements of 1859, Beust talked vaguely of 'the idea of the trias', without further specification, and in his proposal of October 1861 he envisaged a directorate of three, made up of Prussia, Austria and – in all likelihood – Bavaria; and at the Frankfurt *Fürstentag* of 1863, Franz Joseph suggested a five-person directory of the three largest states, plus two places allotted by rotation.[202] The aim of the directory's sponsors was to create greater coordination amongst the largest sovereign states in order better to fulfil the objectives of the German Acts of Confederation (1815), which were broad in theory – including 'the maintenance of the external and internal security of Germany' (Article 2) – but which were constrained in practice by increasing recognition of states' own powers. It was obvious, wrote Beust in 1856, 'that a *Bund* of states with equal rights, whose character and purpose largely rests on the securing of the independence of the individual states in respect of their free and particular development, cannot at the same time incorporate and allow to unfold those elements which would be suited to lending such a *Bund* organism the vigour of a standing government of the *Bund*'.[203]

The same priority of states' jurisdictions and powers was present in governments' discussion of a representative assembly for the Bund, combined with distaste for 'democracy'. At Dresden, the debate about a representative assembly had been bitter, marked by Wihelm I of Württemberg's leaked accusation that Vienna was not interested in the setting up of a confederal *Volksvertretung*. Beust argued that such an assembly was 'a real need' as long as it did not take on 'the nature of a parliament with the right of approval etc.':

If the suggested assembly of delegates of the estates is only convened in individual, exceptional cases, if it only has to consider bills put before it by the *Bundesversammlung*, if each and every initiative is constitutionally removed from it, if it has nothing to do with a responsible ministry, and if, finally, its sessions do not take place in public, such an assembly will have to be remarkably lucky if it is to become a second Paulskirche.[204]

In 1855, Beust had suggested 'a form of representation of the chambers of the different states in the *Bundestag*' or 'a strengthening of

Table 4.2   Number of votes in the Engerer Rat of the Bundestag and population

	1852	1865
Virilstimmen		
1. Empire of Austria (area within the Confederation)	12,919,300	13,865,000
2. Kingdom of Prussia	12,937,228	14,785,000
3. Kingdom of Bavaria	4,559,452	4,815,000
4. Kingdom of Saxony	1,987,832	2,354,000
5. Kingdom of Hanover	1,819,253	1,926,000
6. Kingdom of Württemberg	1,733,269	1,752,000
7. Electorate of Hesse-Cassel	755,350	754,000
8. Grand Duchy of Baden	1,356,943	1,429,000
9. Grand Duchy of Hesse-Darmstadt	854,314	854,000
10. Duchies of Holstein and Lauenburg	550,000	
11. Grand Duchy of Luxembourg	394,262	395,000
Kuriatstimmen		
12. Grand Duchy of Saxony-Weimar	262,524	1,037,000*
Duchy of Saxe-Coburg-Gotha	150,451	–
Duchy of Saxony-Meiningen	166,364	–
Duchy of Saxony-Altenburg	132,849	–
13. Duchy of Braunschweig	267,177	295,000
Duchy of Nassau	429,060	466,000
14. Grand Duchy of Mecklenburg-Schwerin	542,763	555,000
Grand Duchy of Mecklenburg-Strelitz	99,750	

the *Bundestag*', but largely as a means of acting 'against the disturbing condition of the chambers in individual lands' and of reducing 'the importance of the business of the chambers'.[205] Although he did not wish to create 'a break with the existing representative system and the overthrow of existing constitutions', the Saxon Foreign Minister was convinced that assemblies in the German states had 'overstepped the correct mark'.[206]

By 1859, under pressure from the *Nationalverein* and the 'Gotha party', the Bavarian Foreign Minister Schrenk, whose predecessor Pfordten had opposed reform throughout much of the 1850s, urged his counterparts 'in no way to reject' the idea of a Bund assembly composed of delegates of individual chambers, since it

Table 4.2   continued

	1852	1865
15. Grand Duchy of Oldenburg	285,226	302,000
Duchy of Anhalt-Dessau	111,759	
Duchy of Anhalt-Köthen	–	
Duchy of Anhalt-Bernburg	52,641	
Principality of Schwarzburg-Sonderhausen	74,956	
Principality of Schwarzburg-Rudolstadt	69,032	
16. Principality of Hohenzollern-Hechingen	–	
Principality of Hohenzollern-Sigmaringen		
Principality of Liechtenstein	7,000	
Principality of Reuss, older line	114,720	
Principality of Reuss,, younger line	–	
Principality of Lippe-Detmold	106,615	
Principality of Schaumburg-Lippe	29,000	
Principality of Waldeck	59,697	
County of Hesse-Homburg	24,921	
17. Free City of Lübeck	48,425	
Free City of Frankfurt a. M.	73,150	
Free City of Bremen	88,000	
Free City of Hamburg	211,250	269,000
(Miscellaneous)		(817,000)
Total	43,286,116	47,689,000

*Note: * This figure corresponds to the population of the Thuringian states in their entirety.*
Source: J. Angelow, Von Wien nach Königgrätz (Munich, 1996), 323; idem, Der Deutsche Bund, 117.

could help to harmonise and constrain the activities of state parliaments.[207] The subsequent agenda of the Würzburg conference of the same year, though, made no mention of a representative assembly, merely resolving to publish the proceedings of the existing *Bundesversammlung* and to establish a confederal court.[208] Only after the Grand Duke of Baden had introduced a bill at Frankfurt to turn the *Bund* into a *Bundesstaat* in August 1860 and, in conjunction with the liberal leader Roggenbach, had begun to agitate for Prussian leadership and a national *Volksvertretung* did Beust revive the plan of the Weimar envoy to Dresden, Carl Friedrich von Fritsch, to create a confederal government, assuming the competencies of the *Engerer Rat*, and a *Bundesrat* made up of delegates from states' assemblies, proportionate to population, and from governments, with one for each of the 36 administrations.

In later versions of the plan in 1861, the Saxon minister proposed that the *Bundestag* be convened twice annually, once in North Germany, once in South Germany, that it retain the representation of the *Engerer Rat*, and that it be composed of ministers, not power-less delegates. This stronger, but still confederal, 'highest power' was to be supplemented by a chamber of 128 deputies from the assemblies of each state, where they existed, with Austria and Prussia receiving 30 seats each. Finally, partly in response to Bismarck's call for a directly elected German parliament, Franz Joseph and Rechberg outlined an assembly of 302 delegates of states' assemblies to the *Fürstentag* in 1863, together with an advisory *Engerer Rat* and an active *Fürstenversammlung*, which could block the proposals of the *Abgeordnetenversammlung*. The governments intended all such representative assemblies to be conservative, by avoiding direct election, by carefully limiting competencies and by drawing delegates from both the upper and lower houses of indi-vidual states. With a weak assembly and no executive, the reformed *Bund* would remain a *Staatenbund*, very different from the national, constitutional *Bundesstaat* designed at Frankfurt in 1848–49.

Beust himself, the main advocate of confederal reform, betrayed the defensive and conservative character of the proposed changes to the *Bund*. Radowitz had attempted in 1850 to introduce a *Bundesstaat*, wrote the former Saxon Minister-President and Habsburg *Reichskanzler* in his memoirs. Since the Habsburg monar-chy, according to Radowitz, had 'no place in a *Bundesstaat*', for those who 'wanted to continue the confederal community with Austria, it followed, with compelling logic, that there could be, once and for all, no talk of a *Bundesstaat* and its like, but the *Staatenbund* must be maintained and sanctioned anew'.[209] Prussia's demand of complete obedience had ensured that 'one was, at times and mostly with reluctance, "anti-Prussian" in Munich and Stuttgart, as in Dresden and Hanover'.[210] Prussia's supposed penchant for uniformity and exclusion ran against the grain of Beust's aristocratic upbringing in Saxony and his university educa-tion in Leipzig and Göttingen, where he had been taught law by Eichhorn, history by Heeren, and politics by Sartorius, all of whom were supporters of the cultural and political patchwork of the *Bund*. From a reading of his later recollections, the young son of a relatively impoverished noble official, born in 1809, seems to have

been troubled by the complicated and well-intentioned manoeuvring of King Friedrich August I, who had elected to back
Napoleon at the battle of Leipzig in 1813 – witnessed by the five-
year-old boy from the family estate outside the city – in order to
avoid the French treating Saxony 'as a conquered land', if they had
won.[211] Ludwig Senfft von Pilsach, a neighbour of the Beust family
at their estate of Zöpen, had decided to transfer to the Austrian
diplomatic service rather than to return from Prague with
Friedrich August, but he had nevertheless warned Beust in the
1840s not to 'judge the king too severely', since allegiances and
calculations had been so finely balanced during the Napoleonic
wars. To an extent, this sense of the intricacy of dynastic and Court
politics had been confirmed by the future Foreign Minister's entry
into the Saxon diplomatic corps in 1831 at the age of 21.

In the gilded world of diplomacy, dominated by Metternich,
whom Beust later met and always greatly admired, war with Austria,
as was contemplated after 1850, had been inconceivable: 'who
would have dared even to think such a thing, not to say articulate
it!'[212] The machinations and power-political calculations, against a
backdrop of war and regular crisis meetings of foreign ministers
travelling rapidly by train to their respective capitals and resorts,
had been difficult to imagine at the start of the young diplomat's
career in the 1830s, as he made the five-day trip by carriage to
Munich to arrange the engagement of the Prince Regent with
Princess Maria of Bavaria. His chief of mission, who travelled in top
hat and tails, insisted on setting up a formal 'cercle' every morning
and having a full dinner and supper on every evening of the voyage,
reminding the Saxon diplomat of 'the old Court life of the previous
century'.[213] Nobility, with Beust proud of his family's 64 quarter-
ings, concern for etiquette and disdain for long trousers in the
1830s, and loyalty to one's monarch, with King Johann's praise of
the young Foreign Minister's steadfastness in the May uprising of
1849 constituting the 'most honourable proof' of his service, all
unobtrusively circumscribed the actions and outlook of the first
minister.[214] Although ministers considered it natural to pursue the
interests of their own dynasty and land, to the point where Beust
'never raised objections' to being labelled an 'anti-Prussian particularist and reactionary', they unthinkingly stopped short of actual
conflict.[215] Prussia, where the Legation Secretary was stationed
between 1836 and 1838, was seen to be one of the pillars of such
cabinet politics, 'the seat of the strictest legitimacy'.[216]

1848 undermined the workings of cabinet diplomacy and reset the terms of the debate about 'Germany'. The 'European party of movement' had already noticed 'the weakness of the larger governments' in 1847, adumbrating 'the bankruptcy of the Metternichian system'.[217] After 1849, it proved difficult to reinstall the old order, with observers like Beust conscious of its artifice. His distance from the 'reaction', of course, did not result exclusively from a change of view during and after the revolution, but derived in part from his enlightened education, overseen by his highly educated mother, from his experiences as an assiduous scholar at university and from his postings in Paris (1838–41) and London (1846–48), which he viewed as 'a second *Heimat*', reinforcing the 'liberal' attitudes of his Göttingen days in the 'English' state of Hanover.[218] Although such Anglophilia was arguably rooted in an overestimation of the powers of the monarch, the aristocracy, and the Court, where he was well acquainted with Prince Albert, together with a realistic assessment of Britain's limited franchise and an appreciation of its relative tranquillity in 1848–49, the Saxon Foreign Minister's 'liberalism' certainly made it easier for him to countenance the creation or maintenance of representative assemblies and the use of national rhetoric in Germany after 1849. 'We have never forgotten to recognise that the national question is the upshot of a real need, and is thus a lasting and practical one, which must be brought into line with existing conditions, wrestled free from the revolution and solved on the ground of the *Bund*', wrote Beust in 1851.[219]

Since the Confederation was 'a young institution in the state order of Germany', it required 'more time to embed itself in the legal consciousness of the nation (*Nation*)', he declared in 1858.[220] The Bund, after all, had presided over a period of national prosperity and peace, which warranted a reassessment of its successes: 'In the period of time which belongs to *it*, there has been no reduction of German territory, during *its* existence no German armies have fought against each other, and no German land has made an alliance abroad against another German land.'[221] At the very least, the Confederation had not inhibited Germany's 'steady progress'.[222] As Beust told the audience at the fiftieth anniversary of the battle of Leipzig in 1863, 'the princes of Germany and their governments not only recognise and comprehend the upturn that a general German consciousness has benefited from ... they also sincerely welcome it, because they have learned to recognise in this development of German sentiment the best point of support for their own endeavours'.[223] The Foreign Minister even went as far as to imply, in a memorandum of 1861, that the founding of the *Bund* in 1815 had given rise to 'the first expression' of the striving for national unity in Germany.[224] The Confederation was more likely to succeed if it could be recast as a national institution.

The Saxon Minister-President knew, however, that his own conception of a national Confederation was viewed sceptically by much of the population, as part of a 'reaction' which was 'mostly understood as a type of conspiracy' directed 'through secret intrigues and then with open violence against the progressive institutions and liberal elements in the state'.[225] Beust was conscious that his plans were widely associated with 'petty statehood (*Duodezstaaterei*), small-state misery, *Bundestag* mismanagement (*Bundestagswirthschaft*), Confederation-of-the-Rhine-ism (*Rheinbündelei*) etc.' The *Bund* was not popular, he confessed in 1861, not least because the principle of nationality was generally associated with the revolution and with the idea of a constitutional *Bundesstaat*, a central executive and a directly elected National Assembly, not with a loose organisation of semi-sovereign states within a confederation.[226] A confederal nation was different from a federal one:

It would be blindness not to see that the German *Bund* has never put down deep roots in the heart of the German *Volk*, and that the two are not connected by a firmer tie than that of habit, indeed that the feeling of indifference with which it is linked has made way for a worse feeling.

It is true that the revolutionary ideas, whose mother is not Germany but Europe, have contributed to this ... One is inclined, in general, to trace this phenomenon back to two things: first, to the *resistance which the long-lasting police regime of the* Bund *elicited*, and then to *an unsatiated national consciousness, which demands a united action for Germany as a European power.*

The push for national unity, the demand for national power in Germany are, of course, older than the nationality principle, preached in the West for three years now ... Only... as the revolution ... broke out ... did the ideals of the German *Bundesstaat*, the German title of *Kaiser*, and the German parliament see the light of day. A revolution can call them once again into being.[227]

Most, if not all, governments of the third Germany agreed with Beust that the *Bund* had to be presented, in light of public opinion since 1848, as a national institution. There was some disagreement about the specific content of a reform of the *Bund*, but not about its national foundation, with even Pfordten searching for a form in which 'the effective exercise of government power' could be combined 'with free development of the spirit of the *Volk* through a national representation for the good of the whole'. [228] 'Bavaria should work not only towards the maintenance, but also as much as possible towards the development of the German Bund', urged Pfordten in December 1864: 'The *Mittelstaaten*, especially the central and southern German ones, are the natural allies (*Bundesgenossen*) of Bavaria, and we must immediately try once more to unite them in common action with Bavaria. The same interest in survival and the same duty towards the fatherland as a whole (*Gesammtvaterland*) binds them together.'[229] The Confederation was the only means of coordinating the actions of the individual states and of securing public support, reported the Hanoverian envoy in Frankfurt in 1852: 'For, if one doesn't want to base the account on the results of great catastrophes, on revolution or a general war, the *Bund* is the only possible tie linking Germany.'[230]

Some ministers pushed for more thoroughgoing reform than others. Notably, the government of Saxe-Coburg-Gotha, which became the main sponsor of the *Nationalverein* in 1859, believed that its aim of establishing a *Bundestaat* and of 'strengthening national ties' matched 'the wishes of the great majority of the nation'.[231] Most were much more cautious. Thus, although Roggenbach argued in August 1860 that 'German development must progress from the form of a *Staatenbund*, which the Acts of Confederation and Vienna Final Acts laid down, to that of a *Bundesstaat*', the Badenese government had traditionally contended that a confederation was 'the form which corresponded to the historical and legal relations' of Germany': 'In the further construction of common institutions (e.g. of military institutions, of forts, etc.), in the rapprochement, if not identification, of the relations of civil society lies both the mettle and the strength of the national idea. Raised and strengthened by the governments themselves, this would unfold more and more relentlessly and give healthy nourishment to the sense of solidarity.'[232] The Badenese Foreign Minister, Ludwig Rüdt von Collenberg, was consequently content to back Bavaria's moderate proposals for legal convergence alone in 1855, albeit on clear national grounds: 'In this way, the common interests of the German nation would be considerably furthered, public opinion would without doubt be satisfied, as far as it deserves consideration, and an enhanced, consensual effect internally, and therefore a greater position of power externally, would be achieved.'[233] Such national but conservative aims could be discerned in Württemberg, where Wilhelm I had backed the idea of a German parliament in 1851: 'If we are to withhold from the nation (*Nation*) its deserved part in the highest affairs of its state life as a whole, we cannot hope to reconcile it with the constitution of the *Bund* and, just as little, bring the revolution in Germany to a standstill.'[234] Yet, as in Baden, the government generally supported the view that the *Bund* was a confederation with the principal task of serving, in a 'political and national context', as 'an indissoluble connection abroad' rather than as an agent for change or reform at home.[235] The demands of a national-minded opposition were unlikely to be met by such limited proposals.

Dalwigk, like Beust, acknowledged the risks of attempting to harness popular nationalism, but saw little alternative for the states of the third Germany during the 1850s. Unlike 'democracy', with which it was often paired, 'the national idea has nothing to do with the form of the state' and 'can just as well become prominent in a monarchy as in a republic, and there were and are enough states in which the aristocracy respectively was or is the principal carrier of national thought'.[236] Whereas democracy was predicated on the notion of equality and tended towards republicanism and revolution, nationalism could be combined with different regimes and was, 'by nature, positive in content and, as far as it rests on tradition and history, conservative'.[237] Indeed, national feeling 'originates from the same source as one's sense of family or *Heimat*': 'For just this reason, national sentiment is very well suited to serving as the foundation for a strong government and healthy political life (*Staatsleben*),' noted the Hessian Minister-President in 1861.[238] Whilst democracy was cosmopolitan, spreading 'throughout the whole world', nationalism was exclusive, serving to cement feelings of internal belonging against a hostile external set of rivals: 'Each *Volk* has its own particular national policy, which exists for the most part in the pursuit of specific interests at the cost of other *Völker*.'[239] Any feeling of sympathy for Poles, Italians and others could quickly be extinguished, finding satisfaction in the fact 'that these peoples will be subordinated to German power'.[240] Such feelings could be exploited by the states of the third Germany, especially, since they alone were 'purely German', in a common phrase of the 1850s.

Moreover, the *Mittel-* and *Kleinstaaten* could take advantage of the circumstance that national belonging was cultural and ethnic, not political. 'National consciousness in no way demands a unitary state,' asserted Dalwigk: 'It does not exclude the feeling of tribal particularity, uniqueness, for it flows from the same source. One should, above all, not confuse consciousness of national unity, i.e. of belonging, as a result of the same descent, language, customs etc. with the demand for political unity.'[241] This cultural unity was built on the diversity of the whole, as could be witnessed in the national festivals of the period, involving Schiller, shooting, choral, gymnastics and other associations. It was also compatible with 'a confederal tie'.[242]

The problem, of which Dalwigk was aware, was that democracy and nationalism had been pushed together as a consequence of government repression before 1848, which had not distinguished between the different types of 'opposition'.[243] 'In the revolutionary movements of Germany, democratic and national tendencies have always been united,' continued Dalwigk in 1861: 'The *Bundestag* succumbed to a united attack by both elements in 1848. Today, too, the governments face a united front, and even if the present opposition movement has not nearly regained the intensity of those of 1848 and 1849, its scope – one cannot deny this – has grown considerably; it has extended to circles from which it previously was distant.'[244] Although, in the event of an uprising, order could be restored, given that the army remained loyal, it would not be 'a lasting tranquillity'.[245] It was necessary for the reactionary governments to divide and rule, seeking to separate nationalism and democracy and to qualify the particular interests of Austria and Prussia by appealing to overarching national interests, but such an undertaking was not bound to succeed, not least because Dalwigk and his counterparts continued to view nationalism as a 'means', not an 'end'.[246]

As was to be expected, the individual states failed to reform the *Bund* and to establish it as a popular national organisation. For a while, 'in the period between the ending of the Italian war of 1859 and the outbreak of the German war of 1866, there were many attempts made, in part by Austria, in part by the *Mittelstaaten*, especially by Bavaria and Saxony,' recorded the Saxon Finance and Interior Minister Richard von Friesen, 'to turn the constitution of the German *Bund* into one which better corresponded to the real relations of power of its members and, at the same time, to shape

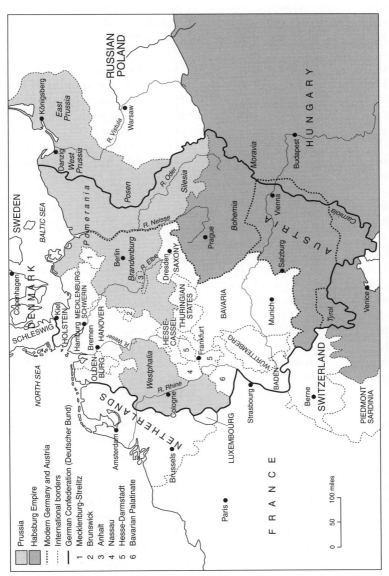

Map 4   The German Confederation in 1848
Source: Adapted from

national ideas and endeavours, which are emerging ever more decisively, in a more satisfying way by means of a mutual agreement
amongst the participating governments, strictly by means of the law,
and to order them on a new basis'.[247] Yet such a project was bound
to fail because of Prussian and public opposition:

> Incidentally, all those attempts, and indeed not only the different
> reform plans of the *Mittelstaaten* but also the negotiations of the
> Frankfurt *Fürstentag*, remained completely within the bounds of
> theoretical ideas and considerations; these ideas themselves ...
> remained without any practical success ... Prussia ... did not at all
> want a reform with the retention of the confederal character of
> the constitution and with the participation of Austria, as Austria
> itself and the *Mittelstaaten* alone desired and – through agreeable
> talks – could accept; rather it aimed solely at a complete dissolu-
> tion of the *Bund* and its replacement by a *Bundesstaat* with a
> Prussian leadership and with the exclusion of Austria.[248]

Bismarck, who merely followed the policies of his predecessors
with greater ruthlessness, had the 'clear intention, without any
regard for Austria ... of lowering the German *Bund* in public
opinion and making it feel its actual impotence'.[249] A three-way
relationship had come into being between the German
Confederation, the *Mittelstaaten* and the Habsburg monarchy, which
rapidly unravelled in the 1850s, contended Friesen. 'The opaque,
perpetually vacillating and contradictory policy which Austria
followed after 1849 abroad and at home – all this destroyed almost
every sympathy for Austria in the public opinion of Germany and
led, more than all the efforts of Prussia, to alienate the German
people from Austria and drive them into the arms of Prussia', noted
the Saxon minister, before explaining that 'the power and status of
Austria in Germany depended entirely on the trust and dependency
of the governments of the German *Mittelstaaten*, which in part had
already become very mistrustful and in truth could only be moved
to support Austria by the fear of being raped by Prussia'.[250] In turn,
the 'significance of these *Mittelstaaten* rested exclusively on the
German *Bund*'; 'if this common tie, which encompassed them all,
were destroyed, then all of them, with each standing on its own,
were meaningless, and could no longer be a support for Austria'.[251]
In effect, this house of cards looked likely to collapse throughout
the 1850s and early 1860s.

The individual states proved incapable of cooperating with each other in the interests of a greater national good or mere self-defence. Despite successfully standardising important components of commercial law and practice, German governments failed to reform the *Bund* itself.[252] Prussia had been forced to accept the Confederation at Olmütz and Dresden, but it generally used confederal institutions to oppose Vienna and block cooperation between the other states, as Friesen recognised. The Prussian cabinet had 'only gone back to the *Bund* in a coerced way' and welcomed 'each failure with a kind of *Schadenfreude*', lamented one Bavarian diplomat in November 1851.[253] Austrian administrations, although deploring Bismarck's cynical disregard for the legality of the *Bund* and his predecessors' obstructionism, tended to ridicule the inefficacy and powerlessness of what Schwarzenberg had called 'the old, downtrodden, despised *Bundestag*', 'an unwieldy, used-up thing, in no way sufficient for current conditions'.[254] Austrian attempts to reform the *Bund* in 1863 came too late to convince many contemporary observers that Vienna's position was genuine. For their part, the governments of many small states feared 'mediatisation', or a forced merger with the larger states, as a consequence of any reform. 'We come off best if as little as possible changes in the old constitution of the *Bund*', wrote the plenipotentiary of Nassau at the start of the Dresden conferences, prior to the full restoration of the Confederation.[255] The governments of other, liberal, small states such as Sachsen-Weimar opposed an extension of the powers of the *Bund* because they viewed it as an agent of reaction: 'One must remember ... that Germany is not a *Bundesstaat* but a *Staatenbund*, and that all measures going beyond this constitutional form will shake its foundations.'[256]

More importantly, Bavaria, the largest and most powerful middling state, blocked reform of the Confederation until the early 1860s on the grounds that it endangered Bavaria's independence as a first-rank German power. As Pfordten asserted in a memorandum of 1852, 'the individual German states can be divided into two classes in their relationship to the *Bund*; namely, into those through which the *Bund* exists, and those which exist through the *Bund*. Certainly, Austria, Prussia and Bavaria belong in the first class, all the rest probably in the second.'[257] Though it was true that Bavaria was not like Prussia and Austria, as European Great Powers and with some of their territories outside the *Bund*, its constitution had been predicated on its continuing independence. With Vienna and

Berlin pitted against each other, concluded Pfordten, Bavaria's need to retain its independence in order to use 'its weight according to its interest', to increase its influence, and to tip the balance one way or the other.[258] Bavaria could 'allow the German *Bund* no more incursive intervention in its internal affairs than could Prussia', wrote Pfordten to Max II in October 1856.[259] To Ludwig von Montgelas, it was natural that this freedom be extended to all the *Mittelstaaten*.[260] The result, as Bavaria began to reconsider its policy on a reform of the Confederation around 1860, was that 'one was fully unclear and clueless about the means to solve this problem', with little prospect of ending the 'many-headedness', 'the unwieldiness' and the 'envy' which characterised confederal politics, in the opinion of the Bavarian envoy to Stuttgart.[261] 'The individual states are setting themselves up again,' reported his Badenese counterpart in Berlin: 'A common feeling for the *Bund* can only be talked of as far as the latter can be used for certain particular ends.'[262] Even the 'conservative party' – 'i.e. the governments' – frequently seem to have believed that such 'particularism' prevented any national reform of the German Confederation.[263]

Much of the German press and most political parties were critical of the *Bund*, rejecting it as a viable and effective structure for national politics. The hope 'that something other than the old *Bundestag*' would emerge from the revolution and its immediate aftermath had been disappointed, lamented the Saxon *Constitutionelle Zeitung* in its annual review on 31 December 1851.[264] The period had not witnessed anticipated reforms, concurred the Bremen *Weser-Zeitung*, but 'the completion of a merely *negative reaction*'.[265] By the time of the Crimean War, when the *Bund* was first tested, as many parties came to oppose the pro-Russian 'neutrality' of Prussia, there was a 'sharply defined impression in public opinion', wrote Beust, that the *Bundesverfassung* was 'only an empty form' and that 'the other German states constituted a sort of second contingent beside the two Great Powers, destined to be put at the disposal of both powers'.[266] To the *Weser-Zeitung* in 1854, the *Bund* had already proved that it was 'fully unsuited' to dealing with the crisis and representing Germany abroad.[267] The 'material side of national unification' had occurred by the end of 1856, asserted the newspaper, but 'political unification' was still 'an ideological phantom': 'The sole advances which Germany has made towards unification had nothing to do' with the Confederation.[268] 'The matter of national progress is in the following state: the only

national institute that we have in Germany has done nothing positive for national progress', concluded the report.[269] Even previously
supportive publications such as the *Kasseler Zeitung* believed that it
remained to be proved that the Confederation was 'a European
potency, equipped with all the requisites for survival', 'not merely a
fictional constitutional concept'.[270]

Beust's claim in 1858 that a German *Bundesstaat* with a stronger
executive and a National Assembly was incompatible with the
monarchical system was roundly rejected by newspapers like the
Constitutionelle Zeitung, which contended that the Saxon minister was
opposed to 'German unity' in favour of '*the full sovereignty* of the
German *Kleinstaaten*', and the Nuremberg *Korrespondent von und für
Deutschland*, which declared that his statement was a 'break' 'with all
national hopes' and 'the declaration of insolvency of a German
policy'.[271] In the Franco-Austrian War of 1859, the same newspaper
printed – without objection – the opinion of the *Preussisches
Wochenblatt* that small and medium-sized states had used the
Confederation to gain influence beyond their actual significance
and to act – or to block actions – 'at the cost of the majority of the
German *Volk*'.[272] In spite of some initial support for the *Bund*, it was
widely accepted that it had not worked effectively during the
crisis.[273] Throughout the period, the refusal of the governments of
the individual states to introduce a directly elected National
Assembly was condemned in the press, with the suggestion in 1862
and 1863 to set up an assembly of delegates from the upper and
lower chambers being dismissed as a 'deception', in the words of the
official *Karlsruher Zeitung*.[274] Looking back in 1865, the Heidelberg
liberal Ludwig Häusser, writing in the *Preussische Jahrbücher*, maintained that the *Bund* had done nothing, especially in respect of the
main national question for the previous 20 years in Schleswig-
Holstein.[275] The German Confederation, he went on, relied on the
states of the third Germany, which were internally divided and were
mistrusted by the German *Volk*, in part because they had traditionally been contemptuous of public opinion.[276] As a result, the *Bund*
had been weak and ineffective since its restoration.

Prominent liberal publications, particularly in North and Central
Germany, agreed with Häusser's diagnosis. The Confederation not
only had a history of oppression, wrote the *Grenzboten* in 1850, it also
lacked any connection with the German nation.[277] The Congress of
Vienna in 1815 had created Germany from a series of small states,
in opposition to the wishes of Prussia, which had proposed a united

German *Bundesstaat* with a central administration, continued the same publication in 1855.[278] The *Bund* which emerged, rather than binding the individual states, constituted 'a loosening of German ties'.[279] It was designed to prevent civil war, countering the divisions caused by the Reformation and the French Revolution, not to 'make possible a positive policy for Germany'.[280] Small states in the Confederation were unlikely to exercise full sovereignty or to take military action in the manner of Austria or Prussia, which helped to safeguard peace, but they also diminished 'the productive power of the *Volk*' as a corollary of their lack of coordination and obstruction.[281] Like the Holy Roman Empire, which 'did and could do nothing for Germany', even to the point of failing 'to prevent alliances of the German princes with the hereditary enemy' of France, the *Bund* could not be reformed: 'Further development of this constitution is not conceivable, least of all through the well-meaning but absurd means of a representative assembly in the *Bundestag*. True development, for the moment concerning only material questions, takes place outside the *Bundestag*, in the *Zollverein*, treaties about currency, weights, and so forth.'[282]

Beust's plan for a *Bund* assembly in 1858 seemed disingenuous and unrealistic to the *Grenzboten*, given the minister's unwillingness to introduce a strong executive and to coordinate the separate bureaucracies of the individual states. 'The German *Bund* is not a confederation (*Föderation*) of the different German "tribes", of the Austrians, the Prussians, the Hanoverians, the Hessians, and so on, but a confederation of the princes and cities, declared sovereign by the Acts of Confederation, in which certain rights were guaranteed to the former Reich princes', continued another article in 1858.[283] The Confederation was unable to intervene 'to protect the rights of subjects against the powers of the government' and it had 'few means to represent the great awareness and rise of, and enthusiasm for, the nation'.[284] With the geographical and historical division of Germany between North and South, together with the self-interest of the individual states, there was little chance of reforming the Confederation, claimed one correspondent in 1859: 'True, no *Bundesstaat's* official policy takes issue in principle with the necessity of a *Bundesreform*; but with the passing of each year, the wonderful agreement of their leaders is strengthened in the assurance that "the right moment" has not yet come.'[285] By the early 1860s, it was obvious, declared the *Grenzboten*, that the *Bund* was not defending Germany; Prussia, Austria and, even, Bavaria were.[286] Although

Prussia's desire to annex Schleswig-Holstein in 1864 was probably illegal and counterproductive, it demonstrated a willingness to act on behalf of the nation, whereas 'the *Bund* has done next-to-nothing'.[287] Many had accepted Austria's proposed reform of the Confederation in 1863 only half-heartedly, as a stop-gap, because of the inadequacy of existing arrangements:

> It is true that the *Bund* richly deserves the neglect with which the governments regard it in private and the contempt which works against it in the *Volk* ... The old *Bund* was, as an unpopular institution condemned by governments and public opinion, perfectly designed to prepare the ground and struggle for a well-organised *Bundesstaat* for the national party. It was anachronistic, its faults obvious; it was powerless even in obstruction.[288]

To publications like the *Grenzboten*, the German Confederation was beyond reform.

Few political parties championed a *Bundesreform* with any zeal. In Prussia, only ultra-right-wing reactionaries and Catholics treated the Confederation sympathetically. To Ludwig von Gerlach, the *Bund* was both enduring and legal, having been sidelined unconstitutionally by the 'anti-confederal events of March'.[289] With the Confederation restored, he went on in December 1850, 'we are now uniting and founding *Germany*, creating our old alliances – the power and status of *Prussia* in *Germany* and in *Europe* – these are the goals by which we now set our compass'.[290] If the individual states desired, asserted the reactionary *Neue Preussische Zeitung* in March 1850 in direct opposition to Radowitz's Erfurt Union plan, they could construct a strong *Bund*: the only alternative was a unitary republic, since a centralised German nation-state was incompatible with the continuing existence of German princes and with the monarchical principle.[291] The Franco-Austrian War in 1859 merely confirmed that there was nothing with which to replace the Confederation, after the moderate conservative government of the 'New Era' had stood aside while Austria – in the name of Germany – was defeated.[292] In the opinion of the camarilla, such inactivity demonstrated Prussian ministers' 'liberal and Gotha-style *Tendenzpolitik*'.[293] Although the reform of the *Bund* had been dogged by abstraction, reported the newspaper in 1863, it had achieved some of its goals, not least the defence and coordination of the 'facts' of Germany; namely, its diversity and particularity, its confessional division, and its tribes.[294] Within such a loose 'republic' (*res publica*), which described even the Holy Roman Empire, some type of confederal structure was needed in order to maintain order.[295]

Many Prussian Catholics agreed. There was a danger, argued August Reichensperger in 1864, that 'the overwhelming majority in our *Abgeordnetenhaus*' had been led astray by French constitutional theory and the model of Young Italy, prompting them to see 'in multiple statehood a thoroughly serious, scarcely surmountable obstacle' rather than the natural complement of Germany's diversity: 'Monotone, more or less abstract unity contravenes Germanic sensibilities, which strive for harmony – that is, for difference in unity, in which is based an awareness that only here the forces and attributes of our *Volkstum* can fully unfold.'[296] The Confederation, which allowed the inclusion of the largely Catholic power of Austria in Germany, was still the assumed framework for what Hermann von Malinckrodt called 'the national task of the German *Volk*': 'This task demands harmony and a firmer unification (*Einigung*) of all the parts (*Glieder*) of Germany, it demands a reform of the *Bund* and the founding of a central power, but it does not allow the destruction of the *Bund* and the fragmentation of the nation in the name of a closer connection of its parts.'[297] Although most calls to form a 'Catholic party' during the 1850s made little mention of the Confederation, in common with other 'purely political questions' in which 'freedom of conscience' was the rule, they generally appear to have assumed its continuing existence.[298]

Nevertheless, Catholic leaders such as the Reichensperger brothers remained sceptical of the *Bund* and seem to have doubted at times whether it could be reformed. Despite the fact that the improvement of the Confederation was one of 'Germany's Next Tasks', as one of their pamphlets put it in 1860, the *Bund* had 'unfortunately done nothing since its foundation' and had 'failed in many things'.[299] *Kleinstaaterei*, which – it was believed – 'owed its existence exclusively to the German Confederation', was held to constitute 'an insuperable obstacle for the greatness and development of the power of the fatherland', to the point where even the Reichenspergers were not willing to plead that 'the continuation of 35 *Bundesstaaten*, without any exceptions,' was 'a European or also merely a German necessity'.[300] It was not obvious, in such circumstances, how 'the organic extension and reconstruction of the confederal constitution' would occur: the Catholic deputies were left little option but to hope for a renewal of the German spirit and the emergence of new German leaders akin to those of 1813, which might introduce 'more movement and alacrity through a greater unity of organisation' in the *Bund*.[301]

Other political leaders in Prussia were much harsher in their criticisms and more pessimistic in their appraisals of future reform, as August and Peter Reichensperger acknowledged. The liberal party of Gotha and the *Nationalverein* had risen to prominence precisely because of 'the previous failures of the external and internal aspects of German policy'.[302] Thus, though a handful of democrats – with Jakob Venedey the most well-known – went on supporting a *grossdeutsch* and confederal solution to the German question, a large majority of Prussian liberals and radicals were critical of the *Bund*. At the *Abgeordnetentag* of August 1863, which was intended by its old liberal architects as a form of *Vorparlament* to overshadow the *Fürstentag*, most of the 319 participants, including a majority of the 26 democratic and 58 Prussian deputies, were willing to rule out reform of the Confederation by setting unacceptable conditions for Austria, Saxony and other proponents of a *Bundesreform*; namely, a National Assembly directly elected according to the law of 1849 and with the right to sanction any reform of the *Bund*, the parity of Prussia and Austria in the envisaged directory, and the inclusion of East Prussia and Posen.[303] The bill of the standing committee on the question of a *Bundesreform*, which was approved unanimously, welcomed the Austrian initiative almost sarcastically as 'a happy sign of a belief, victorious everywhere, in the inadequacy of the existing form of the *Bund* and of the pressing necessity of its restructuring'.[304] 'Now, as previously, the *Abgeordetentag* can hope for the complete satisfaction of needs only from a federal unity (*bundesstaatliche Einheit*), as it found its legal expression in the German constitution of 28 March 1849, which offers the German nation both freedom and unity, security and power', read the resolution, before conceding that the assembly of deputies could not afford, given internal crises and external threats, to treat the Austrian proposals for a '*Staatenbund* with a closer collegial executive and with a representative assembly' 'simply negatively'.[305] The effect and intention of the resolution was, however, merely negative.

Liberals, especially, believed that the Confederation had failed and was likely to fail again. They were joined by a significant number of radicals, including socialists, and by moderate and governmental conservatives. The 'small Germans' had become dominant, wrote the Lassallean *Social-Democrat* in January 1865, by convincing democrats, amongst other things, that there had been no growth in Germany under the Confederation.[306] The *Bund* was rotten and ineffective, concurred conservatives, leading Bethmann-Hollweg to push Friedrich Wilhelm IV to accept the title of *Kaiser* in 1849, gossiped Ludwig von Gerlach to the Queen in January 1853.[307] 'The Confederation, which should be a pledge of the nation's unity and power vis-à-vis the external world, is in truth the cause of its fragmentation and weakness', reported the *Preussisches Wochenblatt* seven years later.[308] Manteuffel himself had argued, in the Prussian *Abgeordnetenhaus* in 1852, that there were better options for Germany than the *Bund*, even if they were not possible, for the time being, 'without great martial catastrophes'.[309] In Prussia, across the political spectrum, the Confederation found little support.

In the rest of Germany, parties and the press were occasionally more sympathetic towards the *Bund*, but they recognised that they were in a minority. Beyond government circles, the most supportive publication was the *Allgemeine Zeitung*, which argued that the 'political unit of the Confederation' should act on behalf of the German nation in the Crimean War, the Franco-Austrian War and the Schleswig-Holstein War.[310] At the same time, the newspaper conceded in 1854 the 'necessity of the improvement' of the *Bund* and admitted in 1859 that its military constitution was 'flawed'.[311] By the time of the Danish War, despite the publication's hope in 1864 that 'the rest of Germany, resting on the joyful self-sacrifice of the *Volk*, will show the astonished world that it is a great power even without the two Great Powers', the Confederation was seen to have demonstrated its weakness, pushing the *Allgemeine Zeitung* to countenance backing Prussia despite the 'setback' that this would cause the 'confederal system' (*Föderativsystem*): the 'German group of states', which had to be the 'principal representatives and supports of the confederal system', had proved incapable of acting.[312]

'Opposition' political parties in the third Germany rarely took issue with such a judgement. At the Frankfurt *Abgeordnetentag* in August 1863, deputies from the German *Klein-* and *Mittelstaaten* had made up 82 per cent of the total, joining forces – in effect – to vote against Austria's planned reform of the *Bund*.[313] In Bavaria, the Chamber of Deputies had already toyed with the idea, put forward by the ex-Frankfurt liberal Peter Ernst von Lassaulx in September 1855, of sponsoring 'a rebuilding (*Neugestaltung*) of the German *Bund* in accordance with the needs of the time', including a National Assembly and supreme *Bundesgrericht*, before finally accepting Pfordten's call for moderation.[314] When the Bavarian diplomat again became Foreign Minister in November 1864, he was obliged to admit that the state's parties and public opinion were against his policies in favour of the Confederation.[315]

In Württemberg, deputies had spoken out earlier and more forthrightly than in Munich, criticising the strict neutrality of the *Bund* in the Crimean War and calling for 'national' backing of Austria and the West.[316] In August 1864, the Chamber of Deputies adopted a bill demanding the fulfilment of 'the long recognised and increasingly pressing need, as a result of recent experiences, for the rebuilding of the public and legal relations of Germany in the direction of unity and the active participation of the German *Volk* in the leadership of its common affairs'.[317] Politicians complained vociferously in accompanying debates that the Confederation had done nothing 'for the unity of the nation at home' or for 'the position of Germany in external affairs'.[318] Such complaints surfaced at other times. In May 1862, for instance, a number of bills demanded the creation of a '*Volksvertretung*' and the 'transformation of the *Bundesverfassung* with a National Assembly'.[319]

Finally, in Saxony, deputies who had hesitated to speak on German affairs until 1858 came to criticise the cautious *Bundesreform* proposals of their own minister, Beust. At the very least, declared the conservative *Rittergutsbesitzer* Carl August Rittner in the main debate in February, 'the German *Bund* has to come to the conviction that, if it gradually succeeds in uniting German material interests, it *must* also move to lead the German peoples to agreement (*Einigkeit*), if not unity (*Einheit*), in the *political* sphere'.[320] The moderate democratic deputy Christian Gottlieb Riedel was less guarded, accusing the Confederation of merely protecting 'the rights of the dynasties inside Germany' and of ignoring 'the rights of the *Völker*'.[321] Notwithstanding a polite word of 'thanks to His Majesty' at the end of the session, the second chamber had refused to back Beust, with the *Constitutionelle Zeitung*'s sarcastic 'sincere thankyou to the *Staatsminister*' for his 'open explanation', which would have 'a doubly significant effect', much closer to the overall tone of the debate.[322] The Minister of State was similarly unsuccessful in harnessing party support in the early 1860s, despite transient cross-party support for the *Bund* – as in other states – during the early stages of the Schleswig-Holstein crisis in 1864.[323] As the Progressive politician Carl Heyner, who met Beust in February 1864, put it, the policy of *Mittelstaaten* such as Saxony had 'nothing, not even their own *Volk*, behind it', and could not have, 'after it [had] given it cause for mistrust over 14 years and [had] suppressed every initiative'.[324] An ineffectual *Bund* and unpopular state governments were seen by opposition deputies to have combined in stymieing national unification.

The force of such arguments could be witnessed in the shifting stance of the Bavarian and Catholic *Historisch-politische Blätter*, whose anti-Prussian and *grossdeutsch* leanings initially encouraged it to take the Confederation seriously. Prussia, argued one article in 1862, constituted merely one-third of the *Bund*'s population.[325] With the third Germany united, except for Baden, it matched the Prussian state's population and exceeded its resources, leading it to favour some sort of trias, possibly within a reformed Confederation.[326] Yet the periodical harboured doubts about confederal institutions from the start, lamenting that Germany was capable of more than the *Bund* allowed as early as 1850.[327] Contemplating the 'interregnum' of 'reaction' from the standpoint of 1858, the publication admitted that the Confederation had failed as a national organisation, especially in the military sphere.[328] By 1862, some correspondents denied that a *Bundesreform* was feasible, despite its promising origins, in 1815, when 'one could imagine the *Bund* however one wanted'.[329] In fact, the Vienna Final Acts had turned the *Bund*, via an international treaty, into an inter-state confederation. Thus, what was necessary was not 'reform', but complete reconstruction: 'What one could call the reform of the *Bund* satisfies no party today,' asserted the correspondent: 'Reform presupposes the retention of the original character of the institution which is to be reformed; but precisely in this character lies the obstacle to the fulfilment of the German *Bund*'s tasks.'[330] 'When Germans really demand the unity of the fatherland, *they demand the* Bundesstaat *instead of the* Staatenbund, *and if they don't want this, they want nothing at all*', the article continued.[331] It was difficult to see how the demands of the age – a constitution, the participation of the *Völker*, a National Assembly, a stronger executive tied to the 'life of the *Volk*' – could be combined with the existing structure of the Confederation.[332] The *Bund* could no longer simply defend Germany against external enemies; it had to harness the country's internal, national energies and establish itself as a Central European Great Power.[333] There were doubts, however, whether this would be possible, given the narrowness and international character of the Confederation, and the inability or unwillingness of the states – especially Prussia – to cooperate.[334]

Partly because of these doubts about the *Bund*, partly because of a long-standing fascination with the '*Reich*', the *Historisch-politische Blätter* put forward its own solution to the German question – the '*Kaiseridee*'.[335] Such a greater German *Kaisertum* was designed to be more effective than the *Bund*, with one leader not a directory, and to allow the incorporation of a German parliament, the dynasties, and Austria. Some Catholic authors desired the restoration of the Holy Roman Empire, but the principle of nationality had necessarily moved the focus of power from Rome and Vienna to Germany itself, asserted one article in 1862.[336] Unlike liberal conceptions of *Kleindeutschland* or the individual states' notion of a trias, the '*grossdeutsche Kaiseridee*' allowed Germany to become a world power at the centre of Europe, now that the artificial settlement of 1815 had come to an end.[337] Catholics differed from liberals in viewing the reform or replacement of the *Bund* not as a domestic constitutional problem but as the main foreign-policy question of the century.[338] Yet it soon became apparent, by 1864 at the latest, that neither *Grossdeutschland* nor a *Bundesreform* was likely in the near future, given that they were only supported by particular sections of Prussia's Catholic population, with many Catholics backing the Progressives' national programme.[339] After Prussia's successful war in Schleswig-Holstein, Berlin's resurrection of the 1849 *Reichsverfassung* plan to establish a German *Bundesstaat* with parliamentary rule under the Prussian crown – a plan which was championed by the *Nationalverein* – had few, if any, rivals.[340] The *Bund*, which had seemed to be a superior, national alternative to the Holy Roman Empire 46 years earlier, was widely believed by the mid-1860s to be weak and incorrigible.[341] Contemporaries mistakenly believed that the transition to a national *Bundesstaat* would be straightforward, opined the *Historisch-politische Blätter* in 1866, but there seemed to be no other possibility in view. Such despair was the culmination of scepticism about the *Bund*, even on the part of the main Catholic and Bavarian periodical, since its restoration in 1850.

Few contemporary politicians or journalists believed in the viability of the German Confederation or in the possibility of coordinating the states of the third Germany. To the Munich academic Riehl, who had lingered so long in the patchwork of *Klein-* and *Mittelstaaten*, power had shifted from the fertile historical core of Germany to the harsh, monotonous and exposed plains of the North, where a Prussian military monarchy had had little choice but to expand and to defend itself in order to survive. Many of the political parties which had developed during and after the revolution, adopting – at the very least – the national rhetoric of those years, had been obliged to criticise or abandon both Austria and the *Bund* as the focus of popular expectations of a German nation-state. Quite a few contemporaries remained fearful or sceptical of Prussia but, given the poor reputation of particularist governments, the Confederation and the Habsburg monarchy, they found it more difficult to deny the Hohenzollern state a major role in unifying Germany. The next chapter investigates how that role was defined, limited and reconciled with the parties' other objectives.

5 Prussia, the Nation and the Constitution

Prussia was singled out by liberals and democrats, meeting in Eisenach and Hanover on 17 and 19 July 1859 to discuss the establishment of a national association, as the only source of a 'strong and lasting central government of Germany' and of 'a German National Assembly'. It was also agreed that, 'should Germany in the near future again immediately be threatened from abroad, leadership of German military forces and external diplomatic representation are to be transferred to Prussia, until the definitive constitution of a German central government'.[1] A day later, an article appeared in the Hanoverian *Zeitung für Norddeutschland* proclaiming that 'we direct our hope towards Prussia's government, which – through the change of system voluntarily introduced last year – has shown its *Volk* and the whole of Germany that it has recognised it as its task to bring the latter's interests into line with those of its own land, and it doesn't shy away from sacrificing its full powers and adopting a new and difficult course towards such an end. The aims of Prussian policy largely coincide with those of Germany.'[2] Apart from revolution, 'the most natural way' for Germany to attain a reform of its constitution and to save itself 'from internal and external dangers' was for 'one of the two great German governments to undertake to bring to life the reform of our *Bund* constitution'.[3] 'Austria is not in a position to do so' because of its domestic preoccupations, the article continued: 'A great part of Germany – and we, too – harbour the expectation, therefore, that Prussia will take the initiative of introducing a unified and free *Bundesverfassung* as quickly as possi-

221

ble in the period of calm and preparation, which is perhaps only granted to us now for a short time.'[4] Such statements were remarkable from the founders of an organisation which aimed to appeal to supporters of *Grossdeutschland* as well as *Kleindeutschland* and, in its later inaugural statement of 15–16 September, to 'let the goals and means of the movement, which had spread over our entire fatherland, enter the consciousness of the *Volk* more and more clearly'.[5] What was more, the declarations of support for Prussia were made immediately after the defeat of Austria in the Franco-Austrian war, in which much of the public – particularly in the South – had been supportive of Vienna and critical of Berlin's inaction. For many members of the new *Nationalverein*, it appeared that only Prussia could introduce reform and unify Germany.

Such claims were contested at the time and have been challenged since.[6] To the Hanoverian historian Onno Klopp, there had been a systematic and successful, if not always conscious, attempt to achieve 'the alienation of Germans from Austria'.[7] Given that both the Habsburg monarchy and the German Confederation had been widely discounted as bases of a German nation-state, nationalists had to look elsewhere – most obviously, to Prussia – for sources of support.[8] The temptation to look to Prussia, irrespective of previous opposition, occurred from the elevated circles of the princes to the ranks of disaffected and exiled radicals. Ernst II of Saxe-Coburg-Gotha, 'as a German patriot', was 'above all interested in the unity of Germany', whichever 'way it comes into being'.[9] His many trips to Vienna to persuade 'Austria to put itself at the head of Germany', after Friedrich Wilhelm IV had turned down the title of *Kaiser* in 1849, 'met with no approval at all', for 'the idea was too great for the rulers there', who wanted 'only to have to do with themselves'.[10] As a consequence, he 'again and again came back to the belief that it [unification] can only come about through Prussia'.[11] At the other end of the political spectrum, the radical forty-eighter Ludwig Simon, who had been in exile since 1849 and had been condemned to death by Prussian authorities in his absence, likewise supported the *Nationalverein*'s 'goal of achieving German unity through the influence and strength of the Prussian state'.[12] Although he remained attached to a 'republic as a higher and more beautiful expression of human life together than a monarchy', he acknowledged that 'the conditions of political effectiveness are completely different today compared to 1848', with the 'ten-year reality of princely sovereignty, which has completed its reactionary course everywhere and without interruption', replacing 'the short dream of theoretical popular sovereignty'.[13] In such circumstances, it seemed to Simon,

> Prussia recommended itself as the greatest predominantly German state, as the Protestant bulwark of religious enlightenment, in which even – or in particular – Catholics enjoy equal rights, as the founder of the *Zollverein* and pioneer of a lowering of tariffs, and as the *Heimat* of a young but not hopeless constitutional life; in short, because of its entire historical position, on the strength of which it has become interwoven more and more with Germany, whereas Austria has increasingly grown apart from Germany.[14]

Certainly, it would have been better, continued the democrat, if 'the goal of German unity' could have been attained 'through the strength of the German *Volk* alone, without any aftertaste of a specific Prussianness and dynastic interests', but this appeared unlikely, leaving only 'a joining of forces with the respectable kernel of orderly Prussian power'.[15]

The principal question for such conditional supporters of Berlin was the extent to which Prussia would remain a constitutional regime, after Bismarck's acceptance of the Minister-Presidency in 1862 in the midst of a deadlock between Wilhelm I's government and the Chamber of Deputies over a reform of the army. How far could the Prussian administration be influenced by public opinion and to what extent did it genuinely desire national unification rather than Prussian aggrandisement? How significant was unification compared to other domestic and foreign-policy goals for governments, political parties and public opinion? In particular, how important were economic and financial imperatives deriving from membership of the *Zollverein*? Lastly, would a Prussian-led unification of Germany lead to a recognisably liberal and constitutional nation-state? Even if there were no alternative means of unifying Germany over the short term, was it advisable to withdraw support from Prussia and to await future events?

New Era, Old Politics

The period after the accession of Wilhelm, Friedrich Wilhelm IV's brother, to an unlimited regency in October 1858, and eventually to the throne itself in 1861, witnessed the rapid re-emergence of a

national political sphere which transformed the means and significance of government and party intervention. At the time, some
contemporaries, such as the Saxon editor of the *Weimarer Zeitung*
Karl Biedermann, were optimistic that the 'instalment of the
"Ministry of the New Era", as well as its agreed and published political programme', had awoken 'new and apparently more reliable
hopes for an improvement of Prussian and German affairs than at
the time of the succession of 1840'.[16] Others such as Georg
Gottfried Gervinus, Ludwig Häusser, Heinrich von Gagern and
Friedrich von Römer thought it 'highly risky', in the words of one of
Biedermann's Bavarian correspondents in June 1859, 'to take up
the question of the German constitution now'.[17] Biedermann
himself believed that 'a stronger political pulse-beat of public
opinion was first felt as ... the rather certain prospect of war
between France and Austria, a war immediately on Germany's
borders and with a threat to the territory of one of the German
Great Powers, came before the German people', yet he also learned
on a visit to Berlin in 1859 that there was 'no thorough understanding or even a lively, active interest in grasping the German
question', merely a preoccupation with domestic affairs or disinter-
est and *Schadenfreude* at the plight of Austria.[18]

Responses to a Prussian-inspired 'New Era' were mixed. In states
like Bavaria, there was a parallel movement towards greater openness and more liberal policies, with a stronger opposition – a consequence of the elections of December 1858 – criticising censorship
and delays in the completion of judicial and administrative reforms.
Eventually, in the spring of the following year, Maximilian II ceded
to calls for Pfordten's resignation, arguing, 'I want to have peace
with my people and with the chambers; that is why I have dismissed
the ministry.'[19] Similarly, in Baden, after a dispute about the newly
signed Concordat in 1859, the Grand Duke replaced the existing
government with the leaders of the opposition in 1860. By contrast,
the reactionary Minister-President Ferdinand von Beust remained
in office in Saxony and the coup of 1855 remained in force in
Hanover. Nevertheless, in Germany as a whole, 'a movement came
gradually into existence which was directed at the common goal of
pooling all the powers of non-Austrian Germany under the leadership of Prussia in the event of a war with France'.[20] There were two
important changes after 1858. First, national associations and
parties emerged, despite the continuance of the *Bund* decision of
1854 outlawing affiliations of parties and other organisations,

largely because Prussia was no longer willing to enforce the confederal interdiction. In the opinion of Gustav Freytag, even the government of Saxe-Coburg-Gotha, where the *Nationalverein* was eventually domiciled, was anxious about the enforcement of the 1854 law, although conscious that Berlin would probably oppose it.[21] Second, democrats reassumed a political role in both the *Nationalverein* and *Fortschrittspartei*, with some forty-eighters returning from exile and other radicals entering politics for the first time.

Between 1858 and 1863, an interlocking network of national organisations had developed which dominated the political landscape of Prussia and a number of smaller states. It had ramifications throughout Germany. The *Kongress deutscher Volkswirte* (founded in March 1859), the German *Nationalverein* (September 1859), the *Deutscher Juristentag* (1860), the *Deutscher Handelstag* (May 1861), the *Fortschrittspartei* (June 1861), the *Abgeordnetentag* (1862), the *Deutscher Journalistentag* (1863) and the *Deutscher Protestantenverein* (1863) were established within five years by an elite of middle-class notables, many of whom were deputies in *Landtage*. According to one study, 68 per cent of leaders of the principal national associations had seats in state assemblies; 36 per cent were members of more than one national committee; 83 per cent were Protestants; 83 per cent were university-educated, the majority of them lawyers; and 96 per cent had experienced 1848 as adults.[22] Many members of the governing committee of the pivotal national organisation of the 1860s, the *Nationalverein*, were also on the boards of other organisations, including the Danzig merchant and manufacturer Heinrich Behrend (*Handelstag* 1861–64, *Abgeordnetentag* 1862), the Hanoverian politician and judge Rudolf von Bennigsen (*Kongress deutscher Volkswirte* 1858–59, *Abgeordnetentag* 1862–67), the Bavarian journalist Karl Ludwig Theodor Brater (*Abgeordnetentag* 1862–67), the owner of the *Volks-Zeitung* Franz Duncker (*Abgeordnetentag* 1862–67), the Weimar lawyer Hugo Fries (*Abgeordnetentag* 1862–67), the Göttingen lawyer and later mayor of Osnabrück Johannes Miquel (*Abgeordnetentag* 1862–67), the Cassel lawyer and returned exile Friedrich Oetker (*Abgeordnetentag* 1862–67), the Heidelberg academic and journalist Eduard Pickford (*Kongress deutscher Volkswirte* 1858–59, *Abgeordnetentag* 1862–67), the Berlin former lawyer and publicist Hermann Schulze-Delitzsch (*Kongress deutscher Volkswirte* 1858–66, *Abgeordnetentag* 1862–67), the Coburg journalist and lawyer Fedor Streit (*Abgeordnetentag* 1862–67), the Berlin railway entrepreneur Hans-Viktor von Unruh (*Abgeordnetentag* 1862–67) and the Frankfurt doctor Johann Georg Varrentrapp (*Abgeordnetentag* 1863–66). They represented the notable circles of almost all the *Landtage* and many of the largest cities in Germany, mobilising the political elites of their localities and reactivating the national networks of 1848–49 in order to create a series of overlapping national professional, commercial and political organisations.

The *Nationalverein*, which was designed to have a political platform and an electoral role from its inception, was the largest party organisation of the period, with 5,369 members by 1860, 20,000–25,000 by 1862, 18,000 in 1864, and 5,314 in 1866 (see Table 5.1). Its followers largely belonged to the *Wirtschafts-* and *Bildungsbürgertum*, and they were spread across the German lands, with 8,421 members in Prussia (1861), 1,416 in Hessen-Darmstadt, 1,173 in Baden, 847 in Hamburg and Bremen, 664 in Hanover, 559 in Weimar and Saxe-Coburg, 513 in Nassau, 478 in the small states of Thuringia, 428 in Frankfurt, 386 in Württemberg, 355 in Bavaria, 337 in Schleswig-Holstein, 228 in Saxony, and 609 in exile. A list of 587 *Nationalverein* members in Berlin compiled by Adalbert Delbrück, an agent of the association, revealed that 29 per cent were merchants, 10 per cent manufacturers, 8 per cent doctors, 5 per cent academics, 3 per cent teachers, 4 per cent lawyers, 1 per cent journalists, 22 per cent from the '*neuer Mittelstand*', and 11 per cent from the petty bourgeoisie, mainly master artisans.[23] The *Abgeordnetentag*, whose aims and membership coincided with that of the leadership of the *Nationalverein* but whose origins could be traced back to the scepticism of constitutionalists and South German liberals and democrats with regard to the National Association's purportedly pro-Prussian and democratic stance, was similarly national in scope, attracting 490 deputies from virtually all Germany's state assemblies at its height in December 1863: 21.8 per cent came from Bavaria (1863), 14.9 per cent from Frankfurt, 9.8 per cent from Württemberg, 9.4 per cent from Prussia, 9 per cent from Baden, 8.6 per cent from Hessen-Darmstadt, 6.3 per cent from Hessen-Kassel, 4 per cent from Nassau, 3.3 per cent from Hamburg and Bremen, 2 per cent from Saxony, and 1.8 per cent from Hanover (see Table 5.2). Together, such deputies provided links, in addition to the centralised organisation of the *Nationalverein*, to nearly all German states and many cities. They comprised an almost exclusively liberal or democratic political elite.

National associations' activities, although difficult to assess, could have a decisive political effect. This was demonstrated most saliently

Table 5.1   Regional membership of the Nationalverein

	1861	1862	1863	1864	1865
Prussia	3,073	8,421	8,355	4,399	2,358
Baden	433	1,173	752	583	302
Bavaria	193	355	264	97	59
Braunschweig	142	307	224	129	101
Bremen	191	300	708	400	1
Coburg-Gotha	282	293	306	158	2
Frankfurt	98	428	342	174	25
Hamburg	163	547	802	529	399
Hanover	194	664	1,157	964	707
Hesse-Darmst.	32	1,416	1,383	1,039	462
Hesse-Cassel	–	2	278	243	c. 184
Lübeck	–	–	183	125	100
Mecklenburg	3	18	87	–	–
Nassau	109	513	493	256	66
Österreich	–	7	1	23	7
Oldenburg	113	111	265	160	87
Saxony	124	228	454	193	47
Thuringian sts	297	478	784	605	157
Weimar	95	266	235	160	13
Württemberg	45	386	82	38	8
Schleswig-H	178	337	326	229	108
Ausland	36	609	380	177	121
Total	5,801	16,859	17,861	10,681	5,314

Source: A. Biefang, Politisches Bürgertum in Deutschland 1857–1868 (Düsseldorf, 1994), 104

in the rapid rise of the *Fortschrittspartei* in Prussia, drawing heavily on national elites as well as on longer-established relationships within the Prussian *Landtag* to gain 104 out of 352 seats (29.5 per cent) in December 1861, 133 seats (37.8 per cent) in May 1862 and 141 (40.1 per cent) seats in October 1863. In the so-called *Konfliktslandtag* of 1862, 230 deputies (65.3 per cent) belonged to the Progressives or, like Heinrich von Sybel, to the 'left centre', the members of which were also closely tied to national organisations. According to one estimate, at least 46 per cent of the leaders of the different national organisations became leading members of the *Fortschrittspartei*.[24] They included many of the most prominent figures in the national-

Table 5.2   Participants in the Abgeordnetentag according to their state of origin

	Sept. 1862	Aug. 1863	Dec. 1863	Oct. 1865	May 1865
Baden	14 (2)	21 (2)	44 (8)	18 (1)	36 (5)
Bavaria	8	11	107 (2)	80	14
Braunschweig	5	3	6	3	–
Bremen	4	3	8	–	3
Coburg-Gotha	19	12	10	2	1
Frankfurt	4	64	73	37	37
Hamburg	–	3	8	2	1
Hanover	9 (1)	8	9	10	3
Hesse-Darmst.	5	32	42	22	30
Hesse-Cassel	12	27	31	6	30
Mecklenburg	3	3	–	–	4
Nassau	7 (3)	14 (2)	20 (6)	21 (8)	34 (10)
Oldenburg	–	2	5	–	1
Austria	–	–	7	1	–
Prussia	46 (1)	58 (1)	46	7	17
Saxony	15	11 (1)	10	9 (1)	2
Schleswig-H.	1	4	4	19	30
Weimar	36	16	6	2	1
Württemberg	12	15	48	27	2
Miscellaneous	10	12	6	5	4
Total	210 [45]	319 [52]	490	271	250 [33]

Source: A. Biefang, Politisches Bürgertum, *245.*
Note: The number of members of upper chambers is given in round brackets, the number of former members of the Frankfurt Parliament in square brackets.

ist milieux of the different German states, including the Erlangen lawyer Marquard Barth, the Wiesbaden lawyer Karl Joseph Wilhelm Braun, the Trier merchant Karl Philipp Cetto, the Cologne businessman Johann Classen-Kappelmann, the Nuremberg manufacturer Karl Crämer, the Frankfurt journalist Karl Julius Faucher, the Elbing lawyer Max von Forckenbeck, the Stuttgart administrator Julius Hölder, the Prussian landowner and official Leopold von Hoverbeck, the Deidesheim wine-grower Ludwig August Jordan, the Leipzig lawyer and estate-owner Hermann Gottlob Joseph, the Munich manufacturer and newspaper owner Julius Knorr, the Frankfurt journalist and former radical Georg Friedrich Kolb, the

Wiesbaden official Friedrich August Lang, the Berlin journalist Otto Michaelis, the Stuttgart lawyers August Ludwig Reyscher, Adolf Seeger, Karl August Fetzer and Johann Friedrich Gottlob Tafel, the Augsburg lawyer Josef Völk, and the Rostock lawyer Moritz Wiggers, in addition to other well-known leaders of the *Nationalverein* and *Abgeordnetentag* such as Behrend, Bennigsen, Brater, Franz Duncker, Miquel, Schulze-Delitzsch and Unruh.

The geographical spread of the *Fortschrittspartei*'s leadership itself suggests that the Progressives were more than a protest party reacting against Wilhelm I and Bismarck. The party's origins, of course, were Prussian, resulting from the discussions in late 1861 and early 1862 of Forckenbeck, Behrend, Hoverbeck and Brämer – all leaders of the *Nationvalverein* – with other members of Vincke's moderate liberal faction in the Prussian *Landtag*, with the intention of giving the liberal programme greater coherence and of limiting the powers of the faction's leaders. When the majority of the faction voted against a 'German policy in the sense of that of the *Nationalverein*', though agreeing with the other elements of a joint liberal programme, Heinrich Ancker and ten other deputies seceded on 2 March 1861 to form a separate group, for which, as the Frankfurt liberal newspaper *Zeit* later put it, 'the policy of the liberal era was inadequate, and inadequate primarily on national grounds'.[25] After Schulze-Delitzsch joined the faction on 15 March, having gained a seat in a by-election, the *Nationalverein* became involved in organising the faction into what Schulze termed a 'national party'.[26] The name eventually agreed, after a meeting of Schulze, Hoverbeck and Forckenbeck from the faction with Unruh, Mommsen, Virchow and the editors of the *National-Zeitung* and the *Volks-Zeitung*, which served as the principal organs of the *Nationalverein*, was the '*Deutsche Fortschrittspartei*', embodying the national and progressive aims of its founders. Although its initial organisational task was to prepare for the December elections in Prussia, the first point in its founding programme of 6 June 1861 – and its ideological priority – imitated that of the National Association, calling for the 'secure unification of Germany' with 'a strong central power in the hands of Prussia' and a 'common German national assembly (*Volksvertretung*)'.[27] To Schulze and other leaders, the Progressive Party and the *Nationalverein* were complementary. In March 1862, the two organisations even convened their committee meetings in the same Berlin hotel.[28]

Table 5.3   Meeting places and dates of Annual General Meetings

	Kongress Deutscher Volkswirte	Nationalverein	Deutscher Handelstag	Abgeordnetentag
1858	Gotha (20–23 Sept.)			
1859	Frankfurt (12–15 Sept.)			
1860	Cologne (10–14 Sept.)	Coburg (3–5 Sept.)		
1861	Stuttgart (9–12 Sept.)	Heidelberg (23–24 Aug.)	Heidelberg (13–18 May)	
1862	Weimar (8–11 Nov.)	Coburg (6–7 Oct.)	Munich (14–18 Oct.)	Weimar (28–29 Sept.)
1863	Dresden (14–16 Sept.)	Leipzig (16 Oct.)	Frankfurt (21–22 Aug., 21 Dec.)	Frankfurt (1 Oct.)
1864	Hanover (22–25 Sept.)	Eisenach (31 Oct.–1 Nov.)		
1865	Nuremberg (28–31 Aug.)	Frankfurt (29 Oct.)	Frankfurt (25–28 Sept.)	
1866				Frankfurt (20 May)
1867	Hamburg (26–29 Aug.)	Cassel (11 Nov.)		

Source: A. Biefang, Politisches Bürgertum, 304.

The national question was not simply appended to the professional, commercial and political programmes of the mushrooming associations of the 1860s, it was intrinsic to them. To Schulze-Delitzsch, all the associations belonged to a wider 'national movement' or, even, 'national party'.[29] They were part of an attempt to coordinate the liberal and democratic parties and broader social milieux in support of a common national cause (see Table 5.4). 'Within a few months', proclaimed the first pamphlet of the

Nationalverein, written by Schulze in December 1859, 'we have achieved what could not even be imagined in the course of the previous decade: the unification of the liberal parties, the joining of forces of constitutionalists and democrats from the most diverse individual German states through the constitution of a national party'.[30] Against the socialist Stephan Born's charge at the Heidelberg meeting of the *Nationalverein* on 24 August 1861 that Germans were too used to waiting, 'in all matters, for impulses from above', Schulze countered that the London exile had 'left his residence in the fatherland and, therefore, he could not know of the important transformation which had taken place in Germany in this respect over recent years and which alone made the establishment of the *Nationalverein* possible'.[31] In his 'defence of the national movement as well as of the German *Volk*', the Berlin leader of the National Association and *Fortschrittspartei* pointed out to those who had left Germany in 1848 that 'things no longer stand as they did at the time when they left us', with the 'great signs of the times which are declared in associations and free cooperatives, which are manifest in all spheres of public life'.[32] Politics in its entirety was to be considered in a national light. In the foundation of the Progressive Party, 'the German *Volk*, which can be alienated from the Prussian government but no longer from the Prussian *Volk*, knows that the future of Prussia can only lie in free development, and that this must be secured in Prussia for the whole of Germany,' ran the declaration of the central electoral committee in March 1862: 'The current of public opinion is favourable to this development, and the Prussian people has an opportunity to do something for the cause of progress in Europe.'[33]

As Unruh declared in a famous essay – 'Was hat Preussen zunächst in der deutschen Sache zu tun?' – in the *Deutsche Jahrbücher* in September 1861, it was obvious that the 'current condition of Germany and of Prussia' was 'completely unsustainable in the long term':

> The Holy Alliance created these conditions, and with the dissolution of the Holy Alliance by Louis Napoleon, the artificial, unnatural edifice of Germany strained and snapped in all its joints ... Only Prussia can construct the new building, and it has the sacred duty of doing so ... The urge of the German *Volk* towards state unity, power and security is not revolutionary, but moral and justified. The right to be a *Volk* again is so primordial,

so timeless and inalienable, of such divine origin, that the right of princes to keep Germany fragmented and dependent on foreign lands cannot oppose it ... The German *Volk* demands nothing new, something which never existed; it is asking for that which it possessed for a thousand years ... Without Germany, there is no political future for Prussia and the Hohenzollern dynasty, and without Prussia, Germany will succumb unfailingly to the fate of Poland ... The most daring policy is the most certain and least dangerous for Prussia.[34]

To the founders of the *Fortschrittspartei*, the interests of the Prussian people, like those of other German populations, were identical to those of Germany. The *Abgeordnetentag* intended to unite these populations through their party representatives in a form of German *Vorparlament*. In a similar vein, the free-trade *Kongress deutscher Volkswirte* aimed, in the words of one of its leaders, to represent, 'not single estates, but the economic interests ... of the entire German fatherland', and the *Deutscher Handelstag*, which was a federal organisation of individual chambers of commerce, hoped to achieve 'unity in a commercial context', since economic unity, unlike its political counterpart, did not affect the sovereign rights of the German princes', in the estimation of its founder.[35] As in 1848, leaders anticipated the creation of a German market, National Assembly and central power.

The striking confidence of liberal leaders in advancing their national claims after 1858, in contrast to their hesitancy during the 1850s, was partly the corollary of large-scale democratic participation in politics for the first time since 1849. Accordingly, new national associations could claim with greater conviction that they represented the entire *Volk* against bureaucratic 'absolutism' and the sectional interests of what Unruh termed 'the successors of the feudal estates' at the Court.[36] As Schulze-Delitzsch – a democratic-leaning left liberal himself – wrote to Biedermann in June 1859, 'the introduction of the *Reichsverfassung* [of 1849] would be right in my opinion; the whole democratic party in Prussia, with the exception of a few radicals who scarcely come into consideration, could be won over'.[37] For his part, Biedermann believed that democrats as well as liberals in both the North and the South constituted 'the voice of the nation (*Nation*)', legitimating the policies of the *Nationalverein*.[38] As long as the association did 'not leave the path of legality', it was assured 'the support of public opinion in Germany',

both democratic and liberal.[39] While it is true that membership
dues of 1.45 Gulden excluded the majority of the lower orders and
students, ensuring that it was dominated by men 'at the centre of
political life', in Bennigsen's phrase, the National Association
nonetheless went to considerable lengths to foster and protect
workers' organisations, subsidising the *Verband Deutscher
Arbeitervereine* and paying for a delegation of workers to go to the
World Exhibition in London in 1862, for example.[40] Similarly, it
sought to represent other mass-membership national associations
such as those of gymnasts, marksmen and choristers in the belief
that 'it is not their job to concern themselves with politics', as
Miquel put it at one regional *Turnfest* in 1863.[41] Despite the social
exclusivity of their leadership, with 40 per cent of Prussian deputies
of the *Fortschrittspartei* in 1862 coming from the civil service, 20.7
per cent from the liberal professions, and 9.6 per cent each from
estate-owners and merchants and manufacturers, national organisations could not afford – in terms of their finances and their legitimacy – to ignore wider society. For this reason, wrote
Schulze-Delitzsch to Freytag in October 1859, the *Nationalverein*
could not be a secret society, as the Duke of Saxe-Coburg-Gotha had
proposed; rather, it had to be 'an open form of association', if it
were 'to achieve a practical, enduring effectiveness'.[42] Openness
was essential for the association because it nurtured 'the feeling of
justification and of trust in our cause' and because it obliged 'the
Volk' to 'show the necessary moral strength to avail itself, in the face
of unpopularity, of its legal rights, within legal limits':

> The association is a test both upwards and downwards. Our *Volk*
> must get used to such agitation in the fullest openness and legal-
> ity, and namely also bring along the necessary means, without
> which the lasting pursuit of such aims is impossible. Not a revo-
> lution, but a cash-box! Either something important will come
> from the seed sown or nothing at all; there is no middle way for
> me, and I only desire to be in a position to devote all my time and
> energy to the movement.[43]

The 'national movement' had to be popular and democratic in the
broad sense of the words.

The re-entry of large numbers of democrats into German assemblies after 1858 signalled the return of popular politics, recalling
the fact that they had come to dominate the Frankfurt parliament

Table 5.4 Committee members of national associations

	Kongress Deutscher Volkswirte	National-verein	Deutscher Handelstag	Abgeord-netentag
Albrecht, S. W. (Hanover)	✖			
Barth, K. (Erlangen/Augsburg)				✖
Barth, M. (Erlangen)				✖
Baudissin, E. (Friedrichshof)				✖
Beckerath, H. von (Krefeld)			✖	
Behrend, H. (Danzig)		✖	✖	✖
Bennigsen, R. von (Bennigsen)	✖	✖		✖
Bering, M. (Leipzig)		✖		
Biedermann, K. (Leipzig)	✖			
Billing, C. (Munich)	✖			
Bluntschli, J. K. (Heidelberg)				✖
Bockelmann, J. C. (Retwischhöh)				✖
Böhmert, V. (Bremen)	✖			
Brater, K. (Frankfurt)		✖	✖	
Braun, K. (Wiesbaden)	✖			✖
Carnall, D. von (Breslau)	✖			
Cetto, K. (St Wendel)		✖		✖
Christmann, R. (Dürkheim)				✖
Cichorius, T. (Leipzig)				✖
Classen-Kappelmann, J. (Cologne)	✖	✖	✖	
Crämer, K. (Nuremberg)		✖		✖
Delbrück, A. (Berlin)		✖		
Deneke, K. (Magdeburg)			✖	
Dietrich, G. (Berlin)			✖	
Duncker, F. (Berlin)		✖		✖
Faucher, J. (Frankfurt)	✖			
Fetzer, K. A. (Stuttgart)				✖
Feustel, F. (Augsburg)				✖
Finckh, K. (Reutlingen)			✖	
Forckenbeck, M. (Berlin)		✖		
Francke, K. (Coburg)	✖			
Fries, H. (Weimar)		✖		
Georgii, T. (Esslingen)		✖		
Godeffroy, A. (Hamburg)				✖
Götte, K. (Hamburg)		✖		
Golden, K. (Zweibrücken)				✖
Gourdé, L. (Wiesbaden)		✖		

Table 5.4   Continued

	Kongress Deutscher Volkswirte	National- verein	Deutscher Handelstag	Abgeord- netentag
Grumbrecht, A. (Harburg)	✖			
Haberkorn, L. (Camenz)				✖
Hänle, L. (Munich)			✖	
Häusser, L. (Heidelberg)				✖
Hansemann, D. (Berlin)			✖	
Hansen, A. (Grumbye)				✖
Henneberg, F. W. (Gotha)				✖
Hertel, A. von (Augsburg)			✖	
Heyner, J. (Leipzig)				
Hölder, J. (Stuttgart)				
Hopf, J. (Heidelberg)		✖		
Hoverbeck, L. (Nickelsdorf)				✖
Hurtzig, F. (Hanover)	✖			
Jacoby, J. (Königsberg)		✖		✖
Jessen, P. (Altona)			✖	
Jordan, L. A. (Deidesheim)		✖		✖
Joseph, H. (Leipzig)		✖		
Jung, J. G. (Cologne)			✖	
Jungermann, W. (Cassel)				✖
Kerstorff, (Augsburg)				✖
Knies, K. (Heidelberg)		✖		
Knorr, J. (Munich)	✖			
Ladenburg, L. (Mannheim)				✖
Lammers, A. (Bremen)	✖			
Lang (Plauen)		✖		
Lang, F. (Wiesbaden)		✖		
Lehmann, T. (Kiel)				✖
Lette, W. A. (Berlin)		✖		✖
Leue, F. G. (Cologne)		✖		
Liebermann, B. (Berlin)	✖			✖
Limburger, B. (Leipzig)		✖		
Lorenz, M. (Leipzig)			✖	
Löwe-Calbe, W. (Berlin)			✖	
Lüning, O. (Rheda)		✖		
Macowiczka, F. (Erlangen)		✖		✖
Mammen, F. A. (Plauen)		✖		✖
Mayer, G. (Leipzig)	✖			

Table 5.4   Continued

	Kongress Deutscher Volkswirte	National-verein	Deutscher Handelstag	Abgeord-netentag
Meier, H. H. (Bremen)				✖
Metz, A. (Darmstadt)		✖		
Michaelis, O. (Berlin)			✖	
Miquel, J. (Göttingen)		✖		
Molinari, T. (Breslau)	✖			
Moll, E. (Mannheim)		✖		✖
Müllensiefen, T. (Crengeld.)		✖		
Müller, G. (Stuttgart)			✖	
Müller, S. (Stuttgart)		✖		
Nagel, L. (Frankfurt)	✖			
Nebelthau, F. (Cassel)	✖	✖	✖	
Niebour, A. (Oldenburg)		✖		
Oberländer, L. (Coburg)				✖
Oberleithner, K. (Schönberg)		✖		
Oetker, F. (Cassel)				✖
Passavant, F. E. (Frankfurt)			✖	
Patow, R. von (Berlin)		✖		✖
Pauli, F. (Cologne)				✖
Pfeiffer, F. (Bremen)	✖			
Pickford, E. (Konstanz)				✖
Planck, G. (Göttingen)				✖
Preetorius, C. (Alzey)	✖			
Prince-Smith, J. (Berlin)				✖
Puscher, W. (Nuremberg)		✖		
Reincke, T. (Altona)	✖			
Rentzsch, H. (Dresden)			✖	
Reuter, F. W. (Braunschweig)			✖	
Reventlow, L. (Kiel)				
Rewitzer, F. X. (Chemnitz)				
Reyscher, A. L. (Cannstatt)	✖			
Riesser, G. (Hamburg)			✖	
Rochau, L. A. (Heidelberg)		✖		
Röpell, K. (Danzig)	✖			
Rose, M. (Leipzig)		✖		
Ross, E. D. (Hamburg)		✖		

Table 5.4   Continued

	Kongress Deutscher Volkswirte	National-verein	Deutscher Handelstag	Abgeord-netentag
Rückert, K. (Coburg)		✖		
Rückert, L. (Coburg)	✖			
Sattler, J. (Schweinfurt)		✖		
Schenck, F. (Wiesbaden)			✖	
Scherbius, G. (Frankfurt)		✖		
Schramm, K. A. (Dresden)		✖		
Schröder, G. F. H. (Mannheim)			✖	
Schubert, F. W. (Königsberg)		✖		
Schulze-Delitzsch, H. (Potsdam)			✖	
Seeger, A. (Stuttgart)			✖	
Seeger, L. (Stuttgart)	✖			
Soetbeer, A. (Hamburg)	✖			
Sonnemann, L. (Frankfurt)	✖	✖		✖
Stahlberg, P. J. (Stettin)		✖		✖
Steinbeis, F. (Stuttgart)				✖
Strackerjahn, L. (Oldenburg)	✖		✖	
Streit, F. (Coburg)	✖			
Sybel, H. von (Bonn)			✖	
Tafel, G. (Stuttgart)	✖			
Twesten, K. (Berlin)	✖			
Unruh, H. V. (Berlin)		✖		✖
Varrentrapp, G. (Frankfurt)			✖	✖
Veit, M. (Berlin)				✖
Vieweg, E. (Braunschweig)				✖
Völk, J. (Augsburg)		✖		✖
Weigel, H. (Breslau/Cassel)	✖			✖
Wertheim, F. von (Vienna)		✖		
Wesenfeld, K. L. (Elberfeld)				✖
Wichmann, N. D. (Hamburg)				✖
Wiggers, E. (Rendsburg)	✖		✖	
Wiggers, M. (Rostock)			✖	
Wirth, M. (Frankfurt)			✖	
Wolff, O.	✖			

Source: Compiled from data taken from A. Biefang, Politisches Bürgertum, *448–55.*

in 1848–49. Before the revolution, contended the Catholic *Historisch-politische Blätter* in 1858, liberals had been weak, requiring an alliance with democrats in order to appear popular and legitimate, only to be abandoned by radicals in 1848 after failing to harness revolutionary forces.[44] In the political turmoil of the revolution and the early 1850s, the *Grenzboten* had remarked in 1854, party affiliations and labels had been conflated, with many democrats going into exile and those who remained in Germany adopting different names, such as '*Mittelpartei*'.[45] After 1858, it seemed to many contemporaries, the old boundaries between parties would be re-established. Whereas liberals appeared to the Leipzig periodical to have no principles, returning democrats were unambiguously in favour of universal suffrage and popular sovereignty, attempting – in the opinion of the old liberal Constantin Rössler – to secure the predominance of a popular assembly by purely mechanical means.[46] Other publications pointed out that democrats tended to be proponents of *Grossdeutschland*, contrasting with the 'small German' proclivities of liberals.[47]

By the 1860s, such radicals, it appeared, were closely connected to the *Nationalverein*, the *Fortschrittspartei* and the left-wing factions of many individual *Landtage*. Of the 88 democratic deputies of the National Assembly who went on to serve in *Landtage* and the *Reichstag* between 1849 and the 1880s, at least 36, or 41 per cent, were active between 1858 and 1866, including Gabriel Riesser (Hamburg), Bruno Hildebrand (Saxony-Weimar), Georg Friedrich Kolb (Bavaria), Johann Jacoby (Prussia), Wilhelm Löwe-Calbe (Prussia), Moriz Mohl (Württemberg), Friedrich Rödinger (Württemberg), Friedrich Siegmund Jucho (Frankfurt), and Jodokus Temme (Prussia).[48] At least 16 radical forty-eighters were actively involved in the establishment of the *Nationalverein* – Biedermann, Freudentheil, Grumbrecht, Heldmann, Julius Hoffmann, Jacoby, Joseph, Ludwig Müller, Nauwerck, Nicol, Riesser, Schaffrath, Christian Schüler, Titus, Venedey and Ziegert – with others such as Wigard, Vogt, Nägele and Fetzer joining later. Many more young democrats also participated. A similar number of radicals were active in the committee of the *Abgeordnetentag*.[49] In the absence of clarity over liberal doctrine, they were believed by some observers to have become the dominant force on the left, 'driven by the attraction of the new towards changes' and opposed by conservatives, 'who support the old and the inherited'.[50] Other commentators, such as the liberal Robert von Mohl, did not believe that democrats had eclipsed the liberals, but they thought that radicals had remained separate, creating fear within the *Bürgertum* by their courting of the 'masses'.[51] The number of republicans, Mohl asserted, had actually increased by 1859, compared to 1848.[52] Conservatives like Constantin Frantz, who had been employed by Manteuffel, were less guarded in the identification of 'democracy' as a distinct and menacing enemy, promoting centralisation, espousing a levelling equality and seeking to revolutionise the state.[53]

To many contemporaries, the distinction between democrats and liberals was blurred. Certainly, a radical such as Ludwig Bamberger, in exile in Paris but making regular trips to Germany, considered the political struggles of the 1860s, of which he felt himself a part, a liberal matter – 'the great fight of the Prussian liberals' – and an educated, middle-class one: 'In the first half of the 60s, Germany and especially Prussia still stood under the banner of the military conflict [with the Bismarck administration], but, in spite of all the prosecutions of the press and breaches of the constitution, how free and lively the excitement of minds was, what an ideal impulse affected the whole of the educated *Bürgertum*.'[54] Bamberger's contacts in Germany – Unruh, Oetker, Karl Mayer, Heinrich Simon, Jacoby – were liberal as well as democratic. As Jacoby spelled out in his two speeches on 'the foundations of Prussian democracy' in November 1858, radicals were compelled, not 'to chase unattainable political ideals', but to work 'within the monarchical and constitutional form of government in the way offered by the constitution of the Prussian land'.[55] Other democrats such as Benedikt Waldeck agreed, abiding by the Prussian constitution and joining the *Fortschrittspartei*.[56] The main political division, it seemed, ran through the liberal camp, pitting – as Rössler lamented – 'old liberals' against Progressives, or it served to unite liberals and democrats against a common conservative foe, which backed Bismarck and Wilhelm I against the *Abgeordnetenhaus*.[57] To the *Grenzboten*, in 1861, it was evident that the liberal parties were split, as in 1848, and that the *Fortschrittspartei* had come to oppose 'the previous liberal majority' as 'a collection of traitors' or 'academics', 'who know a lot, but desire little'.[58] The old distinctions were further confused by the fact that the liberals and some democrats, but not all, were monarchists.[59] From the other side of the traditional divide, the *Social-Demokrat* acknowledged that both liberals – 'Gotha' – and democrats in North Germany had united behind *Kleindeutschland*, reversing the 'greater German' democratic majority of 1849.[60] They were also eventually joined, the same newspaper conceded in January 1865, by South German democrats, leaving the 'greater Germans' a weak, right-wing rump.[61] The only radicals still supporting *Grossdeutschland* were old democrats from central Germany, claimed the social-democratic publication.[62] Despite alluding to different sources of disagreement between middle-class liberals and populist democrats, the *Historisch-politische Blätter*, which was initially in favour of 'greater Germany', likewise recognised that the two camps – democratic and liberal – had temporarily been reconciled in a joint renunciation of revolution, the princes and the notion of *Grossdeutschland*.[63]

Democrats and liberals cooperated in the early 1860s by resurrecting their constitutional and political plan for a nation-state of 1849. For radicals such as Ludwig Walesrode, writing to Ferdinand Lassalle in July 1860, it was essential for '*die Demokratie*' to 'force the *Gothaer*' towards 'recognition of the revolution of 1848'.[64] The main foundation for such recognition, as a circular to democrats from Tafel, Adolph Rossmässler, Kolb, Christian Heldmann, Rudolf Christmann and Ludwig Reinhard in the summer of 1862 spelled out, was the *Reichsverfassung* of 1849, which was held still to be in force and legally binding:

In view of the attempt taking place to build an assembly, which is to be a *Vorparlament* in all but name, and in view of the entire situation of the fatherland, the challenge faces those members of parliament who are still in legal possession of their mandate to unite again, initially for a private conversation.

We are still the only ones who have received a mandate directly from the German nation. Not only is this mandate not yet formally dissolved, not only do we possess a special external right, before all others, to concern ourselves with the affairs of the fatherland – but it is also, after all that has happened and namely after a special parliamentary decision (from 30 April 1849...), our special duty carefully to keep all the political changes of the time in view and to this end to remain on alert.[65]

Although the plan came to nought, Löwe, Heinrich Bernhard Oppenheim and other radicals 'not only returned to Germany', with such ambitions in mind, 'but to participation in a newly-awoken political life', remarked Bamberger.[66] To Heinrich Simon shortly before his death in 1860, democrats should openly champion the

Reich constitution of 1849 in order to alter the *Nationalverein*'s defensive stance: 'it is ... our duty to hold the banner high, around which all friends of the fatherland should unite. It was dearly won in the years 1848 and 1849: *the German Reichsverfassung!*[67] 'Until the German *Volk* has spoken in its second parliament', there could be no other 'legitimate banner for Germany', he continued: '*every* other tends, consciously or unconsciously, towards particularist betrayal (*Sonderbündelei*), not towards the unification of Germany.'[68] After consulting with Jacoby and Tafel as surviving members of the Rump Parliament's committee of fifteen 'for implementing the *Reichverfassung*', the leadership of the *Nationalverein* reported to the general meeting of 4 September 1860 that the time had not yet arrived to put forward 'the Reich constitution as a banner'.[69]

The majority of liberals, like the committee of the National Association, were well disposed towards a revival of the agreement of 1849, however, with even conservative-minded liberals such as Hermann Baumgarten and Karl Francke speaking in favour of its inclusion in the *Nationalverein*'s programme.[70] At the end of May 1860, Fedor Streit, although still not personally convinced of the wisdom of adopting the constitution, admitted that it 'rests on a compromise of all parties', that it was legally binding, that 'no party can put up serious opposition to it (including the Prussians) in the current situation', that it allowed the *Nationalverein* a way out of the 'fatal question of [Prussian] hegemony', and that 'the masses' would see it as a 'shibboleth', 'if they should be put into motion'.[71] Schulze-Delitzsch had written to Biedermann as early as June 1859 that the introduction of the Reich constitution would be 'quite right', in his opinion.[72] To Adolf Seeger, it was tantamount to a Magna Carta of the German people.[73] As Vienna, together with assorted *Grossdeutsche*, attempted to organise a meeting in 1862, which even the radical critic of Berlin Jakob Venedey discounted as 'an anti-parliament', Streit and other leaders of the *Nationalverein* began to champion the *Reichsverfassung*: 'They put forward an assembly of delegates – we demand the Reich constitution of 1849.'[74] In October 1862, the National Association adopted the reintroduction of the revolutionary constitution as its policy:

Only one thing corresponds to the legal consciousness of the nation and its demand for power and freedom: the implementa-tion of the *Reichsverfassung* of 28 March 1849, complete with basic rights and electoral law, as they were decided by the legally

elected representatives of the German *Volk*. To press, with seriousness and force, for the realisation of this law, above all the
convocation of a parliament, elected according to the regulations
of the Reich electoral law, is the task of the national party.[75]

Copies of the constitution were disseminated throughout Germany,
along with 25,000 pamphlets on its history and actual significance.
Meetings to publicise its adoption were held in Frankfurt, Stuttgart,
Nuremberg, Munich, Bremen, Osnabrück, Braunschweig,
Hamburg, Breslau, Danzig, Frankfurt an der Oder, Königsberg,
Stettin, Leipzig, Nassau, Heidelberg, Giessen, Mannheim,
Pforzheim, Darmstadt, and Mülheim. The memory of 1849 was still
vivid in 1862.

From a liberal point of view, democrats had come fully to accept
the terms of their revolutionary agreement in March 1849.[76] In
return for a German nation-state, a National Assembly, universal
manhood suffrage, a German central government, and a merely
suspensive veto for the Kaiser, the majority of radicals were willing
to countenance the continuance of monarchy, a degree of federalism, the primacy of Prussia, and a constitutional regime of checks
and balances vis-à-vis the executive. All of these elements had been
present in March 1849, as the Frankfurt Parliament had voted for
the *Reich* constitution and a Prussian *Kaiser*, but they had been
opposed by a majority of democrats, as the *Reichsverfassung* scraped
through a second reading by 267 votes to 263. Now, the agreement
of most democrats appeared more whole-hearted, noted Unruh in
August 1859. The talks at Eisenach leading to the foundation of the
Nationalverein 'conspicuously documented the greatest advances in
political education and political tact in Germany':

> By designating themselves members of the earlier democratic
> party and by outlining a programme which every friend of the
> fatherland can join, the men who met in Eisenach wanted not
> only to get closer to other free-thinking parties, but to join
> together in a great national party ... The difference between now
> and 1848 was clear for all to see: no theorising, no dogmatic
> adherence to abstract principles, above all no phrase-making, just
> moderation in the judgement of diverging opinions, a powerful
> desire and an acute apprehension of factual conditions. One
> recognises without contradiction that the old dispute about *Gross-*
> and *Kleindeutschland* is completely impractical, that only the unifi-

cation of Germany through the leadership of Prussia, with the exclusion of Austria and its German provinces, can be striven for.[77]

In Unruh's opinion, democrats – and public opinion more generally – could be persuaded to tolerate a Prussian-led unification of Germany, in all likelihood during wartime.[78]

Radicals themselves were often more sceptical than the liberal leader realised, continuing to express 'empathy' for 'the greater German standpoint', in the words of the forty-eighter and mayor of Harburg August Grumbrecht.[79] Yet most conceded 'realistically', like Grumbrecht, that schemes to include the Habsburg monarchy in Germany were 'fantasies'.[80] When pressed, the leaders of the *Nationalverein* had explained that Austria was not formally excluded from Germany, but that it did not appear to wish to be included.[81] Likewise, the organising committee of the *Abgeordnetentag*, which included members with democratic backgrounds such as Hugo Fries, August Metz, Julius Hölder and Moritz Wiggers, allowed its moderate Badenese liberal chair Johann Kaspar Bluntschli to work towards the voluntary exclusion of Austrian deputies in 1862 because it could not see how Habsburg territories could take part in German unification. The majority of democrats, most of whom supported the *Abgeordnetentag*, effectively sanctioned this decision, with the radical press in states such as Württemberg coming to label the organisation '*freisinnig*' rather than '*kleindeutsch*', as in the past, and the meetings of the *Reformverein* '*reaktionär*' instead of '*grossdeutsch*'.[82] The symbols of the *Abgeordnetentag*, especially the assembly of August 1863 in the huge exhibition hall of the Frankfurt *Museumsgesellschaft*, were deliberately reminiscent of the Frankfurt Parliament, with speakers flanked by two large black, red and gold flags. It was referred to by Bennigsen in 1862 as the *Staatenhaus*, with the *Nationalverein* as the *Volkshaus*, of the future German *Bundesstaat* envisaged in the *Reich* constitution of 1849.[83]

The career of Ferdinand Lassalle reveals the extent to which democrats had compromised with liberals. The later founder of the *Allgemeiner Deutscher Arbeiterverein (ADAV)*, who changed his name from 'Lassal' to 'Lassalle' in homage to the French revolution, was contemptuous of the 'bourgeoisie' and of liberalism, partly as a reaction to his father, who was a liberal Jewish manufacturer in Breslau: 'He wants to let me study and outlines the pervasive holy idea that *he* calls liberalism! As if it was not precisely this which pushes me to study, this which I want to fight and without which I would have rather stayed what I am!'[84] As soon as the 'iron pressure' of the reaction relented slightly in 1858, the 'people here swarm for the new era and a conscientious prince and the law-abiding administration which has now come into being', he wrote to Karl Marx.[85] Even the *Volks-Zeitung*, 'the sole half-democratic paper', had become a government mouthpiece: 'All that expresses itself is this bourgeois cretinism', ran his report to Marx, who was, 'by the by, extraordinarily pleased' by it.[86] Liberals like 'Herr Julian Schmidt, der Literaturhistoriker', in the title of his satirical essay of March 1862, were typical of the 'mob of literati' which controlled the press and, therefore, political expression: they were 'a band of unknowing and thoughtless *Buben*, too ignorant to be elementary school teachers, too incapable and lazy to be postal clerks, and thus believing themselves called upon to pursue literature and the education of the *Volk*! They all too often dictate the great words of literature and politics, in newspapers and journals.'[87] To Lassalle, Wilhelm Adolf Lette, the President of the Prussian second chamber whom the radical had met at the Berlin Philosophical Society in 1857, characterised the weakness of liberal 'opposition': 'I could not depict our entire misery in the chamber more clearly in microcosm than in this well-meaning, waffling, weak little man.'[88]

Liberals seemed superficial and ineffective, without principles or a sense of historical movement. Like Marx, with whom he collaborated on the radical *Neue Rheinische Zeitung* in the late 1840s and with whom he corresponded in the 1850s and early 1860s, Lassalle was convinced by his reading of Hegel that history would move with certainty to an absolute end, benefiting a universal class of producers. 'I especially, who have been schooled in the Hegelian school, know best how one must, above all, wait for the right time', he ruminated in the 1840s, asserting that 'an individual can contribute to the quickening of an event in no other way than by spreading education and philosophy'.[89] Like other left-wing Hegelians, he doubted that the real or extant was rational, preferring to question the legitimacy of existing institutions and to test commonplace assumptions. Thus, his *System der erworbenen Rechte* (1861) showed how property and other 'rights' in positive law, all of which were condoned by liberals, were neither natural nor unalterable, but were contingent on society and historical development, to be superseded by 'will', power and the actions of a revolutionary state. As Lassalle accepted the logic of this position and took up the offer of Leipzig workers to form what became the *ADAV*, he recognised that he might become 'a dead man' to liberals and democrats, with the *Fortschrittspartei* rejoicing over his decision, 'since the bourgeoisie is very clear about it'.[90]

Lassalle's break with liberal and democratic milieux only occurred in 1863, however. Before making his decision, he canvassed the opinion of the democrat Franz Ziegler and the correspondent of the *National-Zeitung* Lothar Bucher: the former – 'only a political revolutionary and otherwise bourgeois' – advised him against leaving democratic circles within the *Nationalverein* and *Fortschrittspartei* on pain of becoming 'a dead man' and ruining himself forever; the latter was more circumspect, but he had already made up his own mind by moving towards the right, prior to being employed as an adviser by Bismarck in 1864.[91] Until the previous year, Lassalle had maintained contact with those on the democratic left and had generally referred to himself as a democrat.[92] He was critical of the Communist League's 'game of revolution with the workers', which 'serves no purpose' other than awakening 'their worst appetites' without any prospect of success, as he noted retrospectively in 1860.[93] Although disdainful of liberals, Lassalle was willing to join them in a common opposition. In 1848–49, he was – between spells in jail (February–August 1848, November 1848–July 1849) as a result of his involvement in the custody battles and divorce proceedings of Sophie von Hatzfeld – part of a broad democratic movement in Düsseldorf which included civil servants, artists such as the painter Lorenz Clasen, and merchants like Lorenz Cantador, who led the democrats. Meetings were moderate and national in tone, taking place under a black, red and gold banner, not republican or communist, as the *Düsseldorfer Journal* remarked:

> Herr Ferdinand Lassalle explained in the name of the *Volksklub* that he considered it necessary strenuously to deny the rumour that the *Volksklub* wanted to use the current crisis for the purpose of a red republic. At the present moment, it is a question of something quite different, it is a question of the protection of common freedoms, for the maintenance of which all parties must work together.[94]

Until 1854, he was largely preoccupied with the protracted defence of Hatzfeld, which he had taken up at the age of 20 in 1846 at the instigation of the Jewish democrat Felix Alexander Oppenheim, against an unjust legal system and an oppressive noble husband. He subsequently lived off the fees agreed by the Countess, in conjunction with funds from his father, briefly living with her in Düsseldorf between 1856 and 1857. The relationship, which was viewed as a distraction by socialists, helped to cement Lassalle's reputation as a parvenu and dilettante, dismissed by Marx and Engels as 'Baron Itzig', a 'Jewish baron or baroneted Jew (probably by the Countess)', and a 'Jewish nigger', 'descended from negroes' according to the evidence of 'the construction of his head and the growth of his hair'.[95]

During the 'New Era', after he had finally received permission to reside in Berlin indefinitely in 1859, Lassalle continued to cultivate his democratic contacts, living for a time with the radical publisher Franz Duncker – the brother of the head of the Prussian 'literary bureau', Max – and distancing himself from Marx's accusation in 1860 that the democratic leader Carl Vogt was a Bonapartist spy. Unlike Marx, he was willing to appear in the *Demokratische Studien*, published by the Hamburg radical Ludwig Walesrode, alongside Vogt and other democrats such as Heinrich Bernhard Oppenheim. Walesrode's aim, which he spelled out to Lassalle in 1860, was to prompt liberals to recognise the revolution and to 'join us on the ground of the *Reichsverfassung*', allowing 'the German *Volk* to become one through its basic rights' and encouraging the promotion of unity by 'the decidedly democratic press'.[96] Despite opposing the Reich constitution for its espousal of the principle of hereditary monarchy and for perpetuating a cult of legality, obscuring the fact that law merely reflected temporary relations of power, Lassalle went along with Walesrode's project and, if later rumours are to be believed, even toyed with the idea of standing as a Progressive deputy.[97] Certainly, he had entertained the possibility of standing as a democratic candidate for Düsseldorf in the Prussian second chamber in 1858, confident of winning the whole of the third class of voters and three-quarters of the second class, as he put it to Hatzfeld in a moment of self-delusion.[98] Whether in his unsuccessful attempt to persuade the liberal publishers Hermann and Eduard Brockhaus to resurrect the *Neue Rheinische Zeitung* in 1862 or in the identification of what Marx termed 'a dwarf like Schulze-Delitzsch' as 'the central point of his agitation' on behalf of the committee of Leipzig workers in 1863, Lassalle continued to define himself with reference to 'democracy' and the 'national opposition'.[99]

On important questions concerning the establishment of a German nation-state, Lassalle concurred with many liberals and democrats. The main statement of his position was a treatise on *Der italienische Krieg und die Aufgabe Preussens* (1859), by means of which he sought to signal his entry into Prussian and German politics. Tellingly, he published the pamphlet anonymously as 'a voice from democracy'. Like many of his counterparts, Lassalle found it difficult to use the crisis as a national rallying-point, given disagreements about whether to support Austria and whether to go to war. His argument about the legitimacy of Italian nationalism was widely shared in democratic circles, and beyond them, but its primacy in dictating German states' foreign policies was usually contested, except by radicals such as Arnold Ruge.[100] Many, including some from the South such as Karl Blind and others from the Rhineland such as Jakob Venedey, matched Lassalle's distaste for the Habsburg monarchy, recalling its role in propping up the repressive system of Metternich before 1848, but they balked at supporting France under Napoleon III, who was seen as an heir of the revolution and a champion of national independence by Lassalle. Nevertheless, the Düsseldorf radical replicated those central national tenets of German liberalism and democracy which had ensured that differences of emphasis had not derailed the national movement after 1859. Freedom and unity, he contended, were complementary: 'The principle of free, independent nationalities is therefore the basis and source, the mother and root of the very concept of democracy.'[101] 'This inner, conceptual relationship between the principle of free nationalities and democracy has expressed itself historically and tangibly often enough', he went on, accounting for the success of 1813 and the Prussian reform era, and the failure of 1848, when the defeat of one principle had undermined the viability of the other.[102]

Nations would, in the spirit of Mazzini, whom Lassalle much admired, coexist naturally, as powerful national cultures – activated by a coherent *Volksgeist* – imposed themselves through assimilation and, if necessary, by force at the expense of weaker entities. The Habsburg monarchy had failed in this respect and was doomed to disintegrate, ending a damaging dualism in Germany and making way for a Prussian-led nation-state. 'We have a striking example of how Austria is capable of assimilation,' Lassalle asserted: 'We refer to Bohemia's suffocated *Volksgeist*! What has become of this land, the mother of Protestantism, the cradle of the wars of the Hussites, the birthplace of the thirty-years' war of faith, what has become of it after hundreds of years of possession? The answer is: 'A suffocated, cowed *Volksgeist*.'[103] Although he acknowledged that 'in modern times' – 'when subjectivity and individualism, education and scepticism etc. have loosened this strict unity and convergence of the moral views of the *Volksgeist* present in individuals' – 'the ethical awareness of individuals belonging to the same state' had become fragmented and reliant on the hazard of reason and chance achievements instead of a 'general ethos of the *Volk*', he visibly regretted its absence and sought to shore up a national collectivity.[104] What was needed, he declared in a lecture 'Über Verfassungen' in April 1862, was to 'transform the real, actual relations of power in the land, to intervene in the executive, to intervene so much and transform it to such an extent that it will never again on its own be able to stand against the will of the nation – that was what was required at that time [in 1848 in Prussia], and what had been needed beforehand, so that a written constitution can endure'.[105] Since he was doubtful that simply sending 'a national parliament to Frankfurt again' would be able 'to make the impossible possible', he came to back the use of the Prussian state, even exalting a figure such as Friedrich the Great, to unify Germany or, at least, to entangle it in a war with France from which democracy would emerge stronger and 'the forces of the *Volk*' would be needed by the state.[106] Whereas 'Austria destroys Germany, Prussia and Germany complement each other', Lassalle concluded, echoing many other democrats and the majority of liberals.[107]

Liberals and liberalism dominated the revival of politics in German states after 1858 by promoting the establishment of a German nation-state according to a plan agreed in 1848–49. Even sceptical left-wing democrats such as Lassalle were convinced by these national elements of the liberal programme. Liberal notables such as Bennigsen, Bluntschli, Lette, Hansemann and Beckerath ran the principal national associations – the *Nationalverein*, the *Abgeordnetentag*, the *Juristentag*, the *Kongress Deutscher Volkswirte* and the *Deutscher Handelstag* – and liberal activists were preponderant in the organisations' committees. Their domination of national politics appeared to be social, political and economic. Sociologically, both the leadership and membership of the national associations and liberal parties came largely from the *Bürgertum*, granting them coherence, education and increasing wealth. At least 70 per cent of *Fortschrittspartei* deputies in 1862 were drawn from the civil service, liberal professions or commerce. One consequence was that the national and liberal milieu as a whole was perceived to be middle-class (see Table 5.5). Even during the revolution, the *Grenzboten* had noted in 1850, liberalism had been founded on the objectives of a single stratum whereas 'so-called democracy' had tried to represent those of several strata, leading to contradiction and conflict.[108] Party affiliations had been confused during and after the revolution, claimed the same publication in 1854, but anti-noble sentiment in the middle classes was deeply entrenched, helping to define liberalism, and class conflicts between middle-class liberals and lower-order democrats dictated policy and political oppositions in cities such as Leipzig.[109] After 1858, as liberal organisations began to cast themselves in a more inclusive light, such comments became less frequent in the liberal press, although they were concealed in injunctions to new, purportedly liberal ministries to oppose both feudal – or noble – and anarchist – or working-class – forces.[110]

In private, liberals were more candid, with Elben admitting of Stuttgart, for example, that 'the party system was very simple' in the 1850s, consisting of 'a victorious reaction' opposed by 'a liberal *Bürgertum*'.[111] The latter was 'newly strengthened' in the 'New Era', sometimes called 'liberal' and sometimes 'progressive', but its composition remained fundamentally unaltered (see Tables 5.5 and 5.6).[112] Those outside liberal circles confirmed such facts in a less flattering fashion. 'At the beginning of the constitutional system in Prussia, this inner division of the *Volk* into *bourgeoisie* and *people* did not yet exist, or at least not in the same measure as today,' remarked the *Historisch-politische Blätter* in 1855:

> Then, subordinate circles viewed the merchant, the factory lord and the great landowner as their natural representatives, because of their greater education and familiarity with their relations; they expected from these the representation of their own interests, and they joined without a second thought their liberal tendency and constitutional policy in the belief that these matters and endeavours were true and were also good for the *Volk* and its real needs. This opinion has gradually changed.[113]

Liberals' pursuit of the 'egoistic class interests' of the *Bürgertum* had estranged them from the rest of the population, rejoiced the Catholic publication, 'so that they no longer truly live in the *Volksgemeinschaft*.'[114] Gotha, repeated the publication ten years later,

Table 5.5 Social and occupational background of elected deputies in the Württemberg Landesversammlung (%)

	1849	1850	1851	1851–54	1856–61	1862–68	Zoll-parl.	1868–70
State official	17.1	20.0	18.5	29.7	22.5	25.00	5.55	23.0(17)
Communal official	15.6	15.7	17.0	22.6	30.1	23.80	16.70	19.2 (24)
Merchants, manufacts and bankers	6.2	8.6	9.2	9.5	14.0	12.50	33.30	16.6 (17)
Lawyers	21.9	20.0	23.1	16.6	18.3	21.20	27.80	11.5 (10)
Graduates (excl. civ.servs)	1.6	2.9	3.1	6.0	3.2	2.50	5.55	2.6 (7)
Priests	7.8	8.6	6.1	–	–	2.50	–	–
Teachers, professors	18.7	15.7	15.4	1.2	–	2.50	5.55	2.6 (3)
Editors	1.6	1.4	–	1.2	1.1	–	–	2.6
Landowners	1.6	1.4	1.5	6.0	3.2	2.50	5.55	6.4 (4)
Higher employees	–	–	–	2.4	1.1	–	–	– (2.9)
Bürgertum	**92.1**	**94.3**	**93.9**	**95.2**	**93.5**	**92.50**	**100.00**	**84.5**
Farmers	1.6	–	–	–	1.1	1.25		–
Innkeepers	4.7	1.4	1.5	1.2	–	–		6.4 (6)
Manual workers	–	4.3	4.6	3.6	4.3	1.25		2.6 (3)
Primary teachers	–	–	–	–	–	1.25		1.3 (1)
Master artisans	–	–	–	–	1.1	1.25		1.3 (1)
Kleinbürgertum	**6.3**	**5.7**	**6.1**	**4.8**	**6.5**	**5.00**		**11.6**
Ret. officers	1.6	–	–	–	–	1.25		2.6
Unknown	–	–	–	–	–	1.25		1.3

Sources: D. Langewiesche, Liberalismus und Demokratie in Württemberg zwischen Revolution und Reichsgründung (Düsseldorf, 1974), 225; H. Brandt, Parlamentarismus in Württemberg 1819–1870 (Düsseldorf, 1987), 68.
Note: Figures in brackets are from the latter's analysis of both chambers.

had become detached from the *Volk*, limited to civil servants and other members of the middle classes, yet it got on with no one precisely 'because it wants to be all in everything'.[115] To this end, the 'bourgeoisie' was even prepared to profit from the Prussian three-class franchise, which had given all 'political influence to one class, and indeed to the greediest and most unreliable one'.[116] Liberals appeared to have benefited from the class solidarity and increasing prosperity of the German middle classes. To their opponents, such class solidarity was likely in future to lead to isolation. To liberal supporters, solidarity facilitated the extension of the universal claims of the *Bürgertum* – particularly civil servants – to society as a whole.

Such claims to universality on the part of liberals were manifested, even critics agreed, in their national policy. The connection between the two creeds was not natural, remarked the *Historisch-politische Blätter* in 1858, but opportunistic, with national feelings to be found 'in the depths of the soul', close to the sources of religiosity and contradicting the superficial rationality of liberalism.[117] 'The national feeling of the Germans was suppressed but not extinct' during the Restoration after 1815, being reignited by France's threat to the Rhine in 1832, when

> the national feeling of the Germans re-emerged forcefully, as it always surfaces and imposes itself when a crisis breaks out. The liberals recognised this and they therefore immediately strengthened themselves through their sentiment for the fatherland. Such sentiment had no representatives, and as the liberal party put itself forward as such, it was quickly forgotten that it had earlier not recognised *German interests*. From then on, it soon appeared to the masses (*die Masse*) to be the opponent of arbitrariness, the protector of freedom and the representative of the national unity of the Germans, and it was joined by thousands upon thousands of highly honourable men, whose noble disposition outweighed the sharpness of their reason. Here lay the greatest strength of the party from now on.[118]

The fortunes of the liberal party subsequently waxed and waned, with liberals failing to harness the revolution in 1848 but benefiting from the unpopularity of particularism during 'The Interregnum of the Reaction', as one article put it in 1858.[119] Nationalism had been a mere theory in the early nineteenth century: liberals had popularised it and extended it to the realm of the state, with officials

Table 5.6 Social composition of the Prussian Abgeordnetenhaus, 1862

	Progressives		Other Liberals		Catholics		Conservatives		Total
Civil servants	54	40.0	74	49.3	15	45.4	7	63.6	43.2
Municipal	7	5.2	8	5.3	–	–	–	–	4.3
Admin.	2	1.5	17	11.3	3	9.1	7	63.6	8.2
Judges	34	25.2	43	28.7	11	33.3	–	–	25.6
Retired	11	8.1	6	4.0	1	3.0	–	–	5.1
Free professions	28	20.7	15	10.0	11	33.3	–	–	16.8
Professors, *Gymnasium*	6	4.4	4	2.7	3	9.1	–	–	3.7
Clergy	1	0.7	6	4.0	7	21.2	–	–	5.4
Lawyers	12	8.9	4	2.7	–	–	–	–	4.5
Graduates	9	6.7	1	0.6	1	3.0	–	–	3.1
Farmers (of which	28	20.7	43	28.7	5	15.2	4	36.4	27.2
landowners)	13	9.6	22	14.7	1	3.0	4	36.4	14.2
Artisans	3	2.2	2	1.3	–	–	–	–	1.4
Manufact.	6	4.4	1	0.6	–	–	–	–	2.0
Merchants	7	5.2	7	4.7	–	–	–	–	4.0
Rentiers	6	4.4	5	3.3	1	3.0	–	–	3.4
Unknown	3	2.2	3	2.0	1	3.0	–	–	2.0
Total	135	99.8	150	99.9	33	99.9	11	100.0	100.0
% of total		38.4		42.6		9.4		3.1	

Source: A. Hess, Das Parlament, das Bismarck widerstrebte (Cologne, 1964), 65–7; D. Langewiesche, Liberalism in Germany (Basingstoke, 2000), 118–19.

becoming liberal instruments in the process.[120] Since the states of the third Germany were not 'capable of life', the liberal party had backed Prussia from the revolution onwards, using its old foil of an impotent German Confederation with increasingly devastating effect 'because the national feeling of the Germans is more defined and more powerful than it was before'.[121] In a parallel movement, liberal parties had gained power state by state after 1830, first in the South and then in the North, partly by exploiting national phrase-ology in a demagogical and cynical way.

Having conquered the individual German lands through the ballot box, it was now in the liberal interest to demand a national assembly, which would give it power in the whole of Germany, declared the *Historisch-politische Blätter* in 1864.[122] To the Catholic periodical, this rise of liberalism was the result of chance, not histor-ical inevitability: liberals had gained support because of opposition to absolutism, the mistakes of individual governments, the lack of alternative organised parties, middle-class anxiety about revolution and democracy after 1848, criticism of particularism, fear of a French invasion in the 1850s and, especially, 'the most pressing desire of each German who loved his fatherland and who had a feeling for the honour of his nation (*Nation*)' that Germany 'would become strong and powerful, that the tribes would unite, and that the federal states would fashion themselves into one power'.[123] None of these events, or their exploitation by liberals, were inevitable, noted an article in 1866, yet they had ensured that liber-alism had come to the fore throughout Germany during the New Era.[124] Although emphasising the natural affinity between liberal and national ideas, most of the liberal press concurred with the substance of this analysis: liberals had become politically dominant by the late 1850s because of their support for a 'small German' nation-state.[125] In the critical election of 1861 in Prussia, both the *Grenzboten* and the *National-Zeitung* agreed with the decision of the 'out-and-out liberals' to put the nation-state first: 'We fully agree that the German question is placed at the top of the agenda; the centre of gravity of Prussian Progress is to be found here.'[126]

The *Zollverein* and the Economics of Unification

Prussia, it seemed to many liberals, could merge with Germany without colonisation or annexation. In the economic sphere, such

integration appeared to have long been in train after the establishment of the German Customs' Union (*Zollverein*) in 1833. Two sets
of renegotiations had taken place, one in 1852–53, when Vienna's
attempts to form a single customs area had been rebutted with the
postponement of discussions about a unification of tariffs until at
least 1860, and the other between 1862, after the signature of a
Franco-Prussian free-trade agreement, and 1865, when the *Zollverein*
was renewed without Austrian involvement. To Gustav Schmoller,
who was still an official in Württemberg in 1862 prior to being
appointed to a professorship in Halle two years later, Austria's entry
into the German Customs' Union was inconceivable.[127] Many others
agreed. In 1853 and 1865, the governments of the *Mittelstaaten* had
reluctantly acceded to Prussian terms after Austria had failed to
create a viable alternative market – given that the monarchy's
imports and exports in the early 1850s were only half the size of
those of the Prussian-led *Zollverein* – or to produce a reliable alternative source of revenue from tariffs, which was seen by administrations to be vital because of its independence of parliamentary
approval. Whereas Prussia received slightly less revenue from the
Custom's Union than was actually raised on Prussian goods, Bavaria
gained nearly three times and Hanover and Württemberg about two
times more than their imports and exports merited. Moreover, trade
between the Habsburg monarchy and the German Customs' Union
was more significant to the former than to the latter; in 1864,
Austrian exports to the *Zollverein* amounted to 70 million Taler and
imports from it 57 million Taler.[128] In purely economic terms, even
critics of Berlin such as the Tübingen national economist and deputy
Albert Schäffle recognised the inevitability of the *Zollverein*, the value
of the Franco-Prussian free-trade agreement and the strength of
Prussia's economic position.[129] Such facts seemed crucial to contemporaries – including Schäffle, who wanted to reconcile them with the
greater national good of *Grossdeutschland* – because economic and
political affairs had become more closely connected. 'It is a question
of shaping Germany – on the grounds and through the further
development of the existing *Handelsbund* – into an economic unit
and power which is designed to become a *Bundesstaat* or, in case this
comes about in another way, to dissolve it within the *Bundesstaat* and
to put at its disposal the means for its military, diplomatic and other
needs', commented the *Grenzboten* in 1860.[130]

Economic cooperation, promoted by Prussia, appeared to
presage national unity. For this reason, the writings of the econo-

mist Friedrich List provided an 'arsenal of weapons for one of today's parties, but also for the others', since his aim was 'to educate the nation until it could stand at the side of the other nations with the same rights'.[131] List had argued for free trade within a protected German market until German goods could compete with those of neighbouring states, after which point free trade could be extended across Europe. 'Thus, the tariff and toll borders in the interior of Germany, which treat the inhabitants of the other German states and of foreign states equally, must be regarded as constraints which allow the emergence neither of national well-being nor of national sentiment', ran an article in the same periodical in 1863: 'The freeing of indigenous industry, its rise to the level on which England stood, whose superiority List enviously admired rather than detested, was the practical goal of all his efforts which he saw in conjunction with – and as almost identical to – the political unification of the fatherland.'[132] The economist, continued the *Grenzboten*, had given 'the general, in many respects unclear, urge towards progress a real, practical content, and vague, for the most part Frenchifying, liberalism a genuinely national foundation', prophesying 'that economic unification must necessarily lead to national unity'.[133] The converse, however, was also true: economic ties were in themselves meaningless and fragile without a nation-state to protect and harness them. 'What are all these efforts worth, whether we are rulers or the ruled, from the aristocratic or *bürgerlich* order, soldiers or civilians, manufacturers, agriculturalists or merchants, without nationality and without a guarantee of the continuation of our nationality!', the article asked rhetorically.[134]

However 'imposing' and 'full of life' Austria was, it did not share 'our spirit, our interests, our background and education, our hopes and desires'; Prussia, by contrast, had the potential to extend a '*Zollverein* to the whole of Germany', to create a navy and a German parliament.[135] Most commentators concurred that the purpose of Prussia's championing of the *Zollverein* was political: to opponents such as Anton Edmund Wollheim da Fonseca, employed by the Austrian government, Berlin was acting cynically towards the political end of its own aggrandisement in Germany, damaging the industry and commercial interests of many German states without strengthening their 'material forces' and safeguarding 'their political independence'; to supporters such as the liberal deputy and *National-Zeitung* journalist Otto Michaelis, speaking on behalf of the Prussian *Landtag* commission on trade, finances and tariffs in 1862,

Prussia was acting 'as a state and as a *Volk*' with 'a German vocation'; likewise, to conservative correspondents of the *Kreuzzeitung*, Prussia alone was powerful enough to consolidate the links between the German states, to prop up an ailing *Bund* and to create German organisations outside the Confederation such as the Customs' Union.[136] Even publications like the *Berliner Revue* which did not believe that Germany could be unified, so different were the North and the South, nevertheless acknowledged that the Prussian government had created an internal market 'because it was believed that the basis of a future political unity could be found in the *Zollverein*'.[137]

Public opinion in most German states, although hardly uniform, backed a Prussian-led *Zollverein* as a matter of economic interest and as a precursor of national unity. Although the economic 'rise' of Prussia was not clear-cut, on the basis of statistics published at the time, the impression that the Habsburg monarchy was in economic difficulty or decline was widely believed (see Table 5.7). Public opinion was supported in its convictions about the economy by the German *Handelstag*, the *Kongress deutscher Volkswirte* and the *Nationalverein*, whose *Wochenschrift* declared in 1860 that the creation of a German market 'must, in return, have a unifying and reinforcing effect on the union of German state politics'.[138] North German states like Bremen, Hamburg, Mecklenburg and Hanover, which had joined the Customs' Union as late as 1854 for financial reasons, seemed to have little option but to back Berlin, however sceptical some sections of their populations were of Prussia.[139] 'As in the national question, so in the tariff question, the German nation will have to transfer leadership to Prussia, for without Prussia's powerful support it will have to postpone its hopes of victory indefinitely,' wrote the democrat Moritz Wiggers from Rostock: 'Luckily, in this question too, the interests of Prussia go hand in hand with those of the German nation.'[140] Badenese opinion seems to have followed the pro-Prussian line of its government.[141] Saxon deputies, despite opposition from protectionist landowners, supported the stance of the Interior Minister Richard von Friesen, trusting that he would 'do everything to maintain the *Zollverein*' in 1852.[142] Friesen's superior, the Foreign Minister and later Minister-President, Ferdinand von Beust was more critical of Prussia, but he acknowledged – according to his recollections – 'the disadvantages, indeed the impossibility, of withdrawing from the *Zollverein* with Prussia'.[143] In 1862, the debate was much more one-

Table 5.7   Economic Potential of Prussia and Austria, 1860–66

	Prussia	Austria
Population (millions)	19.3	37.5
Agricultural population (%)	45	70
Grain harvest (millions of tons)	0.8	0.7
Number of steam engines (millions of horsepower)	15,000 (0.8)	3,400 (0.1)
Coal production (millions of tons)	12	5.7
Pig iron production (millions of tons)	0.85	0.46
Railways (km)	3,698	6,895
Gross state income (millions of Thaler)	240	292
State debt (millions of Thaler)	290	1670
Military budget (millions of Thaler)	45	51
Education:		
Primary-school pupils (1860)	2,778,000	1,656,000
Secondary-school pupils (1860)	172,900	36,700
University students (1860)	12,400	8,000

Note: Figures refer to 1865–66, unless stated otherwise.
Source: H. Lutz, Zwischen Habsburg und Preussen. Deutschland 1815–1866 (Berlin, 1985), 330; J. Breuilly, Austria, Prussia and Germany, 1806–1871 (London, 2002), 100–2.

sided, with the majority of deputies following the lead of the government – since Beust and Friesen now agreed with each other – in recognising the Franco-Prussian free-trade agreement in advance of other German states. As the liberal forty-eighter Robert Georgi put it in his report on behalf of both chambers of the Saxon parliament, Austria was not prevented by the agreement from entering the German Customs' Union, but if it was not in a position to do so, which seemed likely, 'the material loss for the Zollverein and especially for Saxony would not be very significant' because 'reciprocal trade, even now, is not at all extensive'.[144] Although Saxon leaders were surprised in 1862 when Württemberg and Bavaria did not follow suit and back Prussia's trade agreement with France, with the majority of the public supporting their respective governments, they were reassured by later divisions of opinion – with four out of seven of Württemberg's delegates at the Deutscher Handelstag in October 1862 voting for the agreement – and by resigned public acceptance of the continuation of the Zollverein on Prussian terms, for want of a better alternative.[145]

Certainly, from his vantage point, the Saxon Finance Minister Friesen saw no reason to doubt that Prussia's policy on the Customs' Union would be accepted on the part of governments and publics alike:

The reputation which Austria still enjoyed at that time, its entire influence over German affairs, rested simply on the existence of the German *Bund*. The purely negative policy of Emperor Franz in the last phase of his government, whose main aim was to leave everything as it was domestically and to arrest – as much as possible – the new ideas, which preoccupied the world, at the Austrian border; the later, so light-headed financial policy of Bruck, who did virtually nothing to increase the productive forces of Austria ... looking on calmly at the relentlessly advancing financial collapse of the Reich instead ... finally, the unclear, perpetually vacillating and contradictory policy which Austria pursued after 1849 both abroad and at home – all this destroyed almost every sympathy for Austria in the public opinion of Germany and, more than all the efforts of Prussia, led to the alienation of the German people (*Volk*) from Austria and its movement towards an embrace with Prussia, which alone could be trusted to be capable of reasonably promoting the material interests of Germany and of having the power to realise national ideas.[146]

Even to a minister in one of the most pro-Austrian governments of the middling states, which constituted the principal source of opposition to Berlin in the 1850s and 1860s, there seemed to be little economic and political alternative to Prussian leadership in Germany over the long term. Such a realisation, however reluctant, characterised most sections of public opinion throughout the German lands. It could be seen in the muted and ambiguous public criticism of 'Prussia' during the rancorous constitutional crisis of the 1860s.

Bismarck and the Constitutional Crisis

Prussia was the object of most national reformers' hopes throughout the 1850s and early 1860s, in spite of Friedrich Wilhelm IV's rejection of a German imperial crown in 1849, the abandonment of the Erfurt Parliament in 1850 under pressure from Vienna and the subsequent emergence of the 'bureaucratic' and 'absolutist' administration of Manteuffel. The need for Prussian participation in the unification of Germany had been accepted by the majority of deputies – with a large number of radical dissenters – in the Frankfurt Parliament. The post-revolutionary decade reinforced such acceptance, given the opposition of the Habsburg monarchy, the weakness and confederal preoccupations of the *Mittelstaaten*, and the inefficacy and anachronism of the *Bund*. By the early 1860s, as a network of national organisations revived the agreements of 1848–49 and made use of a pre-existing German public sphere, as well as the national-minded factions and *Landtage* of the individual states, attention was increasingly focused on Berlin. Most of the enthusiasm about the 'New Era' related to a putative change of guard in Prussia, where Wilhelm had sworn an oath on 26 October 1858 to the Prussian constitution of 1850 shortly after accepting a regency of unlimited duration and had replaced the Manteuffel ministry with one led by the liberal Rudolf von Auerswald, who had been Minister-President of Prussia between June and September 1848. The Regent's message to the assembled ministry on 8 November concluded with the injunction for Prussia 'to make moral conquests in Germany through wise legislation in its own right, through the raising of all ethical elements and through the seizure of unifying elements, such as the tariff union, which must be subject to reform'.[147] 'The world must know that Prussia is ready to defend the law everywhere,' he continued: 'A firm, consistent and, when necessary, energetic conduct in politics, paired with intelligence and common sense, must create the political reputation and position of power for Prussia that it is not in a position to attain by means of its material power alone.'[148]

Little over a year later, the introduction by the Prussian War Minister Albrecht von Roon of a bill to increase the size of the army, lengthen military service to three years and disperse the more civic-spirited *Landwehr*, which was rejected by the *Abgeordnetenhaus* and then imposed by royal decree, appeared to have brought Prussia's liberal, constitutional and national credentials into question. The escalation of the crisis in 1860 and 1861 helped the opposition to victory in the elections of December 1861, with the liberals gaining 141 seats and the newly formed *Fortschrittspartei* 109, and in those of May 1862, in which the left centre, Progressive Party and other opponents of the government won 285 seats out of 352 seats (see Table 5.8). It also precipitated the fall of the liberal-conservative

Table 5.8   Political composition of the Prussian Abgeordnetenhaus, 1858–63

Party	1858 Seats	%	1861 Seats	%	1862 Seats	%	1863 Seats	%
Conservatives	47	13	14	4.0	11	3	35	10
Progressives	–		104	29.5	133	38	141	40
Other liberals:								
Vincke/Mathis	195	55	–		–		–	
Grambow	–		91	26.0	–		–	
Constitutionals	–		–		19		–	
Left Centre	–		48	14.0	96	27	106	30
Catholics	57	16	54	15.0	28	8	26	7
Poles	18	5	23	6.5	22	6	26	7
No faction	35	10	18	5.0	43	12	18	5
Total	352		352		352		352	

Source: H. Lutz, Zwischen Habsburg und Preussen, *428; W. Fischer et al.,*
Sozialgeschichtliches Arbeitsbuch I *(Munich, 1982), 238.*

ministry of Auerswald in March 1862 and the eventual appointment
of the ultra-reactionary Otto von Bismarck-Schönhausen in
September with the intention of pursuing the reform of the military
– according to Bismarck's recollection of his interview with the King
– 'even if against the majority of the *Landtag* and its decisions'.[149]
The Bismarck administration and the *Abgeordnetenhaus* remained
locked in conflict until the Minister-President's Indemnity Bill of
July 1866, during the war against Austria, which signalled a return
to constitutional government in exchange for a parliamentary
renunciation of retribution vis-à-vis the ministry. The question was:
how seriously did these events damage Prussia's reputation as a
champion of unification? How were the Prussian government and
Prussian society perceived, and how were national-minded and
liberal 'public opinion' and political parties viewed by Bismarck and
other ministers? Since the debate about the constitution of a
national polity had become the pivotal component of German unification after 1848, it was imperative that Prussia could be conceived
of as a constitutional state.

There were reasons to doubt the Hohenzollern monarchy's constitutional credit. Wilhelm, born in 1797 and therefore 61 on assuming the regency in 1858, had enjoyed a reputation as a reactionary in March 1848, advising the military suppression of the revolution. Although he changed his opinion in exile in Britain during the early summer, returning to be elected to the National Assembly in Berlin and professing his allegiance to the principles of a constitutional monarchy, he remained a conservative figure, eschewing any 'break with the past now or ever'.[150] In the words of his first speech as Regent to the new ministry in November 1858, he merely wished to act against arbitrary practices which ran counter to 'the needs of the time'.[151] His main task was to maintain the 'healthy, strong, conservative foundations' of Prussia and to counter the 'deliberately overwrought ideas' of the liberals.[152] By 1863, at the height of his battle with the parliamentary opposition, the King demonstrated the extent of his frustration with its overwrought ideas, as the Crown Prince Friedrich Wilhelm noted in his diary, after a private argument with his father:

Crown Prince:	I didn't want to express my doubts yesterday in front of the ministers. But what about the future?
King:	Repeated dissolutions, one after the other.
C. P.:	But to what end shall these measures finally lead?
King:	Obedience in the country, scaffold, possibly a rupture of the constitution by barricades in the streets and then naturally suspension of the same.
C. P.:	In Gastein, Bismarck spoke of the untenability of the constitution and of the coming necessity of its abandonment.
King:	The Kaiser of Austria and I are both convinced that in twenty years there will be no more constitutions.
C. P.:	What then?
King:	I don't know. I won't be alive then. But this abominable constitutional system can't continue; it will only bring about the destruction of royal authority and the introduction of a republic with a president as in England. The

> scoundrels of the opposition, like Schulze-
> Delitzsch, have to be shown who is King of
> Prussia.[153]

Wilhelm was shaped by his education in the army, which he had entered at the age of ten. In 1849, he had been made Governor General of the Rhineland and, in 1854, Governor of the *Bund* fortress of Mainz. According to Article 108 of the Prussian constitution of 1850, the army was not to take an oath to the constitution, but continued to swear 'a bodily oath' to the flag, pledging to serve the King of Prussia 'in all cases'.[154] The military sphere remained separate from politics in Wilhelm's mind as a solely royal prerogative. It was no coincidence that constitutional conflict in Prussia, which drove the new King to the point of abdication in 1862 rather than giving in to what he considered illegitimate parliamentary incursions into the jurisdiction of the monarch, centred on the reform of the army. The Regent's voluntary oath to the constitution in 1858, which Friedrich Wilhelm IV had advised against, in no way altered such a state of affairs, in Wilhelm's opinion, since the military was not a constitutional matter.

Bismarck concurred with the King that the ministers of Auerswald's administration had unjustifiably 'subjected themselves and [Wilhelm] to a parliamentary majority'.[155] In his interview with Wilhelm in September 1862 at Babelsberg, he was anxious to portray the conflict – even if with some exaggeration as a result of hindsight – as more than a party squabble over the extent of parliamentary scrutiny and the royal power of command over the army: 'I succeeded in convincing him that it was not a conservative or liberal question for him, of this or that hue, but concerned a monarchical regime or parliamentary rule, and that the latter was of necessity to be avoided, also by means of a period of dictatorship.'[156] Bismarck would 'rather fall with the king', 'even if Your Majesty should order something which I did not hold to be right', than 'leave Your Majesty in the lurch in a struggle with parliamentary rule'.[157] This fear of a 'parliamentary regime' had initially prompted Roon in June 1862, with the sanction of the King, to write to Bismarck in Paris, where he was a Prussian envoy, and to enquire about his willingness to become a minister.[158] Bismarck's reply on 2 July affirmed that he would remain true to his Prince 'up to and into the Vendée' of counter-revolution.[159] He believed that the Prussian government had been too 'liberal' and 'constitutional' at home and too 'legitimistic' abroad; his advice was to stand up to the opposition and 'to break with the chamber', dissolving it in order 'to show the nation how the king stands with respect to the people (*zu den Leuten*)'.[160] Promising to depart for Germany immediately, he refrained from 'putting on paper much of what I want to say', probably because it was more extreme.[161]

Bismarck was already by that time well-known in conservative circles for his unorthodoxy, having been a more traditional reactionary during the revolution. His admission to Roon that his anti-legitimist 'way of thinking' in foreign policy was 'so distant from that of our most gracious ruler' as to disqualify him from office went back to a dispute with the Gerlachs in the mid-1850s about the merits of Napoleon III.[162] Although he justifiably protested to Leopold von Gerlach that he was not a 'Bonapartist' wishing to combine new social forces in a plebiscitary fashion on the basis of the revolution, he was willing to cooperate with Napoleon diplomatically, against the 'legitimate' conservative powers of Austria and Russia, and to consider novel domestic alliances and forms of government. Certainly, he had given up his earlier hope of acting as the representative of a restored aristocratic, corporate, divine-right monarchy, cleansed of bureaucracy and absolutism, and he was willing, as his discussions with King Wilhelm showed, to contemplate the possibility of 'dictatorship'. 'One can accomplish a great deal even under a constitution by such ordinary means as fear, enticement and the like,' Bismarck declared to Ludwig von Gerlach in November 1862: 'If nothing avails, one can still resort to a *coup d'état*.'[163] During his first year in office, the Minister-President attempted to discipline 'political' civil servants, including the 40 per cent of Prussian deputies who were officials in 1862, to prevent soldiers from voting, and to muzzle the liberal press through the royal edict of June 1863, which granted the administration the power to ban – after two warnings – publications displaying a 'general attitude' 'dangerous to public welfare'.[164] To the liberal Crown Prince, who had publicly criticised Bismarck's press edict, the Minister-President lamented that the King believed in his oath to the constitution and that ministers acted 'conscientiously' in adhering to the letter of the *Verfassung*. 'What if conscience bids me not to respect it?' he asked provocatively.[165] Such a modern and unpredictable – but still uncompromisingly royalist and Prussian – stance understandably worried national-minded constitutionalists and liberals.

The conduct of Bismarck, Wilhelm and Roon during the crisis over the reform of the Prussian army during the 1860s seemed unconstitutional. Although it was true that increases in conscription, length of service and the role of the *Landwehr* lay within the traditional royal power of command, the rise in expenditure which they occasioned brought them within the purview of the chambers. When parliamentary approval was made conditional on the retention of a two-year – not three-year – military service and on the continued inclusion of a separate *Landwehr* in the army proper, Wilhelm introduced the full reforms by royal decree. The *Abgeordnetenhaus* avoided outright conflict over the issue in 1860 and 1861 by means of temporary financial legislation to cover the army's increased costs, but it refused any more increases in September 1862, after the pro-liberal and anti-government election results of December 1861 and May 1862. The Auerswald administration openly doubted whether it was authorised to govern on the basis of the existing budget, which the King believed continued to obtain in perpetuity. These were the circumstances in which Bismarck was appointed Minister-President and Foreign Minister, averting the abdication of the monarch and promising to support Wilhelm without reference, in the last resort, to the law or the constitution.

The new minister withdrew the budget for 1863 from parliamentary scrutiny, arguing publicly that the King had the right in an emergency, which had resulted from the lack of constitutional provision for the failure of an administration and the chambers to agree a budget, to avail himself of all the powers that had not specifically been allocated to other organs of state. As Bismarck put it on 27 January 1863, after the lower chamber had been dissolved in October of the previous year, in cases where compromise between the three law-giving powers of the monarch, *Herrenhaus* and *Abgeordnetenhaus* proved impossible, 'conflicts take its place, and conflicts ... become questions of power'.[166] 'Whoever has power in his hands then goes ahead in his own way, since the life of the state cannot, even for a moment, stand still', he went on.[167] For the Minister-President, this was a struggle between the 'Prussian monarchy', which had 'not yet fulfilled its mission' and which was not yet 'ready to become a purely ornamental decoration' of the 'constitutional edifice', and a 'parliamentary regime', in which the monarchy was destined to become 'a dead component in the mechanism'.[168] Lacking the legislation – despite a general reference in Article 61 of the constitution – to impeach ministers, the

Chamber of Deputies replied to Bismarck's actions with a belligerent address on 22 May 1863, having 'no means of reconciling itself
with this ministry' and withdrawing 'its joint responsibility for the
present policy of the government'.[169] Every negotiation had
convinced the majority of the house, continued the address, that 'a
rift exists between the advisers of the Crown and the country, which
can only be filled by means of a change of personnel and, even
more so, by means of a change of system'.[170] The popular assembly
had respected the rights and interests of the Crown, the statement
concluded, but 'the most important rights of the *Volksvertretung* have
been disrespected and injured'.[171] Bismarck governed until 1866
without submitting a budget to the chambers, dissolving the lower
house prematurely in May 1863 and February 1866. In the latter
instance, the Minister-President had prorogued the session himself
after parliamentary censure of an unconstitutional conviction of
Karl Twesten and John Peter Frentzel – upheld by a supreme court
packed with two conservative 'relief judges' – for speeches in the
Abgeordnetenhaus.[172] The government of Prussia, it appeared, was
acting illegally and was ill-suited to lead a constitutional reunifica-
tion of Germany.

The majority of Prussian politicians criticised Bismarck's break
with the constitution and refused to cooperate with the government. To Twesten, speaking in one of the main debates about the
reform of the army on 16 September 1862, a few days before the
Parisian envoy's appointment as Minister-President, it was already
evident that the government 'wants subjugation *sans phrase* to its will
or it desires a conflict'.[173] In liberal circles too, he contended, it was
said that the constitution should be put to the test, even at the risk
of its failure. When Bismarck had attended the budget committee of
the *Abgeordnetenhaus* on 30 September, having accepted the minister-presidency on 22 September, he had spoken informally, partly in
an attempt to ingratiate himself with the deputies, digressing in
what Roon called 'witty sallies' and revealing his anti-liberal
Realpolitik at the same time as hinting at a domestic truce through
the inclusion of moderate liberals in government, a possible two-
year period of military service and a renunciation of the lower
chamber's budgetary control over the army:

It is not to Prussia's liberalism that Germany looks, but to its
power; let Bavaria, Württemberg and Baden indulge in liberalism, no one will give them Prussia's part for that; Prussia must

collect and keep its strength for the right moment, which has
been missed several times already; Prussia's frontiers as laid down
by the Vienna treaties are not conducive to a healthy national
life; it is not by means of speeches and majority resolutions that
the great issues of the day will be decided – that was the great
mistake of 1848 and 1849 – but by iron and blood.[174]

The Minister-President's fabricated levity and forthrightness was
interpreted by deputies – and liberals outside parliament – as crude-
ness, cynicism and reaction. 'You know how passionately I love
Prussia', wrote Heinrich von Treitschke to his brother-in-law: 'But
when I hear so shallow a country squire as this Bismarck bragging
about the "iron and blood' with which he intends to subdue
Germany, the meanness of it seems to me to be exceeded only by
the absurdity.'[175] Inside the committee room, the academic and
liberal grandee Rudolf Virchow accused Bismarck of trying to attain
his impliedly reactionary domestic aims through the distractions of
foreign policy and the exercise of power. The Minister-President was
forced to backtrack, protesting – too loudly – that 'to seek conflicts
abroad in order to get over difficulties at home ... would be frivo-
lous; he was not looking for deals; he was talking about conflicts that
we would not be able to avoid, without our having sought them'.[176]
   Such denials merely reinforced the sense of liberals like Max von
Forckenbeck, the chair of the budget committee, that Prussia faced
the 'rule of the sword at home' and 'war abroad' under Bismarck,
as he predicted on 24 September, as news of the new Minister-
President was published in the press.[177] This belief that the Prussian
government was acting unconstitutionally, although varying in
intensity, remained in place until the Austro-Prussian war of 1866.
'We ought not to maintain any longer that the constitution is still in
effect,' wrote Twesten in that year, concurring with Leopold von
Hoverbeck that 'force has destroyed the law' and with Eduard
Lasker that 'in almost every respect the country is being governed
absolutely in the true sense of the word'.[178] To Twesten and many
other liberals and democrats, the constitutional crisis was underpinned by a conflict 'between *Junkertum* and *Volk*', with a feudal,
'closed and decisive representation of the interests of a small party'
of conservative landowners, willing to contravene the law, pitted
against the *Bürgertum,* which 'represents the material and ideal
interests with which the working and thinking *Volk* is filled, the
classes of the *Volk* which have been in the process of rising since the

end of the Middle Ages and which have always had moral power and which sooner or later will, in our state too, also have political power in their hands'.[179] Bismarck, it seemed to the opposition, did not embody the anticipated civic and constitutional politics of a German nation-state.

Observers outside Prussia, who were often already wary of Berlin, were even more sceptical of Bismarck than their Prussian counterparts. In Baden, the traditional support of Prussia in the South, the pro-Prussian liberal Foreign Minister Franz von Roggenbach warned his envoy at the *Bundestag* Robert von Mohl on 3 October 1862 that 'the man and the system must be attacked without quarter'.[180] 'The only thing left for us to do is to keep alive the national idea and to give it greater substance in the convictions of the nation, in spite of its complete rejection by the Prussian government,' wrote Karl Samwer to Roggenbach on 17 October: 'In this respect, I believe your plan to oppose the vacuous ideas of reform of the Austrians and the *Mittelstaaten* with the image of the *Reichsverfassung* of 1849 to be excellent.'[181] After the rebuttal of the Grand Duke's attempt to warn Wilhelm, who was celebrating the birthday of the Queen at Baden-Baden, about Bismarck and Prussia's change of course, the official *Karlsruher Zeitung* spelled out the Badenese government's 'Position vis-à-vis the Prussian Constitutional Crisis' on 22 October: although the Prussian administration had been entrusted by nationalists with 'our political rebirth' since 1859, 'a government which does not respect its own parliament cannot create a German parliament, and without the will of the German *Volk* German unity will not be founded'.[182] Although Roggenbach was subsequently won over by Bismarck's policy in Schleswig-Holstein and Germany more generally, he was unable to convince the Grand Duke and was opposed by Georg Ludwig von Edelsheim and the majority of Badenese liberals, prompting him to stand down as Foreign Minister and Minister of State on 7 October 1865. Edelsheim replaced him a fortnight later.

Liberals and democrats in other South German states, traditionally less well disposed to Prussia, were more forthright in their criticism of the Prussian Minister-President. In Württemberg, for instance, the Prussian *Legationsrat* in Stuttgart had already warned Berlin in April 1862 that 'Bismarck as a minister would, with one blow, isolate Prussia in Germany.'[183] After his appointment, not only the democratic *Beobachter* was scathing about the new Bismarckian era, even accusing the Prussian Progressives of having been 'most profoundly altered and corrupted' in their 'whole sense of legality', moderate liberal newspapers like the *Schwäbische Zeitung* and the *Schwäbischer Merkur* were also suspicious of the new administration, though not averse to its 'unheard-of recognition that power is power', portraying its leader as a 'fantasist in the grand style' without the 'tough stamina' of a great statesman.[184] Bismarck, noted the owner of the *Merkur* Otto Elben, was seen as a 'real Junker' who had alienated 'all liberals of the old school from Prussia' through measures such as the press edict.[185] Notwithstanding its call for a 'German Cavour', a 'powerful and liberal statesman in Austria or Prussia', the *Schwäbische Volkszeitung* did not discern such a figure in Bismarck, discounting him as 'personified presumption and immorality'.[186] These antipathies, together with long-standing South German sympathy for Austria, informed the call of the *Volkszeitung* and *Merkur* for a policy of armed neutrality on the part of the third Germany on the eve of the Austro-Prussian war. Supporters of Prussia such as Gustav Rümelin, who had written to his brother-in-law Gustav Schmoller that the 'expansion of Prussia's power and size' was 'historically grounded, natural and desirable, even in terms of German interests', rejected Bismarck's bellicose policy.[187] Friedrich Notter wrote in his diary on 29 June 1866, two days after Prussia's setback in the battle of Langensalza, that, 'as much as I am for Prussia, I have a sort of joy over this defeat, because it will hopefully summon forth the alteration of a mad Bismarckian policy. It is just the same for most friends of Prussia, the number of whom is greater than I had thought, as for me.'[188] For its part, the *Schwäbische Chronik*, the supplement of the *Merkur*, held that the victory of Prussia under Bismarck's leadership would lead to the 'moral decline of Germany'.[189]

By contrast, 'Prussia' without Bismarck, although not popular in many parts of the South, was usually seen by liberals – and by many others – to be compatible with a German nation-state. To some South German observers, the constitutional crisis of the Hohenzollern state had served to emphasise the difference between a reactionary government and a liberal populace and public sphere, creating sympathy for the latter. 'The advantages of the changed situation, too, cannot be overlooked,' commented the *Karlsruher Zeitung* after Bismarck's appointment in 1862:

> The struggle of the Prussians for their constitution wins over the sympathies of the whole of liberal Germany more easily and more

surely than anything else, and in Prussia the conviction impresses itself more deeply by the day that internal freedom there will only be secured against an overpowerful *Junkertum* when the anachronisms of Kurbrandenburg will have become forever impossible within a great German *Bundesstaat*.[190]

Not all South German publications were so sympathetic. One of the most critical was the Bavarian and Catholic periodical, the *Historisch-politische Blätter*. Yet, even here, there was increasing, if still grudging, support for Prussia between 1862 and 1866, in spite of the constitutional crisis. In the past, Prussia had been viewed as an expansionist, centralised, martial, Protestant state and an enemy of the third Germany and the *Bund*.[191] The Crimean and Franco-Austrian wars had demonstrated that Prussia, playing the part – in the words of the Austrian note of 5 November 1861 – of 'the egotistically calculating spectator', was intent on stymieing the unification of Germany, noted one correspondent in February 1862: 'Who in the world would believe in the reality of German unity, as long as these conditions persist ...?'[192] 'Prussia is the big question mark in Germany, and the so-called German question is merely an imprecise term for the Prussian question,' continued the article, because unification could not occur against the wishes of Berlin, but the Prussian government showed no sign of desiring to cooperate with the other German states.[193] Moreover, 'no other party in Prussia offers the remotest hope that this power [Prussia] will ever depart from the status quo of the *Bund* to join a reform of the Confederation which would suit Austria and the *Mittelstaaten*'.[194]

A 'political wilderness' had been created in Prussia, which made a conflict between Berlin, Vienna and the other German states seem likely, to the benefit of France, lamented the mouthpiece of South German political Catholicism.[195] After 1862, however, the *Historisch-politische Blätter* gave a more positive appraisal of Prussia, as it became frustrated with the *Mittelstaaten*, the Confederation and Austria. 'Greater Germans' had failed to address the questions of territorial and cultural integrity and political sovereignty posed by unification, preferring to blame Berlin in order to obscure the responsibility of the third Germany.[196] Even in 1859, it now seemed to the Catholic periodical, the sins of the middling states had exceeded those of the Hohenzollern monarchy.[197] Loyal to Germany before Catholicism, the publication preferred to back the German state of Prussia rather than to risk a resurrected

Confederation of the Rhine, in which the weak, particularist states of the third Germany would be dominated by the Bonapartist regime of France.[198] When there was 'no other choice', ran an article in 1863, it was better to be 'Prussian-imperial' than 'Rhine-confederal':

> Many guileless souls will say that this is self-evident, but they are decidedly wrong. Thus, it is the most pressing duty of all of us, for whom the well-being of Germany and of the church – but otherwise nothing – is close to our hearts, not to allow ourselves to be drawn towards blind embitterment against the second German power, and not to talk ourselves unawares into a hateful mood, in the course of which even the renewal of a French protectorate over our states must appear in a milder light, as a desirable alliance against the hated policy of Berlin.[199]

Consequently, the *Historisch-politische Blätter* warned against the misuse of the *Bund* and the misdirection of public opinion towards an antagonism with the Prussian state.[200] Such warnings came at the height of the constitutional crisis and before Prussia's victory over Denmark at the battle of Düppel on 18 April 1864.

There were many reasons why Bismarck's appointment as Minister-President of Prussia failed to deter contemporaries from seeing the kingdom as the pivot of a liberal and constitutional, if not peaceable, unification of Germany. The 47-year-old Junker, who had lived abroad as Prussia's envoy in Frankfurt and St Petersburg for most of the preceding decade, was an unknown quantity outside conservative circles, having briefly enjoyed a national reputation as a young firebrand – in his early thirties – and as an ultra in 1848–49. During his opening public performance as Minister-President, before the budget committee on 30 September 1862, some witnesses found him nervous and abrupt, his hands shaking and his speech oscillating between bluster and indiscretion.[201] Others believed him to be the last of the reactionaries, betraying the desperation of the monarch and his advisers. 'With the employment of this man, the last and most powerful bolt of the "by-the-grace-of-God" reaction has been shot,' wrote Rochau: 'Even if there is much that he has learned and unlearned, he is in no way a fully fledged statesman but merely an adventurer of the commonest sort, concerned only with what the next day may bring.'[202] On several occasions, Bismarck himself complained that he had been unable to recruit talented or established ministers. As a result, few outside government predicted that the ministry would last long. To Freytag and to Sybel, it seemed necessary for liberals to take a pause, in the opinion of the former, 'not of indolence and exhaustion, but for gathering strength', in the expectation that they would reassume office.[203] According to the latter, liberals should raise their 'voice, unsparingly and fearlessly, against the false advice of the counsellors of the throne' in order to save the King for the land and the land for the King.[204] As early as February 1863, the diarist Theodor von Bernhardi reported that 'all think that Bismarck's government is finished and they are convinced that he cannot hold on any longer'.[205] If the elections of October 1863 failed to produce a Chamber of Deputies 'which concurs with the current ministry, then it is the constitutional duty of the current ministers to make way for men with whom the new *Abgeordnetenhaus* can agree', wrote the economist and deputy John Prince-Smith.[206] In a similar vein, remarked the editor of the *Preussische Jahrbücher* Rudolf Haym, it was common for liberals to argue that 'the storm' would soon 'blow over'.[207] Within government, Bismarck, too, at times appeared to anticipate an early end to constitutional deadlock, albeit on different grounds, with the ministry emerging victorious after deputies had tired of the affair and the public had become bored.[208] From either point of view, it appeared that the constitutional crisis would soon be over.

Bismarck's opportunism and unorthodoxy, although they also suited his temperament and outlook, were the corollary of his weak position. In conservative ranks, he had been labelled a 'democrat' by counter-revolutionaries such as the chief of the military cabinet Edwin von Manteuffel, who favoured a *coup d'état*. In addition, like all ministers, he was dependent on the monarch, who appointed the executive, making it imperative that he demonstrated as emphatically as possible that he was the servant of the King not parliament. 'In the palace the King heard from every side insinuations to the effect that I was a democrat in disguise,' he wrote later: 'I could gain his complete trust only by showing him that I was not afraid of the chamber.'[209] To this end, Bismarck deliberately exaggerated his willingness to contravene the constitution, playing the part of a 'Junker reactionary' in order to head off criticism from the right.[210] At court, this tactic seems to have been quite well understood, with Wilhelm himself pointing out to the Crown Prince that 'Minister v. Bismarck's utterance that we could reach the point of dispensing with the constitution' was merely '*one* of the eventualities which lie within the range of possibility'.[211] It was not the sole 'goal of his efforts'.[212]

In fact, as contemporary commentators were aware, Bismarck was a 'chameleon to whom every party lays a claim', switching from one position to another in order to garner support and head off attacks, in the words of the liberal chief of the Prussian literary bureau Max Duncker.[213] What was characteristic of the Minister-President at the beginning of his period of office was his malleability and unpredictability, as Kurd von Schlözer, a friend from the embassy in St Petersburg, recorded after a rendezvous on 3 October 1862:

> We drank a lot of champagne, which loosened even more his naturally loose tongue. In the *Herrenhaus* he paints the reaction he plans in colours so black that, as he puts it, the lords themselves are becoming anxious about the conditions he says he will bring about if need be. Before the gentlemen of the second chamber he appears at one moment very unbending, but in the next hints at his desire to mediate. Finally, he intends to make the German cabinets believe that the King is hard put to restrain the Cavourism of his new minister. There is no denying that until now people are impressed by his spirit and his brilliance.[214]

There is little evidence that, outside government, contemporaries were as impressed as Schlözer intimated. Rather, they seem to have been bemused by and sceptical of Bismarck, knowing that it was in the minister's interest to portray the struggle as one between the monarchical principle and a parliamentary regime. As such, the Minister-President's strategy was already well established, resting on a distinction elaborated and popularised by Friedrich Julius Stahl and taken up by the reaction as a means of discrediting the opposition. Thus, when Twesten had threatened in January 1863 that the lower chamber would not support the government if it went to war against Denmark, there was an element of ritual in Bismarck's retort in the *Abgeordnetenhaus*, over the loud protests of the assembled deputies, 'that, if we find it necessary to carry on a war, we shall do so with or without your consent'.[215] The prerogatives of the monarch and the executive, particularly in the sphere of the military and foreign policy, would not be subjected to a parliamentary diktat, he implied.

In the event, Bismarck and the King often proved willing to abide by the tenets of a constitutional system of government, in which the monarch appointed the executive and retained important prerogatives, and parliament exercised a sanction over legislation and scrutinised the budget. In his attempt to frighten the Crown Prince in order to weaken the hold of the liberal coterie around Friedrich Wilhelm at court, the Minister-President had contended that a 'constitutional regime' was 'untenable', equating it with parliamentary rule and the collapse of the monarchy; yet Friedrich Wilhelm had refused to be intimidated, replying that Bismarck was indulging in 'peculiar talk', given that he continued to govern under the constitution.[216] The latter was forced to admit that he would continue to obey the law, reduced to hinting darkly that this might not be the case in future. As has been seen, the King subsequently dismissed such scare-mongering: although he, too, occasionally raged against 'this abominable constitutional system', his actions and his professions of loyalty to the constitution proved that he was not against every form of constitutional monarchy – just the excesses, as he perceived it, of the existing one in Prussia – and that he did not consider the Prussian system of government to have been reduced to that of a republic with a president, as had occurred in Britain.[217]

Likewise, liberals and democrats, despite labelling the regime 'an already-extant administrative absolutism', in the phrase of the constitutional lawyer and deputy Rudolf Gneist, continued to distinguish, according to the precedent set in the revolution, between a constitutional regime and a parliamentary one, where a popular assembly dominated, and effectively nominated, the executive.[218] '"No parliamentary regime" was always the battle-cry of the reaction, and the old liberals often concurred, without perceiving the scope of the magic word,' Lasker had written in the *Deutsche Jahrbücher für Politik und Literatur* in 1862:

> Monarchical or parliamentary: this was the question of judgement which ministries laid before the voting *Volk* in order to gain a safeguard from a loyal chamber, which might have wanted to exercise a certain control over the actions of the government. And yet the constitution knows nothing of this opposition, and the fundamental concept of constitutional government is an intimate merger of monarchical and parliamentary power. For the government in a constitutional state is nothing other than the extension of the state order, which rests on the harmony of king and *Volk*.[219]

Democrats in Prussia, proclaimed Wilhelm Löwe in 1863, had 'carefully avoided purely theoretical questions', in particular 'the question of parliamentarism or a personal regime of the king', since it was not relevant in the circumstances of the early 1860s.[220] 'Acknowledgement of the principle of constitutionalism and democracy' now existed, declared the radical publication *Der Beobachter* in April 1866, and it could not be 'wiped from history'.[221] The problem in the early 1860s, as Lasker recognised, was not whether a constitutional monarchy should exist, but whether monarchical and parliamentary competencies and powers could be reconciled when the assembly and the government failed to agree: 'The inescapable precondition of every constitutional government is the capacity to create agreement between king and parliament.'[222] The most obvious area of contention or gap, which the constitution of 1850 failed to address, concerned the army. In this sense, the constitutional crisis in Prussia was a genuine one – and not simply a subterfuge for a return to absolutism – which had implications for the constitution of a German nation-state.

Reform of the army was controversial but not clear-cut. Like the *Reichsverfassung* of 1849, which stated that 'the Kaiser disposes over the army', the Prussian constitution of 1850 was unequivocal in its maintenance of monarchical authority in the military sphere, but it also vested in the *Abgeordnetenhaus* the power to block budget increases. One unresolved constitutional question was the extent to which budgetary scrutiny permitted a substantive parliamentary discussion of military affairs; another asked what should be done when the different organs of state failed to agree a budget – who should rule and with what financial means? Bismarck's answer, presented in the debate about the House of Deputies' address on 27 January 1863 condemning the government's breach of the constitution, was that the King, as head of state and guarantor of the executive, had to ensure order and the continuity of government in the event that the three legislative authorities – the administration, the *Herrenhaus* and the *Abgeordnetenhaus* – could not agree a budget in a constitutional manner, for 'none of those authorities can *coerce* the others into submission'.[223] His charge was a legal one: 'This address demands from the royal house of Hohenzollern its constitutional rights of government in order to transfer them to the majority in this House.'[224] 'When no budget comes into being, then we have a *tabula rasa*', the Minister-President had proclaimed to the budget commission on 30 September 1862: 'the constitution offers no way out, for, here, one interpretation stands against another.'[225] Bismarck was, in the words of an article by Ludwig von Gerlach in the *Kreuzzeitung* in May 1862, ruling 'without the law', but not 'against' it.[226] In May 1863, after another parliamentary address had refused cooperation in reforming the army, the King replied in similar terms to those of his Minister-President, accusing politicians of trying 'to prepare the ground for an unconstitutional dictatorship of the House of Deputies'.[227] Although both Wilhelm and Bismarck had, at various points, threatened to exceed the constitution, which had united liberals and democrats against them, they continued to make a parallel constitutional case. Financially, the Minister-President had told the parliamentary commission on 30 September 1862, the constitution of 1850 did not specify that budgets should be passed in advance, but merely estimated in advance, allowing the government to rule without their enactment. Such constitutional ambiguity combined with differences of opinion about the role of the army in Prussia and in a future German nation-state to set limits on resistance to Bismarck's government, even though it had become 'unpopular to a degree scarcely seen before in Prussia', according to the Minister-President's banker Gerson Bleichröder.[228]

While it is true that there was broad support for the civilian and bourgeois *Landwehr* and the German volunteers of 1813, whose national successes – as 'men of action, of daring', in favour of a 'war of life and death' and opposed to 'narrow-minded dynastic egotism' – were celebrated in 1863, there was also widespread scepticism of the *Bund*, whose military constitution had undergone only minor reform despite glaring inadequacies, and there was reluctant support for Prussia as the most likely basis of a German army.[229] As a result, a large majority of commentators concurred, it was important that the Hohenzollern state further improved its military. 'The new organisation is a good thing for the country, as King Wilhelm ceaselessly assures us', wrote the *Historisch-politische Blätter* in 1863, concurring 'that the previous disorder of the *Landwehr* was in need of reform, since there was, given an unusually expanded population, general conscription in name only, and a heavy burden fell on those affected'.[230] 'Democracy now rules in Prussia, but only via the military question; without this heavy imposition on the pecuniary resources of the *Volk*, we would never have seen all the votes of the chamber save three dozen go to the united Progressive Party,' an article in the same publication had noted a year earlier: 'This chamber pushes the government to the most extreme degree; it is demanding the impossible, for it is, on a hundred grounds, unthinkable that the army reform will now be reversed again.'[231] Liberals and even some democrats converged in their backing of an expansion of the Prussian army on national grounds. 'We, too, desire a restructuring of the army organisation, but in the spirit of Scharnhorst and Gneisenau', declared the radical Johann Jacoby to voters in November 1863, before going on to champion the *Landwehr*, which alone corresponded 'to the basic conditions of a constitutional state order'.[232] To Schulze-Delitzsch, one of the main democratic critics of Bismarck, Germany needed 'Prussia as the most militarily capable state, deploying the whole strength of its *Volk* to take the lead in these struggles' against its many enemies, 'France in the West, Russia in the East, perhaps Italy in the South, Denmark and Sweden with England in the North'.[233] All German tribes were 'belligerent', but Prussia had seen such belligerence develop 'advantageously' over the course 'of a long history'.[234] Despite the vociferousness of the struggle against Bismarck's ministry, Prussia was vital for Germany's 'national existence'.[235]

For many opponents of Bismarck, the Prussian constitutional crisis of the 1860s did not rule out the Hohenzollern monarchy as a fulcrum of unification. 'From a certain side' – that of the *Grossdeutschen* – 'it has been seen to be desirable to draw a comparison between the governments of Austria and Prussia,' wrote Schulze in October 1863: 'I am glad to take up this comparison, and you know that I take a very impartial position in this respect precisely because we stand in opposition to our government and because we have never given them any quarter in the treatment of this question, and shall not give them any in future.'[236] Nevertheless, even though Bismarck was reprehensible, the fact that there was a crisis in Prussia showed that the state was fundamentally different from Austria, where absolutism was accepted by the political public:

> Look at the powerful revolt of the *Volksgeist* and of legal awareness in Prussia against the current Prussian [press] edict, and this edict temporarily introduces conditions – but truly not for the duration – which are completely in order in Austria. Thank God we are making a fuss, and I accept, at best, that other Germans will see it as a turning-point and will press for improvement. But why, I ask myself, are such demands also not made of Austria for the removal of similarly poor conditions? Because it is known

throughout Germany that nothing would be achieved by it. At least we in Prussia should take such a challenge to heart and, it is believed in Germany, we have the means to effect improvements.[237]

The press edict of June 1863, which Bismarck had introduced to such outcry after the dissolution of the lower chamber, was immediately repealed by the *Abgeordnetenhaus*, using its constitutional powers, after the return of a large liberal majority in autumn of the same year. In a similar way, the Minister-President's pursuit of judges and civil servants had proved ineffective. Although, according to the estimate of one liberal deputy, up to a thousand functionaries could have been affected by government harassment, the ministry's actions had little, if any, impact on the polls, in spite of Bismarck's warning that officials revealing their 'oppositional views' would be treated as 'opponents of the government'; what was more, the involvement of twenty deputies, including nine judges, appears to have consolidated liberal opposition in the lower chamber rather than cowing deputies into submission.[238] In their darker moments, some liberals and democrats toyed with the eventuality that Bismarck's government would use force against its own population. Sybel, for example, warned Baumgarten in May 1863 that he doubted that 'a *coup de main* such as 1848 would be possible here today', 'where a disciplined army of 200,000 men holds together as a result of training and discipline'.[239] Yet few contemporaries appear to have envisaged a reversion to absolutism or even reaction in Prussia.

Sybel's purpose in discussing force was to head off Baumgarten's call for Prussian deputies to make 'the whole land rise up'.[240] When Max Duncker raised the spectre of a *coup d'état* in January 1864, in the same rhetorical spirit as Sybel, Bernhardi dismissed the suggestion: 'I don't believe in a *Staatsstreich* or an imposed electoral law in our case'.[241] Unruh, the only leader of the *Nationalverein* who knew Bismarck personally, had been anxious from the beginning to dispel the idea that the Minister-President was merely a member of the camarilla, unable to compromise with liberals and unwilling to work with the institutions of representative government: 'I said to my old Prussian and new German friends, they were in error if they saw Bismarck simply as a reactionary or even as an instrument of reaction. Certainly, he doesn't belong to the liberals, but he has ideas and plans in mind which are quite different from those of

278 NATIONALISM IN GERMANY

Manteuffel and his colleagues.'[242] Bismarck was 'a very original and
skilled character of great energy', whose intentions were unclear
but who was capable of cooperating with the forces of liberalism,
Unruh explained to the members of the *Nationalverein* at Coburg in
October 1862.[243] It was a mistake, wrote the Berlin liberal to
Bennigsen in October 1865, 'to lump the *state* of Prussia and its
population together with its government', for 'Prussia is the good
half of Germany, it has significance and history as a state', deserving
support in spite of its 'sad internal conditions', against which
Prussian liberals continued to fight.[244]

In the South, conceded Viktor Böhmert to Bennigsen on 29
October 1864, it had proved more difficult 'to come to terms with
Prussian leadership' than in the North, where there was 'no choice',
since 'I prefer the unity of Germany over a couple of Prussian constitutional paragraphs, which – in the end – can only be resolved by a
German parliament', and since 'doubt about Prussian leadership
constitutes a return to political nothingness for us'.[245] Yet at least
some southerners, including liberal opponents of Prussia such as
Robert von Mohl, were also prepared to dismiss the long-term
consequences of the constitutional crisis. 'It would have been childish to declare oneself against Prussia because its government was,
momentarily, a violent one, inimical to freedom, and sought to
achieve greater unity not through moral but through physical
conquests', wrote the Heidelberg constitutional lawyer, deputy and
Badenese envoy in his memoirs.[246] What had stopped Mohl from
backing Prussia was a belief in the cultural and political benefits of
'fragmentation into so many states'.[247] Nevertheless, he admitted
that 'the feeling of weakness and negligibility in all European questions, on the one hand, and the wretchedness, the unnecessary
expenses, the narrow points of view of *Kleinstaaterei*, as well as the
constantly repeated difficulty of bringing general institutions into
being, on the other, had gradually made the desire for unity the
dominant goal, and almost a passion, of a great part of the nation'.[248]

Even for many proponents of *Kleindeutschland*, opposition to
Prussia on constitutional grounds was not considered 'childish'. Yet
such opposition tended to promote quiescence on the national
question rather than support for Austria, the *Bund* or the
Mittelstaaten. Bennigsen refused to join the ranks of 'lazy pessimists',
who thought 'revolution impossible, a national initiative of the
Prussian government without prospects' and 'energetically concentrated Prussian particularism' the only option, but he nonetheless

lamented the fact that 'the Bismarckian tendency, that is the worship of military power and diplomatic successes' had gained, 'in a shocking way, the upper hand'.[249] In the heated committee meeting of the *Nationalverein* on 28 October 1865, which finally agreed to the readoption of the programme of 1860 and an interim transfer of the central authority to Prussia during unification, Bennigsen maintained that,

> in the period of struggle which lies before us, we should not allow ourselves to be deflected by a justified feeling of embitterment about the regime in Berlin and by passionate irritation from the course that the national party has recognised as the right one for the political development of Germany; still less, though, should we allow ourselves to be bribed and seduced by those voices which seek salvation in an increase in power for the greatest purely German state at the cost of the highest ideal goods of the nation. No *Volk* can work towards the growth of external power alongside the suspension of legal sensibility, a feeling of freedom and moral goods without the great danger of destroying their innermost core.[250]

The only alternative was to trust in 'a great people', which would 'sacrifice itself' even 'in terrible times'.[251]

As war with Austria approached, the majority of the committee of the *Nationalverein* rejected, on 13–14 May, Bismarck's offer of a directly elected constituent assembly – a German parliament – to reform the Confederation in April 1866. 'Should the German Volk support a parliament and a reform of the *Bund*, it must be put forward in the precise form which the history of the years 1848 and 1849 has given it, and, above all, the government which wants to refashion the whole constitution of the nation must have given completely different proofs of its constitutional disposition and loyalty to the constitution than has hitherto been the case on the side of the Prussian government,' ran the *Nationalverein*'s statement, framed by Rochau, on 14 May: 'As long as the *Prussian* constitution is a dead letter, our nation will never believe in a *German* constitution placed in view by Prussia, not to mention be set in fundamental motion by such a view.'[252] At the same committee meeting, a majority of Prussians refused to support Bismarck if a Austro-Prussian war were to break out; they were backed – it was said – by most of the population in the South, though not in North and

Central Germany. Oetker, one of a minority of Bismarck's admirers in the National Association leadership, recalled the tone of the meeting:

'The man is not at all worthy of taking the German question in hand,' cried Schulze-Delitzsch and others repeatedly: 'Not a Pfennig should be approved for him!' I, however, wrote in the *Morgenzeitung*: 'If Prussia puts itself, by means of a decisive and prospectively successful action, at the head of the nation in order to a free *Bundesstaat* into being, then on the national side no aid would be too large, no sacrifice too heavy.'[253]

Against the wishes of the committee, Bennigsen went to meet Bismarck, having already asked Roggenbach to inform him of 'Bismarck's plans, his resources, his position vis-à-vis the King and his intention of binding himself to others, in addition to the conservatives'.[254] Like many other leaders of national organisations, Bennigsen was undecided about which line to take in 1866, remaining neither for nor against the Prussian Minister-President: 'Even so clear and calm a figure as R. von Bennigsen had not yet freed himself of the general antipathy towards Bismarck,' recorded Oetker in May 1866: 'He agreed with me that the perpetual empty negation of the Prussian *Abgeordnetenhaus* was reproachable and damaging; but he had not yet come to acknowledge Bismarck fully.'[255]

One of the best-known evaluations of liberals' attitude to the Prussian ministry was produced by the academic and journalist Hermann Baumgarten. His 'Self-Critique' of German liberalism, which he completed in October 1866, is usually seen as a description of liberalism's real weaknesses and tactical mistakes rather than a polemic, published in the *Preussische Jahrbücher*, by a moderate liberal, dissatisfied by the 'doctrinairism' of the Prussian Progressive Party. The essence of Baumgarten's case was that the *Fortschrittspartei*, initially backed by the majority of public opinion, had failed to take the opportunity to govern effectively between 1858 and 1862 or to collaborate with Bismarck after 1862. 'A politically experienced man, who looked at the position of the Prussian state impartially, would have to say that the favourableness of the circumstances' between 1858 and 1862 'was not fully exploited, that liberal ministers could have given their edifice firmer foundations, that they could have better used and more carefully consolidated their relationship with the throne', contended Baumgarten in 'Der deutsche Liberalismus'.[256] The constitutional crisis had been a 'turning-point' for German liberalism, creating 'new aims', 'new methods' and a new 'outcome'.[257] Thus, although Bismarck, on entering office, had 'suggested a compromise to liberal leaders, which would have meant a liberal turn for the government at important points, above all in the army question', they had thrown it back at him 'quite demeaningly', seeing him 'as the worst incarnation of the most objectionable Junkerdom' and ignoring 'his diplomatic achievements' and 'the meaning of his entire personality'.[258]

Instead of exploring the possibility of working with the Minister-President, liberals were bent on pushing him to contravene the constitution in order to create a backlash against him and secure his resignation or dismissal. Having subsequently discovered that they could not remove Bismarck, the *Fortschrittspartei* should then have reached a compromise: 'Not disposing of the means to distance Herr v. Bismarck, they should have gone along with his initiatives.'[259] Later, they were forced to reach agreement with the ministry on worse terms, leading to public disillusionment. 'In the first great political struggle undertaken on German soil without the help of revolution', the Progressive Party, when it pushed to extremes, found that 'the advantage of power was unconditionally on the side of their opponent'.[260] By 1865, 'Prussia and Germany had had a series of the most significant experiences, which countered the original conditions of the *Fortschrittspartei* in general and in particular with devastating force.'[261] Even though the Progressives had been joined by liberals in the *Mittelstaaten*, who had opposed Prussia's Great Power policy in Schleswig-Holstein, they remained 'impotent' in their rejection of 'the hated Bismarckian regime'.[262] According to Baumgarten, 'everyone who counted as a political force in Germany stood in phalanxes against Bismarckian policy', but Bismarck's ministry nevertheless 'strode towards its goal calmly and surely, barely hindered by its countless opponents'.[263] From a reading of the Karlsruhe historian's account, it appeared that nearly all liberals had stood in opposition to the Prussian Minister-President in a dogmatic, pointless and unsuccessful struggle.

In fact, many liberals had been willing to accept aspects of Bismarck's rule and few were ready to act against his ministry. Baumgarten himself was a protagonist in a dispute which divided some liberals before 1866 and unsettled many others. In particular, after victory in the war against Denmark in 1864, 'a man of rare strength and cleverness' stood before the nation, showing it 'the right way'.[264] 'A lucky star lit up Prussian power, but an unfavourable wind was blowing against Prussian freedom: was there a point in merely chasing after the latter and sacrificing the former?', asked the liberal publicist rhetorically:

> How long had one sighed in liberal circles for a man who would finally lead Prussia forward! ... And, in fact, there were a hundred reasons to give Prussian policy a turn from that intended years beforehand. Nothing stood in the way of a really healthy, free development apart from the incompleteness of its own growth. Complete freedom rests only on complete power. A state which always has to work at the outer limit of its strength in order to secure its existence remains in the shackles of its need. In addition, there was the fact that, in Prussia, certain absolutist, aristocratic and bureaucratic traditions dominated the inherited state body, which it was best to push back if one wanted to place the whole state on a new basis. In the rest of Germany, which had to be won over, these traditions could not become powerful ... Things were still not yet so. A resolution of the internal conflict was still of considerable importance to the fortunate minister. He didn't hide the fact that he was ready to make not inconsiderable sacrifices for such a resolution.[265]

Baumgarten's call for cooperation with Bismarck was all the more remarkable because of his earlier stance. Born in Braunschweig in 1825, he had, as a student, been an active member of a *Burschenschaft* in Jena, before being drawn by Young Hegelianism to Halle. Later, he became a follower of Gervinus, whom he joined in Heidelberg as an historian during the 1850s. In the middle of the decade, he defended his master against charges of treason for the publication of *Einleitung in die Geschichte des neunzehnten Jahrhunderts* (1853), which predicted that democracy would be the state form of the future. Despite his caution in some respects and his desire to demonstrate his pragmatism in 'Selbstkritik', Baumgarten had advised greater agitation and resistance to Bismarck as late as 1863.[266] Baumgarten to Sybel, 22 May 1863, in Fenske (ed.), *Reichsgründung*, 273–5. Though a Borussian historian and a supporter of *Kleindeutschland* who wrote for the *Preussische Jahrbücher* and edited the *Süddeutsche Zeitung*, which was opposed to the *Allgemeine-Zeitung*, he was nonetheless sympathetic to southern points of view, having transferred to Karlsruhe in 1861, where conditions were better than in the North, with the Grand Duke's 'heart-felt' backing of German liberalism, a strong and talented liberal government, the 'almost unanimous enthusiasm of the public', the absence of a potentially resistant aristocracy, a workable bureaucracy and favourable external conditions.[267] The fact that Baumgarten's earlier hopes of German liberalism were subsequently disappointed betrays the divisions within the party, especially by 1866, when 'Selbstkritik' was written. All the same, the Heidelberg historian's own support for the opponents of Wilhelm I and Bismarck in the constitutional crisis also showed the liberals' strength until 1866.[268] Even in 'Selbstkritik', he admitted – as a 'duty of fairness' – that the tactical opposition of the Progressive Party to the Prussian government 'corresponded to the dominant views and opinions in Prussia and Germany at that time', which would have made cooperation with Bismarck seem like an 'unworthy weakness'.[269] This helped to explain the circumstance, left without comment by Baumgarten, that the Prussian Minister-President had, until a late date, been prepared 'to make not inconsiderable sacrifices' for a resolution of the constitutional crisis.

Bismarck, of course, was never likely to overstate his debt to party and public opinion. In the spring of 1863, he had written to an American university friend that 'I hate politics ... At this moment, my ears are full of it. I'm compelled to listen to unusually silly speeches from the mouths of unusually childish and excited politicians ... *querelle d'allemand* ... the babblers cannot rule Prussia ... They have too little wit and too much self-satisfaction, are stupid and impudent.'[270] Such private ranting, however, was indicative of the Minister-President's frustration, betraying the plausibility of a return – as in 1858 – to a liberal government. Bismarck had to pay attention to parties and the press, and at times to court them, because of the weakness of his position, which was exacerbated by his stand-off with the *Abgeordnetenhaus*. His wife Johanna, fearing for the health of her husband as a result of 15-hour stints of work and unrelenting headaches, wrote in January 1863 that he started his day by skimming through the newspapers and then divided his time between correspondence, the King, the ministerial council and 'the monstrous Chamber'.[271]

Bismarck needed Wilhelm in order to act, but the King's assent was hardly automatic, not least because the Minister-President had promised to be his vassal. The monarch had felt free to reject

Roon's and Bismarck's revised plan for a reform of the army in October 1862, because it seemed not to insist on three-year military service, and he had similarly refused to accept a potentially workable military reform initiated by deputies, and again accepted by the Minister-President and Army Minister, in 1865. Irritatingly, the King was influenced by both ultra-conservatives and liberals who were beyond Bismarck's control. Thus, he was advised by the camarilla, especially the Chief of the Military Cabinet Edwin von Manteuffel until his appointment – at Bismarck's instigation – as Governor of Schleswig in 1865. Such advice from ultras prompted the Minister-President to exaggerate his criticism of the constitution and of liberalism.

Yet the King was also surrounded by moderates such as Robert von der Goltz and Albrecht von Bernstorff, diplomats linked to the *Wochenblatt* party, Alexander von Schleinitz, Minister of the Royal Household and former Foreign Minister, his sister the Grand Duchess of Mecklenburg-Schwerin, his son-in-law Grand Duke Friedrich of Baden, his wife Queen Augusta, and his son and daughter-in-law, Crown Prince Friedrich Wilhelm and Vicky, the daughter of Queen Victoria, most of whom were involved in the so-called 'Coburg intrigue' to depose Bismarck on the eve of the Austro-Prussian war. The continuing hold of these circles over the King almost certainly led Bismarck to limit his attacks on liberals and to stress his legal and constitutional credentials. As he told the Italian negotiator as the war with Austria broke out in June, 'If I could do what I wanted with the King, I could always have him by me, if I could sleep with him like the Queen, everything would be fine.'[272] But he could not. He despised the Crown Prince, as an 'impudent nonentity' and a 'cretin', but he had to humour him, giving him *Vorträge* at the request of the King, and he was obliged to take him into account, as part of a liberal clique with close relations with Britain and with the most progressive German states.[273] Doing so, despite the Minister-President's distaste, was advantageous. Adherence to constitutional principles and cooperation with the main political parties had the dual benefit of appeasing liberals at Court and giving Bismarck an external lever to use against the Court, if required.

The Minister-President recognised the strength of the liberals, even though he also lamented it. 'It is a mistake to trace Prussia's significance back to its representation of national and liberal ideas', he replied in June 1863 to the Prussian envoy Prince Heinrich VII Reuss, who had passed on Napoleon III's claim that the

Hohenzollern monarchy had declined after it had ceased to act on behalf of a 'German nationality': rather, the kingdom's significance 'does not rest on Prussia's liberalism, but on its army and its *financial* powers and on the intelligence of its own population. Other German states have always been more liberal than Prussia without, *for this reason*, attaining a leading influence in Germany.'[274] Indeed, 'one can claim, on the contrary, that the influence of Prussia in Europe has declined in the same measure as that of our liberalism has increased'.[275] Nonetheless, Bismarck did not challenge the notion that the liberals' influence had grown and would endure. Even before the Progressive Party's successes at the polls in December 1861, May 1862 and October 1863, the diplomat was in no doubt that liberals were 'the opponents who – in practice – come into question for now'.[276] Furthermore, he acknowledged that most were moderate, eschewing the 'dirt' of a republic and of revolution or a taxpayers' strike, which at once made them easier to work with and more difficult to demonise.[277] 'In the whole of Prussia, you will not find a single person who does not hold open violence to be an act of folly and a crime', wrote Sybel to Baumgarten in 1863.[278][7] 'No one here wants to precipitate revolution', he reported on 11 September.[279]

While it is true that the Minister-President was always willing to exploit the liberals' weaknesses, most notably their justified fear of 'reaction' and their anxiety about the collapse of their vote, he was unsuccessful in this endeavour, with his repressive acts and threats merely serving to consolidate a single liberal and democratic opposition which survived a victorious war in Schleswig-Holstein, the offer of a National Assembly and the spectre of a war against Austria more or less intact.[280] Progressives and other liberals rejected the government's reform of the army and criticised its contravention of the constitution, but they continued to cooperate in the formulation of policy in other respects, for example by supporting the ministry's exclusion of Austria from the *Zollverein* in 1865. Such cooperation and moderation, together with widespread suspicion of the Minister-President's motives and inconsistency, had militated against the realisation of Bismarck's prophesy in June 1862 that 'the longer the affair is drawn out the more the chamber will sink in public esteem', forcing it to come to a settlement.[281] Given the reality of continuing liberal strength, the Minister-President had little option but to contemplate compromise. Despite his pathos-laden discussions with Wilhelm of Polignac, Strafford, Louis XVI and the prospect of a heroic death on a revolutionary scaffold at the start of his ministry, Bismarck found it impossible to cast the liberals as revolutionaries and he was unwilling to launch a *coup d'état* himself.[282]

On constitutional and national grounds, the Minister-President had long anticipated that agreement might be feasible, as he had explained to a close friend in September 1861:

> In any event, I don't see why we *shy away so whimperingly from the idea of a Volksvertretung, either in the Bund or in a Zollvereinsparlament.* We can't fight an institution which plays a legitimate part in each German state and which we conservatives, even in Prussia, cannot do without! In the national sphere, very moderate concessions have to date still been recognised as worthwhile. One could create a genuinely conservative National Assembly and still be thanked for it, even by liberals.[283]

Bismarck, of course, remained an advocate of the 'monarchical principle' in the tradition of Stahl, according to which it was pitted against 'parliamentary government'. Yet, in common with many conservatives after 1848, he had renounced a return to a noble-dominated society of estates and monarchical rule without representative institutions. He recognised 'the principle of the struggle against the revolution' as his own, he had assured Ludwig von Gerlach in 1857, but he intended to act within the new post-revolutionary parameters of politics, including working with the principal parties of the *Landtag*, to the extent that the government supposedly had little room to manoeuvre:

> The course that a Prussian ministry can take is not so very wide; whoever stands on the far left will have to move to the right when he becomes a minister; and whoever stands far to the right will have to move to the left when he becomes a minister, and there is no room for the far-ranging digressions of doctrine, which can be developed by speakers and deputies, on this narrow path on which the government of a great land can stroll.[284]

Gerlach himself had converted to the idea of political parties during the revolution and he continued to abide by the constitution in the crisis of the 1860s, arguing in an essay on 'Prussia's Struggle against Democracy' in January 1863 that 'the government, by continuing to rule *in accordance with the constitutional declaration,* stands on ... the rights of the king entrenched in the *constitutional declaration*. The usurpations are on the side of democracy, which is interfering with the constitutional declaration against the *Herrenhaus* and the Crown.'[285] Bismarck was not an advocate of 'constitutional monarchy' or 'parliamentarism', as defined by his adviser Lothar Bucher in 1855, but he was ready to abide by the constitution and to cooperate with representative institutions.[286] In 1858, he had merely suggested 'more energetic activity on the part of the land's assembly'.[287] By 1861, he was proposing 'a German *Gesammtvertretung*' to deal with the military, tariffs and trade, with delegates chosen from individual state assemblies, not directly elected, in order to safeguard 'the intelligence and conservative stance' of the chamber.[288] Such an offer, 'as a first step towards better institutions', Bismarck wrote in the same memorandum, would make 'a profound impression in Germany and, in particular, it would ease considerably the task of the Prussian government at home in respect of the elections and chambers'.[289] Finally, by the time of the Frankfurt *Fürstentag* in 1863, the Minister-President was willing to concede a directly elected German parliament – a gesture that he repeated early in 1866. Universal suffrage was less dangerous in the Hohenzollern state than in Britain, he contended in 1866, because 'in England only the higher classes are dependent on the monarchy and constitution, which extend *their* privileges and *their* domination over the land. The masses are raw, uneducated, and their loyalty to the Crown is not akin to that in Prussia.'[290] Whereas in Britain 'the very idea of universal suffrage is terrifying', in Prussia and Germany it was an acceptable risk, proposed Bismarck in 1866. Likewise, he refused to compare its effects in France, which was 'without a monarchical tradition', in the phrase of a marginal comment in 1866, with its likely consequences in the German lands.[291] However cynical his motives, the Prussian Minister-President had few qualms about implementing these plans for a German parliament, electorate and constitution.

Bismarck's constitutional concessions were designed, above all, to strengthen Prussia's position in Germany. He remained, first and foremost, a diplomat, pursuing 'the Great Power position of Prussia which had been fought for with the heavy sacrifices of the *Volk*'s goods and blood', as he put it to the *Abgeordnetenhaus* in January 1864.[292] Serving as the Prussian envoy to the Bundestag in the 1850s, Bismarck had become sceptical of the historical traditions and legal legitimacy of a weak Confederation and of particularist

German states, leading him to espouse a doctrine of state interests and state power which made him seem 'not completely reliable', in Ludwig von Gerlach's estimation in 1854.[293] To his former opponent in Frankfurt and ally in Vienna, the Austrian first minister Rechberg, the Prussian Minister-President was 'a man who admits his political cynicism so openly,' that he dismissed any maintenance of the Confederation and defence of the 'well-established rights of the German princes' with the 'hair-raising' comment that Berlin and Vienna should pursue their own interests on the basis of cabinet policy, not nationalism.[294] In conservative circles, even in the Prussian Foreign Office, such cynical and naked pursuit of Prussian interests meant that 'they don't like him there ... [since] he makes his own policy', in the words of Bismarck's friend in St Petersburg Schlözer in 1860.[295] A similar image of the Minister-President was also adopted in liberal and democratic ranks, as Bismarck openly derided their self-interested and unrealistic nationalism, declaring to the lower chamber in January 1864:

> There must be a peculiar magic in this word 'German'. It can be seen that everyone seeks to win the word for himself and each calls what is useful to him, what gives his party standpoint an advantage, 'German', to be altered according to need. Thus, it has come about that it has, at times, been called 'German' to rise up against the *Bund* and, at other times, it is held to be 'German' to take the side of the *Bund*, which has suddenly become progressive. Thus, it can easily happen that we are reproached, that we want to know nothing of Germany apart from our private interests. I can return this reproach to you with complete justification. You want to know nothing of Prussia because it suits your party standpoint either not to let Prussia stand or to let it exist as a domain of the *Nationalverein* ... You put your party standpoint above the interests of the country; you say, 'Prussia can exist as we want it to or, if not, it can fall.' ... This shows how far you stand from the actual *Volk*, how you have become ensconced in coteries of like-minded people, and how you have allowed yourselves to be deceived about the real state of affairs by a press which is dependent on you.[296]

Bismarck's purpose in such speeches was to defend his policies – on the army, Schleswig-Holstein, the navy, and the Confederation – against liberal criticisms. It is worth noting that, even on these occa-

sions, he took the national idea seriously and confronted the notion
that Germany and the *Bund* took precedence over Prussia.
Unification would require Prussia because of 'evil conditions',
'which derive from the unnatural multitude of borders in the interior of Germany and which are reinforced by the height, unknown
in earlier times, to which the consciousness of sovereignty of the
individual states has risen', recorded Bismarck in 1861.[297] Prussia
alone, it seemed, could overcome particularism and fend off the
Great Powers, including Austria. In this sense, he wrote in a memorandum for Wilhelm on 30 March 1858, 'there is nothing more
German than the development of Prussia's particularist interests,
correctly understood'.[298] Although he refused to subordinate the
interests of the Hohenzollern monarchy to those of 'Germany',
Bismarck had accepted the reality and utility of a national idea
which had been largely formulated by liberals. In part, this was the
response of a young Junker, involved in the organisation of a new
'conservative party', to the national preoccupations of liberal and
democratic revolutionaries in 1848–49. During the revolution itself,
Bismarck had already identified Prussia as the 'best bulwark of
German power'.[299] In 1851, he had indicated his willingness to
conclude 'separate treaties on tariffs, law, and the military' outside
the Confederation.[300] In 1859, he confessed to Schleinitz, 'in these
private reflections', that his views diverged 'from those approved on
high, and indeed not in the direction of the *Kreuzzeitung*, but
surprisingly towards the Italian side', since he was not alienated by
Italian nationalism and he perceived Prussian and German advantages from cooperating with the 'national' powers – Italy and France
– against Austria.[301] By the early 1860s, he was ready to add a
German parliament to his list of national offerings, all of which
coincided with the aims of many liberals and their rejection of
Austria and the *Bund*. Prussian interests could be seen to have
converged with those of liberals in the *Klein-* and *Mittelstaaten*:
whereas 'the humiliating feeling of lack of worth and security
abroad' and 'the limitedness of political circles' was 'dominant' in
the smaller states, 'the Prussian *Volk*' felt let down by Austria and
hemmed in by the Confederation, prevented from realising its
potential. For its part, the German *Volk* was condemned, as 'a great
and powerful nation', 'by the shortcomings of its constitution for
the whole (*Gesammtverfassung*) not only to renounce the place in
Europe that it deserves, but also to live in constant fear of attack by
its neighbours'.[302]

All parties, it appeared, would benefit from unification under Prussian leadership. The Prussian Minister-President, despite his criticism of nationalists' idealism, had accepted – or, at least, had not rejected – many of their tenets on principle and in practice, partly because he was, as Rechberg noted in 1858, 'ambitious', demonstrating 'on many occasions, that he understands that he has to adapt his views to circumstances'.[303] Abroad and, to a more limited extent, at home, such adaptation to the national demands of liberals could be advantageous. The use of 'the army for a policy in the sense of the *Nationalverein*' would dissolve 'the resistance of the majority on the military question', Bismarck had told Disraeli in June 1862.[304] The next chapter examines the extent to which this actually occurred.

6 The Struggle for Germany in Schleswig-Holstein

It was no coincidence that Bismarck first used the Prussian army in Schleswig-Holstein. Ten days after his appointment on 22 September 1862, the new Minister-President asked the Chief of the General Staff Helmuth von Moltke to investigate the possibility of a war with Denmark.[1] The struggle between Germans and Danes in Schleswig had been going on for the last 500 years, Georg Waitz had written a decade earlier, and it would certainly continue.[2] The duchies, which were joined by a personal union of the monarch to the Kingdom of Denmark, had become the most famous national cause in Germany after Christian VIII had decreed in 1840 that Danish was to be used in the schools, courts and churches of North Schleswig. 'Our *Volk* has been brought up politically on the Schleswig-Holstein question,' declared the Badenese liberal Franz von Roggenbach: 'It was the first one in which the nation (*Nation*) participated again with insight, with conscience, after a long period of indifference. This question must be led to a happy end, otherwise the German *Volk* will lose its belief in itself.'[3] Until 1840, German had been the official language throughout the territory, even though at least half of Schleswig's population of 400,000 – and a large majority in the North – spoke a dialect of Danish. The duchies became a flashpoint not only because of the size and proximity of the German 'diaspora' there, accounting for about 700,000 of a total population of 900,000 in 1860, but also because Holstein was part of the German Confederation and because the charter of 1460, signed by the King of Denmark on being elected to what became –

in 1474 – the Dukedom of Schleswig-Holstein, had decreed that the two territories should remain independent of the kingdom and closely tied to each other. These 'old rights' had been maintained, with separate estates, separate laws of male-only succession and a separate chancellery run by German officials in Copenhagen, as a consequence of Denmark's inability to incorporate the duchies over the next three and a half centuries.

From a German point of view, such rights appeared to have been ignored by Christian's 'open letter' (*Aabene Bref*) of 1846, in which he had proposed that the eventual inheritance of the crown by his younger sister Charlotte – since he and Crown Prince Frederik were heirless – also applied to Schleswig, but not to parts of Holstein. In response, the Holstein estates protested to the German Confederation that Denmark was interfering illegally with the relationship between the two duchies, compounding the impression in Copenhagen, after the German majority of the Schleswig estates had voted in 1846 to join the *Bund*, that the entire territory was gravitating away from the Danish kingdom and towards Germany. The introduction of a new liberal constitution for the whole of the Helstat, including Schleswig and Holstein, in the spring of 1848 gave Germans the impression that the duchies were finally being incorporated into Denmark. When the duchies' estates insisted on a separate constitution and the entry of Schleswig into the Confederation, Frederik – who had succeeded Christian in December 1847 – replied by appointing a new ministry containing prominent national liberals such as Orla Lehmann and by proclaiming that Schleswig, as part of Denmark, would have the same constitution as the rest of the kingdom, which in turn prompted the establishment of a potentially secessionist provisional government in Kiel.

Prussia had taken up the provisional government's appeal to the *Bundestag* for protection, occupying the duchies and invading the rest of Denmark in April, May and June 1848, before being pressured by Russia, Britain and France into abandoning the 'revolution' and concluding the armistice of Malmö in July. A series of measures after the war finally ended in July 1850, including the sole use of Danish in schools and joint use in the civil service and church in the mixed areas of Central Schleswig as well as in the North, the imposition of constitutions on both duchies in 1854, and the introduction of a common constitution covering foreign policy, the military, trade and finance throughout the Helstat in 1855, all ensured that Schleswig-Holstein remained the principal site of national contention for both Germans and Danes. Young Germans like Otto Elben often made Schleswig-Holstein a point of pilgrimage on their tours of Europe, marvelling at the loyalty and suffering of their fellow countrymen. The *Volk* in the duchies was 'fully German-minded, moved by a firm will not to leave the German fatherland', wrote Elben on a trip just before the revolution, having completed his law degree at Tübingen.[4]

This chapter examines the 'German war' in Schleswig-Holstein and its consequences between 1864 and 1866, before the outcome of the Austro-Prussian War (1866) allowed the establishment of a new framework for German politics in the form of the *Norddeutscher Bund* (1867). The conflict with Denmark involved the national movement, the individual German states, Prussia, Austria and the European states' system. It reinforced the impression in some quarters that the national and constitutional questions were interrelated, a fact which appeared to have been proved by the Polish uprising of 1863, when liberals had had to choose – after Bismarck had agreed in the Alvensleben Convention (February 1863) to cooperate militarily with tsarist Russia against the Poles – between opposing the government or giving it conditional support in the face of a 'national threat' to supposedly exposed German communities in the East. In a similar – and much more emphatic – fashion, the conflict between Germans and Danes in Schleswig and Holstein revealed the character of the relationships between the different parties vis-à-vis the national question, with entanglements and after-effects, particularly those involving Berlin, Vienna and the administration of the duchies, which lasted – via the Gastein Convention (1865) – until the outbreak of war between the two Great Powers in 1866.

A War of Independence

The breadth and depth of support for a national war in Schleswig-Holstein in the early 1860s took many contemporaries by surprise, despite the long-running nature of the dispute. Even Bismarck, noted Theodor von Bernhardi in May 1864, 'was pushed into the affair against his will'.[5] All regions, a majority of political parties and large sections of the population appeared to have been affected. About 900 Schleswig-Holstein committees were established through-

out Germany.[6] According to Sybel's calculation, 84.4 per cent of
Landtag deputies in the third Germany, 53.4 per cent in Prussia and
7.6 per cent in Austria signed the petition for the duchies' 'rights'
in 1864.[7] Amidst the celebrations of the half-centenary of the battle
of Leipzig, wrote Elben, the unambiguous cause of Schleswig-
Holstein had surfaced to unite the German *Volk*:

> In great enthusiasm, the mood of the people immediately burst
> into flames, especially in South Germany. There had been no
> such movement since 1848; not even in 1859 at the time of the
> Italian war had such unanimity manifested itself. The gatherings
> of the years of the reaction had actually only encompassed party
> members; now, the whole *Volk* once again flowed together when
> they were called on to advise about the events of the day. As soon
> as a Schleswig-Holstein committee was formed, it contained, in
> fact, all relevant political points of view.[8]

Unexpectedly, the 'small German' *Nationalverein* and the 'greater
German' *Reformverein* had converged in a common national cause,
criticising Prussia, Austria and the Confederation. On 21 December
1863, members of the two organisations met in a specially convened
assembly at Frankfurt comprised of 490 deputies. 'Just beforehand,
on the occasion of the *Fürstenkongress* in Frankfurt, the
"Grossdeutsche" and the "Kleindeutsche" had strongly opposed
each other,' wrote Karl Biedermann: 'now they both united in the
national cause.'[9] Although members of the *Reformverein* subsequently left the assembly, they continued to cooperate in regional
Schleswig-Holstein committees throughout Germany. The movement for the duchies, which was coming to an end by October 1864,
reported one correspondent in the *Wochenschrift des Nationalvereins*,
had not merely been an aside but a complete act in the drama of
Germany's national development, creating a unity of purpose on
the part of the previously inimical National and Reform
Associations which was not to be squandered.[10] 'The *Volk* is united
to a man in the Schleswig-Holstein affair,' commented the
Wochenblatt des Deutschen Reformvereins on 29 November 1863: 'This is
the great favourite bet for the many small German squabbles and
German disunity. They completely dissolve in it.'[11]

During the crisis before war had broken out in January 1864, the
Reformverein had passed resolutions – in May 1863 – similar to those
of its 'small German' counterpart:

1. The *grossdeutsch* association recognises a considerable infraction of the rights of Germany in the measures of Denmark, which aim to bring about a complete division of Schleswig from Holstein and make the former into a Danish province; 2. The greater German association articulates the expectation that all German governments … will energetically oppose this step … 3. *Der grossdeutsche Verein* finds in the attempt of Denmark to withdraw from its duties towards Germany new grounds for pointing out the necessity of a *Bundesreform*, which in particular will consider the creation of a more unified and effective military organisation of the forces of the *Bund* resting on the military constitution of the German Confederation.'[12]

Later statements backed 'Friedrich von Schleswig-Holstein-Sonderburg-Augustenburg' as the heir to the duchies; they claimed that Denmark had forfeited the terms of any treaty by injuring 'the rights of Germany' through the 'signature of the common constitution for Denmark and Schleswig'; they pointed out the 'inadequacy of the constitution of the *Bund*'; and they criticised Austria and Prussia for making a mockery of the nation's rights.[13] The *Nationalverein* made the same points, albeit with more pronounced criticism of Austria and the third Germany, but with no greater leniency towards Prussia.[14] Both parties were confident that their stance on Schleswig-Holstein was justified on historical, moral, legal, political and national grounds. 'The Schleswig-Holstein affair is a struggle for law and right against usurpation, of honesty against lies, a struggle for freedom against arbitrariness and tyranny, for nationality against foreign domination,' declared a *Nationalverein* pamphlet in October 1863: 'But it is also a struggle for the interests and position of power of Germany, for the future of the German *Volk*, for the honour of the German tribe.'[15]

The war against Denmark in 1864 was popular, opposed only by a handful of radicals, wrote the liberal historian and forty-eighter Ludwig Häusser in the *Preussische Jahrbücher*, because Schleswig-Holstein had been the principal national question for the preceding twenty years.[16] Many 'patriots', complained Treitschke, had thought 'for years' that 'the Schleswig-Holstein question [was] the German question itself; whoever solves one will bring the other to an end'.[17] There had been broad agreement in 1848–49 that most, if not all, the territories of the duchies should be incorporated into the Reich and there was a corresponding sense of humiliation and dishonour, recalled a retrospective article in the *Grenzboten* in 1864, when Schleswig-Holstein was handed back over to Denmark in 1850.[18] Austria's treacherous support for Denmark, Prussia's self-interested actions as a Great Power, withdrawing from Jutland by the time of the armistice of Malmö in July 1848, the weakness of the Frankfurt Parliament and the inability or unwillingness of the political parties to act all seemed from the perspective of 1864 to have been responsible for Germany's failure to incorporate the duchies and to protect the German diaspora there in 1848–50.[19] Such a reading of history was widely shared, with much of the press concurring with Arndt's appraisal at the time – published in the *Kölnische Zeitung* – that Schleswig-Holsteiner were 'fighting for their German life and for their old right of a fatherland'.[20] 'They stand, fight and bleed not for themselves alone, but for all Germans, for the whole of Germany', he continued.[21] The North German liberal *National-Zeitung*, the South German liberal *Allgemeine Zeitung*, and the conservative and Catholic *Deutsches Volksblatt* all agreed in 1850 that the fight for Schleswig-Holstein was a just national cause on which the fate of Germany itself depended, thwarted by the actions of self-interested Great Powers anxious to perpetuate the fragmentation and impotence of the German lands at the centre of Europe.[22]

The interpretation of events in the duchies provided by a *kleindeutsch* periodical such as the *Grenzboten* was predictable: the *Bund* had rightly contended that Schleswig and Holstein should not be divided, with the territories belonging by education and culture in a progressive Germany rather than a poor, backward and isolated Danish 'sham state', or *Scheinstaat* (1849); discussion of the duchies by the Great Powers at London in 1852, after Prussia had stood down definitively in 1850, was more significant for the area's history than 1848 had been, with Denmark effectively mocking a divided Germany despite the risk of revolutionising German public opinion, ignoring the fact that Germans dominated both the state and the culture of Denmark, and sealing off Schleswig-Holstein as a bridge for the spread of German culture to the North (1852–53); the 'occupation' of Schleswig-Holstein by Denmark in the 1850s had been the result of German, not merely Prussian, powerlessness, with the duchies – Schleswig in particular, since it was most endangered – remaining an open national sore and a source of dishonour for large sections of the public, notwithstanding the continuing dominance and expansion of German culture (1856–61); and the reopening of the Schleswig-Holstein question, when it occurred in the early 1860s, had been the consequence of public agitation in the face of Prussia's and Austria's unreliability as Great Powers, the Confederation's continuing ineffectiveness, and international hostility (1863–64).[23] More striking than such a North German liberal narrative of Schleswig-Holstein's history was that of the South German Catholic *Historisch-politisch Blätter*, which shared many common elements with that of the *Grenzboten*, including the notion that the duchies were part of a natural German organism, that they had been a source of German shame since 1848, when they had been left to fend for themselves against Danish nationalism and centralisation, that they had exposed the inefficacy of German institutions, and that they had suffered from Berlin's and Vienna's contraventions of the national interest.[24] Cross-party support for a beleaguered Schleswig-Holstein as a German '*Lebensfrage*', as various correspondents put it, had a long pedigree.[25]

Historians from the region – Dahlmann, Waitz, Wihelm Beseler, Droysen, Theodor Mommsen – had done much to establish the historical reality, legal rights and national culture of the duchies in the public imagination. The peninsula was portrayed as a 'German arm' reaching out to dominate the North and Baltic seas, extending 'German life, influence and education' to the British Isles, Scandinavia and the world.[26] It was also the battleground between Scandinavians coming South and Germans advancing to the coast and to the North: 'The archipelago, whose southern half comprises the duchies of Schleswig and Holstein, is the bridge over which the Scandinavian North is connected with the South, with the rest of Europe. Again and again, the Danes – the people of the northern tribe which is furthest forward – have tried to gain both domination of the Baltic and possession of the land up to the Elbe.'[27] 'The struggle between the Germans and the Danes here is almost as old as our knowledge of history', asserted Waitz, underlining the momentousness of contemporary events and national conflicts.[28]

In the modern era, the duchies had gradually become more unified, despite Danish tutelage.[29] Since the seventeenth century, at the latest, they had shared estates, a common law and legal system, and other institutions, much as Prussia and Brandenburg had done: Denmark's tie to Schleswig-Holstein was no greater than that of the King of Prussia to Poland, proposed Waitz in 1852.[30] The relationship had begun to change in the nineteenth century, as Denmark had sought to expand to the South, conflicting with long-established links – presented as if they were in a chain – between

Map 5   Schleswig-Holstein in 1864
Source: Adapted from

Schleswig and Holstein, and between Holstein and Germany.[31] 'In
Schleswig as in Holstein, one lived in full consciousness of the
linkage with the German *Volk* ... in many respects perhaps too cut
off and closed in on themselves, but still advancing along the path
of national development', wrote Waitz more than a decade later.[32]
In part, such a shift was the corollary of Danish expansionism, with

the Danes succeeding in 'drawing the different *Völker* and states in
their vicinity towards their sphere of power and tying them to their
fate', in Droysen's words.[33] More importantly, it was a result of
inevitable national conflicts which, after the revival of 'the old
struggle between Danes and Germans' and after attempts by the
majority 'Eiderdane party' to incorporate both duchies into
Denmark in the 1840s, had become incontrovertible by January
1848, as Beseler explained.[34] 'A state is always a state, to which –
according to modern thinking and practice – individual parts or
provinces must be subordinated,' he continued: 'One foresaw with
certainty that the profound enmity of the two nationalities, the
conflict of their contradictory interests, would make a harmonious
life together impossible and allow no reconciliation to be found;
one foresaw that the government would soon see itself forced into
taking embittering coercive measures against the duchies.'[35]

The war which broke out in 1848 was seen to be a defensive and
a just one, but 'Austria was against the cause of the duchies', Prussia
'was afraid of bearing the burden alone' and was pushed around by
the other Great Powers, and the National Assembly in Frankfurt
'lacked absolute decisiveness and power'.[36] After Prussia had
submitted to 'Austrian policy' at Olmütz, concluded Waitz,
Copenhagen had attempted 'the building of a Danish *Gesammtstaat*'
in the 1850s, treating the duchies like 'subjugated provinces'.[37]
When the Danish common constitution had failed, it had tried to
incorporate Schleswig, repressing and persecuting inhabitants 'with
brutal violence' in the northern duchy, and in 'somewhat more
accommodating forms' in the southern one.[38] 'It required no
particular political acuity to foresee the immediate effects of these
catastrophes,' wrote Beseler: 'Danes and Schleswig-Holsteiner have
no particular political, social and material interests in common; in
almost all spheres of these interests, they face each other as
enemies.'[39] 'The fate of the duchies is and remains chained to
Germany,' he continued: 'The bonds which nature has created are
sacred and indissoluble.'[40] Schleswig-Holstein was small and easily
overlooked, but its *Volk* was 'immortal', containing a 'higher life
force' and offering Germany the enticing prospect of national
redemption.[41]

The small and middling states, acting through the *Bund*,
appeared to be the most reliable defenders of Schleswig-Holstein in
the early 1860s. In Häusser's opinion, the states of the third
Germany had proved themselves more national-minded than

Prussia or Austria, and the Confederation, at the start of the crisis, had acted correctly.[42] In February 1858, the *Bundestag* refused to recognise Denmark's common constitution of 1855 or Holstein's constitution of the previous year, since they had not been submitted to the estates as required by federal law. Instead, it made a formal request, on pain of federal execution, for a return to the independent status promised to Holstein – and to the small Duchy of Lauenburg – by King Frederik's proclamation of January 1852, which had offered Holstein, Lauenburg and Schleswig separate constitutions, ministries and estates. When Denmark promptly suspended the common constitution in the two confederal territories and referred the matter to the estates, the latter called for the restoration of the administrative and legislative union of Schleswig and Holstein which had existed before 1848 and solicited the help of the *Bund*, Prussia and Austria, complaining that Denmark's different treatment of the duchies presaged a definitive partition. After twice postponing action in 1860 and 1861, following Danish concessions, the *Bundestag* decided to proceed on 1 October 1863 with a federal execution against King Frederik as the Duke of Holstein and Lauenburg, since he was threatening to divide the duchies in contravention of the royal proclamation of 1852, having confirmed in April that all legislation passed by the monarch and the *Rigsraad*, not merely the common constitution, would in future be binding in Schleswig, whereas no legislation would be binding in Holstein without its estates' consent, in line with the liberal constitution granted on 30 March.

When Frederik died on 15 November, succeeded by Christian von Glücksburg as Christian IX in accordance with the terms of the Treaty of London (1852), the *Bundestag* refused on 28 November by 14 votes to 2, against Prussian and Austrian objections, to recognise him as the Duke of Holstein, which had a male-only law of succession, and it ruled that an enquiry should determine whether Christian had a claim not only to Holstein, but also to Schleswig and Lauenburg. Berlin and Vienna narrowly managed – by 8 votes to 7 – to prevent the federal 'occupation' from going ahead on this basis by threatening to take military action against the *Bund*, only to be overruled by 11 votes to 5 on 14 January 1864 in favour of Hesse-Darmstadt's motion to occupy Schleswig, in addition to Holstein, 'until the current pending issues' – that is, the succession question as well as the constitutional one – 'are resolved'.[43] Prussia and Austria, which had agreed in the Treaty of London – along with the other Great Powers, but without the involvement of the Confederation – to guarantee the succession of Christian, declared jointly on 16 January that they would act on their own 'to make effective the rights of Germany' by forcing Denmark to revoke its common constitution within 48 hours and to put forward proposals to make good the pledges of the royal proclamation of 1852, if the *Bund* persisted in interfering in the succession to the Duchy of Schleswig, which lay outside its jurisdiction.[44] The Great Powers added that, once they had occupied the duchies, they would not allow demonstrations of support for Duke Friedrich von Augustenburg, who had established an unofficial Court in Kiel. 57,000 Prussian and Austrian troops entered Holstein on 21 January 1864, superseding the existing confederal occupying force of 12,000 Hanoverian and Saxon soldiers, and they invaded Schleswig on 1 February, preventing the Confederation from doing the same on different – and less internationally acceptable – grounds. After defeating the Danish army at Düppel on 18 April and failing to come to an agreement at the London Conference in May and June, the contending powers signed an armistice on 20 July and the Treaty of Vienna on 30 October, placing the duchies under joint control and, with the Gastein Convention of August 1865, under separate Austrian and Prussian administrations in Holstein and Schleswig respectively.

Public opinion and the political parties sided largely with the *Mittelstaaten* and the German Confederation as war approached, since they had championed the popular causes of Augustenburg and an independent Schleswig-Holstein, but few saw the *Bund* and the states of the third Germany in a fundamentally new light. Initially, individual governments such as that of Bavaria had coincided in their aims with the most important sections of the political public, especially with what the editor of the *Historisch-politische Blätter* Joseph Edmund Jörg termed 'dominating liberalism'.[45] To the Bavarian Foreign Minister Karl von Schrenck, the Schleswig-Holstein affair was a 'holy cause' and the Schleswig-Holstein-Verein was 'their association', 'composed of very solid people', which aspiring officials like Chlodwig zu Hohenlohe-Schillingsfürst were advised to join, as 'this was the means to become a minister'.[46] The 'question was able to gain so great a significance' in the first instance because of its legal ramifications, and 'the Germans are a legal people', wrote Hohenlohe to Queen Victoria on 4 May 1864: 'Yet, apart from this, everyone in Germany felt the deeper signifi-

cance of the Schleswig-Holstein question for our internal conditions. Everyone knows that in this question the German question
will be decided.'[47] What was more, it appeared to both the ministry
and the public 'at the start', 'as if the German *Mittelstaaten*, the truly
pure German states, could gain greater political weight through the
Schleswig-Holstein affair,' he continued: 'Here is the reason why
this question has called forth a larger movement in the lands
outside Prussia and Austria.'[48] The Bavarian government, parties
and public opinion had grasped that the defence and formation of
an independent, medium-sized Schleswig-Holstein, the most
popular national cause since the 1840s, might offer other
Mittelstaaten and the *Bund*, as the principal champions of
Augustenburg and the duchies, a more central role in a recon-
structed Germany.

Partly because they could more easily imagine themselves in the
position of the Schleswig-Holsteiner, partly because they were more
threatened by the seemingly imminent resolution of the German
question, many Bavarians reacted strongly to the occupation of the
duchies, to the distaste of self-confessedly more 'conservative' and
'federative' onlookers like Dalwigk, who hinted in March 1864 that
the former Bavarian Foreign Minister Pfordten had put 'the subordinate Schleswig-Holstein question' above 'the continuation of the
German Confederation' and the states' relationship to Austria and
Prussia.[49] This was also the tenor of much early and some later press
reportage and pamphleteering, which depicted the Treaty of
London as a brutal act of violence and called for the establishment
of 'Schleswig-Holstein as an independent German land' in 'the
interests and for the honour of Germany'.[50] The Augsburg
Allgemeine Zeitung reported in similar terms that the German states,
the Confederation and 'the German *Volk*' should regulate their
'internal affairs' and fight Danish aggression with 'iron and blood',
not just words, albeit in a 'nobler sense' than Bismarck.[51] 'The
German question does not hinge on Prussia or on Austria, but it has
its pivot in the pure German states', declared the Munich periodical
Chronik der Gegenwart, before proceeding to outline its scheme for a
'West German federation' of middling states, for which Prussia
would need to give up the Rhineland.[52] The thrust of Bavarian
policy towards Schleswig-Holstein should be to create a counterweight in the *Bund* to the Great Power pretensions of Prussia, wrote
the prominent liberal and founder of the Bavarian *Reformverein*
Gustav von Lerchenfeld as late as March 1866: on the solution of the

question 'rests the continuation or dissolution of the Confederation, the position of its members vis-à-vis the *Bund* authority and amongst themselves; the question of federalism or hegemony, or, more clearly expressed, of complete subjugation and incorporation of the confederal states which are not Great Powers ... whether *grossdeutsch* or *kleindeutsch* or, better, *grosspreussisch*, whether through freedom to unification and, temporarily at least, to unity'.[53] To many contemporaries, Schleswig-Holstein seemed, in Hohenlohe's phrase, to be an '*Existenzfrage*' for Bavaria.[54]

Support for the Bavarian state and the *Bund* was fragile and quickly metamorphosed into criticism. According to Hohenlohe, the reason for initial euphoria and subsequent pessimism was the same, resting on a sense of inferiority and powerlessness:

> Whoever has carefully observed the upheavals which have moved Germany in the last fifty years will find that their real motive can be found in the discontentment of the inhabitants of the *Mittelstaaten* and *Kleinstaaten*, a population of about 19 million people, which sees itself excluded from participation in the fate of Europe. This population of the middling and small states of Germany can be seen in the condition of mature men, from whom the administration of their own affairs is reserved ... In order to escape these conditions, one strove in 1848 for so-called German unity. This movement began in South West Germany. It proved to be impractical, since neither Austria nor Prussia could subject themselves to an ideal power.
>
> The German *Volk* has made progress in its political education since 1848, and has in particular learned to wait ... It is, though, in this state of affairs and by the completely dominant mood in Germany inevitable that the consequences of a solution of the Schleswig-Holstein question which injures the legal conscious-ness of the people will have the most serious consequences for Germany and, in particular, for the existence of the *Mittelstaaten* and the *Kleinstaaten*.
>
> Statesmen also fully recognise this, which explains why conser-vative men like Beust and Pfordten have joined the party of move-ment in this question.[55]

Many of Pfordten's actions over Schleswig-Holstein betrayed feel-ings of insecurity. Like Hohenlohe, he was not at all certain that the small and medium-sized states would survive. In October 1864, for instance, Dalwigk found him 'very pessimistic about politics': he 'is convinced that in fifty years' time all German *Mittel-* and *Kleinstaaten* will be mediatised'.[56] When the Hessian first minister had met him in April, he

> was very embittered about the course of German affairs. He said Bavaria should leave the German Confederation. It would then play a completely different role. The Great Powers would then have good words to say to a state which has five million inhabitants and could easily have double the number of inhabitants if it wanted to change its legislation concerning marriage and freedom of profession.[57]

As sections of public opinion began to criticise the government, Pfordten turned on the *Bund*, already complaining as early as March 1864 that 'Germany has ceased to exist' and threatening that 'Bavaria should leave the Confederation.'[58] 'If the *Bund* were to dissolve itself,' Pfordten told the Saxon envoy in Munich, 'then Bavaria would "not come out of it badly."'[59] The Foreign Minister was increasingly convinced of the ineffectiveness of the Confederation and the bankruptcy of Austria, pushing him – almost despite himself – further towards Prussia, which he portrayed in April 1866 as 'a young, upwardly striving state, whose urge to strengthen and enlarge itself in order to match its vocation is not unjustified'.[60] Consequently, the Hohenzollern monarchy, negotiating from a position of power, was held to be 'more flexible in the Schleswig-Holstein question' and a more likely partner than Austria, which had proved itself 'unreliable in all respects'.[61] Even on the eve of the Austro-Prussian war, Pfordten thought that he could persuade Berlin not to annex Schleswig-Holstein by offering it the military command of North Germany within the Confederation.[62]

If the Schleswig-Holstein affair was a 'legal question' for the people, wrote Hohenlohe in May 1864, it was a '*Machtfrage* for the governments and an *Existenzfrage* for the Confederation'.[63] Once it had reverted to a 'question of power and influence between Prussia and Austria', the states of the third Germany seemed to have little option but to watch events unfold, not least because the 'present state of the German *Bund*' was one of 'the most ineluctable confusion'.[64] All that a state such as Bavaria could do was to continue to try to set up a trias within the Confederation, but it was unlikely to be successful, given the opposition of South and Central German democrats, the 'aversion of Austria and Prussia' and the 'aversion of different dynasties to renounce a part of their sovereignty in favour of the ruling house which would have to take over the leadership of the narrower *Bund*'.[65] At times, lamented Hohenlohe, it appeared 'that the *Mittelstaaten* will be damned to remain, in the future as in the past, in their current condition until they finally fall victim in a great European conflict to necessary territorial alterations'.[66]

Such weakness and inactivity alienated the public, ensuring 'that a feeling of dissatisfaction spread further and further in the South German states in respect of the passive role to which these states were condemned in this question that touches on German interests', noted Hohenlohe.[67] Although 'Schleswig-Holstein is still spoken and written of a lot, the participation of the *Volk* has diminished', meaning 'that the interest in the duchies which manifested itself in such a stormy fashion in the previous year was less for the Schleswig-Holstein question in itself than for the German question, which seemed about to be resolved in this conflict'.[68] As Bavaria and the Confederation proved less and less able to act, overshadowed by Prussia and Austria, many contemporaries appear to have become disillusioned with them. Some parties had been sceptical of them throughout the crisis. A minority of Bavarian liberals who were in favour of *Kleindeutschland* were convinced that 'the unworthy role' of the *Mittelstaaten* had been one of 'self-interested denial of national duties' and 'mean-heartedness, incapacity and vacillating cowardice'.[69] For its part, the *Bund* had again shown itself to be merely the instrument of the German Great Powers: 'There is only a Prussian and an Austrian, no *German* policy, in which the *strength of the whole* nation (*Nation*) could be realised', wrote Karl Brater, the editor of the *Süddeutsche Zeitschrift*, co-founder of the Bavarian *Fortschrittspartei* and one of the leading *kleindeutsch* deputies in the Bavarian *Landtag*:

> Even the most stupid today grasp the necessity of a unitary central power and an ordered and constitutional *Volksvertretung* … Soon the German dynasties will seek the ultimate guarantee of their own security against all the uncertainties of the future in a German parliament, in the necessary limitation of their sovereign rights … The *Bundesverfassung* is the impotence of the small states under the hypocritical appearance of sovereignty; a *Reichsverfassung* secures for each single member a worthy place in the great organism of the whole.[70]

Although liberal politicians like Brater were critical of Prussia as a self-interested Great Power and of Bismarck as a violent adventurer 'without greatness', they believed that 'the German powers [had] been pushed to victory by the pressure of public opinion': 'Through the pressure of the popular movement the allied army was led to Schleswig; under the pressure of military victories Berlin's policy has been obliged to increase its diplomatic demands.'[71] The Prussian Minister-President himself, claimed Brater, had been forced, 'after long toing and froing, to satisfy the desires of the popular assembly and leave the reprehensible path of the policy of 1850. A powerful *liberal* government would have come to the same decisions *without* hesitation.'[72]

The mouthpiece of the Bavarian Progressive Party echoed such sentiments, arguing that a Prussian victory 'consolidates the rule of the Junkers' and 'encumbers the internal struggle for freedom', but it was also more dismissive of the 'Austrian *Gesammtstaat*', whose interest was 'not a German interest'.[73] According to this reading of events, 'the nation (*Nation*), as is the essence of cabinet politics, stands beyond the fighting parties'.[74] One part of the democratic party in the South and Central German states, which was made up of 'conscious or unconscious republicans', concurred with such a reading and was similarly detached, waiting for a time 'when a democratic Continental storm would bring down thrones and bring back the happy times of a constituent National Assembly'.[75] The other faction of South German democracy, wrote Hohenlohe, belonged 'in part to the *Nationalverein* and is striving for the organisation of a German *Bundesstaat* under the leadership of Prussia. They hold the government of Herr von Bismarck for a temporary evil, after whose dismissal the idea [of *Kleindeutschland*] would still be implemented.'[76] A proportion of the liberal and democratic milieux of Bavaria – more than is suggested by the 16 deputies of the *Fortschrittspartei* elected in 1863 – rejected Austria's claims and had lost faith in the *Mittelstaaten* and the *Bund*. In such circumstances, cooperation with – or lack of resistance to – Prussia, although an object of contempt under Bismarck, could seem to be the lesser evil.

The *Historisch-politische Blätter* demonstrated the ambivalence of Bavarian political Catholicism, which constituted – in an undefined form – the second largest political grouping after the liberals, towards the German question between 1863 and 1866. Although its editor Edmund Jörg went on to found the *Bayerische Patriotenpartei* in 1868 and to oppose national unity under Prussian leadership in

1870, the periodical was highly critical of particularist *Mittelstaaten*, which appeared to have forged a *de facto* alliance with liberals and Progressives in support of Augustenburg and against the German Great Powers.[77] All Germans were justified on legal and national grounds in resisting Denmark's illegitimate attempt to annex the duchies and to oppress their German populations.[78] Yet Progressives had sought to gain a demagogic party advantage from the affair, even mouthing the arguments of monarchical legitimacy in their quest for a revolution of the relations within and between German states.[79] The centralising logic of liberalism – the 'fault of the all-powerful liberal *Zeitgeist*' – on both sides of the border meant 'that German demands for Holstein are simply incompatible with the essence of the constitutional order of a *Gesammtstaat*'.[80] The Confederation and the middling states had been pushed into a federal execution by the end of 1863 which would be difficult to reverse, 'not least because an ascendant liberalism feels the undemonstrable need to make a hero-ically active entry somewhere and therefore must hold up the Danish king each time because it believes that it has least to fear from him'.[81] Caught in such a contradictory position, the *Bundestag* and the individual states had been unable to act, merely proving that the Confederation could not work.[82] 1864 had proved three things: 'First, the European states' system no longer exists. Second, the hope that the whole of Germany (*Gesammtdeutschland*) would throw itself into the breach as a European balance has as good as disappeared ... Third, the *status quo* of the German *Bund* is also no longer sustain-able and must, in one way or another, become something else', observed Jörg in 1865.[83]

By contrast, Austria and Prussia, to whose actions the periodical gave its blessing on 24 January 1864, had bypassed the machinery of the *Bund* in pursuit of more realistic, internationally acceptable goals, motivated by their own self-interest.[84] 'It was our view from the start that the snatching of the duchies would be at the cost of a war of conquest against half of Europe and that one would not mount such a war in order to found a new little middling state à la Baden or Coburg for the sphere of domination of the liberal-demo-cratic party and to transfer to a puppet of this party the watch over the most difficult border in Germany,' commented Jörg on 24 April 1864: 'If a great war is to be carried out for Schleswig and Holstein, then it must have the goal of incorporating both lands in Prussia.'[85] The Confederation and the states had naively put themselves at the head of the liberal and national movement, only to fail to achieve their aims in the face of opposition from the Great Powers. Their decisions had left Prussia dominant in Germany. The advice of the *Historisch-politische Blätter* was to allow Berlin to annex the duchies in order cheaply to satisfy the Prussian state's hunger to expand.[86] Austria, it was held, secretly desired the *status quo ante bellum* and did not need to be appeased.[87] The prospect of *Grossdeutschland*, espoused in the past by Catholics such as Peter Reichensperger, was no longer worth entertaining.[88] The periodical continued to claim that 'an honest German *Bundesreform*' would 'be very well worth a small world war', but it was by no means optimistic that such a reform would come about.[89] In current conditions, it had little sympathy for a weak *Bund* and feckless *Mittelstaaten*.

A shift from a near-consensus over Schleswig-Holstein in 1863, which was framed against Berlin and Vienna, to splintered criticism of one's own government and of the Confederation after mid-1864 was characteristic of most middling and small German states. By that date, before the Gastein Convention (1865) signalled his demise by ensconcing the administration of the Great Powers and adumbrating the annexation of the duchies, Augustenburg's popularity had already begun to wane, commented Jörg.[90] With a victorious Prussian state continuing to defy its own *Landtag*, to uphold the Treaty of London's guarantee of the succession and to refuse to set up an independent state of Schleswig-Holstein, disillusionment with the *Mittelstaaten* and the *Bund* was never likely to redound straight-forwardly to Berlin's advantage, even if it had not been further confused by the diverse and complex formation of parties and political milieux in the individual states. 'The unity with which the German *Volk* initially stood by the side of the Schleswig-Holstein uprising was dissolved; whereas we in South Germany held that the handing over of the duchies to the Duke of Augustenburg was the sole possible solution, ever greater sources of confusion were introduced into the whole affair: the common administration of Prussia and Austria proved impossible; it became ever clearer that the German question was contained within the Schleswig-Holstein question,' wrote the Stuttgart liberal Elben in the summer of 1864, after making his fifth trip to the duchies: 'How should everything be solved? Nowhere was there any clarity. If the *Nationalverein* had correctly characterised the end-point, and the national-minded here had also signed up to it in principle, the conduct of Prussia was fundamentally designed to destroy every predilection and all trust.'[91] As always, continued the newspaper owner, 'such conditions provided the ground for the creation and splitting of parties', with the once-united Schleswig-Holstein committee abandoned by the conservatives, spawning a new democratic *Volkspartei* and pushing the *Grossdeutsche* to the left.[92]

A similar pattern could be seen in Saxony, where Beust, who also served as the external representative of the *Bund*, had rejoiced that public opinion and the policy of the government had naturally coincided over the duchies, and where Biedermann had marvelled that 'this movement of the people for the right of Schleswig-Holstein found ... an unexpectedly powerful echo in ruling circles right up to the throne', to the point at which the former radical worried that the third Germany might manage to refashion Germany without Prussia into a form of '*Klein-Klein-Deutschland*'.[93] As in other states, 'the victorious deeds of the Prussian army ... which showed what Prussia could do ... and which also cast light on the army reform that had in the meantime been set into motion, gave another direction to public opinion', which was more favourable to Berlin, although 'the general German question, the question about its future form,' remained 'open'.[94] With the signing of the peace treaty in October 1864, 'Prussia's victory was confirmed, not only over Denmark, but also over the German Confederation and over Austria', wrote the Finance Minister Richard von Friesen in his memoirs, aided by Vienna's vacillating and contradictory policy after 1849, which had 'alienated the German *Volk* from Austria and led it into the arms of Prussia'.[95] As in Württemberg, actual conversions in Saxony to support for Prussia were complicated, haphazard and limited in scope.[96] Nevertheless, it was also true that there was little support for Beust's alternative strategy of a *Bundesreform*. The Schleswig-Holstein crisis, although resolved 'by the weapons and diplomacy of the two Great Powers', had fomented a genuinely national, if only briefly united, movement, in which 'public opinion in Germany' had had 'an indirectly shaping effect' on events, in Biedermann's estimation.[97] The main effect of the crisis outside Prussia was to remove plausible alternatives to a *kleindeutsch* federal state.

The Forces of Progress

Some democrats took exception to the involvement of Prussia under Bismarck in the future unification of Germany. Their objections drew on a broader antipathy towards the Hohenzollern monarchy in the *Mittelstaaten* and rested on a long-established debate, prominent in 1848, about the precedence of freedom or unity. Neither set of objections, however, seriously undermined the case for a small German *Bundesstaat*, as it had been outlined in the *Reichsverfassung* of 1849. Thus, the effects of the formation of the *Demokratische Volkspartei* which resulted from the division of liberals and democrats, as well as splits within democratic ranks, were largely limited to Württemberg, even though the party attracted members from other states such as Georg Friedrich Kolb, Franz Tafel (Palatinate), Jakob Venedey (Baden), Johann Jacoby (Prussia), Adolph Rossmässler, Christian Schüler, Wilhelm Michael Schaffrath and Franz Wigard (Saxony). The *Volkspartei*, which was set up in 1864 from within Progressive ranks by the returning radical forty-eighters Carl Mayer, Ludwig Pfau and Julius Haussmann, quickly gained supporters and standing in the South German state, assuming control of the *Beobachter* and gaining 1,700 members by 1866, partly because it was able to benefit from the residual popularity of radicalism in the South West, and partly because it acted as a conduit for popular anti-Prussian feeling heightened by the Schleswig-Holstein crisis. 'Freedom must dissolve Prussia into its tribes and incorporate them in the great federation', ran one of its founding statements.[98] Yet, although it shaped the political landscape of Württemberg, supporting the state's stand against Berlin in the Austro-Prussian war and provoking the creation by 1866 of an opposing German Party composed of remaining democrats and liberals, the *Volkspartei* had little impact elsewhere, especially in Prussia, whose radicals and liberals it accused of hypocrisy: 'The Prussian faction of the German *Fortschrittspartei* and the *Nationalverein* never ceases to thunder against the person of Herr v. Bismarck, but it accepts the successes of his *violent, specifically Prussian politics* as useful.'[99] Even in Württemberg, a single parliamentary liberal-democratic faction, which counted at least 44 deputies out of a total of 93, continued to exist until after the Austro-Prussian war, despite the creation of the *Volkspartei* and the *Deutsche Partei* beforehand.[100] As one greater German member of the faction wrote to Julius Hölder, leader of the German Party, in October 1866: 'The left should not forget that it belongs together because of temporary differences about the way to our common goal.'[101]

In the rest of Germany, the incipient division of the democratic and liberal milieu in Württemberg, which caused a drastic fall in

Nationalverein membership there, was part of a wider revolt against Prussia in the South, which issued in a meeting of the *Abgeordnetentag*, designed to protest against the Gastein Convention, on 1 October 1865. Democrats and Southerners played a prominent role, after a meeting of Prussian Progressives, including Unruh, Twesten, Mommsen and Schulze-Delitzsch, had publicly announced that they would not attend in order to try to deflect criticism from Prussia and to avoid displaying 'the splits of the liberal German party'.[102] Of the 268 deputies at the Frankfurt meeting, called a 'Rump Parliament' by the *Grenzboten* because it compared badly to the 490 at the meeting of December 1863, there were only 7 Prussians, as opposed to 79 Bavarians (29 per cent), 37 Frankfurters (14 per cent) and 27 Württembergers (10 per cent).[103] Bennigsen, who opposed the convening of the meeting, could merely hope, on 4 September, that 'those, too, who have decided in favour of a consciously radical and anti-Prussian tendency will soon have to convince themselves that South West Germany, with its democratic plans, can gain no advantage, but will run a great risk, if the assembly seals the rift between the South and the North Germans'.[104] In the event, the *Abgeordnetentag* passed off without incident, restricting itself to 'mere words', in the view of the Württemberg radical Carl August Fetzer.[105] Although democratic parties were mooted, none, apart from the *Volkspartei*, was successfully founded. Many well-known democrats remained members of the *Nationalverein*, *Abgeordnetentag* and *Fortschrittspartei*.

The many divisions and disputes on the left over the German question could be misleading. 'How hard it must be to agree on the German question', Fetzer wrote to Venedey in September 1865, 'if friends, who wish each other well and who strive for the same goal by largely similar means, need to use so many words in order to understand each other.'[106] With few organisational restraints to keep them in check, democrats and radicals disagreed about the nature of the army or militia, the desirability of a monarchy or republic, the political significance of the social question and economics, and the practicality of popular agitation and revolution. As the controversy surrounding speeches given by Ludwig Simon and Ludwig Bamberger at the German *Turnfest* in Paris on 27 May 1865 evinced, there were also differences of opinion about unitary and federal government: the former, attacked by Georg Friedrich Kolb in the *Neue Frankfurter Zeitung* and by Carl Mayer in the *Beobachter*, defended the ideas of 1789 against 'German freedom', contending that 'France from time to time sacrifices its liberty in order to bind itself together in unity and power'; the latter argued, using the American Civil War as a warning, that 'Germany's salvation can only come about ... under the banner of a strictly unified Germany, without federalist half-measures.'[107]

Mayer replied to Bamberger in a long article in the *Beobachter* in which he identified a four-party system in Germany, with two of the groupings on the left: particularists who strove to maintain the *status quo*; 'Gothaer', or liberals who wanted to submit to 'the *Pickelhaube* of Prussian Caesarism'; 'revolutionary centralists and unitarians' such as Bamberger; and democratic federalists like himself, who 'negate both Great Powers ... and who, through the temporary coalition of small and middling states ... strive for a lever ... for the bringing about of a democratic and naturally integrated, real *Bundesstaat*'.[108] At the same time, Mayer distanced himself from the trias put forward in *Theorie der Politik* (1864) by Julius Fröbel, begging the question of what, exactly, he meant by 'federalism'. Its precondition was freedom, the entrenchment of whose 'essence and being' guaranteed 'that the victory of federalism is decided in advance'.[109] Such trust in freedom took precedence over everything else, in Mayer's opinion, even loyalty to the nation, as he spelled out in the *Beobachter* in February 1864: 'Today, the national question has come into the foreground; but where nationality and freedom come into conflict, our paper will stand on the side of freedom.'[110] To the leader of the *Volkspartei*, the policy of the *Nationalverein*, which was prepared to back the exercise of power for the attainment of a German nation, was 'myopic':

> We ideal politicians [pursue] our goal of a free German federal state (*Föderativstaat*), with the princes or without them, by trying to remove the obstacles which hinder democratic and national progress. Our way is the way of freedom, not violence ... If the path of freedom also only leads to the goal after years ... we shall take our time and can do enough good in the service of freedom and the *Volk*, even if we do not ourselves reach the last goal.'[111]

Yet how many democrats shared Mayer's view or, in contrast to 1848, believed that freedom and unity were separable?

At the beginning of the Schleswig-Holstein crisis, radicals reacted in a manner redolent of 1848. Karl Blind wrote from exile in

Britain on 30 January that Prussia and Austria had committed treason, as in the first Slesvig war, and that 'Not Bavaria and Saxony, not Baden, Coburg and Augustenburg can now be the solution, but the independence of the land of Schleswig-Holstein brought about by the sovereign German nation! ... Germany's fate will now be decided on open ground.'[112] From the United States, Gustav Struve returned to print in a series of memoirs which linked his recollections of 1848 to the present crisis: 'The obstacles which stand in the way of a satisfying solution of the Schleswig-Holstein question are the same as those which permit neither freedom nor unity to emerge in the whole of Germany.'[113] The sun of freedom was in the ascendant, rejoiced the radical forty-eighter: the German nation itself had the right to resist and overcome, 'through iron and blood', the despotic dynastic regimes of Prussia and of Austria, as had occurred in Italy.[114] In Germany, radical forty-eighters such as Kolb, Ruldolf Christmann, Franz August Mammen and Wilhelm Löwe were instrumental at the Frankfurt meeting of deputies on 21 December 1863 in the establishment of a standing '36-committee', typical of the revolution, to coordinate the campaign to free the duchies.

Some radicals such as Venedey suspected, again in a manner recalling the revolution, that democrats, many of whom had not got seats in state assemblies because of restrictive franchises, were being kept away from Frankfurt deliberately since their presence 'would disturb the unanimity of the Gotha fuddle', yet they appealed to acceptable revolutionary precedents for the most part: 'The plan of Häusser & Co., who have taken you in tow ... *does not aim for a German parliament*, but for a Schleswig-Holstein *German central committee.*'[115] Venedey's criticism of the majority of the Prussian *Fortschrittspartei*, which was '*dealing with Herr v. Bismarck*', and his call for a militia of 100,000 gymnasts to expel the Danes from the duchies and for a popular uprising against the 'Junker' regime – for 'if the millions in Prussia ... take to the streets and speak, then no resistance would be offered *to the command of millions*' – found an echo in radical circles, but it was ignored by most democratic leaders.[116] In general, they advanced more realistic proposals, which met with agreement in liberal quarters. Löwe, the spokesman of democrats in the Progressive Party who later mediated between the organisers of the 1865 *Abgeordnetentag* and the Prussian boycott, had gone as far as to suggest, in April 1863, that any pledge from Bismarck guaranteeing 'that the important interests of the nation are at least passively protected' might have been enough to appease the *Fortschrittspartei*.[117] In the crucial debates of December 1863 in the Prussian *Abgeordnetenhaus*, he had called on democrats, 'if the great war should come', to 'do your duty', so 'that you do not now dam the current of the national movement, but that you let it become stronger and stronger' in order to get rid of 'this poor government with the first blow of a real storm': 'For if the great war should come, then the *Volk* will rise up triumphantly.'[118] Löwe's demand for a war to achieve an independent Schleswig-Holstein, backed by the *Mittelstaaten* and resting on the German *Volk*, was widely shared by democrats throughout Germany. His contention in December 1863 that it was better for 'the *Volk*' to be 'under a German government governed by feudalism' than to be under a Danish one governed 'in accordance with free principles' was rarely articulated, but his emphasis on nationality was barely contested.[119] Very few radicals thought that Schleswig-Holstein should remain under a free Danish constitution rather than a restricted one under Augustenburg and the estates.

The majority of democrats, with the exception of exiles such as Bamberger and Ruge, converged on the national question between 1863 and 1866. Even those most sympathetic to Prussia refused to countenance Bismarck's annexation of the duchies: Löwe, who had toyed with the idea of annexation in 1864, backed the independence of Schleswig-Holstein unambiguously in June 1865; Biedermann, who had advocated a return to the National Association's founding objective of a 'German *Bundesstaat* under Prussian leadership' at its fifth general assembly on 31 October 1864, continued to oppose annexation, becoming embroiled as a result in a public spat with Treitschke.[120] Such democrats did not have to decide between unity and freedom, since none considered giving up their campaign against Bismarck's tyranny in Prussia or giving back Schleswig or Holstein to Denmark. There were, of course, fierce arguments between radicals and liberals about whether to give limited backing or no support at all to the Prussian government. The most well-known debate took place in the Prussian *Abgeordnetenhaus* on 1 and 2 December 1863 between the old revolutionary Benedikt Waldeck, one of the spokesmen of the left, and Karl Twesten, who had confessed that he placed the 'integrity of the German fatherland' above opposition to Bismarck.[121] Before the liberal leader spoke, Waldeck had already restated his position from 1848:

Gentlemen, if this question is certainly a German one, and if it is quite certain that Prussia, as the first German state, has a self-evident interest in every German question, now, gentlemen, you surely don't mistake, above all things, that statement which I had already uttered repeatedly in 1848–49, which I have impressed on you since 1861 from this tribune and elsewhere, and which has now found general recognition and which has become, I would say, a trivial statement, namely that Prussia can do nothing at all for German freedom and unity as long as it is tied up internally in its own constitutional struggles, as long as it has not achieved freedom internally. (*Hear! Hear! Left*). That is the job that we have to do for Germany, and that we have to do with all our strength![122]

The fact that the Prussian ministry was a 'feudal, bureaucratic and military absolutism' intent on destroying the constitution meant that its policies had to be opposed in their entirety.[123]

Waldeck's stance, which contradicted the carefully circumscribed opposition of most Progressives, was opposed by other democrats, however. Thus, Schulze-Delitzsch warned him in the same debate not to let 'the internal situation overwhelm him'; instead, the chamber had to show 'that the internal constitutional turmoil does not cloud its free and clear view, so that it can take up a position against an external enemy for the honour and the right of the German nation (*Nation*)'.[124] Johann Jacoby, for his part, agreed that Virchow's and Stavenhagen's bill, which asked the government to follow a series of national policies in the duchies, could be accepted as a declaration of sympathy for 'our brothers in Schleswig-Holstein'.[125] The *Abgeordnetenhaus* was in no position genuinely to help the duchies, he continued, since the ministry was in charge. This was still more obviously the case after Prussia's and Austria's occupation of the territories, leaving democrats, like liberals, little choice but to continue to refuse to cooperate with the government on financial matters and to criticise its policy towards Schleswig-Hostein. As the *Social-Demokrat* remarked from the margins of 'democracy', professing in December 1864 to be 'bored' by the Schleswig-Holstein affair, all Germans could be pleased that a German land had been freed, albeit by Prussia and Austria.[126] The other decisions affecting the territories, which would probably lead to their incorporation into the Hohenzollern monarchy, would be taken in Berlin's and Vienna's corridors of power, not in popular

meetings, the press or state assemblies, leaving democrats – fortu-
nately, in the socialist paper's opinion – as more or less helpless
onlookers.[127]

Such democrats were no doubt relieved, as Mayer had hinted,
that they were not obliged to choose between cooperation with
Bismarck for the sake of German unification and the continuation
of their struggle for constitutional freedom. Many radicals sought to
challenge these assumptions, but they simultaneously emphasised
elements of consensus. Like the *Social-Demokrat* and other workers'
leaders, Friedrich Engels declared that he stood 'outside the actual
conflict' at home and abroad, as 'in all conflicts between reaction
and the *Bürgertum*', allowing him to judge it 'in cold blood and
impartially', 'scientifically, historically … [and] anatomically': 'the
German proletariat will never trouble itself with Reich constitutions,
Prussian leadership, a trias and so forth, except to get rid of them',
he announced in 1865, yet workers were to support the bourgeoisie,
'as long as it remains true to itself', in its struggle against reaction,
since 'every conquest which the bourgeoisie makes over the reaction is all, under these conditions, to the good of the working
class'.[128] Venedey had denounced Bismarck's Progressive collabora-
tors and raised the cry for a popular uprising against Prussia in
1864, but he concurred with most other radicals that Schleswig-
Holstein should be part of Germany on national grounds, that 'the
crossing of the German border by foreign troops should silence all
internal disputes and unite all parties in the fight against the
foreigner', that the Great Powers had acted in a self-interested, trai-
torous and un-German way, and that Germany needed to be saved
'from the "simply anarchic" conditions of the German
Confederation'.[129]

Fröbel backed the plan for tripartite leadership of a reformed
Bund and argued controversially that Germany would need to enter
an alliance against Prussia and Austria in order to avoid a partition
by the German Great Powers, but his preoccupation with the principle of nationality, his stress on the interests of Germany as a whole
rather than those of the Great Powers, and his scheme for a democratic and federal nation-state were not thought to clash irreconcil-
ably with other versions of a national *Bundesstaat*.[130] Likewise, in his
influential *Andeutungen zur gegenwärtigen Lage* (1864), the radical
forty-eighter Carl Vogt candidly considered the feasibility of a
federal constitution, not merely for Germany but for all the
Germanic states in Europe, and he recommended an alliance

between the *Mittelstaaten* and Bonapartist France, which had defeated 'Austria as a *Großstaat*' in 1859 in the name of national rights, to break the repressive grip of the Habsburg and Hohenzollern monarchies on Germany. He also doubted whether the people of Schleswig-Holstein would be freer under Augustenburg, given the liberal nature of the various Danish constitutions. Yet his criticism of the Great Powers, his refusal to cooperate with Bismarck unless he gave up his anti-national and illiberal policies at home, and his advocacy of the principle of nationality all met with democratic approval: Schleswig-Holstein was 'simply a question of whether a German *Volksstamm* should be under Danish rule or whether it should decide to leave it in accordance with free self-determination.'[131] Like most other democrats – or so the *Social-Demokrat* believed – Vogt assumed that the resolution of the Schleswig-Holstein crisis would provide an answer to the German question.[132]

Some democrats blamed liberals for dividing the national camp. The Prussian army's successes in the Danish war, followed by Bismarck's outmanoeuvring of Austria between the Treaty of Vienna in October 1864 and the Gastein Convention in August 1865, encouraged certain North German liberals to propose Prussia's annexation of Schleswig-Holstein. Such approval of Berlin's foreign policy appeared subsequently to have softened liberals' attitudes to Bismarck's constitutional, army and German policies. The former dispute reached its climax at the Frankfurt assembly of deputies in October 1865, the latter at the Frankfurt *Abgeordnetentag* in May 1866. Both involved more or less open rifts between democrats and liberals, and between North and South. The first meeting was called by the *Engerer Ausschuss* of the Schleswig-Holstein associations, which were preponderantly located in the third Germany, especially in the South West. The resolution which was to be put to the assembly on 1 October criticised the Gastein Convention and demanded self-determination for the duchies. It ended the 'Berlin Compromise' agreed by the associations, the 36-Committee and deputies on 26 March, which had insisted on the establishment of Schleswig-Holstein under Augustenburg, but which also granted Prussia control of the duchies' military. The leaders of the Prussian *Fortschrittspartei* decided to boycott the assembly, publishing letters explaining their actions in the *National-Zeitung*. Theodor Mommsen declared that the purpose of the meeting had been met, with the separation of Schleswig-Holstein from Denmark, and he demanded the disbanding of the 36-Committee: he would only attend the Frankfurt assembly of deputies if it decreed 'the definitive, perpetual subordination of all the middling and small states under the Prussian *Großstaat*' in advance.[133] Earlier in the year, the ancient historian and Progressive deputy had already announced in a pamphlet in favour of annexation that he had changed his mind about the duchies, having previously believed that 'the honour and interest of Germany' demanded their independence.[134] In his own letter, Twesten claimed that Prussia's position of power had not been recognised and that the resolution was aimed at the Prussian state rather than at its current government. The letters provoked strong reactions to Prussia's 'hegemonic absence', which threatened to split North Germany from the South.

The second meeting in Frankfurt on 20 May 1866 was convened by supporters of Prussia in order to discuss the impending war between the German Great Powers and Bismarck's proposal for a reform of the *Bund* on 9 April, with a National Assembly elected directly by universal manhood suffrage. The resolution of the *Abgeordnetentag*'s committee backed the call for a parliament elected according to the election law of 1849 and it condemned the coming 'dynastic' war and called for neutrality, with *Landtage* being asked to tie war credits to purely defensive actions. Partly because the invitation was sent out on 12 May, only 14 deputies came from Bavaria and 2 from Württemberg; 36 deputies out of 250 came from Baden, 34 from Nassau, 30 from Kurhessen, 30 from Hesse-Darmstadt, and 17 from Prussia. The committee's resolution was passed by a large majority: Rochau estimated that it was opposed by between 50 and 70 deputies. It was widely seen to vindicate Prussia's reform plans and to safeguard its pre-war position in Germany.

Increasingly forceful backing of Prussia lay behind such actions. In public, most pro-Prussian liberals were still circumspect, with the exception of mavericks such as Treitschke, who advised readers in January 1865 to 'leave the ground of the law' and to carry out 'the *Anschluss* of the small states to Prussia' in order to achieve 'Germany's unity'.[135] One month later, he was calling it 'the first duty of the German patriot to defend and increase the power of this state', as he reiterated the case for Berlin's annexation of Schleswig-Holstein.[136] The majority of liberals were more cautious. Rudolf Haym, Treitschke's colleague from the *Preussische Jahrbücher*, organised the first public petition by Prussian liberals in support of Bismarck – the Halle Declaration – as late as 26 April 1866. In private, pride, triumphalism and admiration of Bismarck were more common, together with a disdain for *Klein-* and *Mittelstaaten*. 'I am not making up an "ideal Prussia" for myself, as the article which you send me claims,' wrote Duncker to a correspondent in Kiel about a piece in the Viennese *Neue Freie Presse* on 26 April 1865: 'My heart is attached to the "real Prussia", whose whole history since 1640 has meant the saving of the German nation and German existence with all its strengths and weaknesses, with its suffering, emergencies and struggles.'[137] Germany's freedom would be created by Prussia's power: 'You know that I don't just want power and success for Prussia's sake; every strengthening of Prussia is a considerable relief for the solution of the German question,' he went on: 'The stronger Prussia has become, the less resistance Austria will necessarily offer, the more easily the merger of the smaller German states will occur. To hinder Prussia's growth at a certain point in time so that it can later form an entire *Bundesstaat* is a false doctrine.'[138] If Schleswig-Holstein were made independent, he concluded, it would have a life-long problem with Prussia and particularism.[139] Annexation was desirable, Duncker told Theodor von Bernhardi in January 1866, even if it was necessary to delay it until Hungary seceded from Austria.[140]

Droysen, another dinner guest of Bernhardi's, was equally ebullient, declaring 'in a raised voice' in May 1864 that 'the taking of Düppel is ... one of those events which are epoch-making in the life of a nation'.[141] 'The army has won such confidence, such trust in itself, that it is now equal to any enemy; it now knows what it can do. The population has developed a love for and trust in the army; it has shown what part it can play in the public realm, in the honour of Prussian arms,' he went on: 'A swing in favour of Bismarck has certainly taken place. Bismarck, too, has truly significant attributes. He [Droysen] had recently said to Gruner: "If you were at the helm, we would still be standing at the Eider! Bismarck's impertinent, even cocky, attitude to foreign powers has its advantages."'[142] When Bernhardi took the opportunity to aim a blow at 'Samwer and his like', referring to the Badenese liberal as a cipher for small-state, southern parochialism, Droysen's response was 'Quite right!' [143] Such a liberal, proclaimed the Berlin diarist and go-between, was 'completely wrong about these things':

he is a *Kleinstaatler* and has no idea of the self-confidence of the population of a large state, which has a glorious history closely

tied to the life of the *Volk*. He has no other picture other than
that of a population, whose current state conditions are matters
of indifference or disfavour, which could and would – in part
gladly, in part without resistance – be transferred to the first and
best other state, and which imagines that Prussia can be worked
into a progressive Germany more or less in the same way as
Lippe-Detmold.[144]

In such accounts, it could seem that Prussia was different in kind
from other German states, entitled to annex Schleswig-Holstein and
to expand, even under the ministry of a reactionary Junker, with
little reference to the rest of Germany. Southern German liberals,
from this point of view, could be portrayed as compensating 'for the
narrowness and impoverishment of their political conditions with
the dreams of *Grossdeutschland*' appealing to 'poetic fantasy' but
repellent to 'a political mind', in Baumgarten's summation.[145]
Liberals in the third Germany rightly worried about 'the fate of
Schleswig-Holstein', conceded the Karlsruhe historian, fearing that
their own states might be annexed next.[146]

Pro-Prussian, North German newspapers made such views known
to a wider public. Initially, publications like the *National-Zeitung* and
the *Grenzboten* represented the broad sections of the reading public
which clamoured for an undivided, independent Schleswig-Holstein
under Augustenburg. As in 1848, the press regularly contended that
both duchies were 'German' and should therefore be incorporated
into the *Bund*. 'A partition of Schleswig according to nationality is
nothing other than an illusion of those who comprehend nothing
of the matter, for there are not two nationalities in the land but one,
even if two dialects are spoken', reported the *National-Zeitung* in
March 1864.[147] In North Schleswig, the only area which was not
clearly German, Danish-speaking rural communities existed alongside German towns and a German culture, noted the *Grenzboten*
after the failure of the London Conference, but did Danish-speak-
ers really want to belong to Denmark rather than to Germany?[148]
Whereas the German Great Powers ignored the principle of nationality in pursuit of their own interests, the German *Volk* recognised
and came to the aid of their brethren intuitively, it was suggested.[149]
'As long as the possibility of a national act still lies before us, which
cannot happen without Prussia since it alone can really vouch for
the reinvigoration and renewal of Germany', the Hohenzollern
monarchy had the chance to lead the national movement, but it

seemed not to want to do so, mired in its own 'deep humiliation', the *Preussische Jahrbücher* had remarked in August 1863.[150] As early as November of the same year, the periodical had already advised the Prussian *Abgeordnetenhaus* 'to place all the means at the state's disposal which it needs for its ethical elevation (*Erhebung*)'.[151]

When the Prussian state did act, much of the liberal press, notwithstanding doubts about the Great Power's motives and its refusal to adopt the objectives of the national movement, nonetheless came to support it. By the summer of 1864, the *Grenzboten* was openly considering the possibility of Prussia's annexation of Schleswig-Holstein, concluding that it had a moral right and an actual opportunity to do so, given the impotence of the Confederation and the *Mittelstaaten*.[152] By January 1865, the periodical was still undecided about what to do, declaring grandly that the essence of liberalism was 'to think well of humanity' and to emphasise 'the self-determination of *Völker*' everywhere.[153] 'The final mystery of our strength lies in our respect for the will of the *Volk*', continued the journal, before recommending a very carefully circumscribed referendum offerering a choice between annexation or merger.[154] Constantin Rössler asked the same leading question in the *Preussische Jahrbücher* in March.[155] In either event, the duchies were to join Prussia, as the *National-Zeitung* had hinted in August 1864, while still formally backing their independence: 'We rejoice in the yearned-for freedom of Schleswig-Holstein, but we cannot think that this new state will allow the conditions in which it was born to be forgotten'; '"so-called rights" without power' were a 'mere claim and wish'.[156] The *Grenzboten* had already been much blunter a month beforehand: Bismarckian policy 'coincides, in the main, with the truly national'.[157] It was Prussia's right, intimated important sections of the liberal press, to merge with Schleswig-Holstein, and later with Germany, on its own terms.

The widely perceived arrogance of Prussia over Schleswig-Holstein, combined with animosity towards Bismarck, helps to explain the fluctuating opinions of liberals in the South German states. Whereas the *Landtage* of Hanover, Braunschweig, Hesse-Darmstadt, Weimar and Nassau complied with the *Abgeordnetentag*'s request for a declaration of neutrality, which benefited Prussia, in May 1866, those of Bavaria, Württemberg and Baden, all of which had liberal majorities, did not. 'Neutrality was preached among us', wrote Elben of the Swabian monarchy, 'but in vain: blind passion against Prussia was too powerful in the leading circles.'[158] The experience of Badenese liberals is arguably most illuminating, since they not only dominated the *Ständeversammlung* but also ran the government between 1861 and 1866, and they were, until the resignation of Franz von Roggenbach in September 1865, the most consistent proponents of *Kleindeutschland*. On taking up his office, backed by the liberal-minded Grand Duke Friedrich, Roggenbach had outlined his plan for a reform of the *Bund* in a circular dispatch on 28 January 1862, resurrecting most of the elements of the *Reichsverfassung*; the idea of a narrower and a wider *Bund* to overcome the dualism between Prussia and Austria; extensive federal competencies for the individual states; a strong central power; and a National Assembly. As in 1848, he warned Beust, whose *Bundesreform* he was criticising, there was a 'great societal-political movement' towards a German parliament and a *Bundesstaat*:

> The danger of the return of similar uprisings is not ruled out, as long as the deep unrest about the lack of any national achievement can blacken the present order with the reproach that it is to blame. Should such shocks not fail to occur, then it is to be feared that their consequences could be serious for the throne as well as for the existence of the individual states.[159]

Five days later, Austria sent out its own note, in which it spelled out its opposition to all small German plans to reform the Confederation. On 11 February, the Grand Duke sent an authorised letter to his father-in-law Wilhelm I to find out what Prussia intended to do and to offer assistance in reconciling the monarch and the Prussian population, since the constitutional crisis seemed likely to push the Prussian Court and government to the right, endangering Roggenbach's scheme for *Kleindeutschland*. The King of Prussia replied curtly that 'concessions which run against my principles of government ... will not come from me'.[160] When the Grand Duke sent a second letter, Wilhelm's reply was much fuller, claiming that the *Abgeordnetenhaus* was fomenting 'revolution and civil war in Germany', and protesting that 'time must have an effect and do its work, and reason gradually forge a path'.[161] It was the first of a series of blows dealt to Friedrich I and Roggenbach by the Prussian government.

When Bismarck was made Minister-President, Roggenbach's response was that 'the man and the system must be attacked pitilessly'.[162] Prussia's conduct in Schleswig-Holstein, just prior to the conflict, was traced by the Grand Duke to 'Bismarck's treason'.[163] The Gastein Convention in August 1865 adumbrated, as Wilhelm and Bismarck hinted at a meeting with Roggenbach in Baden-Baden at the end of the month, the annexation of the duchies and, the Foreign Minister was sure, war between Prussia and Austria. 'Whether a development towards a *Bundesstaat* can still be kept in view, given these tendencies of Prussia, is very doubtful,' he wrote on 1 September: 'the situation seems, rather, to be assuming such a form that the German states must make a decision whether they dare to make an ultimate push for their own independence or whether they want to give a fillip to a completely new development of the fatherland with considerable sacrifices of their own independence.'[164] Roggenbach eventually decided to back Prussia's 'completely new development', the outcome of which was difficult to predict. Unlike many of his counterparts, he accepted the logic of his belief 'that the position of Austria has become impossible in Germany, and that the German *Bund* in its existing shape is no longer the correct expression of the fundamental political relations which now obtain in Germany'.[165] Friedrich I refused to follow him, helping to precipitate the Foreign Minister's resignation later that month.

The Grand Duke refrained until late May 1866, when it was too late, from contemplating the other choice – independence through a war against Prussia – which Roggenbach had put before him. By that time, his own Foreign Minister Ludwig von Edelsheim had already agreed with the other ministers of the *Mittelstaaten* to the *Bund*'s intervention on the side of Austria, provided that Vienna allowed the *Bundestag* to decide the succession to the duchies, which it did on 1 June. 'I was in Karlsruhe over the last few days,' wrote Robert von Mohl to his brother on 11 May: 'The Grand Duke is vacillating and not at all a man for clear decisions. There is no real unity; namely, my new minister Edelsheim is going much further towards Austria than is the case with any of his colleagues.'[166] Many Badenese liberals were as disunited, indecisive and confused as their monarch and some of their ministers. On 11 April 1866, the second chamber voted almost unanimously – with only three votes against – in support of Bismarck's proposal to reform the *Bund*, which was later rejected even by the *Nationalverein*. The measure's Bismarckian provenance was not enough to deter deputies from voting for it, as Carl Eckhard and Friedrich Kiefer, the leaders of the

Fortschrittspartei, made plain: 'First let us have this, then we want to have done with the Junker Bismarck.'[167] On 29 May, the second chamber voted unanimously for war credits for the Badenese government as it prepared to enter the war on Austria's side. The decision, however, did not imply an outright rejection of a Prussian-led small German *Bundesstaat* on the model of 1849, much less an acceptance of a confederal or Austrian solution to the German question. Despite beginning his speech with the statement that virtually no one in the chamber or in the land was in favour of Baden's neutrality or an *Anschluss* with Prussia, Eckhard went on to claim that there was also no desire in liberal ranks to join an illiberal Austria: rather, it was vital that the individual states ally with each other and with the national movement to create – immediately – a *Volksarmee* and a *Volksvertretung*, elected in accordance with the law agreed in 1849. Kiefer added that, only a few weeks ago as the Prussian *Bundesreform* was put to a vote, he had seen Bismarck as a German Cavour, but he had been disabused of this belief by the current arming of Prussia in order to fight a *Bruderkrieg*: nevertheless, he still saw in the Hohenzollern monarchy, if it would give up its present policy, the power which could solve the German question.

There were compelling reasons why the majority of Badenese liberals, apart from a small group of hardened pro-Prussian deputies led by Roggenbach, Karl Mathy, Julius Jolly and Hermann Baumgarten, failed to back Prussia in 1866. Liberal deputies had traditionally adhered to a truce on the national and confessional questions, tolerating differences of opinion for the sake of party unity. Roggenbach had exploited this political space, which was typical of many states with their strict interpretation of *raisons d'état* and cabinet diplomacy, in order to formulate a *kleindeutsch* policy largely insulated from party opinion. Likewise, his successor Edelsheim, who was a university friend and former *kleindeutsch* protégé of Roggenbach, was able to design and implement his own policy, 'with the *Bund*, at present, as the sole national bond of the German nation, despite some transient internal tumult'.[168] As the former Badenese envoy to Vienna, he was willing to court the Habsburg monarchy to a much greater degree than any of his contemporaries and to present the ministry and second chamber with a series of *faits accomplis*, including agreements with other German ministers to go to war in 1866. Partly as a result of such agreements, Edelsheim was able to argue in the debate on 28–29

May that a small border state such as Baden had no option but to act in concert with the other *Mittelstaaten*. Any other decision would mean that the state would be completely isolated in Germany as a whole, surrounded by enemies. Even *kleindeutsch* opponents of the Foreign Minister's claims such as Bluntschli were obliged to admit in May 1866 that neutrality would be a contravention of the law of the *Bund*. He was therefore obliged to contend that confederal law was no longer valid. 'Although Baden, too, has at all times loyally met its obligations to the Confederation and will do so in future, it cannot regard formal confederal law as the highest law at that moment when the entire existence of the present constitution of the *Bund*, which is seen on all sides as untenable, is itself in question', the constitutional lawyer told the first chamber on 14 May, 'and when a break between the two German Great Powers destroys the foundations on which the present law of the *Bund* rests. Rather, in this case, Baden must reserve the right to take its own free decisions as an independent state.'[169]

Given the uncertainty surrounding the decision to go to war in 1866, liberal deputies would have required a strong predisposition towards Prussia to ignore the legally binding decisions of the Confederation. With Bismarck in charge in Berlin, the majority of deputies were not sufficiently predisposed towards Prussia to take such a momentous step. As Eckhard had pointed out on 29 May, echoing Roggenbach's earlier admission in September 1865, support for the Hohenzollern monarchy in the war might entail an actual merger, or *Anschluss*, with Prussia within a new form of state, the details of which were not known in advance. With a despised, aggressive figure such as Bismarck at the head of a state widely known for its rule of violence and its military tradition, few liberals were confident about a German future dictated by Berlin after a victorious war. By contrast, sanctioning the probable mobilisation of the *Bund*'s forces against Prussia did not seem to presage an *Anschluss* with Austria – a point made by Eckhard as if it were self-evident – for even those most sceptical of the Hohenzollern state appeared to have viewed the Habsburg monarchy not as the harbinger of an alternative vision of Germany but as a means of delaying any decision. This attitude had already been articulated in April 1865 by Robert von Mohl, one of Edelsheim's confidants. Although he was pleased that 'the carrying out of the old Gotha plans cannot be considered now or for a long time', he was not, as a consequence, in favour of *Grossdeutschland* or Austria:

I see the whole *Grossdeutschtum,* whether it is in a direct relationship to Austria or through a *Sonderbund* under Bavarian hegemony, simply as a barely concealed ultramontanism, that is,
subjection to a principle which I hold for the most damaging of
all; or, on the part of democrats, as a concealed revolutionary
means to arrive at a republic. I don't know which result I would
dislike most ... at least, we have been spiritually free in Germany
until now, if also politically powerless.[170]

Mohl's recommendation was to give up the idea of German unity
altogether, having lived through 'the school of 1848 and 1849 and
now the experience of the last four years': 'I am no enthusiast of
German unity.'[171] Few Badenese liberals, less independent and original than the academic and diplomat, were willing to go so far. They
agreed, however, that it was better to wait and see on the side of
Austria, which stood a good chance of winning the war, than to await
an uncertain future, even if victorious, on the side of Prussia.

The actions of Bismarck's ministry at home and abroad placed
great strain on Germany's national movement. After eight years of
reaction and four years of the New Era, the liberals who had created
the movement were confronted, over the next four years, with a
constitutional crisis in Prussia which seemed to endanger the
centrality of the *Reichsverfassung* as the basis of a German nation-
state, with a cabinet war in the national heartland of Schleswig-
Holstein, and a conflict in 1866 between 'brothers' in the
Confederation, the Habsburg and Hohenzollern monarchies, the
anticipation of which had cast a shadow over politics in the preceding year. It is remarkable in such circumstances that liberal and
national organisations, despite their novelty, continued to play a
central role in the German public sphere, disposing of mass
memberships, contacts in the press, extensive links with each other
and with the *Landtage,* and influence over governments. Thus, when
Bismarck sought, in 1866, to canvass support for his proposed
reform of the *Bund* and to ensure the states' neutrality, his officials
met Baumgarten, Bluntschli, Jolly and Roggenbach in Baden and
the Progressive leaders Karl Braun and Friedrich Lang in Nassau,
who requested the convening of an *Abgeordnetentag.* 'If Bismarck
wins with the emphatic support of popular forces, then liberal
Prussia wins,' wrote Baumgarten on 11 May: 'If it wins, whilst the
liberal *Volk* joins in with the howling of the *Kölnische Zeitung* and the
Jewish *Volkszeitung,* then the Prussian *Volk* will turn its back on liber-

alism.'[172] On the same day, Roggenbach wrote to Bennigsen, the leader of the *Nationalverein*, about 'which of the two *Großstaaten* will in future determine and dominate the fate of Germany – on which side the wishes of the German people must stand seems to me beyond doubt' – and about the course of the *Bundesreform*: 'I would very much regret it, if the aversion against the current regime could lead to the German *Volk* preferring to renounce such a reform than to back one in which Bismarck participates ... the current regime is working under high pressure, which lets it take decisions that many other regimes would shrink away from.'[173]

On 14 May, the second day of the *Nationalverein* committee meeting called in preparation for the *Abgeordnetentag* in Frankfurt a week later, Bismarck invited Bennigsen in person to a meeting at nine o'clock in the evening. Bernhardi, who was the intermediary, hinted at the reasoning of both sides. Bismarck had to promise a reform of the *Bund* and to offer a German parliament as the price of the war for other parties, an offer which 'old liberals' like Bernhardi thought was worth accepting.[174] Bennigsen desired the measures, but he was opposed to Bismarck, deciding in the end neither to accept nor refuse the Minister-President's proposals; he was 'very concerned in respect of the chances in a war'.[175] The Berlin diarist reassured him that the Prussian army was in 'an outstanding state and good spirit' and that Bismarck was capable of leading Prussia to victory; indeed, and 'this is also Roggenbach's opinion', 'only he can', since a liberal ministry 'would never overcome ... the resistance of the Austrian-leaning party in the personal entourage of the king'.[176] For his part, the Minister-President was characteristically contemptuous when confronted with the commonplace idea 'that he cannot conduct a war at all because he has public opinion against him': 'One doesn't shoot with public opinion, but with gunpowder and lead.'[177] Yet he was visibly interested in the stance of the *Nationalverein* and other national organisations, admitting that he was 'not happy about Bennigsen's statements' on 28 April.[178] The Minister-President's initiation of talks with liberals after that date betrays the extent of his concern.[179]

The *Nationalverein* and *Abgeordnetentag* maintained a coherent and more or less consensual line in 1866 under considerable pressure from German governments and from its own heterogeneous membership. Immediately after meeting Bismarck, Bennigsen reiterated the mantra, published in the *Wochenschrift des Nationalvereins* on 17 May, that the German nation could not believe in a German constitution, especially given 'the uncertainty of its content', put forward by 'a system of government' which had contravened and suppressed its own constitution in Prussia.[180] Any public announcement of the National Association's willingness to reach an agreement with Bismarck while the constitutional crisis in Prussia remained unresolved would have led to dissent, resignations and, even, secessions. The *Nationalverein*'s membership had, after all, declined from approximately 21,000 in 1863 to 10,681 in 1865, although such a fall was offset by a switch of members' activities to the Schleswig-Holstein committees in 1864 and it was concealed by higher figures published for 1864 and 1865 at the time.[181] Rather than collapsing, organisations like the National Association and the *Fortschrittspartei* remained prominent in public life, maintaining a sufficiently consistent and acceptable stance during the various crises to safeguard their integrity and their role.

The *Nationalverein*'s strategy in May 1866 was to ignore Bismarck's proposals for a *Bundesreform*, restating the need for a German parliament elected by the law of 1849, and to criticise Berlin's policy on Schleswig-Holstein at the same time as guaranteeing the neutrality of states hostile to Prussia, by asking liberal-dominated *Landtage* to refuse them war credits except for purely defensive purposes. The resolutions submitted by the committee of the *Abgeordnetentag* to the general meeting on 20 May were almost identical. They proved unobjectionable to both supporters and opponents of Prussia. 'The core point of the resolutions advanced today' was the neutrality of the third Germany, reported the Prussian envoy in Frankfurt Karl Friedrich von Savigny: 'the other declaration, partly directed against the Prussian policy in Schleswig-Holstein, is only intended to marshal all those towards an acceptance of the core point who have absorbed the widely-held diatribes against Prussia over the years into their political catechism'.[182] Despite a heated discussion about an alternative resolution which was more critical of Prussia's annexationism, about 170 of the 220 votes cast supported the committee's wording: the entire delegation from Schleswig-Holstein, who desired a clearer statement of the duchies' independence, made up a good proportion of the fifty or so deputies who voted against the resolution. A similar pattern had been discernible at the general assembly of the National Association in October 1865, where the resolution, again opposed by about fifty votes, had repeated the organisation's adherence to the *Reichsverfassung* and had given its continuing support to the constitution of a state in Schleswig-

Holstein under Augustenburg, but with Prussian control of its military. This concession to Prussia had been agreed in the so-called 'Berlin compromise' between liberal and national leaders in March 1865 and was a watered-down version of the 'February demands' outlined by Bismarck, which had required economic as well as military cooperation if a separate state were to be set up. As in May 1866, when the terms of the compromise had altered, the *Nationalverein*, after a full-blooded debate, secured the backing of a large majority for its position.[183]

Despite the fragmentary effects of Bismarck's policies on German politics, why did national, liberal and democratic organisations and milieux not splinter and break apart, as had begun to occur in Württemberg? First, they had benefited from the wave of support for Schleswig-Holstein in, and before, 1863. It was founded not only on national grounds, although these were the most important, but also on historical and legal ones, prompting a slew of expert opinions from prominent liberal constitutional lawyers and historians, which underlined the moral legitimacy of the cause.[184] Notwithstanding the difficulties caused by Prussian and Austrian policy, this moment of national awakening had long-lasting consequences, which the *Nationalverein* and *Abgeordnetentag* harnessed by refusing to accept annexation.

Second, Schleswig-Holstein was seen by the majority of liberal and democratic nationalists as the German question 'writ small', as Treitschke sarcastically put it.[185] As efforts to gain the independence of the duchies stalled because of the opposition of Prussia and Austria, the attention of many contemporaries was deflected to the German question writ large, with the prospect of a war between the German Great Powers. Once Berlin and Vienna had removed Schleswig-Holstein from the Danish monarchy, a number of solutions surfaced in public discussions of the territories, including referring the problem to the *Bund* or a reconstituted National Assembly, military or economic cooperation with Prussia, and annexation with or without violence. Many liberals, mocked Treitschke, were content to leave it to, 'not Prussia, but the whole of Germany to decide!', to which 'we reply', 'Where is Germany? Where is the legal political organ of our nation?'[186] As the Schleswig-Holstein question became greyer and dimmer, it lost some of its divisive force.

Third, most liberals saw no need to make a choice between freedom and unity. This was even true of Twesten, who had helped to establish the dichotomy in his speech to the Prussian *Abgeordnetenhaus* on 2 December 1863: if presented with the choice whether to extend the Bismarck ministry 'by some time' or give up Schleswig-Holstein 'forever', he would chose the former, but his question was deliberately a hypothetical and leading one.[187] He correctly assumed that he would not be faced with the dilemma: 'I cannot hide it from myself: there is the possibility that the present government will emerge from a European war as a victor and that its duration will be lengthened for some time by a war or by the measures which precede a war', independently of any decision made by deputies in the second chamber.[188] In the event, Bismarck made many of the relevant decisions concerning the duchies, and liberals had little alternative but to look on, either in public protest or private approval.

Fourth, opposition to the Prussian government's contravention of the constitution was a point of agreement in the national movement, not discord, as Twesten had indicated in the same speech: 'I do not, as Herr v. Vincke expressed it in one of the previous sessions, take the gentlemen at the ministerial table to be a temporary embarrassment, but perceive the ministry to be a serious danger and misfortune for the fatherland.'[189] The main difference of opinion concerning Bismarck, notwithstanding Vincke's passing remark, was the degree to which deputies should cooperate with the Prussian ministry in the realm of foreign policy and – for a minority of right-wing liberals – associated war credits, not in constitutional or routine budgetary matters. Few doubted that the constitutional struggle should continue. The *Abgeordnetenhaus* had gone on to reject the government's request for war credits by a large majority shortly after Twesten's intervention. 'There is no higher interest for Prussia than the removal of a system of government which eats away at the marrow of the state and consumes the moral strength of the *Volk*, which dishonours the state and makes the *Volk* despicable in the eyes of the world and in its own eyes,' wrote Rochau, sketching the official viewpoint of the *Nationalverein* in its *Wochenschrift* in February 1865, after the *Abgeordnetenhaus* had again refused the budget: 'For this purpose, no price is too high.'[190]

Finally, liberals in the national movement had grounds to be confident, whatever their other fears, that their constitutional and federal conception of a German nation-state including Prussia was gaining ground, partly because of the perceived self-exclusion of Austria and failure of the *Bund*. Outsiders such as Treitschke, who put the case for a unitary state, recognised that they were arguing against the orthodoxy of a German *Bundesstaat*.[191] When the young Hanoverian liberal Johannes Miquel formulated a similar set of arguments for a Prussian–German *Einheitsstaat* at the committee meeting of the National Association on 28 October 1865, his comments were removed from the record presented to the general meeting. The Reich constitution of 1849 remained the foundation of a liberal German nation-state until 1866.

Conservatism, Bismarckianism and the Nation

Liberals could rightly claim that some conservatives, including Bismarck, had adopted important elements of their national programme: notably, the principle of nationality, legal equality, constitutionalism, a small German parliament, federal government, a strong central authority and even universal suffrage. Circles close to Gerlach, however, vehemently resisted what the founder of the *Kreuzzeitung* had called the 'un-German *Nationalverein*' for its propaganda on behalf of 'a domestic system of revolution' designed 'to push Prussia into the abyss of 1848'.[192] As was to be expected, Gerlach continued to champion the Habsburg and Hohenzollern monarchies as the twin pillars of the German order – stating in 1864 that 'the German Great Powers should not allow themselves to be pushed into the role of *mere* German members of the Confederation' – yet he believed that they should be bound by God, history, law and the *Bund*.[193] The German Confederation had 'great faults', he wrote in May 1866, 'but I don't pulverise my family or my fatherland because they have faults'.[194] With foreign policy closely tied to domestic affairs, in Gerlach's view, the 'Schleswig-Holstein swindle' was above all a pretext for revolution at home and abroad, he declared in two articles – '1848 und 1863!' and 'Die Demokratie und Schleswig-Holstein' – in the *Kreuzzeitung* in December 1863: 'The captivated *crowd* allows itself to be fanaticised for the real or supposed rights and interests of Holstein and Schleswig. But the *leaders* know what they want. The fall of *Prussia* as a Great Power; the *German revolution*; thereby the overturning of *Austria* – those are their aims.'[195] Although Gerlach had supported Bismarck as Prussia and Austria confronted the national movement over Schleswig-Holstein in accordance with the terms of the Treaty of London, heralding Düppel as a defeat for the *Nationalverein* and for those

German states which had been led astray by democrats, he soon
began to distance himself from the Minister-President's departure
from the letter of international treaties and his manipulation of
Austria in the course of 1864 and 1865. It was only on 8 May 1866,
with the publication of 'Krieg und Bundesreform' in the
Kreuzzeitung, that he broke with Bismarck completely, who wrote
back via an intermediary that the article had injured him more seriously than an assassination attempt on the same day.[196] In the field
of politics, diplomacy and war, Gerlach wrote, Bismarck – whom he
did not name in this context – was guilty of 'patriotic egotism', 'as if
these fields had no higher law'.[197] The Minister-President's threat to
go to war against Austria risked dealing a fatal blow to the life-
organs of both parties and his *Bundesreform* proposals of the previous month were condemned as a sign of 'political bankruptcy'.[198]
Gerlach had already been told by Moritz von Blanckenburg on 15
April that the reform was 'not at all ... a mere diplomatic chess
move – it is intended very seriously'.[199] Bismarck's 'Bonapartism',
his ruthless pursuit of self-contained interests of state, and his flir-
tations with 'revolution', or with liberals and nationalists, risked
alienating the conservative party permanently, warned Gerlach.[200]

The question asked by contemporaries of Gerlach was: which
conservative party? Twesten went as far as to suggest that there
would soon be no party at all:

> The conservative party in Prussia is caught in a new instance of
> decomposition, which great but undesired service I attribute to
> Herr v. Bismarck ... such a great service that I in fact believe that
> after Herr v. Bismarck there will be no conservative party in the
> sense of the word to date. Gentlemen, in internal policy it has
> already abandoned everything that they denoted as the tasks of
> conservative policy under Friedrich Wilhelm IV ... They follow
> Herr v. Bismarck, although he denies their previous principles,
> because he is the man through whom they can govern.[201]

Gerlach, too, was worried about the conservative party, which
appeared to have little direction, lapsing unthinkingly into 'war
enthusiasm' at one moment and lethargy the next. 'The dead, cold
self-complacency of the conservatives, their weary defence, indifference vis-à-vis the most important things, their sinful contempt (and
ignorance) of their opponents etc. struck me everywhere', wrote
the reactionary in March 1863.[202] In such circumstances, there was

less of a counterweight to Bismarck – and to his experimentation with national and liberal ideas as well as with acts of force – than many contemporaries believed. Bernhardi's assessment of the strength of the 'Austrian' party around the King was mistaken. The circles close to Gerlach were far less well connected than in the 1850s, so that Gerlach himself complained of being isolated at the *Kreuzzeitung*, which had also largely adopted Bismarck's line in 1865–66, and he was reduced to trying to gain access to the throne via Prince Albrecht of Prussia, one of the King's nephews whom he had taken up as an unlikely protégé. Although he still had meetings with Bismarck, he was so unsuccessful in convincing his former charge that he started writing to the Minister-President's wife, requesting her to read his letters to her husband. His attempts in 1866 to change the King's or the ministry's course were unsuccessful. By that date, Bismarck's own position was much less precarious.

Bismarck's ministry was notorious for its refusal to take national sentiment into account. As early as 1856, the future Minister-President had told his Danish counterpart in Frankfurt, admittedly in part to reassure him of Prussia's *bona fides*, that 'he was no friend of a sentimental or national policy and much too Prussian to make any distinctions in his feelings between Spaniards, Bavarians, or Danes. His only concern was whether Prussia had an interest in quarrelling with Denmark or disrupting the Danish monarchy. For the time being this was not the case.'[203] In different circumstances, Bismarck had said the same thing in 1864 to Rechberg, the Austrian *Staatsminister* and former envoy to the *Bund* in Frankfurt, avowing that he would not be disorientated by the dogmatic 'sentimentalism' of German nationalists.[204] On one level, the Minister-President's policy in 1864 could be understood as the antithesis of a national German one, continuing a traditional policy of Prussian aggrandisement, as Bismarck told Wilhelm at a Crown Council on 3 February, two days after the invasion of Schleswig: 'I reminded the king that each of his immediate forebears, except his brother, had won for the state an increase in territory... and encouraged him to do the same.'[205] This, of course, corresponded to many contemporaries' views of the Prussian ministry. On another level, however, the ministry was in a weak position and was forced to take German nationalism into account. Thus, at the meeting of the Crown Council, Bismarck invoked the glorious record of Hohenzollern expansionism in order to overcome Wilhelm's qualms about the ultimate purpose of Prussia's and Austria's war with Denmark. Like much of the Court, the monarch was at once closer to the position of the *Bund* and of German liberals, who were calling for an independent Schleswig-Holstein. For this reason, Wilhelm added to the protocol of the Crown Council of 3 February that annexation was merely one possible outcome of the war, not Berlin's fixed objective. In his *Gedanken und Erinnerungen,* Bismarck later recalled that his injunction to the King to follow the example of his forebears and increase the size of Prussia's territory 'was missing from the protocol':

> The Geheimer Rat Costenlohe, who was in charge of the protocol, said, when I asked him to comment, that the king had said that I would prefer it if my disclosures were not recorded in the protocol; His Majesty seems to have believed that I had talked under the Bacchanalian influence of a good breakfast and would be happy to hear nothing further of the matter. I insisted, however, on their inclusion, which did indeed occur.[206]

Opposition to the Minister-President's stance was not limited to the monarch. During the council, Bismarck went on, 'the Crown Prince had, as I spoke, raised his hands to the heavens, as if I had lost my senses; my colleagues remained silent'.[207] Even his own ministers appeared unwilling to back the Minister-President. As in the constitutional crisis, Bismarck's actual position, notwithstanding his bluster, was uncertain.

Such uncertainty did not mean, in itself, that the Prussian Minister-President was influenced by the counsel and criticism of liberals and nationalists between 1864 and 1866. He appears to have been averse to the national enthusiasm surrounding Schleswig-Holstein, referring to its inhabitants disparagingly as 'the old inseparables', who 'must eventually become Prussians', and indicating to Schleinitz in 1861 that 'we have greater concerns and dangers to face than the misdemeanours of Danish overlords in Schleswig, and the Holsteiners are, it seems to me, not favourable to the idea of being saved by German troops'.[208] As he confided to Robert von Keudell at New Year celebrations in 1864, sitting before the fire and – unusually – talking about politics, he 'could not be responsible for shedding Prussian blood to create a new small state, which in the Confederation would always vote against us'.[209] He had already said exactly the same thing to the Prussian envoy in Baden a year before in order to deter Roggenbach from using the duchies to revive the case for *Kleindeutschland*: 'I cannot take it to be a Prussian interest to wage a war to install a new Grand Duke, in the most favourable case, who votes against us in the *Bund* and whose government would be a willing object of Austrian intrigues.'[210] An independent Schleswig-Holstein under Augustenburg would, like Hanover, Saxony and Hesse, be an envious opponent of Prussia within Germany and it would be a bridgehead for an attack against the state's northern flank. However, it was 'as good as clear that H.M., in spite of the danger of breaking with Europe and suffering a worse Olmütz, will give way to democracy and the Würzburger [the *Mittelstaaten*] in order to establish Augustenburg and create a new medium-sized state', he wrote to Roon in January 1864.[211]

In the same letter, he admitted that the refusal of the liberals in the Prussian *Landtag* to back a war loan, in addition to continuing to vote against the budget, was wearing him down: 'I have not slept a wink this night and feel miserable, and don't really know what to tell these people, who will for sure refuse to vote credits.'[212] Unlike their refusal to sanction the budget, which did not impede the collection of taxes, the deputies' rejection of a war loan was likely to affect the government's creditworthiness. When Bismarck accused the *Abgeordnetenhaus* of endangering Prussia's foreign policy for domestic and party ends in the debate on 21 and 22 January, underlining its 'lack of confidence in the present ministry' and seeking 'to establish in Prussia the dictatorship of this House', Virchow retorted – like the Minister-President, for the King's benefit – that Bismarck was turning into a *Kreuzzeitung* man: 'He is no longer the man who joined us with the feeling that he was going to accomplish something with an energetic foreign policy.'[213] Quite possibly piqued, the Minister-President answered:

> I did incidentally, when I came here, cherish the hope that I should find in others besides myself a willingness, should the need arise, to sacrifice the standpoint of party for the overall interest of the country. I shall not, lest I offend anyone, go any further into how far and in whom I have been disappointed in this hope; but disappointed I have been, and of course that affects my political position and relations.[214]

Whether this was Bismarck lifting his mask, betraying his real intention of working with the national movement, is open to debate, since he had an interest in trying to discredit the Augustenburg

cause and 'Schleswig-Holsteinism' – and Wilhelm's and the Court's
sympathy for them – as self-interested party politics.[215]

What is indisputable, though, is that the Minister-President was
acutely conscious of party positions, especially that of the
Progressives, and he often seemed uncertain that he would escape
their logic. As he wrote in his memoirs:

> I saw the situation which I absolutely thought that I must avoid as
> that which was put before public opinion as a programme by our
> opponents – that is, to fight at the head of newspapers, associa-
> tions, volunteers, and the states of the *Bund*, except Austria, for a
> struggle and war on the part of Prussia for the erection of a new
> Grand Dukedom, and without the certainty that the individual
> governments would carry out the thing, whatever the danger. I
> have never faltered in the conviction that Prussia, supported
> purely by the weapons and comrades of 1848, public opinion,
> *Landtage*, associations, volunteers and small contingents in their
> state at the time, would have made a hopeless start and would
> have only found enemies amongst the Great Powers, in England,
> too. I would have seen any minister as a swindler and a traitor
> who had fallen back into the false policy of 1848, 49 and 50,
> which would have prepared a new Olmütz for us.[216]

The Minister-President was determined to steer a course acceptable
to the Great Powers and to avoid the pitfalls of 1848. Yet the fact that
he depicted liberals and public opinion in these terms also revealed
how significant he thought they were.

Bismarck was obliged to pay attention to the public, assemblies
and clubs because of his aims in Germany, where many of the states
were swayed by public opinion, and because of his position at Court
and in government, where he was creating a platform for himself
between the 'absolutism' and would-be 'dictatorship' of the far right
and the liberalism of the Crown Prince's circle and the old
Wochenblatt party in the diplomatic corps. The Minister-President
had, at least, to use liberalism, frequently in an unorthodox fashion,
in both his domestic and foreign policy, as his memoir entries on
'Schleswig-Holstein', whatever their other biases, make plain:

> If German unity could not be produced by *Landtag* resolutions,
> newspapers and shooting festivals, liberalism nonetheless put
> pressure on the princes, which made them more willing to make

concessions for the Reich ... it is unlikely that [Wilhelm I] could have been led onto the path of the Danish and, therefore, the Bohemian wars without his previous experiments and endeavours in a liberal direction, and without the commitments into which he had thereby entered ... The Holstein question, the Danish war, Düppel and Alsen, the break with Austria and the deciding of the German question on the battlefield: he would perhaps never have entered this whole balancing act without the difficult position into which he had been brought by the New Era.[217]

The liberalism of important sections of the Court and foreign ministry was bolstered in the Schleswig-Holstein affair by the legitimism of the succession of Augustenburg, who was an old friend of the Crown Prince from his days at university in Bonn, and by the stance of the German Confederation, which had been a traditional focus of conservative loyalty. In such circumstances, Bismarck opined in January 1864 to Roon, in an attempt to bring Wilhelm back from the brink of a war for Augustenburg, an independent Schleswig-Holstein and the *Bund*, 'I have the premonition that the cause of the Crown against the revolution is lost, for the heart of the King is in the other camp and his confidence rests more with his opponents than with his servants.'[218] 'Bismarck is *unfortunately the only, completely clear, completely* firm man in the government,' wrote the Minister-President's close friend Moritz von Blanckenburg in November 1863: 'All the others are more or less intoxicated and are urging war, the worst is the *furor militaris* which goes up to the *highest* circles.'[219] From this point of view, Bismarck's exchange of letters with Robert von der Goltz, the Prussian ambassador in Paris, adviser to the King and former member of the *Wochenblatt* party, takes on a different complexion. Rather than being a straightforward statement of contempt towards parties and public opinion, the Minister-President's letter of 24 December 1863 was a tactical move in a competition for the opinion of the monarch, the Court and the right, a fact to which Goltz had already alluded in his letter of 22 December as he warned Wilhelm that his own future, 'that of the dynasty, Prussia's position as a Great Power and the existence of the conservative party' all hung on the decision to champion the Schleswig-Holstein movement.[220] Bismarck's verdict that 'the chase after the phantom of popularity "in Germany", which we have been pursuing since the forties, has cost us our position in Germany and in Europe' was designed to convince Goltz and the King that his own Great Power policy in 1864 was the correct one: 'we shall not regain [our position] if we let ourselves be driven by the current in the belief that we are guiding it, but only if we stand firmly on our own feet and are first and foremost a Great Power, and only then a federal state'.[221] 'If we now turn our backs on the Great Powers in order to throw ourselves into the arms of the policy of the small states, which is caught in the net of the democracy of associations, that would be the most wretched situation in which one could bring the monarchy internally and abroad,' he went on, revealing in the process that many German states were in democracy's net, in his opinion: 'We would be pushed instead of pushing; we would support ourselves on elements which we do not control and which are necessarily hostile to us, to which we would have to surrender ourselves unconditionally.'[222]

Bismarck deliberately overstated the menace of democracy, which he knew that Wilhelm believed had advanced too far in Prussia and Germany, but at the same time he acknowledged that many conservatives were prepared to join democrats and liberals in a national cause. 'You believe that there is something in "German public opinion", in the parliaments, newspapers, etc., which could support or help us in a policy aimed at union or hegemony,' he continued, ridiculing the means which Goltz proposed towards their shared end of a Prussian-dominated *Kleindeutschland*: 'I consider that a radical error, a fantasy. Our strength cannot emanate from parliamentary and press politics but only from armed Great Power politics.'[223] His intention was to frighten the King, once again mustering the threat of parliamentary rule, which few contemporaries supported: 'are we a Great Power or simply a German federal state', meaning, 'in the first case, we are to be governed monarchically, or, as would be permissible in the second case, by professors, circuit judges and small-town gossips?'[224] Bismarck had already spelled out on 20 December that 'the more reflective and moderate elements' in the national camp 'form a tiny minority', making 'an open fight against rather than an alliance with the incipient national and revolutionary movement' more likely, at least for the moment; all the same, he was prepared to hint to Goltz that, 'possibly, other stages will yet ensue that are not so far removed from your programme'.[225] For all his posturing in support of his Great Power strategy in Schleswig-Holstein, the Minister-President was conscious that a large majority was in favour of a German national policy and he was, himself, willing to consider such a policy in future.

Bismarck's use of nationalism had important antecedents, dating back to the revolution and the Erfurt Union. On 16 June 1866, two days after the *Bund* had agreed to Austria's request to mobilise its forces against Prussia, Bismarck drafted a proclamation for Wilhelm I entitled 'To the German *Volk*', recalling Friedrich Wilhelm IV's call 'An Mein Volk und an die deutsche Nation' on 21 March 1848. In the manifesto of 16 June, the King of Prussia declared that only the 'living unity of the German nation remained' after the *Bund*, which had been powerless and ineffective for half a century, had committed an illegal act of war by mobilising against Prussia and had therefore caused its own demise. Prussia was fighting for the unrestricted 'national development of Germany', the unity of which required 'a new, vital expression'.[226] This Prussian policy of appealing to the German nation in a struggle against the Confederation, the *Mittelstaaten* and Austria preceded Bismarck's Minister-Presidency. On 7 September 1861, the recently appointed Foreign Minister Albrecht von Bernstorff, a former member of the *Wochenblatt* party, had met Roggenbach along with Wilhelm I at Ostend and had accepted the Baden proposal for a reform of the *Bund*, although disavowing its references to ministerial responsibility and the direct election of a German parliament. The Prussian and Badenese plan was put forward by Bernstorff on 20 December as an immediate rejoinder to one of Beust's schemes for a trias under Austria: only a small German federation within the existing confederation could meet the need for German unity, declared the Foreign Minister, invoking the spirit of Radowitz.[227] When Vienna then took up the question of a *Bundesreform* in 1862, proposing a directory of the governments' representatives, a confederal court and an assembly of *Landtag* delegates, which was presented to the *Engerer Rat* of the *Bundestag* on 14 August, the Prussian envoy Guido von Usedom, with Bernstorff's backing, denounced the plan and challenged the representatives of the other states to join in a genuinely German reform, with a strong executive and a National Assembly – since the Austrians had argued that their chamber of delegates would be purely advisory, in part to avoid the necessity of submitting their proposal to a unanimous vote as an organic change to the confederal constitution.

On acceding to the office of Foreign Minister on 8 October, Bismarck continued to pursue the same national policy as his predecessor, having argued in a memorandum ('Das kleine Buch') to Prince Wilhelm as early as March 1858 that Prussia should use the press and parliaments to stir up the German public against Vienna's policy in the Confederation.[228] Consequently, in response to Austria's refurbished plan for a reform of the *Bund* at the *Fürstentag* in August 1863, which added an assembly of German princes to the previously floated idea of an assembly of *Landtag* delegates, the Minister-President made the institution of a 'true national representative body founded on the direct participation of the entire nation' a condition of Prussian agreement, along with a joint presidency of Prussia and Austria in the proposed directory, and a Prussian and Austrian veto against all but purely defensive confederal wars.[229] He submitted the same proposal to the *Bundestag* on 9 April 1866, again after Vienna had mentioned a 'German parliament', specifying that his proposed German assembly would not only be elected directly but by universal manhood suffrage. His tactic throughout was to call Austria's and the middling states' bluff, knowing that they could not agree to the principal objective of the national movement.[230] If Vienna tried to court the states of the third Germany in the name of the nation, Bismarck would not hesitate 'to rub a bit of black, red and gold under its nose', he boasted to Robert von Keudell in September 1865, shortly after the signature of the Gastein Convention.[231] The same applied to the *Klein-* and *Mittelstaaten*: 'What are the little princes after?' he asked rhetorically in the same year: 'The governments are more reactionary than I – who would even make use of the party of change if it were to Prussia's advantage; they want most of all to stay on their thrones, and while they may be afraid of us they are even more afraid of revolution.'[232] Unlike his counterparts in other German governments, with the exception of those of Baden and the liberal Thuringian states, the Minister-President was prepared to countenance the formation of a representative national *Bundesstaat* in order to give weight to his claim that the 'legitimate power position of Prussia' and the 'legitimate interests of the [German] nation' were closely linked, as he had put it in the *Norddeutsche Allgemeine Zeitung* at the time of the *Fürstentag*.[233] Prussia's and Germany's fates were intertwined. This was the message that Wilhelm and Bismarck gave to the critical Crown Council of 28 February 1866, as they warned the assembled ministers and the Crown Prince – together with the specially invited Generals Moltke and Alvensleben, Goltz as the King's adviser, and Edwin von Manteuffel as the Governor of Schleswig – that the Hohenzollern monarchy was on the verge of a war against Austria: Prussia's 'natural and very justified' mission was to lead Germany, averred the Minister-President.[234]

The standard rejoinder to such utterances was that Bismarck did not believe in the national cause. The Minister-President's Progressive opponents, of course, were well aware of his cynicism. Mistrust, created by the manoeuvrings of a four-year-long constitutional crisis, prevented virtually all liberals and democrats from contemplating – at least in public – a rapprochement with the Prussian ministry. When Bismarck mooted a German parliament, to be elected directly by universal suffrage, in April 1866, there was widespread disbelief. The liberal satirical journal *Kladderadatsch*, the most popular publication of its kind, announced that it would be closing down, since it could not compete with the Minister-President's sense of humour: 'We have been dealt a hard blow ... The Bismarck cabinet appeals to the German nation and supports itself upon the people! Hahahaha! Who's laughing? All Europe and adjacent parts of the world! We aren't up to such competition.'[235] Yet the Minister-President, who was cynical towards all political parties, as reactionaries such as Gerlach recognised, does appear to have taken liberal nationalists seriously, courting them at great length in the build-up to war with Austria. In a series of meetings with Bennigsen, Roggenbach, Bernhardi, Twesten, Unruh and others in April and May, he emphasised his understanding and acceptance of their national point of view, to the extent of claiming improbably to the leader of the *Nationalverein* that reform of the *Bund* and the establishment of a German parliament had been his ambition since 1848–49. At his meeting with Bennigsen on 14 May, Bismarck demonstrated that he fully comprehended his interlocutor's aims, assuring him that his intention, 'as soon as Austria is defeated', was 'to introduce a federal constitution in Germany, with the participation of the population, which should be summoned, with the most extensive electoral system possible, to an assembly to help decide a constitution'.[236] His tone in most of the meetings appears, at times, to have been flippant and insincere, telling his opponents not to worry 'about the little bit of liberalism' that they would forfeit by backing him: 'You will later be able to recoup that within six weeks under the first good liberal cabinet, and in any case a new government will take office under the Crown Prince.'[237] But his main promise of a national reorganisation based on 'a revision of the constitution of 1849', which Bismarck pledged to 'accept with a kiss', was not dismissed out of hand, even though the committee

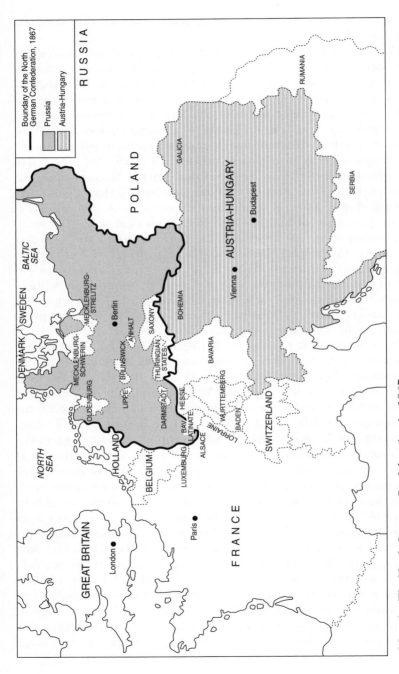

Map 6   The North German Confederation in 1867.
Source: Adapted from J. Breuilly, Austria, Prussia and Germany (London, 2002), xvi

of the *Nationalverein,* after inconclusively canvassing the opinion of its local agents, declined to support the Prussian ministry publicly.[238] The Minister-President's plan, recalled Bennigsen 23 years later, corresponded 'to what was later carried out in the North German *Bund*'s constitution and in the German Reich's constitution. It also corresponds for the most part to what Herr von Gagern, as the Minister-President in 1848–49, put forward as the German *Reichsverfassung* and ... what the *Nationalverein* adopted in its statutes and the resolutions of its programme in 1860 and 1863.'[239]

In the event, as Bennigsen recognised, Bismarck kept his word and introduced a German constitutional *Bundesstaat,* to the surprise and chagrin of the 'anti-German particularists' of the reactionary right.[240] 'The power of the monarchy in Prussia must be supported by a powerful army,' the Minister-President reportedly told Friedrich Wilhelm on 4 July 1866: 'But it must go with the opinion of the nation. It is the duty of every Prussian minister to regard the will of the king as authoritative, but at the same time to let the will of the king be saturated with the opinion of the nation.'[241] The North German Confederation was merely to be a 'stage' on the path to German unity.[242] Doubtless, Bismarck told the liberal Crown Prince what he wanted to hear, just as he had provided an echo of the ideas of liberal leaders a few months earlier. Nationalism had proved useful at home and, especially, abroad. Indeed, from the 1850s onwards, Bismarck had toyed with realigning Prussia with the 'national' and 'revolutionary' power of France, earning himself a reputation as a 'Bonapartist' in conservative circles. His officials and agents had contacted Hungarian and Serbian nationalists in the years before 1866 with a view to undermining an Austrian war effort against Prussia: he later bragged that he would have incited an insurrection in the Habsburg monarchy if it had joined France in July or August 1866 in a two-front war, after its defeat at Königgrätz on 3 July; at the time, he had instructed Goltz, the Prussian ambassador in Paris, to threaten 'a national uprising in Germany', 'the complete ignition of the national spirit', if the Bonapartist regime had attacked the Hohenzollern monarchy.[243] The ambassador was to warn the French government that 'Progressives and democrats' were prepared 'for every sacrifice in a war against France'.[244]

Whatever the short-term diplomatic and domestic advantages of 'nationalism' and 'revolution', it is difficult to explain why Bismarck actually introduced a democratically elected *Reichstag* in 1867 at the height of his power, having been granted – by 230 votes to 75 – an indemnity by the Prussian *Abgeordnetentag* on 3 September for his actions in the constitutional crisis. A month earlier, on 29 July, Friedrich Wilhelm had asked himself the same question: 'Without letting myself be in the least blinded or deceived by Bismarck, I cannot deny that I am astonished at the reasonable liberal views which the man is now putting forward and wants to implement.'[245] Even if the Minister-President hoped that a democratically elected German parliament might eventually produce a rural, conservative majority, why would he take such a risk, had he not already accepted the necessity of establishing a constitutional and federal nation-state in germ form? Certainly, for the majority of German liberal nationalists, who came – between 1866 and 1871 – to endorse Bismarck's actions, the Prussian Minister-President seemed to have reconciled himself with some of their most fundamental beliefs.

Conclusion

The year 1866 saw the implementation of the main components of the national solution to the German question which had been agreed in 1849. Schleswig-Holstein, the principal disputed national territory, was incorporated into Prussia and the North German Confederation; the Habsburg monarchy was excluded from Germany; the *Bund* was abolished; and a prototype of a German constitutional *Bundesstaat*, the most important features of which were transferred to the *Kaiserreich* in 1871, was outlined by Bismarck in a draft constitution for the North German Confederation on the Baltic island of Rügen. In these respects, Prussia's defeat of Austria at the battle of Königgrätz on 3 July, after just over a fortnight of hostilities, appears to be the end of a series of debates about the nation beginning in 1848 rather than a turning-point in itself.[1]

The war between Prussia and the northern *Kleinstaaten*, on the one hand, and Austria and the *Mittelstaaten*, on the other, was rarely seen as a 'civil war'.[2] Few commentators used the word '*Bürgerkrieg*' in 1866, despite the ubiquity of references in the press and elsewhere to the American Civil War only a year beforehand. Occasionally, Catholic or South German journalists deployed the term as a warning, but they were regularly challenged by others who claimed that any 'civil war' was, in fact, a conflict between the nation and the dynasties or the church.[3] A larger number of contemporaries called the conflict a '*Bruderkrieg*', or a war of brothers, acknowledging the consanguinity of their opponents but not their belonging to the same society or country. As such, the term carried an element of prohibition or, even, taboo: if the conflict really were a 'war of brothers', remarked Heinrich von Treitschke in the

Preussische Jahrbücher, it would be 'a crime'.[4] Yet Treitschke's point
was that the war was not a *Bruderkrieg* in the full sense of the word,
not least because it was associated by both sides with the 'cabinet
politics' of Vienna, Berlin, Munich, Stuttgart and Dresden.[5]
Bismarck had, four years earlier, referred to the notion of a 'brothers' war' as 'claptrap'.[6] The *Historisch-politische Blätter* condemned
the actual war as 'light-headed'.[7] The majority of observers had
anticipated the conflict well in advance; many had more or less
accepted its necessity. Although Wilhelm I and Bismarck became
more popular, with one correspondent from the *Social-Demokrat*
reporting on 1 July that thousands had congregated in front of their
residences, there was no sign of the crowds and euphoria in the
major cities that accompanied the declaration of war against France
in 1870.[8] The mood was more often characterised by resignation,
with another correspondent of the social-democratic newspaper,
who was touring South Germany in August, writing of an anti-
Prussian majority in Württemberg, but an anti-Austrian one in
Bavaria.[9] Most were critical of the irresponsible conduct of the war
by their governments and yearned for peace and unification, not
revenge.[10] In such circumstances, the majority of those alluding to
a 'war of brothers' were using a common trope, not anticipating or
describing an unthinkable act of fratricide.[11] Most correspondents
refrained from calling the conflict either a *Bürgerkrieg* or a
Bruderkrieg. It was a regrettable but expected event confirming what
had long been accepted.

The Resolution of the German Question

The first part of the German question formally resolved by the
Austro-Prussian War involved Schleswig-Holstein. Unlike Posen,
where Prussian stewardship was more or less agreed in 1848, with or
without a designation of two-thirds of the territory as 'German', the
northern duchies, which had been claimed on the basis of German
culture and language, with the possible exception of North
Schleswig, had constituted the main border dispute of an envisaged
German nation-state during the 1850s and early 1860s, after
Denmark had regained control under the terms of the Treaty of
London in 1852.[12] The dispute remained unresolved after Prussia's
and Austria's victorious war in 1864, since both states had acted as
Great Powers against the 'national' claims of the *Bund* and the

'German' heir Augustenburg. Rapidly, the crisis had become a five-way struggle between Prussia, which continued to uphold – or so Bismarck's ministry argued – the prerogatives of the Great Powers and appealed directly to the 'nation', the *Mittelstaaten* and the Confederation, which had sent troops to Holstein before Prussia's and Austria's occupation of the duchies in January 1864, German political parties and public opinion, Augustenburg himself, and the Habsburg monarchy, which increasingly courted the *Bund* and hailed Augustenburg as a national hero. After an interim agreement with Austria in the Gastein Convention (1865) to administer Schleswig (Prussia) and Holstein (Austria) separately, the fate of the duchies became interwoven with those of the Hohenzollern and Habsburg monarchies in their putative struggle for Germany. The movement throughout – in the debates of 1848–50, the publicising of the conflict in the 1850s and 1860s, and in the actions of the various parties after 1863 – was towards a greater Prussian role in a pivotal national affair.

With the duchies, according to the Gastein Convention, becoming part of the *Zollverein* and Prussia granted the right to build a canal through Holstein linking the North and Baltic seas, Berlin's intention of dominating the region was obvious. On 23 January 1866, a mass gathering in Altona had called for the convening of the joint estates of Schleswig-Holstein. Playing on Franz Joseph's horror at such radicalism, Bismarck called for Prussian and Austrian action against 'revolutionary' movements in the duchies: Vienna refused in February; Berlin declared its 1864 alliance with Austria invalid and worked towards a 'decisive political preponderance in North Germany', as the Crown Council minutes of 28 February put it.[13] Unconcealed military preparations went on throughout March, April and May, complicated by the entry of Italy into the crisis, after Prussia had signed a three-month offensive alliance with it on 6 April. With Bavaria and Württemberg manoeuvring in the *Bundestag* for a standing-down of all states' armies, the Austrian government replied on 1 June that it was ready to hand over the Schleswig-Holstein question to the Confederation in the face of Prussia's decision to use force there. Since Vienna was deemed to have broken the Gastein Convention by referring the matter to the *Bund*, Prussian forces occupied Holstein on 8 June, supposedly to restore a joint Prussian and Austrian authority in the duchy. On the following day, the Prussian representative in Frankfurt effectively broke with the Confederation, which had no say in the duchies according to the Treaty of London, the Austro-Prussian alliance (January 1864), the Peace of Vienna (October 1864) and the Gastein Convention, by calling for a nationally elected assembly to resolve the Schleswig-Holstein crisis. The Austrian envoy in Frankfurt, Aloys von Kübeck, moved successfully for the mobilisation of all non-Prussian confederal forces on 14 June. When Karl Friedrich Savigny, the Prussian envoy, retorted on the following day that the *Bundestag* had interfered in Schleswig-Holstein without authority, since it was not a party to the Peace of Vienna, and that it had failed to safe-guard the security of Prussia (Article 2) by refusing to act against the arming of other German states despite Berlin's protests, the German Confederation in its existing form had effectively lapsed: Prussia undertook to restructure the organisation fundamentally, relegating Austria to an unspecified wider *Bund*, in the name of the German nation. The proclivity of Berlin's policy in all such events, confirmed by the annexation of the duchies in 1866, was to take control of the region, often on purportedly national grounds. If Austria had defeated Prussia at Königgrätz, it is difficult to imagine much more than the inclusion of an independent Duchy of Schleswig-Holstein in a confederal *status quo ante bellum*.

The exclusion of the Habsburg monarchy from Germany was the second element of the national settlement of 1848–49 which was confirmed in 1866. Technically, the *Reichsverfassung* had left the question open, explicitly providing for a quota of Austrian seats in the upper *Staatenhaus*, but Articles 2 and 3 were widely believed to have set unacceptable conditions of entry for Vienna, with a distinct title for the head of state and a separate administration, assembly and law for 'German' and 'non-German' states. Article 1 stated that 'the German *Reich* consists of the territory of the former German Confederation,' even though it was known that a full or partial severing of Austria's German territories to form *Grossdeutschland* was unacceptable to the Hofburg.[14] Whereas the majority passing this *kleindeutsch* constitution in 1848 was small, albeit for a variety of reasons, the articulation of opposition to – and scepticism of – Austrian participation in any type of German nation-state had become more pronounced by the early 1860s. North German, and some South German, liberals adhered to what became known as the doctrine of 'Gotha', because of liberals' post-revolutionary appro-bation of Prussia at a meeting there in 1849. Democrats, most of whom had been banished or marginalised by the persecution or restrictive franchises of the 'reaction', were much less enthusiastic about *Grossdeutschland* than they had been in 1848. The 'small German' proclivity of the *Nationalverein* and, even, of the Prussian-dominated *Fortschrittspartei* found considerable support and met with little resistance in radical circles. Many Catholics were much more anxious about the loss to Germany of the largest Catholic state and population, but they were unable to formulate a convincing argument for Austria's inclusion, not least because of the detachment and distance of the majority of German Austrians from the affairs of Germany.

What was remarkable in 1866 was the ease with which Austria was 'shut out definitively from any constitutional involvement in the rest of Germany', in the words of the *Historisch-politische Blätter*.[15] Despite the fact that Prussia's victory was 'an unexpected success', with Austria and the *Mittelstaaten* stronger 'on paper' than the Hohenzollern monarchy, the periodical quickly came to terms with the disappearance of the Habsburg monarchy from German politics – 'there will never again be a German Confederation (*Staatenbund*) with two Great Powers' – and with the replacement of Austria by Bonapartist France as 'the first factor in German affairs'.[16] In a long article on 'Austria' immediately after its defeat, the Bavarian publication denied that it had 'advised Austria to withdraw from Germany', as had been claimed in Vienna, yet it admitted to having urged the Austrian government to make 'concessions over Schleswig-Holstein and to refrain from "German interventions" in the question of reform'.[17] It had also warned Vienna not to try to halt the growth of Prussian power in the North.[18] The Austrian ministry's refusal to heed such advice had left Germany's Catholics in an exposed position, contesting claims that 1866 was a victory for Protestantism as well as the German nation, and fending off accusations that Catholicism was tarred by its association with Austria.[19] Nonetheless, the periodical argued with some justification that the Catholic press had adopted a strictly German stance in 1866, not an Austrian one, even if many publications had opposed Prussia's bellicose policy and its alliance with Italy.[20] Catholic newspapers in Prussia such as the *Kölnische Blätter* were much more critical of the Habsburg monarchy, charging it with striving for a war against Prussia and with lacking 'any definition', even during the war itself, of 'Austria's place in Germany'.[21] Defeat had left the Habsburg monarchy, already weak, 'threatened by internal shocks', with 'the friction between nationalities threatening to become more violent than ever'.[22] These were the weaknesses, even a Catholic publication could concur, which had prevented the Habsburg monarchy from taking an active part in German politics in the years before the war.

The conflict between Austria and Prussia had demonstrated that 'the German *Bund* had created and maintained, not the *unity*, but the *fragmentation* of Germany', continued the *Kölnische Blätter*.[23] The dissolution of the Confederation as a result of the defeat of the *Mittelstaaten* and the Habsburg monarchy constituted a third element of the revolutionary national settlement reinstated in 1866, since the *Bund* had previously been disbanded in 1848, only to be revived by Austria in September 1850 and reimposed on Prussia at the Dresden Conferences of January 1851. During the revolution, the governments of the German states had tried to refashion the Confederation into a national institution and 'their communal organ', claiming that they were 'united with the German people in the same love for their fatherland'.[24] During the course of 1848, however, the Confederation was gradually sidelined, with the appointment of the *Reichsverweser* and the establishment of a Central Power in July 1848 on the authority of the National Assembly and, 'in it, the representatives of the German *Volk*', until it was abandoned altogether in the constitution of March 1849, which replaced the confederal structure of the *Bund* with the federal institutions of a national '*Reich*'.[25] After its re-establishment in 1850–51, the Confederation was the subject of a series of proposed reforms during the late 1850s and early 1860s which were initiated by the governments of the *Mittelstaaten*, especially that of Saxony, in order to harness popular support for national organisations. The plans put forward by Beust, Schrenck, Hügel, Platen, Dalwigk and – in 1863 – Schmerling fell far short of public expectations, concentrating on the creation of a confederal court, a weak central authority, typically a 'directory' or 'trias', and – at most – an assembly of delegates from the upper and lower chambers of the *Landtage*, which themselves had restrictive electoral laws. There was no notion that a directory was a standing government – the word 'executive' was avoided – nor that an assembly was a 'parliament' with a right to approve and reject budgets and legislation. As Beust and others made clear, the institutions of a reformed *Bund* were designed to coordinate the activities of the existing states under a more acceptable national guise.

Few contemporaries lamented the passing of the German Confederation. Robert von Mohl, the Badenese envoy in Frankfurt, recorded in his memoirs how it had limped on through the war, after Prussia had left on 15 June. 'Soon the committee meetings became truly painful', receiving bad news daily from the battle-grounds of Bohemia and losing, first, the delegates of the northern states – Hanover, Kurhessen, Saxony and Nassau – and, then, those of all the rest save Bavaria, Württemberg and Liechtenstein, who were by that time housed in temporary accommodation in Augsburg.[26] 'This staying together until the last spark was extin-guished can only have been sad', concluded Mohl, but even he conceded that the Confederation's fate was partly the consequence of its own inactivity.[27] At best, 'improvements of the existing consti-tution of the *Bund* appeared not to be impossible': in backing Austria and the other *Mittelstaaten* in 1866, 'one had to renounce, perhaps for a long time, a long-held desire for improvement, desires pursued for years directly or indirectly, but at least one avoided posi-tive losses', wrote the diplomat and academic.[28] In January of the same year, he had complained to Baden's Foreign Minister that the Confederation had been impotent and ignored in the Schleswig-Holstein affair, which had 'always been seen as a test of whether the German *Bund* has any political significance at all'.[29] It had not been 'what it could under other circumstances and almost must be, a focus of high politics', not least because of the 'internal weakness' of Austria, the 'division' of the *Mittelstaaten* and the 'incredible policy' of Prussia:

> Only when the principal members no longer make the life of the Confederation the object of their opposing envy and prefer systematically to cripple it rather than grant each other advan-tages from it can an independent activity of the *Bund* be imag-ined. Only when the views and needs of the remaining German lands no longer have to be placed automatically behind the two Great Powers' consciousness of their own state and its particular needs is the founding and use of national institutions thinkable. Only when a popular factor can forcefully articulate questions, which have neither their origins nor find favour in the circle of the governments, can a consideration of the desires of the core of the nation be expected and can respect and trust again grad-ually be won for the Confederation and its organs.[30]

For most political parties and much of the public, these political conditions had not been met.

The North German Confederation, the provisions of which had been sketched by Bismarck in the 'Putbus dictates' – named after the owner of the Rügen estate where he was sojourning – on 30 October and 19 November 1866, seemed to continue the tradition of the *Bund*, but it was closer, in reality, to the model of the constitutional *Bundesstaat* outlined in 1849. Bismarck wanted to give the impression of confederal continuity, deliberately relying on 'inherited concepts of the *Bund*' rather than making 'the King of Prussia into an independent factor in the law-making of the Confederation analogous to the monarchy of a constitutional state' in order to overcome residual resistance on the part of the King, the Court and the conservative party in Prussia, to appeal to the South German states, and to appease France.[31] Accordingly, the Prussian proposals for a fundamental reorganisation of Germany referred back, as Rudolph von Delbrück noted in passing in his memoirs, to 'The Principles for a New *Bund* Constitution' presented by Savigny to the *Bundestag* on 10 June 1866.[32] Thus, although the proposals called for 'the exclusion of Austria and the Netherlands' and had 'transferred the legislative power of the *Bund* to the *Bundestag* in conjunction with a National Assembly elected in accordance with the Frankfurt electoral law', the fiction of the continuing existence of a *Staatenbund* similar to the old German Confederation was maintained.[33] In fact, the *Norddeutscher Bund* had crossed the critical boundaries between a confederation and a federal state identified by Waitz: namely, a *Bundesstaat* required a standing government with its own finances, military, powers and jurisdictions formally independent of, although shared with, those of its constituent – state – parts, and it necessitated a direct link between the *Volk* and the *Bund*, or central authority, normally in the form of a directly elected National Assembly.[34] The *Bund* authority and the National Assembly, or *Reichstag*, together had been given control over the basic financial and military means of statehood, constituting 'a unified tariff and trade area' and 'a land and sea power' with the decision 'over war and peace', in Delbrück's words: 'The constitution, which was to be built on this platform, had to order all the affairs transferred to the *Bund*, which were of a fundamental nature, and to create an immediate order, paying attention to the legal position in the individual states, in order to create an entity capable of life.'[35]

The pivotal question concerned what contemporary liberals called the 'executive' in Bismarck's scheme, since it seemed to rest

– as Delbrück had indicated – on a modified version of the *Bundestag*, renamed the *Bundesrat*, in which the governments of the individual states were represented. Yet there were critical differences between the *Norddeutscher Bund* and the old *Bund*. The King of Prussia, in his capacity as 'president' (*Präsidium*) of the *Bundesrat*, exercised control over foreign policy, declarations of war (Article 11), the convocation and dissolution of the *Bundesrat* and the *Reichstag* (Art. 12), the appointment of officials and ministers (Art. 18), and emergency powers in a military context (Art. 19), all carried out on his own authority with the countersignature of the *Bund* Chancellor, who took 'responsibility' for them (Art. 17). The Emperor of Austria, who had presided over the *Bundestag*, had enjoyed none of these powers or responsibilities, since there was no National Assembly or *Bund* court to which he or his representative could be responsible. *Bund* decisions were subject to the vote and veto of individual states in the *Engerer Rat* and – much more rarely – the full *Bundesversammlung*. Whereas Austria had had only 1 vote out of 17 in the majority system of the *Engerer Rat* of the *Bund*, Prussia had 17 votes out of 43 in the *Bundesrat*, plus a decisive influence over most of the small states – Mecklenburg, Schaumburg-Lippe, Oldenburg, Sachsen-Meiningen, Sachsen-Altenburg, Anhalt – surrounded by its territory or on its borders. If anything, the new 'state', as it was widely known, seemed more likely to become unitary in structure than to lapse back into a confederation. Liberals such as Bennigsen and democrats such as Waldeck, though, were confident that it would do neither, referring to it as a 'North German *Bundesstaat*'.[36]

To contemporary politicians and journalists, it went without saying that the provisions of the *Reichsverfassung* of 1849 were less ambiguous, for good or ill, than the clauses of the constitution of the North German Confederation (1867). Democrats and liberals, most of whom had approved of the *Nationalverein*'s adoption of the Reich constitution as the basis of a new nation-state, were critical of the new constitution's lack of clarity. In the main debate of the Constituent Assembly of the North German *Reichstag* on 9 March 1867, Twesten had argued that it had proved impossible 'to draw up a federal (*bundesstaatlich*) constitution as they have, as a rule, been designed and conceived of in political theories', which generally referred to Switzerland and the United States.[37] Although there was no 'monarchical example of such a federal constitution', he went on, 'one could think of an analogy of these constitutions, and the schemes which were worked out in 1849 in Frankfurt and Berlin imagined such an analogy.'[38] In particular, forty-eighters had devised a central power (*Zentralgewalt*) 'which was to be separate from the governments of the individual states' – 'standing above all the states of the German *Bund*' – and 'which was to be constituted in the fashion of a constitutional government'.[39] The executive powers of the 1867 constitution were shared between the individual states in the *Bundesrat*, the King of Prussia as its president, and the *Bundeskanzler* as a supposedly responsible countersignatory of the president's decrees. In such circumstances, complained Sybel, it was misleading to talk of responsibility in the characteristic sense of classic constitutional governments, since the Chancellor had little control over the acts for which he was deemed responsible, unlike the Reich Authority defined so extensively in 1849 (Articles 6–67).[40]

Nonetheless, it was obvious to such liberals that the essential features of 'constitutional monarchy' were preserved within the Prussian government's bill, as they had been in 1849: the King of Prussia had the power to form an 'executive' – the term was used by Bismarck as well as by most other contemporaries – which would be largely independent of both the individual states and of the national assembly. For its part, the *Reichstag* had the right – as in 1849 – to block legislation and to reject the budget – including, in future, that relating to military expenditure, or 90 per cent of overall spending – but not to remove the Chancellor by a vote of no-confidence. Bismarck himself acknowledged in private discussions with Savigny that the constitution, by making the *Bundeskanzler* responsible to a national parliament in military, foreign, fiscal and commercial affairs, would establish German affairs above those of Prussia, even though the two were intertwined:

> Through the responsibility clause the Chancellor has become to a degree – if not legally, yet actually – the superior of the Prussian cabinet ... You are too well acquainted with constitutional law not to realise that the Chancellor thereby receives the power of final decision in the affairs of the Prussian ministries of trade, war, and naval affairs, of the more important parts of the Finance Ministry, and, if the confederal constitution develops correctly, the Ministry of Foreign Affairs ... He receives this authority due to the circumstance that he influences the *Reichstag* by granting or withholding his countersignature. Because of this amendment, therefore, the Chancellor must be

simultaneously president of the Prussian cabinet if the new machine is to function at all.[41]

On 12 March and 15 April 1867, Bennigsen proclaimed to the Constituent Assembly, in contrast to 'many of my colleagues on the left side of this house', that 'the constitutional work' was 'not logical but coherent', 'in need of improvement but also capable of improvement', promising 'many and great advantages' for 'the internal national development of the German *Nation*' and in keeping with 'constitutional development in Germany'.[42] On 16 April, the constitution of the *Norddeutscher Bund* was passed by 230 to 54 votes in the Prussian *Abgeordnetenhaus*, backed by the 80 deputies of the newly formed National Liberal party – created to grant Bismarck indemnity for his role in the Prussian constitutional crisis – and opposed, as Bennigsen had anticipated, by the 'radical left', 'Poles and pessimistic particularists'.[43] For many of the constitution's backers, it seemed possible, in the words of the founding programme of the National Liberal party on 12 June 1867, to bring 'a monarchical *Bundesstaat* into harmony with the conditions of constitutional law' as 'the first and necessary step on the path to a German state, reinforced by freedom and power'.[44]

Revolutionary Nationalism and the Unification of Germany

The national and political legacy of the first unification of Germany in 1848–49 left a significant imprint on the second one after 1866. The revolution had witnessed the emergence of political parties and the rapid development of political networks and milieux, on the one hand, and the unexpected posing of a series of questions about the character, territory and polity of the German nation, on the other. Nationalism and politics were therefore linked together at a crucial moment, as party organisations and doctrines were being created and the nation-state was being designed. 'The foundations of the old political life have been shaken', recorded the welcome address of the *Bundesversammlung* to the Frankfurt National Assembly in May 1848, 'and a new giant has arisen, greeted by jubilation and with the trust of the entire German people (*Volk*): the German parliament.'[45] 'The power of extraordinary events' had transformed political practices and institutions, linking them in new ways to the quest for a nation-state.[46] Rather than the mystical

dreams and cultural yearnings of unpolitical Germans subverting
the idea of the nation, they rapidly yielded to the sudden imperatives of practical politics and state interests, with Arndt's romantic
hope of a German fatherland composed of the lands of the
Confederation, Switzerland, the whole of Austria and beyond being
sacrificed for a realisable set of borders which left Alsace to France,
German areas of the Baltic to Russia, and 'old Austria', Bohemia
and Moravia to the Habsburg monarchy. In this sense, the notion
that there was an enduring and balanced debate between proponents of *Kleindeutschland* and *Grossdeutschland* is misleading: most
contemporaries came to realise in 1848–49 that the Austrian
government, backed by a majority of German Austrians, would resist
the creation of a 'greater Germany' which sought to detach
German-speaking lands from the rest of the monarchy, since such
detachment would probably provoke the state's collapse. The revolution had demonstrated that liberals and others in the Habsburg
territories of the Confederation were, as Schmerling put it, Austrian
first and German second.

A similar statism existed in Germany, limiting the extent of territory in cases where it was necessary to avoid conflict with the Great
Powers, but extending borders as far as possible in Posen and, it was
anticipated, in Schleswig-Holstein, where the claims of national
opponents were not backed by a major state. In 1848–49, many
liberals, democrats and cosmopolitan Catholics and conservatives
had renounced their romantic championing of Polish and Italian
national self-determination, they had given up Mazzini's hope of a
peaceful coexistence of nations during the 'springtime of the
peoples' and they had sought to form as large a territory and population as possible in order to achieve Great Power status in the
states' system. 'In the West and in the East, we have lost valuable old
German land through our own fragmentation, through political
foolishness and false cosmopolitanism,' declared the Catholic
courtier and Frankfurt deputy Radowitz to an appreciative National
Assembly in July 1848: 'should we push away ... our fellow nationals
and transfer them to the dominion of a foreign nation? Such a
suggestion would be inconceivable in the chambers of the other
great European peoples.'[47] Such hard-headed 'realism' preceded
any supposed shift to *Realpolitik* during an era of reaction in the
1850s. It was, above all, a response to the challenges facing an
emerging German nation-state during the revolution: most deputies
had come to believe that such compromises of political principle

were needed to safeguard the state militarily and strategically and to give Germany the place in Europe which it deserved. This territorial and international realism was a product of the revolution, not the reaction, and it characterised both the reactionary 1850s and the more liberal 1860s.

The revolutionary intertwining of nationalism and politics did not lead to a national subversion of liberalism and democracy as much as to the limitation of contemporaries' cultural fantasies of the nation and delusions of national superiority. There was an emancipatory component to German nationalism after 1848 as a consequence of its political origins, with mass support for a nation-state, or a political framework for the German *Volk*, coinciding with the emergence of a democratic party and the rise to power of a nationwide liberal party. These political networks and milieux were restricted by the reaction of the 1850s, particularly through the persecution of radicals and the outlawing of inter-state organisations, but they were not destroyed, with political discourses continuing in the *Landtage*, in the press, in the major cities, and in the more liberal states. The memory of 1848 remained in the forefront of many politicians' and journalists' minds, resurfacing in the programmes of the national and party organisations – the *Nationalverein*, Progressive Party and *Abgeordnetentag* – of the early 1860s. The principal carriers of the national idea in and after the revolution continued to believe, with few exceptions, that freedom and unity were compatible. Although it is true that they – like the majority of their European counterparts – had come to define politics exclusively during the revolution, regularly equating citizenship with nationality, and that they continued to believe in the necessity of a *lingua franca*, assimilation and a hierarchy of cultures, favouring the claims of their own superior nation and emphasising the backwardness of other nationalities, German liberals and democrats had refused to give up what Rochau termed – in 1869 – their 'civic struggle for freedom', winning advantages 'from the princely power and bureaucracy' in the form of 'the most important constitutional questions, press freedom, public judicial proceedings, jury trials, the independence of judicial officials, the separation of justice and administration, in short the majority of civic and bourgeois wishes for which liberalism has deployed its best efforts over the last half century'.[48]

These individual freedoms and 'advances of civilisation (*Zivilisation*)', even a realist like Rochau believed, would temper, order and render human the relations between individuals, of whatever nationality, which in theory were regulated by the same 'final judgement of history' and 'the same law as disputes between states and peoples'; namely, 'that one is stronger' and another weaker.[49] As the maintenance of the constitutional campaign against Bismarck during the war for Schleswig-Holstein demonstrated in 1864, the struggle for emancipation at home was barely compromised by the need for unity abroad. The reorganisation of Germany continued to be a largely liberal and democratic project, with the entrenchment of political freedoms, constitutional and representative government, direct elections and universal suffrage as its main objectives. All 'the citizens of the states which make up the Reich' – or 'the German people' in an open sense – were to be granted 'basic rights', declared the *Reichsverfassung* of 1849, including 'the non-German-speaking people of Germany', who were 'guaranteed their national development, namely, equal rights for their languages, in so far as they exist in their territories, in ecclesiastical matters, in education, in administration of local affairs and of justice' (Article 188).[50] Despite their confused, contested and pragmatic nature, these constitutional provisions continued to be supported by Progressives during the 1860s, echoing the hope of revolutionaries that such individual and collective rights would compensate and integrate minority nationalities.[51]

A largely liberal public and political sphere had been created in Germany during the revolution, resting on the existing political milieux of the larger cities and state assemblies, together with readers of newspapers and periodicals, and tourists, merchants, manufacturers, bankers, journalists and university students who travelled to other German lands. As the liberal leader and newly converted proponent of *Kleindeutschland* Heinrich von Gagern revealed in March 1849, attempting to convince sceptics that he was 'a South German' and not an instrument of Prussia, experiences before the revolution could be surprisingly circumscribed: 'I have lived in the North for little time. I only recently ... saw Berlin for the first time.'[52] Many deputies, arriving in Frankfurt in 1848, gave the impression that they were venturing into a foreign land. By the early 1860s, their counterparts were regularly travelling by train throughout Germany to meet officials, journalists and other politicians and to attend the meetings of the *Nationalverein*, *Handelstag* and *Abgeordnetentag*. To one commentator, it was 'no exaggeration' to say that 'the gulf that separates the years 1873 and 1773' as far as trade

and communications were concerned 'is greater than the gulf separating 1773 and the Phoenicians'.[53] To the politicians of the 1860s,
looking back on the expansion of the public sphere and the
creation of a national network of political centres in 1848–49, at a
time when Frankfurt was only connected by railway to the South
West and Munich was merely linked by train to Augsburg, the linkages between the two periods appeared obvious, as parts of an evolving but – because of the reaction – not linear story of national
progress. With his warnings of the consequences of fragmentation,
foreign domination and national decline, Treitschke could not be
called an optimist, even in the 1860s, but he recognised that the
material and imaginary bases of politics were changing, with
hundreds of thousands from the '*Mittelstand*' reading in their newspapers of the 'reason of universal suffrage' and with Germans
coming into contact with each other 'more regularly from day to
day' as a consequence of 'the immeasurable upswing of transport
and communication'.[54] With borders between small German states
seeming ridiculous to the passengers of trains, theories of the
nation had become 'fashionable', already adhered to 'by a good
part of the half-educated'.[55] Mockery of particularism and
Kleinstaaterei, which very few were prepared to defend, was part of
this wider movement of public opinion. When states such as Saxony,
Württemberg and Hanover attempted to cultivate local patriotism,
they usually did so by demonstrating – or, at least, not denying – its
connection to the heroic and pathos-laden history of Germany.[56]

As the prominent Catholic Bishop of Mainz Wilhelm Emmanuel
von Ketteler conceded in 1862, liberals dominated the press, just as
they dominated politics.[57] Internal critics such as Mohl and external
ones like Stahl agreed that the 'party' had been successful before
1848, dominating 'the party of movement' or the 'opposition' to
government factions.[58] During the revolution, at least 47 per cent of
Frankfurt deputies belonged to the liberal groupings of the centre
left (Württemberger Hof, Westendhalle, Deutscher Hof) and centre
right (Casino, Landsberg, Augsburger Hof). In the 1850s, with the
leaders of the democrats in exile or on the fringes of politics, liberals were preponderant in the oppositions of most German states,
coming briefly to back the governments of the New Era in Prussia
and Bavaria, and to enter government in Baden. Liberals won 55
per cent of the seats in the Prussian *Abgeordnetenhaus* in 1858, 69.5
per cent in 1861, and 70 per cent in 1862 and 1863, despite – or
perhaps because of – the constitutional crisis. Over the same period,

conservatives won between 3 and 13 per cent of seats, and Catholics between 7 and 16 per cent. In the Bavarian lower chamber, liberals held between 58 and 76 per cent of seats from the mid-1850s to the early 1860s, and in Hesse-Darmstadt, between 68 and 84 per cent from 1862 to 1868. These parties and factions were borne, in Rochau's view, 'exclusively by the middle classes': at least 88.4 per cent of Frankfurt deputies came from such strata in 1848–49; and similar figures were recorded for state *Landtage* in the following decades, with Württemberg counting 95.2 per cent of deputies from the *Bürgertum* in the early 1850s (1851–55), for instance, and 92.5 per cent in the mid-1860s (1862–68).[59]

These liberals had no reason to panic in the decades following 1848–49. The revolution, although defeated by the forces of the reaction, had not 'failed', as one of its harsher liberal detractors, Rochau, made clear: 'The measure of success cannot ... be placed on the momentary, but must be placed on the lasting effects of the revolution. It is not a question of how much ground revolution wins in the first instance, but how much ground it wins altogether.'[60] The revolution, went on the liberal publicist and later leader of the *Nationalverein*, had instilled new life into German politics, challenging existing institutions. Liberals like Rochau had weathered the counter-revolution, as they had predicted, and they – together with democrats in the *Fortschrittspartei* – had reassumed a dominant position inside and outside the assemblies of Prussia and most *Mittelstaaten* during and after the New Era, setting up a network of national and other associations and controlling the majority of the biggest-circulation newspapers and periodicals – the *Kölnische Zeitung* (60,000 in 1866), the Berlin *Volks-Zeitung* (22,000 in 1861), *Die Berlinische Zeitung* (13,000), the *National-Zeitung* (8,500), and *Kladderadatsch* (39,000).[61] The seven large liberal papers in Berlin during the constitutional crisis had a joint circulation of 71,000 compared to only 11,330 for the four conservative publications.[62] With such a presence in the public and political spheres, liberals and Progressives had every reason to put forward their political and national demands with confidence, notwithstanding a decline in membership of the *Nationalverein* – which was not widely reported – and anxiety about the loyalties – either Catholic or socialist – of the 'mass of the *Volk*', were it ever to vote in large numbers. For the moment, liberals were in the ascendant. The feeling for the majority was too novel and the task too great to allow of widespread pessimism or defensiveness.

It was in the context of this public and political sphere that liberals and Progressives resurrected the national and political demands of 1849. In doing so, their actions appeared to belie important elements of the traditional – but still widely held – view of German nationalism's role in the process of unification. First, few liberals or democrats thought that the revolution had simply failed.[63] They were thus willing to take up the agreements reached during the revolution itself on the question of borders, the exclusion of Austria, the abolition of the *Bund*, and the establishment of a central Reich authority and a *Reichstag* – the name was used in both 1849 and 1867 – elected by a direct vote and universal suffrage within a federal constitutional monarchy. They also retained many of the revolutionaries' hopes of emancipation, rights, social equality, freedom of expression, political organisation and representation. Second, the reaction did not destroy liberal political milieux, party activity or national aspirations, it merely limited them to individual states and to articulation in the press, despite censorship.[64] Networks of democrats, which were more recent than those of liberals and had grown more dramatically in 1848–49, were disbanded or disrupted in some states, but this dispersal and persecution was seen by some liberals as removing a potential menace. The significance of any hardening of attitudes after 1849 is difficult to gauge: there was certainly pragmatism, an aversion to utopian schemes, and a realistic assessment of the strength of the different states and parties, but it did not imply, even for Rochau, the worship of power or a readiness to sacrifice basic liberal principles. Much of the 'realism' of the 1850s and 1860s dated back to compromises made during the revolution. It is possible that, in some cases, the reaction had the effect of preserving, or delaying full discussion of, the revolutionary settlement. Third, the liberal party was not, in spite of continuing criticism, perceived to be weak or declining in the 1860s.[65] In Prussia, the *Fortschrittspartei* had maintained its opposition to the ministry and monarch during the constitutional crisis and it had, partly as a result, gained votes. Liberals in Bavaria had forced the resignation of Pfordten in 1859, and liberals in Baden had entered government for the first time in 1860, including former revolutionaries like Karl Mathy. Such figures saw no need to give up liberty in order to achieve national unity. Even Baumgarten could ask, in December 1866, 'Is unity not itself a part of freedom?'[66] Fourth, liberalism remained central to the definition of a future German nation-state, existing alongside and overlapping with the rituals and symbols of cultural forms of nationalism perpetuated by large festivals – most notably, the half-centenary of the battle of Leipzig in 1863 – and mass organisations such as the gymnastics, shooting and choral societies.[67] Treitschke regretted that the 'great festival of the fatherland' was necessary in the absence of a German parliament, since 'the vast majority of people believe solely what they experience in person' and 'only in hearty personal contact with much abused neighbouring tribes does the mass of half-educated learn that we belong together', yet he was confident that the 'hollow generalities' and simplifying acclamations of such occasions and associations 'naturally must stop at the point where the political work should first begin'.[68] Party politics and political types of nationalism were not displaced by cultural ones.

Lastly, the political and national claims of liberals and Progressives, which rested on the platform of 1849, set many of the terms of the debate about unification in the 1850s and 1860s, qualifying the notion of a Bismarckian revolution 'from above'.[69] Whatever his other motives, which leaders such as Bennigsen were sure that they would have to confront in future, the Prussian Minister-President appeared to have altered his position since 1849 much more significantly than had liberals and democrats, availing himself of the rhetoric of German nationalism and designing the prototype of a federal and constitutional small German nation-state with a directly and universally elected '*Reich*' assembly. Against opposition from reactionaries, he had also consolidated the *Zollverein* on the basis of free trade, confirmed by Prussia's commercial agreement with France in 1862, and he had tied – in perpetuity – the South German states militarily to the North German Confederation, with the command of southern armies passing to Prussia in the event of war. He had not granted a parliamentary system of government in 1866–67, but few liberals had asked for one. While it is true that the manner in which Bismarck pursued his aims – Great Power diplomacy in Schleswig-Holstein, army reform at the cost of constitutional crisis – and that his ultimate aims – the harnessing of a conservative, rural *Volk* via universal suffrage, Prussian domination in Germany – differed from those of Progressives and other liberals, the actual measures that he put forward and the results that he achieved closely resembled the objectives of liberal nationalists.

Public and party debates about a German nation-state before 1866 had narrowed the range of workable and popular solutions to the German question. The majority of participants in such debates had accepted the exclusion of Austria from a German nation-state, even if it were included in a wider union with Germany, they had given up any hope that the *Bund* could be reformed in a national sense, and they were highly critical of the 'particularism' of the *Klein-* and *Mittelstaaten*. None of these points of political agreement meant that German unification inevitably took the small German, Prussian-dominated form that it did, but they do modify the findings of recent research into unification, which has tended to emphasise the significance of Austria in German affairs until a late date, the plausibility and achievements of the Confederation and the third Germany, and the weaknesses of national organisations in the period immediately before the Austro-Prussian war.[70] Fear, resentment, mistrust and hatred of Prussia were pronounced in the South German states, helping to explain popular support for the Habsburg monarchy in 1866. Liberal milieux in the South had long been divided about the desirability of *Kleindeutschland*, with many preferring to ignore the question altogether, even in Baden, where Roggenbach – as Foreign Minister between 1861 and 1865 – was one of its main advocates. More importantly, democratic organisations in Württemberg and Catholic milieux in Baden and Bavaria were being mobilised in the second half of the 1860s for the first time since 1848–49, creating an anti-Prussian majority in the South in the 1868 elections to the *Zollparlament*, set up by Bismarck to ease the path to unification. About 50 opponents of Prussia were returned out of the 85 seats allotted to southern states; 27 opponents to 12 proponents in Bavaria, with a further 9 deputies undecided, 17 to 0 in Württemberg, 6 to 8 in Baden, and 0 to 6 in Hesse. These results were confirmed by elections to the *Landtage* of Bavaria in 1869 (76 liberals versus 79 Catholics, conservatives, and Bavarian *Patrioten*) and Württemberg in 1868 (30 for the democratic *Volkspartei*, 29 for Catholics and conservatives, and 12 for the pro-Prussian *Deutsche Partei*), though not in Baden in 1869, when the Catholic *Volkspartei* gained only 4 seats.[71]

Such votes reveal division and uncertainty within southern electorates and suggest that the full unification of *Kleindeutschland* remained in the balance. However, the choice facing political elites and voters in Bavaria and Württemberg was, as Helga Grebing has indicated, not one between a Prussian-dominated small Germany and a greater Germany or some other arrangement, but between '*Klein-Deutschland*' and '*Kein-Deutschland*' – that is, no unification at all.[72] Faced with such a choice, deputies and ministers in the two southern states were left to weigh up 'a national linking of the South German states with the North German Confederation' within what the pro-Prussian Minister-President of Bavaria Hohenlohe could still present as a '*Staatenbund*' against the benefits and drawbacks of life alone in their own *Heimat*, which was already tied militarily and economically to the *Norddeutsche Bund*, for any *Südbund* mooted in the Treaty of Prague (1866) was likely to fail because of Badenese resistance and Swabian fear of Bavarian domination.[73] Even for the founder of the Bavarian *Patriotenpartei* Edmund Jörg, the predicament was not a comfortable one, given his previous criticism of particularism and his advocacy of a national '*Reich*'. At the very least, the endless discussions of national unity and unification over the previous two decades, which had been informed by liberals and joined by democrats, Catholics and conservatives, seemed to have closed off alternatives to a small German nation-state which now needed to be reopened. It was difficult to predict how liberals and others would react when confronted with the choice of coming to terms with Prussia or giving up the prospect of inclusion in a German nation-state which many of them had previously supported. In the event, a national war against Germany's long-standing French enemy made their decision easier, but it did not, in itself, preclude actual and later resistance to unification and its consequences, such as happened in Italy. The relative ease with which unification occurred, during and after wartime, was largely the consequence of the debates about a German nation-state which had taken place in the two decades after 1848.

The North German Confederation and the *Kaiserreich*, of course, were not revolutionary regimes.[74] The absence of a declaration of basic rights (*Grundrechte*) in the constitutions of 1867 and 1871 was not merely important symbolically; it also left open the question of the ultimate location of sovereignty, whether popular or monarchical, which remained unresolved throughout the history of the German Empire and even found an echo, albeit within the formal realm of popular sovereignty, in the debates about the emergency powers of the president during the late Weimar era. Nonetheless, to the majority of liberals and many others, the rights promised in the *Reichsverfassung* of 1849 would, it was expected, be consolidated and safeguarded, if far less systematically than in a revolutionary order, within the legal, constitutional and representative polity of the Reich. Although the freedom of religious conscience and associa-

tion seemed to have been restricted during the *Kulturkampf* of the
1870s and the period of anti-socialist legislation between 1878 and
1890, they had been curtailed within legally defined limits and with
the connivance of many liberals. Few contemporaries entertained
the possibility of a return to the reaction of the 1850s or to 'absolutism'. Rather, the German '*Rechtsstaat*' and 'constitutional monarchy' which had been established between 1867 and 1871 appeared
to offer the possibility, within an admittedly precarious and undefined polity during the 1870s, 1880s and 1890s, of individual liberties, regional autonomy and representative government.[75] The
sharing of sovereignty between a monarchical executive and a
popular assembly was intrinsic to this 'constitutionalism', which was
later seen by commentators – including liberals – as a specifically
'German' form of rule, allowing the *Reichstag* to sanction all legislation and increases of expenditure.

Such assumptions and expectations help to explain why National
Liberal and Progressive deputies voted for the North German
Confederation, in spite of the predominance of the Hohenzollern
monarchy within it – made worse by Berlin's annexation of
Hanover, Schleswig-Holstein, Kurhessen and Frankfurt in 1866 –
and despite widespread fears of an emerging 'greater Prussia'.
Many, like Bennigsen, believed that the *Norddeutscher Bund* would be
a staging-post on the way to a fully-fledged German nation-state.
Obviously, there were many opponents and victims – frequently
marginalised as '*Reichsfeinde*' – of the new regime, which carried out,
on repeated occasions, acts of repression and which countenanced
many forms of injustice. The structure of the new order, though,
was broadly liberal, as critics of a German *Sonderweg* have pointed
out.[76] It came into being as a consequence of the complex negotiations and arguments which had taken place within the public
sphere and between parties and governments in the post-revolutionary period. Notwithstanding the justified criticisms of its detractors, the *Kaiserreich* could be seen as the product, not of an invidious
compromise, but of a necessary relationship between nationalism
and the state. The fact that the political unification of Germany
occurred comparatively quickly, without open resistance, after 1871
was the result, amongst other things, of support for a national
system of government outlined in 1848–49, and refined and modified in the years before 1866.

Notes

Introduction

1. L. A. von Rochau, *Grundsätze der Realpolitik* (Frankfurt a. M., 1972), 68.
2. H. Baumgarten, *Der deutsche Liberalismus: Eine Selbstkritik* (Frankfurt a. M., 1974), 52.
3. Ibid., 53.
4. Ibid.
5. H. Lutz, *Zwischen Habsburg und Preussen* (Berlin, 1985); H. Rumpler (ed.), *Österreich und die deutsche Frage im 19. und 20. Jahrhundert* (Munich, 1982).
6. H. Lutz, *Österreich-Ungarn und die Gründung des Deutschen Reiches* (Frankfurt, 1979); H. Lutz, 'Vom Königgrätz zum Zweibund', *Historische Zeitschrift*, 217 (1973), 347–80; H. Lutz, 'Aussenpolitische Tendenzen der Habsburgermonarchie von 1866 bis 1870', in E. Kolb (ed.), *Europa vor dem Krieg von 1870* (Munich, 1987), 1–16.
7. A. Neemann, *Landtag und Politik in der Reaktionszeit. Sachsen 1849/50–1866* (Düsseldorf, 2000); M. Hanisch, *Für Fürst und Vaterland. Legitimitätsstiftung in Bayern zwischen Revolution 1848 und deutscher Einheit* (Munich, 1991); D. Langewiesche, *Liberalismus und Demokratie in Württemberg von der Revolution bis zur Reichsgründung* (Düsseldorf, 1974); L. Gall, *Liberalismus als regierende Partei: Das Grossherzogtum Baden zwischen Restauration und Reichsgründung* (Wiesbaden, 1968); M. John, 'Liberalism and Society in Germany, 1850–1880: The Case of Hanover', *English Historical Review*, 102 (1987), 579–98; M. John, 'National and Regional Identities and the Dilemmas of Reform in Britain's "Other Province": Hanover, c. 1800–c. 1850', in L. Brockliss and D. Eastwood (eds), *A Union of Multiple Identities* (Manchester, 1997), 179–92; M. John, 'Associational Life and the Development of Liberalism in Hanover, 1848–1866', in K. Jarausch and L. E. Jones (eds), *In Search of a Liberal Germany* (New York, 1990), 161–85.

8. J. Müller, *Deutscher Bund und deutsche Nation 1848–1866* (Göttingen, 2005); J. Flöter, *Beust und die Reform des Deutschen Bundes 1850–1866* (Cologne, 2001); A. Doering-Manteuffel, *Die deutsche Frage und das europäische Staatensystem 1815–1871*, 2nd edn (Munich, 2001); J. Angelow, *Von Wien nach Königgrätz* (Munich, 1996); J. Angelow, *Der Deutsche Bund* (Darmstadt, 2003).
9. Michael B. Gross, *The War against Catholicism* (Ann Arbor, 2004) shows how Catholic opposition to liberalism and the perceived Protestantism of Prussia could be combined.
10. D. E. Barclay, *Frederick William IV and the Prussian Monarchy, 1840–1861* (Oxford, 1995); H.-C. Kraus, *Ernst Ludwig von Gerlach*, 2 vols (Göttingen, 1994); W. Füssl, *Professor in der Politik: Friedrich Julius Stahl 1802–1861* (Göttingen, 1998).
11. D. Blackbourn and G. Eley, *The Peculiarities of German History* (Oxford, 1984); H. Grebing, *Der 'deutsche Sonderweg' in Europa 1806–1946. Eine Kritik* (Stuttgart, 1986).
12. C. Jansen, *Einheit, Macht und Freiheit. Die Paulskirchenlinke und die deutsche Politik in der nachrevolutionären Epoche 1849–1867* (Düsseldorf, 2000); A. Biefang, *Politisches Bürgertum in Deutschland 1857–1868: Nationale Organisationen und Eliten* (Düsseldorf, 1994).
13. J. J. Breuilly and R. Speirs, 'The Concept of National Unification', in J. J. Breuilly and R. Speirs (eds), *Germany's Two Unifications* (Basingstoke, 2005), 1–25.
14. V. Valentin, *Geschichte der deutschen Revolution von 1848–49* (Berlin, 1930), vol. 2, 399, 428, 445–6, 492–8.
15. *Historisch-politische Blätter*, 1858, vol. 41, 244.
16. J. Echternkamp, *Der Aufstieg des deutschen Nationalismus 1770–1840* (Frankfurt a. M., 1998), 440–79. On 'opposition', see L. Gall, 'Das Problem der parlamentarischen Opposition im deutschen Frühliberalismus', in K. Kluxen (ed.), *Politische Ideologien und nationalstaatliche Ordnung* (Munich, 1968), 153–70.
17. E. J. Hobsbawm, *Nations and Nationalism since 1780*, 2nd edn (Cambridge, 1994), 14–45; O. Dann, 'Der revolutionäre Weg zum Nationalstaat in Deutschland', in G. Krebs und G. Schneilin (eds), *La naissance du Reich* (Paris, 1995).
18. There are now excellent works on party doctrines, for instance Jörn Leonhard's *Liberalismus* (Munich, 2001).
19. W. Siemann, 'Die Entstehung der Parteien in Deutschland 1848–1870', in A. Schildt and B. Vogel (eds), *Auf dem Wege zur Parteiendemokratie 1848–1989* (Hamburg, 2002), 9–18; D. Langewiesche, 'Die Anfänge der deutschen Parteien', *Geschichte und Gesellschaft*, 4 (1978), 324–61; W. Schieder (ed.), *Liberalismus in der Gesellschaft des deutschen Vormärz* (Göttingen, 1983); G. A. Ritter, *Die deutschen Parteien 1830–1918* (Göttingen, 1985); G. A. Ritter (ed.) *Deutschen Parteien vor 1918* (Cologne, 1983); T. Schieder, 'Die geschichtlichen Grundlagen und Epochen des deutschen Parteiwesens', in T. Schieder, *Staat und Gesellschaft im Wandel unserer Zeit* (Munich, 1970), 133–71; Thomas Nipperdey, *Die Organisation der deutschen Parteien vor 1918* (Düsseldorf, 1961); Thomas Nipperdey,

'Verein als soziale Struktur', in Thomas Nipperdey, *Gesellschaft, Kultur, Theorie* (Göttingen, 1976), 174–205; O. Dann (ed.), *Vereinswesen und bürgerliche Gesellschaft in Deutschland* (Munich, 1984); C. Lipp, 'Verein als politisches Handlungsmuster', in E. François, *Sociabilité et société bourgeoise en France, Allemagne et en Suisse 1750–1850* (Paris, 1986), 275–96.

20. G. Freytag, *Erinnerungen aus meinem Leben* (1886), in *Gesammelte Werke* (Leipzig, n.d.), 576.

21. W. Hardtwig, 'Strukturmerkmale und Entwicklungstendenzen des Vereinswesens in Deutschland 1789–1848', in Dann (ed.), *Vereinswesen*, 11–50.

22. Langewiesche, 'Anfänge', 325; P. Nolte, 'Gemeindeliberalismus', *Historische Zeitschrift*, 252 (1991), 57–93; P. Nolte, *Gemeindebürgertum und Liberalismus in Baden 1800–1850* (Göttingen, 1997); H. Obenaus, *Anfänge des Parlamentarismus in Preussen bis 1848* (Düsseldorf, 1984).

23. *Der Beobachter*, 21 Aug. and 5 Dec. 1847, in Langewiesche, 'Anfänge', 328–9.

24. Nipperdey, 'Verein als soziale Struktur', 174–205

25. *Deutsche Monatschrift*, 1851, vol. 2, 321 and 348–9.

26. W. Boldt, *Die württembergischen Volksvereine von 1848 bis 1852* (Stuttgart, 1970); W. Boldt, *Die Anfänge des deutschen Parteiwesens* (Paderborn, 1971), 44–53.

27. 'Parteien', *Brockhaus Conversationslexikon* (1846), in Boldt, *Anfänge*, 45.

28. *Darmstädter Journal*, 16 Aug. 1849, in Langewiesche, 'Anfänge', 350; W. Schwentker, *Konservative Vereine und Revolution in Preussen 1848/49* (Düsseldorf, 1988).

29. Liebnecht in 1879, in Langewiesche, 'Anfänge', 324.

30. U. Backes, *Liberalismus und Demokratie* (Düsseldorf, 2001). On the 1850s and 1860s, see Chapter 7.

31. See Chapters 4 and 5. On democrats' understanding of the revolution, see Jansen, *Einheit, Macht und Freiheit*, 149–85; C. Jansen, 'Ludwig Simon, Arnold Ruge und Friedrich Wilhelm IV.', in C. Jansen and T. Mergel (eds), *Die Revolution von 1848/49* (Göttingen, 1998), 247–67.

32. K. Tenfelde, 'Die Entfaltung des Vereinswesens während der industriellen Revolution in Deutschland 1850–1873', in Dann (ed.), *Vereinswesen*, 55–114.

33. R. P. Formisano, 'The Concept of Political Culture', *Journal of Interdisciplinary History*, 31 (2001), 393–426; more specifically, G. Eley, 'State Formation, Nationalism and Political Culture: Some Thoughts on the Unification of Germany', in G. Eley, *From Unification to Nazism* (London, 1986), 61–84; M. R. Lepsius, 'Parteiensystem und Sozialstruktur', in Ritter (ed.), *Deutsche Parteien vor 1918*, 56–80.

34. A. Green, 'Intervening in the Public Sphere: German Governments and the Press', *Historical Journal*, 44 (2001), 156–7.

35. The most influential work is, of course, Jürgen Habermas's, *Strukturwandel der Öffentlichkeit* (Frankfurt a. M., 1964).

36. H. Mah, 'Fantasies of the Public Sphere: Rethinking the Habermas of Historians', *Journal of Modern History*, 72 (2000), 153–82; D. Goodman, 'Public Sphere and Private Life', *History and Theory*, 31 (1992), 1–20; M. R. Somers, 'Narrating and Naturalizing Civil Society and Citizenship Theory' and 'What's Political or Cultural about Political Culture and the Public Sphere', *Sociological Theory*, 13 (1995), 229–74 and 113–44; P. U. Hohendahl and M. Silberman, 'Public Sphere and Culture', *New German Critique*, 16 (1979), 89–118; J. L. Brooke, 'Reason and Passion in the Public Sphere', *Journal of Interdisciplinary History*, 29 (1998), 43–67; A. Clark, 'Contested Space', *Journal of British Studies*, 35 (1996), 269–76. A more favourable account is given in G. Eley, 'Nations, Publics, and Political Cultures', in C. Calhoun (ed.), *Habermas and the Public Sphere* (Cambridge, MA, 1992), 289–339; R. Chartier, 'The Public Sphere and Public Opinion', in R. Chartier, *The Cultural Origins of the French Revolution* (Durham, NC, 1991), 20–37; D. Bell, 'The "Public Sphere", the State and the World of the Law in Eighteenth-Century France', *French Historical Studies*, 17 (1992), 912–33.
37. L. E. Lee, *The Politics of Harmony* (Newark, DE, 1980).
38. In Kraus, *Gerlach*, 804.
39. J. M. Brophy, *Popular Culture and the Public Sphere in the Rhineland, 1800–1850* (Cambridge, 2007); J. M. Brophy, 'Carnival and Citizenship', *Journal of Social History*, 30 (1997), 873–904; J. M. Brophy, 'The Politicization of Traditional Festivals in Germany, 1815–1848', in K. Friedrich (ed.), *Festival Culture in Germany and Europe from the Sixteenth to the Twentieth Century* (Lampeter, 2000), 73–106; J. Sperber, *Rhineland Radicals* (Princeton, NJ, 1991).
40. H. von Treitschke, 'Bundesstaat und Staatenbund', in H. von Treitschke, *Historische und politische Aufsätze* (Leipzig, 1865), 465. On national festivals, see J. Sperber, 'Festivals of National Unity in the German Revolution of 1848–49', *Past and Present*, 136 (1992), 114–38; P. Nolte and M. Hettling (eds), *Bürgerliche Feste* (Göttingen, 1993); D. Düding et al. (eds), *Öffentliche Festkultur* (Reinbek, 1988).
41. Green, 'German Governments and the Press, 159. There was a peak in 1850 of 1,102, which stood out from the general trend of slower proliferation of titles.
42. Koch-Gontard to Mittermaier, 22 Mar. 1848, in U. von Hirschhausen, *Liberalismus und Nation* (Düsseldorf, 1998), 315.
43. In Green, 'German Governments and the Press', 165.
44. R. Koselleck, '"Neuzeit"', in R. Kosellek, *Vergangene Zukunft* (Frankfurt, 1979), 300–48.
45. Hirschhausen, *Liberalismus und Nation*, 302.
46. Green, 'German Governments and the Press', 172–3, cites Alfred Hildebrandt's figures from 1862: 54 per cent of Hanoverian papers were controlled by the government, and a further 26 per cent were occasionally influenced by it. On other German states, see Chapter 6.
47. Although it is true that small local papers often took their lead from official publications, it is also the case that the urban centres dictated

the course of political events and it is likely that sections of small-town elites read the liberal press; see, for instance, K. Wappler, *Regierung und Presse in Preussen* (Leipzig, 1935), 60–1, on the dominance of Berlin newspapers in Brandenburg, Posen and surrounding areas.

48. Green, 'German Governments and the Press', 166.
49. J. F. M. O. Meding, *Memoiren zur Zeitgeschichte* (Leipzig, 1881–84), vol. 1, 66–7.
50. Hirschhausen, *Liberalismus und Nation*, 292.
51. This is to temper James Brophy's argument in 'The Common Reader in the Rhineland', *Past and Present*, 185 (2004), 119–58. See also R. Schenda, *Volk ohne Buch*. (Munich, 1977); O. Dann, *Lesegesellschaften und europäische Emanzipation* (Munich, 1981); G. Jäger and J. Schönert (eds), *Die Leihbibliothek als Institution des literarischen Lebens im 18. und 19. Jahrhundert* (Hamburg, 1980); M. Knoche, *Volksliteratur und Volksschriftenvereine im Vormärz* (Frankfurt a. M., 1986); R. Engelsing, 'Zur politischen Bildung der deutschen Unterschichten 1789–1863', in R. Engelsing, *Zur Sozialgeschichte deutscher Mittel- und Unterschichten*, 2nd edn (Göttingen, 1978); R. Pröve and N. Winnige (eds), *Wissen ist Macht* (Berlin, 2001).
52. F. J. Stahl, *Die gegenwärtigen Parteien in Staat und Kirche* (Berlin, 1863), 71.
53. Ibid., 89–90.
54. J. Sperber, *Popular Catholicism in Nineteenth-Century Germany* (Princeton, NJ, 1984), 155, 158.
55. G. Grünthal, *Parlamentarismus in Preussen 1848/49–1857/58* (Düsseldorf, 1982), 415–17, gives the low estimate that liberals won only 12 per cent of seats in Prussia in 1855.
56. O. Elben, *Lebenserinnerungen 1823–1899* (Stuttgart, 1931), 25–7.
57. On distinctions between radicalism and liberalism, see Leonhard, *Liberalismus*, 366–87, 463–7; Backes, *Liberalismus und Demokratie*, especially 55–110.
58. J. J. Breuilly, *Labour and Liberalism in Nineteenth-Century Europe* (Manchester, 1992), 228–72.
59. Ibid., 257; W. E. Ketteler, 'Der moderne Liberalismus' (1862), in W. E. Ketteler, *Werke* (Mainz, 1977), vol. 1, 280; M. B. Gross, *The War against Catholicism*, 74–127; Sperber, *Catholicism*, 99–155; T. Mergel, 'Ultramontanism, Liberalism, Moderation', *Central European History*, 29 (1996), 151–74; T. Mergel, *Zwischen Klasse und Konfession. Katholisches Bürgertum im Rheinland 1794–1914* (Göttingen, 1994) contra W. Altgeld, *Katholizismus, Protestantismus, Judentum* (Mainz, 1992) and W. Altgeld, 'German Catholics', in R. Liedtke and S. Wendehorst (eds), *The Emancipation of Catholics, Jews and Protestants* (Manchester, 1999), 100–21.
60. R. Schöttle, *Politische Theorien des süddeutschen Liberalismus im Vormärz* (Baden-Baden, 1994), 331–2; Breuilly, *Labour and Liberalism*, 249–52. See Chapter 8 below.
61. Lothar Gall, 'Liberalismus und "bürgerliche Gesellschaft"', *Historische Zeitschrift*, 220 (1975), 324–56. Also, R. Koch,

'Liberalismus und soziale Frage im 19. Jahrhundert', in K. Holl et al. (eds), *Sozialer Liberalismus* (Göttingen, 1986); R. Aldenhoff, *Schulze-Delitzsch* (Bonn, 1984); C. Eisenberg, 'Arbeiter, Bürger und der "bürgerliche Verein" 1820–1870', in J. Kocka (ed.), *Bürgertum im 19. Jahrhundert* (Munich, 1988), vol. 2; T. Offermann, *Arbeiterbewegung und liberales Bürgertum in Deutschland 1850–1963* (Bonn, 1979).

62. Backes, *Liberalismus und Demokratie*, 111–374.

63. W. Siemann, 'Parteibildung 1848/49 als "Kampf ums Recht"', in W. Siemann, *1848/49 in Deutschland und Europa* (Paderborn, 2007), 23–55; G. Birtsch, 'Gemässigter Liberalismus und Grundrechte', in W. Schieder (ed.), *Liberalismus in der Gesellschaft des deutschen Vormärz* (Göttingen, 1983), 22–38; W. Boldt, 'Konstitutionelle Monarchie oder parlamentarische Demokratie', *Historische Zeitschrift*, 216 (1973), 553–622 contra M. Botzenhart, *Deutscher Parlamentarismus in der Revolutionszeit 1848–1850* (Düsseldorf, 1977).

64. H. von Treitschke, 'Bundesstaat und Staatenbund', 474.

65. Haym to Hansemann, 17 June 1848, in H. Rosenberg (ed.), *Ausgewählter Briefwechsel Rudolf Hayms* (Berlin, 1930), 45.

66. G. Beseler, *Erlebtes und Erstrebtes 1809–1859* (Berlin, 1884), 58–9.

67. Ibid., 61.

68. Ibid., 57, 60.

69. K. Biedermann, *Mein Leben und ein Stück Zeitgeschichte* (Breslau, 1886), 307–8.

70. Ibid., 321.

71. Rosenberg (ed.), *Briefwechsel*, 37.

72. Ibid., 38.

73. Haym to Hansemann, 6 June 1848, ibid., 43.

74. Haym to Hansemann, 29 May 1848, ibid., 40.

75. Ibid.

76. Haym to his parents, 12 Nov. 1848, ibid., 60.

77. Haym, 18 Mar. 1848, ibid., 35–6.

78. See, for instance, F. D. Bassermann, *Denkwürdigkeiten 1811–1855* (Frankfurt a. M., 1926), 7–122; F. Gilbert (ed.), *Johann Gustav Droysen* (Munich 1933), 131–45.

79. Revolutionary nationalism, of course, is usually associated with France, not Germany: O. Dann and J. Dinwiddy (eds), *Nationalism in the Age of the French Revolution* (London, 1988), 1–36; A. D. Smith, *Nationalism and Modernism* (London, 1998), 18–24, 70–96; M. Hroch, 'From National Movement to the Fully-Formed Nation', in G. Eley and R. G. Suny (eds), *Becoming National* (Oxford, 1996), 60–77.

80. R. von Mohl, *Staatsrecht, Völkerrecht und Politik* (Tübingen, 1860), vol. 2, 333–44.

81. Ibid., 335.

82. Ibid.

83. Ibid., 339.

84. Ibid., 339–40.

85. J. Fröbel, *Theorie der Politik* (Vienna, 1864), vol. 2, 92.

86. Ibid., 93.

87. Ibid., 94.

88. Ibid., 92.
89. J. C. Bluntschli, 'Die nationale Statenbildung und der moderne deutsche Stat', in J. C. Bluntschli, *Gesammelte kleine Schriften* (Nördlingen, 1881), vol. 2, 74.
90. Ibid.
91. Ibid.
92. H. Baumgarten, 'Wie wir wieder ein Volk geworden sind' (2nd edn, 1870), in H. Baumgarten, *Historische und politische Aufsätze und Reden* (Strasbourg, 1894), 309–10.
93. Ibid., 310.
94. M. Hewitson, 'Conclusion', in T. Baycroft and M. Hewitson (eds), *What is a Nation?* (Oxford, 2006), 312–55; J. Breuilly, *Nationalism and the State*, 2nd edn (Manchester, 1993), 1–72, 96–122, 366–424; J. Breuilly (ed.), *The State of Germany* (London, 1992), 1–28; U. von Hirschhausen and J. Leonhard (eds), *Nationalismen in Europa* (Göttingen, 2001), 11–45; J. Snyder, *From Voting to Violence* (New York, 2000), 15–128; L. Scales and O. Zimmer (eds), *Power and the Nation in European History* (Cambridge, 2005), 1–29; J. Echternkamp and S. O. Müller (eds), *Die Politik der Nation* (Munich, 2002), 1–24.
95. B. Anderson, *Imagined Communities*, 2nd edn (London, 1991); E. Gellner, *Nations and Nationalism* (Oxford, 1983); E. J. Hobsbawm, *Nations and Nationalism since 1780*, 2nd edn (Cambridge, 1994); E. J. Hobsbawm and T. Ranger (eds), *The Invention of Tradition* (Cambridge, 1983). More specifically, J. Brophy, *Popular Culture and the Public Sphere*; J. Brophy, 'The Public Sphere', in J. Sperber (ed.), *Germany, 1800–1870* (Oxford, 2004), 185–208; Green, 'German Governments and the Press', 155–75; U. von Hirschhausen, *Liberalismus und Nation*, 285–318; H. Müller, *Liberale Presse im badischen Vormärz* (Heidelberg, 1986); H. Tauschwitz, *Presse und Revolution 1848/49 in Baden* (Heidelberg, 1981); N. Deuchert, *Vom Hambacher Fest zur badischen Revolution* (Stuttgart, 1983); J. Fröhlich, *Die Berliner Volkszeitung 1853 bis 1867* (Frankfurt a. M., 1990), 58–72.
96. O. Zimmer, 'Boundary Mechanisms and Symbolic Resources', *Nations and Nationalism*, 9 (2003), 173–93; A. D. Smith, *The Nation in History* (Oxford, 2000); A. D. Smith, *Nationalism* (London, 2001); A. D. Smith, *Chosen Peoples* (Oxford, 2003); A. D. Smith, *The Cultural Foundations of Nations* (Oxford, 2008); A. D. Smith, *The Ethnic Origins of Nations?* (Oxford, 2009); W. Connor, *Ethnonationalism* (Princeton, NJ, 1993); G. Cubitt (ed.), *Imagining Nations* (Manchester, 1998); M. Guibernau and J. Hutchinson, *History and National Destiny* (Oxford, 2004).
97. The period is missing in the English-language literature, in which most studies concentrate on Bismarck or on localities. The German-language literature has long been much richer. There is no overarching work in German on nationalism in the 1850s and early 1860s.
98. On the supposed transition from liberal to conservative nationalism, see O. Dann, *Nation und Nationalismus in Deutschland 1770–1990*, 3rd rev. edn (Munich, 1996), 85–218; H.-U. Wehler, *Nationalismus* (Munich, 2001), 62–89; H.-U. Wehler, 'Der deutsche Nationalismus

bis 1871', in H.-U. Wehler (ed.), *Scheidewege der deutschen Geschichte* (Munich, 1995), 116–30; H. Schulze, *The Course of German Nationalism* (Cambridge, 1991), 40–101; M. Hughes, *Nationalism and Society: Germany, 1800–1945* (London, 1988), 55–129; J. J. Sheehan, 'Nation und Staat. Deutschland als "imaginierte Gemeinschaft"', in M. Hettling and P. Nolte (eds), *Nation und Gesellschaft in Deutschland* (Munich, 1996), 33–45; B. Giesen, *Die Intellektuellen und die Nation* (Frankfurt, 1993), 163–232. On cultural and ethnic nationalism, H. Kohn, *The Idea of Nationalism* (New York, 1944); T. Schieder, 'Typologie und Erscheinungsformen des Nationalstaats in Europa', in T. Schieder, *Nationalismus und Nationalstaat* (Göttingen, 1991), 65–86; H. James, *A German Identity, 1770–1990* (London, 1989), 34–110; G. Mosse, *The Nationalisation of the Masses* (New York, 1975); L. Greenfeld, *Nationalism* (Cambridge, MA, 1992), 275–396. Other works are more guarded in emphasising the specificity of German cultural nationalism, although this is often implicit: D. Langewiesche, *Nation, Nationalismus, Nationalstaat in Deutschland und Europa* (Munich, 2000), 82–171; D. Düding, *Organisierter gesellschaftlicher Nationalismus in Deutschland 1808–1847* (Munich, 1984); D. Düding et al. (eds), *Öffentliche Festkultur* (Reinbek, 1988); M. Hettling and P. Nolte (eds), *Bürgerliche Feste* (Göttingen, 1993), 7–156; M. Krüger, *Körperkultur und Nationsbildung* (Schorndorf, 1996); S. Goltermann, *Körper der Nation* (Göttingen, 1998), 30–181; B. E. Dencker, 'Popular Gymnastics and the Military Spirit in Germany, 1848–1871', *Central European History*, 34 (2001), 503–30; D. Klenke, 'Nationalkriegerisches Gemeinschaftsideal als politische Religion', *Historische Zeitschrift*, 260 (1995), 395–448; U. Schlie, *Die Nation erinnert sich* (Munich, 2002), 21–38; K. von See, *Barbar, Germane, Arier* (Heidelberg, 1994), 83–160; M. Oergel, 'The Redeeming Teuton', in G. Cubitt (ed.), *Imagining Nations* (Manchester, 1998); M. Oergel, *The Return of King Arthur and the Nibelungen* (Berlin, 1998). On unification from 'above', see D. Langewiesche, '"Revolution von oben"?', in D. Langewiesche (ed.), *Revolution und Krieg* (Paderborn, 1989), 117–33.

Chapter 1

1. *National-Zeitung*, 19 Apr. 1849; on the failure of the revolution, see for instance ibid., 27 Mar. 1849.
2. Ibid., 19 April 1849. *Grenzboten*, 1849, vol. 8, 222, 455; *Kölnische Zeitung*, 13 Apr. and 19 May 1848.
3. *National-Zeitung*, 1 Apr. 1848.
4. Ibid.
5. Ibid., 19 Apr. 1849.
6. *Kölnische Zeitung*, 5 May 1848.
7. In W. J. Mommsen, *1848* (Frankfurt, 1998), 114–15.
8. In W. Siemann, *The German Revolution of 1848–49* (London, 1998),

75.
9. V. Valentin, *Geschichte der deutschen Revolution von 1848–49* (Berlin, 1930), vol. 1, 468. See Map 1.
10. In J. Sperber, *The European Revolutions, 1848–1851* (Cambridge, 1994), 143.
11. Jonathan Sperber's *Rhineland Radicals* (Princeton, NJ, 1991) gives a good sense of overlapping local traditions.
12. Leonhard, *Liberalismus*, 462. Also, G. Hübinger, *Georg Gottfried Gervinus* (Göttingen, 1984), 139.
13. Felix Gilbert (ed.), *Johann Gustav Droysen* (Munich, 1933), 182.
14. Ibid., 144.
15. Ibid., 182.
16. Ibid.
17. Ibid.
18. Leonhard, *Liberalismus*, 431–5.
19. Gilbert (ed.), *Droysen*, 145.
20. H. Laube, *Das erste deutsche Parlament* (Leipzig, 1849), vol. 1, 118.
21. On Julius Fröbel, see R. Koch, *Demokratie und Staat bei Julius Fröbel, 1805–1893* (Wiesbaden, 1978), 171–2; I. Fellrath and R. Muhs, in S. Freitag (ed.), *Die 48er*, 33–44, 81–98; J. H. Schoeps, 'Im Kampf um die deutsche Republik: Karl Blind', in J. H. Schoeps and I. Geiss (eds), *Revolution und Demokratie in Geschichte und Literatur* (Duisburg, 1979), 259–76. On the patriotic majority of workers' representatives, see T. Welskopp, *Das Banner der Brüderlichkeit* (Bonn, 2000), 523–65; W. Schmidt, 'Arbeiterverbrüderung, soziale Emanzipation und nationale Identität', *Beiträge zur Geschichte der Arbeiterbewegung*, 36 (1994), 20–36.
22. F. Thorwart (ed.), *Hermann Schulze-Delitzsch's Schriften und Reden* (Berlin, 1910), vol. 3, 18.
23. J. Jacoby, *Gesammelte Schriften und Reden* (Hamburg, 1872), vol. 2, 11.
24. Ibid.
25. L. Bamberger, *Erinnerungen* (Berlin, 1899), 38.
26. A. Ruge, *Der Patriotismus* (Frankfurt a. M., 1968), 32.
27. In S. Walter, *Demokratisches Denken zwischen Hegel und Marx. Die politische Philosophie Arnold Ruges* (Düsseldorf, 1995), 361.
28. R. Blum (ed.), *Volksthümliches Handbuch der Staatswissenschaften und Politik* (1848–52), 2 vols, in P. Wende, *Radikalismus im Vormärz. Untersuchungen zur politischen Theorie der frühen deutschen Demokratie* (Wiesbaden, 1975), 195.
29. In Jörg Echternkamp, *Der Aufstieg des deutschen Nationalismus 1770–1840* (Frankfurt, 1998), 452.
30. E. Newman, *Restoration Radical: Robert Blum* (Boston, 1974), 49.
31. Bassermann, *Denkwürdigkeiten*, 5.
32. Leonhard, *Liberalismus*, 442–53, on the opposition in some accounts between 'liberalism' and 'radicalism'.
33. R. von Mohl, *Die Geschichte und Literatur der Staatswissenschaften* (Erlangen, 1855), vol. 1, 434.
34. Ibid., vol. 2, 4.
35. Ibid.

36. Echternkamp, *Aufstieg*, 444–52.
37. A. Heuss, *Theodor Mommsen und das 19. Jahrhundert* (Kiel, 1956), 133.
38. M. Botzenhart, *Deutscher Parlamentarismus in der Revolutionszeit 1848–1850* (Düsseldorf, 1977), 156–7.
39. R. Hachtmann, *Epochenschwelle zur Moderne. Einführung in die Revolution von 1848/49* (Tübingen, 2002), 208.
40. W. Siemann, *Die Frankfurter Nationalversammlung 1848/49* (Frankfurt, 1976), 27.
41. Hachtmann, *Epochenschwelle*, 93, 96.
42. Siemann, *German Revolution*, 96.
43. Karl Biedermann, *Mein Leben und ein Stück Zeitgeschichte* (Breslau, 1886), 324.
44. Bassermann, *Denkwürdigkeiten*, 7.
45. *Kölnische Zeitung*, 3 Apr. 1848.
46. Ibid.
47. Elben, *Lebenserinnerungen*, 117. See also the *Dortmunder Anzeiger*, 23 Mar. 1848, in W. Schulte, *Volk und Staat. Westfalen im Vormärz und in der Revolution 1848/49* (Münster, 1954), 251: 'The citizens of Dortmund must now demand that their *Anzeiger* no longer merely provides them with advice on the subject of butter or herrings, but also with advice on how they might act in the best interests of their town and fatherland.'
48. Elben, *Lebenserinnerungen*, 116.
49. Ibid.
50. See, for instance, the *Neue Preussische Zeitung*, 17 and 26 Oct. 1848.
51. In P. Wentzke and W. Klötzer (eds), *Deutscher Liberalismus im Vormärz. Heinrich von Gagern* (Göttingen, 1959), 405.
52. In Kraus, *Gerlach*, vol. 1, 408–9.
53. Hachtmann, *Epochenschwelle*, 210–16.
54. Biedermann, *Mein Leben*, 359–71.
55. F. Wigard (ed.), *Stenographischer Bericht*, 4 May 1849, vol. 8, 6425.
56. S. Berger, *Inventing the Nation: Germany* (London, 2004), 56.
57. See B. Giesen, *Die Intellektuellen und die Nation* (Frankfurt a. M., 1993), 163–99, and G. A. Craig, *The Politics of the Unpolitical* (Oxford, 1995), 125–56, on the ways in which such political engagement had come to affect writers, who were later to become the main critics of such engagement.
58. *National-Zeitung*, 1 Jan. 1849.
59. Ibid.
60. *Neue Preussische Zeitung*, 30 Mar. 1849.
61. Ibid.
62. F. J. Stahl, in Füssl, *Professor in der Politik*, 201.
63. In ibid., 200–1.
64. *Kölnische Zeitung*, 5 May 1848.
65. *National-Zeitung*, 24 Mar. 1849.
66. F. J. Stahl, *Die deutsche Reichsverfassung* (Berlin, 1849), 18.
67. Ibid., 16.
68. In Füssl, *Professor in der Politik*, 183–4.
69. Marginalia on a letter from Senfft von Pilsach, 1 July 1848, in K.

Haenchen (ed.), *Revolutionsbriefe 1848* (Leipzig, 1930), 116–17.

70. Design of royal manifesto, c. 7 Nov. 1848, ibid., 228; marginalia, Dec. 1848, ibid., 260; E. R. Huber (ed.), *Dokumente zur deutschen Verfassungsgeschichte*, 3rd edn, 3 vols (Stuttgart, 1978), vol. 1, 401–2.

71. L. von Gerlach, *Denkwürdigkeiten aus dem Leben Leopold von Gerlachs, Generals der Infanterie und General-Adjutanten Koenig Friedrich Wilhelms IV* (Berlin, 1891), 151.

72. Friedrich Wilhelm IV to E. M. Arndt, Mar. 1849, in Haenchen (ed.), *Revolutionsbriefe*, 393.

73. The extent to which the constitution was accepted is disputed. Füssl, *Professor in der Politik*, 154–5, contends that those in the camarilla who were formally against the imposed constitution played down their opposition. Günther Grünthal, 'Das preussische Dreiklassenwahlrecht', *Historische Zeitschrift*, 226 (1978), 17–66; Günther Grünthal, 'Zwischen König, Kabinett und Kamarilla', *Jahrbuch für die Geschichte Mittel- und Ostdeutschlands*, 32 (1983), 119–74; Günther Grünthal, *Parlamentarismus in Preussen 1848–9–1857/58* (Düsseldorf, 1982), stresses the role of the conservative government in forcing acceptance.

74. See Chapter 2.

75. Ibid., 251.

76. F. J. Stahl, *Das Monarchische Princip* (Heidelberg, 1845), v.

77. F. J. Stahl, *Die Revolution und die constitutionelle Monarchie* (Berlin, 1848).

78. W. Corvinus (ed.), *Radowitz' ausgewählte Schriften* (Regensburg, 1911), vol. 2, 300, 311, 321. On Gerlach's full conversion, see Kraus, *Gerlach*, 261. Radowitz was said by Leopold von Gerlach to have advised the King to opt for the 'constitutional path'; E. Ritter, *Radowitz. Ein katholischer Staatsmann in Preussen* (Cologne, 1948), 137.

79. Wigard (ed.), *Stenographischer Bericht*, 13 Dec. 1848, vol. 6, 4083.

80. J. Jacoby, 'Deutschland und Preussen, 18 May 1848', in J. Jacoby, *Gesammelte Schriften und Reden* (Hamburg, 1872), vol. 2, 11.

81. In Koch, *Demokratie und Staat bei Julius Fröbel*, 109.

82. These and similar figures below come from Jansen, *Einheit, Macht und Freiheit*, 40–1.

83. Ritter, *Radowitz*, 205.

84. Biedermann, *Mein Leben*, 323. Susanne Böhr, *Die Verfassungsarbeit der preussischen Nationalversammlung 1848* (Frankfurt a. M., 1992), 112, notes that no Prussian deputies pushed for a republic, although some on the left did want a figurehead 'democratic monarch'.

85. Wigard (ed.), *Stenographischer Bericht*, 22 Mar. 1849, vol. 8, 5907.

86. Ibid., 27 Apr. 1849, vol. 8, 6313. Contrast his speech against the *Erbkaisertum* on 20 Mar. 1849, vol. 8, 5877–8.

87. Ibid., 20 Mar. 1849, vol. 8, 5883.

88. Gilbert (ed.), *Droysen*, 126.

89. Ibid., 145.

90. Bamberger, *Erinnerungen*, 39.

91. Ibid., 45.

92. In Koch, *Demokratie und Staat bei Julius Fröbel*, 123.

93. Ibid., 112, 171–2.
94. Newman, *Restoration Radical*, 132–5.
95. Ibid., 5905.
96. Wigard (ed.), *Stenographischer Bericht*, 27 Apr. 1849, vol. 8, 6329.
97. Ibid., 26 Apr. 1849, 6319.
98. Ibid.
99. Ibid., 6316.
100. Ibid., 6319–20.
101. *Neue Preussische Zeitung*, 31 Mar. 1849. See also ibid., 30 Mar. 1849.
102. Ibid., 16 Apr. 1849.
103. Ibid., 17 Apr. 1849. See also 22 Apr. 1849.
104. Ibid., 17 Apr. 1849.
105. See Chapter 2 on Gotha, Erfurt and Olmütz.
106. Wigard, *Stenographische Bericht*, vol. 1, 118. The final version of the Reich constitution only mentions language explicitly by referring to the rights of non-German speakers in their own specific spheres, implying that German would be used in all other spheres (Article 188). I am indebted to John Breuilly for making this point.
107. Ibid., vol.7, 5209.
108. Schmerling, 22 Mar. 1849, in Brian Vick, *Defining Germany* (Cambridge, MA), 169.
109. In ibid.
110. Ibid., 168.
111. Ibid.
112. In ibid., 129.
113. Wigard, *Stenographische Bericht*, vol. 7, 5208.
114. Ibid.
115. In Vick, *Defining Germany*, 129.
116. See W. Carr, *Schleswig-Holstein, 1815–1848* (Manchester, 1963), 285.
117. *Grenzboten*, 1849, vol. 8, 89.
118. Carr, *Schleswig-Holstein*, 279–90.
119. Varnhagen von Ense, *Kommentare zum Zeitgeschehen* (Leipzig, 1984), 163.
120. *Grenzboten*, 1848, 496. The article is dated 23 June.
121. Ibid., 1848, 217, 357.
122. Ibid., 356.
123. Ibid., 355.
124. For instance, *Kölnische Zeitung*, 12 Apr. 1848; *National-Zeitung*, 14 May 1848.
125. These figures are taken from Carr, *Schleswig-Holstein*, 70–1.
126. For example, *Kölnische Zeitung*, 12 Apr. 1848.
127. Wigard, *Stenographische Bericht*, 27 July 1848, vol. 2, 1214.
128. Ibid., 1138.
129. *Kölnische Zeitung*, 5 Apr. 1848.
130. Ibid.
131. Ibid.
132. See W. Ribhegge, *Das Parlament als Nation. Die Frankfurter Nationalversammlung, 1848–49* (Düsseldorf, 1998), 49.
133. This is not to suggest that there were no opponents of such policies or that there was consistency on the part of the different factions: as

John Breuilly points out in *Austria, Prussia and Germany, 1806–1871*
(London, 2002), democrats who supported the inclusion of
Schleswig on national grounds opposed the division of Posen, and
conservatives who backed the partition of Posen also sanctioned the
effective surrender of Schleswig via the truce of Malmö, following
the lead of the Prussian government in both cases. Nevertheless, the
majority of deputies at Frankfurt did back maximising national policies in Schleswig-Holstein, Posen, West and East Prussia.

134. *Constitution*, May 1848, in R. Okey, *The Habsburg Monarchy, c.
1765–1918* (Basingstoke, 2001), 145; Palacky, 11 April 1848, ibid.,
144.
135. The position of nationalities in confederal and non-confederal
Habsburg lands, the rights of national minorities, and the relationship of Austria with the rest of Germany and with the Provisional
Central Power were regularly conflated in the debates of both
Austrian and non-Austrian assemblies and public spheres.
136. Löhner, in R. A. Kann, *The Multinational Empire* (New York, 1977),
vol. 2, 12.
137. Welcker in Wigard (ed.), *Stenographischer Bericht*, 12 Mar. 1849, vol. 8,
5667.
138. Ibid.
139. Ibid.
140. Gagern, ibid., 20 Mar. 1849, vol. 8, 5880–1.
141. Ibid., 5880.
142. Mathy, ibid., 25 Apr. 1849, vol. 8, 6289. For Römer, see ibid., 21 Mar.
1849, 5893.
143. Simon, ibid., 20 Mar. 1849, vol. 8, 5875.
144. Ibid., 5874.
145. Ibid., 6312–13.
146. Reichensperger, ibid., 25 Apr. 1849, vol. 8, 6293.
147. Ibid., 6294.
148. Ibid.
149. *Neue Preussische Zeitung*, 26 Oct. 1848.
150. After criticising Austria in 1848, the *Neue Preussische Zeitung* came to
favour a Prussian–Austrian dualism and the restoration of the
German Confederation in some form from December 1848 onwards;
ibid., 8 Dec. 1848, 21 and 24 Jan., 16 Feb., 3 and 17 Mar., and 17 Apr.
1849. Such positions remained contested by conservatives, however.
151. For fuller details of such projects, which are now well known, see G.
Wollstein, *Das 'Grossdeutschland' der Paulskirche: Nationale Ziele in der
bürgerlichen Revolution 1848–49* (Düsseldorf, 1977), especially
266–335.
152. K. O. Conrady (ed.), *Das grosse deutsche Gedichtbuch* (Königstein im
Taunus, 1985), 392.
153. Moering, in Wollstein, *Grossdeutschland*, 268–9.
154. Reichensperger, in Wigard (ed.), *Stenographischer Bericht*, 24 Apr.
1849, vol. 8, 6293.
155. Ibid.
156. Biedermann, *Mein Leben*, 369.

157. E. M. Hucko (ed.), *The Democratic Tradition: Four German Constitutions* (Oxford, 1987) , 79.
158. M. Duncker, *Politischer Briefwechsel aus seinem Nachlass*, ed. J. Schultze (Stuttgart, 1923), 7.
159. Duncker to his wife, 9 Jan. 1849, ibid., 10.
160. Wollstein, *Grossdeutschland*, 304.
161. Ibid.
162. Ibid., 276, 298.
163. *Beobachter*, 9 July 1848, in Langewiesche, *Liberalismus und Demokratie*, 184.
164. Vischer to Strauss, 3 Apr. 1849, ibid., 190.
165. On 12 Dec. 1848, the Austrian Foreign Minister noted that 'Hanover, Bavaria, and Saxony could already be counted on', in T. Kletecka (ed.), *Die Protokolle des österreichischen Ministerrates, 1848–1867*, vol. 2, 13.
166. F. Oetker, *Lebenserinnerungen*, 3 vols (Stuttgart, 1877–85), vol. 3, 161.
167. Ibid.
168. Duncker, *Politischer Briefwechsel*, 7.
169. Ibid.
170. Oetker, *Lebenserinnerungen*, vol. 3, 162.
171. Welcker, in Wigard (ed.), *Stenographischer Bericht*, 12 Mar. 1849, vol. 8, 5667.
172. Ibid., 5666.
173. Ibid.
174. Ibid., 5667.
175. Ibid.
176. Gagern, ibid., 20 Mar. 1849, 5885.
177. Ibid.
178. Ibid.
179. Ibid.
180. Droysen, 25 Oct. 1848, in Gilbert (ed.), *Droysen*, 173. See also W. Hock, *Liberales Denken im Zeitalter der Paulskirche. Droysen und die Frankfurter Mitte* (Münster, 1957).
181. Gilbert (ed.), *Droysen*, 173.
182. Ibid., 174.
183. Droysen, 6 Jan. 1849, ibid., 190.
184. Ibid., 180.
185. Ibid., 187.

Chapter 2

1. W. Siemann, *Gesellschaft im Aufbruch* (Frankfurt, 1990), 25–6.
2. U. E. Koch, *Der Teufel in Berlin* (Cologne, 1991), 415.
3. *Constitutionelle Zeitung*, 10 Oct. 1850, in Gilbert (ed.), *Droysen*, 286.
4. 12 Dec. 1850, ibid., 291.
5. Ibid.
6. Ibid., 337.

7. Ibid., 336.
8. Ibid., 336–7.
9. Ibid., 292.
10. This is true of more traditional, preponderantly diplomatic histories of German unification as well as of the societal histories of the 'Bielefeld school'. For summaries of the literature, see J. J. Breuilly, *The Formation of the First German Nation-State 1800–1871* (London, 1996), 5–11; A. Doering-Manteuffel, *Die deutsche Frage und das europäische Staatensystem 1815–1871*, 2nd edn (Munich, 2001), 53–118.
11. Siemann, *Gesellschaft im Aufbruch*, 171–89, stresses 1859.
12. This is the gravamen of Heinrich Lutz's case in *Zwischen Habsburg und Preussen*. It has also been stated recently by John Breuilly in *Austria, Prussia and Germany*, 64–5, strengthening the claims advanced in *The Formation of the First German Nation-State*, 19–20, which placed more emphasis on the destabilising impact of the Crimean War.
13. A classic text in this literature remains F. Meinecke, *Radowitz und die deutsche Revolution* (Berlin, 1913).
14. As a result, most historians pay less attention to the 1850s than to the 1860s. Even those who do examine the 1850s, such as Wolfram Siemann, tend to stress that it was an era of 'reaction', closely related to rivalries between the German states. See W. Siemann, *Vom Staatenbund zum Nationalstaat. Deutschland 1806–1871* (Munich, 1995), 389–425.
15. Gerlach, *Denkwürdigkeiten*, vol. 1, 567.
16. Ibid., 565. See A. Schwarzenberg, *Prince Felix zu Schwarzenberg: Prime Minister of Austria, 1848–1852* (New York, 1946), 156–63, for more details on the meeting.
17. R. Kiszling, *Fürst Felix zu Schwarzenberg* (Graz, 1952), 155. On Kempen, see J. K. Mayr (ed.), *Das Tagebuch des Polizeiministers Kempen von 1848 bis 1859* (Vienna, 1931), 194.
18. On Schwarzenberg, see R. A. Austensen, 'The Making of Austria's Prussian Policy', *Historical Journal*, 27 (1984), 873.
19. In Schwarzenberg, *Felix zu Schwarzenberg*, 161.
20. This case has been made most forcefully by historians of the Habsburg monarchy. In addition to the works of Roy Austensen, who concentrates on the Dresden conferences rather than Olmütz, see K. W. Rock, 'Felix Schwarzenberg, Military Diplomat', *Austrian History Yearbook*, 11 (1975), 95.
21. Schwarzenberg to Prokesch, 19 Dec. 1850, in Schwarzenberg, *Felix zu Schwarzenberg*, 163.
22. Prokesch to Metternich, 1 Dec. 1850, in Austensen, 'The Making of Austria's Prussian Policy', 872.
23. Hübner to Metternich, 5 Dec. 1850, ibid., 873.
24. In Barclay, *Frederick William IV*, 210.
25. Gerlach, *Denkwürdigkeiten*, vol. 1, 568.
26. Ibid., 565.
27. O. von Manteuffel, *Unter Friedrich Wilhelm IV. Denkwürdigkeiten*

(Berlin, 1901), vol. 1, 348.
28. Gilbert (ed.), *Droysen*, 291.
29. Aegidi, 23 Jan. 1851, in Duncker, *Verfassungsgeschichte*, 48.
30. Duncker to his wife, 8 Jan. 1851, ibid., 45–6.
31. Gagern to Duncker, 10 Jan. 1851, ibid., 46.
2. On the 'German question', see W. D. Gruner, *Die deutsche Frage* (Munich, 1985); J. Becker and A. Hillgruber (eds), *Die Deutsche Frage im 19. und 20. Jahrhundert* (Munich, 1983); H. Rumpler (ed.), *Deutscher Bund und deutsche Frage 1815–1866* (Vienna, 1990).
33. Palmerston to Cowley, 22 Nov. 1850, in Mosse, *The European Powers and the German Question 1848–71* (New York, 1969), 38.
34. Ibid.
35. Palmerston to Russell, 26 Nov. 1850, ibid.
36. Palmerston to Cowley, 22 Nov. 1850, ibid.
37. Meyendorff to Nesselrode, 9/21 Apr. 1851, ibid., 45.
38. Russell to Palmerston, 18 Nov. 1850, in F. J. Müller, *Britain and the German Question* (Basingstoke, 2002), 153.
39. Palmerston to Westmorland, 13 July 1849, ibid., 117. On Palmerston's policy, see also G. Gillessen, *Lord Palmerston und die deutsche Einigung* (Hamburg, 1961).
40. Ibid., 129.
41. W. J. Orr, Jr, 'British Diplomacy and the German Problem, 1848–1850', *Albion*, 10 (1978), 228.
42. Morier to Russell, 26 Jan. 1861, in Müller, *Britain and the German Question*, 184.
43. Russell to Prince Albert, 24 Apr. 1850, ibid., 130.
44. Palmerston to Westmorland, 3 Dec. 1850, in Mosse, *The European Powers and the German Question*, 40–1.
45. Cowley to Palmerston, 21 May 1850, in Müller, *Britain and the German Question*, 138.
46. Palmerston to Drouyn de Lhuys, 22 July 1849, ibid., 120.
47. Palmerston to Russell, 26 Nov. 1850, ibid., 38.
48. The precariously reconstituted axis of Russia, Austria and Prussia was referred to disparagingly as the 'Holy Alliance' by British diplomats. See especially A. Doering-Manteuffel, *Vom Wiener Kongress zur Pariser Konferenz* (Göttingen, 1991).
49. For British diplomats' views of 'public opinion', see Müller, *Britain and the German Question*, 157–200.
50. In M. Behnen, *Das Preussische Wochenblatt 1851–1861* (Göttingen, 1971), 199.
51. *Preussisches Wochenblatt*, 1853, vol. 8, 1858, vol. 16, 1860, vol. 21, and 1861, vol. 10, ibid., 232–3.
52. *Preussisches Wochenblatt*, 1853, vol. 8, and 1861, vol. 10, 'Die italienische Einheit und die Interessen Frankreichs', ibid., 231. The quotation comes from 1860, vol. 21.
53. *Preussisches Wochenblatt*, 1853, vol. 51, and 1853 vol. 50, ibid., 199.
54. *Neue Preussische Zeitung*, 25 Aug. 1859.
55. *Grenzboten*, 1850, vol. 3, 425.
56. Ibid., 1859, vol. 1, 437 and 313.

57. Ibid., vol. 2, 315.
58. Ibid., 477.
59. *Historisch-politische Blätter*, 1863, vol. 51, 141.
60. Ibid., 150.
61. A. B. Spitzer, 'The Good Napoleon III', *French Historical Studies*, 2 (1962), 325.
62. Napier to Russell, 30 Dec. 1863, in Mosse, *The European Powers and the German Question*, 165.
63. Ibid., 85.
64. Ibid., 64, 59.
65. Palmerston to Russell, 7 Apr. 1863, ibid., 119.
66. Queen Victoria's journal, 21 June 1864, ibid., 205.
67. Ibid., 47.
68. Ibid., 53.
69. Ibid., 56.
70. Russell to Clarendon, 23 Apr. 1855, ibid., 62.
71. Esterházy to Buol, 6 July 1854, ibid., 58.
72. Seymour to Clarendon, 8 Sept. 1856, ibid., 70.
73. Ibid., 88.
74. Ibid.
75. Stanley to Buchanan, 28 July 1866, reporting a conversation with Brunnow, ibid., 244.
76. Talleyrand to Drouyn, 14 Aug. 1866, ibid., 248.
77. Napier to Russell, 11 May 1864, ibid., 195.
78. Alexander II marginalia, 1 Feb. 1864, ibid., 179.
79. Ibid., 95.
80. Ibid.
81. Ibid., 70.
82. Tsar's marginalia, 22 Aug./3 Sept. 1863, ibid., 133.
83. Napier to Russell, 30 Dec. 1863, ibid., 165.
84. Ibid.
85. Gorchakov to Olga Nicolaevna, 6 July 1861, ibid., 100.
86. Ibid., 52.
87. In P. W. Schroeder, *Austria, Great Britain, and the Crimean War* (Ithaca, NY, 1972), 395.
88. H. Rumpler (ed.), *Die Protokolle des österreichischen Ministerrates 1848–1867* (Vienna, 1970), vol. 3, 428.
89. Ibid.
90. Buol, 29 May 1854, ibid., 444.
91. Schroeder argues that these elements of the Concert, as opposed to a defunct Holy Alliance, continued to exist until their destruction during the Crimean War: P. W. Schroeder, 'The Nineteenth-Century International System', *World Politics*, 39 (1986), 1–26.
92. Buol, 22 Mar. 1854, in Rumpler (ed.), *Protokolle*, vol. 3, 429.
93. Friedrich Wilhelm IV, in R. Müller, *Die Partei Bethmann-Hollweg und die orientalische Krise 1853–1856* (Halle, 1926), 39.
94. In Barclay, *Frederick William IV*, 266.
95. L. Gall, *Bismarck* (London, 1986), vol. 1, 120.
96. In Kraus, *Gerlach*, vol. 2, 632.

97. Ibid., 633.
98. Ernst Ludwig Gerlach, 15 Oct. 1854, ibid., 636–7.
99. Usedom to Bunsen, 25 Dec. 1853, in Müller, *Die Partei Bethmann-Hollweg*, 45.
100. Clarendon to Malet, 22 Mar. 1855, in Müller, *Britain and the German Question*, 160.
101. *National-Zeitung*, 9 Oct. 1850, in N. Buschmann, *Einkreisung und Waffenbruderschaft* (Göttingen, 2003), 186.
102. *National-Zeitung*, 3 Jan. 1852, ibid., 209.
103. *National-Zeitung*, 3 Nov. 1850, ibid., 206.
104. Buschmann, *Einkreisung und Waffenbrudenschaft*, 206–40.
105. *Preussisches Wochenblatt*, 18 and 25 Feb. 1854, in Müller, *Die Partei Bethmann-Hollweg*, 76, 78.
106. *Kölnische Zeitung*, 2 Jan. 1854, ibid., 208.
107. See, for instance, *Grenzboten*, 1854, vol. 13, 111–16, and 1855, vol. 14, 34–8, which advocated a war against the Russian 'enemy' that might make a return to the national conditions of 1848 possible.
108. *Allgemeine Zeitung*, 16 Apr. 1854, ibid., 210.
109. Ibid., 7 Dec. 1854, ibid., 213.
110. *Historisch-politische Blätter*, 1858, vol. 2, 20. Droysen agreed, talking of a 'revolution of the European states' system' during the Crimean War: Gilbert (ed.), *Droysen*, 331.
111. Ibid.
112. A. Palmer, *Metternich* (London, 1972), 326.
113. This constitutional dilemma is examined in Chapter 4.
114. Schwarzenberg to Schmerling, 4 Feb. 1849, in S. Lippert, *Felix Fürst zu Schwarzenberg* (Stuttgart, 1998), 286–7.
115. Schwarzenberg, *Felix zu Schwarzenberg*, 129.
116. Bernstorff's summary, ibid., 324.
117. Schwarzenberg to Thun, 22 July 1850, ibid., 325.
118. Invitation, 12 Dec. 1850, ibid., 347.
119. Schwarzenberg to Trauttmannsdorff, 24 Jan. 1849, ibid., 286.
120. Schroeder, *Austria, Great Britain and the Crimean War*, 157–8.
121. Buol, 22 Mar. 1854, in W. Heindl (ed.), *Die Protokolle des österreichischen Ministerrates 1848–1867* (Vienna, 1970–2003), vol. 3, 431.
122. Buol to Schönburg, 5 Feb. 1859, in Müller, *Deutscher Bund und deutsche Nation*, 279; Austrian resolution, 2 May 1859, ibid., 286.
123. R. B. Elrod, 'Bernhard von Rechberg and the Metternichian', *Journal of Modern History*, 56 (1984), 433.
124. Memorandum on the Polish question, Mar. 1863, ibid., 447.
125. Rechberg to Schrenk, the Bavarian Foreign Minister, 3 Jan. 1862, ibid.
126. Rechberg to Richard Metternich, 18 Feb. 1862, ibid.
127. Austensen, 'Austria and the "Struggle"', *Journal of Modern History*, 52 (1980), 218.
128. Metternich to Kübeck, Elrod, 'Rechberg', 431.
129. L. Höbelt (ed.), *Österreichs Weg zur konstitutionellen Monarchie. Aus der Sicht des Staatsministers Anton von Schmerling* (Frankfurt, 1994), 231–2.
130. See E. E. Kraehe, 'Austria and the Problem of Reform in the German

Confederation, 1851–1863', *American Historical Review*, 56 (1951), 283–94.

131. Müller, *Deutscher Bund und deutsche Nation*, 349.
132. In Lutz, *Zwischen Habsburg und Preussen*, 445.
133. Schmerling memoirs, in Höbelt (ed.), *Österreichs Weg*, 239.
134. Ibid., 245.
135. See Map 3.

136. Ibid., 237.
137. Ibid., 232.
138. Ibid., 241.
139. Ibid., 238.
140. Lippert, *Schwarzenberg*, 279.
141. Ibid., 289, 309. See also T. Kletecka (ed.), *Protokolle* , vol. 1, 739.
142. Ibid., 316–17.
143. Schwarzenberg to Prokesch, 8 Mar. 1850, ibid., 318.
144. Schwarzenberg memorandum, 3 Oct. 1851, ibid., 391.
145. Buol to Appony, 10 Oct. 1855, in Müller, *Deutscher Bund und deutsche Nation*, 203.
146. The first quotation dates from Jan. 1865, the second from 28 Aug. 1861, in Elrod, 'Rechberg', 442–3.
147. Council of Ministers, 11 Feb. 1861, ibid., 438.
148. Hübner to Rechberg, 14 Nov. 1862, ibid., 455. For Buol, see Schroeder, 'Bruck versus Buol', *Journal of Modern History*, 55 (1968) and Schroeder, *Austria, Great Britain and the Crimean War*.
149. Buol, 25 Mar. 1854, in Heindl (ed.), *Protokolle*, vol. 3., 437.
150. Schwarzenberg to Schmerling, 9 Mar. 1849, Lippert, *Schwarzenberg*, 290.
151. Ibid.
152. Ibid., 323, 349.
153. 'Allgemeine Instructionen', 20 Dec. 1850, in Austensen, 'Struggle', 206.
154. An article by Bruck, sanctioned by Schwarzenberg, in the *Wiener Zeitung*, 26 Oct. 1849, Lippert, *Schwarzenberg*, 312.
155. Austensen, 'Struggle', 213.
156. Ibid., 221.
157. Rechberg, 23 Apr. 1862, in S. Malfèr (ed.), *Protokolle*, vol. 5, 408.
158. Ibid.
159. Rechberg, 11 Apr. 1862, ibid., 393.
160. For example, 25 Apr. 1863, ibid., 396.
161. Biegeleben, 22 July 1863, ibid., 196.
162. Rechberg, 23 Apr. 1862, ibid., 408.
163. Bernstorff, 24 Apr. 1865, ibid., 278.
164. Schwarzenberg to Thun, 22 July 1850, in Lippert, *Schwarzenberg*, 325.
165. Schwarzenberg to Franz Joseph, 1 Jan. 1851, ibid., 350.
166. Buol, 22 Mar. 1854, in Heindl (ed.), *Protokolle*, vol. 3, 431.
167. Ibid., 432.
168. Bruck, 28 May 1859, in Malfèr (ed.), ibid., vol. 4, 23; Rechberg, 28 June 1859, ibid., 61.

169. Rechberg to Bohuslav Chotek, 14 Aug. 1864, in Elrod, 'Rechberg', 443.
170. Rechberg to Karolyi, 30 Dec. 1859, ibid., 444.
171. Rechberg, 6 Apr. 1861, in H. Brettner-Messler (ed.), *Protokolle*, vol. 5, 257.
172. Rechberg to Schrenk, 3 Jan. 1862, in Elrod, 'Rechberg', 447.
173. Ibid., 451.
174. 10 Jan. 1864, in T. Kletecka and K. Koch (eds), *Protokolle*, vol. 5, 190.
175. Rechberg, 27 Feb. 1864, ibid., 259.
176. Schwarzenberg, *Felix zu Schwarzenberg*, 130.
177. Buol to Bruck, 16 Oct. 1854, in Schroeder, 'Bruck versus Buol', 212.
178. Pfordten to Max II, 3 Nov. 1854, in S. Meiboom, *Studien zur deutschen Politik Bayerns in den Jahren 1851–59* (Munich, 1931), 87.
179. Rechberg to Franz Joseph, 12 Feb. 1864, in Elrod, 'Rechberg', 443.
180. Kempen, 20 Oct. 1855, in Mayr (ed.), *Tagebuch*, 375.
181. Elrod, 'Rechberg', 445.
182. Schwarzenberg to Buol, 31 Dec. 1848, in Lippert, *Schwarzenberg*, 282.
183. See, for instance, the pamphlet of the chief of the *Unterrichts- and Kultusabteilung* of the *Staatsministerium*, Joseph Alexander von Helfert, *Time is Money!* (Prague, 1862), in H. Rosenberg, *Die nationalpolitische Publizistik Deutschlands* (Munich, 1935), 237.
184. C. von Czoernig, *Oesterreichs Neugestaltung, 1848–1858* (Stuttgart, 1858), 23.
185. Ibid., 27.
186. Mayr (ed.), *Tagebuch*, 16–21.
187. In H. Rumpler, 'Die rechtlich-organisatorischen und sozialen Rahmenbedingungen für die Aussenpolitik der Habsburgermonarchie 1848–1918', in A. Wandruszka and P. Urbanitsch (eds), *Die Habsburgermonarchie 1848–1918* (Vienna, 1989), vol. 6, 91.
188. D. Bertsch, *Anton Prokesch von Osten* (Munich, 2005), 353.
189. Ibid., 34.
190. Ibid.
191. J. von Hammer-Purgstall, ibid., 32.
192. Prokesch to his wife, 5 Mar. 1849, ibid., 327; Prokesch to Buol, 18 Jan. 1854, ibid., 354.
193. Prokesch, diary, 3 Feb. 1853, ibid., 349.
194. Prokesch to Warsberg, 12 Jan. 1872, ibid., 326.
195. Ibid., 354–5. Prokesch came to believe that the German Confederation would not change.
196. Schmerling memoirs, in Höbelt (ed.), *Österreichs Weg*, 234.
197. Ibid., 97.
198. P. Judson, *Exclusive Revolutionaries* (Ann Arbor, 1996) is the main text. See also R. A. Kann, *The Multinational Empire* (New York, 1977), 2 vols.
199. G. Franz, *Liberalismus. Die deutschliberale Bewegung in der habsburgischen Monarchie* (Munich, 1955), 324; B. Sutter, 'Die politische und rechtliche Stellung der Deutschen in Österreich 1848 bis 1918', in Wandruszka and Urbanitsch (eds.), *Habsburgermonarchie*, vol. 3, 187.

200. O. B. Friedmann, *Zehn Jahre österreichischer Politik 1859–1869* (Vienna, 1879), 339–40.
201. Franz, *Liberalismus*, 330.
202. *Die Presse,*, 12 Dec. 1860, ibid., 325.
203. Ibid.
204. Höbelt (ed.), *Österreichs Weg*, 236.
205. Ibid., 240–1.
206. Ibid., 241.
207. J. Fröbel, *Deutschland und der Friede von Villafranca* (Frankfurt, 1859), in Rosenberg, *Publizistik*, 126–7.
208. J. Fröbel, *Die Forderungen der deutschen Politik* (Frankfurt, 1860), ibid., 430.
209. Ibid.
210. Ibid.
211. J. Fröbel, *Österreich und die Umgestaltung des deutschen Bundes* (Vienna, 1862), ibid., 416.
212. Ibid., 415.
213. Fröbel, *Deutschland, Österreich und Venetien* (Munich, 1861), ibid., 303.
214. H. von Perthaler, *Neun Briefe über Verfassungs-Reformen in Österreich* (Leipzig, 1860), ibid., 215.
215. Franz, *Liberalismus*, 328.
216. O. Lorenz, *Österreichs Politik in Italien und die wahren Garantien seiner Macht und Einheit* (Vienna, 1859), in Rosenberg, *Publizistik*, 53.
217. H. Reschauer, *Die Aufgaben Deutschösterreichs nach dem 26. Februar 1861* (Vienna, 1861), ibid., 231.
218. O. B. Friedmann, *Zur Einigung Österreichs* (Vienna, 1862), ibid., 248–9.
219. Ibid., 250.
220. Ibid.
221. Ibid., 249.
222. See A. Fischhof and J. Unger, *Zur Lösung der ungarischen Frage* (Vienna, 1861), who talks of the very existence of the *Gesamtstaat* being in question, not just its constitutional character.
223. J. N. Berger, *Zur Lösung der österreichischen Verfassungsfrage* (Vienna, 1861), Rosenberg, *Publizistik*, 247.
224. Ibid., 248.
225. C. Giskra, *Wahlrede für die Landtags-Candidatur des II. Bezirks in Brünn im Augarten-Saale am 21. März 1861* (Brünn, 1861), ibid., 233.
226. Ibid.
227. Ibid.
228. See the former auditor, Franz Joseph Öhri, *Die Weltordnung und die Aufgaben Österreichs und Deutschlands* (Vienna, 1862), ibid., 235–6.
229. Ministerial conference, 18 Mar. 1864, in Malfèr (ed.), *Protokolle*, vol. 5, 302.
230. 22 July 1863, Kletecka and Koch (eds.), *Protokolle*, vol. 5, 202.
231. 7 Oct. 1864, ibid., 200.
232. *Reform*, 1862, in Rosenberg, *Publizistik*, 693.
233. 'Deutschland und die Deutsch-österreicher', *Reform*, Aug. 1862, 1025–30, ibid., 252; F. Schuselka, *Gesamt-Petition der Völker Österreichs*

an Seine Majestät den Kaiser (Leipzig, 1861), ibid., 238–9.
234. Ibid., 239.
235. 'Kann Österreich dualistisch organisiert werden?', *Reform*, Nov. 1862, 1441–4, ibid., 253; F. Schuselka, *An Franz Deak* (Vienna, 1861), ibid., 242.
236. *Reform*, Aug. 1862 and 28 July 1864, ibid., 252 and 785.

Chapter 3

1. H. Schulze-Delitzsch, *Flugblätter des Deutschen Nationalvereins* (Gotha, 1860), in Rosenberg, *Publizistik*, 146.
2. H. von Sybel, *Die deutsche Nation und das Kaiserreich* (Düsseldorf, 1862), 125.
3. R. von Dalwigk, memorandum of Feb. 1861, in W. Schüssler (ed.), *Die Tagebücher des Freiherrn Reinhard v. Dalwigk zu Lichtenfels aus den Jahren 1860–71* (Osnabrück, 1967), 53. The first quotation is from 1864, ibid., 144.
4. R. von Friesen, *Erinnerungen aus meinem Leben* (Dresden, 1880), vol. 2, 101.
5. Ibid.
6. Sybel to Duncker, 9 Feb. 1861, in Duncker, *Politischer Briefwechsel*, 262–4.
7. Ibid., 262–3.
8. See, for instance, Langewiesche, *Liberalismus und Demokratie*, 290–306.
9. O. Klopp, *Das preussische Staatsministerium und die deutsche Reformfrage* (Hanover, 1863), in Rosenberg, *Publizistik*, 668.
10. O. Klopp, *Die gothaische Auffassung der deutschen Geschichte und der Nationalverein*, 2nd edn (Hanover, 1862), 48–50.
11. Ibid., 61.
12. Ibid., 55.
13. Ibid.
14. H. Langwerth von Simmern, 'Für Östreich' (Frankfurt, 1866), in Rosenberg, *Publizistik*, 934.
15. O. Klopp, *Briefe über Grossdeutsch und Kleindeutsch* (Hanover, 1863), ibid., 644.
16. A. Schäffle, 'Realpolitische Gedanken aus der deutschen Gegenwart', *Deutsche Vierteljahrsschrift*, vol. 3 (1859), 261–319, ibid., 70.
17. A. Schäffle, 'Die politischen Bestrebungen der Gegenwart und Deutschlands wahres Bedürfnis', *Deutsche Vierteljahrsschrift*, vol. 4 (1859), 224–87, ibid., 118.
18. A. Schäffle, 'Rechtsphilosophische Zeitgedanken über die politische Bedeutung der Nationalität, historisches Recht, Autonomie und Polizeistaat', *Deutsche Vierteljahrsschrift*, vol. 1 (1861), 288–389, ibid., 351.
19. Ibid.

20. A. Schäffle, 'Die Wiener Zollkonferenzen', *Deutsche Vierteljahrsschrift*, vol. 3 (1858), 255–333, ibid., 560.

21. Ibid., 561. See also A. Schäffle, 'Der preussisch–französische Handelsvertrag, volkswirtschaftlich und politisch betrachtet', *Deutsche Vierteljahrsschrift*, vol. 3 (1862), 254–378; A. Schäffle, 'Die Zolleinigung mit Österreich', *Deutsche Vierteljahrsschrift*, vol. 4 (1862), 297–376; A. Schäffle, 'Die Zolleinigung mit Österreich', *Wochenblatt des Deutschen Reformvereins*, vols 1, 4, 18–20, 22, 28–33 (1863).

22. *Wochenblatt des Deutschen Reformvereins*, 10 Jan. 1863, in Rosenberg, *Publizistik*, 630.

23. Ibid.

24. *Allgemeine Zeitung*, 12 and 25 Sept. 1859, in W. Gebhardt, *Die deutsche Politik der Augsburger Allgemeinen Zeitung* (Diss., Dillingen-Donau, 1935), 50.

25. For details of the relevant newspapers, see Table 3.1.

26. The 1855 report of the Austrian *Presseleitungskomitee* is reproduced in K. Paupié, *Handbuch der österreichischen Pressegeschichte 1848–1959* (Vienna, 1960), vol. 2, 23–53.

27. Zerzog to Cotta, 2 Mar. 1859, in Gebhardt, *Politik*, 20.

28. *Grenzboten*, 2 (1859), 277.

29. 'Die nationale Bewegung und ihr Ziel', *Stimmen der Zeit*, 1 (1859), 316–20, in Rosenberg, *Publizistik*, 31.

30. *Bayrische Wochenschrift*, 16 Apr. 1859, vol. 3, 19–22, ibid., 41.

31. Ibid., 41.

32. Ibid., 91.

33. Ibid., 89, 99.

34. For the circulation figures, see K. Wappler, *Regierung und Presse* (Leipzig, 1935), 46–7.

35. Paupié, *Handbuch*, vol. 2, 23.

36. Ibid., 25.

37. Ibid., 24.

38. H. von Sybel, *Die Fälschung der guten Sache durch die Augsburger Allgemeine Zeitung* (Frankfurt, 1859), in Rosenberg, *Publizistik*, 105.

39. Anon., *Die deutsche Frage und die Allgemeine Zeitung* (Leipzig, 1859), ibid.

40. Kolb to Cotta, 18 June 1857, in Gebhardt, *Politik*, 14.

41. Orges to Cotta, 26 June 1859, ibid., 27.

42. Orges in the *Allgemeine Zeitung*, 1 Oct. 1859, ibid., 50.

43. Orges in the *Allgemeine Zeitung*, 31 Jan. 1859, ibid., 24.

44. Ibid., 33.

45. Ibid., 39.

46. Altenhöfer to Cotta, 19 Aug. 1861, ibid., 54.

47. Kolb to K. von Cotta, 6 June 1863, ibid., 70.

48. H. Simon, *Don Quixote der Legitimität oder Deutschlands Befreier?* (Zurich, 1859).

49. N. M. Hope, *The Alternative to German Unification* (Wiesbaden, 1973), 61, gives details of reports in the *Mainzer Journal* to this effect.

50. *Historisch-politische Blätter*, 1863, vol. 51, 155.

51. Ibid., 156.

52. 'Wo stehen wir? Die innere Lage Deutschlands', ibid., 963.
53. Ibid., 964.
54. 'Zur Geschichte des Liberalismus', ibid., 1866, vol. 58, 182.
55. Ibid., 183.
56. Ibid., 1856, vol. 37, 7.
57. Ibid.
58. Ibid., 6.
59. Respectively, ibid, 1859, vol. 43, 951; 1858, vol. 42, 332; 1857, vol. 40, 714.
60. See, for example, ibid., 1859, vol. 44, 159.
61. Ibid., 1862, vol. 49, 357.
62. Ibid., 1861, vol. 47, 301.
63. Ibid., 306.
64. Ibid.
65. Ibid.
66. Ibid., 302.
67. Ibid., 308.
68. Ibid., 308–9.
69. Ibid., 309.
70. Ibid., 1861, vol. 48, 765.
71. Ibid., 770.
72. Ibid., 774.
73. Ibid., vol. 51, 1863, 16.
74. Ibid., 15–16.
75. Ibid., 20.
76. Ibid., 150.
77. Ibid., 141.
78. Respectively, ibid., 1864, vol. 53, 634, and 1866, vol. 58, 298.
79. Ibid., 1863, vol. 52, 977, and 1862, vol. 49, 856.
80. See, for instance, ibid., 1862, vol. 49, 948, and 1863, vol. 52, 977–8.
81. Orges to Cotta, 26 June 1859, in Gebhardt, *Politik*, 27.
82. Paupié, *Handbuch*, vol. 2, 25.
83. Cotta to Zedlitz, 9 Oct. 1851, in E. Heyck, *Die Allgemeine Zeitung, 1798–1898* (Munich, 1898), 285.
84. Cotta to Stein, 29 May 1862, ibid., 298.
85. Zedlitz to Cotta, 24 Nov. 1849, ibid., 281.
86. Zedlitz to Cotta, 19 Oct. 1851, ibid. 286.
87. See, for example, Zedlitz to Cotta, 23 Aug. 1857, ibid., 289–90, where he even accuses Orges of being pro-Prussian.
88. Ibid., 296.
89. Schäffle's autobiography, in Gebhardt, *Politik*, 63–4.
90. Lerchenfeld to Edel, 30 Oct. 1865, ibid., 84.
91. Altenhöfer to Lerchenfeld, 27 Mar. 1865, ibid., 82.
92. Kolb, in Heyck, *Allgemeine Zeitung*, 117.
93. Kolb to Liebig, 17 May 1859, ibid., 127–8.
94. Kolb to Lerchenfeld, 9 Feb. 1863, in Gebhardt, *Politik*, 70.
95. Kolb to Cotta, 6 June 1863, ibid.
96. Ludwig Steub on Kolb, ibid., 123–4.
97. See W. Real, *Der deutsche Reformverein. Grossdeutsche Stimmen und Kräfte*

zwischen Villafranca und Königgrätz (Lübeck, 1966).

98. F. Curtius (ed.), *Denkwürdigkeiten des Fürsten Chlodwig zu Hohenlohe-Schillingsfürst* (Stuttgart, 1907), vol. 1, 124.
99. Ibid., 117, 123–4.
100. Biefang, *Bürgertum*, 276–7.
101. Paupié, *Handbuch*, vol. 2, 23–47, and K. Wappler, *Regierung und Presse*, 46. The figures are from the mid-1850s.
102. Gall, *Liberalismus*, 61.
103. Ibid., 150–1.
104. Curtius (ed.), *Hohenlohe*, vol. 1, 114.
105. Hohenlohe, 18 Aug. 1863, ibid., 130.
106. Hohenlohe, 18 Jan. 1862, ibid., 117.
107. 26 Sept. 1862, ibid., 126.
108. This is the reluctant conclusion of Nicholas Hope's meticulous study, *The Alternative to German Unification* (Wiesbaden, 1973), in which each chapter ends with a section on the failure of the greater German movement or *Reformverein*.
109. Ibid., 29.
110. Fröbel to Lerchenfeld, 28 Oct. 1861, ibid., 25.
111. Fischer-Goullet to Lerchenfeld, 14 Mar. 1863, ibid., 54.
112. Paupié, *Handbuch*, vol. 2, 32.
113. Ketteler to Hahn-Hahn, 20 Feb. 1862, ibid., 65,
114. Heydenreich, 17 July 1863, ibid., 134.
115. Löning to Lerchenfeld, 23 Sept. 1862, ibid., 30.
116. Fröbel to Lerchenfeld, 28 Oct. 1861, ibid., 26.
117. Ibid., 25.
118. *Franfurter Zeitung*, 12 Sept. 1863, in K. Stoll, *Die politische Stellung der Frankfurter Zeitung in den Jahren 1859 bis 1871* (Frankfurt 1932), 34.
119. *Neue Frankfurter Zeitung*, 2 May 1861, in Hope, *Alternative*, 250.
120. *Volksfreund*, 31 Oct. 1862, ibid., 45.
121. Ibid.
122. *Neue Frankfurter Zeitung*, 21 Aug. 1863, ibid., 249.
123. *Deutsches Wochenblatt*, 39, ibid., 275.
124. Büchner, 26 May 1866, ibid., 289.
125. J. B. Schweitzer, *Zur Deutschen Frage* (Frankfurt, 1862), in Rosenberg, *Publizistik*, 365–6.
126. *Nordstern*, 6 Apr. 1861, ibid., 705.
127. J. B. Schweitzer, *Widerlegung von Carl Vogt's Studien zur gegenwärtigen Lage Europas* (Frankfurt, 1859), 42.
128. J. B. Schweitzer, *Der einzige Weg zur Einheit* (Frankfurt, 1860), 18.
129. Ibid., 42, 44.
130. J. B. Schweitzer, *Die österreichische Spitze* (Leipzig, 1863), 107.
131. Ibid., 37.
132. Ibid., 99, 116.
133. J. B. Schweitzer, 'Der bevorstehende Abgeordnetentag', *Social-Democrat*, 17 Sept. 1865, in F. Mehring (ed.), *Politische Aufsätze und Reden von J. B. v. Schweitzer* (Berlin, 1912), 92–4.
134. J. B. Schweitzer, 'Die Partei des Fortschritts als Trägerin des Stillstands', speech at the *Allgemeine Deutsche Arbeiterverein* in Leipzig,

13 Oct. 1863, in Rosenberg, *Publizistik*, 528.

135. Schweitzer, *Weg*, 23.
136. C. Vogt, *Studien zur gegenwärtigen Lage Europas* (Geneva, 1859), in Rosenberg, *Publizistik*, 37.
137. Ibid., 38.
138. Simon, *Don Quixote*, 23.
139. See also A. Ruge, *Die drei Völker und die Legitimität oder die Italiener, die Ungarn und die Deutschen beim Sturze Östreichs* (London, 1860).
140. L. Bamberger, *Juchhe nach Italia* (Frankfurt, 1859), in L. Bamberger, *Gesammelte Schriften* (Berlin, 1913), vol. 3, 168.
141. F. Lassalle, *Der italienische Krieg und die Aufgabe Preussens. Eine Stimme aus der Demokratie* (Berlin, 1859).
142. Ibid., 30.
143. *Social-Democrat*, 25 Apr. 1866.
144. Ibid., 28 May 1866.
145. Oetker, *Lebenserinnerungen*, vol. 3, 163.
146. Ibid, 165.
147. Ibid.
148. Ibid., 172.
149. Ibid.
150. Biedermann, *Mein Leben*, vol. 2, 137.
151. Ibid., 138.
152. Ibid., 140.
153. Sybel to Duncker, 9 Feb. 1861, in Duncker, *Politischer Briefwechsel*, 262–3.
154. Mevissen, election speech, 5 Feb. 1850, in J. Hansen (ed.), *Gustav von Mevissen* (Berlin, 1906), vol. 2, 611.
155. L. K. Aegidi, *Preussen und der Friede von Villafranca* (Berlin, 1859), 27.
156. C. Rössler, *Sendschreiben an den Politiker der Zukunft vom preussischen Standpunkte* (Berlin, 1858), in Rosenberg, *Publizistik*, 7.
157. Ibid.
158. Häusser to Baumgarten, 14 May 1859, in J. Heyderdorff (ed.), *Deutscher Liberalismus im Zeitalter Bismarcks* (Bonn, 1925), vol. 1, 35.
159. Ibid., 35–7.
160. Miquel, 23 Aug. 1861, in W. Schultze and F. Thimme (eds), *Johannes von Miquels Reden* (Halle, 1911), vol. 1, 30–1.
161. Pfizer to Gagern, 7 Sept. 1859, on the subject of Gagern's biography of his brother, killed in 1848, in G. Küntzel (ed.), *Politische Aufsätze und Briefe von Paul Achatius Pfizer* (Frankfurt, 1924), 60–3.
162. See P. A. Pfizer, *Zur deutschen Verfassungsfrage* (Stuttgart, 1862).
163. Pfizer, 8 July 1849, in Küntzel (ed.), *Aufsätze*, 45.
164. Ibid.
165. *Schwäbische Chronik*, 11 Jan. 1850, ibid., 46.
166. Ibid., 48.
167. Ibid.
168. Pfizer, *Verfassungsfrage*, 15.
169. Ibid., 14.
170. Ibid., 13.
171. Ibid.

172. Ibid., 12.
173. Ibid.
174. *Grenzboten*, 1860, vol. 19, no. 37, 403.
175. Ibid.
176. Ibid, 1851, vol. 9, 86.
177. Ibid., 311.
178. Ibid., 1862, vol. 21, no. 52, 482.
179. Ibid., 1863, vol. 22, 78.
180. Ibid.
181. Ibid.
182. Ibid., 437.
183. Ibid., 1853, vol. 12, 108–9, and 1863, vol. 22, 331.
184. Ibid., 399–400. See also ibid., 1851, vol. 9, 313.
185. Ibid., 1863, vol. 22, 400.
186. Kraus, *Gerlach*, 534.
187. *Neue Preussische Zeitung*, 27 May 1849.
188. 11 Sept. 1850, Gerlach, *Denkwürdigkeiten*, vol. 1, 529.
189. In O. Pflanze, *Bismarck and the Development of Germany: The Period of Unification, 1815–1871* (Princeton, NJ, 1963), 74.
190. O. von Manteuffel, *Unter Friedrich Wilhelm IV*, ed. H. von Poschinger, vol. 1, 233.
191. In Kraus, *Gerlach*, 528.
192. Ibid., 524.
193. Füssl, *Professor in der Politik*, 254.
194. Ibid., 216.
195. Ibid., 245–7.
196. Stahl memorandum, 8 May 1850, ibid., 256.
197. Manteuffel, *Unter Friedrich Wilhelm IV*, vol. 1, 384.
198. Grünthal, *Parlamentarismus*, 395.
199. Leopold to Ernst Ludwig von Gerlach, Kraus, *Gerlach*, 531.
200. Gerlach diary, 2 Nov. 1850, in Barclay, *Frederick William IV*, 208.
201. Ibid., 209.
202. Meinecke, *Radowitz*, 495.
203. K. A. Varnhagen von Ense, *Tagebücher*, 14 vols (Leipzig, 1861–70), vol. 10, 464.
204. Ibid.
205. 23 May 1854, Gerlach, *Denkwürdigkeiten*, vol. 2, 155.
206. Ibid., 154.
207. Prokesch to Buol, 26 Aug. 1854, in Bertsch, *Prokesch*, 352.
208. Prokesch to Buol, 9 Aug. 1854, ibid., 335.
209. *Preussisches Wochenblatt*, 28 Jan. 1854, in Müller, *Die Partei Bethmann-Hollweg*, 51.
210. Ibid., 55–6.
211. Behnen, *Wochenblatt*, 234.
212. *Neue Preussische Zeitung*, 24 Aug. 1859.
213. Ibid., 25 Aug. 1859.
214. Prokesch to Buol, 26 Aug. 1854, in Bertsch, *Prokesch*, 352.
215. Prokesch, 24 July 1854, in Gall, *Bismarck*, vol. 1, 123.
216. In Elrod, 'Rechberg', 450–1.

217. *Kreuzzeitung*, 13 Nov. 1850, in Gall, *Bismarck*, vol. 1, 77.
218. Ibid., 106.
219. Ibid.
220. Bismarck to Manteuffel, 15 Feb. 1854, ibid., 123; Bismarck to Auerswald, 1860, in Pflanze, *Bismarck*, vol. 1, 136.
221. In Gall, *Bismarck*, vol. 1, 214.
222. Bismarck to Karolyi, 4, 12, 18 and 26 Dec. 1862, ibid.
223. Ibid., 215.
224. See above. Also, L. A. von Rochau, *Grundsätze der Realpolitik* (Stuttgart, 1859); W. Schulz-Bodmer, *Entwaffnung oder Krieg* (Leipzig, 1859); F. G. Leue, *Preussen und Österreich gegen Frankreich* (Leipzig, 1859); A. W. Stiehler, *Die Politik und das Verhalten Frankreichs und Russlands gegen Deutschland* (Leipzig, 1859); F. von Raumer, *Zur Politik des Tages* (Leipzig, 1859); A. Peez, *Deutschland am Wendepunkt seiner Geschicke* (Wiesbaden, 1859); F. W. Schaaff, *Ein Wort über Preussens Politik* (Heidelberg, 1859); F. W. Schaaff, *Preussen und die Übereinkunft von Villafranca* (Heidelberg, 1859); E. Fischel, *Die Despoten als Revolutionäre* (Berlin, 1859); R. Marggraff, *Vor und nach dem Frieden von Villafranca* (Leipzig, 1860); J. Venedey, *Der italienische Krieg und die deutsche Volkspolitik* (Hanover, 1859).
225. Paupié, *Handbuch*, vol. 2, 23–53. Some newspapers were seen to be unaligned, of course.
226. *Freiburger Zeitung*, 23 Jan. 1859, and *Badische Landeszeitung*, 17 Feb. 1859, in F. Fischer, *Die öffentliche Meinung in Baden waehren der italienischen Krise 1859 und in der anschliessenden Diskussion um die Bundesreform bis 1861* (Berlin, 1979), 52–3.
227. *National-Zeitung*, 27 May 1859; *Grenzboten*, 1859, vol. 18, 277.
228. Usedom to Bernhardi, 28 Apr. 1859, in T. von Bernhardi, *Aus dem Leben Theodor von Bernhardis* (Leipzig, 1893), vol. 3, 194.
229. *Grenzboten*, 1859, vol. 18, 277–8.
230. Ibid., 276.
231. Ibid., 278.
232. Ibid., 402–8.
233. See Rosenberg's survey of periodicals, *Publizistik*, 84–103. The *Deutsches Museum* and *Königsberger Sonntagspost* were also anti-Austrian. The *Volksblatt für Stadt und Land*, *Bremer Handelsblatt*, *Deutsche Vierteljahrsschrift* (Stuttgart), *Stimmen der Zeit* (Gotha), *Historisch-politische Blätter*, *Bayrische Wochenschrift*, *Deutsche Blätter* and *Glocke* (Leipzig and Dresden) all backed Austria.
234. Mayr (ed.), *Tagebuch*, 510.
235. W. Beseler, *Zur östreichischen Frage* (Leipzig, 1860), 22.
236. The article in *Das Jahrhundert*, 1859, 14, is attributed by Rosenberg to Ruge, in Rosenberg, *Publizistik*, 33. See also Simon, *Don Quixote*; C. Vogt, *Studien zur gegenwärtigen Lage Europas*; H. B. Oppenheim, *Deutschlands Noth und Ärzte* (Berlin, 1859); H. B. Oppenheim, *Deutsche Begeisterung und Habsburgischer Kronbesitz* (Berlin, 1859).
237. Bamberger, *Juchhe nach Italia!*, in Rosenberg, *Publizistik*, 83.
238. K. Blind, *Kriegsgefahr! Deutsche National-Vertretung! Männer von Deutschland!* (Frankfurt, 1859), ibid., 42.

239. Venedey, *Der italienische Krieg*, especially 34–55.
240. For instance, Ruge, in Rosenberg, *Publizistik*, 33.
241. Droysen to Duncker, 8 June 1859, in H. Fenske (ed.), *Der Weg sur Reichsgründung* (Darmstadt), 161.
242. Ibid., 106.
243. C. Rössler, *Preussen und die italienische Frage* (Berlin, 1859), 36.
244. See also Aegidi, *Preussen und der Friede von Villafranca.*
245. T. von Bernhardi, 'Frankreich, Österreich und der Krieg in Italien', *Preussische Jahrbücher*, 1859, vol. 4, 179–97, 229–52, 457–94, 571–612.
246. Bernhardi, *Leben*, vol. 3, 194–5.
247. W. Beseler, *Das deutsche Interesse in der italienischen Frage* (Leipzig, 1859), 14–15.
248. Kraus, *Gerlach*, 706–7.
249. On cultural hegemony, see the democrat Johann Berger, *Zur Lösung der österreichischen Verfassungsfrage*, in Rosenberg, *Publizistik*, 248; Perthaler, *Neun Briefe*, ibid., 215.
250. Bruck, *Die Aufgaben Österreichs*, ibid., 213.
251. 'Die Conferenz und die Nationalitäten', *Ost und West*, 20, 30 Apr. 1864, 787–91, ibid., 772.
252. *Historisch-politische Blätter*, vol. 50, 1862, 87–108.
253. *Stimmen der Zeit*, vol. 1, 1861, 513–19, in Rosenberg, *Publizistik*, 257.
254. *Historisch-politische Blätter*, vol. 50, 1862, 108.
255. L. K. Aegidi, *Der deutsche Kern der italienischen Frage* (Leipzig, 1859), 25.
256. Ibid, 26–7.
257. Beseler, *Zur österreichischen Frage*, 13.
258. Ibid., 12.
259. Ibid., 6–7.
260. Ibid., 8.
261. Ibid., 15.
262. Ibid.
263. Ibid., 17–18.
264. Rössler, *Preussen und die italienische Frage*, 36.
265. *Historisch-politische Blätter*, vol. 50, 1862, 87–108; ibid., vol. 47, 1862, 392–416.
266. Miquel, 23 Aug. 1861, in Fenske (ed.), *Reichsgründung*, 218.
267. Ibid., 219.
268. Ibid.
269. E. Fischel, *Deutsche Federn in Österreichs Doppeladler* (Berlin, 1860), in Rosenberg, *Publizistik*, 223.
270. K. Blind, 'Was sollen unsre Österreichischen Bundesprovinzen thun?', *Flugblätter des Vereins 'Deutsche Einheit und Freiheit' in England*, 1, 1860, ibid., 228.
271. J. E. Jörg, 'Österreich und abermals Österreich', *Historisch-politische Blätter*, vol. 47, 1861, 392–416.
272. Oetker, *Lebenserinnerungen*, vol. 3, 164.
273. Friesen, *Erinnerungen*, vol. 2, 101.

Chapter 4

1. W. H. Riehl, *Die Naturgeschichte des deutschen Volkes*, abr. edn (Leipzig, 1934), 83.
2. Ibid.
3. Ibid., 86.
4. Ibid., 87.
5. Ibid., 89.
6. Examples of the former include A. Green, *Fatherlands* (Cambridge, 2001), and Hanisch, *Fürst*. For the latter, see especially J. Müller, *Deutscher Bund und deutsche Nation 1848–1866* (Göttingen, 2005), and J. Flöter, *Beust und die Reform des Deutschen Bundes 1850–1866* (Cologne, 2001).
7. For the figures above, see Jansen, *Einheit, Macht und Freiheit*, 65–72.
8. W. Siemann, *Deutschlands Ruhe, Sicherheit und Ordnung* (Tübingen, 1985), 260.
9. Siemann, *Gesellschaft im Aufbruch*, 55.
10. Biedermann, *Mein Leben*, vol. 2, 26.
11. Gerlach, Jan. 1851, in Kraus, *Gerlach*, 549.
12. Ibid.
13. 2 Sept. 1856, Varnhagen von Ense, *Tagebücher*, vol. 13.
14. Ibid.
15. See, for instance, *Grenzboten*, 1850, vol. 9, 28, which argues that the reaction after 1848 was not a repeat of 1819.
16. Elben, *Lebenserinnerungen*, 124–5.
17. The Habsburg monarchy, Hessen-Homburg and Fürstentum Reuss älterer Linie remained 'absolutist'.
18. G. Waitz, *Grundzüge der Politik* (Kiel, 1862), 41.
19. G. Waitz, 'Das Königthum und die verfassungsmässige Ordnung', ibid., 129.
20. Ibid., 148.
21. R. von Mohl, *Staatsrecht, Völkerrecht und Politik* (Tübingen, 1860), vol. 1, 394.
22. The number of *Wahlmänner* is for 1852; the percentages of voters is for 1849.
23. For example, Mohl, *Staatsrecht*; Rochau, *Grundsätze der Realpolitik*; J. Fröbel, *Theorie der Politik* (Vienna, 1861–4), 2 vols; C. Frantz, *Kritik aller Parteien* (Berlin, 1862); F. J. Stahl, *Die gegenwärtigen Parteien in Staat und Kirche* (Berlin, 1863).
24. See Chapter 8.
25. H. Brandt, *Parlamentarismus in Württemberg 1815–1870* (Düsseldorf, 1987),159, 630, 668.
26. Neemann, *Landtag*, 113–15.
27. M. L. Anderson, *Windthorst: A Political Biography* (Oxford, 1981), 64–6.
28. Ibid., 77.
29. M. John, 'Liberalism and Society in Germany, 1850–1880: The Case of Hanover', *English Historical Review*, 102 (1987), 579–98.

30. Grünthal, *Parlamentarismus*, 395–413.
31. Schüler to Venedey, 12 Oct. 1853, in Jansen, *Einheit, Macht und Freiheit*, 64.
32. Wuttke to Paur, 16 July 1858, ibid.
33. Ibid., 62.
34. Ibid., 82.
35. Bamberger to Hartmann, 1 June 1867, ibid., 89.
36. Walter, *Denken*, 364–8.
37. Simon to Mayer, 22 Mar. 1853, in Jansen, *Einheit, Macht und Freiheit*, 91.
38. Oetker, *Lebenserinnerungen*, vol. 3, 114.
39. L. Gall, *Bürgertum in Deutschland* (Berlin, 1989), 331–2.
40. Haym to Duncker, 30 Mar. 1852, in Rosenberg (ed.), *Briefwechsel*, 134.
41. Jan. 1851, ibid., 132.
42. Ibid.
43. Ibid.
44. Baumgarten, *Liberalismus*, 55. *Grenzboten*, 1852, vol. 11, 121, commented that the reaction in Prussia was characterised not by its bloodiness but by its legality.
45. Baumgarten, *Liberalismus*, 55.
46. Green, *Fatherlands*, 49.
47. Siemann, *Deutschlands Ruhe*, 260. Even the Prussian total had dropped to 180, compared to 558 in the previous year.
48. Lamey, 1876, in Gall, *Liberalismus*, 77. Also, P. Nolte, 'Gemeindeliberalismus. Zur lokalen Entstehung und sozialen Verankerung der liberalen Partei in Baden 1831–1855', *Historische Zeitschrift*, 252 (1991), 57–93.
49. John, 'Liberalism and Society', 585–90; M. John, 'National and Regional Identities and the Dilemmas of Reform in Britain's "Other Province": Hanover, *c.*1800–*c.*1850', in L. Brockliss and D. Eastwood (eds), *A Union of Multiple Identities* (Manchester, 1997), 179–92; R. Lembke, *Johannes Miquel und die Stadt Osnabrück* (Osnabrück, 1962).
50. D. Bellman, 'Der Liberalismus im Seekreis 1860–1870', in G. Zang (ed.), *Provinzialierung einer Region* (Frankfurt, 1978); Langewiesche, *Liberalismus und Demokratie*; Neemann, *Landtag*; A. Neemann, 'Models of Political Participation in the Beust Era', in J. Retallack (ed.), *Saxony in German History* (Ann Arbor, 2000), 119–34; T. Offermann, 'Preussischer Liberalismus zwischen Revolution und Reichsgründung im regionalen Vergleich: Berliner und Kölner Fortschrittsliberalismus in der Konfliktzeit', in D. Langewiesche (ed.), *Liberalismus im 19. Jahrhundert* (Göttingen, 1988), 109–35; B.-C. Padtberg, *Rheinischer Liberalismus in Köln während der politischen Reaktion in Preussen nach 1848/49* (Cologne, 1985); U. Krey, 'Vereine zwischen Bürgertum und Unterschichten in Westfalen 1840–1854', *Jahrbuch zur Liberalismus-Forschung*, 1 (1989), 9–24.
51. Soiron to Haym, 25 Dec. 1850, in Rosenberg (ed.), *Briefwechsel*, 127.
52. Haym to Treitschke, 28 Oct. 1857, ibid., 143.
53. Haym's correspondents between the end of the revolution and the 'New Era' included Hermann Hartung, Georg Waitz, Heinrich von

397

Gagern, Alexander von Soiron, Max Duncker, Joseph Lehfeldt, Georg Beseler, Karl Francke, Eduard Simson, Friedrich Christoph Dahlmann, Gustav Pfizer, Hermann von Beckerath, Karl Ludwig Aegidi, Georg Gottfried Gervinus, Klaus Groth, Otto Jahn, Eduard Zeller, Friedrich Theodor Vischer, Heinrich von Treitschke, Justus von Gruner, David Friedrich Strauss, Rudolf Schleiden, Karl Neumann, Karl Biedermann, Robert von Mohl, Johann Kaspar Bluntschli and Theodor Mommsen. See Rosenberg (ed.), *Briefwechsel*, 81–171.

54. In H. Oncken, *Rudolf von Bennigsen* (Stuttgart, 1910), vol. 1, 258.
55. For example, 22 Feb. 1852, ibid., 205.
56. Ibid.
57. Bennigsen to his mother, Dec. 1842, ibid., 82.
58. Ibid., 82–3, 88.
59. Bennigsen to his father, 8 Dec. 1844, ibid., 112.
60. 5. Mar. 1848, ibid., 146.
61. Bennigsen to his father, 23 June 1848, ibid., 156.
62. 9 June 1849, ibid., 174.
63. Bennigsen to his mother, 31 Mar. 1849, ibid., 165.
64. See the royal proclamation of 25 Apr. 1849, ibid., 175.
65. 22 Oct. 1850, ibid., 190.
66. 12 Apr. 1858, ibid., 307.
67. Bennigsen to his mother, 22 Oct. 1855, ibid., 274.
68. 28 July 1859, ibid., 332.
69. Ibid.
70. Bennigsen speech, 15 Jan. 1895, ibid., 281.
71. Ibid.
72. Bennigsen to his father, 9 Dec. 1856, ibid., 283.
73. See Hanisch, *Fürst*, 125–6, 217–49, and Neemann, *Landtag*, 143–9.
74. Hanisch, *Fürst*, 125.
75. See Chapter 2.
76. In Oncken, *Bennigsen*, vol. 1, 277.
77. Friedrich Wilhelm IV to E. von Manteuffel, 13 Sept. 1853, in Barclay, *Frederick William IV*, 229.
78. Ibid., 228.
79. Ibid., 240.
80. Kraus, *Gerlach*, 586–606.
81. Ibid., 588. On the perceived proximity of Manteuffel and the Gerlachs at the time of Olmütz, see Gerlach, *Denkwürdigkeiten*, 11 Dec. 1850, 571.
82. *Kreuzzeitung*, 9, 1850, in H. Walter, *Die innere Politik des Ministers von Manteuffel und der ursprung der Reaktion in Preussen* (Berlin, 1910), 140.
83. 'Protokoll der Vernehmung Techens', 30 Jan. 1856, in W. Baumgarten (ed.), *Akten zur Geschichte des Krimkriegs* (Munich, 1990–1), vol. 2, 805–8.
84. Gerlach to Friedrich Wilhelm IV, 20 Feb. 1853, in Kraus, *Gerlach*, 614.
85. Wagener to E. L. von Gerlach, 21 July 1852, ibid., 613.

86. Gerlach to Wagener, 22 July 1852, ibid.
87. Perthes, 13 Mar. 1852, in Behnen, *Wochenblatt*, 63.
88. *Wochenblatt* party statement, 1852, in Müller, *Die Partei Bethmann-Hollweg*, 7.
89. Bethmann on the holiness of the constitution in the *Abgeordetenhaus*, 9 Dec. 1852, and R. von der Goltz, *Ideen über die Reorganisierung des Deutschen Bundes* (1848), in W. Schmidt, *Die Partei Bethmann Hollweg und die Reaktion in Preussen 1850–58* (Berlin, 1910), 100, 146.
90. Ibid., 151.
91. Ibid., 146.
92. Perthes, in Behnen, *Wochenblatt*, 63.
93. Quehl to Manteuffel, 15 Nov. 1852, ibid., 49.
94. 6 Dec. 1856, ibid., 50.
95. Bismarck to Manteuffel, 29 Sept. 1851, ibid., 62.
96. Ibid.
97. Manteuffel reporting the position of Friedrich Wilhelm IV, ibid., 45.
98. See, in particular, M. Gross, *The War against Catholicism: Liberalism and the Anti-Catholic Imagination in Nineteenth-Century Germany* (Ann Arbor, 2004) on Catholic missions and liberals' responses.
99. Reichensperger to Steinle, 6 Dec. 1852, in L. Bergstrasser (ed.), *Der politische Katholizismus* (Munich, 1921), 190.
100. Ibid.
101. Anon. (Peter Reichensperger), *Die Wahlen zum Hause der Abgeordneten in Preussen* (1858), ibid., 225–6.
102. J. Sperber, *Popular Catholicism in Nineteenth-Century Germany* (Princeton, NJ, 1984), 107.
103. Ibid., 110–11.
104. K.-E. Lönne, *Politischer Katholizismus im 19. und 20. Jahrhundert* (Frankfurt, 1986), 136.
105. H. von Lerchenfeld-Koefering, *Erinnerungen und Denkwuerdigkeiten* (Berlin, 1935), 32–3.
106. In Bergstrasser (ed.), *Katholizismus*, 192.
107. Ibid., 193.
108. *Die Ministerial-Erlasse vom 22. Mai und 16 Juli in der zweiten Kammer* (Paderborn, 1853), ibid., 211. Contributions were largely anonymous.
109. Ibid., 198.
110. Ibid., 207.
111. Ibid., 208.
112. Reichensperger, in U. von Hehl (ed.), *Peter Reichensperger 1810–1892* (Paderborn, 2000), 66–7.
113. Manteuffel to Rochow, 3 July 1851, in R. Kohnen, *Pressepolitik des Deutschen Bundes* (Tübingen, 1995), 34.
114. Siemann, *Gesellschaft*, 67–77.
115. Biedermann, *Mein Leben*, vol. 2, 116.
116. Pfordten to Schrenck, 10 Oct. 1857, in Kohnen, *Pressepolitik*, 121.
117. L. Kuppelmayr, 'Die Tageszeitungen in Bayern 1849–1972', in M. Spindler (ed.), *Handbuch der bayerischen Geschichte* (Munich, 1975), vol. 4, 1147.

118. Kohnen, *Pressepolitik*, 185.
119. Münchhausen to Schele, 14 July 1851, and Rüdt to Marschall, 12 July 1851, in Müller, *Bund*, 97–8.
120. 21 Mar. 1854, Varnhagen von Ense, *Tagebücher*, vol. 11, 1.
121. 10 May 1854, ibid., 63–4. Hinckeldey was, according to Varnhagen, also acting to get his own back for unpunished attacks on him by the *Kreuzzeitung*, but he made the argument only because it was credible.
122. Wappler, *Regierung und Presse*, 59.
123. See Table 3.1.
124. *Wappler, Regierung und Presse*, 59.
125. R. Engelsing, *Analphabetentum und Lektüre* (Stuttgart, 1973).
126. Wappler, *Regierung und Presse*, 60.
127. All the figures below come from 1854, in Wappler, *Regierung und Presse*, 46–76, and Paupié, *Handbuch*, vol. 2, 27–53.
128. In Hanisch, *Fürst*, 139.
129. In Green, *Fatherlands*, 272.
130. *Leipziger Zeitung*, 8 Mar. 1850, ibid., 272.
131. *Neue Hannoversche Zeitung*, 27 Oct. 1859, ibid.
132. *Staats-Anzeiger für Württemberg*, 5 Feb. 1861, ibid., 271.
133. Green, *Fatherlands*, 284–5.
134. *Staats-Anzeiger für Württemberg*, 1 July 1860, ibid., 281.
135. *Staats-Anzeiger*, 14 July 1850, and *Dresdner Journal*, 4 Sept. 1859, ibid., 275.
136. Hanisch, *Fürst*, 170–4.
137. Rochau, *Gründsätze der Realpolitik*, 176. This section of the work was published in 1853.
138. Ibid., 178.
139. Ibid., 175, 70–1.
140. Ibid., 73.
141. Ibid., 70.
142. Ibid.
143. In the immediate aftermath of the revolution, Rochau backed advocates of the *Bundesstaat* such as Bodelschwingh and opposed critics such as Stahl; L. A. von Rochau and G. Ölsner-Monmerqué, *Das Erfurter Parlament und der Berliner Fürsten-Congress* (Leipzig, 1850), 176, 185.
144. Rochau, *Gründsätze der Realpolitik*, 78.
145. In L. R. Ping, *Gustav Freytag and the Prussian Gospel* (Bern, 2006), 21.
146. Freytag, *Erinnerungen*, 578.
147. Ibid., 577.
148. *Grenzboten*, 1854, vol. 1, 441–2.
149. Ibid., 441, 444.
150. Ibid., 442–3.
151. Ibid., 1859, vol. 2, 37.
152. Ibid.
153. Ibid., 37–8.
154. Ibid., 144.
155. Ibid., 1850, vol. 4, 27–8.
156. Ibid., 1849, vol. 1, 362; ibid., 1850, vol. 1, 499–501; ibid., 1858, vol. 3,

153–5; ibid., 1860, vol. 1, 205; ibid., 1863, vol. 4, 318.

157. Ibid., 1858, vol. 3, 155.
158. This is a point made by Abigail Green, *Fatherlands*, 268. Only Bavarian leaders talked of 'Bavarian national feeling'; the term 'national' was avoided with reference to Saxony, Hanover and Württemberg.
159. Haym to Treitschke, 28 Oct. 1857, in Rosenberg (ed.), *Briefwechsel*, 143.
160. *Grenzboten*, 1861, vol. 3, 121–2, 131.
161. Ibid., 131.
162. Ibid., 132.
163. Ibid.
164. Ibid.
165. Ibid., 133.
166. 'Deutsche Interessen und Deutsche Politik', *Preussische Jahrbücher*, 1858, vol. 2, 2.
167. Ibid., 1860, vol. 6, 148.
168. Ibid., 149.
169. *Neue Preussische Zeitung*, 5 Sept. 1863.
170. Ibid.
171. Ibid.
172. *Historisch-politische Blätter*, 1850, 477–96.
173. Ibid., 609–22, 679–99.
174. Ibid., 610.
175. Ibid., 695.
176. Ibid., 1856, 6.
177. Ibid., 1858, 75.
178. Ibid., 81.
179. Ibid., 81–2.
180. Ibid., 1859, 955–6.
181. Ibid., 957.
182. Ibid.
183. Ibid.
184. Ibid., 1865, 747.
185. Ibid., 1860, 161–6.
186. Dalwigk memorandum for the Archduchess, 6 Jan. 1861, in Schüssler (ed.), *Dalwigk*, 48. See also, Beust memorandum, Feb. 1854, in Müller, *Bund*, 169: 'Only the collective, united stand of the other German governments, in particular the *Mittelstaaten*, can achieve any significance.'
187. Schüssler (ed.), *Dalwigk*, 48.
188. Dalwigk draft programme for the Würzburg conference, Feb. 1861, ibid., 53.
189. Memorandum, 18 Nov. 1861, ibid., 63.
190. Dalwigk diary, 5 Oct. 1864, ibid., 145.
191. F. F. von Beust, *Aus drei Viertel-Jahrhunderten*, 2 vols (Stuttgart, 1887), vol. 1, 275.
192. Ibid., 294.
193. Ibid., 324.

194. See Flöter, *Beust.*
195. Dalwigk, 18.   Nov. 1861, in Schüssler (ed.), *Dalwigk,* 57–8.
196. 6 Jan. 1861, ibid., 47.
197. 18 Nov. 1861, ibid., 61.
198. Ibid., 61–2.
199. Meysenbug memorandum, Nov. 1855, in J. Müller (ed.), *Quellen zur Geschichte des Deutschen Bundes* (Munich, 1998) vol. 3, no. 2, 399.
200. *Karlsruher Zeitung,* 11 Jan. 1863, in Müller, *Bund,* 344.
201. Schüssler (ed.), *Dalwigk,* 64.
202. Flöter, *Beust,* 241, on Beust in 1859.
203. Beust memorandum, June 1856, in Müller (ed.), *Quellen,* vol. 3, no. 1, 460.
204. Special report, 19 Apr. 1851, ibid., 457, 460. On the nature of the envisaged parliament, Carl von Weber, diary, 2 Mar. 1851, in Flöter, *Beust,* 78–9.
205. Blittersdorf to Buol, 17 Oct. 1855, in Flöter, *Beust,* 167.
206. Beust, June 1856, in Müller (ed.), *Quellen,* vol. 3, no. 1, 465–6.
207. Schrenk to Maximilian II, 23 Sept. 1859, in Flöter, *Beust,* 242.
208. Ibid., 254–5.
209. Beust, *Aus drei Viertel-Jahrhunderten,* vol. 1, 122.
210. Ibid., 123.
211. Ibid., 11.
212. Ibid., 25.
213. Ibid., 22.
214. Ibid., 4, 23, 75.
215. Ibid., 111.
216. Ibid., 24.
217. Ibid., 37–8.
218. Ibid., 33, 12.
219. Beust to Nostitz, 7 July 1851, in Müller, *Bund,* 77.
220. Ibid., 274.
221. F. W. Ebeling, *Friedrich Ferdinand Graf von Beust* (Leipzig, 1870), vol. 2, 7–8.
222. Ibid.
223. Beust, *Aus drei Viertel-Jahrhunderten,* vol. 1, 324.
224. Ibid., 281.
225. Ibid., 81.
226. Ibid., 80.
227. Beust, *Aus drei Viertel-Jahrhunderten,* vol. 1, 281–2.
228. In Müller, *Bund,* 55, 370.
229. Ibid.
230. Bothmer to Georg V, 8 Sept. 1852, in Müller, *Quellen,* vol. 3, no. 2, 282.
231. In Müller, *Bund,* 133.
232. Roggenbach to Grand Duke Friedrich I, 25 Aug. 1860, ibid., 325; Meysenbug memorandum, Nov. 1855, in Müller, *Quellen,* vol. 3, no. 2, 410.
233. Rüdt to Marschall, 28 Dec. 1855, ibid., 418–19.

402 NOTES

234. Wilhelm I to Schwarzenberg, 18 Jan. 1851, ibid., 161.
235. Hügel to Beust, 29 Aug. 1856, ibid., 475.
236. Dalwigk promemoria, 18 Nov. 1861, in Schüssler (ed.), *Dalwigk*, 62.
237. Ibid., 62–3.
238. Ibid., 63.
239. Ibid., 64.
240. Ibid.
241. Ibid.
242. Ibid.
243. Ibid., 63.
244. Ibid.
245. Ibid.
246. Ibid., 91.
247. Friesen, *Erinnerungen*, vol. 2, 90.
248. Ibid., 91.
249. Ibid., 98.
250. Ibid., 101.
251. Ibid.
252. See Müller, *Bund*, 391–564, on successful forms of cooperation.
253. Lerchenfeld to Max II, 5 Nov. 1851, in Meiboom, *Politik*, 9–10.
254. Schwarzenberg to Prokesch, 29 Mar. 1851, in Lippert, *Schwarzenberg*, 359 and in Müller, *Quellen*, vol. 3, no. 1, 388. For Rechberg's assessment of Bismarck, see Elrod, 'Rechberg', 351.
255. Dungern to Duke Adolf, 27 Dec. 1850, in Müller, *Bund*, 70.
256. Watzdorf to Fritsch, 31 July 1851, in Müller, *Quellen*, vol. 3, no. 2, 72.
257. Pfordten, 2 Mar. 1852, ibid., 729.
258. Ibid., 730–1.
259. Pfordten to Max II, 20 Oct. 1856, in Meiboom, *Politik*, 27.
260. Montgelas to Max II, 5 Nov. 1856, ibid.
261. Reigersberg to Max II, 16 Sept. 1859, ibid., 126.
262. Meysenbug to Rüdt, 30 July 1851, in Müller, *Quellen*, vol. 3, no. 2, 692.
263. Lerchenfeld to Max II, 5 Nov. 1851, in Meiboom, *Politik*, 9.
264. In Müller, *Bund*, 88.
265. *Weser-Zeitung*, Jan. 1852, ibid., 89.
266. Müller, *Quellen*, vol. 3, no. 2, 793.
267. *Weser-Zeitung*, 14 June 1854, in Müller, *Bund*, 188.
268. *Weser-Zeitung*, 30 Dec. 1856, in Müller, *Quellen*, vol. 3, no. 2, 505.
269. Ibid., 506.
270. *Kasseler Zeitung*, 28 Aug. 1854, ibid.
271. *Constitutionelle Zeitung*, 26 Feb. 1858, and *Korrespondent von und für Deutschland*, 4 Mar. 1858, ibid., 642–5.
272. 7 Dec. 1859, in Müller, *Bund*, 306.
273. See, for instance, the cross-party analysis of Fischer, *Die öffentliche Meinung in Baden*, 157–63.
274. *Karlsruher Zeitung*, 20 Aug. 1862, ibid., 340.
275. *Preussische Jahrbücher*, 1865, 84–6.
276. Ibid., 91–3.
277. *Grenzboten*, 1850, vol. 1, 37–8.
278. Ibid., 1855, vol. 1, 67–74.

279. Ibid., 74.
280. Ibid., 1857, vol. 1, 48.
281. Ibid., 45.
282. Ibid., 47–8.
283. Ibid., 1858, vol. 1, 441.
284. Ibid., 443.
285. Ibid., 1859, vol. 2, 144.
286. Ibid., 1862, vol. 2, 14.
287. Ibid., 1864, vol. 3, 432.
288. Ibid., 1863, vol. 4, 398.
289. June 1850, in Kraus, *Gerlach*, 536.
290. Ibid.
291. *Neue Preussische Zeitung*, 1 Mar. 1850. See also ibid., 29 Mar. 1850.
292. Ibid., 31 Aug. 1859.
293. Ibid., 24 Aug. 1859.
294. Ibid., 5 Sept. 1863.
295. Ibid.
296. In Bergsträsser (ed.), *Katholizismus*, 260–2.
297. Ibid., 249.
298. Article by an 'important person' in the *Kölnische Zeitung* in 1853, ibid., 192. See also 'Die Fraktion des Zentrums', ibid., 234–47.
299. A. and P. Reichensperger, *Deutschlands nächste Aufgaben* (Paderborn, 1860), 84.
300. Ibid., 84–5.
301. Ibid., 86. See also *Historisch-politische Blätter*, 1862, vol. 49, 422, which claimed that even Prussian Catholics did not support either the *Bund* or Austria.
302. Ibid., 84.
303. Biefang, *Bürgertum*, 220–47, 279–87; Jansen, *Einheit, Macht und Freiheit*, 431–43.
304. Resolution of 21 Aug. 1863, in Fenske (ed.), *Reichsgründung*, 282.
305. Ibid., 282–3.
306. *Social-Demokrat*, 4 and 18 Jan. 1865.
307. Gerlach to the Queen, 22 Jan. 1853, in Schmidt, *Bethmann-Hollweg*, 155–6.
308. *Preussisches Wochenblatt*, 1860, vol. 25, in Behnen, *Wochenblatt*, 224.
309. Ibid., 191.
310. *Allgemeine Zeitung*, 22 Feb. 1854, in Müller, *Bund*, 166; *Allgemeine Zeitung*, 12 July 1859, in Gebhardt, *Politik*, 34; *Allgemeine Zeitung*, 1, 2, 18, 19 Jan., 5, 6, 21 Feb., 1–4, 6, 8, 31 Mar. 1864, in *Gebhardt Politik*, 74.
311. *Allgemeine Zeitung*, 22 Feb. 1854, in Müller, *Bund*, 166; *Allgemeine Zeitung*, 12 July 1859, in Gebhardt, *Politik*, 34.
312. *Allgemeine Zeitung*, 31 Mar. 1864 and 12 Nov. 1865, ibid., 74 and 86.
313. Biefang, *Bürgertum*, 245.
314. Lassaulx, 25 Sept. 1855, in Müller, *Quellen*. Vol. 3, no. 2, 326.
315. Pfordten to Dalwigk, 12 Nov. 1864, in Schüssler (ed.), *Dalwigk*, 151.
316. In Müller, *Bund*, 197.
317. Müller, *Quellen*, vol. 3, no. 2, 312.

318. Ibid., 312, 314.
319. Müller, *Bund*, 338.
320. Müller, *Quellen*, vol. 3, no. 2, 636.
321. Ibid., 618–19.
322. In Neemann, *Landtag*, 440.
323. Ibid., 444, 467.
324. Petermann to Wuttke, 14 Feb. 1864, ibid., 475.
325. *Historisch-politische Blätter*, 1862, vol. 49, 383–7.
326. Ibid., 1861, vol. 48, 774–6.
327. Ibid., 1850, vol. 25, 488.
328. Ibid., 1858, vol. 41, 81–3, 111.
329. Ibid., 1862, vol. 49, 348.
330. Ibid., 349.
331. Ibid.
332. Ibid., 350–1.
333. Ibid., 352.
334. Ibid., 371–2, 416–40; ibid., 1863, vol. 51, 141–5.
335. Ibid., 1862, vol. 50, 673–4; ibid., 1863, vol. 51, 969–85.
336. Ibid., 1862, vol. 50, 674–6.
337. Ibid., 676–82.
338. Ibid., 1863, vol. 51, 963–4.
339. Ibid., 1864, vol. 53, 137–49.
340. Ibid., 1866, vol. 57, 190–2.
341. Ibid., 264–6.

Chapter 5

1. In Huber (ed.), *Verfassungsgeschichte*, vol. 2, 104–5.
2. Declaration of a '*freisinniger Vaterlandsfreunde*', *Zeitung für Norddeutschland*, 20 July 1859, in Fenske (ed.), *Reichsgründung*, 174.
3. Ibid., 173.
4. Ibid., 173–4.
5. Huber (ed.), *Verfassungsgeschichte*, vol. 2, 105.
6. Two good examples, in addition to those listed in the previous chapter, are J. Breuilly, *The Formation of the First German Nation-State 1800–1871* (Basingstoke, 1996), and H. Lutz, *Zwischen Habsburg und Preussen. Deutschland 1815–1866* (Berlin, 1985).
7. Klopp, *Die gothaische Auffassung*, 18.
8. For scepticism about Austria and the *Bund*, see Chapters 3 and 4.
9. Diary of Theodor von Bernhardi, 8 Aug. 1858, in T. von Bernhardi, *Aus dem Leben Theodor von Bernhardis* (Leipzig, 1893), vol. 3, 54–5.
10. Ibid., 55.
11. Ibid.
12. L. Simon, 'Deutschland und seine beiden Grossmächte' (1860), in Fenske (ed.), *Reichsgründung*, 193.
13. Ibid., 190–1.
14. Ibid., 193.

15. Ibid.
16. Biedermann, *Mein Leben*, 135. See also R. Prutz, 'Preussische Briefe', *Deutsches Museum*, 1860, vol. 1, 89–94, 621–6, 721–30, 810–16, 873–81, 944–7; A. Blumroeder, *Ansprache an das Deutsche Volk* (Leipzig, 1859); F. Harkort, *Eine Stimme aus dem Volke* (Berlin, 1859), all in Rosenberg, *Publizistik*, 178, 161–3.
17. Biedermann, *Mein Leben*, 143. Also, L. Simon, 'Der preussische Constitutionalismus', *Demokratische Studien*, 1861, 1–33; 'Die Aussichten in Preussen', *Stimmen der Zeit*, Nov. 1858, 215–32; L. von Gerlach, *Der Ministerwechsel im November 1858* (Berlin, 1859); H. Wagener, *Was wir wollen* (Berlin, 1859), all in Rosenberg, *Publizistik*, 183, 160–5.
18. Ibid., 140.
19. In H. Rall, 'Die politische Entwicklung 1848–1871', in Spindler (ed.), *Handbuch*, vol. 4, 245.
20. Ibid., 151.
21. Schulze to Bennigsen, 1 Nov. 1859, in Thorwart (ed.), *Hermann Schulze-Delitzsch's Schriften und Reden*, vol. 3, 147–8.
22. This and most statistics below come from the seminal work of Andreas Biefang, *Politisches Bürgertum in Deutschland 1857–1868* (Düsseldorf, 1994), 298–309. The figures are based on membership of the committees of the *Nationalverein*, *Abgeordnetentag*, *Kongress deutscher Volkswirte*, and *Handelstag*.
23. Ibid., 109.
24. This calculation is taken from Biefang's list of the members of a functional national elite, *Bürgertum*, 436–47,
25. *Zeit*, 10 Dec. 1861, ibid., 194.
26. Schulze to Bennigsen, 15 Apr. 1862, ibid.
27. Gründungsprogramm der Deutschen Fortschrittspartei, 6 June 1861, in Fenske (ed.), *Reichsgründung*, 212.
28. For annual meetings of national associations, see Table 5.3.
29. Thorwart (ed.), *Hermann Schulze-Delitzsch's Schriften und Reden*, vol. 3, 136–424.
30. Ibid., 153.
31. Ibid., 183.
32. Ibid.
33. 'Aufruf des Zentralwahlkomitees der Fortschrittpartei', 14 Mar. 1862, in Fenske (ed.), *Reichsgründung*, 243.
34. H. V. von Unruh, 'Was hat Preussen zunächst in der deutschen Sache zu tun?' (1861), ibid., 221–5.
35. Biefang, *Bürgertum*, 49.
36. Unruh, 'Preussen', in Fenske (ed.), *Reichsgründung*, 223.
37. Biedermann, *Mein Leben*, vol. 2, 146.
38. Ibid., 151–2.
39. Ibid., 153.
40. In Oncken, *Bennigsen*, vol. 1, 468.
41. Biefang, *Burgertüm*, 108.
42. Schulze to Freytag, 8 Oct. 1859, in Thorwart (ed.), *Hermann Schulze-*

Delitzsch's Schriften und Reden, vol. 3, 144.
43. Ibid., 144–5.
44. *Historisch-politische Blätter,* 1858, vol. 41, 738–9.
45. *Grenzboten,* 1854, vol. 13, 441–50.
46. Ibid., 1858, vol. 17, 153. C. Rössler, *Die bevorstehenden Krisis der preussischen Verfassung* (Berlin, 1862).
47. See, for instance, *Der Social-Demokrat,* 4 Jan. 1865, and *Historisch-politische Blätter,* 1861, vol. 20, 371–87.
48. This figure is calculated from the table in Jansen, *Einheit, Macht und Freiheit,* 619–20.
49. Christmann, Crämer, Franz Duncker, Fetzer, Jacoby, Joseph, Georg Friedrich Kolb, Löwe-Calbe, Lüning, Mammen, Metz, Schulze-Delitzsch, Streit, Tafel, Völk, and Moritz Wiggers.
50. Anon., *Demokraten und Conservative* (Potsdam, 1862), in Rosenberg, *Publizistik,* 492. *Historisch-politische Blätter,* 1862, vol. 50, 696, claimed that Progressives were doctrinaire democrats for the most part.
51. R. von Mohl, *Staatsrecht, Völkerrecht und Politik* (Tübingen, 1860), vol. 2, 13.
52. Ibid., vol. 1, 388.
53. C. Frantz, *Kritik aller Parteien* (Berlin, 1862), 128–38.
54. Bamberger, *Erinnerungen,* 499, 501.
55. J. Jacoby, *Die Grundsätze der preussischen Demokratie* (1859), 13.
56. B. Waldeck and A. F. J. Riedel, 'Zwei Wahlreden' (1861), ibid., 189.
57. Welcker's memorandum on *Der preussische Verfassungskampf* (Frankfurt, 1863) suggests this, opposing the 'Prussian *Volk* and its deputies', on the one hand, to the 'most extreme injustice', on the other, in Rosenberg, *Publizistik,* 508.
58. *Grenzboten,* 'Die neue Fortschrittspartei', 1861, vol. 20, 76, 78.
59. Ibid., 78.
60. *Social-Demokrat,* 4 Jan. 1865.
61. Ibid., 20 Jan. 1865.
62. Ibid. See also ibid., 22 Jan. 1865.
63. *Historisch-politische Blätter,* 1861, vol. 48, 365–87; ibid., 1862, vol. 50, 668–700; ibid., 1863, vol. 52, 62–5; ibid., 1864, vol. 53, 621–36.
64. Walesrode to Lassalle, 8 July 1860, in Biefang, *Bürgertum,* 249.
65. Bamberger, *Erinnerungen,* 511.
66. Ibid., 512.
67. In Jansen, *Einheit, Macht und Freiheit,* 344.
68. Ibid.
69. Ibid., 345.
70. Biefang, *Bürgertum,* 252.
71. Streit to Bennigsen and Fries, 23 May 1860, ibid., 149.
72. Biedermann, *Mein Leben,* 146.
73. Biefang, *Burgertüm,* 258.
74. Streit to Bennigsen, 23 Sept. 1862, ibid., 248.
75. The text of the association's policy was prepared by Brater, Unruh and Metz, ibid., 253.
76. *Grenzboten,* 1853, vol. 12, 261, already expressed satisfaction about changes which had taken place within '*die Demokratie*'.

77. Unruh to Duncker, Aug. 1859, in Duncker, *Politischer Briefwechsel*, 167.
78. Ibid., 168.
79. In Jansen, *Einheit, Macht und Freiheit*, 401.
80. Ibid.
81. *Historisch-politische Blätter*, 1861, vol. 48, 72.
82. Biefang, *Bürgertum*, 239.
83. Ibid., 252.
84. In S. Na'aman, *Lassalle* (Hanover, 1970), 18.
85. Ibid., 275.
86. Ibid.
87. Ibid., 453–4. See also F. Lassalle, *Die Feste, die Presse und der Frankfurter Abgeordnetentag* (Düsseldorf, 1863), which attacks the bourgeoisie and the liberal press.
88. Na'aman, *Lassalle*, 269.
89. Ibid., 28.
90. Ibid., 570.
91. Ibid.
92. See F. Lassalle, *Macht und Recht* (Zurich, 1863), in which he continues to champion 'democracy'.
93. Na'aman, *Lassalle*, 199.
94. Ibid., 157–8.
95. Ibid., 498. The terms come from Marx.
96. Walesrode to Lassalle, July 1860, ibid., 328.
97. Ibid., 328.
98. Ibid., 270.
99. Ibid., 560. See F. Lassalle, 'Offnes Antwortschreiben an das Central-Comité zur Berufung eines Allgemeinen Deutschen Arbeiter-Congresses zu Leipzig' (1863), in which his main targets are Schulze-Delitzsch and the *Fortschrittspartei*.
100. For radical positions vis-à-vis Austria in 1859, see Chapter 3.
101. Na'aman, *Lassalle*, 307.
102. Ibid., 310.
103. Ibid., 308.
104. Ibid., 352.
105. F. Lassalle, 'Über Verfassungen' (1862), in Rosenberg, *Publizistik*, 484.
106. Na'aman, *Lassalle*, 312–14.
107. Lassalle, *Der italienische Krieg*, 30.
108. *Grenzboten*, 1850, vol. 9, 351.
109. Ibid., 1854, vol. 13, 443.
110. Ibid., 1858, vol. 17, 354–5.
111. Elben, *Lebenserinnerungen*, 125.
112. Ibid.
113. *Historisch-politische Blätter*, 1855, vol. 36, 983.
114. Ibid., 984.
115. Ibid., 1863, vol. 51, 381. Also, ibid., 1865, vol. 56, 741–51; ibid., 1866, vol. 58, 35.
116. Ibid., 1863, vol. 51, 383.

117. Ibid., 1858, vol. 41, 731.
118. Ibid., 731–2.
119. Ibid., 71–112, 219–45.
120. Ibid., 82–3.
121. Ibid., 242.
122. Ibid., 1864, vol. 53, 621–36.
123. Ibid., 1865, vol. 56, 746.
124. Ibid., 1866, vol. 58, 38.
125. See, for example, *Grenzboten*, 1858, vol. 17, 392–6; 1859, vol. 18, 196–200; 1861, vol. 20, 75–8; 1862, vol. 21, 323–6, 521–4.
126. Ibid., 1861, vol. 20, 75, summarising and commenting on a *National-Zeitung* report.
127. G. Schmoller, *Der französische Handelsvertrag und seine Gegner* (Frankfurt a. M., 1862); Otto Michaelis, in *Bericht der vereinigten Kommissionen für Handel und Gewerbe* (Berlin, 1862); Ludwig Karl Aegidi, *Vorwände und Thatsachen. Ein Beitrag zur Kritik der Opposition gegen den Handelsvertrag vom 2. August 1862* (Berlin, 1862).
128. A. Bienengräber, *Statistik des Verkehrs und Verbrauchs im Zollverein für die Jahre 1841–1864* (Berlin, 1868), 462.
129. A. Schäffle, 'Die Wiener Zollkonferenzen', *Deutsche Vierteljahrsschrift*, 1858, 255–33, in Rosenberg, *Publizistik*, 560; H. Rosenberg, 'Die Zolleinigung mit Österreich', *Wochenschrift des Deutschen Reformvereins*, 1863, vols 1, 4, 18–20, 22, 28–33, ibid., 596–7; H. Rosenberg, *Sonderachten des Abgeordneten Schäffle über den preussisch-französischen Handelsvertrag* (1864), ibid., 598.
130. *Grenzboten*, 1860, vol. 20, 1–11, 41–53, ibid., 568.
131. *Grenzboten*, 1863, vol. 22, 322–3.
132. Ibid., 325–6.
133. Ibid., 329.
134. Ibid., 331.
135. Ibid.
136. A. E. Wollheim da Fonseca, *Einige politische Betrachtungen* (1862), in Rosenberg, *Publizistik*, 790; Michaelis, *Bericht*, ibid., 571–2; *Neue Preussische Zeitung*, 14 Apr. 1850.
137. *Berliner Revue*, 1858, vol. 13, 519–26, in Rosenberg, *Publizistik*, 561–2.
138. 'Die Bedürfnisse und Bedingungen der deutschen Handelspolitik', *Wochenschrift des Nationalvereins*, 8 May 1860, ibid., 567.
139. See, for instance, the editor of the *Bremer Handelsblatt* Arwed Emminghaus, *Entwicklung, Krisis und Zukunft des Detuschen Zollvereins* (Leipzig, 1863); A. Emminghaus, 'Die Zollvereinsfrage', *Unsere Zeit*, 1863, vol. 7, 465–514; anon., *Denkschrift für Handelsfreiheit an den zweiten deutschen Handelstag in München* (Hamburg, 1862); M. Wiggers, *Die mecklenburgische Steuerreform, Preussen und der Zollverein* (Berlin, 1862); and Onno Klopp, *An die Wähler des Königreichs* (Hanover, 1863), putting forward the government's case against that of the Progressive Party, but concurring in the importance of the *Zollverein*.
140. Wiggers, *Steuerreform*, 142.
141. W. Köster and L. A. Baum, *Denkschrift des Mannheimer Handelsvereins*

(1862); H. Schröder, *Über die handelspolitische Lage Deutschlands. Rede, gehalten in der Versammlung der Mitglieder des deutschen Nationalvereins zu Mannheim* (1862), in Rosenberg, *Publizistik,* 601–2.
142. Friesen, *Erinnerungen,* vol. 1, 338–9.
143. F. von Beust, *Erinnerungen zu Erinnerungen* (Leipzig, 1881), 35.
144. Georgi, June 1862, in Neemann, *Landtag,* 420.
145. For Württemberg, see Langewiesche, *Liberalismus und Demokratie,* 226–31, 424–43; on Bavarian public opinion's initial resistance, see W. Neuffer, *Einige Worte über den preussisch-französischen Handelsvertrag* (Regensburg, 1863); G. F. Rothenhöfer, *Fünf handelspolitische Briefe über die Entwicklung des Zollwesens und insbesondere des Zollvereins in Deutschland* (Munich, 1863); J. Haller, *Handelsvertrag und Zollverein* (Munich, 1863); G. Heinzelmann, *Altes und Neues aus der Handelsgeschichte von Deutschland, Österreich, England, Frankreich, Russland, Schweiz, den Ver. Staaten von Nord-Amerikas und über den preussisch-französischen Handeslvertrag* (Nördlingen, 1863).
146. Friesen, *Erinnerungen,* 100–1. See also Bernhardi, *Leben,* vol. 6, 101–2, who believed that once Saxony had backed the *Zollverein,* the North German customs' union was complete, and Bavaria and Württemberg could be left to their own devices, only to join the union later.
147. Fenske (ed.), *Reichsgründung,* 136.
148. Ibid.
149. O. von Bismarck, *Gedanken und Erinnerungen* (Essen, 2000), vol. 1, 116.
150. Fenske (ed.), *Reichsgründung,* 134.
151. Ibid.
152. Ibid.
153. Pflanze, *Bismarck,* vol. 1, 208–9.
154. Huber, *Verfassungsgeschichte,* vol. 3, 76.
155. Bismarck, *Gedanken,* vol. 1, 116.
156. Ibid., 117.
157. Ibid.
158. Ibid., 100.
159. Ibid., 102.
160. Ibid.
161. Ibid.
162. Ibid. Also, Gall, *Bismarck,* vol. 1, 132–5.
163. In Pflanze, *Bismarck,* vol. 1, 207.
164. Ibid., 204.
165. Ibid., 207.
166. In Huber (ed.), *Verfassungsgeschichte,* vol. 2, 57.
167. Ibid.
168. Ibid., 60.
169. Fenske (ed.), *Reichsgründung,* 278.
170. Ibid.
171. Ibid.
172. See Pflanze, *Bismarck,* vol. 1, 313.
173. Fenske (ed.), *Reichsgründung,* 263.

174. In Gall, *Bismarck*, vol. 1, 206.
175. Treitschke to Nokk, 29–30 Sept. 1862, ibid.
176. Reported by the *Berliner Allgemeine Zeitung*, ibid., 205.
177. Ibid., 202.
178. Pflanze, *Bismarck*, vol. 1, 311.
179. Twesten speech in the *Abgeordnetenhaus*, 22 Feb. 1866, in H. A. Winkler, *Preussischer Liberalismus und deutscher Nationalstaat* (Tübingen, 1964), 18.
180. In Gall, *Bismarck*, 206.
181. Samwer to Roggenbach, 17 Oct. 1862, in Gall, *Liberalismus als regierende Partei*, 223.
182. *Karlsruher Zeitung*, 22 Oct. 1862, ibid., 224–5.
183. Zschock to Duncker, 12 Apr. 1862, in Duncker, *Politischer Briefwechsel*, 332.
184. *Schwäbische Volkszeitung*, which replaced the *Schwäbische Zeitung* in 1865, 29 July 1865, in Langewiesche, *Liberalismus und Demokratie*, 379.
185. Elben, *Lebenserinnerungen*, 136.
186. *Schwäbische Volkszeitung*, 22 Mar. 1866, in Langewiesche, *Liberalismus und Demokratie*, 380.
187. Ibid., 381.
188. Ibid.
189. *Schwäbische Chronik*, 28 June 1866, ibid.
190. *Karlsruher Zeitung*, 22 Oct. 1862, in Gall, *Liberalismus als regierende Partei*, 225.
191. On Prussian expansionism, see *Historisch-politische Blätter*, 1857, vol. 40, 713–14, ibid., 1859, vol. 44, 160, ibid., 1862, vol. 50, 674; on centralisation, see ibid., 1857, vol. 39, 7, ibid., 1861, vol. 47, 335; on the state's Protestant nature, see ibid., 1852, vol. 30, 86–7, ibid., 1856, vol. 37, 657–8, ibid., 1856, vol. 38, 1123, ibid., 1861, vol. 48, 379–80; on militarism, see ibid, 1862, vol. 49, 369, 377; on Prussia's opposition to the third Germany and the *Bund*, see ibid., 1858, vol. 41, 242, ibid., 1861, vol. 48, 781–4, ibid., 1863, vol. 51, 146, 155.
192. Ibid., 1862, vol. 49, 419.
193. Ibid.
194. Ibid., 422.
195. Ibid., 435.
196. Ibid., 1862, vol. 50, 521–2.
197. Ibid., 524.
198. Ibid., 1863, vol. 51, 22.
199. Ibid., 141.
200. Ibid., 141–4.
201. See Pflanze, *Bismarck*, vol. 1, 174.
202. In Gall, *Bismarck*, vol. 1, 202. See also, Oetker, *Lebenserinnerungen*, vol. 3, 334.
203. Pflanze, *Bismarck*, vol. 1, 215.
204. Ludolf Parisius, 'Ein freies Wort an die preussischen Wähler' (1863), in Rosenberg, *Publizistik*, 508.
205. Bernhardi, *Leben*, vol. 5, 37.
206. J. Prince-Smith, 'An die Wähler zu Stettin' (1963), in Rosenberg,

NOTES

Publizistik, 508.
207. Pflanze, *Bismarck*, 215.
208. Ibid., 195.
209. In ibid., 198.
210. Ibid.
211. Ibid., 219.
212. Ibid.
213. Duncker to the Crown Prince, 22 September 1862, in Duncker, *Politischer Briefwechsel*, 340.
214. In Pflanze, *Bismarck*, 172.
215. Ibid. 196.
216. Ibid., 208.
217. See note 151.
218. R. Gneist, 'Rede des Abgeordneten Professor Dr. Gneist, gehalten in der 40. Plenarsitzung des Abgeordnetenhauses am 7. Mai 1863', in Rosenberg, *Publizistik*, 499.
219. E. Lasker, 'Über Verfassungsgeschichte und Fragen des Staatsrechts in Preussen', *Deutsche Jahrbücher für Politik und Literatur*, 1862, vol. 4, in Fenske (ed.), *Reichsgründung*, 255.
220. Jansen, *Einheit, Macht und Freiheit*, 446.
221. *Beobachter*, 14 Apr. 1866, in Langewiesche, *Liberalismus und Demokratie*, 380.
222. Fenske (ed.), *Reichsgründung*, 256.
223. In Gall, *Bismarck*, vol. 1, 223.
224. Ibid.
225. In H. Brunck, *Bismarck und das Preussische Staatsministerium 1862–1890* (Berlin, 2004), 98.
226. Kraus, *Gerlach*, 757–8.
227. Gall, *Bismarck*, vol. 1, 227.
228. In F. Stern, *Gold and Iron* (London, 1977), 29.
229. *Gartenlaube*, 1864, vol. 45, in Buschmann, *Einkreisung*, 149. On the paucity of reforms in the military constitution of the Confederation, see J. Angelow, *Von Wien nach Königgrätz* (Munich, 1996).
230. *Historisch-poliitsche Blätter*, 1863, vol. 51, 378.
231. Ibid., 1862, vol. 50, 687.
232. Jacoby, 'Rede' (1863), in Rosenberg, *Publizistik*, 509.
233. Schulze, speech to *Nationvalverein*, 16 Oct. 1863, and 31 Oct. 1864, in Thorwart (ed.), *Schulze-Delitzsch's Schriften und Reden*, vol. 3, 212 and 233.
234. Ibid., 233.
235. Ibid., 227.
236. Schulze, 16 Oct. 1863, ibid., 213.
237. Ibid.
238. Bismarck to Senfft-Pilsach, 17 Sept. 1863, in W. Windelband and W. Frauendienst (eds), *Bismarck. Gesammelte Werke* (Berlin, 1933), vol. 14, 653. Also, Pflanze, *Bismarck*, vol. 1, 199.
239. Sybel to Baumgarten, 26 May 1863, in Fenske (ed.), *Reichsgründung*, 276.
240. Baumgarten to Sybel, 22 May 1863, ibid., 274.

241. Bernhardi, *Leben*, vol. 5, 331.
242. In Oncken, *Bennigsen*, vol. 1, 574.
243. Ibid.
244. Unruh to Bennigsen, 26 Oct. 1865, ibid., 678.
245. Böhmert to Bennigsen, 29 Oct. 1864, ibid., 647.
246. R. von Mohl, *Lebenserinnerungen 1799–1875* (Stuttgart, 1902) 265.
247. Ibid., 263.
248. Ibid.
249. Bennigsen to Böhmert, 9 Nov. 1864, in Oncken, *Bennigsen*, vol. 1, 647–8.
250. Ibid., 683.
251. Ibid.
252. Ibid., 709.
253. Oetker, *Lebenserinnerungen*, vol. 3, 423.
254. Bennigsen to Roggenbach, 8 May 1866, in Oncken, *Bennigsen*, vol. 1, 706.
255. Oetker, *Lebenserinnerungen*, vol. 3, 423.
256. Baumgarten, *Liberalismus*, 107.
257. Ibid., 105.
258. Ibid., 110.
259. Ibid., 115.
260. Ibid., 118.
261. Ibid., 123.
262. Ibid.
263. Ibid., 124.
264. Ibid., 130.
265. Ibid., 130–1.
266. Ibid., 98.
267. Baumgarten to Sybel, 22 May 1863, in Fenske (ed.), *Reichsgründung*, 273–5.
268. A. Birke, 'Einleitung', ibid., 9.
269. Ibid., 110–11.
270. In Pflanze, *Bismarck*, vol. 1, 197.
271. K. A. Lerman, *Bismarck* (Harlow, 2004), 75–6. See, generally, 63–113.
272. In ibid., 72.
273. Ibid., 68.
274. In A. Kaernbach, *Bismarcks Konzepte zur Reform des Deutschen Bundes* (Göttingen, 1991), 189.
275. Ibid.
276. Bismarck to Below-Hohendorf, 18 Sept. 1861, in O. von Bismarck, *Deutscher Staat. Ausgewählte Dokumente* (Munich, 1925), 578.
277. Ibid.
278. Pflanze, *Bismarck*, vol. 1, 216.
279. Ibid.
280. On liberal fears of the population and reaction, see, for instance, Hoverbeck, ibid, 278: 'Are our people independent and perspicacious enough to find out by themselves what is right and especially in the face of such pressure? One could doubt it. It is very possible that through intimidation the reaction will conquer.'

281. Ibid., 195.
282. Bismarck, *Gedanken*, vol. 1, 129.
283. Kaernbach, *Bismarcks Konzepte*, 189.
284. Bismarck, *Deutscher Staat*, 277.
285. Kraus, *Gerlach*, 764.
286. L. Bucher, *Der Parlamentarismus wie er ist* (Berlin, 1855).
287. In Kaernbach, *Bismarcks Konzepte*, 133.
288. Bismarck, memorandum on the German question, July–Oct. 1861, in O. von Bismarck, *Die gesammelten Werke* (Berlin, 1924–32), eds G. Ritter and R. Stadelmann, vol. 3, 147.
289. Ibid., 269.
290. Kaernbach, *Bismarcks Konzepte*, 222.
291. Marginalia on Goltz to Bismarck, 13 Apr. 1866, ibid., 222.
292. Bismarck, *Deutscher Staat*, 210.
293. Gerlach, diary, 13 May 1854, in Kraus, *Gerlach*, 713.
294. In E. Feuchtwanger, *Bismarck* (London, 2002), 117.
295. Ibid., 69.
296. Bismarck, 22 Jan. 1864, in Bismarck, *Deutscher Staat*, 209–10.
297. Memorandum, July–Oct. 1861, in Stadelmann and Ritter (eds), *Bismarck. Gesammelte Werke*, vol. 3, 266.
298. Ibid., vol. 2, 317.
299. In Kaernbach, *Bismarcks Konzepte*, 133.
300. Bismarck to Manteuffel, 29 June 1851, ibid., 135.
301. Stadelmann and Ritter (eds), *Bismarck. Gesammelte Werke*, vol. 3, 147.
302. Ibid., 267.
303. Rechberg to Buol, 17 Mar. 1858, in Kaernbach, *Bismarcks Konzepte*, 133–4.
304. Feuchtwanger, *Bismarck*, 76.

Chapter 6

1. A. Bucholz, *Moltke and the German Wars, 1864–1871* (Basingstoke, 2001), 77.
2. G.Waitz, *Der neueste dänische Versuch in der Geschichte des Herzogthums Schleswig* (Göttingen, 1852), 1.
3. In Gall, *Liberalismus als regierende Partei*, 226.
4. Elben, *Lebenserinnerungen*, 73.
5. Diary, 14 May 1864, Bernhardi, *Leben*, vol. 6, 100.
6. Biefang, *Bürgertum*, 332.
7. Jansen, *Einheit, Macht und Freiheit*, 482.
8. Elben, *Lebenserinnerungen*, 136.
9. Biedermann, *Mein Leben*, 221.
10. 'Was nun weiter?', *Wochenschrift des Nationalvereins*, 6 Oct. 1864, in Rosenberg, *Publizistik*, 797.
11. 'Deutschlands Pflicht', *Wochenblatt des Deutschen Reformvereins*, 29 Nov. 1863, in ibid., 733.
12. J. Bärens, 'Schleswig-Holstein und Bundesreform' (Hanover, 1863), ibid., 710–11.

13. O. von Wydenbrugk, 'Die endgültige Lösung der schleswig-holsteinischen Frage', *Wochenblatt des Deutschen Reformvereins*, 22 Feb. 1863; 'Generalversammlung des Grossdeutschen Vereins zu Hannover am 24. November 1863', 'Deutschlands Pflicht', 'Schleswig-Holstein's Recht und dei Dritte Machtgruppe' and 'Zu Neujahr 1865', *Flugblatt des deutschen Reformvereins*, ibid., 707–8, 718–19, 733, 751, 809.

14. L. A. von Rochau, 'Wochenbericht', *Wochenschrift des Nationalvereins*, 11 Feb. 1864, 'Aus Mitteldeutschland', ibid., 31 Mar. and 16 June 1864; K. Brater, 'Politischer Bericht', *Flugblätter des deutschen Nationalvereins*, 31 Oct. 1864; 'Bismarck der Grosse', *Wochenschrift des Nationalvereins*, 19 Jan. 1865; 'Unsere Aufgabe', *Flugblatt des deutschen Reformvereins*, 29 Jan. 1865; Rochau, 'Wochenbericht', *Wochenschrift des Nationalvereins*, 9 Feb. 1865; 'Der Kampf in Preussen, der deutsche Liberalismus und Schleswig-Holstein', ibid., 16 Feb. 1865; 'Die liberale Partei in Preussen', *Wochenblatt des Nationalvereins*, 31 Aug. 1865; 'Wochenbericht', ibid., 31 Aug. 1865; 'Aus Süddeutschland', ibid., 31 Aug. and 7 Sept. 1865; 'Politischer Bericht', *Flugblätter des Deutschen Nationalvereins*, 29 Oct. 1865; 'An die Mitglieder des Nationalvereins', *Wochenblatt des Nationalvereins*, 17 May 1865, all in Rosenberg, *Publizistik*, 754, 766, 775–6, 804–5, 814–15, 816–18, 843, 850–1, 854–5, 935.

15. Anon., *Dänische Keckheit und deutsche Schwäche. Ein Mahnruf an das deutsche Volk* (Coburg, 1863), ibid., 717.

16. *Preussische Jahrbücher*, 1865, vol. 15, 85.

17. H. von Treitschke, 'Herr Biedermann und die Annexion' (1865), in H. von Treitschke, *Zehn Jahre Deutscher Kämpfe* (Berlin, 1874), 30.

18. *Grenzboten*, 1864, vol. 23, 161–76.

19. Ibid., 161–76, 201–14, 260–96.

20. *Kölnische Zeitung*, 15 Sept. 1850, in Buschmann, *Einkreisung*, 243.

21. Ibid.

22. *National-Zeitung*, 15 Sept., 18 and 28 Oct. 1850; *Allgemeine Zeitung*, 16 and 21 Oct. 1850; *Deutsches Volksblatt*, 18 and 21 July, 2 and 7 Aug. 1850, ibid., 244–8.

23. *Grenzboten*, 1849, vol. 8, 215–18, 355–7, 432; 1852, vol. 12, 225–7; 1853, vol. 13, 41–63; 1856, vol. 15, 14, 210–13; 1857, vol. 16, 397–8; 1858, vol. 17, 66–71, 330–3, 440–4, 481–97, pt. 2, 353, 481–90; 1859, vol. 18, 117, 479, pt. 2, 36–9, 78, 356–9; 1861, vol. 20, 341–7; 1864, vol. 23, 34–6, 77–80, 112–18, 356–60, 518–20, pt. 2, 76–80, 281–7, 348–53, 431–6.

24. *Historisch-politisch Blätter*, 1856, vol. 38, 1121–35; 1857, vol. 40, 693–714; 1858, vol. 41, 244–5; 1861, vol. 47, 4–23, 222–40.

25. For instance, *Grenzboten*, 1864, vol. 23, 116, or *Preussische Jahrbücher*, 1861, vol. 8, 428.

26. G. Waitz, *Kurze Schleswigholsteinische Landesgeschichte* (Kiel, 1864), 3. See Map 5.

27. Ibid., 4.

28. Ibid.

29. Ibid., 141–7.

30. Waitz, *Geschichte des Herzogthums Schleswig*, 5–10.
31. This is the thesis of J. G. Droysen, *Die Herzogthümer Schleswig-Holstein und das Königreich Dänemark*, 2nd edn (Hamburg, 1850), for instance.
32. Waitz, *Landesgeschichte*, 166.
33. Ibid., 3.
34. Ibid., 169.
35. W. Beseler, *Zur Schleswig-Holsteinischen Sache im August 1856* (Braunschweig, 1856), 59–62.
36. Waitz, *Landesgeschichte*, 179.
37. Ibid., 184–91.
38. Ibid., 191. Also, J. G. Droysen, 'Der Vertrag vom 8. Mai 1852' (1863), in J. G. Droysen, *Kleine Schriften zur Schleswig-Holsteinischen Frage*, 2nd edn (Berlin, 1863), 97, who dates attempts at incorporation back to the Treaty of London.
39. Beseler, *Sache*, 122.
40. Ibid., 149.
41. Ibid., 151.
42. *Preussische Jahrbücher*, 1865, vol. 15, 87–90.
43. In W. Carr, *The Wars of German Unification* (London, 1991), 74. Beust, *Aus drei Viertel-Jahrhunderten*, vol. 1, 338, rightly insisted that the action was not an execution because of the open-ended nature of the enquiry.
44. Carr, *Wars of German Unification*, 75. This point was made by the Austrian envoy to Dalwigk, 14 Jan. 1864, in Schüssler (ed.), *Dalwigk*, 159.
45. 'Die Geschichte der Bundesexekution gegen Dänemark und ihre europäische Umstände', *Historisch-politische Blätter*, 1863, vol. 52, 698–726.
46. Hohenlohe-Schillingsfürst, 18 Feb. 1864, in Curtius (ed.), *Denkwürdigkeiten*, vol. 1, 134.
47. Hohenlohe to Queen Victoria, 4 May 1864, ibid., 141.
48. Ibid.
49. Schüssler (ed.), *Dalwigk*, 164.
50. *Flugblätter des schleswig-holsteinischen Vereins zu Erlangen*, 1863, vol. 1; 1864, vols. 3, 4 and 5; *Verhandlungen der am 28. Februar 1864 zu Erlangen abgehaltenen bayerischen Landesversammlung für Schleswig-Holstein* (1864), in Rosenberg, *Publizistik*, 725, 759–61, 757.
51. *Allgemeine Zeitung*, 25 Nov. and 2 Dec. 1863.
52. 'Die Politik des deutschen Volkes', *Chronik der Gegenwart*, 1865, 289–97; J. Strobel, *Vorschläge zur Neugestaltung Deutschlands oder die deutsche Frage und ihre Lösung* (Munich, 1865), originally published in *Chronik der Gegenwart*, 1865, 913–14.
53. G. von Lerchenfeld, *Das Verfahren der deutschen Grossmächte gegen Schleswig-Holstein und den Bund* (Jena, 1866), 1–2.
54. Hohenlohe, 18 Feb. 1864, in Curtius (ed.), *Denkwürdigkeiten*, vol. 1, 134.
55. Ibid., 141–3.
56. Dalwigk, 5 Oct. 1864, Schüssler (ed.), *Dalwigk*, 145.
57. 16 Apr. 1864, ibid., 137–8.

58. 2 Mar. 1864, ibid., 136.
59. Friesen, *Erinnerungen*, vol. 2, 118.
60. 22 Apr. 1866, Schüssler (ed.), *Dalwigk*, 205.
61. Ibid.
62. 23 Apr. 1866, ibid., 206.
63. Hohenlohe to Queen Victoria, 4 May 1864, in Curtius (ed.), *Denkwürdigkeiten*, vol. 1, 143.
64. Hohenlohe to Victoria, 15 Apr. 1865, ibid., 144–5.
65. Ibid.
66. Ibid., 145.
67. Ibid., 144.
68. Ibid.
69. K. Brater, *Preussen und Bayern in der Sache der Herzogthümer* (Nördlingen, 1864), 2.
70. K. Brater, *Flugblätter des deutschen Nationalvereins* (1864), in Rosenberg, *Publizistik*, 804–5.
71. Brater, *Preussen*, 3, 10.
72. Brater, *Flugblätter*, in Rosenberg, *Publizistik*, 804.
73. *Wochenschrift der Fortschrittspartei in Bayern*, 30 June 1866, ibid., 969.
74. Ibid.
75. Hohenlohe, 15 Apr. 1865, in Curtius (ed.), *Denkwürdigkeiten*, vol. 1, 144.
76. Ibid.
77. 'Ungezählte Fragezeichen zum dritten Deutschland und zur französischen Allianz', *Historisch-politische Blätter*, 1864, vol. 53, 222–38. On Jörg's later career, see E. Fink, 'For Country, Court and Church: The Bavarian Patriots' Party and Bavarian Regional Identity in the Era of German Unification', in Speirs and Breuilly (eds), *Germany's Two Unifications*, 155–71, and F. Hartmannsgruber, *Die Bayerischer Patriotenpartei 1868–1887* (Munich, 1986).
78. *Historisch-politische Blätter*, 1864, vol. 53, 621–36.
79. Ibid.
80. 'Die Geschichte der Bundesexekution gegen Dänemark und ihre europäischen Umstände', ibid., 1863, vol. 52, 698–726.
81. Ibid.
82. Ibid., 1864, vol. 53, 148–9.
83. Ibid., 1865, vol. 55, 1–25.
84. Ibid, 1864, vol. 53, 222–38.
85. 'Deutschland vor der Londoner Conferenz und der Congress-Ära der Zukunft', ibid., 731–52.
86. Ibid., 474–7.
87. Ibid., 458–79.
88. Ibid., 137–53.
89. Ibid., 731–52.
90. Ibid.
91. Elben, *Lebenserinnerungen*, 140.
92. Ibid.
93. Beust, *Aus drei Viertel-Jahrhunderten*, vol. 1, 410–11; Biedermann, *Mein Leben*, 221–2, 226–8.

94. Ibid., 229.
95. Friesen, *Erinnerungen*, vol. 2, 100–1.
96. Neemann, *Landtag*, 464–87.
97. Biedermann, *Mein Leben*, 230.
98. Langewiesche, *Liberalismus und Demokratie*, 318.
99. Jansen, *Einheit, Macht und Freheit*, 492.
100. See Figure 4.1.
101. Langewiesche, *Liberalismus und Demokratie*, 353.
102. Schulze to Biedermann, in Biedermann, *Mein Leben*, vol. 2, 254.
103. Biefang, *Bürgertum*, 382.
104. Bennigsen to Nagel, 4 Sept. 1865, ibid., 376
105. Jansen, *Einheit, Macht und Freiheit*, 523.
106. Fetzer to Venedey, 22 and 27 Sept. 1865, ibid., 523.
107. Ibid., 515–16.
108. *Beobachter*, 4 and 5 July 1865, ibid., 516.
109. Ibid., 115.
110. *Beobachter*, 10 Feb. 1864, ibid., 318.
111. Ibid., 528–9.
112. K. Blind, 'An den Sechsunddreissiger Ausschuss zu Frankfurt', *Hermann: Deutsches Wochenblatt aus London*, 30 Jan. 1864.
113. G. Struve, *Diesseits und Jenseits des Oceans* (Coburg, 1864), vol. 2, in Rosenberg, *Publizistik*, 744.
114. Ibid., 744, 773–4.
115. In Jansen, *Einheit, Macht und Freiheit*, 454.
116. Ibid., 478.
117. Ibid., 445.
118. Ibid., 463.
119. Ibid., 462.
120. Treitschke, 'Herr Biedermann und die Annexion', 29–30.
121. C. Twesten, 2 Dec. 1863, in Fenske (ed.), *Reichsgründung*, 288.
122. B. Waldeck, 1 Dec. 1863, ibid., 285.
123. Ibid.
124. See Winkler, *Preussischer Liberalismus und deutscher Nationalstaat*, 45.
125. Ibid., 46.
126. *Social-Demokrat*, 21 Dec. 1864.
127. Ibid., and 27 Jan. 1865.
128. F. Engels, *Die preussische Militärfrage und die deutsche Arbeiterpartei* (Hamburg, 1865), in R. Dlublek and M. Steinke (eds), *Karl Marx Friedrich Engels Gesamtausgabe*, vol. 20 (Berlin, 2003), 75, 97, 107.
129. J. Venedey, 'Rede zur Begründung der Freiburger Zusätze zu den Frankfurter Vorschlägen für die Ostermontag-Versammlungen', *Wochenschrift des Nationalvereins*, 28 Mar. 1864; J. Venedey, *Rettung aus den 'einfach anarchischen' Zustände des deutschen Bundes* (Mülheim, 1864), in Rosenberg, *Publizistik*, 765–6, 753–4.
130. J. Fröbel, *Theorie der Politik* (Vienna, 1861–4), vol. 1, 142–58, vol. 2, 87–109, 225–45. See Chapter 6.
131. C. Vogt, *Andeutungen zur gegenwärtigen Lage* (Frankfurt, 1864), 28–32.
132. *Social-Demokrat*, 21 Dec. 1864.

133. Biefang, *Bürgertum*, 377.
134. In A. Heuss, *Theodor Mommsen und das 19. Jahrhundert* (Kiel, 1956), 173–5; T. Mommsen, *Die Annexion Schleswig-Holsteins* (Berlin, 1865).
135. H. von Treitschke, 'Die Lösung der schleswig-holsteinischen Frage', 15 Jan. 1865, in Treitschke, *Zehn Jahre*, 10, 25.
136. Treitschke, 'Herr Biedermann und die Annexion', 22 Feb. 1865, 29.
137. Duncker to Francke, 6 May 1865, in Duncker, *Politischer Briefwechsel*, Schultze, 388.
138. Ibid., 389.
139. Ibid., 390.
140. Diary, 28 Jan. 1866, Bernhardi, *Leben*, 225–6.
141. 17 May 1864, ibid., 110–11.
142. Ibid., 111–12.
143. Ibid., 111.
144. Ibid.
145. Baumgarten, *Liberalismus*, 101.
146. Ibid., 129.
147. *National-Zeitung*, 3 March 1864.
148. *Grenzboten*, 1864, vol. 23, 401–18, 456.
149. See, for instance, ibid., 112–18, 201–7.
150. 'Was gehört zur Lösung der schleswig-holsteinischen Frage?', *Preussische Jahrbücher*, 1863, vol. 12, 156–78.
151. 'Die Entscheidung der schleswig-holsteinischen Sache', ibid., vol. 4, 316–18.
152. *Grenzboten*, 1864, vol. 23, 431–6.
153. 'Annexion oder Anschluss der Herzogthümer', ibid., 1865, vol. 24, 77–80.
154. Ibid.
155. C. Rössler, 'Preussische Probleme für 1865', *Preussische Jahrbücher*, 1865, vol. 15, 316–25.
156. *National-Zeitung*, 3 Aug. 1864.
157. *Grenzboten*, 1864, vol. 23, pt 3, 1–9.
158. Elben, *Lebenserinnerungen*, 141.
159. Roggenbach, 28 Jan. 1862, in Gall, *Liberalismus als regierende Partei*, 217.
160. In H. Oncken (ed.), *Grossherzog Friedrich I. von Baden und die deutsche Politik von 1854–1871* (Stuttgart, 1927), vol. 1, 323.
161. Wilhelm I to Friedrich I, 2 Apr. 1862, ibid., 329–30.
162. Roggenbach to R. von Mohl, 2 Oct. 1862, in J. Heyderdorff (ed.), *Deutscher Liberalismus im Zeitalter Bismarcks* (Bonn, 1925), vol. 1, 118.
163. Friedrich I to Roggenbach, 5 Dec. 1863, in Gall, *Liberalismus in regierende Partei*, 251.
164. Oncken (ed.), *Friedrich*, vol. 1, 490–2.
165. Ibid.
166. R. von Mohl to J. Mohl, 11 May 1866, in Gall, *Liberalismus in regierende Partei*, 346.
167. Ibid., 348–9.
168. Ibid., 346.
169. Bluntschli, *Denkwürdiges aus meinem Leben* (Nördlingen, 1884), vol. 3,

137–9.
170. Mohl to Edelsheim, 30 Apr. 1865, in Gall, *Liberalismus in regierende Partei*, 347.
171. Ibid.
172. Baumgarten to Sybel, 11 May 1866, in J. Heyderhoff (ed.), *Deutscher Liberalismus im Zeitalter Bismarcks* (Bonn, 1925–6), vol. 1, 281–3.
173. Roggenbach to Bennigsen, 11 May 1866, in Oncken, *Bennigsen*, vol. 1, 707.
174. Bernhardi, *Leben*, 28 Apr. 1866, vol. 6, 299.
175. Ibid., 302.
176. Ibid., 302–3.
177. Diary, 28 Apr. 1866, recounting a meeting with Bismarck that evening, ibid., 304.
178. Ibid.
179. Andreas Biefang makes this point in *Bürgertum*, 400.
180. In ibid., 401.
181. Ibid., 101. The figure for 1866 of 5,314 was affected, to an extent, by the Austro-Prussian war.
182. Ibid., 401–2.
183. Biefang, *Bürgertum*, 310–430, emphasises the challenges posed by the debates more than the actual votes cast, in line with his thesis about the crisis and disintegration of the movement.
184. G. Waitz, *Das Recht des Herzogs Friedrichs von Schleswig-Holstein* (Göttingen, 1863); G. Waitz, *Über die angeblichen Erbansprüche des königlich-preussischen Hauses an die Herzogthümer Schleswig-Holstein* (Göttingen, 1864); G. Waitz, *Über die gegenwärtige Lage der schleswig-holsteinischen Angelegenheit* (Berlin, 1864); J. G. Droysen, 'Der Vertrag vom 8. Mai 1852', 94–101; H. A. Zachariä, *Staatsrechtliches Votum über die schleswig-holstein'sche Successionsfrage und das Recht des Augustenburgischen Hauses* (Göttingen, 1863); G. Beseler, *Der Londoner Vertrag vom 8. Mai 1852 in seiner rechtlichen Bedeutung geprüft*, 2nd edn (Berlin, 1863); H. Hälschner, *Staatsrechtliche Prüfung der gegen das Thronfolgerecht des Augustenburgischen Hauses erhobenen Einwände* (Berlin, 1864).
185. Treitschke, 'Herr Biedermann und die Annexion', 30.
186. H. von Treitschke, 'Die Parteien und die Herzogthümer' (Sep. 1865), in Treitschke, *Zehn Jahre*, 37.
187. Twesten, 2 Dec. 1863, in Fenske (ed.), *Reichsgründung*, 288.
188. Ibid.
189. Ibid.
190. Rochau, 'Wochenbericht', *Wochenschrift des Nationalvereins*, 2 Feb. 1865, in Rosenberg, *Publizistik*, 817.
191. This is implicit in both the tone and the argumentative strategy, more or less ignoring the possibility of a *Staatenbund*, of H. von Treitschke's 'Bundesstaat oder Einheitsstaat', in Treitschke, *Aufsätze*, 445–511.
192. In Kraus, *Gerlach*, 774.
193. L. von Gerlach, *Schleswig-Holstein* (Berlin, 1864), in Rosenberg, *Publizistik*, 748.

194. Kraus, *Gerlach*, 804.
195. Ibid., 775. '1848 and 1863!', *Neue Preussische Zeitung*, 16 Dec. 1863.
196. Kraus, *Gerlach*, 806.
197. *Neue Preussische Zeitung*, 8 May 1866.
198. Ibid.
199. Kraus, *Gerlach*, 802.
200. *Neue Preussische Zeitung*, 8 May 1866.
201. Twesten, ibid., 17 Apr. 1866.
202. Kraus, *Gerlach*, 785.
203. In Pflanze, *Bismarck*, vol. 1, 237.
204. Feuchtwanger, *Bismarck*, 117.
205. Pflanze, *Bismarck*, vol. 1, 246.
206. Bismarck, *Gedanken*, vol. 1, 164.
207. Ibid.
208. Feuchtwanger, *Bismarck*, 106, 101.
209. Ibid., 106.
210. Bismarck to Flemming, 22 Dec. 1862, in Gall, *Liberalismus in regierende Partei*, 228.
211. Feuchtwanger, *Bismarck*, 108.
212. Ibid., 107.
213. Gall, *Bismarck*, vol. 1, 245–6.
214. Ibid., 246.
215. This is the claim advanced by Gall, ibid.
216. Bismarck, *Gedanken*, vol. 1, 165.
217. Ibid., 165–6.
218. Feuchtwanger, *Bismarck*, 107.
219. Blanckenburg to Gerlach, 26 Nov. 1863, in Lerman, *Bismarck*, 100.
220. Gall, *Bismarck*, 246.
221. In Lerman, *Bismarck*, 97.
222. Ibid., 98.
223. Ibid.
224. Feuchtwanger, *Bismarck*, 103.
225. Ibid., 102. Gall, *Bismarck*, 247.
226. In Pflanze, *Bismarck*, vol. 1, 298.
227. Ibid., 148.
228. O. Pflanze, 'Bismarck and German Nationalism', *American Historical Review*, 60 (1955), 551.
229. In Gall, *Bismarck*, vol. 1, 232.
230. Pflanze, *Bismarck*, vol. 1, 299.
231. Bismarck to Keudell, 21 Sept. 1865, in Gall, *Bismarck*, 278.
232. Ibid.
233. Ibid., 232.
234. Pflanze, *Bismarck*, vol. 1, 284.
235. Ibid., 315. Also, Koch, *Teufel*, 460–2.
236. In Oncken, *Bennigsen*, vol. 1, 712.
237. Pflanze, *Bismarck*, vol. 1, 319–20.
238. Ibid., 320.
239. Ibid.
240. Bismarck used the term partly for the benefit of the Crown Prince,

ibid., 323.
241. Ibid.
242. Bismarck, 4 July 1866, ibid., 324. See Map 6.
243. Ibid., 305. On Austria, Pflanze, 'Bismarck and German Nationalism', 553–4.
244. Pflanze, *Bismarck*, vol. 1, 305.
245. Friedrich Wilhelm to his mother, 29 July 1866, in Lerman, *Bismarck*, 125.

Conclusion

1. In H. A. Winkler, '1866 und 1878. Der Machtverzicht des Bürgertums', in H. A. Winkler and C. Stern (eds), *Wendepunkte deutscher Geschichte 1848–1945* (Frankfurt, 1979), 37–60; K.-G. Faber, 'Realpolitik als Ideologie', *Historische Zeitschrift*, 203 (1966), 1–45.
2. This interpretation differs from the widely cited thesis about a German Civil War put forward by James Sheehan, *German History, 1770-1866* (Oxford, 1989), 899–911.
3. *Historisch-politische Blätter*, 1866, vol. 58, 953–72; *Preussische Jahrbücher*, 1866, vol. 17, 684. The term 'civil war' was sometimes used strategically after the event. See, for instance, Bennigsen on 12 Mar. 1867: 'It was not a great popular movement but a civil war which removed the old conditions', in Oncken, *Bennigsen*, vol. 2, 46. Likewise, the Crown Prince used the term just before war broke out, but mainly to deter the King of Prussia from backing a bellicose policy, in Lerman, *Bismarck*, 104.
4. *Preussische Jahrbücher*, 1866, vol. 17, 573. Buschmann, *Einkreisung*, 269–307, argues that taboo was the dominant element.
5. The accusation was levelled at opponents: *Preussische Jahrbücher*, 1866, vol. 17, 687; *Neue Preussische Zeitung*, 21 June and 11 July 1866; *Social-Demokrat*, 8 July 1866. In May 1866, the *Abgeordnetentag* had 'damned the threatening conflict as a cabinet war serving only dynastic interests', in Pflanze, *Bismarck*, vol. 1, 319.
6. Bismarck to Karolyi, Dec. 1862, in Gall, *Bismarck*, vol. 1, 214.
7. *Historisch-politische Blätter*, 1866, vol. 58, 781.
8. *Social-Demokrat*, 1 July 1866.
9. Ibid., 10 Aug. 1866.
10. Ibid.
11. Ibid., 16 Aug. 1866.
12. Article 1 of the *Reichsverfassung* stipulated that 'the position of the Duchy of Schleswig remains to be determined', Hucko (ed.), *Tradition*, 79.
13. In W. Carr, *The Origins of the Wars of German Unification* (London, 1991), 127.
14. Hucko (ed.), *Tradition*, 79.
15. *Historisch-politische Blätter*, 1866, vol. 58, 315.
16. Ibid., 323, 318.

17. Ibid., 625–6.
18. Ibid., 782.
19. Ibid., 786.
20. Ibid., 782–3.
21. *Kölnische Blätter*, 18–19 June 1866.
22. Ibid., 1 Aug. 1866.
23. Ibid.
24. Wigard (ed.), *Stenographischer Bericht*, vol. 1, 4.
25. Huber (ed.), *Verfassungsdokumente*, vol. 1, 341–2.
26. Mohl, *Lebenserinnerungen*, vol. 2, 269, 274, 277.
27. Ibid., 277.
28. Ibid., 266.
29. Mohl to Edelsheim, 20 Jan. 1866, in Müller, *Bund*, 375.
30. Ibid., 376–7.
31. Bismarck spelled out the two 'systems', one 'constitutional', the other an adaptation of the *Engerer Rat* of the *Bundestag*, which would give the King of Prussia and himself similar powers, in the second 'Putbus dictate' on 19 Nov. 1866, in Fenske (ed.), *Reichsgründung*, 341–3.
32. R. von Delbrück, *Lebenserinnerungen* (Leipzig, 1905), vol. 2, 378.
33. Ibid.
34. See Chapter 7.
35. Delbrück, *Lebenserinnerungen*, 378–9.
36. Hanoverian National Liberal election committee, 31 Dec. 1866, in Oncken, *Bennigsen*, vol. 2, 15; Waldeck speech in the Constituent Assembly, 9 Mar. 1867, in Fenske (ed.), *Reichsgründung*, 352.
37. Twesten, 9 Mar. 1867, Fenske, *Reichsgründung*, 347.
38. Ibid.
39. Ibid., 347–8.
40. Sybel speech to the Constituent Assembly, 23 Mar. 1867, ibid., 360–3.
41. Pflanze, *Bismarck*, vol. 2, 131.
42. Oncken, *Bennigsen*, vol. 2, 59, 48.
43. Bennigsen to his wife, 3 Mar. 1867, ibid., 29.
44. National Liberal programme, 12 June 1867, ibid., 81.
45. Wigard, *Stenographische Bericht*, vol. 1, 4.
46. Ibid.
47. Radowitz, 27 July 1848, ibid., vol. 2, 1156.
48. Rochau, *Grundsätze der Realpolitik*, 228.
49. Ibid., 225.
50. Hucko (ed.), *Tradition*, 105, 114.
51. Vick, *Defining Germany*, 110–38.
52. Gagern, in Wigard (ed.), *Stenographischer Bericht*, 20 Mar. 1849, vol. 8, 5885.
53. Otto Gildemeister, in D. Blackbourn, *Germany, 1780–1918* (London, 1997), 272.
54. Treitschke, 'Bundesstaat', 471.
55. Ibid.
56. This is one of the main theses of Abigail Green's *Fatherlands*.
57. Ketteler, 20 Feb. 1862, in Paupié, *Handbuch*, vol. 2, 65.

58. Mohl, *Staatsrecht*, vol. 2, 7; Stahl, *Parteien*, 71.
59. Rochau, *Grundsätze der Realpolitik*, 228; Langewiesche, *Liberalismus und Demokratie*, 225. See L. Gall, 'Liberalismus und "bürgerliche Gesellschaft"', *Historische Zeitschrift*, 220 (1975), 324–56.
60. Rochau, *Gründsätze der Realpolitik*, 53.
61. K. Koszyk, *Deutsche Presse im 19. Jahrhundert* (Berlin, 1966), 143.
62. Brophy, 'The Public Sphere', 206.
63. R. Hachtmann, *Epochenschwelle zur Moderne* (Tübingen, 2002); W. Schieder, '1848/49: Die ungewollte Revolution', in C. Stern and H. A. Winkler (eds), *Wendepunkte deutscher Geschichte 1848–1990* (Frankfurt, 1994), 17–42; D. Blackbourn and G. Eley, *Mythen deutscher Geschichtsschreibung* (Frankfurt a. M., 1980); J. J. Breuilly, 'The Failure of the Revolution of 1848', *European Studies Review*, 1 (1981), 103–16; T. Nippedey, 'Kritik oder Objektivität?', in T. Nipperdey, *Gesellschaft, Kultur, Theorie* (Göttingen, 1976), 259–78; D. Langewiesche (ed.), *Die deutsche Revolution von 1848/49* (Darmstadt, 1983).
64. Siemann, *Deutschlands Ruhe, Sicherheit und Ordnung*; Siemann, *Gesellschaft im Aufbruch*, 25–88.
65. This is one of the principal conclusions of the nuanced works of Winkler, *Liberalismus*, Gall, *Liberalismus*, and Langewiesche, *Liberalismus und Demokratie*. The latter has modified his view in *Liberalism in Germany* (Basingstoke, 2000), 56–120.
66. In Winkler, '1866 und 1878', 44.
67. D. Langewiesche, 'Kulturelle Nationsbildung im Deutschland des 19. Jahrhunderts', in Langewiesche, *Nation, Nationalismus, Nationalstaat*, 82–102.
68. Treitschke, 'Bundesstaat', 465.
69. D. Langewiesche, '"Revolution von oben"?', 117–33. E. Fehrenbach, 'Bonapartismus und Konservatismus in Bismarcks Politik', in K. Hammer and P. C. Hartmann (eds), *Der Bonapartismus* (Munich, 1977), 39–55; L. Gall, 'Bismarck und der Bonapartismus', *Historische Zeitschrift*, 223 (1976), 618–32; H.-U. Wehler, 'Bonapartismus oder charismatische Herrschaft', in H.-U. Wehler, *Gegenwart als Geschichte* (Munich, 1994), 72–83.
70. Lutz, *Zwischen Habsburg und Preussen*, 227–486; H. Lutz and H. Rumpler (eds), *Österreich und die deutsche Frage im 19. und 20. Jahrhundert* (Munich, 1982); H. Rumpler (ed.), *Deutscher Bund und deutsche Frage 1815–66* (Munich, 1990); Müller, *Bund*; Flöter, *Beust*; Green, *Fatherlands*; Hanisch, *Fürst* ; Biefang, *Bürgertum*, 357–435.
71. Gall, *Liberalismus*, 460.
72. H. Grebing, *Der 'deutsche Sonderweg' in Europa 1806–1946* (Stuttgart, 1986), 102.
73. Hohenlohe, in Huber (ed.), *Verfassungsdokumente*, vol. 3, 683.
74. In the modified position of the 'Bielefeld school', the *Kaiserreich* is still seen as a contradictory, polycratic and repressive regime of authoritarian and charismatic rule. The classic statement is Hans-Ulrich Wehler's *Deutsche Gesellschaftsgeschichte*, the relevant volume of which – revealingly – runs from 1849 to 1914, linking a 'German

double revolution' before 1871/73 – the industrial revolution and the 'political revolution of the *Reichsgründung* "from above"' – to the consolidation of the German Empire after 1871.

75. For the relevant legal and political literature, see M. Hewitson, 'The *Kaiserreich* in Question', *Journal of Modern History*, 73 (2001), 725–80.

76. See Introduction. Also, M. Jefferies, *Contesting the German Empire* (Oxford, 2008); J. Kocka, 'Nach dem Ende des Sonderwegs', in A. Bauernkämper et al. (eds), *Doppelte Zeitgeschichte* (Berlin, 1998); C. Schönberger, 'Die überholte Parlamentarisierung', *Historische Zeitschrift*, 272 (2001), 623–66; M. L. Anderson, *Practicing Democracy* (Princeton, NJ, 2000); G. Eley (ed.), *Society, Culture and the State in Germany* (Ann Arbor, 1996); K. Jarausch and L. E. Jones (eds), *In Search of a Liberal Germany* (Oxford, 1990); J. R. Dukes and J. Remak (eds), *Another Germany* (Boulder, CO, 1988).

Select Bibliography*

Primary Sources

PRESS

Allgemeine Zeitung
Frankfurter Zeitung
Die Gartenlaube
Germania
Die Grenzboten
Hermann
Historisch-politische Blätter
Kölnische Blätter
Kölnische Zeitung
Kölnische Volkszeitung
National-Zeitung
Neue Preussische Zeitung
Neue Rheinische Zeitung
Preussische Jahrbücher
Rheinische Volkshalle
Der Social-Demokrat

TREATISES AND ARTICLES

L. K. Aegidi, *Preussen und der Friede von Villafranca* (Berlin, 1859).
—, *Der deutsche Kern der italienischen Frage* (Leipzig, 1859).
—, *Vorwände und thatsachen* (Berlin, 1862).
L. Bamberger, *Juchhe nach Italia* (Frankfurt, 1859), in L. Bamberger, *Gesammelte Schriften* (Berlin, 1913), vol. 3, 168–7.
H. Baumgarten, *Historische und politische Aufsätze und Reden* (Strasbourg, 1894).

---

* For a full bibliography, see the author's website, http://www.ucl.ac.uk/german/aboutus/staff/hewitson.htm

—, *Der deutsche Liberalismus* . *Eine Selbskritik* (Frankfurt a. M., 1974).

L. Bergsträsser (ed.), *Der politische Katholizismus* (Munich, 1921), vol. 1.

— (ed.), *Das Frankfurter Parlament in Briefen und Tagebüchern* (Frankfurt a. M., 1929).

G. Beseler, *Der Londoner Vertrag vom 8. Mai*, 2nd edn (Berlin, 1863).

W. Beseler, *Zur östreichischen Frage* (Leipzig, 1860).

—, *Zur Schleswig-Holsteinischen Sache im August 1856* (Braunschweig, 1856).

M. A. von Bethmann-Hollweg, *Reaction und Sonderthümlerei* (Berlin, 1848).

A. Bienengräber, *Statistik des Verkehrs und Verbrauchs im Zollverein für die Jahre 1841–1864* (Berlin, 1868).

R. Blum, *Volkstümliches Handbuch der Staatswissenschaften und Politik*, 2 vols (Leipzig, 1848–51).

—, *Politische Schriften* (Nendeln, 1979), vol. 6, ed. S. L. Gilman.

J. C. Bluntschli (ed.), *Deutsches Staatswörterbuch*, 11 vols (Stuttgart, 1857–70).

—, *Charakter und Geist der politischen Parteien* (Nördlingen, 1869).

—, 'Die nationale Statenbildung und der moderne deutsche Stat', in J. C Bluntschli, *Gesammelte kleine Schriften* (Nördlingen, 1881), vol. 2.

K. Brater, *Preussen und Bayern in der Sache der Herzogthümer* (Nördlingen, 1864).

L. Bucher, *Der Parlamentarismus wie er ist* (Berlin, 1855).

L. Camphausen, *König Friedrich Wilhelms IV. Briefwechsel mit Ludolf Camphausen*, ed. E. Brandenburg (Berlin, 1906).

G. Cohn, *Über die Bedeutung der Nationalökonomie und ihre Stellung im Kreise der Wissenschaften* (Berlin, 1869).

W. Corvinus (ed.), *Radowitz' ausgewählte Schriften* (Regensburg, 1911), vol. 2.

C. von Czoernig, *Oesterreichs Neugestaltung, 1848–1858* (Stuttgart, 1858).

F. C. Dahlmann, *Die Politik* (Frankfurt a. M., 1997).

— and G. Waitz (eds), *Quellenkunde der Deutschen Geschichte*, 4th edn (Göttingen, 1875).

—, *Kleine Schriften und Reden* (Stuttgart, 1886).

J. C. Droysen, *Politische Schriften*, ed. F. Gilbert (Munich, 1933).

—, *Aktenstücke und Aufzeichnungen zur Geschichte der Frankfurter Nationalversammlung*, ed. R Huebner (Osnabrück, 1967).

—, *Die Herzogthümer Schleswig-Holstein und das Königreich Dänemark*, 2nd edn (Hamburg, 1850).

—, *Kleine Schriften zur Schleswig-Holsteinischen Frage*, 2nd edn (Berlin, 1863).

F. Engels, *Die preussische Militärfrage und die deutsche Arbeiterpartei* (Hamburg, 1865), in R. Dlublek and M. Steinke (eds), *Karl Marx Friedrich Engels Gesamtausgabe*, vol. 20 (Berlin, 2003).

H. Fenske (ed.), *Der Weg zur Reichsgründung* (Darmstadt, 1976).

J. Ficker, *Das Deutsche Kaiserreich in seinen universalen und nationalen Beziehungen* (Innsbruck, 1862).

A. Fischhof and J. Unger, *Zur Lösung der ungarischen Frage* (Vienna, 1861).

C. Frantz, *Die Konstitutionellen*, 3rd edn (Berlin, 1851).

—, *Kritik aller Parteien* (Berlin, 1862).

—, , *Literarisch-politische Aufsätze* (Munich, 1876).

G. Freytag, *Bilder aus der Deutschen Vergangenheit*, 7th edn, 4 vols (Leipzig, 1872–3).

J. Fröbel, *System der sozialen Politik*, 2nd edn (Mannheim, 1847).

—, *Theorie der Politik*, 2 vols (Vienna, 1861–4).

H. von Gagern, *Das Leben des Generals Friedrich von Gagern*, 3 vols (Leipzig, 1856–7).

L. von Gerlach, *Von der Revolution zum Norddeutschen Bund*, ed. H. Diwald, 2 vols (Goettingen, 1970).

G. G. Gervinus, *Einleitung in die Geschichte des neunzehnten Jahrhunderts* (Leipzig, 1853).

—, *Geschichte des neunzehnten Jahrhunderts seit den Wiener Verträgen*, 8 vols (Leipzig, 1855–66).

R. Gneist, *Berliner Zustände* (Berlin, 1849).

J. Haller, *Handelsvertrag und Zollverein* (1863).

L. Häusser, *Denkwürdigkeiten zur Geschichte der badischen Revolution* (Heidelberg, 1851).

D. Hansemann, *Das Preussische und Deutsche Verfassungswerk* (Berlin, 1850).

F. Hecker, *Die Erhebung des Volkes in Baden für die deutsche Republik im Früjahr 1848* (Basel, 1848).

A. H. L. Heeren, *Ideen über die Politik*, 4th edn (Berlin, 1826).

G. Heinzelmann, *Altes und Neues aus der Handelsgeschichte von Deutschland, Österreich, England, Frankreich, Russland, Schweiz, den Ver. Staaten von Nord-Amerikas und über den preussisch-französischen Handelsvertrag* (Nördlingen, 1863).

E. R. Huber (ed.), *Dokumente zur deutschen Verfassungsgeschichte*, 3 vols (Stuttgart, 1961–6).

V. A. Huber, *Bruch mit der Revolution und Ritterschaft* (Berlin, 1852).

—, *Die Machtfülle des altpreussischen Königthums und die conservative Partei* (Bremen, 1862).

E. Iserloh (ed.), *Wilhelm Emmanuel von Ketteler 1811–1877* (Paderborn, 1990).

J. Jacoby, *Gesammelte Schriften und Reden*, 2 vols (Hamburg, 1977).

—, *Die Grundsätze der preussischen Demokratie* (1859).

W. E. von Ketteler, *Deutschland nach dem Kriege von 1866* (Mainz, 1867).

—, 'Der moderne Liberalismus. Absolutismus unter dem Scheine der Vernunft' (1862), in W. E. von Ketteler, *Werke* (Mainz, 1977), vol. 1.

O. Klopp, *Die gothaische Auffassung der deutschen Geschichte und der Nationalverein*, 2nd edn (Hanover, 1862).

K. Knies, 'Die Wissenschaft der Nationalökonomie seit Adam Smith bis auf die Gegenwart', *Gegenwart*, 1852, vol. 7.

—, *Die politische Ökonomie vom Standpunkte* (Braunschweig, 1853).

G. F. Kolb, *Culturgeschichte der Menschheit*, 2 vols (Leipzig, 1869–70).

G. Küntzel (ed.), *Politische Aufsätze und Briefe von Paul Achatius Pfizer* (Frankfurt, 1924).

E. Lasker, *Zur Verfassungsgeschichte Preussens* (Leipzig, 1874).

F. Lassalle, *Der italienische Krieg und die Aufgabe Preussens* (Berlin, 1859).

—, *Die Feste, die Presse und der Frankfurter Abgeordnetentag* (Berlin, 1863).

—, *Macht und Recht* (Berlin, 1863).

H. Laube, *Das erste deutsche Parlament*, (Leipzig, 1849).

H. Leo, *Nominalistische Gedankenspäne* (Halle, 1864).

—, *Vorlesungen über die Geschichte des deutschen Volkes und Reiches*, 5 vols (Halle, 1854–67).

—, *Studien und Skizzen zu einer Naturlehre des Staats* (Halle, 1833).

G. von Lerchenfeld, *Das Verfahren der deutschen Grossmächte gegen Schleswig-Holstein und den Bund* (Jena, 1866).

W. Liebknecht, *Leitartikel und Beiträge in der Osnabrücker Zeitung 1864–1866* (Hildesheim, 1975).

R. von Mohl, *Die Geschichte und Literatur der Staatswissenschaften*, 3 vols (Erlangen, 1855–8).

—, *Politische Schriften* (Cologne, 1966).

—, *Staastrecht, Voelkerrecht und Politik*, 3 vols (Tübingen, 1860–9).

—, *Encyclopädie der Staatswissenschaften* (Tübingen, 1859).

T. Mommsen, *Die Annexion Schleswig-Holsteins* (Berlin, 1865).

W. Neuffer, *Einige Worte über den preussisch-französischen Handelsvertrag* (Regensburg, 1863).

H. B. Oppenheim, *Deutschlands Noth und Ärzte* (Berlin, 1859).

—, *Deutsche Begeisterung und Habsburgischer Kronbesitz* (Berlin, 1859).

A. Peez, *Deutschland am Wendepunkt seiner Geschicke* (Wiesbaden, 1859).

P. A. Pfizer, *Zur deutschen Verfassungsfrage* (Stuttgart, 1862).

—, 'Nord- und Süddeutschland in ihrem Verhältniss zur Einheit Deutschlands', *Germania*, 1 (1851).

J. Prince-Smith, *Gesammelte Schriften*, 3 vols (Berlin, 1877).

F. von Raumer, *Zur Politik des Tages* (Leipzig, 1859).

R. von Raumer, *Vom Deutschen Geiste* (Erlangen, 1866).

A. and P. Reichensperger, *Deutschlands nächste Aufgaben* (Paderborn, 1860).

W. H. Riehl, *Die Naturgeschichte des deutschen Volkes*, abr. edn (Leipzig, 1934).

L. A. von Rochau, *Grundsätze der Realpolitik* (Frankfurt a. M., 1972).

— and G. Ölsner-Monmerqué, *Das Erfurter Parlament und der Berliner Fürsten-Congress* (Leipzig, 1850).

W. Roscher, *Grundlagen der Nationalökonomie* (Stuttgart, 1854).

C. Rössler, *Preussen und die italienische Frage* (Berlin, 1859).

—, *Die bevorstehenden Krisis der preussischen Verfassung* (Berlin, 1862).

G. F. Rothenhöfer, *Fünf handelspolitische Briefe über die Entwicklung des Zollwesens und insbesondere des Zollvereins in Deutschland* (Munich, 1863).

A. Ruge, *Der Patriotismus* (Frankfurt a. M., 1968).

—, *Die drei Völker und die Legitimität* (London, 1860).

F. Rümelin, *Aus der Paulskirche* (Stuttgart, 1892).

—, *Reden und Aufsätze*, 3 vols (Freiburg, n.d.).

A. Schäffle, *Das gesellschaftliche System der menschlichen Wirtschaft*, 3rd edn (Tübingen, 1873), vol. 1.

J. Scherr, *Deutsche Cultur- und Sittengeschichte*, 5th edn (Leipzig, 1873).

J. Schmidt, *Geschichte der deutschen Literatur seit Lessings Tod*, 5th edn (Leipzig, 1867), vol. 3.

G. Schmoller, *Der französische Handelsvertrag und seine Gegner* (Frankfurt a. M., 1862)

H. Schulze-Delitzsch, *Gesammelte Schriften und Reden*, 5 vols (Berlin, 1909).

J. B. Schweitzer, *Widerlegung von Carl Vogt's Studien zur gegenwärtigen Lage Europas* (Frankfurt, 1859).

—, *Der einzige Weg zur Einheit* (Frankfurt, 1860).

—, *Die österreichische Spitze* (Leipzig, 1863).
H. Simon, *Don Quixote der Legitimität oder Deutschlands Befreier?* (Zurich, 1859).
F. J. Stahl, *Die gegenwärtigen Parteien in Staat und Kirche* (Berlin, 1863).
—, *Das Monarchische Princip* (Heidelberg, 1845).
—, *Die Revolution und die constitutionelle Monarchie* (Berlin, 1848).
—, *Was ist die Revolution?* (Berlin, 1852).
—, *Die Philosophie des Rechtes*, 2 vols (Heidelberg, 1854–6).
—, *Die deutsche Reichsverfassung nach den Beschlüssen der deutschen Reichsversammlung und nach dem Entwurf der drei königlichen Regierungen* (Berlin, 1849).
L. von Stein, *Zur preussischen Verfassungsfrage* (Darmstadt, 1961).
—, *System der Staatswissenschaft*, 2 vols (Stuttgart, 1856).
G. Struve, *Geschichte der drei Volkserhebungen in Baden* (Berne, 1849).
H. von Sybel, *Die deutsche Nation und das Kaiserreich* (Düsseldorf, 1862).
—, *Über den Stand der neueren deutschen Geschichtsschreibung* (Marburg, 1856).
—, *Vorträge und Aufsätze* (Berlin, 1874).
—, *Kleine historische Schriften* (Munich, 1863).
H. von Treitschke, *Die Gesellschaftswissenschaft* (Leipzig, 1859).
—, *Zehn Jahre Deutscher Kämpfe 1865–1874* (Berlin, 1874).
—, *Historische und politische Aufsätze* (Leipzig, 1865).
K. Twesten, *Woran uns gelegen ist* (Kiel, 1859).
—, *Was uns noch retten kann* (Berlin, 1861).
J. Venedey, *Der italienische Krieg und die deutsche Volkspolitik* (Hanover, 1859).
C. Vogt, *Studien zur gegenwärtigen Lage Europas* (Geneva, 1859).
W. Wachsmuth, *Geschichte deutscher Nationalität* (Braunschweig, 1860), vol. 1.
G. Waitz, *Grundzüge der Politik* (Kiel 1862).
—, *Der neueste dänische Versuch in der Geschichte des Herzogthums Schleswig* (Göttingen, 1852).
—, *Kurze Schleswigholsteinische Landesgeschichte* (Kiel, 1864).
—, *Das Recht des Herzogs Friedrichs von Schleswig-Holstein* (Göttingen, 1863).
—, *Über die angeblichen Erbansprüche des königlich-preussischen Hauses an die Herzogthümer Schleswig-Holstein* (Göttingen, 1864).
—, *Über die gegenwärtige Lage der schleswig-holsteinischen Angelegenheit* (Berlin, 1864).
T. Waitz, *Anthropologie der Naturvölker*, 2nd edn (Leipzig, 1877).
C. T. Welcker (ed.), *Staatslexikon*, 3rd edn, 14 vols (Leipzig, 1856–66).
—, *Die letzten Gründe von Recht, Staat und Strafe* (Giessen, 1813).
M. Wiggers, *Die mecklenburgische Steuerreform, Preussen und der Zollverein* (Berlin, 1862).
L. Windthorst, *Ausgewählte Reden des Staatsministers a.D. und Parlamentariers Dr Ludwig Windthorst*, 2 vols (Osnabrück, 1901–2).
A. Wuttke, *Deutsche Volksaberglaube der Gegenwart*, 2nd edn (Berlin, 1869).

MEMOIRS AND CORRESPONDENCE

E. M. Arndt, *Briefe*, 3 vols (Darmstadt, 1972–5).
—, *Ein Lebensbild in Briefen*, ed. H. Messner (Berlin, 1898).
—, *Meine Wanderungen und Wandelungen mit dem Reichsfreiherrn Heinrich Karl Friedrich von Stein*, 2nd edn (Berlin, 1858).

L. Bamberger, *Erinnerungen*, ed. P. Nathan (Berlin, 1899).

F. D. Bassermann, *Denkwürdigkeiten 1811–1855* (Frankfurt a.M., 1926).

W. Baumgarten (ed.), *Akten zur Geschichte des Krimkriegs* (Munich, 1990–1), vol. 2.

A. Bebel, *Aus meinem Leben*, 3rd edn (Berlin, 1961).

T. von Bernhardi, *Aus dem Leben Theodor von Bernhardis*, 2 vols (Leipzig, 1897).

E. Bernstein, *My Years of Exile* (London, 1921).

G. Beseler, *Erlebtes und Erstrebtes 1809–1859* (Berlin, 1884).

F. F. von Beust, *Drei Viertel-Jahrhunderten*, 2 vols (Stuttgart, 1887).

——, *Erinnerungen zu Erinnerungen* (Leipzig, 1881).

K. Biedermann, *Erinnerungen aus der Paulskirche* (Leipzig, 1849).

——, *Mein Leben und ein Stück Zeitgeschichte*, 2 vols (Breslau, 1886–7).

O. von Bismarck, *Die gesammelte Werke*, 15 vols (Berlin, 1923–33).

——, *Gedanken und Erinnerungen*, 3 vols (Essen, 2000).

——, *Deutscher Staat* (Munich, 1925).

J. C. Bluntschli, *Denkwürdiges aus meinem Leben*, ed. R. Segerlen, 3 vols (Nördlingen, 1884).

S. Born, *Erinnerungen eines Achtundvierzigers*, ed. J Schütz (Berlin, 1978).

M. von Bunsen, *Georg von Bunsen* (Berlin, 1900).

M. Busch, *Tagebuchblätter*, 3 vols (Leipzig, 1899).

W. Cahn (ed.), *Aus Eduard Laskers Nachlass* (Berlin, 1902).

R. von Delbrück, *Lebenserinnerungen 1817–1867*, 2 vols (Leipzig, 1905).

G. von Diest, *Aus dem Leben eines Glücklichen* (Berlin, 1904).

I. von Döllinger, *Briefwechsel 1820–1890*, ed. V. Conzemius, 4 vols (Munich, 1963–81).

——, *The Pope and the Council* (Boston, 1870).

J. C. Droysen, *Briefwechsel*, 2 vols (Stuttgart, 1929).

A. Duckwitz, *Denkwürdigkeiten aus meinem öffentlichen Leben von 1841 bis 1866* (Bremen, 1877).

M. Duncker, *Politischer Briefwechsel aus seinem Nachlass*, ed J. Schultze (Stuttgart, 1923).

J. von Eckhart, *Lebenserinnerungen*, 2 vols (Leipzig, 1910).

O. Elben, *Lebenserinnerungen, 1823–1899* (Stuttgart, 1931).

H. von Feder, *Die Revolution und die Partei des gesetzlichen Fortschritts in Baden* (Karlsruhe, 1850).

G. Freytag, *Erinnerungen aus meinem Leben* (Leipzig, 1887).

O. B. Friedmann, *Zehn Jahre österreichischer Politik 1859–1869* (Vienna, 1879).

Friedrich Wilhelm IV, *Aus dem Briefwechsel Friedrich Wilhelms IV. mit Bunsen* (Leipzig, 1873).

——, *König Friedrich Wilhelms IV. Briefwechsel mit Ludolf Camphausen* (Berlin, 1906).

R. von Friesen, *Erinnerungen aus meinem Leben*, 2 vols (Dresden, 1880).

J. Fröbel, *Ein Lebenslauf*, 2 vols (Stuttgart, 1890–1).

H. von Gagern, *Briefe und Reden 1815–48* (Göttingen, 1959).

E. L. von Gerlach, *Aufzeichnungen aus seinem Leben und Wirken 1795–1877*, ed. J. von Gerlach, 2 vols (Schwerin, 1903).

——, *Politik und Ideengut der preussischen Hochkonservativen: Tagebuch 1848–1866* (Göttingen, 1970), vol. 1, ed. H. Diwald.

L. von Gerlach, *Denkwürdigkeiten aus dem Leben Leopold von Gerlachs, Generals der Infanterie und General-Adjutanten Koenig Friedrich Wilhelms IV* (Berlin, 1891).

—, *Briefe des Generals Leopold von Gerlach an Otto von Bismarck*, ed. H. Kohl (Stuttgart, 1912).

G. G. Gervinus, *Leben, von ihm selbst* (Leipzig, 1893).

K. Haenchen (ed.), *Revolutionsbriefe 1848* (Leipzig, 1930).

J. Hansen (ed.), *Rheinische Briefe und Akten zur Geschichte der politischen Bewegung*, 2 vols (Osnabrück, 1967).

M. Hartmann, *Revolutionäre Erinnerungen*, ed. H. H. Houben (Leipzig, 1919).

R. Haym, *Ausgewählter Briefwechsel Rudolf Hayms*, ed H. Rosenberg (Stuttgart 1930).

—, *Aus meinem Leben. Erinnerungen* (Berlin, 1902).

W. Heindl (ed.), *Die Protokolle des österreichischen Ministerrates 1848–1867*, 19 vols (Vienna, 1970–2003).

M. Herwegh (ed.), *Briefe von und an Georg Herwegh* (Munich, 1896).

J. Heyderdorff, and P Wentzcke (eds), *Deutscher Liberalismus im Zeitalter Bismarcks*, 2 vols (Bonn, 1925–6).

H. Hirsch, *August Bebel* (Reinbek, 1973).

L. Höbelt (ed.), *Österreichs Weg zur konstitutionellen Monarchie* (Frankfurt a. M., 1994).

Prinz Kraft zu Hohenlohe-Ingelfingen, *Aus meinem Leben*, 4 vols (Berlin, 1897–1907).

C. zu Hohenlohe-Schillingsfürst, *Denkwürdigkeiten*, 2 vols (Stuttgart, 1907).

E. Ippel (ed.), *Briefwechsel zwischen Jacob und Wilhelm Grimm, Dahlmann und Gervinus*, 2 vols (Berlin, 1885–6).

J. Jacoby, *Briefwechsel 1816–1849* (Hanover, 1974).

J. E. Jörg, *Briefwechsel 1846–1901*, ed. D. Albrecht (Mainz, 1988).

Johann, König von Sachsen. *Briefwechsel zwischen König Johann von Sachsen und den Königen Friedrich Wilhelm IV und Wilhelm I von Preussen*, (Leipzig, 1911).

—, *Lebenerinnerungen des Königs Johann von Sachsen* (Göttingen, 1958).

F. Kapp, *Vom radikalen Frühsozialisten des Vormärz zum liberalen Parteipolitiker des Bismarckreichs*, ed. H.-U. Wehler (Frankfurt, 1969).

W. von Klopp, *Onno Klopp* (Osnabrück, 1907).

G. F. Kolb, *Lebenserinnerungen eines liberalen Demokraten 1808–1884*, ed. L. Merckle (Freiburg, 1976).

H. Langwerth von Simmern, *Aus meinem Leben*, 2 vols (Berlin, 1898).

F. Lassalle, *Reden und Schriften*, ed. F. Jenaczek (Munich, 1970).

—, *Ferdinand Lassalle*, ed. H. J. Frederici (Berlin, 1991).

H. von Lerchenfeld-Koefering, *Erinnerungen und Denkwürdigkeiten* (Berlin, 1935).

F. Lewald, *Erinnerungen aus dem Jahre 1848*, ed. D. Schäfer (Frankfurt a. M., 1969).

O. von Manteuffel, *Unter Friedrich Wilhelm IV*, ed. H. von Poschinger, 3 vols (Berlin, 1901).

L. von der Marwitz (ed.) *Vom Leben am preussischen Hofe 1815–1852* (Berlin, 1908).

K. Mathy, *Aus dem Nachlass von Karl Mathy* (Leipzig, 1898).

J. K. Mayr (ed.), *Das Tagebuch des Polizeiministers Kempen von 1848 bis 1859* (Vienna, 1931).

J. F. M. O. Meding, *Memoiren zur Zeitgeschichte* (Leipzig, 1881–4).

R. von Mohl, *Lebenserinnerungen 1799–1875*, 2 vols (Stuttgart, 1902).

J. Müller (ed.), *Quellen zur Geschichte des Deutschen Bundes* (Munich, 1998), vol. 3.

F. Oetker, *Lebenserinnerungen*, 3 vols (Stuttgart, 1877–85).

H. Oncken (ed.), *Grossherzog Friedrich I von Baden und die deutsche Politik von 1854–1871*, 2 vols (Stuttgart, 1927).

C. H. A. Pagenstecher, *Lebenserinnerungen*, 3 vols (Leipzig, 1913).

J. von Radowitz, *Nachgelassene Briefe und Aufzeichnungen zur Geschichte der Jahre 1848–53* (Stuttgart, 1922).

—, *Gesammelte Schriften*, 5 vols (Berlin, 1852–3).

—, *Ausgewählte Schriften und Reden*, ed. F. Meinecke (Munich, 1921).

L. von Ranke, *Tagebücher*, ed. W. P. Fuchs (Munich, 1964).

—, *Das Briefwerk*, ed. W. P. Fuchs (Hamburg, 1949).

F. von Raumer, *Lebenserinnerungen und Briefwechsel*, 2 vols (Leipzig, 1861).

—, *Briefe aus Frankfurt und Paris 1848–49* (Leipzig, 1849).

W. Real (ed.), *Karl Friedrich von Savigny*, 2 vols (Boppard, 1981).

—, *Katholizismus und Reichsgründung. Neue Quellen aus dem Nachlass Karl Friedrich von Savigny* (Paderborn, 1988).

P. Reichensperger, *Erlebnisse eines alten Parlamentariers im Revolutionsjahre 1848* (Berlin, 1882).

A. L. Reyscher, *Erinnerungen aus alter und neuer Zeit 1802–1880* (Freiburg, 1884).

A. von Roon, *Denkwürdigkeiten*, 3 vols (Breslau, 1897).

K. Rosenkranz, *Politische Briefe und Aufsätze, 1848–1856*, ed. P. Herre (Leipzig, 1919).

A. Ruge, *Briefwechsel und Tagebuchblätter aus den Jahren 1825–1880*, 2 vols (Berlin, 1886).

J. Schondorff (ed.), *Varnhagen von Ense, Friedrich Fürst Schwarzenberg* (Munich, 1960).

K. Schorn, *Lebenserinnerungen*, 2 vols (Bonn, 1898).

H. Schröter (ed.), *Briefe Ludwig Windthorsts an seinen Schwager Ferdinand Engelen 1834–1868* (Hanover, 1954).

H. Schulze-Delitzsch, *Schriften und Reden*, ed. F. Thorwart, 5 vols (Berlin, 1909–13).

W. Schüssler (ed.), *Die Tagebücher des Freiherrn Reinhard von Dalwigk zu Lichtenfels aus den Jahren 1860–1871* (Stuttgart, 1920).

L. F. Seyffardt, *Erinnerungen* (Leipzig, 1900).

W. von Siemens, *Lebenserinnerungen* (Berlin, 1892).

A. Struve, *Erinnerungen aus den badischen Freiheitskämpfe* (Hamburg, 1850).

G. Stüve (ed.), *Johann Carl Bertram Stüve nach Briefen und persönlichen Erinnerungen*, 2 vols (Hanover, 1900).

—, *Briefwechsel zwischen Stüve und Detmold in den Jahren 1848 bis 1850* (Hanover, 1903).

J. C. B. Stüve, *Briefe*, ed. W Vogel, 2 vols (Göttingen, 1959–60).

J. D. H. Temme, *Erinnerungen* (Leipzig, 1883).

R. von Thadden-Trieglaff, *Erinnerungen an den Fürsten Bismarck*, ed. E. Marcks et al. (Berlin, 1924).

H. V. von Unruh, *Erinnerungen* (Stuttgart, 1895).

—, *Erfahrungen aus den letzten drei Jahren* (Magdeburg, 1851).

—, *Skizzen aus Preussens neuester Geschichte* (Magdeburg, 1849).

K. A. Varnhagen von Ense, *Tagebücher*, 14 vols (Leipzig, 1861–70).

—, *Kommentare zum Zeitgeschehen* (Leipzig, 1984).

R. Virchow, *Briefe an seine Eltern 1839 bis 1864*, ed. M. Rahl, 2nd edn (Leipzig, 1907).

C. Vogt, *Aus meinem Leben* (Stuttgart, 1896).

H. Wagener, *Erlebtes*, 2 vols (Berlin, 1884).

K. Wappler, *Regierung und Presse* (Leipzig, 1935).

J. Wiggers, *Aus meinem Leben* (Leipzig, 1901).

Wilhelm I., *Briefe an seine Schwester Alexandrine und Grossherzog Friedrich Franz II* (Berlin, 1928).

Secondary Sources

The principal introductions to the period are by Wolfram Siemann, *Gesellschaft im Aufbruch* (Frankfurt, 1990) and *Vom Staatenbund zum Nationalstaat* (Munich, 1995), both of which draw on his earlier work, *Deutschlands Ruhe, Sicherheit und Ordnung* (Tübingen, 1985). General works with an emphasis on the 1850s and 1860s include H. A. Winkler, *Der lange Weg nach Westen* (Munich, 2000); C. Clark, *Iron Kingdom* (London, 2006); T. Nipperdey, *Deutsche Geschichte 1800–1866* (Munich, 1983); E. D. Brose, *German History, 1789–1871* (Providence, RI, 1997); W. J. Mommsen, *Das Ringen um den nationalen Staat* (Berlin, 1993); H.-U. Wehler, *Deutsche Gesellschaftsgeschichte 1849–1914* (Munich, 1995), and the classics by T. S. Hamerow, *Restoration, Revolution, Reaction* (Princeton, NJ, 1958) and *The Social Foundations of German Unification, 1858–1871*, 2 vols (Princeton, NJ, 1969–72). For further reading on 1848, see R. Hachtmann, *Epochenschwelle zur Moderne* (Tübingen, 2002) and *Berlin 1848* (Bonn, 1997), W. Siemann, *The German Revolution of 1848–49* (London, 1998), and F. L. Müller, *Die Revolution 1848/49* (Wiesbaden, 2002).

On the diplomatic context of German nationalism, W. E. Mosse, *The European Powers and the German Question, 1848–71* (New York, 1969), H. Friedjung, *The Struggle for Supremacy in Germany, 1859–1866*, reissued edn (New York, 1966), and P. W. Schroeder, *Austria, Great Britain and the Crimean War* (Ithaca, NY, 1972) are now complemented by A. Doering-Manteuffel, *Die deutsche Frage und das europäische Staatensystem 1815–1871*, 2nd edn (Munich, 2001); F. R. Bridge, *The Habsburg Monarchy among the Great Powers, 1815–1918* (Oxford, 1990); J. Angelow, *Vom Wiener Kongress zur Pariser Konferenz* (Göttingen, 1991); N. Buschmann, *Einkreisung und Waffenbruderschaft* (Göttingen, 2003), and F. J. Müller, *Britain and the German Question* (Basingstoke, 2002). The 'German question' and German Confederation are treated extensively: J. Müller, *Deutscher Bund und deutsche Nation 1848–1866* (Göttingen, 2005); J. Angelow, *Der Deutsche Bund*

(Darmstadt, 2003) and *Von Wien nach Königgrätz* (Munich, 1996); J. Flöter, *Beust und die Reform des Deutschen Bundes 1850–1866* (Cologne, 2001); H. Müller, 'Deutscher Bund und Deutsche Nationalbewegung', *Historische Zeitschrift*, 248 (1989), 51–78; H. Rumpler (ed.), *Deutscher Bund und deutsche Frage 1815–1866* (Vienna, 1990) and *Die deutsche Politik des Freiherrn von Beust 1848–50* (Vienna, 1972); B. B. Hayes, *Bismarck and Mitteleuropa* (Rutherford, NJ, 1994); H.-W. Hahn, *Geschichte des Deutschen Zollvereins* (Göttingen, 1984), and W. Real, *Der Deutsche Reformverein* (Lübeck, 1966). On the wars of unification, see A. Bucholz, *Moltke and the German Wars, 1864–1871* (Basingstoke, 2001); W. Carr, *The Wars of German Unification* (London, 1991); S. Förster and J. Nagler (eds), *On the Road to Total War* (Cambridge, 1997); G. A. Craig, *The Battle of Königgrätz* (Philadelphia, PA, 1964); G. Wawro, *The Austro-Prussian War* (Cambridge, 1996) and *The Franco-Prussian War* (Cambridge, 2003), and M. Howard, *Franco-Prussian War*, 2nd edn (London, 2001).

A good literature exists on individual states, with notable gaps: A. Green, *Fatherlands* (Cambridge, 2001); G. Grünthal, *Parlamentarismus in Preussen 1848/49–1857/58* (Düsseldorf, 1982); H. A. Winkler, *Preussischer Liberalismus und deutscher Nationalstaat* (Tübingen, 1964); M. Levinger, *Enlightened Nationalism* (Oxford, 2000); J. Brophy, *Capitalism, Politics, and the Railroads in Prussia, 1830–1870* (Columbus, OH, 1998); B.-C. Padtberg, *Rheinischer Liberalismus in Köln während der politischen Reaktion in Preussen nach 1848/49* (Cologne, 1985); H. Brandt, *Parlamentarismus in Württemberg 1815–1870* (Düsseldorf, 1987); D. Langewiesche, *Liberalismus und Demokratie in Württemberg von der Revolution bis zur Reichsgründung* (Düsseldorf, 1974); L. Gall, *Liberalismus als regierende Partei* (Wiesbaden, 1968); S. Wolf, *Konservatismus im liberalen Baden* (Karlsruhe, 1990); M. Hanisch, *Für Fürst und Vaterland* (Munich, 1991); T. Schieder, *Die kleindeutsche Partei in Bayern in den Kämpfen um die nationale Einheit 1863–1871* (Munich, 1936); A. Neemann, *Landtag und Politik in der Reaktionszeit* (Düsseldorf, 2000) and 'Models of Political Participation in the Beust Era', in J. Retallack (ed.), *Saxony in German History* (Ann Arbor, MI, 2000), 119–34; N. M. Hope, *The Alternative to German Unification* (Wiesbaden, 1973); M. John, 'Liberalism and Society in Germany, 1850–1880', *English Historical Review*, 102 (1987), 579–98, and 'National and Regional Identities and the Dilemmas of Reform in Britain's "Other Province"', in L. Brockliss and D. Eastwood (eds), *A Union of Multiple Identities* (Manchester, 1997), 179–92, and M. Ritter, *Die Bremer und ihr Vaterland. Deutscher Nationalismus in der Freien Hansestadt 1859–1913* (Berlin, 2004).

The Habsburg monarchy is one of the main foci of Heinrich Lutz, *Zwischen Habsburg und Preussen* (Berlin, 1985). On diplomacy and government, see the various articles of Roy Austensen, especially 'Austria and the "Struggle for Supremacy in Germany", 1848–64', *Journal of Modern History*, 52 (1980), 195–225; P. W. Schroeder, 'Bruck versus Buol', *Journal of Modern History*, 55 (1968), 193–217; P. J. Katzenstein, *Disjointed Partners* (Berkeley, CA, 1976); S. Lippert, *Felix Fürst zu Schwarzenberg* (Stuttgart, 1998), and H. Rumpler, (ed.), *Österreich und die deutsche Frage im 19. und 20. Jahrhundert* (Munich, 1982). On domestic politics and nationalism, see R. Okey, *The Habsburg Monarchy, c. 1765–1918* (Basingstoke, 2001); P. Judson, *Exclusive Revolutionaries* (Ann Arbor, MI, 1996); R. A. Kann, *The Multinational Empire,*

2 vols (New York, 1977); J. Boyer, *Political Radicalism in Late Imperial Vienna* (Chicago, 1981); E. Somogyi, *Vom Zentralismus zum Dualismus. Der Weg der deutschösterreichischen Liberalen zum Ausgleich von 1867* (Wiesbaden, 1983), and G. Stourzh, *Die Gleichberechtigung der Nationalitäten in der Verfassung und Verwaltung Österreichs 1848–1918* (Vienna, 1985).

Some political parties and milieux are better covered than others. Prussian conservatism is treated extensively from various points of view: D. E. Barclay, *Frederick William IV and the Prussian Monarchy, 1840–1861* (Oxford, 1995); D. Blasius, *Friedrich Wilhelm IV 1759–1861* (Göttingen, 1992); O. Pflanze, *Bismarck and the Development of Germany*, 3 vols (Princeton, NJ, 1963), and 'Bismarck and German Nationalism', *American Historical Review*, 60 (1955), 548–66; Gall, *Bismarck*, 2 vols (London, 1986) and 'Bismarck und der Bonapartismus', *Historische Zeitschrift*, 223 (1976), 618–32; K. A. Lerman, *Bismarck* (Harlow, 2004); E. Feuchtwanger, *Bismarck* (London, 2002); A. Kaernbach, *Bismarcks Konzepte zur Reform des Deutschen Bundes* (Göttingen, 1991) and 'Bismarcks Bemühungen um eine Reform des deutschen Bundes 1849–1866', in O. Hauser (ed.), *Preussen, Europa und das Reich* (Cologne, 1987), 199–221; H.-C. Kraus, *Ernst Ludwig von Gerlach*, 2 vols (Göttingen, 1994); W. Füssl, *Professor in der Politik: Friedrich Julius Stahl 1802–1861* (Göttingen, 1998); E. Trox, *Militärischer Konservatismus* (Stuttgart, 1990); G. A. Craig, 'Portrait of a Political General: Edwin von Manteuffel', *Political Science Quarterly*, 66 (1951), 1–36, and L. Dehio, 'Edwin von Manteuffels politische Ideen', *Historische Zeitschrift*, 131 (1925), 41–71.

Liberal thought and programmes in the 1850s and 1860s have been examined in U. Backes, *Liberalismus und Demokratie* (Düsseldorf, 2001); A. Lees, *Revolution and Reflection* (The Hague, 1974); J. J. Breuilly, *Labour and Liberalism in Nineteenth-Century Europe* (Manchester, 1992), and J. J. Sheehan, *German Liberalism in the Nineteenth Century* (Chicago, 1978), as well as through a large number of biographies. On liberal parties and milieux, the seminal work, particularly for its examination of liberal nationalism, is Andreas Biefang, *Politisches Bürgertum in Deutschland 1857–1868* (Düsseldorf, 1994); also, G. Eisfeld, *Die Entstehung der liberalen Parteien in Deutschland 1858–1870* (Hanover, 1969); D. Langewiesche, *Liberalism in Germany* (Basingstoke, 2000); L. Gall, *Bürgertum in Deutschland* (Berlin, 1989), 'Der deutsche Liberalismus zwischen Revolution und Reichsgründung', *Historische Zeitschrift*, 228 (1979), 98–108, and 'Liberalismus und "bürgerliche Gesellschaft"', *Historische Zeitschrift*, 220 (1975), 324–56; V. Hentschel, *Die deutschen Freihändler und der volkswirtschaftliche Kongress 1858 bis 1885* (Stuttgart, 1975); S. Na'aman, *Der Deutsche Nationalverein* (Düsseldorf, 1987), and L. O'Boyle, 'The German Nationalverein', *Journal of Central European Affairs*, 16 (1957), 333–52.

On radicalism and democracy, see the work of Christian Jansen, especially *Einheit, Macht und Freiheit* (Düsseldorf, 2000), and Jonathan Sperber, *Rhineland Radicals* (Princeton, NJ, 1991), in conjunction with relevant biographies. For further reading on the early socialist and labour movement, see S. Berger, *Social Democracy and the Working Class in Nineteenth and Twentieth-Century Germany* (London, 2000). See also W. Conze and D. Groh, *Die Arbeiterbewegung in der nationalen Bewegung* (Stuttgart, 1966); H. Mommsen, *Arbeiterbewegung und nationale Frage* (Göttingen, 1979); H.-U.

Wehler, *Sozialdemokratie und Nationalstaat* (Göttingen, 1971), and D. Groh
and P. Brandt, *Vaterlandslose Gesellen* (Munich, 1992). On political
Catholicism, see J. Sperber, *Popular Catholicism in Nineteenth-Century Germany*
(Princeton, NJ, 1984); M. Gross, *The War against Catholicism* (Ann Arbor, MI,
2004); E. Heinen, 'Das katholische Vereinswesen in der Rheinprovinz und
in Westfalen 1848–1855', in W. Becker and R. Morsey (eds), *Christliche
Demokratie in Europa* (Cologne, 1988), 29–58; K.-E. Lönne, *Politischer
Katholizismus im 19. und 20. Jahrhundert* (Frankfurt, 1986), and T. Mergel,
Zwischen Klasse und Konfession (Göttingen, 1994).

The public sphere has recently attracted attention: J. Brophy, *Popular
Culture and the Public Sphere in the Rhineland, 1800–1850* (Cambridge, 2007),
'The Common Reader in the Rhineland', *Past and Present*, 185 (2004),
119–58, and 'The Public Sphere', in J. Sperber (ed.), *Germany, 1800–1870*
(Oxford, 2004), 185–208; A. Green, 'Intervening in the Public Sphere',
Historical Journal, 44 (2001), 155–175; G. Eley, 'Nations, Publics, and
Political Cultures', in C. Calhoun (ed.), *Habermas and the Public Sphere*
(Cambridge, MA, 1992), 289–339. On the press, see U. von Hirschhausen,
Liberalismus und Nation. Die Deutsche Zeitung 1847–1850 (Düsseldorf, 1998);
J. Fröhlich, *Die Berliner Volkszeitung 1853–1867* (Frankfurt a. M., 1990); M.
Behnen, *Das Preussische Wochenblatt 1851–1861* (Göttingen, 1971); K.
Belgum, *Popularising the Nation* (Lincoln, NE, 1998); J. C. Struckmann,
*Staatsdiener als Zeitungsmacher. Die Geschichte der Allgemeinen Preussischen
Staatszeitung* (Berlin, 1981); R. Kohnen, *Pressepolitik des Deutschen Bundes*
(Tübingen, 1995), and K. Koszyk, *Deutsche Presse im 19. Jahrhundert* (Berlin,
1966).

The foundational work on early nineteenth-century nationalism is Jörn
Echternkamp, *Der Aufstieg des deutschen Nationalismus* (Frankfurt a. M.,
1998) and, on 1848, Brian Vick, *Defining Germany* (Cambridge, MA, 2002).
The theses of M. Hughes, *Nationalism and Society* (London, 1988); H. James,
A German Identity, 1770–1990 (London, 1989), and H.-U. Wehler, 'Der
deutsche Nationalismus bis 1871', in H.-U. Wehler (ed.), *Scheidewege der
deutschen Geschichte* (Munich, 1995), 116–30, can be balanced against S.
Berger, *Germany: Inventing the Nation* (London, 2004); E. Fehrenbach,
Verfassungsstaat und Nationsbildung 1815–1871 (Munich, 1992); H. Schulze,
Der Weg zum Nationalstaat (Munich, 1985); J. J. Breuilly, *Austria, Prussia and
Germany, 1806–1871* (London, 2002), *The Formation of the First German
Nation-State, 1800–1871* (London, 1996) and (ed.), *The State of Germany*
(London, 1992); O. Dann, *Nation und Nationalismus in Deutschland
1770–1990* (Munich, 1993), (ed.), *Nationalismus und sozialer Wandel*
(Hamburg, 1978), (ed.), *Vereinswesen und bürgerliche gesellschaft in
Deutschland* (Munich, 1984), and 'Der revolutionäre Weg zum Nationalstaat
in Deutschland', in G. Krebs und G. Schneilin (eds), *La naissance du Reich*
(Paris, 1995); D. Langewiesche, *Nation, Nationalismus, Nationalstaat in
Deutschland und Europa* (Munich, 2000); G. Eley, 'State Formation,
Nationalism and Political Culture', in G. Eley, *From Unification to Nazism*
(London, 1986), 61–84. On individual questions, see A. Fahrmeir, *Citizens
and Aliens* (New York, 2000) and 'Nineteenth-Century German Citizenship',
Historical Journal, 40 (1997), 721–52; D. Gosewinkel, *Einbürgern und
Ausschliessen* (Göttingen, 2001); H. C. Meyer, *Mitteleuropa in German Thought*

and Action, 1815–1945 (The Hague, 1955); A. Wandruszka, 'Grossdeutsche und kleindeutsche Ideologie 1840–1871', in R. A. Kann and F. E. Prinz (eds), *Deutschland und Österreich* (Vienna, 1980), 110–42; M. Hettling and P. Nolte (eds), *Bürgerliche Feste* (Göttingen, 1993); D. Düding et al. (eds), *Öffentliche Festkultur* (Reinbek, 1988); S. Goltermann, *Körper der Nation* (Göttingen, 1998); B. E. Dencker, 'Popular Gymnastics and the Military Spirit in Germany, 1848–1871', *Central European History*, 34 (2001), 503–30; H. Gramley, *Propheten des deutschen Nationalismus* (Frankfurt, 2001), and B. Giesen, *Die Intellektuellen und die Nation* (Frankfurt, 1993).

Glossary

Abendland	West
Abgeordnetenversammlung	assembly of deputies
Abgeordnetenhaus	Chamber of Deputies
Allgemeine Deutsche Arbeiterverein	General German Workers' Association
Anschluss	merger or fusion
Anzeiger	advertiser or newspaper
Arbeiterbildungsvereine	workers' education associations
Ausland	abroad
Bildungsbürgertum	educated middle classes
Bruderkrieg	war of brothers
Bundesgebiet	territory belonging to the German Confederation
Bundesgenossen	fellow member of the Confederation
Bundesgericht	confederal court
Bundeskanzler	Chancellor or representative of the Confederation
Bundeskrieg	war involving the Confederation
Bundesrat	Federal Council in the North German Confederation and German Empire
Bundesreaktionsbeschluss	reactionary decree of the Confederation
Bundesreform	reform of the Confederation
Bundesstaat(en)	federal state
bundesstaatlich	federal
bundesstaatliche Einheit	federal unity
Bundestag	Diet of the Confederation, meeting at Frankfurt, usually referring to both the plenary and inner councils
Bundesverfassung	constitution of the Confederation
Bundesverhältniss	confederal relationship
Bundesversammlung	assembly of the Confederation, usually referring to the full assembly rather than the inner council (*Engerer Rat*)

438

Bündnis	alliance
Bürgerkrieg	civil war
Bürgerlich	civic or bourgeois
Bürgertum	middle classes or bourgeoisie
Burschenschaft(en)	student association/s
Constitution	constitution
constitutionell	constitutional
Demokratie	democracy
Deutsche Fortschrittspartei	German Progressive Party
Deutsche Partei	German Party
Deutscher Handelstag	German Trade Association
Deutscher Journalistentag	German Association of Journalists
Deutscher Juristentag	German Association of Lawyers
Deutscher Protestantenverein	German Union of Protestants
Deutschland	Germany
Dreikönigsbündnis	Three Kings' Alliance
Einheit	unity
einheitlich	united
Einheitstaat	unitary state
Einigung	unification
Engerer Rat	inner council of the Confederation
Erbkaiserlichen	supporters of a hereditary German emperor
Erbkaisertum	hereditary emperorship
Erhebung	uprising
Existenzfrage	existential question or crisis
Föderation	confederation
föderativ	confederal
Föderativstaat	confederal state
Föderativsystem	confederal system
Fortschrittspartei	Progressive Party (see German Progressive Party)
freisinnig	liberal or progressive
freisinniger	liberal supporters of the fatherland
Vaterlandsfreunde	
Fürstenkongress	congress of princes
Fürstentag	Congress of Princes (1863)
Geheimbund	secret society
Geldaristokratie	aristocracy of wealth or finance
Gemeinschaft	community
Gesamtdeutschland	the whole of Germany
Gesamteintritt	entry of the Habsburg monarchy in its entirety into the *Zollverein* or Confederation
Gesamtkörper	a body in its entirety
Gesamtministerium	full ministry

Gesamtmonarchie	Habsburg monarchy in its entirety
Gesamtstaat	state in its entirety
Gesamtvaterland	whole fatherland
Gesamtverfassung	constitution for all of Germany
Gesamtvertretung	assembly for the whole of Germany
Gleichberechtigung	equality of rights
Glieder	organs (of a state or nation)
grossdeutsch	greater German
Grossdeutscher	advocate of greater Germany
Grossdeutschland	greater Germany
Grossdeutschtum	greater Germanness
Grossösterreich	greater Austria
Grossösterreicher	supporter of a greater Austria
Grosspreussisch	greater Prussia
Grundrechte	basic rights
Handelsbund	commercial union
Handelstag	see *Deutscher Handelstag*
Heimat	home region
Heimatland	homeland
Herrenhaus	House of Lords
Hofapotheke	apothecary (by royal appointment)
Hofkriegsrat	royal war council
Intelligenzblätter	newspapers
jeder Deutsche	every German
jeder Staatsangehörige	every citizen
Junkerparlament	'Junkers' parliament' (convened during the revolution of 1848-49 in Prussia)
Junkertum	Junkerdom
Kadettenschule	cadet school
Kaiser	emperor
Kaiseridee	the idea of emperorship
Kaiserreich	empire
Kaiserstaat	imperial state
Kaisertum	emperorship
Kleindeutsch	small German
Kleindeutschland	small Germany
Kleinstaaten	small states
Kleinstaaterei	petty statehood
Kleinstaatler	supporters of small or petty states
Klerikale	clerics or the clerical party
Konfliktslandtag	'conflict assembly' (in Prussia during the early 1860s)
Kongress deutscher Volkswirte	Congress of German Economists
Konstituierung	constituting (of)

Kreis	local administrative unit
Kreuzzeitungspartei	conservatives in Prussia close to the
Kreuzzeitung	newspaper
Kulturkampf	'cultural struggle' of liberals and officials against the Catholic church in Germany during the 1870s
Kulturvolk	a cultured or civilised people or nation
Kultusminister	Minister of Religious Affairs
Kuriatstimmen	the votes of small states within curia or electoral colleges in the Confederation
Landesversammlung	assembly of a land or state
Landmannschaft	regionally defined student association
Landrat/Landräte	regional official/s
Landtag(e)	state assembly/assemblies
Landwehr	territorial army or civil guard
Lebensfrage	a question of life or death
Legationsrat	counsellor in an embassy
Lied	song or poem
Losungswort	password
Machtfrage	question of power
Märzvereine	March associations (from the early revolution in 1848)
Menschenart	human species
Ministerialrat	ministerial counsellor
Ministerrat	ministerial council
Mitte	centre
Mitteldeutschland	Central Germany
Mitteleuropa	Central Europe
Mitteleuropäischer Staatenbund	Central European confederation of states
Mittelpartei	centrist party
Mittelstaaten	medium-sized states
Mittelstand	middling strata, especially artisans and other small property-owners
Museumsgesellschaft	museum association
Nation	nation
Nationalität	nationality
Nationalpatriotismus	national patriotism
Nationalstaat	nation-state
Nationalverein	National Association
Naturvolk	a natural or indigenous people
neuer Mittelstand	new middle class
Neugestaltung	new form or reshaping
Neuigkeiten	novelties or news
Norddeutscher Bund	North German Confederation

Obergerichtsadvocat	lawyer of the high court
Obrigkeit	authority
öffentliche Meinung	public opinion
Öffentlichkeit	public sphere
Österreich	Austria
Partei	party
Particularismus	particularism
Patrioten	patriots
Patriotenpartei	(Bavarian) Patriotic Party
Pfaffenverein	priests' association
Plenum	plenum
Politik	politics or policy
Polizeipräsidium	police authority
Polizeiverein deutscher Staaten	police association of the German states
Präsidium	presidency
Presseleitungskomittee	(Austrian) committee for influencing the press
Preussentum	Prussianness
Rasse	race
Rassegemeinschaft	racial community
Reaktionär	reactionary
Reaktionsausschuss	confederal committee of the 'reaction'
Realpolitik	realistic policy or the politics of realism
Rechtsstaat	legal or law-governed state
Reformverein	Reform Association
Regierungsrat	government counsellor
Reich	empire
Reichsfeinde	enemy of the empire
Reichskanzler	imperial Chancellor
Reichsrat	imperial counsellor
Reichsritterschaft	imperial knights (of the Holy Roman Empire)
Reichstadt	imperial city
Reichstag	imperial assembly of deputies (in the constitution of 1848 or 1871)
Reichsverfassung	imperial constitution
Reichsverweser	imperial regent
Rettung	salvation
Rheinbund	Confederation of the Rhine
Rheinbündelei	involvement in ideas or practices recalling the Confederation of the Rhine
Rittergutsbesitzer	owner of noble estates
Ritterschaft	knighthood (of the Holy Roman Empire)
Rundschau	review
Schadenfreude	delight in the misfortune of others
Scheinstaat	sham state
Sonderbund	special or divisive union

Sonderbündelei	countenancing the idea of a *Sonderbund*
Sonderweg	special path (of German history)
Sonderwesen	special entity
Sprechsaal	forum
Staatenbund	confederation
Staatenhaus	assembly of state representatives
Staatsangehörige	citizen
Staatsleben	public affairs
Staatsminister	minister of state
Staatsministerium	state ministry
Staatswesen	state body or state
Staatswissenschaftler	scholar of state affairs or politics
Stamm/Stämme	tribe/s or kinship group/s
Stammeseigenthümlichkeit	particularity of a tribe
Stammesverwandtschaft	tribal or kinship tie
Ständeversammlung	assembly of estates or orders
ständische Monarchie	monarchy based on estates
Statthalter	governor
Stockpreussentum	Prussian stock or archetypal Prussianness
Südbund	southern union (of German states)
Süddeutschen	southern Germans
Tendenzpolitik	biased or tendentious policy
Teutsch	German (anachronistic)
Turnfest	gymnastics festival
Unheil	evil or misfortune
Unterrrichts- und	department of education and religious affairs
Kultusabteilung	
Vaterlandsliebe	love of the fatherland
Verband Deutscher	Union of German Workers' Associations
Arbeitervereine	
Verein für König und	Association for King and Country
Vaterland	
Verein(e)	association/s
Vereinigung	unification
Verfassung	constitution
Verfassungspartei	constitutional party
Vertretung	representative assembly
Vielvölkerreich	multi-ethnic empire
Vierköngisbündnis	Four Kings' Alliance
Virilstimmen	single votes for states in the Confederation
Volk/Völker	people/s or nation/s
Völkchen	small or petty people or nation
völkerrechtliches Bündnis	international alliance
Volkerschaften	peoples
Völkerverband	league of peoples or nations

Völkerwanderung	migration of peoples in antiquity and the Dark Ages
Volksarmee	popular army or militia
Volksblätter	popular newspaper
Volksgeist	national spirit
Volksgemeinschaft	national community
Volkshaus	popular assembly
Volksklub	popular club
Volksmasse	the masses
Volksparlament	popular parliament
Volkspartei	people's party
Volkstamm/Volkstämme	tribe/s
Volkstum	ethnicity
Volkstümlich	ethnic
Volksvertretung	popular assembly
Vormärz	pre-March era or the 1840s, before the revolution in March 1848
Vorparlament	pre-parliament, prior to the election of the Frankfurt Parliament
Vortrag/Vorträge	lecture/s
Wahlmänner	voters in an electoral college
Wirtschaftsbürgertum	commercial or economic bourgeoisie
Wochenblattspartei	faction around the *Preussisches Wochenblatt*, a liberal-leaning conservative newspaper
Zeitgeist	spirit or atmosphere of the time
Zentralgewalt	central power
Zentralmärzverein	Central March Association, the largest organisation of the 1848–49 revolution, set up by democrats
Zentralstelle für Pressangelegenheiten	Central Organisation for Press Affairs in Prussia
Zentraluntersuchungskommission	Central Commission of Enquiry in the Confederation
Zivilisation	civilisation
Zolleinigung	unification of tariffs
Zollunion	a customs' union
Zollverein	Customs' Union, founded in 1834
Zollvereinsparlament/ Zollparlament	parliament of the Customs' Union

Index

choral societies 36, 233, 362
Christian VIII, King of Denmark
291–2
'*Aabene Bref* (1846) 292
Christian IX, King of Denmark 300
Christian August, Duke of
Augustenurg 51
Christianity 84, 124, 191
Christians 82
Christmann, Rudolf 240, 313
Chronik der Gegenwart 302–3
Cicero 136
citizenship 19, 21, 28, 48, 95, 357
civil servants 10, 248–9, 277
civil war 194, 212, 345–6
'war of brothers' (*Bruderkrieg*)
324, 345–6
Clasen, Lorenz 245
Classen-Kappelmann, Johann 228
Coblenz 85
Coburg 307, 313
coffee houses 12
Colbert, Charles 136
Cologne 12, 46, 169
Committee of Fifteen 25
Committee of Fifty 25
Committee of Seven 25–6, 51
Committee of Seventeen 29
Communist League 245
Concert of Europe 67, 81–3, 85,
108, 148–9, 194–5, 293, 307
confederation (*Staatenbund*) 21, 63,
95, 106, 116, 186–7, 189, 193,
195–220, 352
Confederation of the Rhine 63, 77,
101, 203, 270
Congress of German Economists
(*Kongress deutscher Volkswirte*)
225, 232, 248, 256
conservatism 6, 39–43, 143–50,
152, 175–8, 213–16, 258–90,
302–4, 331–44
conservative associations 34
conservative party 37, 41, 332–3
conservatives 8, 37–43, 56–58, 69,
75, 82–3, 111, 130, 143–51,
156–7, 166–7, 175–8, 213–16,
258–90, 331–44, 363–4
Constantinople 102
Constitution (Vienna) 54

constitutionalism 14–15, 24, 32,
38–46, 115, 125–6, 139, 142,
221–3, 255–90, 331, 343–4,
359–60, 365
constitutional associations 34
constitutional government 16–17,
30, 43–4
constitutionalists 29, 34, 38, 231
constitutional monarchy 60, 287,
365
Constitutionelle Zeitung 71, 210–11
Copenhagen 292, 299
corporations 10, 27
Cotta, Georg 117, 122, 127, 129
counter-revolution 28, 41, 64, 144–7
coups d'état 163, 261–3, 271, 277,
286
Cowley, Henry Wellesley, Earl 74–5
Crämer, Karl 228
Crimean War (1854–56) 67, 76–84,
99, 101, 117, 124, 127, 129,
148–50, 176, 192, 194, 210, 217,
269
Croatia 48, 92
Croats 49–50, 54
culture 28, 39, 47–64, 110, 189, 247,
357
customs' union (*Zollverein*) 14, 87,
95–9, 111, 116, 143, 212, 223,
253–8, 285–6, 347, 362–3
Custozza, battle of 28
Czechs 54, 67, 105–7, 109–10
Czoernig, Carl von 102

Dahlmann, Friedrich Christoph 16,
297
Dalmatia 92
Dalwigk von Lichtenfels, Reinhard
von 89, 114, 193–6, 205–6, 302,
304, 350
Danes 20, 291, 297–9, 333
Danube 84, 116, 118
Danzig 242
Darmstadt 36, 242
Darmstädter Zeitung 132
Darmstädter Journal 8
Delbrück, Rudolph von 352
democracy 6, 14, 45, 94, 233–48,
253, 275
democratic associations 34

Schaffenhausenschen Bankverein 169
Schäffle, Albert 115–17, 254
Schaffrath, Wilhelm Michael 238, 310
Scharnhorst, Gerhard von 276
Schaumburg-Lippe 353
Schele, Eduard August von 165, 195
Scherer, Wilhelm 108
Schiller Association 32
Schlehdornpartei (conservative faction) 145
Schleinitz, Alexander von 73, 284, 28, 334–5
Schleswig 20, 50–2, 99–100, 284, 291–321
  population 52
Schleswig-Holstein 22, 48, 50–3, 73–5, 77, 80, 85–6, 89, 111, 124, 128, 141, 213, 216–17, 226, 267, 285, 288, 291–321, 323, 326, 328–31, 335–8, 346–9, 351, 356, 358, 365
  constitutions of 1854 292
  Estates 68
  Governor 68
  Landesversammlung 68
  population 291
  provisional government 50–1
Schleswig-Holstein committees 293–4, 313, 317, 328
Schlözer, Kurd von 272, 288
Schmerling, Anton von 49–50, 57, 86, 89–92, 105–7, 126, 350
Schmidt, Julius 244
Schmoller, Gustav 254, 268
Schneller, Julius Franz 103–4
Schopenhauer, Arthur 134
Schrenk, Karl von 195, 301, 350
Schüler, Christian 167, 238, 310
Schulze-Delitzsch, Hermann 31, 113, 225, 229–33, 241, 246, 276, 280, 311
Schuselka, Franz 111
Schwäbische Volkszeitung 268
Schwäbische Zeitung 268
Schwäbischer Chronik 141, 268
Schwäbischer Merkur 12, 183, 268
Schwarzenberg, Felix zu 28–9, 49, 56–8, 66–70, 78, 86–7, 89, 92, 94–103, 106, 127, 142, 146, 149–52, 197

Schwarzenberg, Karl von 103–4
Schweitzer, Johann Baptist von 134–7
  Der einzige Weg zur Einheit (1860) 135
  Die österreichische Spitze (1863) 135
  Österreichs Sache ist Deutschlands Sache (1859) 135
  Widerlegung von Carl Vogt's Studien zur gegenwärtigen Lage Europas (1859) 135
  Zur Deutschen Frage (1862) 134
Schwerin 71
Second Empire (France) 76, 147–8
secret society 128
secularism 14
Seeger, Adolf 229, 241
seigneurial dues 27
Senfft von Pilsach, Ludwig von 201
separation of church and state 14, 27
Sepp, Johann Nepomuk 59–60
Serbia 87
  Serbian nationalism 343
Serbs 54
shooting clubs 36, 135, 233, 362
Silesia 146, 182, 187–8
Simon, Heinrich 44, 136–7, 239–41
Simon, Ludwig 44, 50, 57, 167, 222–3, 311
  Aus dem Exil (1855)
Simson 71
Slavs 59–60, 84, 102, 115, 141–2, 147, 154–5
  South Slavs 94
Slovaks 49–50, 54
Slovenians 54
small Germany (*Kleindeutschland*) 2, 5, 20, 57, 61, 64, 85–6, 106–9, 113–17, 122, 126–7, 130–2, 135, 187–8, 211, 222, 238–43, 278, 282–3, 294–6, 303, 305–6, 309, 321–6, 331, 335, 338–44, 348–9, 356, 358, 363
small states (*Kleinstaaten*) 31, 79, 99–101, 167, 189–95, 216–17, 219, 289, 299, 303–4, 319, 338, 340, 345, 363
social democracy 13, 134–7, 243–8